For Jyoti –
With all best
wishes.
Lan Cao
2018

AF772343

CULTURE IN LAW AND DEVELOPMENT

Culture in Law and Development

NURTURING POSITIVE CHANGE

Lan Cao

OXFORD
UNIVERSITY PRESS

OXFORD
UNIVERSITY PRESS

Oxford University Press is a department of the University of Oxford. It furthers the University's objective of excellence in research, scholarship, and education by publishing worldwide. Oxford is a registered trademark of Oxford University Press in the UK and certain other countries.

Published in the United States of America by Oxford University Press
198 Madison Avenue, New York, NY 10016, United States of America.

Library of Congress Cataloging-in-Publication Data

Names: Cao, Lan, 1961- author.
Title: Culture in law and development : nurturing positive change/Lan Cao.
Description: New York : Oxford University Press, 2016. | Includes bibliographical references and index.
Identifiers: LCCN 2015042566 | ISBN 9780199915231 ((hardback) : alk. paper)
Subjects: LCSH: Culture and law. | Law and economic development.
Classification: LCC K487.C8 C36 2016 | DDC 340/.115—dc23 LC record available at http://lccn.loc.gov/2015042566

9 8 7 6 5 4 3 2 1

Printed by Edwards Brothers Malloy, United States of America

Note to Readers

This publication is designed to provide accurate and authoritative information in regard to the subject matter covered. It is based upon sources believed to be accurate and reliable and is intended to be current as of the time it was written. It is sold with the understanding that the publisher is not engaged in rendering legal, accounting, or other professional services. If legal advice or other expert assistance is required, the services of a competent professional person should be sought. Also, to confirm that the information has not been affected or changed by recent developments, traditional legal research techniques should be used, including checking primary sources where appropriate.

(Based on the Declaration of Principles jointly adopted by a Committee of the American Bar Association and a Committee of Publishers and Associations.)

To Harlan Margaret Van Cao

Contents

Acknowledgments

IN DOING THE research on which this book draws, I had support from the summer research programs of the Marshall-Wythe School of Law at the College of William & Mary and the Dale E. Fowler School of Law at Chapman University. I was also very fortunate to receive exceptional research help from Sherry Leysen, research librarian at Fowler School of Law. I would also like to thank the following research assistants whose contributions merit special mention here: from Marshall-Wythe School of Law, Laura Deneke, Laura Bain, Polina Zvyagina-Tabor, Nicole Hartz, Josh Stiff, Gowri Janakiramanan, and Shana Hofstetter; from Fowler School of Law: Jay Yu, Veronica Borenstein Buckels, Kristin Cavert, Geoffrey Hersch, and Vivan Kalu. Different drafts of this book were presented at Columbia Law School, Center for Gender & Sexuality Law, Cornell Law School, Clarke Program in East Asian Law & Culture, SUNY Buffalo Law School, Baldy Center for Law & Social Policy, Chicago-Kent College of Law, Mount Holyoke College, Politics Department. In writing this book, I much appreciate the works of as well as suggestions from Alexander Boni-Saenz, Amy Chua, Jane Stromseth, Madhavi Sunder, and William Van Alstyne. I also thank the editors at and associated with Oxford University Press involved in the acquisition, editing, and production of the book: Kevin Pendergast, Blake Ratcliff, Alden Domizio, Arun Kumar Vasu, and the copyeditor, Mary Rosewood.

Introduction

Somewhere in a small hamlet in the Mekong Delta in South Vietnam, a woman prepared for a lavish wedding ceremony. The groom held in his hands a platter of betel nut and betel leaves and lime paste—the traditional wedding arrangement that signified everlasting fidelity and love. Along the wedding route, girls with baby brothers and sisters straddled against their hips watched the ritual from their front steps. Even the earth, replenished by months of monsoon water, rumbled festively under the renewed activities of tadpoles and bougainvilleas. And so the wedding ceremony began and ended with the woman and her groom performing the requisite three bows before the altar.

That night, in the black stupor of her husband's house, in a village three full days and nights away by horse-drawn carriage, she lay lifeless against a bed of bleached white cotton. The following morning, fresh blood, three drops, dotted the pristine landscape of white. The morning after that, in full fanfare, to her astonishment and fear, she found herself seated in a freshly painted carriage being driven along the winding dirt path back to her family house.

Although she didn't know it then, red had become a life fluid for her and her family. The woman was returning to her village, fortunately, as an accidental victor in a very old war. Old men and women lined the dirt street and cheered as her wagon passed by. In their hands, strips of white cloth large as bedsheets waved like miniature flags hoisted by a conquered land. An open cart with a red roasted pig led the way, its two plump ears proudly intact, triangular and solid like pyramids pointing at the sky—thanks to the red virginal blood of the wedding night. Along the route, people cried "The bride is home," and "The pig has two ears." The moment her parents saw the pig's uncut ears, they quickly dropped to their knees and knelt gratefully before the family altar.

They had not warned the woman beforehand of the possible doom that might befall the family had she not been able to produce the three drops of blood on her wedding night. Fear and anxiety, they had heard, may cause all the blood, even in a virginal body, to gather in the brain, in which case there might not be any left for the wedding night.

They remembered only too well what had happened many years ago to another village girl. She was "all white and no red," as people said, like a rotten egg with too much white and not enough yolk. Her husband's family had thrown her on an old wagon, the kind used to cart animals and dead wood. Next to her, hanging from a pole pierced through its body, was a giant roasted pig, both its ears shamefully shorn into two little stumps.

When the wagon passed their houses, the villagers had thrown rocks at the wagon and spat in the girl's direction. Several village elders chased after the cart and cursed her karma with hexes they claimed would last generation after generation.

That night, villagers torched the family's barn and drove all their farm animals and livestock into the fields. Flames leapt into the air, lapping up everything with their fiery tongues. With sledgehammers and scythes, the villagers slashed every animal in sight, and the flesh that hung from the carcasses bled pools of red into the soil. The next morning, the body of the bride was found by an old stream, her blood turning the water the bright color of her wedding-red dress. All the animals were killed except the pigs. The pigs were spared, so that their ears could be slashed as a warning to bad daughters who ventured beyond the traditional circle of virtue.[1]

The above passages are excerpts from a novel I wrote. The description of the wedding and the ritual after are based on actual events surrounding my mother's wedding to the groom (not my father whom she married later). Years later when she recounted the story to me, I could sense the fear she must have felt when she discovered the fate that could have awaited her had she not been deemed a virgin by her husband.

Does this story have anything to do with law and development?

I argue that it does, although the standard law and development agenda would in all likelihood consider this traditional practice to be outside its purview. Assuming the incident involving the ill-fated girl (and other similar incidents) even garnered the attention of law and development, the conventional approach would be to ask if there is a law that addresses this objectionable practice and the acts following therefrom (criminal assault, trespass, destruction of private property). If not, perhaps the necessary laws could be drafted, passed, and implemented. Perhaps lawyers could be trained in the necessary causes of action, maybe tort or trespass, against the perpetrators. Or prosecutors could be persuaded to bring a criminal case against the attackers. However, the fact that the ritual

[1] Lan Cao, Monkey Bridge 49–50 (1997).

and the violence surrounding it are seamlessly part of the cultural fabric of that hamlet and hence difficult to regulate by passing a law outlawing such practice would, in all likelihood, not be considered a significant factor in the conventional law and development analysis.

Indeed, to view this story as merely about garden-variety criminal or tortious assaults or destruction of private property to be remedied, if at all, by laws and lawyers and courts is to miss at least half, and I would argue, the more significant half of the story. This is also, in vital parts, a story about victimization and voicelessness and a mindset that encouraged a village, village elders and villagers alike, to support the perpetration of such oppressive practices. The fact that the objectionable virginity ritual is part of a cultural tradition of gender relations should make it no less subject to a law and development inquiry. Cultural issues are critically important for law and development and as such should be embraced, not marginalized, by the discipline.

However, integrating culture into law and development will be an uphill battle, as I will explain in this book. Lawyers and legal scholars in the field of law and development have long failed to understand that law is peripheral, not central, to the development objectives of developing countries. The central role "law" has historically played in law and development has meant that the field views the establishment of the "rule of law" as singular and indispensable to development. This view has Weberian roots—Weber argued that a rational legal system was crucial to the economic development of the Protestant West by promoting transparency and predictability in individual market transactions. This view has moreover been affirmed in a number of studies showing a correlation between the rule of law and economic growth.[2]

Thus, without doubt, rule of law is now central to the law and development project, edging out other important considerations, such as, I argue, culture. Though there is little consensus for a working definition of the rule of law, scholars generally agree on some important attributes. Rachel Kleinfeld Belton discussed what she calls an ends-based definition of the rule of law and institutional-based approach to the rule of law. With reference to the first, she enumerated five generally accepted end-goals: (1) government bound by law; (2) equality for all before the law; (3) stable law and order; (4) predictable judicial rulings; (5) respect for human rights.[3] Kleinfeld also set forth what most scholars consider to be the three main rule of law institutions that must be reformed in order to achieve the stated rule of law end-goals: (1) a comprehensive body of laws; (2) a well-functioning

---

[2] Max Weber, Max Weber on Law in Economy and Society (Edward A. Shils & Max Rheinstein eds.,1954); *see, e.g.*, Stephen Knack & Philip Keefer, *Institutions and Economic Performance: Cross-Country Tests Using Alternative Institutional Measures*, 7 Econ. & Pol. 207 (1995), *as republished in* Munich Personal RePEc Archive 1 (MPRA Paper, Paper No. 23118, June 8, 2010), *available at* http://mpra.ub.uni-muenchen.de/23118/; Daniel Kaufmann, Aart Kraay & Massimo Mastruzzi, *Governance Matters IV: Governance Indicators for 1996–2004* (World Bank Policy Research, Working Paper No. 3630, June 2005).

[3] *See generally* Rachel Kleinfeld Belton, *Competing Definitions of the Rule of Law: Implications for Practitioners* (Carnegie Endowment Int'l Peace, Paper No. 55, Jan. 2005).

judiciary that is knowledgeable, efficient, and independent; (3) law-enforcement agencies capable of executing judgments and maintaining public peace and safety.[4]

Despite the lack of consensus over basic definitions and even objectives,[5] "rule of law" has become a mantra. Who can be against a robust rule of law foundation, however conceptualized and defined, for developing countries?[6] The rule of law mantra continues to be proclaimed and repeated and pursued even as law and development scholars and practitioners bemoan the continuing failures of their pursuits. Ironically, even as legal scholars in other fields increasingly recognize the need to study norms and the interaction of norms and law,[7] law and development scholars remain seemingly blind to this phenomenon, clinging to law predominantly if not exclusively. Thus "rule of law," it is assumed, is the same as law and development, as if one can achieve "development" by establishing "rule of law." The "law" in law and development has practically marginalized its "development" counterpart. As this book will establish, rule of law is not the same as development because development is not only about establishing a legal system or even a legal culture. Development is broader than rule of law, as I will show in my discussion of works by development scholars.

Within this broader (and increasingly accepted) conception of development, promulgating formal laws, though necessary, is hardly sufficient to achieve development objectives. This book looks at why law and development has failed and argues that *even if* its objective is to establish "rule of law" alone, norms, or more controversially, culture matters and must be factored into the equation. Law is not enough for even "just" "rule of law," and it most certainly is not enough for something more multi-pronged as "development." Rather, law and development requires a multilayered, long-term commitment to the countries involved because the institution of law can only be a first-step in a complex, time-consuming, and ultimately culture-bound endeavor.

In this book, I seek to uncover the relationship between culture and law and development. By no means do I claim a causal relationship. However, there is undoubtedly a connection between the two, and it is "multiple and complex."[8] Although culture should

---

[4] *Id.* at 16.

[5] Jane Stromseth, David Wippman, & Rosa Brooks, Can Might Make Rights?: Building the Rule of Law After Military Interventions 56 (2006) (describing how the phrase "the rule of law" has been defined to include "a rather vague cluster of concepts: fairness, justice, predictability, equality under law.... More concretely, we may think of the rule of law as having something to do with certain kinds of institutions and structures: well-functioning, respected courts, judicial review, fair and adequate legal codes, well-trained lawyers, and so on.").

[6] Katharina Pistor, *The Future of Law and Development: There Is No Single Field of Law and Development*, 104 Nw. U. L. Rev. 168, 168 (2009) ("The beauty of the 'law and development' ideal and the 'rule of law' ideal is that hardly anybody can disagree with the goal of building a neutral and universally accessible institutional framework that is meant to benefit all people irrespective of race, gender, social status, or membership in a particular clan or group.").

[7] Lan Cao, *Looking at Communities and Markets*, 74 Notre Dame L. Rev. 841, 857–74 (1999) (examining law/norm interaction).

[8] Hela Yousfi, *Culture and Development: The Continuing Tension Between Modern Standards and Local Contexts*, *in* Culture, Institutions, and Development: New Insights into an Old Debate 20, 55–56 (Jean-Philippe Platteau & Robert Peccoud eds., 2011).

not be privileged over other factors that affect development, it should not be ignored or deemed either irrelevant or too thorny to examine and evaluate. This book seeks to integrate culture into the broader development framework "in which culture is seen as intimately connected to different aspects of development issues."[9] In many cases, a blunt assessment is needed in order to understand how certain cultural norms aid or retard the law and development process. Because culture shapes the process of development, the book proposes that the field of law and development pursue the objective of purposive culture change when needed.

Law and development scholars have yet to ask the key question: After so many years of drafting new laws and constructing legal institutions to spur or facilitate development, do poor or failed states need more of the same? As slippery a concept as culture may be and as complex and controversial as the notion of culture change undoubtedly is—particularly given the history of colonialism—it is nonetheless critical to confront head-on, however awkward or unsettling, whether certain cultural attributes in a given society are an impediment to that society's development—economic, social, and political.

This book studies culture change in the field of law and development and thus does not examine culture change in developed countries. Critics of American culture, for example, can point to what they consider to be its many unsavory aspects: obsession with short-term gratification, short-term profits, and quarterly statements, which some argue have a detrimental impact on long-term investment and corporate stability; obsession with rugged individualism, which some argue has hollowed out American commitment to the public good as revealed in substandard childhood education, public transportation, access to health care; obsession with gun culture, which some charge is responsible for the thousands of firearms-related deaths every year; a culture of coziness between regulators and regulated agencies which dilute the effectiveness of regulation. The list can go on but the cultural ills of economically developed countries are not covered in this book. Nor are the prospects of culture change, directed at American culture, or Western culture, part of the book's objectives. Nonetheless, I acknowledge that should there be a culture change project jointly pursued by, for example, US-based and Rwandan women's organizations to transform the culture of violence in the National Football League—given the impressive strides in favor of gender equality in Rwanda since the 1994 Rwandan genocide[10]—I would find such a project to be fully compatible with the gestalt of the proposal set forth herein.

This book, however, only studies the relationship between culture and law and development in developing countries. I will begin by acknowledging considerable opposition to the proposal at the outset. I anticipate that the proposal will be highly controversial

---

[9] *Id.* at 56.

[10] Alexandra Topping, *Rwanda's Women Make Strides Towards Equality 20 Years After the Genocide*, GUARDIAN (Apr. 7, 2014, 05.13 EDT), http://www.theguardian.com/global-development/2014/apr/07/rwanda-women-empowered-impoverished.

for several reasons. First, the proposal, especially if offered by the West, will smack some of arrogance and hubris. This is understandable given that culture is a sensitive issue and critically assessing a cultural practice exposes the critical actor to charges of insensitivity and ignorance. It has been said that Hitler's deputy, Hermann Goering, once remarked, "When I hear the word 'culture,' I reach for my revolver."[11] Cultural issues continue to this day to spark a firestorm.

As noted in a *New York Times* report on poverty and cultural explanations, "[f]or more than 40 years, social scientists investigating the causes of poverty have tended to treat cultural explanations like Lord Voldemort: That Which Must Not Be Named."[12] Within the United States, "ugly battles" erupted after Daniel Moynihan, then an assistant labor secretary in the Johnson administration, introduced the idea of "culture of poverty" into the public discourse, provoking charges that ranged from racism to "blaming the victim." In law and development generally, as "in the overwhelmingly liberal ranks of academic sociology and anthropology the word 'culture' became a live grenade, and the idea that attitudes and behavior patterns kept people poor was shunned."[13]

A few noted academics have observed this entrenched phenomenon in the social sciences. Professor Orlando Patterson, a Jamaican-born American cultural sociologist at Harvard, wrote about the "deep-seated dogma that has prevailed in social science and policy circles since the mid-1960's: the rejection of any explanation that invokes a group's cultural attributes—its distinctive attitudes, values and predispositions, and the resulting behavior of its members—and the relentless preference for relying on structural factors like low incomes, joblessness, poor schools and bad housing."[14] Professor Patterson cautioned that the usual structural explanations that rely on "traditional socioeconomic thinking" do not explain many of the entrenched problems facing black men in the United States. For example, even when the economy produced millions of new jobs during the Clinton administration, "the jobless black youths simply did not turn up to take them. Instead, the opportunity was seized in large part by immigrants—including many blacks—mainly from Latin America and the Caribbean."[15] Moreover, Professor Patterson noted that the usual explanation for why black Americans did not fill those jobs—because they did not offer a living wage—was not convincing. Studies conducted by the sociologist Roger Waldinger of the University of California at Los Angeles, for example, demonstrated that "in New York such jobs offered an opportunity to the

---

[11] Michael Thompson, *Yes, Culture Matters, but in What Way?*, *in* ENVIRONMENT ACROSS CULTURES 39, 39 (Carl Friedrich Gethmann & Eckart Ehlers eds., 2003).

[12] Patricia Cohen, *"Culture of Poverty" Makes a Comeback*, N.Y. TIMES, Oct. 17, 2010, at A1, *available at* http://www.nytimes.com/2010/10/18/us/18poverty.html?pagewanted=all.

[13] *Id.*

[14] Orlando Patterson, Op-Ed., *A Poverty of the Mind*, N.Y. TIMES (Mar. 26, 2006), http://www.nytimes.com/2006/03/26/opinion/26patterson.html?ex=1144126800&en=2152a801b5153f6b&ei=5070&emc=eta1&_r=0.

[15] *Id.*

chronically unemployed to join the market and to acquire basic work skills that they later transferred to better jobs, but that the takers were predominantly immigrants." Clearly, a cultural dimension is needed to more fully understand the problem, although the cultural dimension alone would also be inadequate.

A parallel controversy about the role of culture is also played out in the global arena. In law and development, culture becomes ever more problematic when used as a possible factor in the diagnosis of Third World underdevelopment. This is especially so if the desired cultural attribute is equated with Westernization[16] or with foreign values. For example, even in the urban areas of Afghanistan, democracy is considered by many to be a Western tool; "the vast majority of Afghans still rely on tribal justice, viewing the courts as little more than venues of extortion."[17] A proposed 2013 law aimed at protecting the rights of Afghani women was met with protesters bearing posters that read, "I am a Self-Aware Woman, I Will Not Be Deceived by the Empty Slogans of the West."[18] The country was seized by protests following the introduction of a women's rights bill containing protections already in place via presidential decree—protections against child marriage, polygamy, and violence against women. Students at Kabul University equated the bill with Western culture. "Those who are pushing for the approval of the law, they are doing it to make Westerners happy," one said.[19]

The issue of whether culture influences development was fiercely contested in the 2012 US presidential elections when the Republican nominee Mitt Romney made the following statement during his July 2012 visit to Jerusalem:

> I was thinking this morning, as I prepared to come into this room, of a discussion I had across the country in the United States about my perceptions about the differences between countries. And as you come here and you see the GDP per capita, for instance, in Israel, which is about $21,000, and you compare that with the GDP per capita just across the areas managed by the Palestinian Authority, which is more like $10,000 per capita, you notice a dramatic, stark difference in economic vitality.

---

[16] *See, e.g.*, Mohan Gopalan Gopal, *Law and Development: Toward a Pluralist Vision*, 90 AM. SOC'Y INT'L L. PROC. 231, 233 (1996) ("[T]he law and development movement should set as its main objective the protection of the freedom of states and people to choose their social and cultural norms and values (including their legal systems) in accordance with rules of international law.... It should not be the vehicle for promotion of any particular set of national cultural and social norms."); Makau Mutua, *Savages, Victims, and Saviors: The Metaphor of Human Rights*, 42 HARV. INT'L L.J. 201, 207 (2001) (charging that the "human rights movement is driven by a totalitarian or totalizing impulse, that is, the mission to require that all human societies transform themselves to fit a particular blueprint....").

[17] Azam Ahmed & Habib Zahori, *Despite West's Efforts, Afghan Youths Cling to Traditional Ways*, N.Y. TIMES, July 31, 2013, at A1, http://www.nytimes.com/2013/08/01/world/asia/despite-wests-efforts-afghan-youths-cling-to-traditional-ways.html?pagewanted=all.

[18] *Id.*

[19] *Id.*

And that is also between other countries that are near or next to each other. Chile and Ecuador, Mexico and the United States.[20]

Romney further noted that "[c]ulture makes all the difference. And as I come here and I look out over this city and consider the accomplishments of the people of this nation, I recognize the power of at least culture and a few other things."[21]

Major media outlets characterized these remarks as "gaffes"[22] and responses were swiftly issued. Saeb Erekat, a senior aide to President Mahmoud Abbas of the Palestinian Authority, found Mr. Romney's remarks offensive. "It is a racist statement and this man doesn't realize that the Palestinian economy cannot reach its potential because there is an Israeli occupation. . . ."[23] Jared Diamond, author of *Guns, Germs and Steel*, a book cited by Romney in his speech, lambasted Romney and accused him of "oversimplif[ying] the issue."[24] But Richard Landes, a medieval historian and the son of David Landes, economist and author of *The Wealth and Poverty of Nations*, asserted instead that Israel and the Arab world illustrated "the primacy of culture."[25] Elliott Abrams, a senior fellow for Middle Eastern Studies at the Council on Foreign Relations, also defended Romney, observing that a 2002 UN report penned by Arab authors had made similar points about Arab culture: "culture and values are the soul of development" and "traditional culture and values, including traditional Arab culture and values, can be at odds with those of the globalizing world."[26]

This reluctance to deal with culture is understandable in the internationalist-minded, cosmopolitan world of international law. Take how the prominent law and development scholar, Professor Amy Chua, treated the "culture question" when this issue came up with respect to Malaysia, where the ethnic Chinese are economically dominant and the ethnic, "indigenous" Malay are economically weak. The solution imposed by the government as a way to ameliorate the problematic disparity between the two groups was to

---

20 Ashley Parker & Richard A. Oppel Jr., *Romney Trip Raises Spark at a 2nd Stop*, N.Y. Times, July 30, 2012, at A1, *available at* http://www.nytimes.com/2012/07/31/us/politics/romney-angers-palestinians-with-comments-in-israel.html?pagewanted=all.

21 *Id.*

22 Howard LaFranchi, *Mitt Romney in Jerusalem: Another City, Another Gaffe (or Two)?*, Christian Sci. Monitor (July 30, 2012), http://www.csmonitor.com/USA/Foreign-Policy/2012/0730/Mitt-Romney-in-Jerusalem-Another-city-another-gaffe-or-two; Philip Rucker & Dan Balz, *Mitt Romney Wraps Up Tumultuous Overseas Tour*, Wash. Post (July 30, 2012), http://www.washingtonpost.com/politics/mitt-romney-wraps-up-tumultuous-overseas-tour/2012/07/31/gJQAY2PsNX_story.html

23 Parker & Oppel Jr., *supra* note 20.

24 Jared Diamond, Op-Ed., *Romney Hasn't Done His Homework*, N.Y. Times, Aug. 1, 2012, at A21, *available at* http://www.nytimes.com/2012/08/02/opinion/mitt-romneys-search-for-simple-answers.html.

25 Richard Landes, *Romney Is Right on Culture and the Wealth of Nations*, Wall St. J., Aug. 5, 2012, at A13, *available at* http://online.wsj.com/article/SB10000872396390443866404577566770697427382.html.

26 Elliott Abram, *Culture, Romney and the Press*, Nat'l Rev., Aug. 1, 2012, at 2, *available at* http://www.nationalreview.com/articles/312896/culture-romney-and-press-elliott-abrams?pg=1.

impose quotas against the ethnic Chinese in university admissions and in the percentage of stock ownership the Chinese were allowed to own in companies in Malaysia. Professor Chua saw this as palatable; she observed that "[a]ttempts to inculcate a 'work ethic' . . . have not proved . . . effective. Indigenous elites in developing countries have frequently encouraged their fellow citizens to emulate market-dominant minorities and to become more 'diligent' and 'motivated.'"[27] She noted that efforts by Malaysia's prime minister to get the ethnic Malays to be more like the Chinese have failed because "attempting to change culture from the top down . . . have been notoriously unsuccessful."[28] Moreover, such efforts are hard to defend because "[a]part from the issue of feasibility, there is also a moral question. 'Culture' cannot simply be treated as an inconvenient impediment to free markets."[29]

But development, it should be pointed out, is not just about "free markets" or the pursuit of crass profits and ultradeference to corporate interests. The argument is not that culture should be changed to accommodate corporate profit. It is, rather, that cultural arguments used to justify practices that impede development need to be examined and addressed because development is ultimately about human freedom and human capability.[30] Nonetheless, whatever the rationale, there is no doubt that cultural issues are thorny and efforts to transform culture equally if not even more thorny.

It is true that development was once viewed through a narrow economic lens with an emphasis on GNP,[31] but as I will show, development is now understood in much broader terms that engage broad, substantive rights. Development is not just about economics any more. Neither should it be only about law. Cultural practices that are antithetical to development aspirations should be subject to critical scrutiny. As George Soros has aptly noted, "[i]n many places, laws exist on paper to protect the vulnerable from exploitation, yet informal norms and institutions hold sway, and all too often, these norms and institutions work against the poor and vulnerable, women especially."[32] Indeed, in the universe where law and development operates, formal laws, formal institutions and formal markets are usually weak. By contrast, cultural norms that guide economic and social behavior are strong, sometimes running counter to development objectives and thus must be engaged.[33]

---

27 Amy Chua, World on Fire: How Exporting Free Market Democracy Breeds Ethnic Hatred and Global Instability 266 (2004).

28 *Id.*

29 *Id.* In a subsequent book, however, Chua veers more toward a culturally laden observation of economic success in different immigrant groups, describing certain traits as constituting a "potent cultural package that generates drive. . . ." Amy Chua & Jed Rubenfeld, The Triple Package: How Three Unlikely Traits Explain the Rise and Fall of Cultural Groups in America 1 (2014).

30 Amartya Sen, Development as Freedom (1999).

31 Michael Todaro, Economic Development 77–104 (Andrea Shaw et al. eds., 2000).

32 George Soros & Fazle Hasan Abed, Op-Ed., *Rule of Law Can Rid the World of Poverty*, Fin. Times (Sept. 26, 2012), http://www.ft.com/cms/s/0/f78f8e0a-07cc-11e2-8354-00144feabdc0.html#axzz27foee6wf.

33 Marcel Fafchamps, *Markets and the Diffusion of Institutional Innovations*, *in* Culture, Institutions, and Development: New Insights into an Old Debate 143, 144 (Jean-Philippe Platteau & Robert Peccoud

The point is not that economics (or by inference global markets) should trump culture. It is rather that law is often not enough to effectuate change and culture should not be allowed to reign unchallenged in this void to impede legitimate development (and legal) objectives.[34]

There is a second reason the book's main thesis will be controversial. Its central insight, that culture matters, and the proposal, that it be examined, evaluated, and even changed, runs, from a normative standpoint, counter to the tradition of public and private international law. A culture-embedded law and development endeavor may strike some as odd or heretical precisely because it collides head-on with an international law foundation that is deeply acultural, as well as a rule of law tradition which has incorrectly presented the discipline as merely a legal, technocratic, and acultural endeavor. As discussed in the book, international law, public and private, has eschewed cultural issues and focused on states and markets, respectively. Consciously or unconsciously, law and development, following in the footpath of international law, has embraced and built upon this acultural foundation. Law and development, however, must disassociate itself from this long-standing and deeply embedded tradition in international law.

At the same time that law and development has adopted the acultural traditions of public and private international law, it has also unduly promoted the "rule of law" as if such an approach were merely a standard recipe for development: a dash of this here, a spoonful of that there. This approach has obscured the fact that there is no technical consensus on *the* rule of law needed to bring about development. In other words, the traditional law and development emphasis on legal institution building, policy prescriptions, training judges and lawyers, and writing codes has created the false idea that law and development is essentially about "a domain of expertise, a programme for action . . ."[35] cabined from the wider cultural and political context. Take the World Bank as an example. For many years, this premier international institution charged with promoting development saw its mission in narrow, technocratic terms, refusing calls to broaden its mandate, for example, shrugging off UN requests to cease lending to South Africa and Portugal because of their apartheid and colonial policies, respectively.[36]

While Article I of the Bank's Articles of Agreement states that the purposes of the Bank are to engage in economic and financial activities for the reconstruction of Europe after World War II, Article IV/10 sounds the following cautionary note: "The Bank and its

---

eds., 2011) ("[E]conomists to date have paid less attention to the role that social norms and rules of behaviour play in market performance. Yet laws and courts can accomplish little if societies choose to ignore them.").

[34] What is development and what are development objectives are addressed *infra* notes 116–128 and accompanying text.

[35] David Kennedy, *The "Rule of Law" as Development*, *in* LAW AND DEVELOPMENT: FACING COMPLEXITY IN THE 21ST CENTURY 17, 19 (Amanda Perry-Kessaris & John Hatchard eds., 2003).

[36] Gernot Brodnig, *The World Bank and Human Rights: Mission Impossible?* 4 (Carr Ctr. Hum. Rts., Policy Working Paper No. T-01-05, Dec. 7, 2001), *available at* http://www.hks.harvard.edu/cchrp/Web%20Working%20Papers/BrodnigHR&WorldBank.pdf.

officers shall not interfere in the political affairs of any member; nor shall they be influenced in their decisions by the political character of the member or members concerned. Only economic considerations shall be relevant to their decisions, and these considerations shall be weighed impartially in order to achieve the purposes stated in Article I."[37] But even the World Bank has gradually moved away from this narrow technocratic framework and expanded the development paradigm.[38] For example, it now conditions loans on the recipient countries meeting certain factors, such as good governance, meant to broaden the development inquiry: "accountable and competent public institutions, transparent economic and social policies and practices, a predictable and stable legal framework and participation by affected groups and civil society."[39] This is a step in the right direction for what once was a predominantly if not exclusively economic institution.

However, despite efforts to push against the "law" and the "economic" component of "development," the standard law and development menu remains entrenched in the institutional and technical elements of rule of law, in essence writing off the "development" component of "law and development." So even if the objectives have been expanded beyond economic growth to include good governance, political development, and human rights, the means that law and development employ to achieve such objectives remain rooted in a standard menu of law, law, and more law.

But as this book will demonstrate, although the rule of law is necessary, it must be supplemented by cultural norms that support rule of law objectives. My proposal to embrace culture upsets the simplistic picture of law and development as a predominantly technocratic project—getting governance right, designing the necessary legal institutions, enacting the right laws to support economic transactions, bundling loan packages with the right project, putting into place the right programs to educate the police, and so forth. Adhering to a standard rule of law focus allows rule of law experts to address the legal vacuum by passing laws and building legal institutions and allocating resources toward such efforts in concrete and manageable ways.[40] By contrast, a law and development project

---

[37] Articles of Agreement of the International Bank for Reconstruction and Development, (IBRD), art. I, Dec. 27, 1945, 60 Stat. 1440, 2 U.N.T.S. 134, *as amended* Feb. 6, 1989, *available at* http://web.worldbank.org/WBSITE/EXTERNAL/EXTABOUTUS/ORGANIZATION/BODEXT/0,,contentMDK:20049557~menuPK:64020045~pagePK:64020054~piPK:64020408~theSitePK:278036~isCURL:Y,00.html [hereinafter IBRD]; *id.* at art. IV, § 10; *see generally* Jeffry A. Frieden, Global Capitalism: Its Fall and Rise in the Twentieth Century 58–60 (2006) (discussing the World Bank's original purpose of financing the economic recovery of post–World War II Europe).

[38] IBRD, *supra* note 37, at art. I; *id.* at art. IV, § 10.

[39] Brodnig, *supra* note 36, at 6.

[40] Ronald J. Daniels & Michael J. Trebilcock, *The Political Economy of Rule of Law Reform in Developing Countries*, 26 Mich. J. Int'l L. 99, 107 (2004) ("[T]he general orientation of reform prescriptions entail either more effective or efficient deployment of existing resources devoted to a country's legal system, a re-ordering of a country's domestic priorities and reallocation of resources from other areas of expenditure to the legal system, or the infusion of resources from external donors (in the form of financial assistance, technological assistance, or technical advice and training, etc.")).

that includes culture in its analytical and operational framework seems unmanageably intricate and slippery.[41] Because culture can hardly be reduced to discrete bundles but rather is everywhere,[42] trying to "capture" it and then "do something with it" seems either un-doable or enormously complicated. One can make or pass laws, but how does one make or pass culture? Culture seems so much more opaque and complex than law. As a result, many in law and development prefer to view themselves as engaged merely in a legalistic or technocratic process separate and apart from the more messy cultural realm.

Third, ascribing, even partially, the problems faced by developing countries to culture may allow some to use culture to sidestep various structural inequities in the international economic system. Note this scathing criticism of what a cultural skeptic called a "culturalist explanation [which] is resorted to by those with lazy minds, at least insofar as one has not exhausted the other kinds of social, economic, political and demographic explanation."[43] Critics who reject cultural explanations have argued, for example, that the very concept of culture should be abandoned because focusing on culture "produced the wrong kinds of generalizations, hid history and relations of power, escaped satisfactory definition, smuggled in assumptions about race and gender, and revealed an inaccurately simple and uniform bounded logic."[44] As another critic charged, "[t]he idea that culture is a problem for human rights, that, for example, it stands as a barrier to women's equality, is related to a more general tendency to culturalize problems. This means that it is a way to interpret women's subordination in terms of cultural practices that suppress them rather than the economic or political problems their communities face."[45]

---

[41] Daniel Nielson, Michael Tierny, & Catherine Weaver, *Bridging the Rationalist-Constructivist Divide: Re-Engineering the Culture of the World Bank*, 9 J. Int'l Rel. & Dev. 107, 132 (2006) ("[C]ulture remains a tricky concept—one that is difficult to define, measure, observe, and test.").

[42] Don Mitchell, Cultural Geography: A Critical Introduction xvi (2000) ("[C]ulture is always something to be explained as it is socially produced through myriad struggles over and in spaces, scales, and landscapes. . . . '[C]ulture' is always and everywhere inextricably related to social, political, and economic forces and practices."); *see also* Lawrence Rosen, Law as Culture: An Invitation 3 (2006) (the human "categorizing capacity—the key feature of the concept of 'culture'—was not something that happened *after* we became human but something that actually *preceded* our present speciation. Thus, the acquisition of the capacity for culture, through the selective advantage it offered, contributed enormously to our evolution into *homo sapiens*.").

[43] Jean-Francois Bayart, *Culture and Development: Do Social Struggles Make a Difference?*, *in* Culture, Institutions, and Development: New Insights into an Old Debate 65, 78 (Jean-Philippe Platteau & Robert Peccoud eds., 2011); *see also id.* at 79 (objecting to the influential theories dealing with network espoused by scholars such as Mark Granovetter from the New Economic Sociology School, "the New Economic Sociology . . . inclines to neglect the social and historical relations of power, inequality and territoriality inherent in the economic actors' 'embeddedness'. . . .").

[44] Ilana Gershon & Janelle S. Taylor, *Introduction to "In Focus: Culture in the Spaces of No Culture,"* 110 Am. Anthropologist 417, 418 (2008); *see also* Sally Engle Merry, *Human Rights Law and the Demonization of Culture (And Anthropology Along the Way)*, Pol. & Legal Anthropology Rev., May 2003, at 55, 63 (citation omitted).

[45] Merry, *supra* note 44.

And fourth, adding culture into an already complex mix will likely make the entire endeavor not only more complex but also more costly and more time-consuming. The Nobel Laureate Douglass North made the following fundamental point about formal and informal laws and institutions: "It is the admixture of formal rules, informal norms, and enforcement characteristics that shapes economic performance. While the rules may be changed overnight, the informal norms usually change only gradually."[46] As some commentators have noted, "[w]hile deeply entrenched social values, attitudes, and practices are presumably amenable to change through time, the policy prescriptions entailed in overcoming this class of impediment are not nearly as obvious as in the case of technical or resource-related impediments nor is any impact likely to be immediate or dramatic."[47] Cultural values and beliefs have a way of perpetuating themselves by various means, for example by parents teaching their children what the parents themselves had internalized through their own parents. These norms might have been efficient when they first came into being and are no longer efficient. Still, they may continue to be passed down. Indeed, because cultural influences proceed at a slow pace,[48] adding culture to the law and development menu is likely to mean an even longer time frame.[49]

It is important to keep in mind that even traditional rule of law projects which focus "only" on changing institutions and passing new laws and training judges take time. Regardless, rule of law initiatives are designed to showcase short-term progress. Seminars for judges and lawyers and technical assistance on how to computerize court systems are manageable and can be checked off when completed. Successful completion of projects are rewarded with new funding for additional projects which must also be manageable or technocratically feasible within discrete time frames.[50]

By contrast, culture change along lines compatible with development objectives is complex and requires a definite long-range perspective. "Impacts on social and gender

---

[46] Douglass C. North, *Economic Performance Through Time*, 84 AM. ECON. REV. 359, 366 (1994); *see also* DOUGLASS C. NORTH, INSTITUTIONS, INSTITUTIONAL CHANGE AND ECONOMIC PERFORMANCE 67 (1990).

[47] Daniels & Trebilcock, *supra* note 40, at 108 (citation omitted).

[48] Gerard Roland, *Understanding Institutional Change: Fast-Moving and Slow-Moving Institutions*, 38 STUD. COMP. INT'L DEV. 109 (2004); Brian Z. Tamanaha, *The Primacy of Society and the Failures of Law and Development*, 44 CORNELL INT'L L.J. 209, 224 (2011) (stating that "negative cultural attitudes toward law and judges are slow to change"); *see also Lip-Plates*, MURSI ONLINE, http://www.mursi.org/life-cycle/lip-plates (last visited Nov. 8, 2014) (describing a tradition of the Mursi people of making women unattractive to slave traders by having women wear large ornaments that disfigure their lips, a tradition still practiced today even though the original reason for its emergence is no longer applicable).

[49] Vijayendra Rao & Michael Walton, *Culture and Public Action: Relationality, Equality of Agency, and Development*, *in* CULTURE AND PUBLIC ACTION 3, 25–26 (Vijayendra Rao & Michael Walton eds., 2004) (discussing how tackling "culturally embedded hierarchies" necessitate "more long-term and contextualized approaches than those typically implemented by development agencies."); *see also* Anita Abraham & Jean-Philippe Platteau, *Participatory Development: Where Culture Creeps In*, *in* CULTURE AND PUBLIC ACTION 210, 210 (Vijayendra Rao & Michael Walton eds., 2004).

[50] Tamanaha, *supra* note 48, at 238.

relations is complex; seldom is short-term quantitative data sufficient to demonstrate impact. Assessment of poverty and inequity require more than relative changes in income levels—and assessing results in terms of *empowerment* require more creative approaches to quantitative information, as well as qualitative data.... Monitoring over the long term is required, given the dynamic and complex processes involved in social change."[51]

From a pragmatic, resource-oriented standpoint, then, rich countries that subsidize law and development efforts in poor countries might be reluctant to embrace a mission that seems virtually open-ended. History has shown that such missions antagonize domestic constituents opposed to the diversion of tax dollars from domestic priorities to seemingly elusive foreign ventures. This concern is even more pronounced in law and development scenarios where security has not been established despite continuing military interventions.[52] Support for law and development ventures sharply diminishes when the security in the country at issue deteriorates. For example, while the UN/American Operation Restore Hope in Somalia started out with 84 percent approval, the approval rating quickly fell to 33 percent when the mission became ill-defined and American casualties rose; the prevailing view among analysts is that "Americans have little interest in humanitarian missions and virtually no tolerance for costs, especially casualties, incurred in pursuit of purely humanitarian goals, particularly in Third World countries where American economic and political interests are not directly at stake."[53]

In sum, the obstacles to a cultural approach are many and fall along three general lines: Law and development is part of the discipline of international law and international law is acultural; a culture-focused approach is normatively problematic and is highly charged as it carries sensitive ideological and historical baggage; and such an approach is practically more difficult to implement than a technocratic approach that emphasizes tangible factors such as law and institutions.

Despite these obstacles, if law and development is to be effectively pursued, it cannot deal only with law and sidestep culture either because it believes evaluating culture is normatively offensive or because culture is somehow irrelevant, too complex, or too time-consuming to address. This book will examine the current standard rule of law menu to demonstrate what is wrong and what needs to be altered. Currently, the conventional or standard menu reflects strong, almost orthodox attachment to the formalization of rights and the establishment of a legal apparatus. This generally accepted menu revolves around institutional or technical elements of rule of law development and consists, in short, of

---

[51] Canadian Int'l Dev. Agency (CIDA), Asia Branch, *The Role of Microcredit in Poverty Reduction and Promoting Gender Equity: A Discussion Paper* 15 (June 12, 1997) (prepared by Norman MacIsaac), *available at* http://www.microfinancegateway.org/gm/document-1.9.28404/3247_3247.pdf.

[52] STROMSETH ET AL., *supra* note 5, at 4 ("The electorates of western nations are often loathe to support expensive, risky foreign ventures that offer few clear short-term domestic dividends.").

[53] Carolyn J. Logan, *U.S. Public Opinion and the Intervention in Somalia: Lessons for the Future of Military-Humanitarian Interventions*, FLETCHER F. WORLD AFF., Summer/Fall 1996, at 155, 155.

the following relatively uncontroversial prescriptions: fostering and establishing a transparent governance structure, creating a fair and independent judicial system and criminal law system, training a responsible police force and enacting commercial, property, competition, and other laws necessary for market reform and economic growth.

I do not mean to suggest, however, by my use of the term "conventional menu" or "standard menu" that there is uniformity of opinions in the field. Even within the circumscribed perimeters of this standard law and development template, there are contentious debates. Even a cursory look at the literature reveals scant agreement on basic principles. Development scholars and practitioners contest, to name a few examples, even foundational, first-tier issues such as "what is the rule of law?"[54] That is, is the rule of law to be defined by a thick, substantive approach or a thin, formal approach? Is it to be understood and implemented by reference to "the end purposes it is to serve in society . . . [or by its] institutional attributes—the 'necessary' laws, a 'well-functioning' judiciary, and a 'good' law enforcement apparatus?"[55] Along this vein, a rule of law that aims to achieve an ends purpose with substantive content (human rights, for example) would not view as adequate or meaningful a rule of law that focuses on formal, institutional attributes alone (efficient judiciary, courts, police, a body of laws) unless the institutions at issue yield the desired substantive-based end result.

Other contested issues involve how to implement the rule of law, however defined, and have centered on the questions of the role of prior conditions[56] or the interaction between formal and informal mechanisms and the effect they have on development efforts[57] or whether law (as opposed to nonlegal mechanisms) is even central to economic growth.[58]

---

[54] *See* Brian Tamanaha, *The Rule of Law for Everyone?* 6 (St. John's Legal Studies Res. Paper Series, Working Paper, Feb. 28, 2003), *available at* http://ssrn.com/abstract=312622 (cautioning that despite almost universal acclaim for the rule of law, "the rule of law is strikingly like the notion of the 'good,' in the sense that everyone is for it, but there is no agreement on precisely what it is. Some . . . believe that the rule of law has purely formal characteristics, meaning that the law must be publicly declared, with prospective application, and possess the characteristics of generality, equality, and certainty, but there are no requirements with regard to the content of the law. Others . . . believe that the rule of law also necessarily entails protection of individual rights."); Belton, *supra* note 3, at 5–7 (describing a definition of the rule of law that focuses on the ends and one that focuses on institution building.).

[55] Belton, *supra* note 3, at 6.

[56] Tom Ginsburg, *Studying Japanese Law Because It's There*, 58 Am. J. Comp. L. 15, 17 (2009).

[57] Hernando De Soto, The Mystery of Capital: Why Capitalism Triumphs in the West and Fails Everywhere Else (2000) (arguing that informal arrangements such as squatting be legally formalized so that the poor can become stakeholders with property rights); *see generally* Donald Clarke, *Economic Development and the Rights Hypothesis: The China Problem*, 51 Am. J. Comp. L. 89 (2003) (arguing that in China, informal mechanisms serve as effective substitutes for formal contract enforcement).

[58] Stephen Golub, *Beyond Rule of Law Orthodoxy: The Legal Empowerment Alternative* 9–11 (Carnegie Endowment Int'l Peace, Working Paper No. 41, Oct. 2003); Katharina Pistor, Philip A. Wellons, & Jeffry Sachs et al., The Role of Law and Legal Institutions in Asian Economic Development: 1960–1995, at 2 (1999) (issuing "caution against the use of legal technical assistance programs as an instrument to stimulate and support economic growth and development").

Sequencing—that is, whether economic development and the rule of law on the one hand should precede democratization on the other hand or whether both should be pursued in tandem—has also sparked vigorous debate.[59] A related but different sequencing controversy centers on whether shock therapy, as occurred in Eastern Europe, or a more gradual approach involving incremental and sequential reforms, associated with East Asia,[60] is the more efficacious and "better" model of development.

Despite the infighting within the field, for the most part, the issues that vex the field and its scholars and practitioners center on a seemingly acultural arc of laws, policies, and institutions. Culture remains an understudied area.[61] The central aim of the book is to put forth and defend this main insight—that law and development projects must embody and boldly promote deeper, more substantive conceptions that reflect core, liberal values embedded in the discipline, even if doing so involves critically examining and changing certain cultural attributes.

This is because culture is central to development. It is central even if one were to focus *only* on the rule of law slice of the broader development pie. Moreover, it remains central whether a thick or a thin conception of the rule of law is adopted. Let's start with a thick conception. From a thick, maximalist lens, rule of law is an "extremely complex bundle of cultural commitments and institutional structures that support peace, human rights, democracy, and prosperity."[62] Of course if a thick, substantive definition is used so that rule of law must aim to accomplish a certain array of stated substantive objectives, such as government bound by law or human rights promotion, the centrality of culture to the development project is relatively obvious (though nonetheless sidestepped). The reason culture is critical to a thick understanding of rule of law is simple. To put it bluntly, law is insufficient for development. Even international human rights law is insufficient to deal with international human rights violations. Law alone is inadequate because it must be coupled with the institution and fostering of new norms. As Rachel Kleinfeld Belton aptly noted, "human rights require reforming many rule-of-law institutions, as well as

---

[59] *See* Thomas Carothers, *How Democracies Emerge: The "Sequencing" Fallacy*, 18 J. DEMOCRACY 12, 13 (2007); Edward D. Mansfield & Jack L. Snyder, *The Sequencing "Fallacy,"* 18 J. DEMOCRACY 5, 6 (2007); Comm'n on Legal Empowerment of the Poor & United Nations Development Program (UNDP), Making the Law Work for Everyone: Reports of the Commission on Legal Empowerment of the Poor, Vol. I, at 3 (June 1, 2008), http://www.undp.org/content/dam/aplaws/publication/en/publications/democratic-governance/legal-empowerment/reports-of-the-commission-on-legal-empowerment-of-the-poor/making-the-law-work-for-everyone---vol-i---english/Making_the_Law_Work_for_Everyone.pdf.

[60] Randall Peerenboom, *Rule of Law, Democracy, and the Sequencing Debate: Lessons from China and Vietnam* 12 (Soc. Sci. Res. Network, Working Paper No. 1447051, Aug. 10, 2009), http://ssrn.com/abstract=1447051.

[61] The works of Rachel Kleinfeld Belton (and a few others) are notable exceptions. *See,* e.g., Belton, *supra* note 3, at 14 (aptly noting that rule of law experts who include human rights as a necessary component of rule of law are in fact promoting not just a "technocratic ideal, but a cultural idea with substantive, values-driven content."); *see also* Stromseth et al., *supra* note 5, at 310–46 (discussing how to create rule of law cultures).

[62] STROMSETH ET AL., *supra* note 5, at 4; *see also* Robert S. Summers, *A Formal Theory of the Rule of Law*, 6 RATIO JURIS 127, 135 (1993).

establishing new cultural norms. Laws can and must be established to promote these rights, but laws are among the weakest instruments for protecting human rights."[63] This is because the focus is all too often on compliance with rules. "Human rights law . . . suffers from the problem of rule naïveté—the idea that the public good for any country can be described in the form of simple rules."[64] Ratification of human rights treaties is essentially compulsory. And yet, as Eric Posner observed, this hasn't led to increased human rights observance.[65]

These observations may be startling because as lawyers we are drawn to law and have faith in its ability to promote and protect rights. But David Kennedy's similarly scathing indictment of the human rights movement is equally applicable to the "rule of law" movement: "Human rights offers itself as the measure of emancipation. This is its most striking—and misleading—promise . . . [T]here was the holocaust and then there was the genocide convention, women everywhere were subject to discrimination and then there was CEDAW [Convention on the Elimination of All Forms of Discrimination Against Women]."[66] Analogously, the rule of law movement in law and development also offers itself as the remedy—by equating the passage of more laws as the necessary and virtuous response to underdevelopment. Indeed, people who disagree about which political choices to pursue or which political consequences will ensue when this or that policy is adopted can paper over their differences and rally and unite around the "rule of law."[67] To push the point further, this posture makes the law and development movement *itself* seem redemptive—as if doing something *for the rule of law* was, in and of itself, doing something *against* underdevelopment and poverty.[68]

Thus passing a law or "signing up for a norm—against discrimination—comes to substitute for ending the practice."[69] Again, this is so even when law and development adopts a thick conception of rule of law, as is the case in the international human rights field. Even as lawyers push for state ratification of, for example, CEDAW, research has shown that without more, a law-centric approach focused on state ratification of the treaty has not resulted in state compliance with or implementation of treaty obligations. To the contrary. Countries that ratify a human rights treaty may enjoy the benefit of the treaty's expressive functions, thereby possibly deflecting pressure from the international community for actual improvements in human rights practices, without having to do the

63 Belton, *supra* note 3, at 14.

64 Eric E. Posner, *Against Human Rights*, HARPER'S MAG., Oct. 2014, at 13, 16.

65 *Id.* at 14. Professor Posner suggests that increased freedom in the post–World War II world is due not to human rights law but to economic growth and the collapse of communism.

66 David Kennedy, *The International Human Rights Movement: Part of the Problem?* 15 HARV. HUM. RTS. J. 101, 117–18 (2002).

67 *See supra* notes 54–66 and accompanying text.

68 Kennedy, *supra* note 66, at 118 ("This posture makes the human rights movement *itself* seem redemptive—as if doing something *for human rights* was, in and of itself, doing something *against* evil.").

69 *Id.*

hard work of actual treaty implementation.[70] In fact, "[t]he results suggest that not only is treaty ratification not associated with better human rights practices than otherwise expected, but it is often associated with worse practices. Countries that ratify human rights treaties often appear less likely, rather than more likely, to conform to the requirements of the treaties than countries that do not ratify these treaties."[71]

Because the act of ratification can be so substantively hollow, it has been suggested that ratification be followed by international assistance in building the necessary institutions and drafting the necessary legislation to implement treaty objectives.[72] This is of course necessary, and it should be included in standard law and development directives. But in this book, I argue that one cannot pass a law or ratify a treaty or "sign up for a norm"[73] without taking an additional step toward working to bring the norm into being. True, institutional actions—shoring up the local bar, reforming law enforcement and the judiciary—are necessary. But more is needed—the deployment of what I call a culture change, not just an institution-building, legislation-drafting project so that cultural issues are central to the law and development endeavor.

To summarize then, if it is understood, as it increasingly is, that "creating the conditions for the attainment of human rights is a central and irreducible goal of development,"[74] then this very conception entails the adoption of a thick, substantive view of the development project and, as I argue, a meaningful engagement with cultural norms. But to drive the point further, *even* a *thin* definition of rule of law that is typically concerned only with passing laws and reforming institutions, for example, will implicitly, even if not explicitly, entail engagement with basic cultural questions.

It is hardly controversial to declare that law and culture are intertwined.[75] Indeed, even those scholars who are skeptical of my culture change proposal for law and development admit the obvious: "[F]actors that influence law extend far beyond law itself. Legal institutions and cultural attitudes toward law exist inseparably within a broader milieu that includes the history, tradition, and culture of a society."[76] "[L]aw is connected to every aspect of society."[77] For example, international law—the very discipline that provides the overarching framework for law and development (the ancestor of law and development, so to speak)—is hardly neutral or acultural but is itself embedded in a particular cultural history and tradition of Europe. Given its roots in modern Western culture, in the 1800s

---

[70] Oona A. Hathaway, *Do Human Rights Treaties Make a Difference?*, 111 YALE L. J. 1935, 2002–04 (2002).

[71] *Id.* at 1942, 1988. Studies show that certain variables are associated with poorer versus richer human rights records (wars for the former and democracy for the latter, for example).

[72] *Id.* at 2024.

[73] *See supra* notes 68–72 and accompanying text.

[74] WORLD BANK, DEVELOPMENT AND HUMAN RIGHTS: THE ROLE OF THE WORLD BANK 2 (1998). *See also supra* text accompanying notes 35–55.

[75] *See infra* text accompanying notes 79–99.

[76] Tamanaha, *supra* note 48, at 214 (2011).

[77] *Id.*

the "law of nations," as it was then commonly called, was deemed applicable only to the family of Western nations.[78]

As international law is intertwined with culture, so is law and development. Thus, even a minimalist or thin focus that avoids the issue of substantive rights or end goals, for example, is a cultural-bound endeavor. "Merely" reforming institutions, such as the judiciary, to root out corruption so judges will not accept bribes or so they will treat everyone equally before the law,[79] implicitly entails a cultural agenda and "is highly dependent on cultural factors."[80] An efficient and impartial judicial system—something law and development routinely and uncontroversially seeks to establish—requires a culture that values impartiality and efficiency. Many societies, for example, subscribe to a relationship-based framework, and personal loyalties arising from that framework may trump more impersonal principles of equality or justice. Confucianism valued "patriarchal-feudal social relationships supported by natural economy and blood ties"[81] over abstract principles. As recorded in the Analects of Confucius, for example, the Duke of Sheh boasted to Confucius that his subjects were morally upright: "If their father have [*sic*] stolen a sheep, they will bear witness to the fact." Confucius disagreed. "Among us, in our part of the country, those who are upright are different from this. The father conceals the misconduct of the son, and the son conceals the misconduct of the father. Uprightness is to be found in this."[82]

Similarly, in their initial encounters with China, Western commentators observed that Chinese criminal codes did not reflect the principle of equality before the law but allowed magistrates to take status and relations into account.[83] Chinese magistrates were also endowed with a bundle of executive, legislative, and judicial powers[84] which today's law and development practitioners might work to disaggregate. Other rights that law and development projects now routinely seek to establish in developing countries, such as the right of private property, was not recognized in China as recently as the Qing Dynasty

---

[78] Titus Chih-Chieh Chen, *Extraterritoriality: Expanding Exclusive Internal Jurisdiction*, *in* International Norms and Cycles of Change 141, 148–49 (Wayne Standholtz & Kenneth Stiles eds., 2009) ("International law is the product of the special civilization of modern Europe and forms a highly artificial system of which the principles cannot be supposed to be understood or recognized by countries differently civilized. . . .The nations of Europe and American form a family of states, associated together by community of civilization and religion, by treaties, and by the law of nations. . . .").

[79] Stromseth et al., *supra* note 5, at 70 ("The minimalist conception of the rule of law emphasizes the rule of law's formal and structural components, rather than the substantive content of the laws.") (emphasis omitted).

[80] Belton, *supra* note 3, at 10.

[81] Xiao Jie-Fu, *The Enlightenment of Anti-Neo-Confucian Thought During the Ming-Qing Dynasties*,16 J. Chinese Phil. 209, 218 (1989).

[82] Confucius, Analects ch. 13 (James Legge trans., 1801), *available at* http://china.usc.edu/ShowArticle.aspx?articleID=367.

[83] Chen, *supra* note 78, at 146.

[84] *Id.* (noting that local judicial authorities did not only interpret code provisions but also had the power to create new provisions and punishing violators under such new provisions).

because Confucian principles endowed the emperor with absolute authority over his subjects and their possessions.[85]

What would now be considered the standard law and development agenda—promoting "equality before the law," "due process," and "separation of powers," or establishing the right of private property—could not be only about getting the right laws and institutions in place but must also be about engaging the cultural norms that at the time undergirded the Chinese legal order. Although this book adopts a thick, maximalist account of rule of law (and a robust, expansive notion of development), it is important to note that whether the rule of law is viewed in thick or thin terms, it cannot be extricated from culture. For example, instituting an impartial judiciary—a standard, incontrovertible aim in law and development—has to involve more than simply building a courthouse and training judges in what the law is. It must involve transforming a deeply-embedded, value-laden framework that puts personal history and ties above neutral concepts such as "justice is blind."

To make a broader point which has been observed by many others, law generally—not just international law or law and development—is itself embedded in culture. There is a vibrant anthropolitical literature on law and culture.[86] The preeminent sociologist Clifford Geertz remarked as follows: "[L]aw, rather than a mere technical add-on to a morally (or immorally) finished society, is, along of course with a whole range of other cultural realities . . . an active part of it."[87] Lawrence Rosen elaborated on this idea of law *as* culture in his examination of US, English, Continental, Japanese, and Arab case studies in which he demonstrated, for example, how evidentiary rules reflect cultural presuppositions underlying Japanese, Arab, and US societies.[88] Others have noted a deep connection between culture and other aspects of law, such as dispute resolutions. The African Azande's use of a benge oracle—in which a small dose of poison is fed to a chicken with the chicken's death or survival constituting a litigant's guilt or innocence—cannot be meaningful without understanding the role of witchcraft in that society's culture.[89] Whether "primitive" or "modern," institutions of dispute resolution are culturally embedded. For example, the application of legal rules to facts reflects "methods of science

---

[85] *Id.* (stating that the civil and penal code of the Qing dynasty were framed by neo-Confucian principles that granted the emperor supreme dominion over every person and his possessions; "Civil liberties and private property rights were thus alien concepts to Chinese law. . . .").

[86] *See,* e.g., Paul Bohannan, Justice and Judgement among the Tiv (1989); E. E. Evans-Pritchard, Witchcraft, Oracles and Magic Among the Azande (1976); E. E. Evans-Pritchard, The Nuer: A Description of the Modes of Livelihood and Political Institutions of a Nilotic People (1969); Sally Falk Moore, Law as Process: An Anthropological Approach (1978).

[87] Clifford Geertz, *Local Knowledge: Fact and Law in Comparative Perspective, in* Local Knowledge: Further Essays in Interpretive Anthropology 167, 218, 230 (1983).

[88] Rosen, *supra* note 42, at 94–105 (discussing, for example, cultural assumptions underlying the American evidentiary rule regarding dying declarations).

[89] Jerome S. Bruner, *Foreword* to Oscar G. Chase, Law, Culture and Ritual: Disputing Systems in Cross-Cultural Context xi, ix–x (2005).

that have dominated Western thought since the end of the Middle Ages."[90] Indeed, the very trust Americans place in law and in the adversarial system reflects a particularly American cultural view—mistrust of government bureaucracy coupled with an idealism that believes solutions can be found through decentralized processes such as litigation.[91]

Thus, law's correlative relationship with culture has been amply noted and discussed in various scholarly fields.[92] As observed, "[l]egal systems do not float in some cultural void, free of space and time and social context; necessarily, they reflect what is happening in their own societies. In the long run, they assume the shape of these societies, like a glove that molds itself to the shape of a person's hand."[93] "[I]nstitutions reflect the deeply held normative values, authority relations, and metaphysics of the society that produced them."[94] Similarly, "law is so deeply embedded in the particularities of each culture that carving it out as a separate domain and only later making note of its cultural connections distorts the nature of both law and culture."[95] Relatedly, the question of the degree to which law and culture are interdependent has also been long debated, fueling the comparative law discourse on law and culture, specifically, the following legal transplant controversy: whether law is so intertwined with culture that transferring it from one society to another is impossible or whether such legal transplantation is relatively easy and commonplace.[96]

Yet, in the discipline of law and development, culture has somehow been severed from both law and from development. It is as if the above observations about the relationship between law and culture are only applicable to law but strangely not to law and development. Thus the discipline sees only the need for "change across laws, courts . . . law

---

[90] OSCAR G. CHASE, LAW, CULTURE AND RITUAL: DISPUTING SYSTEMS IN CROSS-CULTURAL CONTEXT 41 (2005).

[91] ROBERT A. KAGAN, ADVERSARIAL LEGALISM: THE AMERICAN WAY OF LAW 15–16 (2001), *quoted in* CHASE *supra* note 90, at 49 ("American adversarial legalism, therefore, can be viewed as arising from a fundamental tension between two powerful elements: first, a *political culture* . . . that expects and demands comprehensive governmental protections from serious harm, injustice, and environmental dangers—and hence a powerful activist government—and, second, a set of *governmental structures* that reflect mistrust of concentrated power. . . .").

[92] *See, e.g.*, David Nelken, *Towards a Sociology of Legal Adaptation*, *in* ADAPTING LEGAL CULTURES 7–54 (David Nelken & Johannes Feest eds., 2001); *see also* KENT GREENAWALT, LAW AND OBJECTIVITY 165 (1992) ("Does law within a society reflect dominant cultural norms? In one sense, to ask this question is to answer it. Unless law is imposed from outside by an alien power, a society's law will reflect its patterns of life and morality."); for a refutation of the mirror thesis, *see* BRIAN Z. TAMANAHA, A GENERAL JURISPRUDENCE OF LAW AND SOCIETY 51–133 (2001).

[93] Lawrence Friedman, *Borders: On the Emerging Sociology of Transnational Law*, 32 STAN J. INT'L L. 65, 72 (1996) (footnotes omitted).

[94] CHASE, *supra* note 90, at 46.

[95] ROSEN, *supra* note 42, at xii.

[96] ALAN WATSON, LEGAL TRANSPLANTS: AN APPROACH TO COMPARATIVE LAW (1974); Pierre Legrand, *The Impossibility of "Legal Transplants,"* 4 MAASTRICHT J. EUR. & COMP. L. 111 (1997); *see also* Duncan Kennedy, *Three Globalizations of Law and Legal Thought: 1850–2000*, *in* THE NEW LAW AND ECONOMIC DEVELOPMENT: A CRITICAL APPRAISAL 19 (David M. Trubek & Alvaro Santos eds., 2006).

enforcement . . . [but not] alterations in the cultural and political fabric."[97] This book argues that law and development assistance should operate from a framework that sees how law reflects a culture and shapes it[98] (and vice versa) and how culture might impede desired legal development. It should operate from a baseline acknowledgment that law is "not an autonomous system that is predominantly the product of insulated specialists and experts. More, [legal institutions] are institutions through which social and cultural life is maintained, challenged, and altered, . . . or 'constituted' or 'constructed.'"[99] As a result, this should mean, in practice, that when the underlying objectives of a law as drafted run counter to a set of values subscribed to by a powerful elite and/or by a significant portion of the society, law and development should be willing to confront the "culture side" of the equation. A law and development project should take on even issues that seem to be part of a particular country's proclaimed cultural or national identity or embedded in its cultural makeup. This is harder to achieve than may appear at the outset.

Take CEDAW as an example. Even though ratification of CEDAW, like ratification of many human rights treaties, does not necessarily translate into better human rights practice,[100] its passage is nonetheless a milestone, symbolic and possibly more, for women's rights. One major reason CEDAW is startling is the fact that it specifically calls for ratifying states to change customary, cultural, and religious laws that are premised upon and perpetuate the inequality of the sexes. The preambular language specifically notes that the state parties are "[a]ware that a change in the traditional role of men as well as the role of women in society and in the family is needed to achieve full equality between men and women."[101] CEDAW then obligates state parties to take all appropriate measures "[t] o modify the social and cultural patterns of conduct of men and women, with a view to achieving the elimination of prejudices and customary and all other practices which are based on the idea of the inferiority or the superiority of either the sexes or on stereotyped roles for men and women. . . ."[102] Article 2 subsection (f) requires state parties "[t]o take all appropriate measures, including legislation, to modify or abolish existing laws, regulations, customs and practices which constitute discrimination against women." Article 3 obligates states to address the cultural field "to ensure the full development and advancement of women, for the purpose of guaranteeing them the exercise and enjoyment of human rights and fundamental freedoms on a basis of equality with men."

Over the years, the CEDAW committee has produced many recommendations to help interpret the meanings of the Convention. General Recommendation 21, issued in

---

97 Belton, *supra* note 3, at 10.

98 Bruner, *supra* note 89, at ix.

99 Chase, *supra* note 90, at 2.

100 *See supra* notes 69–71 and accompanying text.

101 Convention on the Elimination of All Forms of Discrimination Against Women, Dec. 18, 1979, pmbl., *opened for signature* Mar. 1, 1980, 1259 U.N.T.S. 13.

102 *See id.* For a feminist critique of CEDAW, *see* Rosa Ehrenreich Brooks, *Feminism and International Law: An Opportunity for Transformation*, 14 Yale J.L. & Feminism 345, 351 (2002).

1994, further emphasizes CEDAW's distinctive approach, that is, its recognition of "the importance of culture and tradition in shaping the thinking and behaviour of men and women and the significant part they play in restricting the exercise of basic rights by women."[103] General Recommendation 23, issued in 1997, states as follows: "In all nations, the most significant factors inhibiting women's ability to participate in public life have been the cultural frameworks of values and religious beliefs, the lack of services and men's failure to share the tasks associated with the organization of the household and with the care and raising of children. In all nations, cultural traditions and religious beliefs have played a part in confining women to the private spheres of activity and excluding them from active participation in public life."[104]

Such provisions tackling culture head-on are astonishingly radical provisions precisely because women's human rights, unlike other basic rights,[105] have been most susceptible to challenge and most likely to be belittled and negated on cultural grounds.[106] The international community has taken one step toward reversing that trend because it has recognized through CEDAW's explicit language calling for culture change that the status of women cannot be enhanced by the passage of laws alone; indeed, despite comprehensive legal reforms designed to promote women's rights, there is little correlation between women's status and the rule of law.[107] Thus, CEDAW's willingness to battle culture is both bold and unique.[108]

---

[103] Merry, *supra* note 44, at 61 (citation omitted).

[104] *Id.* at 62–63 (citation omitted).

[105] *See* Courtney W. Howland, *The Challenge of Religious Fundamentalism to the Liberty and Equality Rights of Women: An Analysis Under the United Nations Charter*, 35 COLUM. J. TRANSNAT'L L. 271 (1997) (discussing how international law does not allow race discrimination to be justified on religious or cultural grounds); Ann Elizabeth Mayer, *A "Benign" Apartheid: How Gender Apartheid Has Been Rationalized*, 5 UCLA J. INT'L L. & FOREIGN AFF. 237 (2000) (comparing how international human rights law treats race versus gender discrimination).

[106] LOUIS HENKIN ET AL., HUMAN RIGHTS 391 (1999) (discussing how "women's human rights" are undermined by cultural relativism); Berta Esperanza Hernandez-Truyol, *Human Rights Through a Gendered Lens: Emergence, Evolution, Revolution*, *in* 1 WOMEN AND INTERNATIONAL HUMAN RIGHTS LAW 3, 37 (Kelly D. Askin & Dorean M. Koenig eds., 1999) ("Women's rights are especially fragile to a claim of 'culture.'"); Arati Rao, *The Politics of Gender and Culture in International Human Rights Discourse*, *in* WOMEN'S RIGHTS, HUMAN RIGHTS: INTERNATIONAL FEMINIST PERSPECTIVES 167, 169 (Peters & Andrea Wolper eds., 1995) ("No social group has suffered greater violation of its human rights in the name of culture than women."); Madhavi Sunder, *Piercing the Veil*, 112 YALE L.J. 1399 (2003); Thomas M. Franck, *Are Human Rights Universal?*, FOREIGN AFF., Jan.–Feb. 2001, at 191 (noting how universal human rights norms are challenged on cultural grounds).

[107] *See* Katharina Pistor, Antara Haldar, & Amrit Amirapu, *Social Norms, Rule of Law, and Gender Reality: An Essay on the Limits of the Dominant Rule of Law Paradigm*, *in* GLOBAL PERSPECTIVES ON THE RULE OF LAW 241–278 (James J. Heckmann et al. eds., 2009).

[108] CEDAW is an international convention binding on ratifying states. There are also other international law documents that address women's rights and culture, but they are not legally binding treaties. For example, the Declaration on the Elimination of Violence against Women adopted unanimously by the General Assembly of the United Nations in 1993 also incorporates culture into its framework. G.A. Res. 48/104, U.N. Doc. A/RES/48/104 (Dec. 20, 1993). Article 1 of this nonbinding Declaration defines violence against women

In the end, however, CEDAW is badly compromised because it is riddled with reservations that cancel out the very obligations ratifying states had undertaken to adopt. In order to get as many states to ratify CEDAW as possible, signatory states are free to use the opt-out provisions of the treaty to make reservations on the grounds that certain treaty obligations interfere with religious or customary laws, which in turn negate those treaty provisions that ironically also obligate states to alter the very religious or customary laws that reproduce gender inequality. Many Middle Eastern and Islamic countries, such as Bangladesh, Egypt, Iraq, Kuwait, Malaysia, Maldives, and Morocco, justified their reservations on the basis that parts of the treaty were contrary to sharia. India, Israel, and Singapore made similar reservations on general religious grounds. India, Kuwait, Morocco, Niger, Singapore, and Tunisia expressed reservations based on customary laws and cultural mores.[109]

CEDAW, in other words, creates certain obligations on the one hand and then simultaneously nullifies them on the other. Anticipating that many states would not ratify CEDAW if they were obligated to change cultural norms, CEDAW chose the formality of ratification over a culture change obligation. International human rights law might have succumbed to cultural claims for an additional reason—anxiety that pressing the culture button would trigger charges of cultural insensitivity. Indeed, some have charged that "the critique of culture builds on imperial understandings of culture as belonging to the domain of the primitive or backward, in contrast to the civilization of the colonizer. Residues of this understanding of culture emerge in contemporary human rights law."[110]

Despite calls by the United Nations for states to ratify CEDAW without reservations or for states that have ratified with reservations to withdraw their reservations,[111] the

---

broadly to include physical, sexual, and psychological harm or threats of harm in public or private life. It also prohibits invoking custom, tradition, or religious considerations to avoid its obligations. *Id.* at art. 4.

[109] *Declarations, Reservations, and Objections to CEDAW*, http://www.un.org/womenwatch/daw/cedaw/reservations-country.htm (last visited Feb. 20, 2015); *see also* LIESBETH LIJNZAAD, RESERVATIONS TO UN-HUMAN RIGHTS TREATIES: RATIFY AND RUIN? 307 (1995) (describing Bangladesh, Egypt, and Iraq's objections based on sharia law).

[110] Merry, *supra* note 44, at 60.

[111] *See* Report of the Fourth World Conference on Women, ¶ 230(c), U.N. Doc. A/CONF. 177/20 (1995) (calling on states parties to CEDAW to "consider withdrawing reservations . . . [and] ensure that no reservations are incompatible with the object and purpose of the Convention or otherwise incompatible with international treaty law and regularly review them with a view to withdrawing them. . . ."); Press Release, Commission on Human Rights, Commission on Human Rights Takes Up Integration of Human Rights of Women and Gender Perspective, UN Press Release HR/CN/909 (Apr. 13, 1999), *available at* http://www.un.org/News/Press/docs/1999/19990413.hrcn909.html (recommending that "all Governments should ratify, without reservation, the Convention on the Elimination of all Forms of Discrimination Against Women"); *see generally* General Recommendations Made by the Committee on the Elimination of Discrimination Against Women, General Recommendation No. 4 (1987), at http://www.un.org/womenwatch/daw/cedaw/recomm.htm (expressing concern in 1987 over reservations to CEDAW and suggesting "that all States parties concerned reconsider such reservations with a view to withdrawing them").

reservations have remained in place.[112] Not only that, but states that ratified with reservations have gone on the attack, retaliating against their critics by lobbing charges of cultural imperialism.[113]

That CEDAW expects culture-based reservations to be made and then accommodates such reservations is revealing and significant for the purpose of this book. First, the CEDAW example shows that international law and international human rights law, as currently conceptualized, is not equipped to address culture. Both avoid confrontation with it and as a result, end up accommodating or capitulating to it, even when cultural norms are at odds with development values. Rather than focus on getting states to ratify CEDAW for the mere sake of ratification, it is better to work on changing the conditions, whether they be legal or cultural, that would accomplish the objectives of the treaty and enhance the well-being of those the treaty is supposed to protect. Where women's rights are concerned, CEDAW proves how difficult it is for international law, even international human rights law, to avoid "'falling into the trap of cultural relativism . . . ,"[114] as the Algerian-based nongovernmental organization (NGO) Women Living Under Muslim Laws (WLUML) aptly put it. As WLUML observed, "in the name of the right to difference, they are prepared to support any practice, be it totally unjust and against the common understanding of human rights, if so-called 'authentic leaders' of the community justify it by reference to culture or religion."[115]

Second, as I plan to discuss in Chapter 1, law and development must extricate itself from the acultural traditions of international law. It must, for example, embrace CEDAW's call to change cultural norms without submitting this very call to a cultural exception.

Third, it follows then that the law and development agenda should reach beyond legal and economic dimensions conventionally associated with "law" and "development" to promote a broad vision of development that has increasingly been accepted by the human rights and the development communities. American governmental officials at the top echelon, such as Secretary of State Hillary Clinton under the Obama administration,

---

112 Turkey, however, did withdraw reservations based on religion. *See Declarations, Reservations, and Objections to CEDAW*, http://www.un.org/womenwatch/daw/cedaw/reservations-country.htm (last visited June 10, 2015) ("Reservations of the Government of the Republic of Turkey with regards to the articles of the Convention dealing with family relations which are not completely compatible with the provisions of the Turkish Civil Code, in particular article 15, paragraphs 2 and 4, and article 16, paragraphs 1 (c), (d), (f) and (g).... on 20 September 1999, the Government of Turkey notified the Secretary-General of a partial withdrawal.... the Government of the Republic of Turkey has decided to withdraw its reservations made upon [accession to] the Convention on the Elimination of All Forms of Discrimination Against Women with regard to article 15, paragraphs 2 and 4, and article 16, paragraphs 1 (c), (d), (f) and (g).").

113 Mayer, *supra* note 105, at 271 (describing how efforts to achieve ratification of CEDAW without reservations have been characterized as Western attack on Islam and on national cultures); *see* Howland, *supra* note 105 (comparing the refusal to accept religious or cultural justifications for racial apartheid to the easy acceptance of such claims in the case of women's rights).

114 Sunder, *supra* note 106, at 1440.

115 *Id.*

increasingly understand that "development, democracy, and human rights can and must be mutually reinforcing."[116] Indeed it is now generally accepted in many circles that there is a positive linkage between development and human rights, and it is understood that development is intertwined with broader objectives such as human rights promotion.[117] "The world now accepts that sustainable development is impossible without human rights. What has been missing is the recognition that the advancement of an interconnected set of human rights is impossible *without development*."[118] It is also understood that development should be part of a broader framework of political and social institutions that promote basic rights. Studies have also shown a strong empirical link between civil liberties and performance of government projects.[119] Even the World Bank, an institution that once saw its mission in narrow, technocratic terms,[120] adopted a new Comprehensive Development Framework in 1999 that emphasizes a "long-term" and "holistic approach to development" to achieve "a better balance in policymaking by highlighting the interdependence of all elements of development—social, structural, human, governance, environmental, economic, and financial."[121] As I explain below, a cultural loophole such as that permitted by CEDAW would not be compatible with this thicker,

---

[116] Hillary Rodham Clinton, US Sec'y of State, *Remarks to the Center for Global Development*, Washington D.C. (Jan. 6, 2010), *available at* http://www.state.gov/secretary/rm/2010/01/134838.htm ("So those who care about making human rights a reality know that development is an integral part of that agenda."). True, there are states such as China and even post-genocide Rwanda that experience economic growth but not increased political freedom and civil rights. These countries are less politically repressive and more politically open than they were before economic development. Moreover, as Sen argues, political development and human rights are integral to and constitutive of "development." *See* SEN, *supra* note 30, at 146–59.

[117] Ana Palacio, *The Way Forward: Human Rights and the World Bank*, *in* WORLD BANK INSTITUTE, DEVELOPMENT OUTREACH Oct. 2006, at 35; Brodnig, *supra* note 36, at 9 (arguing in favor of integrating human rights objectives with the objectives of the World Bank because "development represents a bundle of interlocking concepts of very broad environmental, socioeconomic, legal and institutional implications, including the protection and promotion of human rights."); *see also* WORLD BANK, HUMAN RIGHTS AND DEVELOPMENT: THE ROLE OF THE WORLD BANK 1998; UNITED NATIONS, COMMON UNDERSTANDING ON A HUMAN RIGHTS BASED APPROACH TO DEVELOPMENT (2003), *available at* http://hrbaportal.org/the-human-rights-based-approach-to-development-cooperation-towards-a-common-understanding-among-un-agencies; WORLD DEVELOPMENT REPORT, EQUITY AND DEVELOPMENT (2006).

[118] WORLD BANK, DEVELOPMENT AND HUMAN RIGHTS: THE ROLE OF THE WORLD BANK 2 (1998).

[119] Jonathan Isham, Daniel Kaufmann, & Lant H. Pritchett, *Civil Liberties, Democracy and the Performance of Government Projects* (1997), 11 WORLD BANK ECON. REV. 219 (1997); *but cf.* ROBERT BARRO, DETERMINANTS OF ECONOMIC GROWTH: A CROSS-COUNTRY EMPIRICAL STUDY (1997); Robert Barro, *Economic Growth in a Cross Section of Countries*, 106 Q. J. ECON. 407 (1991) (discussing research which shows that countries with substantial political and civil rights violations are characterized by lower levels of economic growth).

[120] *See* Belton, *supra* note 3, at 6.

[121] Brodnig, *supra* note 36, at 7. The Bank's Comprehensive Development Framework states that "[w]ithout the protection of human and property rights, and a comprehensive framework of laws, no equitable development is possible." *See also* Lan Cao, *An Evaluation of the World Bank's Comprehensive Development Framework*, *in* PRIVATISING DEVELOPMENT: TRANSNATIONAL LAW, INFRASTRUCTURE AND HUMAN RIGHTS 27, 27–63 (2005).

more robust, and holistic understanding of development that is increasingly accepted by the law and development community.

Against this background, Amartya Sen, the noted Nobel Laureate in economics, has argued eloquently in favor of an expansive understanding of development.[122] For Sen, development means freedom and maximizing well-being, taken broadly to mean maximizing capabilities—to participate freely in the political process, to satisfy hunger, to have access to social networks and connections, reliable information sources and structures.[123] This does not mean a shift from or abandonment of the conventional economic inquiry. To the contrary. Economic growth is all the more necessary to implement such a broad, substantive development agenda.[124] It is not surprising, then, that the author of an empirical study of a number of Asian countries concluded that "[a]lthough money is not everything, it is essential. In the subtle and complex interplay of economics, politics, culture, law and institutions in determining rights performance, what matters most is wealth. Put bluntly if somewhat too simply, if you want better performance across a range of rights and indicators of human wellbeing, *show me the money.*"[125] Indeed, growth can enhance the capacity for development because "increased incomes will increase the range of choices and capabilities enjoyed by households and governments."[126] But economic growth without more is not development. As Sen explained, development includes the capacity of an individual to act as his or her own agent to translate "potential into functionings . . . "and indeed influencing personal and public action in ways that determine the future formation of capabilities."[127] Sen's capability approach has been subsequently endorsed by the philosopher Martha Nussbaum, who sought "to articulate an account of how capabilities, together with the idea of a threshold level of capabilities, can provide a basis for central constitutional principles that citizens have a right to demand from their governments."[128]

Sen's and Nussbaum's groundbreaking work provide a platform upon which law and development can "argue for the place of values in economic analysis and in the politics

---

[122] SEN, *supra* note 30; *see also* AMARTYA SEN, CHOICE, WELFARE AND MEASUREMENT (1992).

[123] *See* SEN, *supra* note 30, at 10 (enumerating five freedoms as "(1) *political freedoms*, (2) *economic facilities*, (3) *social opportunities*, (4) *transparency guarantees* and (5) *protective security*. Each of these distinct types of rights and opportunities helps to advance the general capability of a person. They may also serve to complement each other. Public policy to foster human capabilities and substantive freedoms in general can work through the promotion of these distinct but interrelated instrumental freedoms.").

[124] Randall Peerenboom, *Show Me the Money: The Dominance of Wealth in Determining Rights Performance in Asia*, 15 DUKE J. COMP. & INT'L L. 75, 75 (2004).

[125] *Id.* at 81.

[126] Gustav Ranis, *Human Development and Economic Growth* 1 (Yale Univ. Econ. Growth Ctr., Discussion Paper No. 887, May 2004).

[127] *See also* Rao & Walton, *supra* note 49, at 12.

[128] MARTHA C. NUSSBAUM, WOMEN AND HUMAN DEVELOPMENT: THE CAPABILITIES APPROACH 12 (2000).

of welfare and well-being,"[129] values such as enhancing freedom, dignity, and individual capability. On a different but related note, the anthropologist Arjun Appadurai views such capability in terms of "voice." Using Hirschman's framework laid out in his groundbreaking book, *Exit, Voice, and Loyalty: Responses to Decline in Firms, Organizations, and States*, Appadurai argues that it is especially important in law and development to focus on increasing the capacity of the poor to have their voice heard. Exit is not an option for the world's poor and loyalty is not clear-cut, leaving voice as the only viable and potentially powerful tool to alleviate poverty. For Appadurai, alleviating poverty means working to strengthen the capacity of the poor to exercise their voice,[130] not only because this capacity is tied to democratic principles of inclusion and participation but also because "[i]t is the only way in which the poor might find locally plausible ways to alter . . . the terms of recognition in any particular cultural regime." Appadurai's "terms of recognition" refer to "the conditions and constraints under which the poor negotiate with the very norms that frame their social lives."[131]

"Voice," in other words, is tied to "cultural capacity," that is, the capacity to "engage social, political, and economic issues in terms of ideologies, doctrines, and norms which are widely shared and credible, even by the rich and powerful."[132] In this way, "voice" also affects what Appadurai calls the "capacity to aspire"[133]—to express "wants, preferences, choices, and calculations."[134] The cultural and economic context in which different groups live affect their capacity to aspire, which in turn functions as a "navigational capacity" with the privileged better equipped to use "the map of its norms to explore the future more frequently and more realistically, and to share this knowledge with one another more routinely than their poorer and weaker neighbors."[135]

As others have observed, "the recognition that societies consist of different groups, often structured in hierarchies with unequal social and cultural capital, . . . suggests that mechanisms of inter-group exchange and deliberation need to be set up in a manner that changes the terms of recognition."[136] Inequality and poverty and other issues development is concerned with must be addressed in not just political and economic but also cultural terms. Scholars in other disciplines, development economics and sociology, for example, increasingly understand and acknowledge that "[c]ulture is . . . fundamentally

---

[129] Arjun Appadurai, *The Capacity to Aspire: Culture and the Terms of Recognition*, *in* CULTURE AND PUBLIC ACTION 59, 63 (Vijayendra Rao & Michael Walton eds., 2004).

[130] *Id.* at 63, 66.

[131] *Id.* at 66.

[132] *Id.* at 66–67.

[133] *Id.* at 67.

[134] *Id.; see also* W. ARTHUR LEWIS, THEORY OF ECONOMIC GROWTH 29 (1955) ("[W]ants are limited because the goods that one knows about and can be used are limited.").

[135] Appadurai, *supra* note 129, at 69; *see also* Rao & Walton, *supra* note 49, at 25 ("[T]he subordinate group faces adverse cultural terms of trade that affects its ability to aspire to a better life, while the dominant group faces favorable cultural terms of trade that gives it the ability to maintain its dominant position.").

[136] Yousfi, *supra* note 8, at 29.

linked to the perpetuation of inequality."[137] Economic growth is no longer understood to be sufficient. "Creating an enabling environment to move towards a culturally equitable form of development through social transformation becomes one of the priorities of the development agenda."[138]

From this perspective, development needs to be grounded in Sen's capability approach, incorporating the objective of increasing the poor's voice and the poor's capacity to aspire. I argue that a focus on capability and voice on the one hand necessarily entails a focus on culture on the other hand because the two are linked. Indeed, the capacity to aspire, as Appadurai himself observes, "is by definition an approach to culture, since capacities form parts of sets, and are always part of a local design of means and ends, values and strategies, experiences and tested insights."[139] Because "political cultures [can be] either forces for the reproduction or transformation of inequalities,"[140] increasing the poor's voice necessarily entails an examination of cultural norms. This means that when established norms muffle the capacity of the poor and other marginal groups to exercise "voice," the law and development project must aim toward "achieving more effective poverty reduction through patterns of cultural change that . . . strengthen the voice of poorer groups. . . ."[141] The very process of aspiration and contestation will "change the terms of recognition, indeed the cultural framework itself."[142]

Within this framework that sees capacity and voice as development issues, the rights of women should be a matter of absolute priority for law and development. As Sen noted, women's rights "are important not merely for gender equity (a crucial enough cause even on its own), but also for benefits for all (men, women and children), for example through reduction of child mortality and diminution of high fertility rates. Recent research has brought out the far-reaching role of justice to women which influences nearly every aspect of economic, social, political and legal development, and which call for legal and judicial reform aimed specifically at this objective."[143] For example, the widespread practice of dowries, supported by deeply embedded cultural norms, has economic and human rights implications. Economically speaking, "[d]owry payments are transfers of wealth

---

137 *Id.*

138 *Id.*

139 Appadurai, *supra* note 129, at 70.

140 Rao & Walton, *supra* note 49, at 26–27; *see also* Fernando Calderon & Alicia Szmukler, *Political Culture and Development*, *in* CULTURE AND PUBLIC ACTION 281, 281 (Vijayendra Rao & Michael Walton eds., 2004) (describing how "[t]he political cultures that historically have been dominant in Latin America limit the development of people's and communities' capabilities . . . by emphasizing differences and by stigmatizing and lowering the other (whether poor, woman, indigenous, migrant, black, or mestizo.)").

141 Rao & Walton, *supra* note 49, at 26.

142 Appadurai, *supra* note 129, at 67.

143 Amartya Sen, Address at the World Bank Legal Conference: What is the Role of Legal and Judicial Reform in the Development Process? 20 (June 5, 2000) (transcript available at http://issat.dcaf.ch/Home/Community-of-Practice/Resource-Library/Policy-and-Research-Papers/What-is-the-role-of-legal-and-judicial-reform-in-the-development-process).

from the family of the bride to the groom and his family at the time of marriage."[144] These payments may have a distortionary impact on the way money is spent. Because resources are transferred away from the couple to the older generation who may have "a lower propensity to save or to invest in the education of the couple's children, these marriage practices may slow down the accumulation of physical and/or human capital."[145]

From a women's rights perspective, dowry also has other disturbing consequences: "[F]orward-looking parents may resort to selective abortion or female infanticide in order to avoid dowry payments in the future. Other consequences that have been documented include bride-burning or wifebeating, in case payments from the bridal family are considered insufficient."[146]

As commentators have noted, marriage payments have been outlawed in many countries. Yet in the language of economics, "the reason these norms persist is that they are part of a 'market equilibrium' in which families are the players and strategies of 'conformity' dominate unilateral deviations towards no payments. How to induce an equilibrium switch from the 'everyone pays' to the 'nobody pays' equilibrium is a dramatically important, and still open, question."[147] In other words, these cultural norms need to be changed. How law and development can accomplish culture change is discussed in Chapter 5.

Other damaging practices that are culturally supported include adolescent, and worse, child marriage of girls. Some girls as young as five are married off; ten to twelve million girls suffer from child marriages every year.[148] In Yemen, Afghanistan, Ethiopia, and other countries, the husbands may be much older—young men, widowers, "or even abductors who rape first and claim their victims as wives afterwards."[149] "Forced early marriage thrives in many regions, often in defiance of national laws."[150] The health consequences for girls are severe—torn vaginal walls, internal ruptures called fistulas which usually result in lifelong incontinence. Studies have estimated that "postponing marriage by one year in the age range 11–16 would increase girls' schooling by an average of 0.3 years, and increase adult literacy by 6.5 per cent."[151]

The discussion above shows that in both instances, development as understood by Sen and Appadurai goes beyond the technocratic details associated with establishing

[144] Eliana La Ferrara, *Family and Kinship Ties in Development*, *in* Culture, Institutions, and Development: New Insights into an Old Debate 107, 111 (Jean Philippe-Platteau & Robert Peccoud eds., 2011).

[145] *Id.* at 113 (citation omitted).

[146] *Id.*

[147] *Id.*

[148] Cynthia Gorney, *Too Young to Wed: The Secret of Child Brides*, Nat'l Geographic Mag. (June 2011), http://ngm.nationalgeographic.com/2011/06/child-brides/gorney-text/1.

[149] *Id.*

[150] *Id.*

[151] Ferrara, *supra* note 144, at 113.

laws and institutions or increasing economic growth. Development viewed in terms of enhancing freedom, voice, and aspiration requires one to situate the "conditions and constraints under which the poor negotiate with the very norms that frame their social lives."[152] Cultural values and norms become an intrinsic part of the development process. Thus development requires addressing not just contract or property laws or even human rights laws but also cultural norms that are antithetical to development.

Ironically, law and development's kinship and affiliation with the international human rights movement, which has been devoted to critiquing the state and not culture, may be one reason why it has shied from "critiquing, contesting, and remaking culture."[153] As a result, while paying lip service to other values (for example, the broad substantive norms of development), law and development has instead devoted itself to implementing the "rule of law," in essence, immersing itself in the vocabulary of law at the expense of development and culture. In this way, law and development has allowed "law" to overshadow "development." But the two cannot be conflated.

That development is not synonymous with the rule of law has been noted by others. For example, Brian Tamanaha observed that legal development should not be conflated with law and development, arguing that despite failures in law and development, legal development is taking place. Conceptually separating legal development from law and development is important so that the failures of the latter would not be falsely ascribed to the former.[154] I too agree that " 'law and development' is different from 'legal development.' " But my point is that legal development alone is insufficient to establish development.

One could perhaps defend law and development's decision to narrowly focus on legal expertise this way. By hitching law and development to the "rule of law" movement, proponents might believe that the *norms and values* underlying the laws and legal institutions deemed conducive to development would be transmitted via law generally and human rights laws in particular. Law would be established, and the norms embedded in such laws would emerge without having to undertake a separate and inevitably more controversial culture change agenda.

Yet because law and development is not only an economic or legal process but also a "cultural process,"[155] culture must be engaged and not just indirectly but directly. To the extent that the rule of law component is addressed in its thin, minimalist, or technocratic dimensions, culture is completely sidestepped. Law and development may, given its limited objective, be only concerned with law's "formal and structural components."[156] Culture would be invisible to that limited mission. But my point is that even

---

[152] Appadurai, *supra* note 129, at 66.

[153] Sunder, *supra* note 106, at 1443.

[154] Tamanaha, *supra* note 48, at 216.

[155] Mariano Grondona, *A Cultural Typology of Economic Development*, *in* CULTURE MATTERS: HOW VALUES SHAPE HUMAN PROGRESS 44, 46 (Lawrence E. Harrison & Samuel P. Huntington eds., 2000).

[156] STROMSETH ET AL., *supra* note 5, at 70.

when the rule of law component is addressed in its thicker, more substantive dimensions (to include human rights, for example), it is not enough to do so on the hope that cultural norms will somehow be automatically transported along with the export of law. That law will foster culture change should not be assumed. Indeed, even in developed countries such as the United States, where the rule of law is established, numerous scholars have questioned the ability of courts and law, as manifested in legislative actions, to reverse entrenched cultural patterns and effectuate social change. For example, some scholars have argued that the ability of courts, even the US Supreme Court, to secure racial gains in areas such as school desegregation is overstated.[157] And even when statutory laws supposedly reflecting majoritarian support for their underlying objectives were enacted, and robustly enforced by courts, the available evidence suggests that "statutes do not necessarily evidence broad cultural support for the regulated matter, making enforcement difficult."[158] Certainly antisegregation legislation was important but as some, relying on historical estimates, have surmised, the antisegregation "campaign would need seventy years of cultural and political change to achieve the necessary convergence of both black and white support to achieve success."[159]

With the purpose of proposing an explicit, upfront culture change agenda, the book examines specific instances in which culture change projects have been pursued, provides a comprehensive assessment of the pitfalls inevitably bound up in such endeavors, and evaluates their overall success and failure. The book draws from a wide array of examples in its examination of culture change projects. Some fall squarely within what most people associate with a human rights framework but also implicate development, for example, female genital mutilation, footbinding, caste, and restrictions on educating girls. These practices constrict freedom and voice. They are included in the book because they undermine the values of law and development and constrict women's capabilities. Yet other practices arguably fit a more market-oriented view of law and development. Examples of the latter include the prohibition on charging interest because it is an essential part of the "Islamic way of life"; personalistic and group-focused relationships as well as patterns of authority that discourage individual wealth accumulation, especially by those not from the traditional ruling elites; deeply entrenched community conservatism that enforces strict redistributive practices and utilizes ostracism and other terror tactics (including inflammatory charges of witchcraft) to punish those, especially women, who defy patriarchal authority and manage nonetheless to accumulate private wealth. Note that in referring to some practices as falling more squarely within a human rights versus market framework, I do so with full awareness of the relationship between the market

---

157 Michael J. Klarman, *Brown, Racial Change, and the Civil Rights Movement*, 80 Va. L. Rev. 7 (1994); Michael J. Klarman, *How Brown Changed Race Relations: The Backlash Thesis*, 81 J. Am. Hist. 81 (1994).

158 Davison M. Douglas, *The Limits of Law in Accomplishing Racial Change: School Segregation in the Pre-Brown North*, 44 UCLA L. Rev. 677, 682 (1997).

159 *Id.* at 684.

and freedom itself. As Sen observed, markets have been praised because they generally produce growth and increase living standards, but this focus on utility and wealth should not obscure the market's role in securing freedom of exchange and hence "the central value of freedom itself."[160]

The book advocates confronting not just specific practices but also general inclinations, values, preferences, or mindset that impede development and poverty alleviation. Examples include certain views about authority and dominance, status as an inherited rather than acquired attribute, resulting often in the perpetuation of patriarchal domination as male status is equated with authority, wealth, and power; the relationship between the collective and the individual whereby the well-being of the latter is diminished; superstitions and the tendency to exalt the past; the continuing attachment by marginal groups to "norms and beliefs that directly support their own degradation."[161] As Appadurai observed, the poor are "frequently in a position where they are encouraged to subscribe to norms whose social effect is to further diminish their dignity, exacerbate their inequality, and deepen their lack of access to material goods and services."[162] Thus norms that are problematic for poverty alleviation must be changed. As he explained, "[i]n the Indian case, these norms take a variety of forms: some have to do with fate, luck, and rebirth; others have to do with the glorification of asceticism and material deprivation; yet others connect social deference to deference to divinity; yet others reduce major metaphysical assumptions to simple and rigid rules of etiquette which promise freedom from reprisal."[163]

In essence then, what I am addressing is the cultural framework of development and the need to engage those cultural norms that affect development objectives, broadly understood. In addition to the examples referred to in the preceding paragraphs, a significant portion of the "culture change" discussion of the book is devoted to several country-specific case studies: Japan, Turkey, and Germany—Japan during the 1868–1912 Meiji era and post–World War II era; Turkey after the collapse of the Ottoman Empire; and Germany after World War II. These case studies serve as illustrations of national development and reconstruction with a robust, cultural component. For example, Meiji Japan implemented not only an array of the usual run-of-the-mill rule of law prescriptions but also pursued many of the culture-based measures I advocate in the book. In other words, the Japanese emphasis on reforming existing codes and laws and writing new ones in an effort to modernize fits squarely within today's conventional rule of law agenda. But the Japanese also embarked on a radical and ambitious program to transform traditional Japanese values deemed necessary to successfully promote the much touted modernization campaign. This effort may, in essence, be viewed as part of "an ongoing, managerial process of persuading or teaching the masses to internalize appropriate values"[164] necessary

---

160 SEN, *supra* note 30, at 28; *see also id.* at 25–31.

161 Appadurai, *supra* note 129, at 65.

162 *Id.* at 66.

163 *Id.*

164 SHELDON GARON, MOLDING JAPANESE MINDS: THE STATE IN EVERYDAY LIFE 7 (1997).

for modernization and development. Similarly, Japan's post–World War II experience also involved sweeping cultural changes. During the occupation period under General Douglas MacArthur's command, Japan entered a deep and profound "soul searching" about its militaristic tradition. Many in Japan embraced American efforts to democratize Japan and to instill democratic values into Japanese society. This "cultural revolution from above," however, was also accompanied by a "revolution from below," with enormous grassroots support for a national re-examination of militaristic values in favor of values that promote peace and nonaggression. Indeed, deliberate efforts were undertaken at all levels of society to engage in a thorough examination of Japanese culture—through songs, advertising, magazines—to transform a traumatized and defeated country into a free-market democracy and a stronghold against Communist expansion.

Turkey's modernization also highlighted a cultural shift toward secularism, with legal, economic, and cultural reforms undertaken to promote the modernization of Turkish society. This new secular state ideology came to be known as Kemalism and provided the foundation for modern Turkey. Where the Ottoman Empire had granted significant autonomy to religious communities, including the right to be governed by their own religious and cultural laws,[165] Kemalist reforms meant that recognition to such separate religious enclaves had to be withdrawn. A national law would be applicable to the entire country. Modern Turkey under Atatürk, however, defined a Turk as any citizen of the Turkish Republic, regardless of religion, culture, or ethnicity. This section in the book looks at the cultural framework in which a national identity was created and nurtured, transcending religious and ethnic divisions. Atatürk's goal was to mold a nation that would be an equal to that of the West, not a subordinate to be colonized. To that end, his reforms consisted of ridding the country of the vestiges of old systems and ideals and adopting modern customs, even down to replacing the fez with a Western brimmed hat and replacing Arabic script with Latin script as the dominant alphabet.

Post–Second World War Germany is often hailed as one of the greatest and most successful examples of nation-wide reconstruction by an external actor. The Allies, and most significantly the United States in the eastern half of Germany, managed to transform this former fascist nation into the democratic and prosperous "engine of Europe." In the years following World War II, the allies embarked on an ambitious mission defined by four goals, known as the "4 Ds": democratization, denazification, demilitarization, and decartelization. In order to achieve each of these goals, the Allies recognized that they could not simply pass laws and expect Germany to transform overnight. Instead, the Allies tackled the cultural underpinnings of the nation which had led to Hitler and National Socialism. In particular, the Americans used film and popular culture to undermine the traditional German military culture and to sell the idea of democracy to the German

[165] Each separate religious community was called a millet, and separate millets were established for Muslims, Greek Orthodox Christians, Armenian Apostolic Christians, Syriac Orthodox Christians, and Jews.

people. The Americans particularly viewed the transformation of the German economy to a capitalist society as an integral and inseparable part of the nation's democratization. However, one of the most remarkable aspects of the German transformation is that, while the main outlines of the project were drafted and imagined outside of the country, it was the Germans who eventually implemented and reshaped these policies into something uniquely their own. The Germany today is the product of collaboration between the Germans themselves and the Allies. Many of the policies enacted by the Allies were taken and shaped in unexpected ways by the reactions, interpretations, and biases of the German populace. The book will explore the ways the external and internal policy makers used culture as a tool for change outside the realm of pure lawmaking.

While these experiences may be of interest to scholars in Japanese, Turkish, and/or German history or scholars of comparative law generally, I propose that they be studied not only for their historical or comparative interest but also for law and development purposes. Some critics may view these examples as being far afield from contemporary law and development challenges. I disagree. Postconflict societies such as Japan and Germany can serve as positive examples for law and development projects currently pursued in postconflict societies today. Postconflict societies are not simply smoking ruins or blank slates on which brand new societies can be conceived and constructed. Indeed, it is no easy task to remake postconflict societies, as the examples of the Democratic Republic of Congo, Sudan, and Sierra Leone demonstrate.

Thus, I include these three historical examples although none of the three case studies are formally understood or categorized as rule of law or law and development efforts. In fact, law and development as a discipline or a movement began only in the 1960s, and events that occurred prior to that time would scarcely register as a law and development moment. Nonetheless, all three should serve as interesting case studies of a law and development model that pushes the conventional boundaries and, as proposed in this book, undertakes to examine and alter values, norms, habits, and mindset that are usually associated with the "stuff" we call culture. Although it is possible their particular experiences cannot be precisely replicated in today's environment, nonetheless they speak to those who are skeptical of my proposed culture change project—that is, skepticism about whether deliberate and systematic culture change is even possible (much less normatively desirable). These examples demonstrate that it is.

The book also examines recent law and development experiences such as Kosovo, Iraq, and Afghanistan. All three represent recent law and development efforts, or more precisely, rule of law reform. As I will discuss, the work done in these countries has essentially followed the conventional law-entered path and continues to be guided by the assumption that law is central to the development process. Ironically, the Japan, Turkey, and Germany examples, which I argue better incorporate the culture-focused approach I propose in the book, are not even considered law and development projects per se. By contrast, what passes as actual law and development efforts, past or present, tend to be law-centered and institution-centered, to the exclusion of culture.

The experiences of Kosovo, Iraq, and Afghanistan are worth studying for an additional reason. In recent years, law and development in postconflict countries such as Kosovo, East Timor, Bosnia, Haiti, Somalia, Liberia, Sierra Leone, Afghanistan, and Iraq has become more prevalent because international interventions have proliferated—under the guises not of expansionism or colonialism but democracy promotion, national or international security considerations, and humanitarianism. States nowadays defend their intervention by resorting to a mix of humanitarian and security claims. Imperialism is no longer in vogue and no intervention in today's modern world can be made under its name. Thus, recent interventions have been undertaken within a framework that may be aptly termed "liberal imperialism."[166] Against this background, interveners disavow interest in permanent occupation or resource exploitation and instead must pledge themselves to securing peace and security, protecting the civilian population, providing mundane and basic services such as trash pickup, and fostering democratic institutions. The very legitimacy of the interveners' intervention thus may rest on the success of law and development.

Under such circumstances, law and development becomes more of a pressing need because in today's modern world, "interventionists must generally make a public commitment to building just, democratic, peaceful, and prosperous societies in the areas that they control, if they are to avoid worldwide condemnation."[167] But postconflict reconstruction is bound to be slow and marred by setbacks that might overshadow partial progress (which is why examples drawn from the Germany and Japan case studies can be useful). Postconflict countries tend to be characterized by certain problems unique to a postconflict setting, for example, the need to achieve a minimum level of security and support for the interveners' policies, in addition to the institution of rule of law objectives. UN efforts to establish rule of law institutions in East Timor, for example, cost hundreds of millions of dollars per year.[168] After overseeing the creation of a constitution and the execution of free-and-fair elections, the United Nations declared the mission complete and handed the reins to Timorese leaders.[169] Within four years, East Timor had reverted to a state of violence and instability.[170] The United Nations had given East Timor the institutional "training wheels" of a functioning rule of law democracy, but postconflict societies are particularly fragile and fraught with difficulties. Measuring success by reference to a short-time frame or by the institution of formal institutions can only tell an incomplete and often distorted picture. Alas, it is more often than not that

---

[166] Stromseth et al., *supra* note 5, at 3.

[167] *Id.* at 4 ("Since today's interventionists generally intervene in the name of global order and 'the rule of law,' they must consequently strive to build the rule of law in the societies in which they intervene, at risk of losing their own global credibility.").

[168] Robert McMahon, *Seeking a Patient Path to Nationbuilding*, 83 Foreign Service J., no. 11, Nov. 2006 at 22, 23.

[169] *Id.*

[170] *Id.*

law and development in postconflict states necessitate long-term and often open-ended commitment and as such, are "likely to be less than popular with domestic constituencies concerned about how their tax dollars are spent."[171]

And yet, as already stated, the legitimacy of the intervention itself may be bound up with the success or failure of law and development. Indeed, "military interventions that do not ultimately rebuild the rule of law in post-conflict societies are doomed to undermine their own goals."[172] To effectively promote law and development, culture needs to be incorporated as a component of law and development, and this is the case for post-conflict societies as well.

Throughout the book, the countries selected are varied and eclectic for several reasons. First, I do not intend for the book to have a singular regional focus, whether it be Asia or Europe or Africa or Latin America. Second, the concrete examples are not meant to be country-specific case studies of the kind an expert in the country in question—for example, a China, Japan, or Islamic scholar—might undertake. Rather, the examples are studied within a law and development framework for the limited purpose of pursuing the question set forth in this book: Is culture change possible, and, if so, to what extent and under what circumstances can culture change be pursued in different countries? My aim is to study, through different examples, how a cultural analysis is applicable to a wide range of problematic scenarios implicating practices that have a negative impact on development, understood to encompass human rights and markets, as well as other emerging development objectives such as freedom, voice, and capacity. I also aim to explore how different societies have grappled with these thorny and culturally embedded law and development issues and how culture change may be applicable to law and development in a broad way. Thus, although I intend to study the selected countries with a degree of cultural specificity, I also hope to avoid the all-too-common problem of reifying the particular by selecting countries that are historically, geographically, politically, and economically different. A particularized focus on specific countries balanced against a broad, overarching examination of law and development efforts allows me to identify common conceptual problems across cultures and to engage at the same time in a bit of generalization.

This book proceeds as follows. Chapter 1 briefly sketches the field, its supposed demise and its revival in recent years. This resurrection is due partly to the events of September 11, 2001, whereby law and development is viewed in a new light, in the United States in particular, not just as a do-good effort but as a crucial component in the fight against terrorism. In its brief survey of law and development failures in the past, Chapter 1 suggests the absence of a robust cultural lens as a significant (though clearly not only) reason for such failures. Chapter 1 also distinguishes my proposal from what has been referred to as

---

[171] STROMSETH ET AL., *supra* note 5, at 4.

[172] *Id.* at 7.

"first wave" law and development movement of the 1960s and 1970s, whose focus on the need to change the "legal culture" of developing countries was influenced by modernization theory. Chapter 1 also evaluates "second wave" law and development reform efforts in the 1980s and 1990s to the present, which has focused more on institutions and rules. In the process, I explain why the animating principles that underlie first wave and second wave efforts are insufficient and at times misguided.

Instead, I argue for a different framework for development that incorporates a cultural lens and that accords with new understandings of culture as heterogeneous, hybrid, noninsular, and dynamic. Indeed, the emerging model presented by Amartya Sen and subsequently supported by other noted scholars such as Martha Nussbaum and Arjun Appadurai, offers an opportunity to reinsert culture into development and to legitimize this endeavor, allowing proponents to defend this effort from charges of "blaming the victim," cultural determinism, and cultural imperialism. A key point argued in this chapter is as follows: Development redefined as the process of expanding people's substantive freedoms and enhancing their voice has to encompass not just the political and economic but also the cultural, especially if the latter impedes the development of the former. This is particularly significant if law and development aims to further women's rights, which continue to be undermined by deeply seated cultural practices and beliefs.

Chapter 2 examines how international law has marginalized culture, with public international law concentrated on state issues and private international law on business or commercial issues.[173] Public international law has vacillated between on the one hand defending state interests by promoting state sovereignty and state power and, on the other hand, managing "order between states"[174] and curbing nationalistic flare-ups by restraining state sovereignty. Public international law, in other words, protects as well as limits state sovereignty.

In the latter case (limiting state sovereignty), international law seeks to tame nationalism by imposing a minimum floor of substantive rights, acting thus as a tempering force against the excesses of nationalism. Because it is suspicious of nationalist passion and exaggerated claims of cultural identities, it has devised a variety of legal techniques to tame or harness nationalism, through the principles of self-determination, international

---

[173] Black's Law Dictionary 1230 (6th ed. 1990) (defining public law as consisting generally "of constitutional, administrative, criminal, and international law, concerned with the organization of the state, the relations between the state and the people who compose it, the responsibilities of public officers to the state, to each other, and to private persons, and the relations of states to one another."); compare the definition of private law as "[t]hat portion of the law which defines, regulates, enforces, and administers relationships among individuals, associations, and corporations." *Id.* at 1196. *See* Robert Post, *The Challenge of Globalization to American Public Law Scholarship*, 2 Theoretical Inquiries L. 323, 324, 365 (2001), for a critique of the public/private law distinction. For a critique of the problematic dichotomy between public international law and private international law, *see* Lan Cao, *Law and Economic Development: A New Beginning?* 32 Texas Int'l L.J. 545 (1997).

[174] Brooks, *supra* note 102, at 348.

minority protections, internationalization through international administration, supranational legal integration, mandates, and universal human rights.

At the same time, in its role as protector of state sovereignty, it also cabins certain ethnic and cultural claims within national boundaries, as matters appropriately within the domestic jurisdiction of states and hence beyond international intervention. In this respect, it claims to respect cultural diversity by deferring to the state. International law gives states the right to invoke the principle of self-determination, removing in essence cultural issues from international scrutiny. Either way, whether it protects the state or restrains the state, it is the state, its interests, and its transgressions which are paramount for public international law. Thus, for public international law, the state is central and culture—that which for the most part remains inside the domestic jurisdiction, or to put it another way, inside the "black box" of the state—is marginal. This statist inclination is further reinforced by international relations, which also relegates culture and other norm-based theories to the side so that interest-based issues (power and security) can predominate.

Culture is likewise marginal for private international law. Unlike public international law, which is predominantly concerned about the state, private international law is predominantly concerned about the market, particularly insulating the market from excessive state interference. Private international law furthers market interests and accommodates market desire to transcend national boundaries and bypass nationalistic tendencies. Even more than public international law, private international law stands in direct opposition to nationalism. Private international law seeks to cabin nationalist sentiments by establishing an international economic system that transcends the national or the cultural, which it views as potentially problematic, parochial, and irrational. Whereas the nationalist project is about defending the state as the site for politics and cultures, the private international law project is about overcoming barriers, cultural and otherwise, erected by states and furthering market expansions across national borders. For example, the World Trade Organization (WTO) was established precisely to contain economic nationalism, restrain protectionist impulses, and to maximize free trade. The WTO seeks to minimize cultural bases for protectionist measures and for the most part does not allow states' cultural claims to justify restraints on international trade. Private international law is deployed to ensure that the international economic system functions smoothly and efficiently. Thus, private international law rarely recognizes claims that espouse the need to preserve or protect national cultures if those cultural claims create barriers to trade.

Relatedly, the rise of private international arbitration provides yet another example of how the international market works to separate itself from national cultures. Private international law allows market players to flee the jurisdiction of national courts which private international law fears are rooted in an excess of cultural and nationalistic peculiarities. Market actors can haul states to arbitration and even have foreign arbitration awards enforced in national courts, subject only to a very narrow public policy exception.

Many of the rules of private international law, in other words, are meant to allow market players to escape from national cultures and national politics.

In addition, as the CEDAW example illustrates, even international human rights law—which emerged from the ruins of World War II to insist that state sovereignty cannot be unlimited—has failed to rupture international law's overall statist orientation. Indeed, "human rights law has continued in other ways to insist on the state's centrality."[175] In other words, "[s]tate action has been the *sine qua non* of human rights law violations,"[176] which means that "in this traditional understanding of human rights law, if thousands of men systematically beat or rape thousands of women, this is not a human rights abuse, unless the men are state agents acting on the orders of the state. If the men are merely 'traditional' fathers or husbands, using age-old methods of maintaining their domestic authority, we have, perhaps, a regrettable state of affairs, but no human rights law violation."[177] Thus, although international human rights law has strived to pierce the veil of state sovereignty, so that internal abuses by the state are no longer immune to international scrutiny, it too is preoccupied with states and state action. In that sense it is but an offshoot of public international law and the public international law preoccupation with the state. This means that abuses committed under another name—call it what you will, culture, tradition, norms—are not appropriately the central concern of the discipline. "Human rights abuses that since World War II are no longer acceptable when committed by states are paradoxically tolerated when justified in the name of religion or culture."[178]

Even though international human rights law legitimizes international scrutiny of certain internal matters within a state's territory, its "insistence on the centrality of the state"[179] means that non-state issues, most prominently culture, are understudied and peripheral to the field. Indeed, as aptly observed, "culture . . . represent[s] the New Sovereignty."[180] International law—public, private, or international human rights—has shown little inclination to pierce the veil of cultural sovereignty and has either accommodated or sidestepped culture altogether.

Chapter 3 has two parts. Part A shows how and why law and development has neglected culture. Understanding the depth of and reasons for this resistance is important so that one is aware of potential problems the project will encounter at the outset. First, law and development has inherited and accepted the international law (public international law, private international law, and international human rights) tradition of isolating culture from its discourse. But in the same way that "securing human rights *requires* deconstructing . . .

[175] *Id.*

[176] *Id.*

[177] *Id.*

[178] Sunder, *supra* note 106, at 1401 (citation omitted).

[179] Brooks, *supra* note 102, at 349.

[180] Sunder, *supra* note 106, at 1401.

culture,"[181] securing a robust vision of law and development also entails deconstructing culture and subjecting it to scrutiny and where appropriate, change.

Second, law and development practitioners and scholars are steeped in a cosmopolitan tradition that celebrates "the worldwide community of human beings."[182] A cosmopolitan may forge special ties and give special attention to family or nation, but as Martha Nussbaum, a prominent cosmopolitan remarked, "that should not mean that we believe our own country or family is really worth more than the children or families of other people—all are still equally human, of equal moral worth."[183] A cosmopolitan who embraces differences will tend to discourage critical appraisal of others' cultures, especially given the problematic history of how the West has created and perpetuated misrepresentations of non-Western cultures. Cosmopolitan awareness of this history has resulted in an intellectual backlash against critical evaluation of anybody's culture, much less non-Western culture. Interestingly, however, there is a strand of cosmopolitanism that sees cultures as being in flux and celebrates the notion that individual identities should not be determined by membership in culturally insular and bounded groups. For that strand of cosmopolitan, cultural insularity is unduly restrictive. Because cultures are always changing, absorbing and appropriating bits and pieces from encounters with other cultures, culture change becomes relatively uncontroversial or at least less problematic.[184]

Third, because the work of law and development is not confined to any one region but instead deals with different countries, law and development has forged scholarly connections to anthropology. And anthropology has historically been reluctant to assess cultures because it is premised on and rooted in a foundation of cultural relativism. For example, in 1947, the Executive Board of the American Anthropological Association declined to endorse the UN Universal Declaration of Human Rights because it viewed the Declaration as ethnocentric.

And fourth, law and development is also intellectually associated with economics, and economics too has paid "inadequate attention to culture in investigating the operation of societies in general and the process of development in particular."[185] Generally speaking, economists as a whole "have been tempted by the idea that all human beings behave in much the same way (for example, relentlessly maximize their self-interest defined in a thoroughly insulated way)."[186]

---

[181] *Id.* at 1404 (emphasis added).

[182] Martha Nussbaum, *Patriotism and Cosmopolitanism*, *in* For Love of Country: Debating the Limits of Patriotism 3, 4 (1996). Although the idea of world citizenship need not be antithetical to the special bonds of family, culture, or nation, for cosmopolitans, this can be justified only on the basis that "this is the only sensible way to do good" and not on the basis that "the local is better *per se*." *See* Martha Nussbaum, *Reply*, *in* For Love of Country: Debating the Limits of Patriotism 131, 134–35 (1996) [hereinafter *Reply*].

[183] *Reply*, *supra* note 182, at 131, 136.

[184] *See* Chapter 3.

[185] Amartya Sen, *How Does Culture Matter?*, *in* Culture and Public Action 37, 37 (Vijayendra Rao & Michael Walton eds., 2004).

[186] *Id.* at 40.

Against this background, it is no wonder then that law and development has proceeded along a meek, acultural arc.

After explaining the reasons for the neglect of culture by law and development in Part A, Part B of Chapter 3 argues that the skeptical pose struck by law and development with respect to culture must be remedied. Part B examines select works by sociologists, anthropologists, and economists who have demonstrated that the social structure in which the individual is a part affects and shapes that individual's preferences. In stark contrast to the conventional economic approach, which tends to cast the question of why some people prefer certain goods and outcomes over others as somehow "exogeneous" to economic analysis, these scholars have studied how cultural preferences affect behavior and practices. These culturally enforced preferences may have negative economic consequences because they perpetuate inefficiencies. They may also have negative human rights consequences because they constrict an individual's capability and voice.

Preferences thus should be an important component of the law and development agenda. Although economists have traditionally started with the individual, rather than the group as the unit of study, economists in collaboration with sociologists have begun to look at how preferences are formed and how the culture of a group affects group and individual expectations and preferences. Unlike economists, anthropologists and sociologists "start from a perspective in which a person's belief systems, dispositions, and behaviors are conditioned and embedded within the group to which they belong. In other words, they adhere to 'methodological holism' where the unit of analysis is not an individual but a group."[187] If law and development were to use insights from sociology and anthropology, it would see that individual preference is connected to group preference and that preference formation has both economic and human rights implications.

Pierre Bourdieu, for example, examines how culture affects poverty. Culture, for Bourdieu, is a form of capital that can be accessed by the group. Cultural capital has at least three forms: First, it can be "the ensemble of cultivated dispositions that are internalized by the individual through socialization and that constitute schemes of appreciation and understanding"; second, it can be expressed in the form of books, music, scientific works that are drawn from cultural capital; and third, it can be institutionalized in systems of education.[188] Bourdieu refers to habitus—practices, beliefs, taboos, rituals that imbue individuals with a sense of identity and belonging—and shows how its internalization shapes individual expectations and aspirations and function as a constraining

---

[187] Rao & Walton, *supra* note 49, at 14.

[188] David Swartz, Culture & Power: The Sociology of Pierre Bourdieu 89 (2000), *citing* Pierre Bourdieu, The Logic of Practice (1990); Rao & Walton, *supra* note 49, at 14, 16. Though social capital is also significant in promoting or retarding economic development, it is different from cultural capital, *see id.* at 16 ("Social capital emphasizes the social networks available to people to access and mobilize resources."). For a discussion about different ethnic groups' different access to social capital and the relationship between social capital and economic development, *see* Chapter 3.

preference that perpetuates poverty and inequality.[189] The Hindu caste system, for example, creates external as well as internal constraints that affect how members perceive their status and affect their belief about what is or is not possible.[190] Similarly, "[t]here are striking and significant international commonalities in sex inequality between men and women . . ."[191] which can be fairly described as "a system of caste based on gender,"[192] which, like the Hindu caste system, also creates internal and external constraints.

Furthermore, moving beyond the issue of preferences, Douglass North's work in institutional economics also demonstrates that formal institutions as well as informal institutions, culture, for example, are relevant to the development inquiry because they affect economic choices and performance. In the 1990s, there was great interest in institutions and how they may affect economic development. "[E]ven the World Bank and the IMF which, which used to privilege orthodox economic theory tools, have come round to emphasizing the role of 'institutions' in economic development."[193] Both organizations have begun to examine institutions, such as corporate governance institutions and bankruptcy laws, and to study the process of institutional development. However, the focus was on formal institutions, not informal ones.

North also understood the importance of institutions. "Throughout history, institutions have been devised by human beings to create order and reduce uncertainty in exchange."[194] But institutions "consist of both informal constraints (sanctions, taboos, customs, traditions, and codes of conduct), and formal rules (constitutions, laws, property rights)."[195] Thus, North's study did not neglect informal institutions. He saw them as "informal constraints" which "come from socially transmitted information and are a part of the heritage that we call culture."[196] Informal constraints are part of a "governing structure" that consists of "codes of conduct, norms of behavior, and conventions" that influence our "daily interaction with others, whether within the family, in external social relations, or in business activities."[197]

---

[189] BOURDIEU, *supra* note 188, at 53 (defining habitus as "principles which generate and organize practices and representations that can be objectively adapted to their outcomes without presupposing a conscious aiming at ends or an express mastery of the operations necessary in order to attain them."); Rao & Walton, *supra* note 49, at 15.

[190] LOUIS DUMONT, HOMO HIERARCHICUS: THE CASTE SYSTEM AND ITS IMPLICATIONS (1970); Rao & Walton, *supra* note 49, at 15 ("[P]references derived from the Hindu caste system may create an acceptance of hierarchy and constrain the motivation for mobility, but these beliefs are also simultaneously external constraints.").

[191] Cass R. Sunstein, *Gender, Caste, and the Law*, *in* WOMEN, CULTURE, AND DEVELOPMENT: A STUDY OF HUMAN CAPABILITIES 332, 348 (Martha C. Nussbaum & Jonathan Glover eds., 1995).

[192] *Id.*

[193] Yousfi, *supra* note 8, at 32.

[194] Douglass North, *Institutions*, J. ECON. PERSPECTIVES, Winter 1991, at 97, 97.

[195] *Id.*

[196] NORTH, *supra* note 46, at 37.

[197] *Id.* at 36; Rao & Walton, *supra* note 49, at 13.

According to institutional economists such as North, "the sources of contrasting economic performance lie within the institutional structures of society that define incentives for saving, investment, production and trade."[198] They have also looked at how informal institutions—again, understood to encompass path-dependent cultural practices and norms—perform economically significant functions by addressing entrenched problems of coordination and information asymmetry.[199]

A well-known study by Avner Greif documented the practices of medieval Maghribi traders who relied on commercial agents.[200] In order to overcome the classic principal/agent problem that characterized the relationship between traders and their agents, the Maghribi devised a monitoring mechanism based on reputation, ensuring that no trader would employ an agent who had cheated another trader. Although the Maghribi merchants were not kin or related by blood, they were descendants of Jewish merchants who had emigrated to North Africa a century before. This common cultural and ethnic link functioned as a low-cost way of engaging in transactions—information could be easily conveyed among members; enforcement via ostracism was also effective.

Drawing on the large body of scholarship that explores ways that cultural cohesion promotes cooperation, minimizes defection, solves collective action problems, and lowers transaction costs, Part B also examines the economic enterprise of expatriate minorities such as the Chinese in Southeast Asia, Indians in East Africa, Lebanese in West Africa, and Jews in Europe to show the link between culture and economic success. This particular discussion looks at *positive* cultural norms that marshal trust, cohesion, and community social capital, for example, to produce wealth. Particular attention is devoted to ethnic-based informal savings groups, often referred to rotating credit associations, which rely on community norms to provide members who would not otherwise qualify for bank loans access to informal, community credit wholly outside the purview of the state and the formal banking sector. Indeed, such rotating credit associations have been crucial helping immigrants advance economically and in the economic development of immigrant communities in the United States. Cultural norms do have an effect on social networks and institutions, which in turn affect economic performance.

Part B also explores *negative* cultural norms that hinder capital formation and investment. It looks at various culture-based economic practices that may not enhance efficiency, such as the prohibition in Islam against charging interest or inheritance practices that discourage the emergence of modern industrial corporations. I draw from a rich literature that has emerged following Max Weber's 1905 treatise *The Protestant Ethic and the*

---

[198] Yousfi, *supra* note 8, at 32–33.

[199] *See generally* George Akerlof, An Economic Theorist's Book of Tales: Essays that Entertain the Consequences of New Assumptions in Economic Theory (1984); Rao & Walton, *supra* note 49, at 13.

[200] Avner Greif, *Contract Enforceability and Economic Institutions in Early Trade: The Maghribi Traders' Coalition*, 83 Am. Econ. Rev. 525 (1993).

Spirit of Capitalism, which studied the cultural consequences of the Reformation. Weber argued that the Protestant moral code of abstention and individual self-improvement were particularly conducive to the task of mobilizing capital. There is also an emerging literature that looks at whether certain Islamic tenets are negatively associated with economic growth. For example, according to the economist Timur Kuran, under the law governing Islamic partnerships, any partner could terminate the partnership at will, resulting in successful ventures being terminated because of a partner's death. Productive enterprises thus could come to a sudden halt. As a result, most businesses remained small and were short-lived.[201] Similarly, Islamic inheritance customs resulted in the fragmentation of estates. When a Muslim merchant died, at least two-thirds of his estate must be split among surviving heirs, hindering the formation of capital-intensive businesses. The dearth of large-scale corporations in turn retarded the development of stock markets and other standard commercial practices such as bookkeeping. The private sector was too dwarfed and civil society too weak to challenge the state, state bureaucracies, or state corruption.

Low-trust societies may also result in similarly stagnated economic conditions. Chinese societies, for example, typically reserve trust only for family or clan members and do not customarily extend trust to nonfamily members. As a result, the Chinese tend to create family businesses that do not grow into large-scale, professionally run modern corporations. Such businesses can grow, but only up to a certain point, and then become inefficient and die off because the majority shareholders tend to oppose taking the company public or allowing the company to be run by professional but outside managers. "Familistic societies have greater difficulties creating large economic institutions, and this constraint on size limits the sectors of the global economy in which such businesses can operate."[202] Indeed, "[t]he Chinese difficulty in moving to professional development is related to the nature of Chinese familism."[203]

Other examples of culturally based practices that also have a negative impact on development include India's caste system, schooling restrictions for girls, and kinship norms of solidarity that oppose individual accumulation of wealth especially if such accumulation of wealth challenges local (often male) elites. This discussion shows how such entrenched authoritarian patterns likely conflict with the values of equalities promoted by law and development projects and should, for that additional reason, be altered.

A law and development project of course must include work on formal institutions, such as establishing market initiatives and legal reforms like those already promoted—private property rights, enforcement of contract rules, an impartial and transparent judicial system. But it must also pay attention to informal institutions and include a cultural

---

[201] The discussion on Islamic practices in this paragraph is drawn from Timur Kuran, The Long Divergence: How Islamic Law Held Back the Middle East (2010).

[202] Francis Fukuyama, Trust: The Social Virtues and the Creation of Prosperity 62 (1995).

[203] *Id.* at 75.

component, especially where "cultural lock-in"[204] is a contributing cause of continuing poverty and conflict. In making a case for a "culturally informed perspective," I am by no means endorsing a culturally deterministic approach which views culture as determining economic outcome. Rather, my position is more subtle and nuanced as it sees culture as an important factor that interacts with a host of other factors. This position looks at how relational behavior and the background norms that influence preferences and behaviors affect economic outcome. The purpose of the book is to show that a *culturally* informed framework widens the scope of inquiry and "sees individuals as driven by a culturally influenced set of motives, incentives, beliefs, and identities that interact with economic incentives to affect outcomes." Though Max Weber is often invoked as one of the original proponents of cultural determinism, in fact, he did not claim "a causal relationship between Calvinism and capitalism" but merely noted the "elective affinity" between them.[205] It is this elective affinity between culture and law and development that this book seeks to explore.

After establishing the connection between culture and development in Chapter 3, I begin to lay the foundation for culture change in subsequent chapters. In a nutshell, the purpose of Chapter 4 is to show that although it is indeed the case that international law has generally relegated culture to the margin, international law also has a built-in mechanism that makes space for and accommodates my culture-based argument. Thus, although my argument for a culture-oriented approach to law and development runs against the basic grain in the field, there are also recent developments within the field that create useful openings for a new approach.

Part A of Chapter 4 examines how norms have changed in international law generally, with the aim of drawing some parallels between the evolution of international custom and international norms on the one hand and the development of cultural change on the other. Although it is uncontested that international law and international relations have been quintessentially state-centered, it is also the case that this state-centric model is slowly but surely being eroded in two important ways. First, state actors have been joined by non-state actors that have a role to play in furthering the evolution of norms and custom. Second, state power and state interests still dominate, but there are openings for norms and values in the international system.

There are observable similarities between norm changes in public international law and international relations and my proposed culture change project in law and development. For example, how NGOs have engaged in deliberate projects to change existing norms and custom in international law is salient to my proposal to replicate this endeavor in law and development. How and under what circumstances norm change or customary international law change have occurred, as well as which actors have played an important

---

[204] Timur Kuran, *Cultural Obstacles to Economic Development: Often Overstated, Usually Transitory*, *in* CULTURE AND PUBLIC ACTION 115, 117 (Vijayendra Rao & Michael Walton eds., 2004).

[205] Rao & Walton, *supra* note 49, at 9–10.

role in this process, provide valuable lessons for how law and development may pursue culture change. Moreover, because public international law and international relations have grappled with evolving custom and norm change, my proposal to inject cultural norms in law and development thus should not be viewed as heretical to the international law framework. That international lawyers and international NGOs have forged connections with their counterparts in individual states to transmit international norms to those states should somewhat blunt charges among law and development scholars that the entire process of purposive culture change is offensive or imperialist.

As Chapter 4 discusses, the Hans Morgenthau realist tradition in international relations, which puts states and state power politics at the center of the international order,[206] has been and continues to be challenged and supplemented by other trends in international law. International institutions, networks of non-state actors, individuals, organizations, and movements that transcend national borders have injected new elements of understanding into international relations and international law. The liberal challenge to realism, for example, as manifested in the works of James Rosenau, Robert Koehane, and Joseph Nye, among others,[207] emphasizes a level of interconnectedness or "complex interdependence" that exists among states and between the ordinary practices of non-state actors at one level (national) and their impact on another level (international). Groups of like-minded individuals in one state form alliances with their counterparts in another state to promote new norms or challenge established norms.[208] Even though such non-state actors are not vested with the power and authority to "make" law, they can and do form "interpretive communities"[209] that influence the development of norms and laws; and their practices may have an impact on the lawmaking capabilities of states themselves.[210]

Although this body of work seems disparate, they are linked by a common theme: how various arrangements forged among states and among non-state actors in alliance with each other have enhanced cooperative relations and transnational ties, resulting in the

---

[206] Hans Morgenthau, Scientific Man Versus Power Politics (1946); Hans Morgenthau, Politics Among Nations (1948).

[207] Robert O. Keohane & Joseph S. Nye, Power and Interdependence: World Politics in Transition 23 (1977); James N. Rosenau, The Study of Global Interdependence: Essays on the Transnationalization of World Affairs 1 (1980).

[208] Kathryn Sikkink & Margaret Keck, Activists Beyond Borders: Advocacy Networks in International Politics (1998); Transnational Social Movements and Global Politics: Solidarity Beyond the State (Jackie Smith et al. eds., 1997); Paul Ghils, *International Civil Society: International Non-Governmental Organizations in the International System*, 44 Int'l Soc. Sci. J. 417 (1992).

[209] Robert M. Cover, *The Supreme Court, 1982 Term: Foreword: Nomos and Narrative*, 97 Harv. L. Rev. 4, 40 (1983).

[210] Michel Foucault posits the notion that power is not limited only to the formal, institutional arenas but instead "circulates" as a relational phenomenon through many spheres of life. Michel Foucault, Power/Knowledge: Selected Interviews and Other Writings, 1972–1977 (1980).

erosion of the anarchic, state-centric, and power-focused model of the international system. For example, these works study transnational alliances of non-state actors that transcend state boundaries, international institutions that restrain state power, international regimes such as the European Union and NATO that establish regulatory frameworks for cooperation, social movements around the world that push against and alter preexisting norms. Scholars such as Myres McDougal, Harold Lasswell, and Michael Reisman from the New Haven School of international law[211] and others such as Harold Koh[212] who have studied transnational processes have also pushed back against the dominant state-centered model. Koh's scholarship in particular examines how states have internalized transnational norms whether or not those norms have been produced by the state itself or by outsiders. In addition, there is a large body of scholarship that studies norm-generating communities and their participation in international law. Their works can be used to understand how and why international norms change.[213] These broad developments in public international law have resulted in an enlarged framework in which (1) other actors besides the state can legitimately claim to have a role on the public international law stage, at least in the area of norm change and (2) other issues besides state power and interests can be appropriate subjects of research and study—even in a state-centric subject such as public international law.

In a similar vein, Part A also reviews a discipline within international relations called constructivism and draws on its insights to critically evaluate how culture change in law and development may or may not share constructivism's key features and attributes. Constructivism sharply departs from the core assumptions of neorealism, which for many years reigned as a dominant theory of international relations. Neorealism holds that much in international politics can be explained by the structure of the international system. For example, neorealism's core assumptions are that because the international system is essentially anarchic, states which are formally equal sovereigns in their own right

[211] *See generally* Harold D. Lasswell & Myres S. McDougal, Jurisprudence for a Free Society: Studies in Law, Science and Policy (1992); W. Michael Reisman, Law in Brief Encounters (1999); Symposium, *McDougal's Jurisprudence: Utility, Influence, Controversy*, 79 Am. Soc'y Int'l L. Proc. 266 (1985); Michael Reisman, *A Jurisprudence from the Perspective of the "Political Superior,"* 23 N. Ky. L. Rev. 605 (1996).

[212] Harold Hongju Koh, *How Is International Human Rights Law Enforced?*, 74 Ind. L. J. 1397 (1999); Harold Hongju Koh, *Transnational Legal Process*, 75 Neb. L. Rev. 181 (1996); Harold Hongju Koh, *Why Do Nations Obey International Law?*, 106 Yale L. J. 2599 (1997) (reviewing Abram Chayes &Antonia Handler Chayes, The New Sovereignty: Compliance with International Regulatory Agreements (1995); Thomas M. Franck, Fairness in International Law and Institutions (1995)).

[213] *See, e.g.*, Audie Klotz, Norms in International Relations: The Struggle Against Apartheid (1995); International Norms And Cycles of Change (Wayne Standholtz & Kenneth Stiles eds., 2009); Wayne Sandholtz, Prohibiting Plunder: How Norms Change (2007); John Griffiths, *What Is Legal Pluralism?*, 24 J.L. Pluralism & Unofficial L. 1 (1986); Sally Engle Merry, *Legal Pluralism*, 22 L. & Soc'y Rev. 869 (1988).

must rely on themselves for their own security and for the defense of their own power and interests. International relations is thus a reflection of state interests and power.[214]

By contrast, constructivists claim that significant features of international relations are historically and socially contingent. Constructivists challenge these assumptions by arguing that the neorealist conception of structure is not useful because "it does not predict whether two states will be friends or foes, will recognize each other's sovereignty, will have dynastic ties, will be revisionist or status quo powers, and so on."[215] Alexander Wendt argues that the neorealist story that anarchy constrains states is itself incomplete because it does not look at the way states understand anarchy. In other words, anarchy does not explain an international system based on each state furthering its own interests and relying on self-help for security. Anarchy leads to such a result only if states view security as a competitive, zero-sum concept where a state gains security when another state's security ebbs. In other words, for Wendt and other constructivists, neorealist assumptions and conclusions depend on assumptions about the ways in which the social institutions are constructed and imbued with meaning by states.[216]

Generally speaking, constructivists subscribe to two basic tenets: first, that structures of international relations are determined by social construction and shared ideas, not just material forces as neorealists claim; and second, that the identities and interests of state actors are formed by these shared ideas rather than given by nature.[217] Constructivists, in other words, incorporate norms and their effect on international relations in virtually every significant international domain, from national security to human rights and economic relations. The animating principle that sets constructivism apart from other international relations theories is its immersion in the language of culture, "ideas, norms, knowledge."[218] For constructivists, "[t]he intersubjective (collectively held) transmission of ideas and beliefs as opposed to material factors is the primary source of interaction among humans. Collective intentionality can 'will' the rules of behavior, interactions, or the game of change within and among nations."[219] The bold constructivist assertion is that "[i]f the thoughts and ideas that enter into the existence of international relations change, then the system itself will also change as well."[220]

---

214 *See,* e.g., KENNETH WALTZ, THEORY OF INTERNATIONAL POLITICS (1979).

215 Alexander Wendt, *Anarchy Is What States Make of It: The Social Construction of Power Politics*, 46 INT'L ORG. 391, 396–97 (1992).

216 *Id.*

217 ALEXANDER WENDT, SOCIAL THEORY OF INTERNATIONAL POLITICS 1 (1999); *see also* ROBERT JACKSON & GEORG SORENSEN, INTRODUCTION TO INTERNATIONAL RELATIONS 253 (2003) (declaring that "[t]he international system is not something 'out there' like the solar system. It does not exist on its own. It exists only as intersubjective awareness among people.... It is a set of ideas, a body of thought, a system of norms, which has been arranged by certain people at a particular time and place.").

218 Earl Conteh-Morgan, *Peacebuilding and Human Security: A Constructivist Perspective*, INT'L J. PEACE STUD., no. 1, Spring/Summer 2005, at 72, 72.

219 *Id.*

220 JACKSON & SORENSEN, *supra* note 217.

For example, instead of assuming that states seek security and survival above all, as realists and liberals do, constructivists study how the interests and identities of states influence their views about security and survival. Such interests and identities, in other words, are not assumed to be established but rather the product of specific historical processes and people's attitude toward such processes. States act to further their interests; or conversely states do not act against their interests but their interests change depending on how they understand their interests and their identities. Example: Constructivists understand the breakup of the Soviet Union as a process that entailed material forces (economic stagnation) but also new thinking (glasnost, perestroika).[221]

How new thinking emerges is part of the constructivist inquiry. Evolution and change are central themes for constructivists. Most approaches to international relations assume that state preferences are a given fact, but constructivists question how preferences are socially constructed and how they evolve. Constructivism studies how state preferences can be changed and, most significantly for the purpose of my proposal, it also allows room for non-state actors to influence the norm change process. Indeed, over the years there has been a dramatic transformation in the belief system of states, so that even deeply entrenched norms have been changed and slavery, colonialism, or conquest, which were acceptable, became normatively unacceptable. Works by scholars such as Peter Katzenstein show that even in the high politics area of national security, norms and identities play a significant role.[222] Example: A state may behave differently and view its interests differently if it were a member of the European Union than if it were not (case in point, Turkey).

Part B looks at how other related disciplines have embraced the study of norms and how non-state lawmaking has proliferated in different areas of law. Merchants in the diamond industry, for example, routinely engage in private lawmaking, relying on private industry norms to resolve disputes. International arbitrators arbitrate claims that are resolved outside the state system. International business communities are creating a new private system of transnational governance that relies on state authority to, ironically, evade it.

Part C studies how norm change occurs under various theories of international relations and public international law, specifically constructivism, norm change cycle, and customary international law. Constructivism is discussed in Part A and so Part C focuses on the evolution of custom in customary international law. Customary international law,

---

[221] Wendt, *supra* note 215, at 419, 421 (characterizing Gorbachev's new thinking about the Soviet Union's identity "as one of the most important phenomena in (recent) world politics . . . Gorbachev want[ed] to free the Soviet Union from the coercive social logic of the [C]old [W]ar and engage the West in far-reaching cooperation.").

[222] Peter J. Katzenstein, *Introduction*, *in* The Culture of National Security: Norms and Identity in World Politics 1 (Peter J. Katzenstein ed., 1996).

unlike a treaty, is itself "custom" and as such, like cultural traditions, cannot be located by reference to a text. Customary international law can only be discerned by reference to the conduct of states and their opinions about the legal obligations that bind them to abide by a particular set of conducts. How a particular custom is made, how it changes and evolves or not is often unclear and controversial because custom is not fixed or decreed into being but rather emerges from a continuous process of state interaction.

Part C lays out this process. International law journals are replete with articles assessing how certain events, disputes, judicial decisions, state action, state reaction, state nonaction may be deemed to reinforce existing custom, violate current custom, dislodge it, or form new custom. There is no definitive set of events or moments that define custom formation. Official pronouncements, national legislation, and diplomatic statements, along with soft norms and nonbinding statements at the General Assembly, for example, may all be deemed evidence of state practice. At some point, a process that may seem riddled with internal contradictions reaches a tipping point and a contrary practice somehow ripens into a new rule of customary international law.

Again, my aim is to show how this evolutionary process in customary international law has parallels to the process of cultural change described later in Chapter 5. International law is already familiar and presumably comfortable with custom and its evolution—its vague, amorphous nature and the equally vague and amorphous way in which new custom dislodges old custom. Similarly, constructivist and norm change cycle theory discussed in this Part C also reveal the field's familiarity with the hows and whys of norm change. The crisp delineations that once characterized international law have been blurred. Traditional state-centric tools of international law have been expanded. Norms, values, custom are not only increasingly embraced but equally important for my project, international law and international relations both increasingly endow non-state actors with governance and lawmaking or norm-making capability. In this way, both public international law and international relations have evolved in ways that should accommodate a more culture-based analysis.

Part D discusses several examples of norm change scenarios in which entrenched international norms were changed, with new norms supplanting old ones—often due to the efforts of non-state actors such as the Red Cross and the World Bank. Part D also provides an in-depth study of the alliances forged among states, as well as between states and NGOs to change norms of conquest and slavery.

To sum up, this chapter looks at state and non-state behaviors and norm change. What are the major streams of norm development and how can norm change be triggered? This process can be examined through an international law framework, by looking at the evolution of certain customary international legal norms, or through an international relations lens, by applying the principles of constructivism and norm-cycle theory. Chapter 4, in other words, looks at how interactions, disputes, arguments, in the economic, political, and social sphere, shape and reshape rules of conduct and the norms underlying them.

It is not the purpose of the book to further the discourse on customary international law or constructivism. Rather, my description of how customary international law and constructivism understand norm change in the international system is designed to serve as a springboard for subsequent discussions on culture change for law and development purposes. Although constructivism's main postulates were originally meant to be applied to state-state behaviors in international relations, constructivist insights can also be used to better understand culture change as an *internal* dynamic within a state. Ultimately, my aim is to use the insights developed in the literature on customary international law and constructivism to see if parallels can be made between international norm change and culture change.

Ultimately, this chapter is important for my thesis because it illustrates that despite their entrenched statism, international law and international relations now have sufficient openings to allow into the international framework new normative visions that (1) evolve and change and (2) coalesce around non-state actors, culture, norms, and identity. That public international law and international relations, the progenitors of law and development, have accommodated and accepted a norm-based analytical framework that interacts with non-state actors is, for my purposes, significant for two reasons. First, if public international law and international relations have loosened the state's grip and opened themselves up to the study of norms, norm change, and non-state actors, law and development would not be embarking on a heretical path if it were to do the same. Second, the underlying processes of norm change in public international law and international relations are themselves not much different from the evolution of cultural norms that I argue law and development should be concerned with. Law and development can draw on these processes and work to change cultural norms that are antithetical to development objectives. Constructivists are concerned with state preferences and how background norms influence such preferences. Law and development should be similarly concerned about individual preferences and how cultural norms shape such preferences. Norm change or culture change can occur when dissenters forging international alliances push existing boundaries toward a tipping point.[223]

Chapter 5 builds directly on the foundation established in Chapter 4. Part A of Chapter 5 examines select efforts at culture change that have been pursued by different countries. As I mentioned at the beginning of the Introduction, the book includes countries such as Japan, Turkey, and Germany as case studies to illustrate how culture change was implemented. For example, Japan scholars have written extensively about Japanese history during the Tokugawa and Meiji eras and the post–World War II era, but few have

---

[223] In addition, although this is not the point of Chapter 4, because Chapter 4 draws parallels between customary international law and constructivism, it also represents one of the few scholarly attempts to bridge the growing rift between the two disciplines. *See* David J. Bederman, *Constructivism, Positivism, and Empiricism in International Law: Legal Rules and International Society*, 89 Geo. L.J. 469 (2001) (reviewing Anthony C. Arend, Legal Rules and International Society (1999)).

looked at the Japanese experience as a culturally informed example of law and development. In the 1880s, during what is called the Meiji period, Japan realized it was far behind the West and embarked on a modernization campaign that was notable for its attention to not just promulgating new codes but also to changing what it termed "evil customs of the past."[224] Japan instituted a variety of cultural projects to achieve certain stated objectives, one of which was to get the Japanese people to internalize values necessary for the achievement of development goals.[225] The government marshaled resources drawn from women's groups, village organizations, and other civil society groups to convince the poor and peasants to reject superstitions and increase savings by not spending lavishly on unproductive activities such as weddings and funerals. Moral suasion campaigns, often launched in conjunction with women's organizations, were used to exhort villagers to work hard and save for investment purposes instead.

Interestingly, these efforts dovetail with current debate on the prerequisites of economic development, one of which is the role of capital in economic growth. For example, in his classic and highly influential work, *Economic Development with Unlimited Supplies of Labour*, the Nobel Laureate in economics Sir Arthur Lewis discussed the causes of and solution to underdevelopment[226] and identified surplus labor in the rural sector, low wages, little savings, and hence minimal capital accumulation as a significant obstacle to economic development.[227] The solution, according to Lewis, lay in the ability of agrarian economies to accumulate capital and invest it productively.[228] Notably, Arjun Appadurai also emphasized the importance of savings, though less for economic than for the "moral discipline" inherent in the effort. "In a simple formula: without poor women joining together, there can be no savings. Without savings, there can be no community building.... Thus, the act of savings is an ethical principle which forms the practical and moral core of the politics of patience, since it does not generate large resources quickly."[229]

Despite the new development model that emphasizes broad substantive objectives such as human rights, freedom, voice, and capacity, capital accumulation remains a crucial issue for development purposes. What Chapter 5 demonstrates is its continuing relevance as well as the cultural dimensions that are intertwined with capital and markets.

---

[224] Garon, *supra* note 164, at 20.

[225] *See generally id.*

[226] W. Arthur Lewis, *Economic Development with Unlimited Supplies of Labour*, *in* Paradigms in Economic Development: Classic Perspectives, Critiques, and Reflections 59, 60 (Rajani Kanth ed., 1994).

[227] *Id.* at 72. ("The central problem in the theory of economic development is to understand the process by which a community which was previously saving and investing 4 or 5 per cent. [*sic*] of its national income or less, converts itself into an economy where voluntary saving is running at about 12 to 15 per cent of national income or more.").

[228] *Id.* at 95–97.

[229] Appadurai, *supra* note 129, at 74.

In addition to the country-specific case studies, I also include miscellaneous practices that are problematic from a development standpoint. These practices are organized into three rough categories. The first one comprises development issues in different countries that have been identified and addressed by the government (positively and negatively) through law and culture. The second comprises development issues that have been addressed primarily through law. And the third one comprises development issues that have been identified and addressed by NGOs primarily through culture change efforts.

With respect to category one, examples include traditional preferences against educating girls that exist in many societies. Study after study has shown that this issue is critical from both a human rights and economic growth perspective.[230] It is a widely acknowledged fact in development and human rights circles that denying girls basic education creates negative ripple effects throughout society. For example, a comprehensive study on India concluded "that girl and mother's education i.e., female education, is the single most important determinant of any improvement (change) in living standards in health and education."[231]

Most efforts to rectify the problem, however, have followed the usual conventions—addressing external constraints such as inadequate funding and lack of schools and teachers and textbooks rather than the underlying cultural basis which encourages parents with limited means to focus on educating boys and not girls. Against this backdrop, Korea, for example, took a different path and engaged in a massive cultural campaign to improve the education system based on principles of inclusiveness. Japan also placed a high premium on education. Between 1906 and 1911, Japanese towns and villages spent 43 percent of their budgets on education. By 1913, despite its relative poverty compared to Europe, Japan became one of the largest producers of books in the world, publishing more books than Britain and the United States.[232]

Cultural norms have also been engaged in other ways by governments to implement development objectives. Korea leveraged norms of nationalism and national pride to get its citizens to donate gold to the government in 1997 to alleviate its currency crisis. China, too, has tried to address various development-related economic problems by engaging the cultural realm. To improve the status of women and to improve China's image internationally, the government and various organizations as early as the 1800s embarked upon a culture change campaign to alter the cultural norm that equated women's bound feet with sexual allure and beauty. And because Chinese culture expects sons to take care of their parents in old age, in recent years the government has been giving parents of daughters old-age subsidies to ease the parents' anxieties and to sever the traditional association made between sons and economic security. The government's objective is to provide a

---

[230] Surji S. Bhalla, Suraj Saigal, & Nabhojit Basu, *Girls' Education Is It—Nothing Else Matters (Much)* 2 (World Bank World Development Report, Background Paper, 2004).

[231] *Id.*

[232] Sen, *supra* note 143.

form of old-age insurance for parents in order to alter the traditional preference for girls in Chinese society.

Further, China's One-Child Policy as well as the Chinese Communist Party's (CCP) attempt to abolish traditional relationships and create a society of comradeship can be seen as areas where law has been used in an aggressive and sometimes traumatic way upon the citizenry. In the first instance, the Chinese government forced sterilization and abortions upon the population to enforce the One-Child Policy. Many families in turn resorted to selective abortion to ensure that the one child they were permitted would be male, leading to a gender imbalance in the population. In the second instance, where the party disapproved of friendship and sought to replace it with what it considered a more ideologically palatable form of relationship—comradeship—it did so by imposing harsh sanctions upon violators. Both examples can be viewed as instances of what one might term negative culture change.

With respect to category two, I examine cases where the enactment of laws proved ineffective because traditional cultural norms remain at odds with the objectives of the newly enacted laws. For example, Turkey issued a directive banning forced virginity testing in 2002 as part of its effort to comply with its CEDAW obligations.[233] Turkey's experience in this matter shows that without doing a culture change project, such law is doomed to be ineffective. Similarly, the Indian government responded to the rise in honor killings (also called customary killings) in the northern Indian states of Punjab and Haryana by enacting an amendment to the Indian Penal Code so the killers can be tried for murder. It also tentatively convened a group of ministers to deliberate on the matter, as "honor killings is a sensitive issue"[234] because they implicate traditional mores governing moral standing and appropriate behaviors between social groups, castes, and men and women. Without more, it is unlikely such action will be adequate to address the problem of honor killings. Syria's President Bashar Assad, for example, also decreed that men who kill their daughters and sisters would be punished under a new law. Previously the crime carried no minimum sentence and had a maximum sentence of one year, but the new law would impose a minimum sentence of two years.[235] The new law modified Article 548 of the Penal Code, which exempted men from "the usual sentences for murder and assault if provoked by 'illegitimate sex acts' or 'the suspicious state' of female relatives."[236] Jordan debated the issue, and its lawmakers blocked attempts to impose stiffer penalties on men who kill in defense of honor because it was feared that changes to existing law would encourage adultery.[237] Similarly, efforts by sub-Saharan African countries to reform

[233] Chante Lasco, *Virginity Testing in Turkey: A Violation of Women's Human Rights*, Hum. Rts. Brief, Spring 2002, at 10.

[234] Manasi Kakatlar-Kulkarni, *A Mindset Change to Stop Honor Killings*, Foreign Pol'y Ass'n (July 9, 2010), http://foreignpolicyblogs.com.

[235] *The Law Changes, Will Attitudes?*, The Economist, July 16, 2009, *available at* http://www.economist.com/node/14045284.

[236] *Id.*

[237] *Id.*

inheritance and land rights concerning women have been met with significant challenges because issues such as marriage, divorce, burial, and inheritance rights continue to be governed by customary law even if statutory laws have been enacted to reform custom.[238] Under customary law, women are excluded from property ownership and inheritance,[239] and unless traditional conceptions are altered, statutory law remains ineffective.

With respect to category three, I examine the work of nongovernmental organizations that have strived to effectuate culture change because laws alone have been either detrimental or ineffective with respect to harmful cultural practices. For example, the organization Women Living Under Muslim Laws (WLUML) has worked with women who do not wish to give up their faith but who also do not want to live under oppressive customs that deny them certain rights. Likewise, NGOs have undertaken culture change efforts that directly address the norms underlying the practice of female genital mutilation (FGM) as standard laws have proven ineffective to stop the practice. The FGM discussion focuses on efforts in Egypt and Senegal. Despite initial hostile reactions, the NGOs achieved a 70 percent success rate (with success measured in terms of whether the girls remain uncut past the age of twelve). The NGOs relied on community outreach and educational efforts to change the meaning of the practice (presenting it as a health and family planning issue) and supplemented this work with other community engagement endeavors such as the provision of microloans.[240]

The discussion of microcredit brings Part A of Chapter 5 back to the issue of savings and capital accumulation. From a purely economic standpoint, savings is an important component of the drive to increase capital. As briefly discussed, note how Japan marshaled changes in cultural attitudes in the Meiji era to accomplish the objective of capital accumulation and investment. But from a broader development standpoint, access to capital through savings and credit, especially for historically marginal groups and the poor, is not only about economic growth but also about empowerment, dignity, and self-worth. Thus, I also include in this section a discussion of how microcredit organizations such as the Grameen Bank and others seek to provide women with credit to improve their economic standing and to increase what Sen and Appadurai call their capacity and voice. The Grameen Bank, for example, makes microloans conditioned not on the financial creditworthiness of the borrower (most have no credit history and no collateral) but rather on the borrower's social capital. The bank makes loans not to an individual but to a circle of five borrowers. Lending circles consist of what is called 2, 2, 1 loans. Loans are made to the first two borrowers and subsequent loans to two more borrowers, and finally to the last borrower only if the preceding borrowers have satisfied their debt to

---

[238] Johanna Bond, *Gender, Discourse, and Customary Law in Africa*, 83 S. CAL. L. REV. 509, 514, 532–33, 544 (2010).

[239] Abby Morrow Richardson, *Women's Inheritance Rights in Africa: The Need to Integrate Cultural Understanding and Legal Reform*, HUM. RTS. BRIEF, Winter 2004, at 19, 19.

[240] *See infra* notes 241, 244–46 and accompanying text. *See also* TOSTAN, TOSTAN ANNUAL REPORT (2007).

the bank. Grameen Bank boasts a high success rate, and the loans work because they use peer pressure and a sense of social obligation to ensure repayment. As Appadurai acutely observed, "creating informal savings groups among the poor . . . is a worldwide technique for improving financial citizenship for the urban and rural poor throughout the world . . . . [S]avings has a profound ideological, even salvational status."[241]

But what is uniquely distinctive and interesting about the Grameen Bank is that its loan-making agenda is supplemented by a robust cultural foundation. The provision of loans is supplemented by a concerted campaign to change culturally based attitudes that are antithetical to broad development principles. Borrowers do not have to produce conventional proof of creditworthiness. Instead they must agree to be part of a consciousness-raising regime. The Grameen Bank's so-called "16 decisions" program requires borrowers to commit to essentially changing cultural habits—pledging to educate their children, to not take dowries, to reject the practice of child marriage, to not overspend on weddings and funerals and other unproductive activities, and to save. Interestingly, many of the traditional practices the Grameen Bank work to alter are similar to those Japan undertook to transform in its Meiji era.

Part B of Chapter 5 is devoted to a study of three countries that can serve as high-visibility law and development case studies: Kosovo, Iraq, and Afghanistan. These countries are chosen for several reasons. First, they represent the sort of law and development projects that developed (primarily Western) countries are increasingly involved in, that is, law and development pursued to support and/or justify Western military and/or humanitarian intervention. Countries emerging from military interventions continue to face humanitarian and security problems that require a long-term commitment to rebuilding and reforming institutions. Such a project involves an "extremely complex bundle of cultural commitments and institutional structures that support peace, human rights, democracy, and prosperity."[242] This does not mean that law and development in those countries is categorically different from the usual law and development projects discussed in this book. However, it does mean that there are additional considerations—mostly a continuing lack of security and stability that would make law and development more uncertain and complicated.

Second, given their high-profile status, it is interesting to study law and development efforts in countries that have for a variety of reasons attracted much international and national attention. The stakes are high and thus one would expect law and development in those countries to represent a best effort, presumably well-thought-out and well-financed undertaking. Does law and development in these countries follow the standard, technocratic rule of law agenda or does it include a cultural component?[243]

---

[241] Appadurai, *supra* note 129, at 74.

[242] Stromseth et al., *supra* note 5, at 4.

[243] Relatedly, it is also interesting to note that post–World War II Japan and Germany much more readily accepted culture change brought by the West than Kosovo, Iraq, and Afghanistan. One reason could be that both countries had suffered massive destruction and total defeat and had little choice. But it is possible that the root of acceptance in the historical examples comes from the way in which the societies viewed

Together, these detailed case studies support the central thesis of the book, that law and development is not just a legal and economic endeavor but also a consummately cultural one. As John Norton Moore so aptly remarked, democracy building, for example, "is a goal to be assisted through norm-creation, education, electoral observation, and other modes of peaceful engagement."[244] Similarly, law and development is itself a norm-creating project that must include but at the same time transcend the passage of new laws or the institution of new legal structures. Thus, intimately woven into the chapter is an examination of the *hows* involved in culture change across these markedly different settings. Note that in Chapter 4, I showed how international law has been evolving from its state-centric focus to become more pluralistic. Chapter 5 looks at the many international actors that constructivist theorists in international relations and liberal theorists in international law invited onto the international stage. It analyzes how these non-state actors such as NGOs work to diffuse the liberal norms of human rights globally, through what scholars call networks, webs, and flows of epistemic communities. Increasingly, the international system is seeing a rise in networks of informal interactions between a plurality of actors engaged in political or cultural processes, each united to the other on the basis of shared beliefs and collective identities.[245]

There is also a vibrant literature on the transnational process involved in the diffusion of norms. Actors are engaged in a process of interaction, norm-interpretation, and norm-internalization. Norms are transmitted and translated by "norm entrepreneurs" through webs or networks from a source (an NGO, a social movement, a state) to a target. The contexts in which the norms are diffused will also influence the ways that the norms are received, discussed, and transmitted (or not transmitted). Some norms may need to be modified or translated into the local cultural vernacular in a variety of ways (for example, reframing and altering the model, bundling and solidifying) to make them more locally palatable. In other words, actors, whether local or transnational, need to strategically frame their ideas and proposals in ways that are harmonious with the dominant conceptions of the common good as understood in that community. Framing, for example, is one way that "norm entrepreneurs" or social movements[246] can align their identification

themselves—the Japanese as a backward society needing the intervention of the West and Germany shamed by the scourge of Nazism. While both countries did hybridize some aspects of Western culture to make it their own, the efforts in both of these countries were much more successful than the modern-day scenarios in Afghanistan, Iraq, and Kosovo.

244 John Norton Moore, *Toward a New Paradigm: Enhanced Effectiveness in United Nations Peacekeeping, Collective Security, and War Avoidance*, 37 VA. J. INT'L L. 811, 860 (1997).

245 Mario Diani, *The Concept of Social Movement*, 40 SOC. REV. 1 (1992).

246 William A. Gamson & David S. Meyer, *Framing Political Opportunity*, *in* COMPARATIVE PERSPECTIVES ON SOCIAL MOVEMENTS: POLITICAL OPPORTUNITIES, MOBILIZING STRUCTURES, AND CULTURAL FRAMINGS 275, 283 (Doug McAdam, John D. McCarthy, & Mayer N. Zald eds., 1996) (defining a social movement as "a sustained and self-conscious challenge to authorities or cultural codes by a field of actors (organizations and advocacy networks), some of whom employ extrainstitutional means of influence.").

of a problem (diagnostic framing) and their proposed transformation within an interpretive framework (prognostic framing) that other members will relate to and join.

Chapter 6 is a critical reflection on the ideas set forth in the preceding chapters and directly grapple with countervailing views. Chapter 6 wrestles with a set of core dilemmas—whether the project of culture change is normatively defensible; how new cultural norms can be deliberately introduced, especially those that run counter to patterns of thought and behavior that people have experienced most of their lives; and how this process can be accomplished in not just a strategically effective manner but also a normatively defensible and respectful manner.

A disturbing tension admittedly runs through this project, that is, the tension between universal values on the one hand and local cultural values on the other. This book is a defense of universalism. When law and development promotes development as a project that promotes freedom and maximizes capacity and voice, its task must include changing local cultural norms that are at odds with the maximization of freedom and capacity necessary to "support . . . fundamental functions of a human life."[247] Violence against women, so-called honor killings, widow burning, virginity rites, FGM, systematic denial of education to girls, and the caste system, for example, are practices that fall within this first-order category. In these cases, law and development practitioners should engage in a robust culture change project. Other customary practices may also impede law and development objectives, for example, Islamic prohibition against interest because they increase transaction costs. To the extent that these second-order practices are widely accepted and alternative arrangements have been considered and rejected, and precisely because such practices do not negatively implicate human freedom and capacity, they need not be subject to culture change.

Most of Chapter 6 thus grapples with the tension inherent in changing first-order cultural norms that deny human freedom and capacity. Chapter 6 relies on Martha Nussbaum's extensive writing that defends universalism against relativism. Some scholars of new institutional economics such as Mark Tool also reject the "ethically ambivalent, fundamentally relativist position"[248] that prevails in modern society. Tool's instrumental approach to knowledge is laden with values, and although there is no claim to "Absolute Truth,"[249] Tool stakes his work on principles such as "human rights in foreign policy and the role of education in developing critical and coherent thinking" and the principle of noninvidiousness "to reduce or remove forms of discrimination and disenfranchisement that operate on the basis of rank and prestige—that assess the relative worth of individuals according to race, gender, class, and so on. . . ."[250]

---

[247] Nussbaum, *supra* note 128, at 1.

[248] David F. Ruccio & Jack Amariglio, Postmodern Moments in Modern Economics 180 (2003). *See also id.* at 181.

[249] *Id.* at 181 n.19.

[250] *Id.* at 182.

In this context, the issue of individual or group preference is central and fraught with peril. If the claim is that local cultural norms are widely accepted and/or reflected in formal or informal institutions, who is anyone, especially an outsider, to come in and ask that people subscribe to new ("Western") norms? Given the complexities involved, the objections to universalism need to be individually unpacked. The first objection can be described as a concern about paternalism—overriding the preferences of others. Included in this concern is the issue of participation. How is culture change to be accomplished if the objectionable cultural norm is widely accepted? How much local participation will there be in this effort to change a cultural practice that supposedly reflects the preference of those law and development are trying to help?

Granted, local participation is usually deemed a positive good. For example, the World Bank has initiated a Comprehensive Development Framework which promotes greater local participation in development projects and a sense of greater local ownership of such projects. On the one hand, development ideally should have grassroots participation and support[251] and development objectives should be subjected to "informed choice, aided by public discussion, critical scrutiny, and a participatory political environment."[252] On the other hand, participatory development in communities characterized by entrenched and hierarchical patterns of authority may also be susceptible to capture by the traditional elites themselves, calling for a return to, not surprisingly, traditional, "authentic" culture.

Hardly anyone can disagree with the notion that change, especially if externally promoted or supported, must "honor local conditions and wishes."[253] Yet, at the same time, organizations and institutions that have a stake in the maintenance of certain traditions and norms will oppose the desired change. Indeed, some of the most illiberal traditions and beliefs are held by "grassroots" local organizations and individuals, such as tribal chiefs whose patriarchal power and authority would be diminished by change promoted by the type of law and development project advocated in this book.[254] This is yet another reason why law and development must confront cultural barriers to development. Given the expected resistance that projects that give voice to the poor and the disenfranchised will encounter, research has shown that development must "take[] account of the challenge posed by culturally embedded hierarchies."[255]

Consequently, there are several reasons why "grassroots" and "local" cultural preferences should not be automatically deemed sacrosanct. It is true that Sen's freedom-oriented

---

[251] *See* Cao, *supra* note 121, at 27; *see also* Sen, *supra* note 185, at 53 ("An overarching value must be the need for participatory decision making on the kind of society people want to live in, based on open discussion, with adequate opportunity for the expression of minority positions.").

[252] *Id.* at 55.

[253] Moore, *supra* note 244.

[254] Rao & Walton, *supra* note 49, at 25 (discussing how "threats to the established ascribed patterns of cultural difference are resisted by community leaders. Elites often capture resources and use them to further client-patron relationships with poorer groups.").

[255] *Id.*

perspective emphasizes the importance of "the liberty of all to participate in deciding what traditions to observe . . ."[256] so that presumably, if there is full public discussion and participation on a subject, then the preferences emerging therefrom should be respected and not subject to change. Using Sen's baseline or yardstick, it is easy to conclude that in most developing countries today where women's capability and freedom are radically constricted, women have not had the liberty of participation or discussion. In a world where options are denied to women or the desperately poor, where they are denied education and are illiterate, their consent or preferences do not meet Sen's baseline requirement. Those conditions "should make us reflect before we conclude that women without options really endorse the lives they lead."[257] Part 6 expands on this argument—that under certain circumstances, the satisfaction of private preferences should not be determinative in public policy decisions.

Another reason preferences, especially those that lead to a constriction of freedom and capacity, should be scrutinized is because preferences are culturally and socially determined. A person who is deprived of consciousness about available opportunities will surely have different personal preferences than one who enjoys freedom and has full human capacity. To deny such a person freedom and capacity because the preexisting injustice has distorted her preferences on the basis that it is paternalistic to question her preference is to allow injustice to continue.

One can make this additional observation about preferences and paternalism. As Martha Nussbaum observed, the contested preferences that law and development object to are "themselves highly paternalistic, particularly toward women. They tell them what to do, claiming that they are promoting women's good. They treat women as unequal under the law, as lacking full civil capacity, as not having the property rights, associative liberties, and employment rights of males."[258] How ironic then that a law or a culture project that aims to neutralize such preexisting paternalism against women or the poor would then be accused of paternalism. Any bill of rights or the Indian constitution which prohibits discrimination on the basis of sex or caste would, under this understanding, be charged with paternalism if paternalism means telling people they cannot do something although they want to do it. "[A]ny system of law is 'paternalistic,' keeping some people from doing some things that they want to do. But that is hardly a good argument against the rule of law, or, more generally, against opposing the attempts of some people to tyrannize over others."[259]

Quite apart from whether "true" preferences should be given deference because one is opposed to paternalism, there is also the issue of preference falsification. Professor Timur Kuran's research demonstrates that a certain liberal majority in some Islamic societies

---

[256] SEN, *supra* note 30, at 32; *see also id.* at 242.

[257] NUSSBAUM, *supra* note 128, at 43.

[258] *Id.* at 52.

[259] *Id.* at 53.

are being silenced by a radical few with more aggressively endorsed viewpoints. In that case, preference falsification is a rational tactical response used to avoid sanctions by the dominant group.[260] Thus one cannot blithely assume that vocalized preferences are necessarily genuine or that they reflect uniformity of opinions at the "grassroots" level and that efforts to change those preferences are per se illegitimate.

The phenomenon of preference falsification is ubiquitous and creates a situation in which individuals hide their true proclivities. Preference falsification by individuals make it harder for others similarly situated to express discontent because each individual may believe he or she is alone in his or her true preference. As a result, through individual acts of preference falsification, a false and distorted reality is reproduced in the public domain, making it harder for genuine discussions to take place, whether it be on the drawbacks of existing arrangements or the merits of change.

In certain environments then, if preference falsification is prevalent, it may be quite difficult to distinguish between true and false preferences. This is precisely why, in the quest to assess preferences, "[t]here is thus a strong methodological case for emphasizing the need to assign explicitly evaluative weights to different components of quality of life (or of well-being) and then to place the chosen weights for open public discussion and critical scrutiny."[261] Therefore, "we cannot in general take preferences as given independently of public discussion."[262]

Individuals might hide their true preferences if they know their preferences are maligned and marginalized. Elites who defend the status quo usually embark on two strategies to malign opponents. First, they characterize local culture as pure, homogeneous, and unfractured, thereby minimizing or distorting instances of internal dissent that contests inherited cultural norms and seeks to alter the status quo within the culture.[263] In other words, cultural elites unilaterally decree that local "preferences" as represented by the elites are genuine and grounded in deeply entrenched traditions that cannot and should not be scrutinized or dislodged. Second, they describe the desired change, even if internally motivated and driven, as foreign and illegitimate because it has external or Western roots and thus a threat to the purity of local culture.

One of the most inflammatory charges against culture change is the claim that change is synonymous with Westernization (and by implication, carries with it the baggage of Western imperialism). Yet, as I explore in Chapter 6, the dichotomy set up by cultural purists is itself false. This so-called conflict between Western versus indigenous is not inevitable. I intend to show that culture change is not necessarily synonymous with Westernization. Dipesh Chakrabarty, for example, has criticized this assumption,

---

[260] Timur Kuran, Private Truths, Public Lies: The Social Consequences of Preference Falsification (1995).

[261] Sen, *supra* note 30, at 81.

[262] *Id.* at 153.

[263] Madhavi Sunder, *Cultural Dissent*, 54 Stan. L. Rev. 495 (2001).

which he terms Western historicism—the idea that "progress" and "modernity" must have a Western face. "Historicism is what made modernity or capitalism look not simply global but rather as something that became global *over time*, by originating in one place (Europe) and then spreading outside it."[264] As Chakrabarty puts it, "[t]his 'first in Europe, then elsewhere' structure of global historical time was historicist; different non-Western nationalisms would later produce local versions of the same narrative, replacing 'Europe' by some locally constructed center."[265] Europe is imagined to be "the site of the first occurrence of capitalism, modernity, or Enlightenment."[266] Consequently, under this view, development is understood to result in a singular destination for the world's people. To be a "modern individual" is to become "a European."[267] To be a modern country is to leave the "imaginary waiting room of history" and to be "all headed for the same destination."[268]

But historicism is not predetermined. A culture change project can promote culture change without inevitably imposing a Western cultural construct upon the culture for the obvious reason that no country is a blank slate and every country remains moored to a continuing reality of religion, culture, people, and history. For example, when firms in developing countries adopted suggested administrative reforms that may seem standard or universal, these firms nonetheless "remained profoundly 'traditional' in the way these tools were actually given meaning and interpreted."[269] Culture change does not have to be about "juxtaposing, or compromising between, the modern and the traditional, but creating an intimate union between them."[270]

Moreover, Westernization is itself not the endpoint as aspects of Westernization can also be subject to culture change as well,[271] and the West itself contains its own internal heterogeneity. Varieties of economic behavior exist in the developed world, as reflected

---

264 Dipesh Chakrabarty, Provincializing Europe: Postcolonial Thought and Historical Difference 7 (2000).

265 *Id.*

266 *Id.*

267 *Id.* at 33.

268 *Id.* at 8.

269 Yousfi, *supra* note 8, at 51.

270 *Id.*

271 Although this book is concerned with culture change as a component of the law and development project, which has as its core concern developing countries, culture change may be applicable to developed countries well. For example, one could say that the financial crisis on Wall Street "was symptomatic of a culture, and a governance system, that was seriously out of control." Charles Ferguson, Predator Nation (2012), *as republished in Toxic: Wall Street's Culture and Governance During the Bubble*, Huffington Post (May 21, 2012), *available at* http://www.huffingtonpost.com/charles-ferguson/toxic-finance-wall-street_b_1532520.html. This Wall Street culture of fraud, deception, and extreme recklessness with other people's money should be subject to culture change, for example. Senator Elizabeth Warren has emphasized the need to "fundamentally change the culture at the Fed and in turn the enforcement of regulations through the banking system." *See* Alan Zibel, *Warren Pushes Regulators to Get Tougher on Banks*, Wall St. J. (Apr. 22, 2014), http://online.wsj.com/news/articles/SB10001424052702304049904579517960948902956.

in "the persistence of distinctive cultural traditions even within 'developed countries.' "[272] Within developed countries, firms have adopted different economic models that reflect national and local propensities, revealing "different conceptions of interpersonal and social relations with all their political and moral dimensions."[273] For example, individual Japanese firms may be more embedded in a family of related firms than US firms. The organizational model for a US factory that might be billed as a universal reference for other countries may in fact be "a local product. It reflects a political ideal that corresponds to the notion of a society based on contracts freely entered into by equals."[274] Even a task as seemingly ordinary and universal as performance evaluation—rewarding people for work done—may take on a local tone when implemented locally. In the United States, performance may focus on results. In Jordan, the focus is less about outcome and more about "the extent to which people 'tried to do their best.' "[275] There is growing "evidence of differences in management practices linked to different conceptions of the relations between the individual and society.... These conceptions make the tradition/modernity dichotomy totally obsolete. . . ."[276] Even though the Western experience will remain relevant, "[t]he proposition that societal modernization, once activated, moves inexorably toward establishing a certain type of mental outlook (scientific rationalism, pragmatic instrumentalism, secularism) and a certain type of institutional order (popular government, bureaucratic administration, market-driven industrial economy) irrespective of the culture and politics of a given place is simply not true."[277]

As Chapter 6 shows, this debate is fierce and ongoing—whether modernity is acultural—consisting of a series of progression "toward which all cultures converge, as they go through, one after another, substantially the same changes,"[278] or rather culturally specific—so that the mix and match of sameness and differences resulting from particular civilizational or cultural settings combine to produce "alternative modernities. . . ." For reasons developed in the book, I stake the position of this book on the latter.

In today's globalized world, modernity is "global and multiple and no longer has a governing center or master-narratives to accompany it,"[279] proceeding instead transnationally and transculturally. As noted, this is "a time when non-Western people everywhere begin

---

[272] Yousfi, *supra* note 8, at 55.

[273] *Id.* at 44.

[274] *Id.* (citation omitted).

[275] *Id.* at 52.

[276] *Id.* at 46 (citation omitted).

[277] Dilip Parameshwar Gaonkar, *On Alternative Modernities*, *in* ALTERNATIVE MODERNITIES 1, 16 (Dilip Parameshwar Gaonkar ed., 2001) ("Nor does cultural modernity invariably take the form of an adversary culture that privileges the individual's need for self-expression and self-realization over the claims of the community."). Skeptics may nonetheless charge that claims of universalism are in fact used to mask a Western agenda or conversely that a US or Western model is in fact "not the product of a particular culture, but rather the very expression of a universal rationality applicable across cultural boundaries." Yousfi, *supra* note 8, at 42.

[278] Gaonkar, *supra* note 277, at 17 (internal quotation marks omitted).

[279] *Id.* at 14.

to engage critically their own hybrid modernities."[280] Culture change thus does not necessarily lead to a Western end point but rather to "alternative modernities" that "appear inescapably plural."[281] Change and modernity will come, but from "a specific national/cultural site."[282]

Even as the West is itself evolving and hybrid, so is the non-West. Insisting that such and such a cultural tradition is "authentic" and that it should be protected from change is not only wrong but, in today's global world, anachronistic. This authenticity claim should have "no bite in the modern world, where the ideas of every culture turn up inside every other, through the internet and the media. The ideas of feminism, of democracy, of egalitarian welfarism, are now 'inside' every known society."[283] Chapter 6 critiques the implicit notion that a culture exists in its own separate box and should not be tainted by extraneous elements or that there is a definitive authentic culture to be preserved. I draw on a rich body of literature in law and sociology journals to argue that there is a high degree of porousness between cultures. There is constant borrowing among cultures, and it is difficult to disentangle the different strands and determine which is "indigenous" and "authentic" and which is "foreign" and "inauthentic." Cultures throughout history have evolved and can be traced to many causes, including foreign ones. For example, the term "Indonesian culture" may be used, but it does not mean that Indonesian culture is monolithic. History shows that Indonesia has an Islamic tradition but also strong Hindu, Buddhist, and Confucian cultural influences. Similarly, Hindu nationalists often ignore the fact that Indian civilization has layers of tradition—Hinduism, Buddhism, and Islam.

Besides the fact that a culture might have accumulated centuries of culturally disparate strands and layers, it is also important to acknowledge that modern cultures in particular are marked by robust internal dissension. This means that internal cultural groups are challenging the prevailing views of their own culture from within. Ferment, therefore, is not necessarily externally induced. Consequently, it is inaccurate to present the dominant view of any given cultural practice as the only authentic view because internally there are many dissenting views. Culture is not monolithic but hybrid and constantly evolving. It is normatively better for law and development to align with internal views that accord with the values of law and development projects. Indeed, those who claim to defend authentic cultures often do so under the banner of cultural self-determination. Yet, self-determination is but one among many values—equality, reason, freedom, tolerance, for example. Law and development should not be supporting or acquiescing to traditional practices in deference to the principle of self-determination at the expense of other equally valid principles.

---

280 *Id.*

281 *See* Sudipta Kaviraj, *Filth and the Public Sphere: Concepts and Practices About Space in Calcutta*, PUB. CULTURE, Fall 1997, at 83, 113.

282 Gaonkar, *supra* note 277, at 15.

283 NUSSBAUM, *supra* note 128, at 49.

Law and development cannot submit to the relativist thesis which states that all cultural norms are relative, cannot be criticized, and should be granted moral deference. Even cosmopolitans who value differences can be cosmopolitans but at the same time critical when criticism is called for. Kwame Anthony Appiah criticizes the version of cosmopolitanism that "embraces Difference, with a capital D," in effect refraining from critical assessment of difference. Anthony Appiah observed as follows: "Cosmopolitanism of this sort begins by urging that we should know others, with their differences, and believes that this will lead us to toleration, perhaps even to 'mutual love.' "[284] For Appiah, however, this version has built-in problems:

> This way of making the argument raises an immediate problem, however. For it starts with an acknowledgment that there is good and bad—*le pour et le contre*—in each place. And if that is so, won't treating people in other places as fellow citizens require us, indeed, to love the good but also to seek to eradicate the bad? Why love the French as they are, rather than helping them to become better? Why not take advantage, at the same time, of the ways in which they can improve us? Cosmopolitanism of this variety embraces Difference, with a capital D: but why not embrace the Good, with a capital G? That way, we can learn from other kinds of people and from other societies, just as they can learn from us. This is what we can call a universalistic cosmopolitanism: a celebration of difference that remains committed to the existence of universal standards.[285]

Appiah's universalistic cosmopolitanism provides a good counterargument to those who defend differences even if those differences are against the Good.[286]

As to whether or not a value is Western and legitimate or illegitimate on that basis, one might reply as follows. First, how is one to determine whether a particular value is Western? While it is commonly assumed nowadays that pluralism, tolerance, and freedom of worship are "Western" values, this assumption disregards the fact that Islam too, for example, has had a history that espouses precisely those values. To assert that such and such a value is Western assumes that the world is divided into impenetrable civilizational camps characterized by intrinsically different values. While Europe was riven by the Inquisitions, Akbar, a Muslim emperor of India, preached religious tolerance and freedom of religion.[287] During his reign, he encouraged Muslim scholars to debate religious matters with Hindus, Sikhs, Jains, Jews, and Roman Catholic Jesuits. Akbar was a Sunni Hanafi Muslim and was raised by parents who instilled in him the values of

---

[284] Kwame Anthony Appiah, The Cosmopolitan Scholar (Apr. 5, 2006), http://www.princeton.edu/paw/web_exclusives/plus/plus040506appiah_essay.html.

[285] *Id.*

[286] *Id.; see* Chapter 6.

[287] *See infra* notes 288–89 and accompanying text.

religious tolerance. One of his first official actions as ruler was to eliminate a tax that was imposed only on non-Muslims. His court included many Hindus in high positions of great responsibility. And to show his respect and support for all religions, he decreed that all religious festivals and holidays be observed in the imperial court.

Second, one might declare that the origin of a cultural tradition is irrelevant to a judgment of its value. Admittedly, a value might need to be strategically framed in a way that resonates locally. Yet, the drafters of India's constitution, for example, made a decidedly different choice. Instead of reaching into the reservoir of traditional Indian values, whatever those may be, they incorporated rights and values rooted in different constitutions of the world. The drafters understood that Enlightenment ideals are not necessarily the property of the West alone and were not too troubled by whether a principle is internal or external to India. As India's Nobel Laureate in Literature (1913) Rabindranath Tagore put it, "[w]hatever we understand and enjoy in human products instantly becomes ours, wherever they might have their origin. I am proud of my humanity when I can acknowledge the poets and artists of other countries as my own. Let me feel with unalloyed greatness that all the glories of man are mine."[288] Aristotle said, "[i]n general, people seek not the way of their ancestors, but the good."[289]

It is ultimately on that basis that this book rests its culture change proposal.

To sum up the Introduction, law and development—even if mostly "law" and little "development," supported by either a thick or thin view of the rule of law, with or without a culture focus—*is* already political, meaning its pursuit will inevitably trigger issues that require the adoption of certain political choices which engage political and economic controversies. Thus, bringing a "rule of law" framework to the law and development debate cannot "*itself* be a development strategy" nor can "choosing law . . . substitute for the perplexing political and economic choices . . ."[290] embedded in development. In other words, development is not only about technical or economic adjustment or technocratic expertise but rather has always involved contestable policy prescriptions.[291] There is no one "rule of law" or one systemic modeling from which similarly designed project policies will flow. Development "policy-making breaks eggs, imposes costs, *intervenes* in foreign places with a view to changing them."[292] This is so whether or not law and development adopts an explicit cultural approach to "rule of law."

But to make the point even more forcefully, not only is law and development already political, it is also already immersed in culture. Rule of law is itself political and exporting

---

[288] Amartya Sen, *Poetry and Reason: Why Rabindranath Tagore Still Matters*, NEW REPUBLIC, June 9, 2011, http://www.tnr.com/print/article/books/magazine/89649/rabindranath-tagore.

[289] NUSSBAUM, *supra* note 128, at 49 (quoting ARISTOTLE, POLITICS,1269a3–4).

[290] Kennedy, *supra* note 35, at 17.

[291] *Id.* at 18 (For example, a certain development choice will result in certain groups or interests receiving "more wealth, status, power, than they had before. . . .").

[292] *Id.* at 19.

law through the rule of law mantra is not much different from exporting culture. Indeed, even the first wave law and development reformers knew that in exporting law, cultural shift would (they hoped) eventually follow. As one commentator in the field of anthropology observed, culture is already embedded in and inextricably linked to the work of law and development. It would be a mistake to believe that "villages are full of culture but that there is no culture in the conference halls of New York and Geneva. However, UN meetings are deeply shaped by culture. The transnational elites who populate these halls think they are doing law but they are actually making culture."[293]

Adding cultural considerations explicitly into the mix and engaging in culture change will certainly add complexity to an already complex project. However, it would be grossly inaccurate to see the injection of culture as something that will suddenly turn law and development from a neutral, apolitical effort into a contentious, politicized one.

If culture were included in a law and development framework, culture change would merely be one more contestable idea among the many contestable ideas. In and of itself, this is not extraordinary, as there has always been "contending ideas, contending interests, contested theories, complex unknowables."[294] However complex and contentious, the cultural consideration *is* necessary. As Sen so aptly remarked, "the cultural dimensions of development requires closer scrutiny in development analysis. It is important to investigate the different ways . . . in which culture should be taken into account in examining the challenges of development, and in assessing the demands of sound economic strategies."[295]

In closing this Introduction, I would like to underline the main point made throughout this book. Throughout, the book examines many cultural norms and practices that are economically inefficient and may retard market development. This does *not* mean that I advocate changing all those norms and practices. People have the freedom to choose anti-efficiency norms if that freedom is undergirded by an inclusive and informed decision-making process. Law and development can and should be open to accommodate different cultural values but only if those values do not infringe on other first-order nonnegotiable universal values such as human freedom and human capability.

---

293 Merry, *supra* note 44, at 70.

294 Kennedy, *supra* note 35, at 26.

295 Sen, *supra* note 185.

1

A Brief History of Law and Development and the Emerging New Framework

IN THIS CHAPTER, I examine the two "waves" of law and development that have characterized the movement, describe the characteristics associated with each wave, and propose a new, culturally informed framework for the study of law and development. A primary purpose of this chapter is to provide a brief history of the field, expose its flaws and blind spots—its cursory treatment of culture and heavy emphasis on the technocratic aspects of "rule of law"—and show how these flaws have contributed to the movement's failures. It is not the purpose of this chapter to demonstrate *why* these blind spots exist. That task is taken up in Chapter 2, when I discuss how international law, public and private, and international human rights exclude culture from their conceptual framework; and in Chapter 3, when I apply this tradition of cultural exclusion in international law to law and development itself.

After declaring itself dead, the field of law and development was revived in the 1980s after years of decline and disillusionment.[1] The crisis was partly fueled by the events of the 1960s when Western institutions were deemed flawed[2] and many, particularly those

---

[1] *See* LAW AND CRISIS IN THE THIRD WORLD (Sammy Adelman & Abdul Paliwala eds., 1993); John H. Merryman, *Comparative Law and Social Change: On the Origins, Style, Decline and Revival of the Law and Development Movement*, 25 AM. J. COMP. L. 457 (1977); David Trubek & Marc Galanter, *Scholars in Self-Estrangement: Some Reflections on the Crisis in Law and Development Studies in the United States*, 1974 WIS. L. REV. 1062 (1974).

[2] For a critique of the law and development movement and its self-proclaimed crisis and despair, *see* Brian Z. Tamanaha, *The Lessons of Law-and-Development Studies*, 89 AM. J. INT'L L. 470, 472 (1995) (book review).

intimately associated with the movement, questioned the objectives of law and development[3] and the institution of law itself.[4] In other words, from the perspective of those 1960s so-called first-wave scholars, if law and development aimed to assist poor countries in establishing Western-style markets and laws,[5] and if the integrity of Western laws is questioned, even in developed, Western societies,[6] then the essence of the movement itself must be questioned as well.[7] In this chapter, Part A briefly examines the efforts of the first wave law and development scholars and explores the failures and the disillusionment that follow. Part B describes the second wave and its heavy emphasis on law and institutions, which, whether intentionally or not, presents law and development as primarily a technocratic enterprise. And Part C studies efforts to expand law and development substantively, in a direction that allows the movement to encompass human rights. Part C also shows how noted scholars of development have pushed for an even thicker understanding of development, one that transcends political and economic development to include cultural development. My proposal for a culturally informed law and development incorporates this thicker understanding and argues that culture must play a central role in law and development.

A. First Wave of Law and Development

Scholars and practitioners from the first wave of law and development (1960s and 1970s) were heavily influenced by legal liberalism and saw law in instrumental and purposive terms. Law was seen as a means to an end, which at the time was to effectuate the national development objectives of the state.[8] Although the language of law and development at the time included rhetorical references to human rights, justice, and democracy, the focal

---

[3] David M. Trubek, *Back to the Future: The Short, Happy Life of the Law and Society Movement*, 18 FLA. ST. U. L. REV. 4, 23 (1990) (characterizing the law and development movement as one aimed at "exporting democratic capitalism" to countries "too poor or benighted to grasp the possibilities of this superior form of civilization.").

[4] Trubek & Galanter, *supra* note 1, at 1083.

[5] David M. Trubek, *Toward a Social Theory of Law: An Essay on the Study of Law and Development*, 82 YALE L.J. 1, 7 (1972) (describing how law is necessary to the establishment of markets because law provides predictable, universal rules, thus ensuring that economic activities and fruits generated therefrom will be protected).

[6] Trubek & Galanter, *supra* note 1, at 1083 (pointing out critics' claim that even in the United States, law is instrumental in perpetuating "domination by elite groups" and "arbitrary actions by government."). For a compelling criticism of this self-professed disillusionment of the movement by its founders, *see* Tamanaha, *supra* note 2, at 474–75 (charging that self-estrangement of the movement was homegrown and should have been left at home—disillusionment "had far more to do with events at home than with the situation in developing countries.").

[7] Trubek & Galanter, *supra* note 1, at 1070, 1080 (condemning the liberal-legalism model previously advocated as "ethnocentric and naive" because the model is ignorant of the realities of Third World countries).

[8] David Kennedy, *The "Rule of Law," Political Choices, and Development Common Sense*, *in* THE NEW LAW AND ECONOMIC DEVELOPMENT: A CRITICAL APPRAISAL 95, 102, 117 (David M. Trubek & Alvaro Santos eds., 2006).

point of law and development was on economic growth. As I discuss below, first wave scholars saw law as an instrument for economic growth, which was conducive to the modernization of traditional societies. To the extent that Third World law was not able to facilitate Third World economic development and modernization, first wave reformers sought to modernize Third World traditional legal culture.

A basic assumption of the first wave of law and development was that growth would be a necessary first step to almost everything else. Political democracy and social development would eventually follow economic growth, and to this end, varying degrees of authoritarian rule was tolerated to the extent it was compatible with economic growth.[9] More specifically, law and development scholars supported the establishment in developing countries of capital market programs to foster Western-style regulatory and private property regime.[10] It was hoped that capital markets would result in growth followed by a demand for " 'modern' substantive codes, a more stable and coherent body of laws, a reduction in government ad hoc decisionmaking, judicial reform, rationality in legal thought, and a restructuring of professional organization."[11]

First wave law and development lawyers were also inspired by and drew heavily from the so-called modernization theory, which emphasized, as its name suggests, modernization, as measured by stages of development and corresponding levels of economic growth. Samuel Huntington, one of the primary proponents of modernization theory, remarked that the dual categories of modernity versus tradition were "the latest manifestation[s] of a Great Dichotomy between more primitive and more advanced societies which has been a common feature of Western social thought for the past one hundred years."[12] It was generally assumed that each society had its own separately demarcated cultures; culture was implicitly understood to be " 'a self-contained system of traits which distinguishes one community from another.' This perspective views culture as a relatively stable, homogeneous, internally consistent system of attitudes and values."[13] Different societies subscribe to different sets of cultural values. Societies were distinguished on the basis of traditional versus modern and "differences between modern and traditional societies were explained in terms of deeply embedded cultural traits."[14]

---

[9] David M. Trubek, *The "Rule of Law" in Development Assistance: Past, Present, and Future, in* THE NEW LAW AND ECONOMIC DEVELOPMENT: A CRITICAL APPRAISAL 74, 74–75 (David M. Trubek & Alvaro Santos eds., 2006).

[10] Trubek, *supra* note 5, at 45–46.

[11] *Id.* at 46.

[12] Samuel Huntington, *The Change to Change: Modernization, Development, and Politics*, 3 COMP. POL. 283, 285 (1971).

[13] Hela Yousfi, *Culture and Development: The Continuing Tension Between Modern Standards and Local Contexts, in* CULTURE, INSTITUTIONS, AND DEVELOPMENT: NEW INSIGHTS INTO AN OLD DEBATE 20, 21 (Jean-Philippe Platteau & Robert Peccoud eds., 2011).

[14] *Id.* at 22.

Modernization theory posited that there was a series of successive levels of economic growth through which all countries needed to pass,[15] emphasizing in particular that "development was an inevitable, evolutionary process of increasing societal differentiation that would ultimately produce economic, political and social institutions similar to those in the West. The outcome of this societal evolutionary process would be the creation of a free market system, liberal democratic political institutions, and the rule of law."[16] American economic historian Walt W. Rostow contended that development consisted of the following successive stages: the traditional society, the preconditions for takeoff, the takeoff, the drive to maturity, and the age of high mass consumption.[17] In accordance with this theory, traditional characteristics engrained in the economic, political, and social structures of a society were both a cause and a reflection of underdevelopment.[18] Modernization, in other words, aimed to establish or improve upon what Talcott Parsons termed the four societal institutions: governmental bureaucracy, capitalist economic system, "generalized universalistic legal systems," and democratic political system.[19] Modernization—"diffusion of capital, institutions and values from the First World"—could uplift the Third World.[20]

Modernization theory channeled the teachings of the noted sociologist Max Weber who believed that rationalization and predictability of the legal system were necessary elements to capitalistic enterprise.[21] This rationalization of the law would weaken the grip of the ruling class and allow capitalists to emerge, while the predictability of the legal system would allow capitalists to rely on property and contract rights.[22] The pursuit of gains would bring about economic development.

Note that for first wave scholars, the connection between law and economic development was explicit. The first wave, however, did not directly address the relationship

---

[15] Kevin E. Davis & Michael J. Trebilcock, *The Relationship Between Law and Development: Optimists Versus Skeptics*, 56 Am. J. Comp. L. 895, 900 (2008); Susanne Schech & Jane Haggis, Culture and Development: A Critical Introduction 9–11 (2000).

[16] Tamanaha, *supra* note 2, at 471; *see also* Lan Cao, *Law and Economic Development: A New Beginning?* 32 Tex. Int'l L. J. 545, 549 (1997) (describing how modernization theory views development as a sequential process similar to that experienced by the West).

[17] *See* W. W. Rostow, Stages of Economic Growth: A Noncommunist Manifesto (1960).

[18] Davis & Trebilcock, *supra* note 15, at 900.

[19] Talcott Parsons, *Evolutionary Universals in Society*, 29 Am. Soc. Rev. 339, 356 (1964).

[20] Davis & Trebilcock, *supra* note 15, at 900. Others similarly argued that traditional societies needed to modernize by shedding traditional cultures and adopting traits associated with the West. David C. McClelland, *Business Drive and National Achievement*, *in* Social Change: Sources, Patterns, and Consequences 165, 165–78 (Amitai Etzioni & Eva Etzioni eds., 1964).

[21] Chantal Thomas, *Max Weber, Talcott Parsons and the Sociology of Legal Reform: A Reassessment with Implications for Law and Development*, 15 Minn. J. Int'l L. 383, 387 (2006) (quoting Max Weber, Economy and Society 883 (G. Roth & R. Wittich eds., 1968) ("[T]he rationalization and systematization of the law in general and . . . the increasing calculability of the functioning of the legal process in particular, constituted one of the most important conditions for the existence of . . . capitalistic enterprise. . . .").

[22] *Id.*

between law and social or cultural development; rather scholars implicitly believed that economic growth—induced and supported by legal development—would in time yield social development and democratization. This "spillover" effect would allow first wave scholars to focus on economic growth while authoritarianism would be downplayed as a temporary political structure that would fade away once economic development was realized.[23] In other words, social development and democratization would emerge after the successful establishment of legal development and economic growth. Legal development or rule of law thus became the mantra and that which would follow—social development and democratization and other underlying norms supporting this new social framework—became footnotes to the main rule of law story. Thus social change, or as I call it here, culture change became a veiled subtext that lurked beneath the seemingly more normatively palatable and technocratically manageable rule of law plot.[24]

First wave proponents of modernization theory used rationalization and predictability of a legal system as factors in classifying a society as traditional or modern. For traditional societies, modernists prescribed the implementation of Western institutions and assumed that the economic success that the United States and Western Europe had seen would naturally flow to Third World countries that adopted these institutions.[25] For these assumptions, modernization theory was sharply criticized as ethnocentric and evolutionist.[26] Nonetheless, its main ideas were retained by first wave law and development lawyers and scholars.

Amidst a heightened period of the Cold War—the 1960s—bilateral aid from the United States to the Third World peaked, causing those years to be coined the "development decade."[27] The Cold War had motivated the West to foster economic development and reduce poverty in the Third World, in order to reduce the appeal of Communist revolutions.[28] Initially, American aid agencies placed little importance on legal development, instead deferring to economic and sociological development.[29] But the idea of legal development gained momentum as discussion on the role lawyers could play in development began to penetrate these aid agencies.[30] Lawyers could play a role in development as pragmatic problem solvers who could facilitate state-led growth by helping policy makers

---

[23] Trubek, *supra* note 9, at 76; *see also* Parsons, *supra* note 19, at 353, 355.

[24] It has been noted that legal development is a form of cultural intervention: "yet, despite the emphasis on rule of law, projects by. . . .multilateral institutions are 'often viewed out of context, as isolated abstractions in and of themselves rather than as interventions affecting people who have unique histories, locations, and cultures.'" Mary Packard-Winkler, *Putting the Culture Back into Development*, 13 FLETCHER F. OF WORLD AFFAIRS 251, 253 (1989), *available at* http://dl.tufts.edu/file_assets/tufts:UP149.001.00026.00008.

[25] Tamanaha, *supra* note 2, at 472.

[26] *See infra*, notes 95, 104–107; Francis G. Snyder, *The Failure of "Law and Development,"* 1982 WIS. L. REV. 373, 373–74 (1982) (reviewing JAMES A. GARDNER, LEGAL IMPERIALISM: AMERICAN LAWYERS AND FOREIGN AID IN LATIN AMERICA (1980)).

[27] Trubek & Galanter, *supra* note 1, at 1065.

[28] Jorge L. Esquirol, *The Failed Law of Latin America*, 56 AM. J. COMP. L. 75, 90 (2008).

[29] Trubek & Galanter, *supra* note 1, at 1065.

[30] *See generally* Trubek, *supra* note 9, at 75.

shape and enforce legislation, advising enterprise managers on the best way to accomplish their goals, and counseling private clients to allow them to grow and profit.[31] Agencies began supporting law and development scholarship and recruiting legal scholars to work on reform projects.[32]

First wave law and development can be characterized thus. Law was viewed in instrumental terms, to generate economic growth and in accordance with modernization theory, to serve as an impetus toward modernity. First wave law and development worked from the premise that modern or Western law would be instrumental to Third World modernization and development. The first wave of law and development lawyers exported the rule of law in order to help policy makers in poor countries shape and enforce the policy objectives of the state.

However, these lawyers soon discovered that "the legal cultures of these nations were highly 'formalist,'"[33] that is, characterized by abstract principles or rigid internal rules applied in a mechanical fashion without reference to policy objectives or social needs. These reformers put the blame on Third World legal elites' blind adherence to formal rules. First wave law and development scholars identified the main problem in Third World legal systems as formalism—where rules are "developed, interpreted and applied without careful attention to policy goals."[34] The first wave believed that formalism affected all areas of an underdeveloped country's legal system. Legislatures copied foreign models instead of studying social context and aiming rules toward policy goals.[35] Judges applied rules in a "rigid and mechanical" fashion instead of using the discretion that adjudication entails in the West and instead of giving weight to policy considerations.[36] Law professors taught that law was an abstract system defined by strict rules, without consideration for policy goals and societal impact.[37] These "[b]lind rule following and unimaginative bureaucratic habits were preventing law in the books from realizing its potential in action."[38] Accordingly, first wave development lawyers "sought less to install new social purposes in the legal fabric of developing societies than to encourage the emergence of a new more creative and discretionary sensibility among third world governmental elites. . . ."[39]

As first wave reformers observed, "legal education in almost all developing countries . . . tends to be of a highly formal nature, with little to relate it to the distinctive

---

31 *Id.*

32 Trubek & Galanter, *supra* note 1, at 1068.

33 Trubek, *supra* note 9, at 75.

34 *Id.* at 76.

35 *Id.*

36 *See id.; see also* Kennedy, *supra* note 8, at 112.

37 Trubek, *supra* note 9, at 76; *see also* Amy Cohen, *Thinking with Culture in Law and Development*, 57 Buff. L. Rev. 511, 517 (2009); J. C. L. Merrilat, *Law and Developing Countries*, 60 Am. J. Int'l L. 71, 73 (1966).

38 Kennedy, *supra* note 8, at 112.

39 *Id.* at 121.

needs of a developing society and with little effort to train lawyers to think in terms of processes rather than formal rules."[40] Legal formalism resulted in weak enforcement, rules that were out of touch with society and low legitimacy. Enforcement was ineffective because the rules were so out of touch that they were easily ignored. Legitimacy was low and rules were ignored because they had little to do with the needs of the country.[41] For example, in South America, where local societies were not represented by the legal system, people relied on paralegal alternatives and informal law for relief.[42] Of particular concern to first wave critics was the realization that given the "social stratification and class cleavage"[43] in developing countries, legal rules were likely to benefit the elites and unlikely to be internalized by the majority of the population.[44]

But legal formalism was not the only problem. First wave law and development also saw traditional societies as a problem because it adopted modernization theory's view of traditional legal systems. Traditional legal systems lacked purposiveness and were not rational or conscious, instead deferring to history and custom to shape the law.[45] In many traditional areas, there can be a different form of "law" for each village, tribe, or class.[46] Traditional customs also serve to hinder modern law. Modern law is usually deemed to be autonomous from other sources of normative social order, but law reform in a traditional legal system might face resistance from adherents of traditional norms and customs.[47] For example, in Ethiopia, adherence to the *Fetha Negast* had been "nearly sacred" for generations; implementation of a new civil code met heavy resistance and was nullified in the lesser developed parts of the country that still clung to traditional norms.[48] Traditional norms proved to be a formidable block to the law's penetration. Consequentially, first wave scholars cast traditional legal system as "historically obsolete and culturally inapposite" to their respective societies.[49]

According to first wave reformers, traditional legal systems should be replaced with modern rules and legal institutions. Moreover, such modern rules and legal institutions should not be a result of "blindly transplanting" Western law[50] but rather should be made to account for local needs. Modern law was believed to be the "functional prerequisite

---

[40] Merrilat, *supra* note 37, at 73.

[41] Trubek, *supra* note 9, at 76.

[42] Esquirol, *supra* note 28, at 93; *see also* Rene David, *A Civil Code for Ethiopia: Considerations on the Codification of the Civil Law in African Countries*, 37 TUL. L. REV. 187, 192 (1962–63) (discussing the same problem in Ethiopia).

[43] Trubek & Galanter, *supra* note 1, at 1080.

[44] *Id.* at 1080–81.

[45] Trubek, *supra* note 5, at 5.

[46] *See id.*

[47] David, *supra* note 42, at 203; Trubek, *supra* note 5, at 5.

[48] David, *supra* note 42, at 192, 203.

[49] Esquirol, *supra* note 28, at 92.

[50] Trubek, *supra* note 9, at 76.

of an industrial economy."[51] Fair, rational, and universal rules were needed to supplant traditional forces.[52] Rational law would foster legitimacy and enable the government to impose specific rules and alter norms to achieve development.[53] In this respect modern rules could be viewed as a tool to tailor social change and not merely react to it. The first wave's view on the need for modern rules and institutions would lay the foundation for the next wave of law and development, which as I discuss later, almost exclusively emphasize rules and institutions.

The gestalt of the first wave, however, was less about technocratic change (putting the right rules and institutions in place) and more about modernization. Modernization certainly included modernization of law because modern law was deemed important for establishing rational, modern rules, which in turn were considered important for economic development. But the first wave's overall concern centered on changing traditional societies and modernizing them, using law as a tool to accomplish that objective. Thus, interestingly, the first wave paid attention to law *and* development—both economic and social. In connecting law to economic development, David Trubek, a first wave scholar, outlined two different approaches. In the first, he stressed the role of law in market economies. In congruity with Weber's view that capitalistic market institutions are necessary for economic growth, Trubek believed that modern law was needed to create and maintain markets.[54] Essentially, law should protect and incentivize actors' profit ventures[55] and assure individuals that the fruits of their activities will be protected by predictable, uniformly applied contract and property law.[56] In the second approach, Trubek highlighted the importance of maximizing the effectiveness and penetration of rules. The more a body of law became a rational instrument, the easier penetration would be. If penetration became effortless, then the economic goals of a government could be achieved so long as their relation to the legal system was made transparent.[57]

The objective of modernizing law, however, was not easily implemented because the traditional legal system first wave reformers encountered resisted change. To replace formalism and traditionalism with modernism, first wave scholars worked to construct "a more pragmatic and antiformalist local legal culture . . ."[58] because they believed that change in the legal culture would produce change in law as well as in society. To produce such change through law, law must be reconceived and understood in instrumentalist terms. Again, the underlying rationale was that if formalism was the main reason why the legal system

[51] Trubek, *supra* note 5, at 6.

[52] David, *supra* note 42, at 192, 203; Trubek, *supra* note 5, at 9.

[53] Trubek, *supra* note 5, at 6.

[54] *Id.* at 6–7.

[55] *Id.*

[56] *Id.*

[57] *See id.* at 6–7. *See also* Trubek & Galanter, *supra* note 1, at 1074.

[58] *See* Kennedy, *supra* note 8, at 112; Trubek, *supra* note 9, at 74–75; *see also* Tamanaha, *supra* note 2, at 471–76.

was ineffective, characterized by out-of-touch laws and weak enforcement, then the most important thing to do would be to change the legal culture from formalist to instrumentalist.[59] Thus, efforts were expended to "create a new, more instrumental *legal culture*. . . ."[60] The objective can be stated in this way: Law will be instrumentalist, and society will be modern, rather than traditional. From this instrumentalist perspective, first wave law and development "sees law as a force which can be molded and manipulated to alter human behaviour and achieve development."[61] Law should be an instrument of development, and law and development lawyers should function as social engineers.[62]

According to Lawrence Friedman, legal culture is a significant if not determining factor in "when, why and where people turn to law or government, or turn away"[63] from it. Friedman also identified key factors to consider when characterizing a country's legal culture, such as the attitudes of different populations toward the legal system, the amount of judicial discretion, and the flexibility of the law.[64] Other scholars went further to divide legal culture into internal and external. External legal culture includes the attitude held by people who play no normal role in the legal system, whereas internal legal culture includes the attitudes of people who do have normal roles within the legal system.[65] External legal culture channels and releases social change on the legal system, whereas internal legal culture determines how receptive the legal system will be to the pressure exerted by social change.[66]

Central to first wave thought is the assertion that legal culture will determine the amount of deviance from the law, and, as such, formal reform in law will fail if it does not account for cultural restraints.[67] A legal culture conducive to legal development is characterized by "habits of obedience to law, and respect for law."[68] When legal culture supports a law, compliance and effectiveness come relatively effortlessly, but when legal culture is antagonistic to a law, effectiveness becomes either burdensome or impossible.[69] For

---

[59] Trubek, *supra* note 9, at 76.

[60] *See id.; see also* Tamanaha, *supra* note 2, at 471–76.

[61] Elliot M. Burg, *Law and Development: A Review of the Literature and a Critique of "Scholar in Self-Estrangement,"* 25 AM. J. COMP. L. 492, 505–06 (1977).

[62] Davis & Trebilcock, *supra* note 15, at 901; Robert A. Sedler, *Law Reform in the Emerging Nations of Sub-Saharan Africa: Social Change and the Development of the Modern Legal System*, 13 ST. LOUIS U. L.J. 195, 199 (1968) (stating that "[a] primary function of law may be to engineer the social and economic change necessary to achieve the goals of development"). Interestingly, the critical legal studies movement that emerged after the demise of the first wave also sought social transformation and saw "law as a form of social engineering." RUMU SARKAR, DEVELOPMENT LAW AND INTERNATIONAL FINANCE 30 (2002).

[63] Lawrence M. Friedman, *Legal Culture and Social Development*, 4 LAW & SOC'Y REV. 29, 34 (1969).

[64] *Id.* at 40 (listing questions to ask to characterize a legal culture).

[65] John Henry Merryman, *Law and Development Memoirs II: SLADE*, 48 AM. J. COMP. L. 713, 722 (2000).

[66] *Id.*

[67] Friedman, *supra* note 63, at 41.

[68] Lawrence M. Friedman, *On Legal Development*, 24 RUTGERS L. REV. 11, 61 (1969).

[69] Friedman, *supra* note 63, at 41.

instance, in the United States, the culture mostly supports income tax payment. Income tax collection is relatively easy, and the government can raise taxes without the increased risk of evasion or rebellion. Conversely, adultery laws in the United States do not have the backing of legal culture. The population disapproves of private aspects of life being regulated, and officials feel these laws are not worth enforcing.[70]

First wave scholars sought to change the highly formalist legal culture of developing countries by focusing primarily on legal education and peripherally on creating modern rules and legal institutions. As noted, the first wave sought "to transform legal culture and institutions through educational reform and selected transplant of 'modern' institutions."[71] This is because legal education was seen as the source of the "evils of formalism."[72] First wave reformers worked to inject an instrumental orientation into legal education so that law schools would produce lawyers who could analyze the socioeconomic needs of society and guide the legal system within that framework along the path to development.[73] Scholars assumed that change in legal education was the most effective way to reform the legal system because the legal education system was highly autonomous and influential.[74] Reform in schooling would influence the methods of lawyering, causing lawyers to promote the development goals of the state, which would lead to formation of other legal institutions that were crucial to a modern legal system.[75] So then legal development in the Third World would be brought about by lawyers in these countries learning to "redefine their concepts of law and its function."[76]

There was no shortage of legal education reform, especially in South America.[77] Brazil exemplified all of the major problems that first wave law and development theory had outlined. Laws were frequently imported and out of touch with society and thus were ignored, while lawyers were trained to be overly formalistic and were not able to adapt to the changing social environment or tailor the legal system to Brazil's development needs.[78] When students entered Brazil's law schools, they had had no liberal arts and could not be expected to consider a law's impact in areas like economics or sociology.[79]

---

[70] *Id.* at 42.

[71] Trubek, *supra* note 9, at 76; David Trubek, *Max Weber on Law and the Rise of Capitalism*, 1972 WIS. LAW REV. 720–53 (1972) (first wave reformers drew on Weber's sociological insights to conclude that because rational law was important to the rise of capitalism in the West); Friedman, *supra* note 63, at 42; Esquirol, *supra* note 28, at 76–77.

[72] Trubek, *supra* note 9, at 76.

[73] Cohen, *supra* note 37, at 518; *see* Trubek, *supra* note 9, at 76.

[74] Trubek, *supra* note 9, at 77.

[75] Davis & Trebilcock, *supra* note 15, at 901; Trubek, *supra* note 9, at 76.

[76] Trubek, *supra* note 5, at 10.

[77] Esquirol, *supra* note 28, at 92 (stating that most legal education development was concentrated in Chile, Brazil, and Colombia).

[78] Keith S. Rosenn, *The Reform of Legal Education in Brazil*, 21 J. LEGAL EDUC. 251, 254–55 (1969).

[79] *Id.* at 256.

Additionally, class discussion and debate were rather minimal, with the teaching style of most professors simply presenting rules for the entirety of the class period.[80]

In 1966, the Center of Studies and Research on Legal Education (CEPED) started training lawyers under the guidance of American law and development scholars. The institution's goal was to develop lawyers who could assist in the legal development movement.[81] CEPED held conferences that brought in legal development and education experts from the United States, Chile, and Brazil; it also sent faculty members to top American law schools—notably Harvard University—to discuss teaching methods.[82] CEPED's efforts resulted in Brazilian law school classes that were very similar to their counterparts in the United States. Students were pressed to think hard on problems that frequently had "no clear answer," and class time stressed critical thought and debate.[83]

Although the first wave sought explicitly to modernize only legal culture, it did at least understand the need to engage the cultural realm. In that sense, its scope is broader and deeper than current law and development projects that are more institutional and technocratic in their dimensions. Interestingly, the need to study the role of culture was recognized by some early development economists as well, so the idea that culture is a relevant factor in development is not wholly alien to the field. The most prominent of development economists have opined about the cultural aspects of development, even if only briefly, and have wondered "whether traditional institutions, attitudes and values are likely to block or to promote economic growth."[84] Indeed, their views even echo those expressed by modernization theorists[85] who influenced first wave law reformers. Although development economists such as Gerald Meier and Robert Baldwin wondered about the pace at which traditional culture can and should change, that traditional culture can and should change to be favorable to development was not an issue. "Not only must economic organization be transformed, but social organization . . . must also be modified so that the basic complex of values and motivations may be more favourable for development."[86]

The debate about the relationship between culture and development was at one time ongoing. Some supported what I term culture change but warned about the danger of ethnocentrism.[87] Others believed that traditional culture could coexist and organically

---

[80] *Id.*

[81] *Id.* at 276.

[82] *Id.* at 276–77.

[83] *Id.* at 277.

[84] Jean-Philippe Platteau, *The Role of Culture in Development: An Overview*, *in* CULTURE, INSTITUTIONS, AND DEVELOPMENT: NEW INSIGHTS INTO AN OLD DEBATE 3, 3 (Jean-Philippe Platteau & Robert Peccoud eds., 2011).

[85] *Id.*

[86] *Id.* (quoting GERALD M. MEIER & ROBERT E. BALDWIN, ECONOMIC DEVELOPMENT: THEORY, HISTORY, POLICY 356 (1957)).

[87] *Id.* at 4 (quoting GERALD M. MEIER & ROBERT E. BALDWIN, ECONOMIC DEVELOPMENT: THEORY, HISTORY, POLICY 355 (1957)) ("In considering the social and cultural requirements for development, a

evolve with economic development. Sir Arthur Lewis, for example, stated that "traditional values and attitudes, whenever they are hostile to economic advancement, will eventually adapt themselves to new economic opportunities."[88]

Overall, the first wave was relatively short-lived—ranging from the mid-1960s to the early 1970s. The movement received very little support from bilateral and multilateral aid agencies like the World Bank and Inter-American Development Bank.[89] Tragically, many of the goals of the first wave were hard to implement and many of its assumptions proved to be flawed. Law schools were more resistant to change than scholars had hoped.[90] Penetration was rather insignificant. In Brazil, CEPED's efforts toward legal education reform did not migrate to the major law schools.[91] In some places, legal actors resisted legal reform in an effort to block Western dominance.[92] Ethiopia, for instance, rejected common law principles in an effort to fight Anglo American influence.[93] Reformers concluded that "the structures of law making, law-applying, and practice were quite capable of resisting foreign-inspired cultural change."[94] In addition, the very legitimacy of the movement was called into question by critical scholars who objected to what they perceived to be the movement's ethnocentricism.[95] For them, the hegemony of the Anglo American legal experience was crowding out other approaches.[96]

The movement was marred by other problems as well. From a purely pragmatic standpoint, it became clear that "the transplants did not 'take' at all: some of the new laws promoted by the reformers remained on the books but were ignored in action."[97] More problematic is the fact that the very laws promoted by development scholars were "captured by local elites and put to uses different from those the reformers intended."[98] Indeed, lack of political democracy meant that the instrumentalist conception of law championed by the first wave resulted ironically in law being used as an instrument of the powerful.[99] Some blamed the continuing ineffectiveness of the political system on the political culture that animated such system—the "set of attitudes, beliefs, and sentiments

---

Western student should not make the mistake of ethnocentrism, that is, assuming that, because the West is developed, Western values and institutions are therefore necessary for development").

88 *Id.*

89 Trubek, *supra* note 9, at 78.

90 *Id.*

91 Rosenn, *supra* note 78, at 279–81.

92 Trubek, *supra* note 9, at 78; *see also* David, *supra* note 42, at 192.

93 *See* David, *supra* note 42, at 192.

94 Trubek, *supra* note 9, at 78–79.

95 Snyder, *supra* note 26, at 390.

96 "Does an increasing lack of diversity in legal systems, approaches, and cultures represent true progression forward or simply the 'natural selection' of the Anglo-America approach to law at the expense of other approaches?" SARKAR, *supra* note 62, at 27.

97 Trubek, *supra* note 9, at 78–79.

98 *Id.*

99 Trubek & Galanter, *supra* note 1, at 1076.

which give order and meaning to a political process and which provide the underlying assumptions and rules that govern behavior in the political system."[100]

Not surprisingly, there was never any "spillover" effect that translated legal reform and economic development into democratization. Legalism, instrumentalism, and authoritarianism were not in the least incompatible or unstable.[101] To the contrary, reform was, in fact, strengthening authoritarianism. Reformed law gave authoritarian governments a tool for even smoother control.[102] Stratification, social class gaps, and authoritarian hierarchy were kept in place in lieu of pluralism.[103]

The movement was also branded with the same "evolutionist" tag that modernization theory had been branded with before it. Modernization and the first wave rested upon the same suspect evolution-based assumptions. The premise was that all nations went through the essentially similar successive stages to reach a common end, which was modeled after the United States and Western Europe. Accordingly, the assumption was that developing legal systems were moving toward Western law as the highest evolutionary stage.[104] Indeed, both modernization and first wave law and development accepted that "the typical condition of modernity pertains to the social, political and economic characteristics of Western liberal democracies."[105] Both theories asserted a flawed causal connection between the Western economic success and Western legal systems. They assumed that legal development was a major cause of political and economic transformation in the West on the premise that the modern legal system, the centralized state, and the industrial economy all arose in the West during roughly the same time period.[106] And they extended this assumption further by asserting that this questionable causal chain would be carried into the Third World.[107]

Those criticisms were enough to stop the momentum the movement had been gaining by cutting off prospective support from foundations and aid agencies.[108] By the mid-1970s, the movement began to die. Interest in law and development, however, surged in the 1980s.[109] Although the first wave was short and ineffectual, many of its foundational objectives would be incorporated into the next wave of law and development—the

---

[100] Lucian W. Pye, *Political Culture*, *in* 12 INTERNATIONAL ENCYCLOPEDIA OF THE SOCIAL SCIENCES 218, 218 (David L. Sills ed., 1968).

[101] Trubek, *supra* note 9, at 79.

[102] Tamanaha, *supra* note 2, at 474.

[103] *See id.*

[104] Trubek, *supra* note 9, at 80.

[105] J. P. Nettl & Roland Robertson, *Industrialization, Development or Modernization*, 17 BRIT. J. SOC. 274, 281 (1966).

[106] Trubek, *supra* note 5, at 11.

[107] Esquirol, *supra* note 28, at 92; *see also* Trubek, *supra* note 5, at 11.

[108] Tamanaha, *supra* note 2, at 474; Trubek, *supra* note 9, at 78. ("[T]here was disillusion in the academy, foundation interest declined, and the official aid agencies showed no interest in moving into legal reform. So, for the moment, the . . . movement seemed to have run out of steam.").

[109] John C. Reitz, *Symposium: Export of the Rule of Law*, 13 TRANSNAT'L L. & CONTEMP. PROBS. 429, 431–32 (2003).

second wave, this time, focusing on supplying advanced legal institutions to developing countries.

As I discuss below in Part B, the resurrection of law and development can be traced to the demise of the Soviet Union and the collapse of the Berlin Wall, leading to an increased need to aid transitional or postcrisis countries toward a path of law and development. This "second wave" surge continued well into the 1990s when the world "witnessed a mushrooming of U.S. government-sponsored democracy assistance and of related efforts [which include efforts to strengthen the rule of law] by other governments and by multilateral organizations, foundations, and NGOs."[110] Despite professed concerns and doubts about the project's basic premise—to modernize developing and transitional countries—the thrust of law and development continues to be essentially about modernization,[111] that is, promoting markets, (for some) democracy,[112] and constructing a rule of law framework[113] supportive of modern laws such as property and contract laws.[114] The second wave continues the first wave's concern about establishing modern laws—that is, establishing the "rule of law," though the second wave has not the first wave's aim to transform traditional legal culture.[115]

B. Second Wave of Law and Development

The term "rule of law" sounds deceptively simple and yet it is anything but. The "law" portion of "law and development"—the "rule of law"—has been essentially about instituting laws that further economic development. This is because the "development" portion of "law and development" has been implicitly understood primarily in economic terms.[116] Thus legal development or rule of law is instrumental to or supportive of (economic)

110 *Id.*

111 Brian Z. Tamanaha, *The Primacy of Society and the Failures of Law and Development*, 44 CORNELL INT'L L.J. 209, 215 (2011) ("[T]here is little discernible difference between those supposedly abandoned ideas, and contemporary ideas and approaches to development.... [current law and development work is] modernization theory redux.").

112 Markets and democracy were promoted and linked to the need to establish strong legal institutions. *See* Trubek, *supra* note 9, at 84; *see also* Thomas Carothers, *The Problem of Knowledge*, *in* PROMOTING THE RULE OF LAW ABROAD: IN SEARCH OF KNOWLEDGE 15, 27–28 (Thomas Carothers ed., 2006) (describing how the contemporary international aid movement now sees the "underlying goals of market economics and democracy" as irresistibly connected to the rule of law).

113 *See*, e.g., John Hewko, *Foreign Direct Investment: Does the Rule of Law Matter?* 3 (Carnegie Endowment for Int'l Peace, Rule of Law Series, Working Paper No. 26, 2002); Stephen Holmes, *Can Foreign Aid Promote the Rule of Law?* 8 E. EUR. CONST. REV. 68, 68 (1999). ("Essentially, law is seen as a springboard to economic development," and therefore efforts have been devoted at providing a secure contracts and property framework in order to develop a free market.).

114 Mancur Olson, *Dictatorship, Democracy, and Development*, 87 AM. POL. SCI. REV. 567, 571 (1993).

115 Interestingly, the second wave's disinterest in culture (even legal culture) dovetails with declining interest in culture among development economists. Platteau, *supra* note 84, at 7 ("the relationship between culture and development stopped being a concern of economists during most of the 1970s and 1980s. . . .").

116 SARKAR, *supra* note 62, at 27 ("Weber's concepts are particularly relevant . . . since much of the discourse on development centers around *economic* development . . . .").

development.[117] And indeed, the principle that law is conducive to market development is a historically pedigreed one articulated early on by Max Weber himself.[118] This history, combined with the fall of communism, made market development all the more a rallying call for law and development. In this respect, the standard law and development menu developed by the second wave generally includes laws of corporations and other business associations, securities, antitrust, intellectual property, as well as contract and property rights. Property and contract laws in particular have garnered much attention. Property rights are essential to productive activity because they protect economic players from the rapacious behaviors of others, particularly the state. Property rights also allow people to keep the fruits of their labor and hence encourage the pursuit of productive activity. Contract rights allow economic transactions to be pursued not just between those who know and trust each other but also between strangers who can rely on contract bargains and expectations to be enforced. In fact, the institutions of property and contract are generally deemed prerequisites for law and development programs; the UN Development Program, for example, stated that the two most essential conditions for Vietnam's market development were property and contract laws.[119] This is because private actors are routinely faced with appropriation of their wealth from governments and from other private actors; property law constrains sovereigns from expropriating and contract law constrains private actors. Hence these two institutions are key to the promotion of capital investment.[120]

This agenda is widely supported by law and development organizations. As a result of studies showing a positive correlation between the rule of law and economic development,[121] rule of law work has been funded not just by the World Bank but also by

---

[117] *See*, e.g., Robert C. Effros, *The World Bank in a Changing World: The Role of Legal Construction*, 35 INT'L LAW. 1341, 1344 (2001); Holmes, *supra* note 113, at 68; Paul H. Brietzke, *The Politics of Legal Reform*, 3 WASH. U. GLOBAL. STUD. L. REV. 1, 3–4 (2004); Hewko, *supra* note 113, at 3; Amartya Sen, Address at the World Bank Legal Conference: What Is the Role of Legal and Judicial Reform in the Development Process? 16–17 (June 5, 2000) (transcript *available at* http://issat.dcaf.ch/Home/Community-of-Practice/Resource-Library/Policy-and-Research-Papers/What-is-the-role-of-legal-and-judicial-reform-in-the-development-process).

[118] Trubek, *supra* note 5, at 15. *See supra* note 21.

[119] Tom Ginsburg, *Does Law Matter for Economic Development? Evidence from East Asia*, 34 LAW & SOC'Y REV. 829, 833 (2000) (book review); *cf.* Donald Clarke, Peter Murrell & Susain Whiting, *The Role of Law in China's Economic Development*, *in* CHINA'S GREAT ECONOMIC TRANSFORMATION 375, 376 (Loren Brandt & Thomas C. Rawski eds., 2008) (discussing how China's economic development departed from the conventional rule of law prescriptions); Tom Ginsburg, *Judicial Independence in East Asia*, *in* JUDICIAL INDEPENDENCE IN CHINA: LESSONS FOR GLOBAL RULE OF LAW PROMOTION 247 (Randall Peerenboom ed., 2010) (discussing how a judiciary that lacks independence in political matters as in China can still exercise independence in economic matters and thus provide the requisite certainty and security for economic development).

[120] Olson, *supra* note 114, at 571.

[121] Frank B. Cross, *Law and Economic Growth*, 80 TEX. L. REV. 1737, 1764–71 (2002); *cf.* MARK D. AGRATS ET AL., THE WORLD JUSTICE PROJECT RULE OF LAW INDEX: MEASURING ADHERENCE TO THE RULE OF LAW AROUND THE WORLD 6–7 (2008).

organizations such as the International Monetary Fund (IMF), the US Agency for International Development (USAID) and the Asian Development Bank; by foundations such as the Ford Foundation and the Soros Foundation; and professional organizations such as the American Bar Association's Central and East European Law Initiative. Lawyers now routinely advise foreign governments on the establishment of laws needed to facilitate market reforms, particularly in trade and investment.[122] All these institutions and efforts engage in what is seen as the "export" of the rule of law from developed, democratic states to developing ones.[123]

Indeed, the rule of law is now all the rage. Even undemocratic states extol its virtues. Even as Communist China cracks down on dissidents and subscribes to prison practices universally condemned by human rights observers, it has vowed to establish and be bound by the rule of law. The United Nations signed an agreement with China in 2000 to provide training to Chinese officials on individual rights, and in this respect, to help reform the court, police, and prison systems. It would also monitor China's compliance with two UN treaties which it has signed but not ratified.[124] Communist Vietnam also has signed up to receive rule of law training from the American Bar Association. The term the Vietnamese government uses for "rule of law" is *nha nuoc phap quyen*, which translates to "rules of the state."[125] These governments seem to believe that in this modern, global age, adherence to a rule of law system is viewed by others as a standard to assess governmental legitimacy.

It is not just law and development organizations and authoritarian states that extol the virtues of the rule of law. It is also a common assumption among Western states that the rule of law is a defining characteristic of free societies. The World Bank's own studies show a strong correlation between legal development and other important development indicators.[126] Former World Bank President James Wolfensohn stated unequivocally that "empirical evidence shows a large, significant and causal relationship between improved rule of law and income of nations, rule of law and literacy, and rule of law and reduced infant mortality."[127] The forty-third president of the United States, George W. Bush, pronounced that the rule of law is one of the "non-negotiable

---

[122] Mark Sidel, *New Directions in the Study of Vietnamese Law*, 17 MICH. J. INT'L L. 705, 711–12 (1996) (reviewing VIETNAM AND THE RULE OF LAW (Carlye A. Thayer & David G. Marr eds., 1993)).

[123] Reitz, *supra* note 109, at 432.

[124] Erik Eckholm, *China Signs U.N. Pact on Rights and Rule of Law*, N.Y. TIMES, Nov. 21, 2000, at A4.

[125] *See* AMERICAN BAR ASSOCIATION, RULE OF LAW INITIATIVE: VIETNAM, http://www.americanbar.org/advocacy/rule_of_law/where_we_work/asia/vietnam.html (last visited Jan. 30, 2015). Note that the term the Vietnamese government uses for "rule of law" is *nha nuoc phap quyen*, which translates to "rules of the state." Penelope Nicholson, *Judicial Independence and the Rule of Law: The Vietnam Court Experience*, 3 AUST. J. ASIAN L. 37, 37 (2001), *available at* http://digital.federationpress.com.au/pageview/3aj4a/9mnur/1.

[126] THE WORLD BANK, WHERE IS THE WEALTH OF NATIONS? MEASURING CAPITAL FOR THE 21ST CENTURY 7 (Kirk Hamilton et al. eds., 2006); Robert Danino, Senior Vice President and Gen. Counsel, The World Bank, *The Legal Aspects of the World Bank's Work on Human Rights*, Address at the Human Rights and Development: Towards Mutual Reinforcement Conference 13 (Preliminary Draft, Mar. 1, 2004).

[127] The World Bank, *Rule of Law Central to Fighting Poverty*, Press Release No. 2002/013/S (July 9, 2001).

demands of human dignity."[128] The European Union's Instrument for Pre-accession Assistance declares that its main objective is "to support institution-building and the rule of law, human rights, including the fundamental freedoms, minority rights, gender equality and non-discrimination, both administrative and economic reforms, economic and social development. . . ."[129] As early as 1984, at the London Economic Summit, the "Declaration of Democratic Values," issued by the seven heads of state of the major industrial democracies and the President of the Commission of the European Union invoked the rule of law as among the very first of "values which sustain and bring together our societies. We believe in a rule of law which respects and protects without fear or favor the rights and liberties of every citizen and provides the setting in which the human spirit can develop in freedom and diversity."[130] NATO too has a membership action plan launched in 1999, which includes the rule of law in its roadmap for countries aspiring to NATO membership.[131] Aspirant countries are expected to achieve certain goals in the political and economic fields. These include settling any international, ethnic, or external territorial disputes by peaceful means; and demonstrating a commitment to the rule of law and human rights.[132] In 1996, the IMF adopted a good governance program and in its Declaration on Partnership for Sustainable Global Growth made it an explicit mandate to condition loan grants on rule of law compliance.[133] A known expert on rule of law remarked, "One cannot get through a foreign policy debate these days without someone proposing the rule of law as a solution to the world's troubles."[134]

But since September 11, 2001, law and development has taken on a sense of extra urgency. International security experts have joined market and human rights advocates in trumpeting the rule of law because they view it as a necessary component of terrorism prevention.[135] Some argue that the United States has traditionally combated terrorism by using a "supply-side" only approach that is ineffective. The "supply side" only approach

---

[128] George W. Bush, President of the United States, State of the Union Address, (Jan. 29, 2002) (transcript *available at* http://millercenter.org/president/speeches/detail/4540).

[129] Council Regulation (EC) 1085/2006, Establishing an Instrument for Pre-Accession Assistance (IPA), 2006 O.J. (L. 210) 82, *available at* http://europa.eu/legislation_summaries/enlargement/ongoing_enlargement/e50020_en.htm.

[130] Declaration of Democratic Values *reprinted in "We Believe in a Rule of Law Which Respects and Protects,"* Wash. Post, June 9, 1984, at A14.

[131] NATO's Membership Action Plan, *available at* http://www.db.niss.gov.ua/docs/nato/nato/assets/resources/mod5/m5_i3partners_link.htm (last visited Jan. 28, 2015).

[132] *Id.*

[133] Anton Op de Beke, *IMF Activities to Promote Good Governance and Combat Corruption—An Overview*, World Bank (June 7, 2002) at 1–2, http://info.worldbank.org/etools/docs/library/207469/assessing/pdf/op_de_becke.pdf.

[134] Thomas Carothers, *The Rule of Law Revival*, 77 Foreign Aff. Mar.–Apr. 1998, at 95.

[135] *See, e.g.*, Council on Foreign Relations, Iraq: The Day After (2003); Robert Kaiser, *U.S. Plants Footprint in Shaky Central Asia*, Wash. Post, Aug. 27, 2002, at A1.

is one where terrorism is regarded "as the product of organized groups that could be confronted and destroyed, without regard to their aims or to the reasons that they succeed in recruiting many willing members."[136] This approach is ineffective because it fails to address the underlying reasons for the success of terrorist recruitment, thus only targeting the symptoms and not the root problem. These commentators suggest that the United States should adjust its traditional approach by also engaging the "demand side" of terrorism—that is, understanding that "[p]ublic despair and humiliation are often fertile ground for terror organizers to exploit"[137] and addressing these underlying factors by supporting economic development and political change.[138] One reason among the many complex reasons "the Middle East is a prime target for terrorist recruiters"[139] is "its exceedingly high unemployment rate, evaporating gross domestic product growth, and lack of free markets and stable financial institutions."[140] Part of the solution has to be market reform and political transparency.[141] In this way, we traverse from the security objectives of national defense and return to the well-worn objectives of the law and development project: markets and rule of law.

The idea that economic development is part of a wider political solution is not a new one.[142] But it resonated after September 11 and has been embraced not only by scholars[143] but also by governments and aid agencies. President Barack Obama's 2010 State of the Union Address linked the war in Afghanistan and the fight against terrorism to the success of law and development: "And in Afghanistan, we're increasing our troops and training Afghan security forces so they can begin to take the lead in July of 2011, and our troops can begin to come home. We will reward good governance, work to reduce corruption, and support the rights of all Afghans—men and women alike."[144]

---

136 Shibley Telhami, *Conflicting Views of Terrorism*, 35 Cornell Int'l L. J. 581, 586 (2002).

137 *Id.* at 587.

138 *Id.* at 598.

139 Kevin J. Fandl, *Terrorism, Development & Trade: Winning the War on Terror Without the War*, 19 Am. U. Int'l L. Rev. 587, 599–600 (2004).

140 *Id.* at 599.

141 *Id.* at 600.

142 *See,* e.g., Oren Gross, *Mending Walls: The Economic Aspects of Israeli-Palestinian Peace*, 15 Am. U. Int'l L. Rev. 1539 (2000) (arguing for the inclusion of economic issues as part of the political solution between Israel and Palestine, particularly highlighting the importance of economic development of the poorer Palestinian region).

143 *See,* e.g., Fandl, *supra* note 139, at 608–09 ("Eradicating poverty is the single most potent solution to the problem of terrorism."); Gross, *supra* note 142; Brink Lindsey, *The Trade Front: Combating Terrorism with Open Markets*, 24 Trade Pol'y Analysis 1 (2003), *available at* http://www.freetrade.org/pubs/pas/tpa-024es.html (arguing that the United States should pursue a broad trade strategy as a component in the war on terror); Telhami, *supra* note 136, at 598.

144 Barack H. Obama, President of the United States, State of the Union Address (Jan. 27, 2010) (transcript *available at* http://www.huffingtonpostcom/2010/01/27/state-of-the-union-2010-full-text-transcript_n_439459.html).

Colin Powell, secretary of state in the George W. Bush administration, drew the connection between the national security of the United States and the economic development of poor countries. As Secretary Powell put it, in considering the Bush administration's foreign policy record, there are "issues ... that tend to dominate the headlines, and issues of equal or greater long-term strategic significance that rarely generate as much interest.... Among these latter issues, none is more important than economic development in the world's poorest societies."[145] Although poverty is not a direct cause of terrorism, "[p]overty breeds frustration and resentment, which ideological entrepreneurs can turn into support for—or acquiescence to—terrorism, particularly in those countries in which poverty is coupled with a lack of political rights and basic freedoms."[146] According to Secretary Powell, "[d]evelopment is not a 'soft' policy issue, but a core national security issue.... The United States cannot win the war on terrorism unless we confront the social and political roots of poverty."[147]

Secretary of State Hillary Rodham Clinton in the Obama administration also understood the link between development and the national interests of the United States. In her remarks to the Center for Global Development, she stated:

> The United States seeks a safer, more prosperous, more democratic and more equitable world. We cannot reach that goal when one-third of humankind live in conditions that offer them little chance of building better lives for themselves or their children. We cannot stop terrorism or defeat the ideologies of violent extremism when hundreds of millions of young people see a future with no jobs, no hope, and no way ever to catch up to the developed world.[148]

Accordingly, Secretary Clinton has observed that although "development was once the province of humanitarians, charities, and governments looking to gain allies in global struggles. Today it is a strategic, economic, and moral imperative—as central to advancing American interests and solving global problems as diplomacy and defense."[149] The conflation of development and security can also be seen in the role that Africom, the Pentagon's Africa Command, plays in development-type projects in Africa, which critics fear represents an increasingly disturbing militarization of humanitarian and development objectives.[150] However, President Obama's defense secretary, Robert Gates,

---

[145] Colin L. Powell, *No Country Left Behind*, FOREIGN POL'Y, Jan.–Feb. 2005, at 28.

[146] Thomas Carothers, *The New Aid*, WASH. POST, Apr. 16, 2002, at A19; Powell, *supra* note 145, at 30; *see also* Kaiser, *supra* note 135.

[147] Powell, *supra* note 145, at 30.

[148] Hillary Rodham Clinton, Secretary of State for the United States, *Remarks to the Center for Global Development*, Washington D.C., Jan. 10, 2010 (transcript *available at* http://www.state.gov/secretary/rm/2010/01/134838.htm).

[149] *Id.*

[150] Thom Shanker, *Command for Africa Is Established by Pentagon*, N.Y. TIMES (Oct. 4, 2008), http://www.nytimes.com/2008/10/05/world/africa/05command.html?pagewanted=all&_r=0.

defended this civilian-military partnerships forged among the Defense Department, the State Department, and USAID to address security and development objectives.[151]

Thus, it is not a surprise that since September 11, 2001, US policy has been premised on the notion that "development, democracy, and security [are] inextricably linked."[152] The United States, for example, passed the Export-Import Bank Reauthorization Act of 2001 with new guidelines—in assessing whether to finance a project, the Bank was to take into consideration the cooperation of the host government in the fight against terrorism,[153] thus linking international development projects to terrorism prevention. The USAID, with a history of fighting poverty long before September 11, stated in the post–September 11 world that it aims to have "a major role in minimizing the conditions that foster terrorism, instability, and other global threats."[154] The US National Security Strategy now identifies development assistance as one of the major pillars required for national security.[155] As the White House position paper on national security strategy puts it, "[p]overty does not make poor people into terrorists and murderers. Yet, poverty, weak institutions, and corruption can make weak states vulnerable to terrorist networks . . . within their borders."[156] Promoting market economies and the connection between markets, trade, and development are included as crucial components of the country's National Security Strategy.[157] Indeed, the National Security Strategy paper draws an explicit link between trade liberalization and threat reduction: "We will actively work to bring the hope of democracy, development, free markets, and free trade to every corner of the world. The events of September 11, 2001, taught us that weak states, like Afghanistan, can pose as great a danger to our national interests as strong states."[158]

Accordingly, the United States has actively pursued a strategy of "enhanced engagement"[159] not just in Afghanistan but in other Central Asian countries, such as Uzbekistan and Kazakhstan. The US goal, as articulated by Deputy Assistant Secretary of State B. Lynn Pascoe in testimony to the Senate in 2002, is to push countries in that region toward free markets and democracy in order to bolster them against the tide of Islamic extremism and terrorism.[160] In many ways, this linkage of development with security has

---

[151] *Id.*

[152] Powell, *supra* note 145, at 30.

[153] *See* Export-Import Bank Reauthorization Act of 2002, Pub. L. No. 107–189, 116 Stat. 698 (June 14, 2002); *see also* 148 Cong. Rec. H1773, at H1785 (daily ed. May 1, 2002) (statement of Rep. J.C. Watts from Okla.) ("We must reach out to developing nations across the globe, often beset by forces of terror, and demonstrate how free markets, open trade, and private enterprise under the rule of law can lead to prosperity for their citizens. Our national security improves when global stability prevails.").

[154] US Dep't of State, *USAID Strives to Minimizes [sic] Conditions that Foster Terrorism*, Mar. 26, 2003, *available at* http://wfile.ait.org.tw/wf-archive/2003/030326/epf321.htm.

[155] *Id.*

[156] The White House, The National Security Strategy of the United States of America iv (2002).

[157] *Id.* at 17–23.

[158] *Id.* at iv–v.

[159] Kaiser, *supra* note 135.

[160] *Id.*

historical roots. President John F. Kennedy's Alliance for Progress and President Harry S. Truman's Marshall Plan involved American embrace of financial aid initiatives as a response to security threats.[161]

The US National Security Strategy, implemented after a historic conference in Monterrey, Mexico, six months after September 11, 2001, was aimed at marshaling public and private resources to implement the broad development objectives delineated above. There, the United Nations, the IMF, the World Bank, the World Trade Organization (WTO), and other nongovernmental organizations (NGOs), as well as a large number of private businesses, such as Cisco Systems or the Deutsche Bank, reaffirmed the need to engage with the international economic system and to encourage foreign direct investment and other private capital flows to poor countries in order to achieve the UN Millennium Development Goals.[162] Part of the Monterrey Consensus is that "[u]nderdevelopment and extreme poverty are breeding grounds for violence and despair, thus undermining peace and security for developed and developing countries alike."[163] Consequently, President Bush pledged to raise American official development assistance progressively from 10 to 15 billion dollars, with assistance tied to the recipients' antiterrorism record[164] and establishment of a new Millennium Challenge Account (MCA).[165] The MCA has been hailed as "the most fundamental change to US foreign assistance policy since President John Kennedy introduced the Peace Corps and the USAID in the early 1960s."[166]

This new consensus on development is based upon an emphasis on "private sector-led economic growth"[167] and is reflected in the MCA itself. As Secretary Powell acknowledged, "[a]id can be a catalyst for development, but the real engines of growth are entrepreneurship, investment, and trade."[168] The MCA "offers a contract modeled on the free market itself—that is its genius. Recipients of MCA money have to meet a set of

---

[161] Carothers, *supra* note 146.

[162] The UN Millennium Development Goals include the resolution to halve the proportion of the world's people whose income is less than one dollar a day and the proportion of people who suffer from hunger by 2015. Jens Martens, *Global Development Cooperation After Monterrey, Results and Perspectives from the Financing for Development Process* at 1–2, 7 (Mar. 17, 2002), http://www2.weed-online.org/ffd/texte_e.htm.

[163] International Conference on Financing for Development, Monterrey, Mex., Mar. 18–22, 2002, at 82 A/Conf.198/11 (statement of the President of the General Assembly of the United Nations, Han Seung-soo).

[164] Martens, *supra* note 162, at 6.

[165] Stephen Marks, *The Human Right to Development: Between Rhetoric and Reality*, 17 HARV. HUM. RTS. J. 137, 156–57 (2004); *see also supra* note 156 at, 21–22. On January 23, 2004, the Millennium Challenge Corporation (MCC) was signed into law. The MCC will administer the MCA. Initial funding for the 2004 fiscal year is USD1 billion. *See* MILLENNIUM CHALLENGE CORPORATION, http://www.mcc.gov (last visited Jan. 30, 2015); *see also* Editorial, *The President's Millennium Challenge*, N.Y. TIMES, Nov. 11, 2004, at 32 (hailing the MCA as "a new approach to development aid that links American assistance to a poor country to its progress in key areas" and urging full Congressional funding in this effort).

[166] Marks, *supra* note 165, at 157.

[167] Powell, *supra* note 145, at 31.

[168] *Id.*

eligibility requirements before they get a nickel. Governments must already have in place effective policies to rule justly, invest in their people, and promote economic freedom. They must also agree to achieve measurable results from aid assistance in terms of reducing poverty and generating broad economic growth."[169]

The MCA is administered by the Millennium Challenge Corporation (the MCC).[170] Its board determines eligible countries, relying on sixteen indicators grouped into three categories. Under category one, "Ruling Justly," the indicators include civil liberties, rule of law, and control of corruption. Under category two, "Encouraging Economic Freedom," the indicators include country credit rating, fiscal policy, trade policy, and days to start a business. Under category three, "Investing in People," indicators include public expenditures on health as percent of gross domestic product (GDP), public primary education as percent of GDP, and immunization rates.[171] In determining country eligibility, the MCC Board considers whether a particular country performs above the median compared to its peers on at least half of the indicators in each of the three policy categories.[172] Once a country is identified, the MCC works with potential recipient countries to develop compacts between the United States and the developing country. The compacts establish performance benchmarks to be met. For example, one country passed and enforced laws against corruption to meet eligibility requirements for MCA funds.[173] Areas identified as crucial to achieving economic growth and poverty reduction include agricultural development, education, enterprise and private sector development, governance, health, and trade capacity building.[174] The list, however, is not exhaustive because recipient countries are encouraged to identify their own priorities for achieving economic growth and poverty reduction. The emphasis is on promoting country ownership of the compact to ensure that the program will fit within an individual country's growth and poverty reduction strategies.[175] The MCA thus not only promotes the standard objectives favored by traditional development projects—good governance, adherence to the rule of law, investment in health and education, and market liberalization[176]—but also conditions financial disbursement on the recipient's

---

[169] *Id.*

[170] Millennium Challenge Corp., Report on the Criteria and Methodology for Determining the Eligibility of Candidate Countries for Millennium Challenge Account Assistance in FY 2004, *available at* http://www.mcc.gov/documents/reports/fy04_criteria_methodology.pdf (last visited Jan. 30, 2015) [hereinafter, Millennium Challenge Corp.].

[171] *Id.*

[172] *Id.*

[173] Powell, *supra* note 145, at 31.

[174] Millennium Challenge Corporation, About MCC, https://www.mcc.gov/pages/about (last visited Jan. 30, 2015).

[175] *Id.*

[176] Marks, *supra* note 165, at 157.

implementation of certain prerequisites.[177] Critics, however, have charged that many of the indicators are subject to manipulation.[178]

In addition to the establishment of the MCA as part of its development/antiterrorism agenda, the United States has also promoted a trade agenda as part of its overall strategy for combating terrorism. In the immediate post–September 11 environment, US Trade Representative Robert Zoellick described the Bush administration's trade agenda as integral to the country's counteroffensive against terrorism. "Trade is about more than economic efficiency. It promotes the values at the heart of this protracted struggle."[179] The United States, for example, has been pushing to develop a Middle East Free Trade Area (MEFTA) by 2013.[180] This effort would include economic reforms to facilitate integration of the region into the world trading system and accession to the WTO, along with other core development objectives traditionally promoted by law and development projects, such as "reform of commercial and judicial codes, and improved transparency to fight corruption."[181] The proposed MEFTA has been thus hailed: "The new trade initiative aims to combat terrorism, and the Islamist extremism that underlies it, by promoting economic and political development in the Muslim world."[182] Other initiatives promoted by the United States include bilateral free trade agreements with other Middle Eastern countries—such as Jordan, Bahrain, and Morocco—and plans for eventually integrating them into a single, region-wide free trade area.[183]

In addition to free trade agreements, the United States is also stepping up efforts to negotiate bilateral investment treaties and trade and investment framework agreements in the region. The former is designed to encourage foreign investment by guaranteeing certain rights to foreign investors, and the latter establishes "regular bilateral consultations aimed at strengthening commercial ties."[184]

In other words, the US trade and investment agenda, normally an economic component of law and development, is being developed as part of a wider national security

---

[177] MILLENNIUM CHALLENGE CORP., *supra* note 170.

[178] *See generally* Sheherazade Jafari & Inder K. Sud, *Performance-Based Foreign Assistance through the Millennium Challenge Account: Sustained Economic Growth as the Objective Qualifying Criterion*, 7 INT'L PUB. MGMT. J. 249 (2004).

[179] Robert B. Zoellick, *Countering Terror with Trade*, WASH. POST, Sept. 20, 2001, at A35.

[180] Fandl, *supra* note 139, at 622; Lindsey, *supra* note 143, at 1. The initiative, although enabling the completion of new free trade agreements with Bahrain, Jordan, Morocco, and Oman, fell short of its goal of creating a regional free trade area. In 2011, the Obama administration announced its own "Trade and Investment Partnership Initiative," which similarly aims to increase trade and investment in the Middle East and North Africa. *See* SHAYERAH ILIAS AKHTAR ET AL., U.S. TRADE AND INVESTMENT IN THE MIDDLE EAST AND NORTH AFRICA: OVERVIEW AND ISSUES FOR CONGRESS 1 (CONG. RESEARCH SERV., R42153, 2013).

[181] Fandl, *supra* note 139, at 623.

[182] Lindsey, *supra* note 143, at 1.

[183] Fandl, *supra* note 139, at 600; *see* Lindsey, *supra* note 143, at 1; US Department of State, *Secretary of State Colin. L. Powell at City College of New York*, FDCH FEDERAL DEPARTMENT & AGENCY DOCUMENTS, REGULATORY INTELLIGENCE DATA, Nov. 10, 2003.

[184] Lindsey, *supra* note 143, at 2.

framework. For example, US Trade Representative officials have announced they will not seek a free trade agreement with New Zealand because of its refusal to allow nuclear-armed vessels in its waters, although many critics claimed that this was a shortsighted decision that ran against American interests.[185] These trade initiatives, "through an aggressive policy of bilateral, regionaland multilateral market opening,"[186] should extend-beyond the Middle East[187] and call for "a vigorous assertion of American economic leadership across the board."[188] Besides the benefits that trade may bring to the developing countries themselves, closer commercial relationships can reduce threats to US interests and serve as an olive branch to the poorer world.[189]

As important as trade agreements are to development and security concerns, they take time to negotiate and implement. Thus, some have suggested that a trade strategy "needs to be supplemented with an initiative that is broader in scope and offers immediate results."[190] Such an initiative should, for example, include the removal of "[t]extiles tariffs and quotas, high trade barriers and profligate subsidies for many US farm products, arbitrary and prohibitive protectionism under the antidumping and other trade remedy laws—all of these policies inflict heavy damage on exporters in the world's poorest and most desperate countries."[191] On May 22, 2003, Senators Max Baucus and John McCain introduced the Middle East Trade and Engagement Act, authorizing the president to grant duty-free treatment to eighteen countries in the Middle East, including Afghanistan, Algeria, Azerbaijan, Bahrain, Bangladesh, Egypt, Iraq, Kuwait, Lebanon, Morocco, Oman, Pakistan, Qatar, Saudi Arabia, Tunisia, Turkey, the United Arab Emirates, and Yemen.[192]

As the discussion above shows, after the terrorist attacks on September 11, 2001, law and development has been resurrected and transformed from an important but second-tier-level project to a critical component of the country's national security strategy. Governments have partnered with other multinational organizations to promote a bundle of interrelated objectives. Although law and development enthusiasts now include a wide range of institutions with different goals and interests, they have found common ground around the rule of law mantra. Aid organizations are in favor of the law and development mission—as secure property and contract rights are deemed necessary for the development of a robust, rule-bound market.[193] Indeed, most everyone agrees that

---

[185] *Id.* at 3–4.

[186] *Id.*

[187] *Id.* at 12.

[188] *Id.*

[189] *Id.* at 13.

[190] *Id.* at 9.

[191] *Id.* at 13.

[192] *Id.* at 10.

[193] *See* Hewko, *supra* note 113, at 3; Hernando De Soto, *Preface*, *in* THE LAW AND ECONOMICS OF DEVELOPMENT xiv (Edgardo Buscaglia et al. eds., 1997) ("[S]imply put, formal law is the foundation of the market system, essential to the development of corporations, limited liability contracts and an adequate

"[a] predictable, efficient legal system . . . enables a free market by providing for efficient adjudication of contract disputes," although China's economic development experience may be viewed as an exception to this general principle.[194] Charitable nongovernmental organizations such as Oxfam may disagree about the appropriate strategies for market development and reforms but generally acknowledge that a working market (and the rule of law necessary to support it) is imperative for poverty reduction.[195] The United Nations, which has traditionally been statist in orientation and suspicious of global markets, now recognizes the need to engage the market and promote trade, through greater coordination with the WTO[196] and the international business community. At the 1999 World Economic Forum held in Davos, Switzerland, then UN Secretary Kofi Annan promised that the United Nations would "make the case for and maintain an environment which favors trade and open markets."[197] For example, the UN Millennium Declaration, approved by the largest gathering of states since the United Nations' founding, aims for "greater policy coherence and better cooperation between the United Nations, its agencies, the Bretton Woods Institutions and the World Trade Organization, as well as other multilateral bodies, with a view to achieving a fully coordinated approach to the problems of peace and development."[198] As Kofi Annan remarked, "a fundamental shift has occurred in the UN-business relationship. The United Nations has developed a profound appreciation for the role of the private sector, its expertise, its motivated spirit, its unparalleled ability to create jobs and wealth. . . . In a world of common challenges and common vulnerabilities, the United Nations and business are finding common ground."[199] Even human rights advocates, who have tended to exhibit skepticism toward multinational

---

business environment.") Carothers, *supra* note 134, at 97–98 ("Basic elements of a modern market economy such as property rights and contracts are founded on the law and require competent third-party enforcement. Without the rule of law, major economic institutions such as corporations, banks, and labor unions would not function, and the government's many involvements in the economy . . . would be unfair, inefficient, and opaque. . . . [E]conomic globalization is feeding the rule-of-law imperative by putting pressure on governments to offer the stability, transparency, and accountability that international investors demand.").

194 Rachel Kleinfeld Belton, *Competing Definitions of the Rule of Law: Implications for Practitioners* 13 (Carnegie Endowment for Int'l Peace, Paper No. 55, Jan. 2005), *available at* http://carnegieendowment.org/files/cp55.belton.FINAL.pdf.

195 *See* Oxfam Policy Department, *A Case for Reform: Fifty Years of the IMF and World Bank* 2 (1995) ("There is today a growing consensus that markets have a critical role to play in development, and that chronic budget deficits and balance of payments deficits must be addressed. It is also recognized that, in the creation of the crisis of the 1980s, the impact of external forces was compounded by internal factors, such as ill-conceived forms of State intervention.").

196 UN Millennium Declaration, G.A. Res. 55/2, ¶¶ 29, 30 (Sept. 18, 2000).

197 Rorden Wilkinson & Steve Hughes, *Labor Standards and Global Governance: Examining the Dimensions of Institutional Engagement*, 6 Global Governance 259, 266 (2000) (quoting Press Release, The Secretary-General Proposes Compact on Human Rights, Labour, Environment, in Address to World Economic Forum in Davos, UN Press Release No. SG/SM6881/Rev. 1 (Feb. 1, 1999)).

198 UN Millennium Declaration, *supra* note 196, ¶ 30.

199 Kofi Annan, *Message to the Business Humanitarian Forum* (Jan. 27, 1999), http://www.bhforum.ch/documentation/speeches.aspx?tab=3&nav=2347.

corporations, financial institutions, and markets, have asserted a link between the rule of law and human rights:

> The rule of law revival that we are experiencing today is not just a product of the neoliberal development paradigm but also of the recent triumphs of human rights movement . . . applauded throughout the world. . . . It represents, as Michale Ignatieff has said, a revolution in human consciousness. As part of this revolution, there has been an increasing demand for law, or more specifically, for the treatment of human rights as justiciable claims rather than mere aspirations, and for legal institutions that are able to enforce these claims.[200]

Amnesty International too declared, "The only way to make a break from the past, a time when human rights in Afghanistan were routinely abused, is to establish the rule of law, with the protection of human rights at its center."[201]

One of the more significant developments in international human rights which I argue is especially important for law and development is the emerging recognition that women's rights are human rights. Of course even without this recognition, a discipline such as law and development which is appropriately concerned about poverty should be particularly concerned about the conditions of women, given the fact that women constitute what has been termed "a new global underclass."[202] But the increasing acceptance in the international human rights movement that women's rights are a part of the human rights universe is especially important because this acceptance places women's rights within the core of the international human rights agenda and accordingly also within the ambit of law and development—to the extent that law and development, as discussed below, sees itself as fully compatible with and related to the international human rights movement. Women's rights, in other words, have been recognized as important components of two scholarly disciplines and movements—international human rights and law and development. Neither international human rights nor law and development can afford to ignore women's rights and remain true to their core objectives; as I argue in this book, impediments, cultural or otherwise, that stand in the way of fully achieving equality for women should be addressed.

That the issue of women's rights has been embraced by the international human rights movement is undeniable. For example, at the 1993 UN Conference on Human Rights in Vienna sponsored by the High Commission on Human Rights, a concluding document, the Vienna Declaration and Programme of Action (VDPA), was produced which

---

200 Owen Fiss, *The Autonomy of Law*, 26 YALE J. INT'L L. 517, 521 (2001). Of course for human rights, the incarnation of rule of law must be the thick, rather than the thin one.

201 Amnesty Int'l, *Afghanistan: Police Reconstruction Essential for the Protection of Human Rights*, AI Index: ASA 11/003/2003 (Mar. 2003), at 1, *available at* http://www.amnesty.org/en/library/info/ASA11/003/2003.

202 Mayra Buvinic, *Women in Poverty: A New Global Underclass*, FOREIGN POL'Y, Fall 1997, at 38.

formally recognized women's human rights. Part I, paragraph 18 states unequivocally that the "human rights of women and of the girl-child are an inalienable, integral and indivisible part of universal human rights. The full and equal participation of women in political, civil, economic, social and cultural life, at the national, regional and international levels, and the eradication of all forms of discrimination on grounds of sex are priority objectives of the international community."[203] Article 38 advocates "the elimination of gender bias in the administration of justice and the eradication of any conflicts which may arise between the rights of women and the harmful effects of certain traditional or customary practices, cultural prejudices and religious extremism."

The emphasis on rectifying cultural practices that harm women was further noted in the UN General Assembly Declaration 52/99 concerning Traditional Practices Affecting the Health of Women and Girls.[204] This Declaration stated, for example, that the VDPA had proclaimed "that gender-based violence and all forms of sexual harassment and exploitation, including those resulting from cultural prejudice, are incompatible with the dignity and worth of the human person . . ." and had stressed "the importance of working towards the eradication of any conflicts which may arise between the rights of women and the harmful effects of certain traditional or customary practices."[205]

In 1994, the UN General Assembly unanimously adopted the Declaration on the Elimination of Violence Against Women, linking violence against women to the subordinate position of women and defining violence against women to include "any act of gender-based violence that results in, or is likely to result in, physical, sexual or psychological harm or suffering to women, including threats of such acts, coercion or arbitrary deprivation of liberty, whether occurring in public or in private life."[206] The 1995 Fourth World Conference on Women in Beijing produced a Platform for Action which declares that "[v]iolence against women both violates and impairs or nullifies the enjoyment by women of their human rights and fundamental freedoms."[207]

Today, law and development is deemed to be crucial (for different reasons) by three different constituent groups—market, human rights, and national security advocates. Despite, or perhaps because of, the fact that so many different elements claim interest in and commitment to the rule of law, there is no singular definition of rule of law. Instead, there are varying understandings that defy uniformity or precision. The rule of law is an

---

203 World Conference on Human Rights, June 14–25, 1993, *Vienna Declaration and Programme of Action*, Pt. I, ¶ 18, UN Doc. A/CONF.157/24 (Oct. 13, 1993).

204 Traditional or Customary Practices Affecting the Health of Women and Girls, G.A. Res. 52/99, UN Doc. A/RES/52/99 (Feb. 9, 1998).

205 *Id.* ¶ (d)

206 Declaration on the Elimination of Violence against Women, G.A. Res. 48/104, UN Doc. A/RES/48/104 (Feb. 23, 1994).

207 World Conference on Women, Beijing, Sept. 4–15, 1995, *Report of the Fourth World Conference on Women*, ¶224, UN Doc. A/CONF.177/20/Rev.1.

"essentially contestable concept."[208] Michael Trebilcock and Ronald Daniels wrote that "[t]he rule of law means whatever one wants it to mean. It is an empty vessel that everyone can fill up with their own vision."[209]

As briefly noted in the Introduction,[210] there are thick and thin conceptions of the rule of law[211] and even conceptions such as Trebilcock and Daniels' "procedural definition," which straddle somewhere between the two.[212] For some, the rule of law might mean building or reforming law-related structures and institutions, sometimes also referred to as a minimalist conception of the rule of law.[213]

> The minimalist conception of the rule of law emphasizes the rule of law's formal and structural components, rather than the substantive content of the rule of law. In other words, one can view the rule of law as involving rules and practices that are routinely followed.... [T]he influential British thinker A.V. Dicey emphasized that under the rule of law, no one can be punished except for violating preexisting laws and after sentencing by regular courts; everyone, including government officials, has equal status under law ... and general constitutional principles protecting rights result from ordinary legal processes.[214]

This minimalist conception is meant to capture qualities associated with what we consider "fair" in "law."

Alternatively, the rule of law might mean a system that is aimed toward achieving a cluster of specific end goals[215] and thus reflects "a thicker, more 'substantive' account"[216]

---

[208] Richard H. Fallon, *"The Rule of Law" as a Concept in International Discourse*, 97 COLUM. L. REV. 1, 7 (1997).

[209] MICHAEL J. TREBILCOCK & RONALD J. DANIELS, RULE OF LAW REFORM AND DEVELOPMENT: CHARTING THE FRAGILE PATH OF PROGRESS 13 (2008).

[210] *See* Introduction, text accompanying notes 54–74.

[211] TREBILCOCK & DANIELS, *supra* note 209, at 12–37.

[212] *Id.* at 14, 25, 29–37 (defining their procedural approach as a thinner conception which nonetheless includes process values such as transparency, stability, predictability; institutional values (independence and accountability of institutions); legitimacy values (which includes some basic human rights standards).

[213] JANE STROMSETH et al., CAN MIGHT MAKE RIGHTS?: BUILDING THE RULE OF LAW AFTER MILITARY INTERVENTIONS 70 (2006); Belton, *supra* note 194, at 6 (describing this view of the rule as one with "'institutional attributes.' Creating the proper institutional attributes—the 'necessary' laws, a 'well-functioning' judiciary, and a 'good' law enforcement apparatus—has become, for many practitioners, the goal of rule-of-law reform efforts.").

[214] STROMSETH ET AL., *supra* note 213, at 70.

[215] WORLD BANK, LEGAL AND JUDICIAL REFORM: OBSERVATIONS, EXPERIENCES, AND APPROACH OF THE LEGAL VICE PRESIDENCY 1 (2002).

[216] STROMSETH ET AL., *supra* note 213, at 70; Belton, *supra* note 194, at 6–7 ("[T]here are two very different ways of defining the rule of law.... The first style of definition enumerates the goods that the rule of law brings to society. A society with the rule of law is a society that instantiates these goods or ends, such as law and order, a government bound by the law, and human rights.... Another type of definition describes the institutions a society must have to be considered to possess the rule of law. Such a society would have certain

that serves certain values and purposes.[217] According to the World Bank, "[w]hile defined in various ways, the rule of law prevails where (i) the government itself is bound by the law, (ii) every person in society is treated equally under the law, (iii) the human dignity of each individual is recognized and protected by law, and (iv) justice is accessible to all."[218] Distinctions are also made on a formal versus substantive axis, with those subscribing to the former viewing the rule of law as a legal system that has formal characteristics—for example, "generality, equality, and certainty";[219] those subscribing to the latter believe that the rule of law must provide substantive protections, such as protection of individual or human rights,[220] with the added purpose, for some, of furthering democracy.[221] "A substantive account of the rule of law does not necessarily reject the notion that the rule of law has important structural and formal elements—predictability, universality, nonarbitrariness, and so on—but it insists that true rule of law also requires particular substantive commitments: to human rights, for instance."[222]

Proponents of each view attack the other on multiple grounds.[223] Those who favor a thick, substantive conception of the rule of law argue that a government with the requisite institutional attributes (adherence to comprehensive laws, efficient and well-functioning courts and law enforcement agencies) might nonetheless be unjust. As a Chinese professor remarked, "Chinese leaders want rule by law, not rule of law."[224]

Those who subscribe to a minimalist view of the rule of law argue that the substantive version requires its proponents to engage in the difficult task of choosing between competing principles of justice. For example, can a state that discriminates against women

---

institutional attributes, such as an efficient and trained judiciary, a noncorrupt police force, and published, publicly known laws.").

[217] Fallon, *supra* note 208, at 7–8 ("First, the Rule of Law should protect against anarchy and the Hobbesian war of all against all. Second, the Rule of Law should allow people to plan their affairs with reasonable confidence that they can know in advance the legal consequences of various actions. Third, the Rule of Law should guarantee against at least some types of official arbitrariness."); *see also* F. A. Hayek, The Road to Serfdom 80 (1994) (explaining that the rule of law makes "it possible to foresee with fair certainty how the authority will use its coercive powers in given circumstances and to plan one's individual affairs on the basis of this knowledge.").

[218] World Bank, Legal and Judicial Reform, *supra* note 215, at 1.

[219] Brian Tamanaha, *The Rule of Law for Everyone?* 6 (St. John's Legal Studies Research Paper Series, Working Paper, 2003), *available at* http://ssrn.com/abstract=312622 or http://dx.doi.org/10.2139/ssrn.312622.

[220] *Id.* at 6; Stromseth et al., *supra* note 213, at 71.

[221] Stephen Golub, *Beyond Rule of Law Orthodoxy: The Legal Empowerment Alternative* 8 (Carnegie Endowment for Int'l Peace, Working Paper No. 41, 2003), http://carnegieendowment.org/files/wp41.pdf (The USAID links rule of law with its democracy and governance program.).

[222] Stromseth et al., *supra* note 213, at 71; Tamanaha, *supra* note 219, at 6.

[223] Tamanaha, *supra* note 219, at 6; *see also* Stromseth et al., *supra* note 213, at 72; William W. Van Alstyne, *Civil Rights and Civil Liberties: Whose "Rule of Law?"* 11 Wm. & Mary Bill of Rts. J. 623, 623–24 (2003).

[224] Tamanaha, *supra* note 219, at 6; *see also* Van Alstyne, *supra* note 223, at 632 (describing how the Chinese government reacted to the release by Amnesty International of a report on detention in China that coincided with the anniversary of the Tiananmen Square crackdown—by insisting that "Chinese citizens have the right to exercise their democratic rights in accordance with the constitution. . . .").

be deemed to be in compliance with the basic requirements of a rule of law program?[225] In addition, minimalists contend that minimalism avoids potentially divisive questions about the universality of rights and that formal principles of law, though seemingly devoid of substantive content, nonetheless promote freedom because they constrain state officials. For example, a clear rule, when "objectively interpreted and applied, implicitly limits government."[226] Piling on other values to rule of law, according to critics, also makes the term meaningless because rule of law would simply be a "vacuous shorthand for 'democracy and human rights and other values I happen to like. . . .' " Others sidestep the dichotomy altogether by conflating the two—that is, they assume or hope that structurally independent institutions and well-crafted legislation will create the desired substantive end goals.[227] In the end there is no single definition of "rule of law" that scholars and practitioners both agree upon.[228]

Despite controversy within the field about the meaning of rule of law, it turns out that there is, nonetheless, in practice, a conventional and widely accepted (even if simultaneously widely criticized) rule of law agenda. As observed by Tom Carothers, founder and co-director of the Democracy and Rule of Law Project at the Carnegie Endowment for International Peace, there is the "Rule of Law Assistance Standard Menu," as he coined it, that includes "reforming institutions" such as the judiciary, legislatures, and police and prison system; "rewriting laws," including modernization of criminal, civil, and commercial laws; "upgrading the legal profession through support for stronger bar associations and law schools"; and "increasing legal access and advocacy."[229] What Carothers called the "standard menu" others have termed "rule of law orthodoxy"[230]—an institutional focus that defines "problems and cures narrowly, in terms of courts, prosecutors, contracts, law reform, and other institutions and processes in which lawyers play central roles."[231] The entire effort is state-focused. Much of it is technical in nature.[232] To the extent there is engagement with civil society, "it usually is as a means toward the end of state institutional development: consulting NGOs on how to reform the (narrowly defined) legal system, and funding them as vehicles for advocating reform."[233]

Most standard rule of law projects can be categorized in two ways. The first is by subject matter—writing and enacting "commercial law, criminal law, administrative law,

---

[225] Stromseth et al., *supra* note 213, at 72.

[226] Robert Summers, *The Principles of the Rule of Law*, 74 Notre Dame L. Rev. 1691, 1705 (1999).

[227] Stromseth et al., *supra* note 213, at 72–73; Belton, *supra* note 194, at 17.

[228] Golub, *supra* note 221, at 7 (rule of law "comprises a mélange of goals, assumptions, activities, and strategies. Many of these vary according to context, are ill-defined, or are only implicit.").

[229] Thomas Carothers, Aiding Democracy Abroad: The Learning Curve 165, 168 (1999); Bryant G. Garth, *Building Strong and Independent Judiciaries Through the New Law and Development: Behind the Paradox of Consensus Programs and Perpetually Disappointing Results*, 52 DePaul L. Rev. 383, 384 (2002).

[230] Golub, *supra* note 221, at 10–11.

[231] *Id.* at 9.

[232] Sarkar, *supra* note 62, at 113.

[233] Golub, *supra* note 221, at 10–11.

and the like."[234] The second is concerned with the "depth of reform, with three basic categories."[235] "Type one reform concentrates on the laws themselves: revising laws or whole codes to weed out antiquated provisions,"[236] particularly laws needed for an efficient market. For example, the World Bank and the International Monetary Fund routinely require poor countries to adopt policies considered necessary to establish efficient and transparent markets before bailing them out of financial crises.[237] These structural adjustment programs require countries to open their economies to competition from the international economic system, allowing their currencies to be freely convertible, privatizing government-owned enterprises, addressing budget deficits, instituting a rule of law framework, and so forth.[238] "Type two reform is the strengthening of law-related institutions, usually to make them more competent, efficient, and accountable."[239] Type two reform includes the training of judges, lawyers, the police, and so forth, presumably to respect and obey the newly enacted laws. "Type three reforms aim at the deeper goal of increasing government's compliance with law. A key step is achieving genuine judicial independence."[240]

This conventional or standard menu was uniformly applied to development assistance in many countries.[241] Projects in the Russian Federation, for example, included everything from study visits and continuing-education programs for judges to the coaching of court administrators in docket management and the establishment of alternative dispute-resolution mechanisms. Development efforts have focused on legal codification, the modernization of legal information systems, law-book subsidy and delivery, support for law-school curricular reform, the distribution of human-rights brochures, the production of bench books to summarize high-court decisions for lower-court judges, retraining of procurators, support for local bar associations, and improving public awareness of basic rights. "In particular, enormous sums have been expended on legal commentary and legislative drafting assistance in commercial-law areas, such as securities, bankruptcy, corporate governance, and banking."[242] Notice again that the emphasis is on training judges and lawyers, presumably to prepare them to modernize legal institutions and process, and on the enactment of formal laws.[243]

---

234 Carothers, *supra* note 134, at 99.

235 *Id.*

236 *Id.*

237 Tamanaha, *supra* note 2, at 478–79.

238 *Id.*

239 Carothers, *supra* note 134, at 100.

240 *Id.*; Sarkar, *supra* note 62, at 109.

241 Trebilcock & Daniels, *supra* note 209 (explaining a broad survey of rule of law reforms show predominant focus on these areas: judiciary, police, prosecution, prison, tax, access to justice, etc.).

242 Holmes, *supra* note 113, 68.

243 Sarkar, *supra* note 62, at 126–27.

Despite US efforts to promote rule of law in Russia, "[w]hat we have in Russia today, in short, is an incoherent state tenuously connected to a demoralized society. This pattern explains why there is little of the rule of law, despite foreign efforts to promote it, and why the problems facing legal-development programs seem so immense and intractable."[244] As one of the premier experts on Russian transition noted, "[w]hen Russia launched mass privatization, it was widely believed that it would create a powerful constituency for the rule of law. That didn't happen."[245]

Indeed, "[w]hether we look at Russia or Guatemala, Kosovo or Afghanistan, there is little basis for concluding that following such a 'Rule of Law Assistance Standard Menu,' by itself, has actually produced anything most of us would, in fact, recognize as the rule of law."[246] Past experience has shown that "the rule of law appears mysteriously difficult to establish—one might even say resistant. No one knows quite how to institute and entrench it, or even whether it can be done intentionally."[247] As noted, the slipperiness and vagueness associated with the term "rule of law" may be explained in part by the variety of indicators used to measure it.[248] Referring to the lack of consensus surrounding "rule of law," one scholar observed, "[h]ow can the rule of law be implemented if we don't know what it means?"[249]

Nonetheless, various combinations of this same rule of law template, consisting of writing constitutions and enabling legislation, providing technical assistance, reforming the judiciary, and promoting democratic governance through media and other civil society institutions, have been implemented in the Republic of Congo, Moldova, Kazakhstan, and Poland and other Central and Eastern European countries.[250] As observers have noted, "[f]rom Latin America to the former Soviet States to Bosnia, Kosovo, East Timor and Iraq, most rule of law programs have followed precisely this 'standard menu.'"[251] For instance, the International Platform of Jurists on East Timor that was established to translate "international human rights norms . . . into everyday practice in Timor" after its occupation by Indonesia proved relatively unsuccessful.[252] The Platform was "intended as the link, the site for advocacy which can bring norms established elsewhere—by a yet wider network expressing the commitments of 'the international community'—to bear on the very

[244] Holmes, *supra* note 113, at 69–70.

[245] Karla Hoff & Joseph E. Stiglitz, *After the Big Bang? Obstacles to the Emergence of the Rule of Law in Post-Communist Societies* 2 (Nat'l Bureau of Econ. Research, Working Paper No. 9282, Oct. 2002).

[246] Stromseth et al., *supra* note 213, at 75.

[247] Tamanaha, *supra* note 219, at 7.

[248] Agrast et al., *supra* note 121, at 4; Stephan Haggard, Andrew MacIntyre, & Lydia Tiede, *The Rule of Law and Economic Development*, 11 Ann. Rev. Pol. Sci. 205, 206–09 (2008).

[249] Tamanaha, *supra* note 219, at 7.

[250] Sarkar, *supra* note 62, at 112–16.

[251] Stromseth et al., *supra* note 213, at 74; Wade Channell, *Lessons Not Learned: Problems with Western Aid for Law Reform in Postcommunist Countries*, 7 (Carnegie Endowment for Int'l Peace, Paper No. 57, May 2005).

[252] David Kennedy, The Dark Sides of Virtue: Reassessing International Humanitarianism 90 (2004).

particular site of their ongoing violation."[253] However, the project failed to achieve this goal. David Kennedy explored some of the reasons the Platform failed to accomplish its goals. From Kennedy's perspective, the Platform paid more attention to its own organization and institutional structure than to substantive work. [254] It formed a council modeled on the United Nations, focused on texts, "revised resolutions, elected a board, published polemics, committed to doctrinal interpretations . . ."[255] At the end, the group had created a shell of an organization which would raise money and had adopted a formal resolution complete with a press conference despite serious doubts that these measures would help East Timor.[256] According to Kennedy, the project mistook adoption of vocabulary as solutions in and of themselves.[257]

Similar problems existed in Eastern Europe. Kennedy observed, for example, that Western Europe missed an opportunity to engage in true reform for Eastern Europe—beyond merely imposing the conventional rule of law template on the East when the Berlin Wall fell. Europe could have viewed this moment as "a moment in a long march from feudal centralism to economic democracy. The fall of dictatorships in Spain, Portugal, and Greece only a few years before had been interpreted in precisely this way."[258] But instead, Western Europe and more importantly the European Union viewed the East as developmentally behind and required Eastern Europe to implement rule of law programs before they could join the European Union.[259] Eastern Europe was required to adopt Western trade and regulatory regimes, as policy makers believed these legal rules would spur development.[260] Kennedy suggested such requirements hindered development rather than helped it—claiming that creating such laws before directly aiding economic growth was much like giving people "the regulatory equivalent of a Mercedes when they have not yet developed the capacity to drive a Fiat[.]"[261] Policy makers at this time focused on "establishing a Westward oriented export economy attractive to Western financial investors," ignoring preexisting economic ties to the East and preexisting legal regimes that may have worked just as well now that the Wall had fallen and global trade resumed.[262] Instead, Eastern European governments adopted Western laws, resulting in deregulatory free falls.[263] Kennedy believed that this deregulation hurt the workers,

---

253 *Id.*

254 *Id.* at 96–97 ("It was as if Pedro had become too occupied with organizational detail to see the importance of getting on with the substantive work at hand—his enchantment with means blocking his movement to ends.").

255 *Id.* at 103.

256 *Id.* at 107.

257 *Id.* at 90.

258 *Id.* at 172.

259 *Id.* at 173.

260 *Id.* at 174.

261 *Id.* at 175.

262 *Id.* at 190.

263 *Id.* at 191.

who no longer had job protection now that the market itself was no longer protected.[264] Kennedy also argued that this program of institution building and open trade laws may have slowed economic development in Eastern Europe.[265] According to him, rather than focusing on rule of law programs, the policy makers could have negotiated for trade associations which would have more directly improved trade for Eastern Europe and allowed the economy to adjust before changing the legal regimes. [266]

Whether or not one agrees with Kennedy's critique, the point is that rule of law reform has taken on a uniform, conventional, and technocratic agenda that no doubt contributes to the field's failures. Rule of law and human rights projects have viewed the problems they face too narrowly,[267] have focused too much on the government,[268] have created too many excuses for violations,[269] and have resisted responsibility for their effects.[270] Rule of law programs view the problems they seek to address too narrowly by focusing on form—again, setting up institutions or rewriting laws and assuming this alone solves the problem.[271]

Nonetheless, law and development continues to chug along the same failed path. Twenty something years after the UN-sponsored, US-led intervention in the early 1990s and multiple US efforts to institute rule of law, Haiti remains in crisis.[272] Despite great hopes and rhetorical flourishes combined with considerable financial commitment, it is widely acknowledged that even after billions of dollars in aid spent over the years, law and development has been characterized by more failure than success.[273] Indeed, "USAID spending on democracy and governance programs alone shot up from $671 million in 2002 to $1.2 billion in 2004, but almost all of that increase was devoted to Iraq and Afghanistan."[274] Additionally, the World Bank's expenditures on development have been

---

[264] *Id.* at 191.

[265] *Id.* at 192.

[266] *Id.*

[267] *Id.* at 10–11.

[268] *Id.* at 16.

[269] *Id.* at 24.

[270] *Id.* at 31.

[271] *Id.* at 12. For instance, under many rule of law programs "holding elections can come to substitute for popular engagement in politics." *Id.*

[272] UN Security Council, *Report of the Security Council Mission to Haiti*, Apr. 13–16, 2005, UN Doc. S/2005/402 (2005).

[273] *See* Stephen Golub, *A House Without a Foundation, in* PROMOTING THE RULE OF LAW ABROAD: IN SEARCH OF KNOWLEDGE 105, 105 (Thomas Carothers ed., 2006); Frank Upham, *Mythmaking in the Rule-of-Law Orthodoxy, in* PROMOTING THE RULE OF LAW ABROAD: IN SEARCH OF KNOWLEDGE 75, 95 (Thomas Carothers ed., 2006); Holmes, *supra* note 113, at 68; Linn Hammergren, *Do Judicial Councils Further Judicial Reform? Lessons from Latin America* 1 (Carnegie Endowment for Int'l Peace, Working Paper No. 28, 2002) (finding that efforts to free the judicial system in many Latin American countries of nepotism and corruption have failed).

[274] Peter Baker, *Funding Scarce for Export of Democracy—Outside Mideast, U.S. Efforts Lags*, WASH. POST, Mar. 18, 2005, at A1.

pegged at almost $4 billion.[275] The startling bottom line is that worldwide, one billion people are still in poverty and another billion just slightly above them.[276] Results such as these raise questions as to the efficacy and impact of foreign intervention, particularly when implementing reforms based on "international best practices," which introduce Western laws and institutions on the project country,[277] and, as I argue throughout the book, without any attendant cultural work to support legal development.

C. The Case for Culture in Law and Development

At this point, one might ask, why do rule of law efforts persist in repeating the same mistakes? Why do they continue offering and prescribing the same standard menu if it has been shown not to yield the desired results? One answer may be that the standard menu is manageable and can be done piecemeal. Experts can point to a set of institutions to be reformed and improved. The effort is concrete and pragmatic. Judges need to be trained. Programs can be developed to train them. Law schools, legal institutions, and local bar associations need financial and training support. Western bar associations and law schools can send their lawyers and faculty on exchange missions for one- to two-year stints or, even more conveniently, in the summer.[278] An extremely complex endeavor can be broken into component parts, each with their own respective experts—lawyers for legal reform, police for police reform, judges for judicial reform—and thus becomes more manageable because reform seems achievable via technocratic expertise.

The law and development task becomes understandably more discrete and less daunting "by breaking the concept down into the concrete institutions that needed reforming."[279] But this approach is riddled with problems. First, it is likely to cause conceptual confusion when the necessity of institution building as a practical matter is conflated with and deemed equivalent to the mission of achieving certain designated end goals. Furthermore, even if reformers acknowledge that the rule of law needs to be contextually understood and that end goals need to be normatively identified, "most programs to build the rule of law implicitly define the rule of law by its institutional attributes. Although

---

275 Alvaro Santos, *The World Bank's Uses of the "Rule of Law" Promise in Economic Development*, *in* The New Law and Economic Development: A Critical Appraisal 253, 253 n. 1 (David M. Trubek & Alvaro Santos eds., 2006).

276 Paul Collier, The Bottom Billion: Why the Poorest Countries Are Failing and What Can Be Done About It 3–5 (2007).

277 Randy Peerenboom, *The Future of Rule of Law: Challenges and Prospects for the Field*, 1 Hague J. Rule of L. 5, 5 (2009); *see also* Tamanaha, *supra* note 111, at 225 (describing legal reform efforts in Eastern Europe and describing such efforts involving "wholesale legal transplantation" as likely to fail because "the new laws on paper had little effect on actual rules of conduct") (quoting William Easterly, The White Man's Burden: Why the West's Efforts to Aid the Rest Have Done So Much Ill and So Little Good 94 (2006).

278 Peerenboom, *supra* note 277, at 7–8.

279 Belton, *supra* note 194, at 6.

they cite the rule of law as their ultimate goal, practitioners almost immediately turn to institutions not as means, but as intermediate or measurable ends."[280] It is understandable that reform programs, even if run by well-meaning reformers, will encounter this pitfall, given the enormity of the problem and time and resource constraints. Reformers may understand that law cannot be severed from the broad constellation of societal factors and that it is crucial to engage local conditions because the wider societal context matters.[281] But ultimately, general templates are used and the standard menu is pursued. As a result, it is easy for ends to become conflated with means, either because it is assumed that reformed institutions will provide an effective vehicle through which desired ends can be achieved or because it is simply less wieldy to focus on concrete projects, such as reform of courts, police, and law schools or the passage of specific laws.[282] The societal context, which supposedly matters, recedes into the background.

Second, because institutional reform is parceled out to experts who work on their respective institutions, each field tends to be insulated from the next as each expert focuses "on making each field function 'properly' as an end in itself.[283] As a result, "even if reformers can make a single institution function well, they will not necessarily achieve any rule-of-law ends because each requires reform across *multiple* institutions."[284] What we tend to have is a group of experts working on police reform here, judiciary reform there, commercial law reform further over there, with minimal coordination among the groups and, overall, minimal "understanding of overarching goals."[285]

As a result, the emphasis on institutions and forms has created an atmosphere in which law and development becomes a technocratic process consisting of adopting and implementing standard or uniform templates for developing countries. Hence well-worn templates are perpetuated because experts share a tendency to view the standard institutions they seek to create and the vocabularies they use as benign,[286] rather than considering on a case-by-case basis what would work best in the given area.

Moreover, they often fail to realize that the laws they promote are themselves political choices and have consequences.[287] At other times, they overestimate the impact a legal rule will have—adopting a legal rule is not the same as implementing it into that society.[288] Again, this is where culture and norms must be addressed and considered. Drafting laws

---

[280] *Id.* at 16.

[281] Cynthia Alkon, *The Cookie Cutter Syndrome: Legal Reform Assistance Under Post-Communist Democratization Programs*, 202 J. Disp. Resol. 327, 334 (2002).

[282] Stromseth et al., *supra* note 213, at 74 ("This conflation of the formal and substantive aspects of the rule of law has led to a simplistic emphasis on structures, institutions, and the 'modernization' of legal codes. . . ."); Belton, *supra* note 194, at 17.

[283] Belton, *supra* note 194, at 18.

[284] *Id.* at 17.

[285] *Id.* at 18.

[286] Kennedy, *supra* note 252, at 121.

[287] *Id.* at 115.

[288] *Id.* at 128.

and building governmental structure does not guarantee development or humanitarian results.[289] For example, during the military effort against Al Qaeda, international lawyers insisted that prisoners be tried before international tribunals because their policies prefer international action, but most never questioned whether trials before international tribunals would decrease terrorism, harm the military effort, or actually better protect the defendant's rights.[290] When rule of law programs insist on certain institutions and regimes over others without exploring the consequences in the given scenario, there can be bad consequences which undermine the lofty efforts of the rule of law policy makers.

True, there is some recognition that "social-cultural-historical factors . . . have yielded a set of social values, norms, attitudes, or practices that are inhospitable to even a limited procedural conception of the rule of law."[291] But there is little normative commitment to change in an area outside the scope of the standard menu described above. As a consequence, cultural issues are hardly ever addressed. Thus, as I have discussed, the consequence of adhering to conventional law and development is as follows: (1) a standard menu that is dogged in an institutional focus aimed at reforming institutions and drafting laws without sufficient attention to overarching or intrinsic end goals; (2) a standard menu that works to improve each institution without linking reform within an institution to reform across other related or coordinated institutions; and (3) a blind spot to the need for cultural change.

Let's assume for a moment that the standard menu is tinkered with and improved so that points 1 and 2 above are addressed. Institutions are reformed, laws are drafted with clear, substantive end goals, and both institutional and legal reforms are undertaken in a coordinated manner. This would be an improvement, but it would still be normatively insufficient. Indeed, while it is true that "[r]eform must occur across all primary institutions to achieve any rule-of-law end, . . . even such widespread reform will rarely be enough to ensure real change."[292] This is because law is only part of the picture. Culture is the other part, and as I argue in this book, a crucial part. As observed, "many rule-of-law ends are upheld even when institutional arrangements are far from supportive, if countries have social and political cultures that place a premium on the rule of law."[293] The reverse is also true. "Recalcitrant cultures . . . can undermine even well-organized rule-of-law institutions."[294] I do not mean, however, to suggest that culture is the only other development factor that matters; the influence of history, material resources, geography, economics, and politics, for example, on development and reform is undeniable. History and geography, though a determinant in the law and development equation, are

---

289 *Id.* at 116.

290 *Id.*

291 Trebilcock & Daniels, *supra* note 209, at 39.

292 Belton, *supra* note 194, at 21.

293 *Id.* at 22; *see also* Reitz, *supra* note 109, at 436 (arguing that attitudes supporting rule of law must be widespread throughout society in order to claim that the country is bound by it).

294 Belton, *supra* note 194, at 22.

immutable factors. This book thus focuses on a mutable characteristic—culture—and studies its relationship to law and development.

I begin with the definitional question. What do we mean by culture? Scholars have struggled with varying approximations of what is meant by the word.[295] In the 1950s, Talcott Parson espoused a view of culture that created a dichotomy between values and action, whereby culture was understood to dwell strictly in the realm of values. "This conception of culture sundered values and beliefs from institutions, practices, and political economy."[296] In this way, culture might be understood as the "beliefs, preferences, and behaviors of its members, along with the mechanisms that link these traits to one another."[297] One could call this a "thin" conception of culture—encompassing only "subjective terms as the values, attitudes, beliefs, orientations, and underlying assumptions prevalent among people in a society."[298]

By contrast, the noted anthropologist Clifford Geertz, it has been said, subscribes to a "thick description" of culture, using it "to refer to the entire way of life of a society: its values, practices, symbols, institutions, and human relationships."[299] In this more expansive view, culture encompasses the "capacity for creating the categories of our experience,"[300] broadly connecting "the numerous domains of our lives—economic, kinship, political, legal—binding them to one another."[301] "It does not consist only of beliefs and values but also practices, habits, and commonsensical ways of doing things."[302] Through the common cultural landscape, the collective experience of group members becomes "not only logical and obvious but immanent and natural"[303] because culture makes it possible for us to "create our experience, knit together disparate ideas and actions, and in the process fabricate a world of meaning that appears to us as real."[304] In both cases, culture as beliefs and preferences or culture as a cosmology of experience and logic entails individual and community processes of meaning-making.

---

[295] *See*, e.g., RAYMOND WILLIAMS, KEYWORDS: A VOCABULARY OF CULTURE AND SOCIETY 87 (1985) (noting that "[c]ulture is one of the two or three most complicated words in the English language."); Sally Engle Merry, *Law, Culture, and Cultural Appropriation*, 10 YALE J.L. & HUMAN. 575, 579 (1998) ("Constructing a definition for anthropology's core concept has always been difficult, but at no time more so than the present.").

[296] Sally Engle Merry, *Human Rights Law and the Demonization of Culture (And Anthropology Along the Way)*, Pol. & Legal Anthropology Rev., May 2003, at 55, 64. It is said that this view of culture insulates it from "an ethical critique of a culture since it is simply a system of values and beliefs. Thus, this understanding of culture contributed to the idea of cultural relativism as an inability to judge another culture, since 'culture' was understood only in terms of values, not practices." *Id.* at 64–65.

[297] Timur Kuran, *Cultural Obstacles to Economic Development: Often Overstated, Usually Transitory, in* CULTURE AND PUBLIC ACTION 115, 117 (Vijayendra Rao & Michael Walton eds., 2004).

[298] Samuel P. Huntington, *Foreword: Cultures Count, in* CULTURE MATTERS: HOW VALUES SHAPE HUMAN PROGRESS xiii, xv (Lawrence E. Harrison & Samuel P. Huntington eds., 2000).

[299] *Id.*

[300] LAWRENCE ROSEN, LAW AS CULTURE: AN INVITATION 4 (2006).

[301] *Id.*

[302] Merry, *supra* note 296, at 67.

[303] ROSEN, *supra* note 300.

[304] *Id.*

Another conception of culture was popularized by Franz Boas, whose Germanic notion of *Kultur* served as a counterpoint to the French and English notion of transnational civilization. "In contrast to these societies, Germany claimed that it had a distinct, spiritual essence or Kultur.... While civilization plays down the national differences between peoples and emphasizes what is common to all human beings, Kultur places more stress on national differences and particular identities of groups."[305] Boas's notion of culture as *Volksgeist*, as a set of values and beliefs that makes a people or nation distinctive, appeals to "the need for a nation to define itself, to constitute its boundaries, and to ask how it is different from other groups."[306] Boas's cultural anthropology saw culture as discrete and bounded, rather than, for example, fluid and expansive.

In this Boasian way, culture might be used "to summarize the way in which groups distinguish themselves from other groups."[307] In world politics today, "[e]thnic, tribal, religious, and civilizational identities are increasingly called upon to distinguish communities and explain their political interaction."[308] Culture can be understood thus: the "loose conceptual configuration of all those to whom the particularities of race, religion, ethnicity or nationality are—or are among—the defining elements of their identity."[309] Contrast this German concept of *Kultur* which served as a way to create a distinct national identity with the broader French concept of transnational civilization.[310]

Contemporary understanding of culture, however, is different in at least two significant ways. First, culture is no longer thought of as something that exists in the realm of values and beliefs as Parson did. Second, departing from Boas's view of *Kultur*, contemporary anthropology sees culture as less bounded and more fluid, less defined and more contested, less tradition and more evolution. "Culture is marked by hybridity and creolization rather than uniformity or consistency. Local systems are analyzed in the context of national and transnational processes and are understood as the result of particular historical trajectories. This is a more dynamic, agentic, and historicized way of understanding culture."[311] This modern understanding of culture and how it supports my culture change thesis will be discussed further in Chapter 6.

If culture is central to law and development, why has it not been incorporated as a crucial component of the field? This is hardly a recent insight. Max Weber long ago asserted

---

305 Merry, *supra* note 296, at 65.

306 *Id.*

307 Jacinta O'Hagan, *Conflict, Convergence or Co-existence? The Relevance of Culture in Reframing World Order*, 9 TRANSNAT'L L. & CONTEMP. PROBS. 537, 538 (1999).

308 *Id.* Civilizational identity could arguably be included in one's exploration of cultural identity because civilization transcends state boundaries and as such, includes, again, loosely stated, "shared histories, traditions, values, and beliefs." *Id.* Despite the ethnic and religious differences among European countries, one might observe that "[t]he expansion of the West, as a civilization, has been one of the most significant features of the past millennium." *Id.* at 541.

309 Thomas M. Franck, *The Legal Culture and the Culture Culture*, 93 AM. SOC'Y INT'L L. 271, 271 (1999).

310 *See* Merry, *supra* note 296, at 66.

311 *Id.* at 67.

that institutions alone were insufficient to support modern capitalism and that the latter required a transformation in consciousness associated with the Protestant Reformation.[312] While most rule of law practitioners understand the importance of culture and politics, the standard menu's emphasis on laws and institutions marginalizes culture.[313] "[T]he institutional attributes style of defining the rule of law minimizes the importance of these levers of change and obstructs clear thinking about how to address them."[314] This fact makes it easy for rule of law practitioners to pretend that they are merely engaged in a technocratic or institutional endeavor of writing the right laws or building the necessary institutions and "to deny the fact that their work is inherently about changing the cultural and political values of other countries"[315] Such denial is understandable because as I discussed,[316] somehow it seems more doable to reform institutions and have laws passed than to change attitudes and beliefs. Yet, the former is inextricably linked to the latter. As observed, " 'promoting the rule of law' is an issue of norm creation and cultural change as much as an issue of creating new institutions and legal codes."[317]

Thus drafting laws without a concomitant commitment to the norms underlying those laws will be insufficient for the rule of law to truly take root. For instance, it is all too often assumed in law and development circles that a law decreeing equality of rights between men and women is the correct action to bring about respect for women's rights or that establishing independent courts is what is needed to foster nonviolence in dispute resolution. And yet, even among legal scholars, this is widely acknowledged as insufficient; widespread acceptance reflecting *legitimacy* of the newly drafted laws, or as noted, a cultural commitment to the newly established institutions is needed.[318] Legitimacy may in turn depend on whether or not reform is accepted. And acceptance of reforms in some cases requires a change in values that will make such reforms palatable to and accepted by the local population.[319] Indeed, despite its flaws, first wave law and development reform at least made an effort to engage culture, albeit only legal culture.[320]

The connection between development and culture, replete with concrete examples and case studies, will be explored more fully in Part B of Chapter 3. For now, suffice it to say that neither the first nor second wave of law and development had culture as a

---

312 MAX WEBER, THE PROTESTANT ETHIC AND THE SPIRIT OF CAPITALISM (1930).

313 Ginsburg, *supra* note 119, at 833 (describing the shift away from the cultural factors first wave reformers had sought and turning instead "toward technical institutional arrangements (which provide an environment for individual entrepreneurs). Today's development policy assumes that a country must adopt the proper institutions to facilitate growth and that institutions can be transferred across borders.").

314 Belton, *supra* note 194, at 22.

315 *Id.*

316 *See supra* note 313 and accompanying text.

317 STROMSETH ET AL., *supra* note 213, at 75.

318 Rosa Brooks & Anne-Marie Slaughter, *A Just World Under Law*, 98 AM. SOC'Y INT'L L. PROC. 125, 126–27 (2004).

319 Reitz, *supra* note 109, at 467.

320 Ginsburg, *supra* note 119, at 833; *see also supra* text accompanying notes 58–76.

core component. As a result, values and norms were and remain essentially outside the framework of inquiry. Yet, there are many reasons why they should be integrated into law and development. First, as I demonstrate throughout this book, even if one were to view law and development as essentially about the "rule of law" *only* (so that the development portion is tacitly bypassed), passing laws alone is not sufficient to ensure that the objectives of the laws themselves will take root. A set of culturally supportive conditions is also needed to support legal development. Second (still staying within an exclusive rule of law model), culture is already implicitly engaged whether one views rule of law in thin, minimalist terms or thick, maximalistic terms. Third, even in this law-centered model, increasingly, "rule of law" is understood in thick, maximalist terms. Note that it is not just law and development scholars but also political leaders in recent years who assert that rule of law includes a substantive component—democracy and human rights, for example.[321] If rule of law is understood in those terms, it is all the more vital for law to be situated within a confluence of factors, including cultural factors.

If one were to move beyond a *law*-only frame to include the *development* frame of "law and development," the case for including culture is even stronger. The rest of this chapter is devoted to discussing how recent strands in development scholarship have vigorously pushed for a more expanded, comprehensive understanding of development. As I demonstrate in this chapter below, this expanded conception of development is compatible with a thick, maximalist (rather than thin, formalist) account of rule of law. Viewing "development" within this enlarged frame and viewing "law" in thick, maximalist terms would result, appropriately, in a much needed reorientation of the field of law and development. Law and development would engage *both* law and development rather than assume that (1) legal development is the equivalent of development, or (2) rule of law would spawn economic growth, or (3) economic growth is the same as development. This is so because development would be viewed as a distinct, robust component of law and development, and factors that make up development would be separately evaluated and incorporated into the law and development framework. Law would of course remain important, but it would be situated within an expanded development framework, not function as development's substitute.

In advancing a "thick" evaluative approach to economic development, Amartya Sen demonstrated the welfare realities uncovered when a thin approach is properly broadened. The remainder of this chapter continues the discussion begun in the Introduction about Sen. Sen examined the traditional concentration on "income and wealth" as an indicator of development that, in his opinion, lacks the breadth of scope needed to truly evaluate a country's success in dealing with poverty.[322] Sen promoted a more robust indicator of development, evaluating poverty relief not in terms of income, but in terms of the "[d]eprivation of elementary capabilities . . . reflected in premature mortality, significant

[321] *See supra* notes 128–132.

[322] AMARTYA SEN, DEVELOPMENT AS FREEDOM 19 (1999).

undernourishment (especially of children), persistent morbidity, widespread illiteracy and other failures."[323] To substantiate his claim, Sen compared the mortality rates of certain rich countries with those of "the so-called third world" with surprising results.[324] Specifically, African Americans maintain a significantly lower per capita income than that of the general white population in the United States; however, African Americans are still "very many times richer in income terms than the people of China or Kerala."[325] Despite African Americans' relative wealth, both African American men and women live shorter lives than the men and women of China or Kerala (especially African American men living in the cities of New York, San Francisco, St. Louis, and Washington, D.C).[326] As Sen stated, "it is not only the case that American blacks suffer from relative deprivation in terms of income per head vis-à-vis American whites, they also are absolutely more deprived than the low-income Indians in Kerala (for both women and men), and the Chinese (in the case of men), in terms of living to ripe old ages."[327] This comparison highlights the fact that a thin, technical approach to development based on income, GDP, and so forth overlooks significant elements of the development analysis. Income and wealth metrics certainly do provide important information in this analysis;[328] however, according to Sen, any metric that neglects to incorporate quality of life factors such as longevity and other thick considerations will invariably lead to erroneous conclusions about the state of human welfare in a community.

Evaluating economic development in terms of deprivation of elementary capabilities rather than income represents Sen's attempt to shift development analysis from formulaic metrics to expanded, holistic terms. Sen observed the following: "if the different aspects of development are not simultaneously addressed and considered together for analysis and action, they may each end up 'hanging separately.' "[329] As is clear from above, Sen favors an approach that seeks to "understand[] the interconnections between different aspects of development, and in particular between legal and non-legal features of the process of development."[330] "This involves rejecting a compartmentalized view of the process of development"[331] and adopting a comprehensive view. For Sen, a comprehensive approach should be pursued because there are inherent causal interconnections between the different development domains. Along these lines, law and development should not separate one domain from the other. Note that this approach is starkly

---

323 *Id.* at 20.
324 *Id.* at 21.
325 *Id.*
326 *Id.* at 21–23.
327 *Id.* at 22.
328 *Id.* at 19.
329 Sen, *supra* note 117, at 1.
330 *Id.*
331 *Id.* at 3.

different from the prevailing rule of law approach, which, as already observed, tends to be compartmentalized.

According to Sen, development is a "process of expanding the real freedoms that people enjoy."[332] This is in contrast to "identifying development with the growth of gross national product, or with the rise in personal incomes, or with industrialization, or with technological advance, or with social modernization."[333] For Sen, these technical developments represent important "means to expanding the freedoms enjoyed" by members of a society; however, "[v]iewing development in terms of expanding substantive freedoms directs attention to the ends that make development important, rather than merely to some of the means that, inter alia, play a prominent part in the process."[334] Sen focuses on five necessary freedoms in particular: political freedom, economic capacity, social opportunity, transparency guarantees, and protective security.

If development is viewed in terms expanding real freedoms, the chief aim of development is "the removal of major sources of unfreedom."[335] Sen views these sources of unfreedom as "poverty as well as tyranny, poor economic opportunities as well as systematic social deprivation, neglect of public facilities as well as intolerance or overactivity of repressive states," all of which limit the five freedoms noted above.[336] Removing unfreedom is accomplished by enhancing "people's capability—their freedom—to exercise the rights and entitlements that we associate with legal progress."[337] Development as freedom, then, is about "the expansion of the 'capabilities' of people to lead the kind of lives they value—and have reason to value."[338] Certainly, as noted above, factors such as income and economic growth are likely to expand people's capabilities, but they cannot be the sole yardstick for development. Expanding "capabilities" must be linked to a host of interlocking factors and cannot be reduced to "one homogeneous 'good thing.'"[339] In other words, capability expansion must enhance political freedom, economic capacity, social opportunity, transparency guarantees, and protective security in order to properly guide international development toward improving the lives people hope to enjoy.

The implications of this "capabilities" paradigm are profound. Because development is redefined and focused on expanding people's substantive freedoms or capabilities to lead the lives they value, it zeroes in on an array of "functionings" such as health, literacy, education, and the freedoms of expression and association. These functionings not only form the primary end of development, but its principal means as well.[340] It is only as

332 SEN, *supra* note 322, at 3.
333 *Id.*
334 *Id.*
335 *Id.*
336 *Id.*
337 Sen, *supra* note 117, at 11.
338 SEN, *supra* note 322, at 18.
339 *Id.* at 77.
340 *Id.* at 36.

people's capacity to function improves that they achieve the political freedom, economic capacity, social opportunity, transparency guarantees, and protective security required to thrive. People's capacity to function, however, only improves as these same freedoms are enhanced in the different spheres of political, economic, and social life. Thus, freedom is tied to both the "constitutive" and the "instrumental" roles of development.[341]

This concept of freedom being the constitutive ends and the instrumental means of development suggests that substantive freedoms are interconnected and complementary of one another, and thus must be considered together as a whole. Sen wrote, "[h]eterogeneity of factors that influence individual advantage is a pervasive feature of actual evaluation."[342] As another commentator noted, "development covers the whole range of economic, cultural, social as well as civil and political rights,"[343] each causally dependent on the other. Freedom of association is linked to economic development because the right to participate in decisions that affect one's economic conditions is vital to the process of development.[344] Hence, on one level, development is intertwined with a host of other rights, such as human rights. As Sen explained it, support for a comprehensive approach to development can be justified in this way:

> The claim here is not so much that, say, legal development causally influences development *tout court*, but rather that development as a whole cannot be considered separately from legal development. Indeed, in this view, the overarching idea of development is a functional relation that amalgamates distinct developmental concerns respectively in economic, political, social, legal and other spheres. This is more than causal interdependence: it involves a constitutive connection in the concept of development as a whole.[345]

The conceptual integrity of these different types of development, legal development, economic development, political development, and, as I argue, cultural development, counsels against merely dealing with each type of development as if it were or could be separate from the other. Thus, the idea that development encompasses different spheres that are conceptually integral to the overall process of development also means that political and economic development too cannot be separately conceived. Similarly, one would not be able to argue that "Asian values" facilitate economic development and then justify the lack of political development by pointing to economic growth. Nor can one

---

341 *Id.*

342 *Id.* at 77.

343 Gernot Brodnig, *The World Bank and Human Rights: Mission Impossible?* 10 (Carr Center for Human Rights, Policy Working Paper No. T-01–05), *available at* http://www.hks.harvard.edu/cchrp/Web%20Working%20Papers/BrodnigHR&WorldBank.pdf.

344 *Id.*

345 Sen, *supra* note 117, at 8.

value democracy only by reference to its impact on some other development objective. For example, there may be conflicting evidence that democracy is needed for economic growth or that democracy may even slow down economic growth. But democracy can be defended on its own terms, as a constitutive component of development[346] even if there is no conclusive link between democratization and economic growth. If development were understood in holistic, constitutive terms, questions such as these would simply not be part of the normative equation: "Is true development a speedy economic improvement in the living conditions of as many people as possible or is achieving a democratic society part of the journey towards development? Should development include more than economic prosperity by incorporating the political and social freedoms available to the individual as well?"[347]

Similarly, one could not delink legal development from overall development even if "legal development were not to contribute one iota to economic development."[348] Sen would not conclude that legal development is unnecessary or somehow of questionable value because economic development might be achieved without a rule of law that protects property and contract rights and establishes independent courts. That China's spectacular economic growth might or might not have been accompanied by the full panoply of legal development is neither here nor there.[349] Economic growth is not synonymous with this holistic view of development and cannot be used to justify nondevelopment in other spheres. "It is extremely important to get this point fully accepted, since there is a well-established tradition in development studies and policy making to concentrate exclusively on economic expansion."[350]

Take again, for example, income measurements. Sen noted that while we use "incomes and commodities as the material basis of our well-being," certain variables make clear that income is a "limited guide to welfare and the quality of life."[351] For instance, "[p]ersonal heterogeneities" such as "disparate physical characteristics connected with disability, illness, age or gender" or "[e]nvironmental diversities" such as "variations in environmental conditions, such as . . . temperature ranges, rainfall, flooding" may limit "what a person gets out of a given level of income."[352] Sen identified three more variables that, in addition to further demonstrating the imprudence of the income metric, also allude to the necessity of incorporating culture in development analysis so as to properly account for these variables. First, "[v]ariations in social climate" such as "social conditions, including public educational arrangements, and the prevalence or

---

346 *Id.* at 14.

347 Sarkar, *supra* note 62, at 49.

348 Sen, *supra* note 117, at 10.

349 *See* Sen, *supra* note 117, at 13–14.

350 Sen, *supra* note 117, at 14.

351 Sen, *supra* note 322, at 70–71.

352 *Id.* at 70.

absence of crime and violence in the particular location" can affect the welfare value of income.[353] While Sen specified certain social institutions or social ailments, this variable includes a distinctly cultural component. Namely, cultural attitudes that restrict access to social institutions or prod on violence equally contribute to and limit the quality of life afforded by income.

Second, "[d]ifferences in relational perspectives," which Sen defined as "[t]he commodity requirements of established patterns of behavior [that] . . . vary between communities, depending on conventions and customs," can prevent the "relatively poor in a rich community . . . from achieving some elementary 'functionings' (such as taking part in the life of the community) even though [their] income, in absolute terms, may be much higher than the level of income at which members of poorer communities can function with great ease and success."[354] To illustrate this point, Sen wrote, "[f]or example, to be able to 'appear in public without shame' may require higher standards of clothing and other visible consumption in a richer society than in a poorer one (as Adam Smith noted more than two centuries ago)."[355] The cultural component to this variable is relatively straightforward. Cultural customs and norms establish the commodity requirements that in turn inhibit the relative social value of and prospects afforded by income.

Third, "[d]istribution within the family" of income can "make a major difference to the attainments and predicaments of individual members."[356] Sen explained that since the family is the "basic unit for consideration of incomes from the standpoint of their use . . . the well being or freedom of individuals in a family will depend on how the family income is used in furtherance of the interests and objectives of different members of the family."[357] So, should a family esteem the education of its children, the family will distribute its income to the education needs of its children. However, should the family subscribe to a hierarchical male social system, younger males and women within the family will suffer. Their economic and quality of life prospects dwindle as older male members consume the lion's share of the family income. Once again, the cultural component to this variable is relatively straightforward. Cultural customs and norms instruct family dynamics, which in turn determine the distribution of family income to family members.

As alluded to by Sen's discussion of income variables, Sen's point about freedom being both the ends and means of development goes further than the observation that development is holistic and that the different domains of development are linked. This concept

---

[353] *Id.* at 70–71.

[354] *Id.* at 71.

[355] *Id.*

[356] *Id.*

[357] *Id.*

means that development in one sphere must also support development in another sphere. Sen wrote as follows:

> Political freedoms (in the form of free speech and elections) help to promote economic security. Social opportunities (in the form of education and health facilities) facilitate economic participation. Economic facilities (in the form of opportunities for participation in trade and production) can help to generate personal abundance as well as public resources for social facilities. Freedoms of different kinds can strengthen one another.[358]

Thus, while legal development, or any of the freedoms noted by Sen, are indeed part and parcel of development, legal development alone is not sufficient. The standard rule of law template—whether "thick" or "thin"—hardly meets this notion of development. Sen provided this example: If laws are passed granting women certain legal rights, this would be appropriately considered legal development. However, if this legal development is in fact "hollow" because women cannot meaningfully exercise their rights because of defects in some other sphere, which contribute to women's illiteracy, then the latter defect also needs to be corrected. "If we overlook these constitutive linkages, then we may miss some of the strongest arguments for taking a comprehensive approach, which go well beyond the causal interdependences between separately conceptualized ideas of legal development, social development, political development, and so on."[359]

If developments in different spheres are linked and if law and development must be understood in an integrated, comprehensive and constitutive manner, then, following Sen's thread to its logical conclusion, a legal development (laws supporting women's rights, for example) that is undermined by impediments in another sphere would be dealt with by addressing the impediments in that latter sphere. Thus, norms in the cultural sphere that interfere with or are hostile to development should be challenged by law and development initiatives. By contrast, norms in the cultural sphere that generate supportive conditions for law and development objectives should be incorporated. In this way, "efforts geared to development can hardly ignore the world of culture. Economic and social changes in pursuit of development can certainly influence positively or negatively the opportunities for cultural pursuits. . . ."[360] Sen's understanding of development not only highlights the many spheres of development but also norms and values integral to the law and development framework.[361] Indeed, development as freedom—freedom to

---

[358] *Id.* at 11.

[359] Sen, *supra* note 117, at 11.

[360] Amartya Sen, *Culture and Development*, http://www.scribd.com/doc/6699222/Culture-Development-by-Amartya-Sen (last visited Feb. 11, 2015).

[361] Peter Evans, *Collective Capabilities, Culture, and Amartya Sen's Development as Freedom*, 37 Stud. Comp. Int'l Dev. 54, 55 (2002).

maximize one's capabilities, freedom to lead the lives one values—means the question of culture must be a central part of the inquiry. Sen observed:

> Such an approach also allows us to acknowledge the role of social values and prevailing mores, which can influence the freedoms that people enjoy and have reason to treasure. Shared norms can influence social features such as gender equity, the nature of child care, family size and fertility patterns, the treatment of the environment and many other arrangements and outcomes. Prevailing values and social mores also affect the presence or absence of corruption, and the role of trust in economic or social or political relationships. The exercise of freedom is mediated by values, but the values in turn are influenced by public discussions and social interactions, which are themselves influenced by participatory freedoms. Each of these connections deserves careful scrutiny.[362]

There is little doubt that for Sen, development thus includes a strong cultural component; however, Sen is also quite clear that people must be "allowed to decide freely what traditions they wish or do not wish to follow" rather than being forced to "obey the decisions by religious or secular authorities who enforce traditions—real or imagined."[363] Sen assumed in the passage above that religious and secular leaders enforce certain traditional practices by forcing people to obey religious or traditional strictures. For example, in India, there are "[s]mall but growing and ever more vocal groups of cultural vigilantes . . . attacking anything that does not conform to their notion of purity and morality, from paintings, books and films to modern dress, Western attitudes and even beauty salons."[364] In Saudi Arabia, the morality police, known as the Commission for the Promotion of Virtue and the Prevention of Vice, set up in 1962 to monitor public behavior, regularly patrolled public spaces to enforce dress codes and other strictures. A Saudi judge sentenced a Saudi woman to a month in prison and fifty lashes when she was convicted of " 'cursing the morality police' and calling them 'liars.' "[365] When traditional norms and mores are enforced by vigilantes, many sanctioned by the government, it is hard to determine if someone is freely deciding whether or not to follow a certain practice or being forced to obey the practice deemed correct by the authorities. Sen is rightly fearful of the tendency of authoritarian leaders to use culture and regional values to justify their own authoritarianism.[366] Therefore, culture must be viewed and attended to in terms of freedom, capability, and choice:

> [I]t is up to the society to determine what, if anything, it wants to do to preserve old forms of living, perhaps even at significant economic cost . . . what is crucial

---

362 SEN, *supra* note 322, at 9.

363 *Id.* at 32.

364 Krittivas Mukherjee, *Cultural Bigotry Rises as India Sees Social Change*, REUTERS UK (May 23, 2007), http://uk.reuters.com/article/2007/05/23/uk-india-intolerance-idUKMOL34834320070523.

365 *Lashes for Saudi Woman Who Called Morality Police Liars*, REUTERS US (Aug. 17, 2014), http://www.reuters.com/article/2014/08/17/us-saudi-islam-idUSKBN0GH0DQ20140817.

366 SEN, *supra* note 322, at 231.

> for a rational assessment of such choices is the ability of people to participate in public discussions on the subject. We come back again to the perspective of capabilities: that different sections of the society (and not just the socially privileged) should be able to be active in the decisions regarding what to preserve and what to let go.[367]

Sen thus places importance on choice, the choice to abide by certain traditions, as well as on freedom, that is, maximizing one's capacity to achieve freedom. In the first instance involving the right to choose, one's choice has to be the result of informed decision making or participation in free, public discussion. Sen is clear that political freedom is constitutive of development. A choice cannot be forced or enforced by authoritarian means. For example, a woman who is denied education, is illiterate, poor, uninformed about or deprived of options, and subject to pervasive rule by husband and male relatives, along with morality police, cannot be said to truly prefer this or that traditional practice. Under those circumstances, she cannot be said to have decided to choose anything. Her preference for sons, her decision to not educate her daughter, or to feed her daughter less than her son, or to continue the traditional practice of child bride where her daughter is concerned, should not be insulated from law and development scrutiny.

But let us take an apparently harder case where a choice is not forced by religious elites and is the result of informed decision making. When this choice leads to less, not more freedom, restricts rather than enhances capacity, the question becomes more thorny. One could argue that Sen's work leaves an ambiguous space in which relativism might reign. But as I discussed in the Introduction[368] and will consider more fully in Chapter 6, public deference to private preferences should not be unlimited or unscrutinized when those preferences constrict the capability of a person to perform what Martha Nussbaum calls the "fundamental functions of a human life."[369] Where preferences negatively impact a set of universal norms, that is, a threshold level of basic human capabilities, they do not merit support and should be altered. Again, whether members of a caste are privately satisfied with their lot and with the status quo cannot determine the appropriateness of public policy. Indeed, for reasons further amplified in Chapter 6, "the satisfaction of private preferences, whatever their content and origins, does not respond to a persuasive conception of liberty or autonomy."[370]

---

[367] *Id.* at 241–42.

[368] *See* Introduction, text accompanying notes 255–263.

[369] MARTHA C. NUSSBAUM, WOMEN AND HUMAN DEVELOPMENT: THE CAPABILITIES APPROACH 1 (2000).

[370] Cass R. Sunstein, *Gender, Caste, and Law*, *in* WOMEN, CULTURE AND DEVELOPMENT: A STUDY OF HUMAN CAPABILITIES 332, 350 (Martha Nussbaum & Jonathan Glover eds., 1995).

Sen's view, with its strong cultural core and its emphasis on "mental conditioning and adaptive attitudes,"[371] and Nussbaum's thick capabilities approach, with its insistence on "a universal account to criticize unjust cultural practices,"[372] radically depart from both the first wave and second wave of law and development endeavors. Although Sen's work is groundbreaking, he is not the only development scholar who sees the need to reframe the development debate. Others too view development in holistic terms, including incorporating culture as an important factor in the development process.

As discussed in the Introduction, the noted anthropologist Arjun Appadurai has adopted a similar conception of development—one that conceives of development in terms of one's capacity to aspire, which similarly implicates cultural norms and values. For Appadurai, culture must be understood in terms of the following three key dimensions: "relationality (between norms, values, beliefs, etc.); dissensus within some framework of consensus (especially in regard to the marginal, the poor, gender relations, and power relations more generally); and weak boundaries (perennially visible in processes of migration, trade, and warfare now writ large in globalizing cultural traffic)."[373] Appadurai noted that "the key theorists of the cultural dimensions of globalization . . . foreground mixture, heterogeneity, diversity . . . and plurality as critical features of culture in the era of globalization."[374] Against this backdrop, culture is definitely not habit, tradition, or heritage, all of which suggest entrenchment and fixedness.

Appadurai thus sees culture as dynamic and subject to contestation and change. By acknowledging the existence of cultural obstacles and the need to change cultural norms that impede development, Sen too implicitly subscribes to this view. Others, such as Rao and Walton, have also expounded upon the relational aspects of culture as well as culture's fluidity:

> Culture is concerned with identity, aspiration, symbolic exchange, coordination, and structures and practices that serve relational ends, such as ethnicity, ritual, heritage, norms, meanings and beliefs. It is not a set of primordial phenomena permanently embedded within national or religious or other groups, but rather a set of contested attributes, constantly in flux, both shaping and being shaped by social and economic aspects of human interaction.[375]

---

[371] SEN, *supra* note 322, at 62.

[372] NUSSBAUM, *supra* note 369, at 59.

[373] Arjun Appadurai, *The Capacity to Aspire: Culture and the Terms of Recognition*, *in* CULTURE AND PUBLIC ACTION 59, 62 (Vijayendra Rao & Michael Walton eds., 2004).

[374] *Id.* at 61–62.

[375] Vijayendra Rao & Michael Walton, *Culture and Public Action: Relationality, Equality of Agency, and Development*, *in* CULTURE AND PUBLIC ACTION 3, 4 (Vijayendra Rao & Michael Walton eds., 2004).

This idea of culture as relationality can be explained in this way, which further clarifies why culture is crucially relevant to development. As Rao and Walton observed, "culture not only provides a way to classify *other groups*, but for members of a group to differentiate *themselves* from others."[376] Within this culturally embedded context, groups at the bottom and upper rungs of society might view their relative positions and their mutual relationships as culturally correct and proper. This is yet another reason why personal preferences and personal satisfaction alone cannot determine the correctness of policy. Culture affects how each group views itself, limiting and expanding their respective preferences and social and economic horizons. "The capacity to aspire is a forward-looking cultural capacity that is unequally distributed, with the rich having a greater capacity than the poor."[377] The cultural underpinnings of relationship have development implications. " '[S]mall people' tend to be immersed in a culture that has inculcated in them the values of loyalty, deference, respect and gratitude to the 'big people' who provide for their livelihood."[378] Such patronage relationships may provide a modicum of security but also perpetuate inequalities that laws alone cannot rectify.

In this way, for the social theorist Pierre Bourdieu, "culture, therefore, is a form of capital."[379] Cultural resources, like other resources such as social and symbolic resources, can serve the interests of individuals and groups to maintain their positions in the social order. Resources inherent in social relationships, termed social capital, as well as the capacity to deploy cultural traits play an important role in the reproduction of hierarchical relationships.[380] Bourdieu's notion of cultural capital should be highly relevant to law and development—it is "useful to understand the perpetuation of inequality since it shows that opportunities have a subjective dimension in the sense that they are perceived differently by people occupying different positions in the society.... [P]erceived opportunities are transformed into individual aspirations or expectations that people then internalize in actions and choices. Since these actions and choices themselves tend to reproduce the objective structure of life changes, inequality is reproduced."[381]

As others have noted, "Bourdieu's conception of cultural capital represents an extension of the idea of capital to all forms of culturally derived power."[382] Indeed, "[c]ombining the terminology of Bourdieu and Sen, a group's cultural capital forms part of its

---

376 *Id.* at 15.

377 Yousfi, *supra* note 13, at 30.

378 Platteau, *supra* note 84, at 5.

379 Rao & Walton, *supra* note 375, at 15; Pierre Bourdieu, *The Form of Capital*, *in* HANDBOOK OF THEORY AND RESEARCH FOR THE SOCIOLOGY OF EDUCATION 241–58 (1986).

380 Rao & Walton, *supra* note 375, at 15–17. Cultural capital may be used to justify the rightness and hence perpetuation of caste hierarchy, for example, and is internalized as proper by both the upper and lower castes. *Id.* at 17.

381 Platteau, *supra* note 84, at 3.

382 Rao & Walton, *supra* note 375, at 15.

capability set."[383] Similarly, for Appadurai, culture is tied to one's capacity to aspire. For Sen, it is tied to freedom and capability, which Nussbaum has further developed in her writings. Although the language each scholar uses may be different and although each term may carry different variations and nuances (that are not relevant for the purpose of this book), all are cognizant of the notion that "culture affects power relations within a society and is therefore fundamentally linked with the perpetuation of inequality."[384] Development is "empowerment" and thus must challenge "culturally embedded hierarchies."[385]

A new approach to development that goes beyond the first and second wave must engage the new culturally infused framework initially framed by Sen and expounded upon by others. Cultural norms that marginalize the poor and the powerless, diminish their capacity and freedom, including their capacity to aspire, must be changed. Developing the capacity to aspire requires changing the cultural environment in which aspiration and voice can be expressed. Different ways of enhancing developmental tools may include, as some have suggested, working to connect the poor to decision makers and "understanding people's 'true preferences' "[386] as Timur Kuran urged, or as Sen advocated, providing people with "elementary capabilities" so they can take part in "social decisions."[387]

Although it does not epitomize the propositions advocated in this book, the Kingdom of Bhutan nonetheless provides an interesting example of development efforts that depart from the more conventional models espoused by both the first and second waves of law and development. Bhutan's model incorporates factors that go beyond the preoccupation of the first wave (transforming legal culture) or that of the second wave (institutional and legal reform). Indeed, at first glance, the Kingdom of Bhutan appears to have created an approach to development that reflects, albeit only partially, Sen's philosophy.[388] The monarchy, held by the Wangchuck dynasty since its establishment in 1907, has been the ultimate source of authority in Bhutan.[389] In the 1950s, King Jigme Dorji Wangchuck began the reform process to bring Bhutan into modern times.[390] His reign included both political reform, establishing separate branches of government, and social reform, such as freeing serfs.[391]

---

[383] *Id.* at 28.

[384] *Id.* at 30.

[385] *Id.* at 25.

[386] Yousfi, *supra* note 13, at 30.

[387] *Id.*

[388] Founded on Buddhist principles, the majority of Bhutan's state resources were allocated to support religious institutions. Karma Ura, *Development and Decentralisation in Medieval and Modern Bhutan*, *in* BHUTAN: ASPECTS OF CULTURE AND DEVELOPMENT 25, 26–27 (Michael Aris & Michael Hutt eds., 1994).

[389] Stefan Priesner, *Gross National Happiness: Bhutan's Vision of Development and Its Challenges* 34 (Center for Bhutan Studies: Gross National Happiness, Discussion Paper, 2004), *available at* http://www.bhutan2008.bt/ndlb/typescripts/10/GNH_Ch3_Priesner.pdf.

[390] Ura, *supra* note 388, at 31.

[391] *Id.*

Gross National Happiness (GNH) became the hallmark of the Kingdom's indigenous development process under the fourth king, King Jigme Singye Wangchuck, who ascended to the throne in 1972.[392] This concept remains a stated goal of the Kingdom's development process and a principle state policy per the inclusion of GNH in the Bhutanese constitution.[393] The Bhutanese government promotes GNH as an extension of traditional Bhutanese life and socioeconomic policy.[394] GNH does not refer to economic prosperity alone; instead, it is an amalgam of social and cultural factors drawn from Bhutan's Buddhist and feudal roots.[395] Buddhist philosophy centers on purification, not material consumption, and promotes happiness through the balancing of spiritual and material concerns.[396] Four pillars guide GNH: sustainable and equitable socioeconomic development, conservation of environment, preservation and promotion of culture, and the promotion of good governance.[397] The proposed measurements of this new paradigm include the value of social services, free time and leisure, and the "redistribution of happiness" through the redistribution of income.[398] Based on these characteristics, GNH would seem to illustrate, at least partly, one aspect of the holistic approach to development advocated by Sen.

GNH, however, diverges sharply from Sen's model in its treatment of culture. Whereas Sen advocates an open approach to culture based on choice, GNH is a policy of selective government inclusion. GNH rests on the assumption that the government can identify the worthy elements of modernization and implement them to the exclusion of other elements, including what the government may consider "negative" external cultural influences.[399] For example, the government legalized satellite television in 1999, but later banned certain channels on the grounds that they made the youth too violent in violation of Buddhist philosophy.[400] More recently, the National Council proposed to make religious proselytizing a criminal offense, pointing to reported violence in villages between Christians and Buddhists.[401] This selective policy parallels efforts by the government to

---

392 Priesner, *supra* note 389, at 27.

393 CONST. OF THE KINGDOM OF BHUTAN art. 9, § 2; *see* Jigmi Y. Thinley, *What Is Gross National Happiness?* 3 (Center for Bhutan Studies: Gross National Happiness, Discussion Paper, 2004), *available at* http://www.bhutanstudies.org.bt/pubFiles/8-Rethinking.pdf.

394 CONST. OF THE KINGDOM OF BHUTAN, *supra* note 393; *see* Thinley, *supra* note 393, at 3.

395 Priesner, *supra* note 389, at 27–29.

396 *Id.*

397 Thinley, *supra* note 393, at 6.

398 *Id.* at 7; *see also* Katherine Marshall, *Measuring Happiness in Bhutan*, WASH. POST: ON FAITH BLOG (Aug. 22, 2008), http://newsweek.washingtonpost.com/onfaith/georgetown/2008/08/measuring_happiness.html.

399 Michael Aris, *Introduction*, *in* BHUTAN: ASPECTS OF CULTURE AND DEVELOPMENT 7, 9 (Michael Aris & Michael Hutt eds., 1994).

400 Emily Wax, *A Society on the Threshold of Change*, WASH. POST (Apr. 4, 2008), http://www.washingtonpost.com/wp-dyn/content/article/2008/04/03/AR2008040303869.html.

401 *Buddhist Bhutan Proposes "Anti-Conversion" Law*, RELIGION NEWS BLOG (July 22, 2010), http//www.religionnewsblog.com/24816/buddhist-bhutan-proposes-'anti-conversion'-law.

construct a national identity based on ideas and practices deemed by the government to be uniquely Bhutanese. But as some have noted, observation of a state- prescribed culture, including regulation of architecture and dress, is arguably at odds with the Buddhist notion of the individual quest for enlightenment.[402] Even government officials recognize the limitation on individual choice of identity yet seem to argue that a less rigorous government control of national culture and identity would lead to surreptitious and unwilling change in Bhutanese culture via the forces of modernization and outside cultures.[403]

Nonetheless improvements have been made in important areas such as adult literacy and life span[404]—what Sen deems "functionings." Buddhist values led Bhutan to invest in social facilities early on rather than focusing on industrialization.[405] However, the focus on social programs has masked other issues such as the level of poverty[406] and the growing unemployment among educated youth.[407] Poverty reduction is a primary goal of the current Bhutanese Five Year development plan.[408] The government recently announced an initiative to provide fiscal incentives for small-scale and cottage industry ventures located outside major towns.[409] The terms of the incentive program underscore the government's determination to maintain control of private sector growth under the banner of "balanced economic development."[410] It is potentially telling that the Bhutan Chamber of Commerce, founded by the monarchy, has described one of its goals as becoming "a better partner for the royal government for shaping enabling environment for the development of the Bhutanese private sector."[411] It is not yet clear, though, how GNH will translate into such efforts,[412] as the structural requirements of a functioning and efficient private sector may well clash with the tenets of GNH. Bhutanese officials are worried about this potential collision, as revealed by comments such as "the difficulty, if not the impossibility, of market-led happiness" and the threat of market values to "the factors that lead to happiness."[413] For example, the government has already placed limits on land acquisition in the 1979 Land Law;[414] this law set a minimum and maximum of agricultural acreage

---

402 Aris, *supra* note 399, at 9, 17–18; Thinley, *supra* note 393, at 9.

403 Thinley, *supra* note 393, at 6.

404 Priesner, *supra* note 389, at 36–40.

405 *Id.*

406 Bob Frame, *Bhutan: A Review of Its Approach to Sustainable Development*, 15 DEV. PRAC. 216, 218 (2005).

407 *Id.*

408 UN Development Programme (UNDP), Poverty Eradication and Internationally Agreed Development Goals, http://www.undp.org.bt/poverty.htm (last visited Jan. 25, 2015).

409 *Incentives to Bolster the Private Sector*, BHUTAN TIMES (Apr. 3, 2010), http://www.bhutantoday.bt/?p=3725.

410 *Id.*

411 BHUTANESE CHAMBER OF COMMERCE AND INDUSTRY, ABOUT US, http://www.bcci.org.bt/?page_id=2 (last visited Jan. 28, 2015).

412 Aris, *supra* note 399, at 9, 17–19 ("The greatest challenge will come, surely, from the rapid expansion of a monetary economy rather than from external influences affecting established norms of cultural expression.").

413 Thinley, *supra* note 393, at 5; *see also* Danino, *supra* note 126, at 12–13 (discussing concerns that global markets will have a detrimental impact on human development).

414 Ura, *supra* note 388, at 37.

that could be owned by a household with a large exception for orchard plantations that grow cash crops for export.[415]

Undoubtedly, these new approaches to development (as illustrated by Bhutan's novel, albeit imperfect experience) have pushed against law and development's economic core as well as against the traditional templates of law and development work, whether first or second wave. Sen's work in particular has paved the way toward the "conceptual integration of development and human rights"[416] and the concomitant growth of institutions and NGOs dedicated to the convergence of these two disciplines.[417] The conventional contours of development have been pushed *even at* traditional development agencies. As noted, the UN Global Compact was initiated by Secretary-General Kofi Annan to engage world business leaders in the challenges of development, particularly with regard to its environmental, social, and human rights aspects. The Working Group on the Right to Development also adopts a broad-based understanding of development, calling on the "international financial institutions [to] give the highest priority to an action-oriented approach to the right to development in its multidimensional aspects."[418] As noted, even the World Bank, which has traditionally eschewed noneconomic considerations,[419] now links development to good governance—a term meant to include accountable public institutions, transparent economic and social policies, a predictable and stable legal framework, and civil society participation, all of which constitute an implicit acknowledgment that economic factors are embedded in a wider framework. In 1998, the Bank published *Development and Human Rights*, which emphasized the important contributions of the organization in securing and promoting economic, social, and cultural rights. Thereafter, the Bank redefined its development paradigm with the launching of the Comprehensive Development Framework (CDF), which stresses a multifaceted, holistic approach to development. With surprising flair and boldness, the CDF declares: "Without the *protection of human and property rights*, and a comprehensive framework of laws, no equitable development is possible."[420] World Bank reports unabashedly assert the link between economic development and legal development: "The rule of law is essential to equitable economic development and sustainable poverty reduction.... Vulnerable individuals, including women and children, are unprotected from violence and other forms of abuse that exacerbate inequalities."[421]

Indeed, Sen declared that the CDF complements his own development-as-freedom approach. As Sen remarked, "[t]he CDF approach is institutionally founded, and in

---

[415] *Id.*

[416] Brodnig, *supra* note 343, at 1.

[417] *See* UN Global Compact, https://www.unglobalcompact.org/aboutthegc/ (last visited Jan. 25, 2015).

[418] Comm'n on Human Rights, Rep. of the Intergovernmental Group of Experts on the Right to Dev. on its 2nd Sess., Sept. 29–Oct. 10, 1997 UN Doc. E/CN.4/1998/29 (1998).

[419] *See* Introduction, text accompanying notes 38–39.

[420] Brodnig, *supra* note 343, at 7.

[421] Santos, *supra* note 275, at 276.

many ways, this is a natural extension of the kind of institution-based approach that the World Bank has reason to pursue, except that . . . the coverage is much wider and the domain of institutional interest remarkably broader than in the past."[422] The World Bank's CDF looks at different institutions and work to see how they are linked and integrated with one another, whereas Sen's integrated freedom view "looks at different aspects of human freedom and how they link with each other."[423] Thus both adopt a comprehensive approach to development, but the CDF encourages linkages to be made among institutional spheres while Sen's integrated freedom approach makes linkages between different types of freedoms. Both approaches challenge the dominant assumptions of law and development and depart from the models of the first and second wave.

In short, law and development is surely expanding beyond its purely institutional dimensions and economic growth objective. It is making linkages with human rights. Thus, economic growth and market development, contracts, and property rights now share the same framework as other development objectives. It is being pushed in different directions to broaden its traditional pursuits by scholars and practitioners alike who repudiate its standard menu. To be sure, there is scholarly acknowledgment that culture is relevant and even important in law and development.[424] David Landes, for example, asserted that "[if] we learn anything from the history of economic development, it is that culture makes almost all the difference,"[425] though he hastens to add that "culture does not stand alone . . . [and thus] monocausal explanations will not work."[426] Cultural attributes that contribute positively to development are "thrift, investment, hard work, education, organization, and discipline."[427] Likewise, political development is less likely to thrive in societies marked by hierarchy and obedience to authority.[428] These writings expound on the essential principle that indeed, "culture matters."[429] Even the most perfect model of development, whatever that may be, will encounter impediments or constraints—"the restraints of poverty, the lack of education, and gender, for example, are important impediments to equitable participation in the development process."[430] Again, a cultural lens is necessary to make sense of such constraints.

---

422 Sen, *supra* note 117, at 22.

423 *Id.* at 24.

424 *See,* e.g., Belton, *supra* note 194, at 15; STROMSETH ET AL., *supra* note 213, at 70.

425 David Landes, *Culture Makes Almost All the Difference, in* CULTURE MATTERS: HOW VALUES SHAPE HUMAN PROGRESS 2, 2 (Lawrence E. Harrison & Samuel P. Harrington eds., 2000).

426 DAVID LANDES, THE WEALTH AND POVERTY OF NATIONS: WHY SOME ARE SO RICH AND SOME SO POOR 517 (1998).

427 Huntington, *supra* note 298, at xiii.

428 Anita Abraham & Jean-Philippe Platteau, *Participatory Development: Where Culture Creeps In, in* CULTURE AND PUBLIC ACTION 210 (Vijayendra Rao & Michael Walton eds., 2004); Fernando Calderon & Alicia Szmukler, *Political Culture and Development, in* CULTURE AND PUBLIC ACTION 281 (Vijayendra Rao & Michael Walton eds., 2004).

429 CULTURE MATTERS: HOW HUMAN VALUES SHAPE HUMAN PROGRESS (Lawrence E. Harrison & Samuel P. Harrington eds., 2000).

430 SARKAR, *supra* note 62, at 9.

Different law and development scholars have different views about how culture matters. How it matters and how it should be understood and incorporated in law and development of course is a debatable issue. For example, Hernando De Soto, the noted Peruvian economist, deviated from the rule of law emphasis on formal laws and formal economies and examined instead informal laws and the cultural norms of informal economies. Noting that the majority of the poor in developing countries live in a parallel, "extralegal" universe defined by informality,[431] De Soto urged governments to address the problems of the informal sector—in brief, discover their informal norms and arrangements and "find ways to integrate them into the formal property system."[432] Suffice it to say that De Soto recommended not merely the drafting of new laws—often imposed de novo from the top down by governments with the help of foreign experts[433]—but also the formalization of customary patterns of land use. In other words, he urged law and development experts and government officials to engage with local culture: "listen to the barking dogs" in their own communities and find out what their law should say. Only then will people stop living outside it.[434] As De Soto described it:

> The truth is that lawyers in these countries are generally too busy studying Western law and adapting it. They have been taught that local practices are not genuine law but a romantic area of study best left to folklorists. But if lawyers want to play a role in creating good laws, they must step out of their law libraries into the extralegal sector, which is the only source of the information they need to build a truly legitimate formal legal system. By examining this "people's law" and understanding its logic, reformers can get a sense of what they need to do to create a self-enforcing legal system.[435]

---

431 Hernando De Soto defines an extralegal system as one where many of the world's poor live and work—"outside the official law, using their own informally binding arrangements to protect and mobilize their assets." HERNANDO DE SOTO, THE MYSTERY OF CAPITAL: WHY CAPITALISM TRIUMPHS IN THE WEST AND FAILS EVERYWHERE ELSE 21 (2000).

432 *Id.* at 178.

433 In fact, as noted by Stephen Holmes, often, foreign development experts believe they've achieved great success if "their advice is swallowed whole and the laws they draft are actually passed by parliament." Holmes, *supra* note 113, at 73. Yet, this is often the case if the country at issue is one where formal laws are virtually unenforced.

434 DE SOTO, *supra* note 431, at 178. This approach echoes the sentiment expressed by David Tolbert, who claims "it is important that the society feel that the process is 'theirs' and not the property of outsiders. If the process is seen as primarily imposed or created by foreign donors and experts, the programs are unlikely to be successful." David Tolbert, *United Nations Reform and Supporting the Rule of Law in Post-Conflict Societies*, 19 HARV. HUM. RTS. J. 29, 52–53 (2008).

435 DE SOTO, *supra* note 431, at 186–87.

Whether or not one agrees with De Soto's recommendation to formalize informal arrangements to spur capital formation,[436] what is important is the fact that he goes beyond the emphasis on formal laws and rules that have characterized both the first and second waves of law and development. However, De Soto's focus is almost exclusively on the informal sector, and he does not address the relationship between culture and law and development. In fact, De Soto considers formalization of property rights (more than any other factor) as the key to unlocking the mystery of capital. Culture is secondary to "good political institutions and property law. . . ."[437] For De Soto, instituting a regime of property law is a key component to development. But the institution of this regime should be made, according to him, with particular reference to and perhaps in conformity with the preexisting cultural norms of the informal sector.[438] Thus, if informal, cultural norms prohibit women from owning property, titling property in the formal sector would presumably exclude women from ownership. De Soto does not address this issue. His engagement with culture is limited to the observation that in formalizing property rights, the cultural norms of the informal sector, known to barking dogs but not to lawyers and development practitioners, should be heeded.

Others in law and development (as opposed to economists, philosophers, or anthropologists such as Sen, Nussbaum, and Appadurai) have also rejected the standard law and development menu but have done so obliquely—by referencing the need to include non-law attributes but not necessarily calling for the construction of a culturally informed law and development discipline. Note how Carothers, for example, questioned the centrality of formal rules and institutions in law and development (but did not further tease out the full implications of his own observations):

> Clearly law is not just the sum of courts, legislatures, police, prosecutors, and other formal institutions with some direct connection to law. Law is also a normative system that resides in the minds of the citizens of a society. As rule-of-law providers seek to affect the rule of law in a country, it is not clear if they should focus on institution building or instead try to intervene in ways that would affect how citizens understand, use, and value law.[439]

Elsewhere, Carothers has struck a pessimistic note about the direction of law and development and its continued adherence to the standard menu, arguing without much

---

[436] For a critique of De Soto's ideas, *see,* e.g., David Kennedy, *Some Caution about Property Rights as a Recipe for Economic Development*, 1 Acct. Econ. & L. 1 (2011); Jonathan Manders, *Sequencing Property Rights in the Context of Development: A Critique of the Writings of Hernando De Soto*, 37 Cornell Int'l L. J. 177 (2004); Lan Cao, *Informal Institutions and Property Rights*, 1 Brigham-Kanner Prop. Rts. Conf. J. 263, 264 (2012).

[437] De Soto, *supra* note 431, at 225.

[438] De Soto does not evaluate preexisting cultural norms nor does he address whether they should be changed.

[439] Carothers, *supra* note 112, at 20.

normative or critical analysis, for the insertion of values into the development debate: "The numerous rule-of-law programs carried out in Cambodia after the 1993 elections failed to create values or structures strong enough to prevent last year's coup. Aid providers have helped rewrite laws around the globe, but they have discovered that the mere enactment of laws accomplishes little without considerable investment in changing the conditions for implementation and enforcement. . . ."[440]

Carothers' bleak observations seem quite similar to those by first wave reformers who extolled the need to change legal culture. First wave reformers were critical of the ways Third World lawyers defended law as a set of abstract and rigid internal rules unconnected to the social context of Third World countries and favored the adoption of a more modern law. The focus was on the need to instill favorable cultural attitudes toward law so that legal development would be supported. Note, however, that first wave efforts to instill a new, antiformalist, and pragmatic rule of law culture in poor countries[441] is still essentially a call to reform *law*, not a call to create a culturally informed law and development agenda.

By contrast, Carothers' references to the need to incorporate values suggest a willingness to embrace culture more vigorously. Nonetheless, current scholarship rarely delves into the causes for cultural exclusion or crafts responses that are defensible within the international law tradition. It is the aim of this book to build on the works of scholars who recognize the need to revise the standard rule of law menu and to make culture a central component of the law and development inquiry. My proposal, however, goes beyond a cultural commitment to *legal* institutions[442] or creating a *rule of law* culture or a new *legal* culture. Nor is it an argument designed to promote a view of law *as* culture, law mirroring culture or a cultural analysis of law.[443]

My law and development concerns are broader than *law* and are more in line with Sen's holistic, integrated, and comprehensive framework for *development* or the World Bank's CDF outlook. Although development has been appropriately expanded, this expansion has not included a robust cultural component. Democracy, human rights, and poverty alleviation have been added to development objectives. But "development efforts should no longer focus solely on economic growth and poverty alleviation"[444] because those efforts should be supported by a concomitant culture project.

---

440 Thomas Carothers, *The Rule-of-Law Revival*, *in* PROMOTING THE RULE OF LAW ABROAD: IN SEARCH OF KNOWLEDGE 3, 11–12 (Thomas Carothers ed., 2006).

441 *See supra* note 58; *see also* Ginsburg, *supra* note 119, at 833.

442 Brooks & Slaughter, *supra* note 318, at 126.

443 OSCAR G. CHASE, LAW, CULTURE, AND RITUAL (2005); PAUL W. KAHN, THE CULTURAL STUDY OF LAW: RECONSTRUCTING LEGAL SCHOLARSHIP (1999); ROSEN, *supra* note 300; Paul Schiff Berman, *The Cultural Life of Capital Punishment: Surveying the Benefits of a Cultural Analysis of Law*, 102 COLUM. L. REV. 1129, 1134 (2002) (book review) (arguing for a cultural analysis of law); *see also* BRIAN Z. TAMANAHA, A GENERAL JURISPRUDENCE OF LAW AND SOCIETY (2001).

444 Yousfi, *supra* note 13, at 29.

To recapitulate the fundamental points made in the Introduction and in this chapter, culture is centrally featured in this book on law and development precisely because culture affects development. Again, as used in this book and as used by modern-day anthropologists and sociologists, culture is not monolithic, hegemonic, or insular and self-contained. As discussed further in Chapter 6, "[g]lobalization is calling into question conventional ways of viewing culture.... In fact, the fluidities of global cultural flows undermine the concept of culture as a distinct, discrete and bounded entity—whether conceived of as local, regional, national or global. Instead, 'culture' is more accurately conceived as complex and multidirectional cultural interactions and re-combinations, weaving the local and global together in myriad patterns and configurations."[445] This new understanding of culture and how it may change and be changed in different social, political, economic, and legal contexts is significant for the proposal I am espousing. If culture affects development because "culture is perceived as influencing individual aspirations, as well as the coordination of collective action, the challenge is to redress power inequalities and dominant discriminatory norms in favour of the marginalized."[446] Cultural norms that perpetuate poverty and power inequalities should be studied, evaluated, and, if needed, changed. Indeed, development should take the affirmative step of creating the needed cultural change—"the linkage between culture and development no longer refers to chance historical processes that emerge over time, but rather to the result of conscious efforts that seek specific social transformations."[447] The key here is "conscious"—conscious and deliberate efforts to effectuate cultural change.[448]

Moreover, by seeing culture not as a set of relatively fixed attitudes and beliefs but rather as something "produced essentially by the actors, development occurs as a result of the creation of an enabling environment through which social structure is transformed."[449] Again, my proposal adopts an understanding of culture that emphasizes culture's hybridity, heterogeneity, and capacity for change. In conformity with the emphasis on individual freedom, capacity, aspiration, and empowerment, as supported by Sen, Nussbaum, and Appadurai, among others, this cultural approach to development emphasizes change *plus* individual capacity for effectuating this change.

---

445 *Id.* at 27.

446 *Id.* at 29.

447 *Id.*

448 Others have focused on changing norms that affect market development specifically rather than development generally. Here too it has been noted thus: "Multiple equilibria need not be equivalent in terms of economic efficiency. Some equilibria may dominate others. The question is: how can we move an economy from an inferior equilibrium to a superior one? Since this requires changing social norms, the answer to this question is unclear." Marcel Fafchamps, *Markets and the Diffusion of Institutional Innovations, in* CULTURE, INSTITUTIONS, AND DEVELOPMENT: NEW INSIGHTS INTO AN OLD DEBATE 143, 147 (Jean-Philippe Platteau & Robert Peccoud eds., 2011).

449 Yousfi, *supra* note 13, at 55.

Consequently, my proposal extends beyond law per se and includes cultural changes that go beyond the first wave's interest in changing legal culture. This model includes not just ways of thinking about law or interpreting law but rather practices that have a negative impact on the wider development initiative of empowering individual freedom and aspiration. For example, a cultural exclusion of girls from school does not have any direct connection to traditional or modern ways of thinking about law, whatever those may be (formalist or instrumentalist, for example). Nonetheless, such a cultural exclusion would be relevant to the law and development project as proposed in this book.[450] The question to be grappled with throughout the book is this: If cultural factors are relevant to the law and development project, can and should cultural norms be changed and cultural obstacles removed?[451]

The answer is yes. But the cultural framework I propose in this book is not one that replicates the traditional/modern dichotomy that is characteristic of modernization theory.[452] The crux of a cultural approach is not necessarily to eradicate traditional values and supplant them with modern values, however defined. The crux is to address cultural norms that violate human rights, constrain individual freedom, and suppress individual voice. Cultural norms that hamper economic development or marginalize the poor and perpetuate poverty are also to be considered and evaluated. "[D]evelopment projects should aim to transform social relations in which lack of trust and cooperation, as well as faltering institutions, bar individuals from leading the lives they deem worthwhile. This, at a minimum, requires full adherence to human rights and democratic procedures."[453]

Unlike modernization theory, which was entrenched in the binary opposition posed by tradition versus modernity, this book is more concerned "with the rehabilitation of the role of individuals in shaping their destiny. This approach to culture consciously downplays the understanding of culture as 'essence' in order to focus explicitly on individuals embodying a unique combination of personal, cultural and social experiences."[454] Upholding individual agency may be associated with the modern project but the aim of my proposal is not to bring about modernism per se. Rather, my aim is to make culture an ally of an emergent model of development that starts with rule of law, human rights, and poverty alleviation but also includes at its core the notion of development as individual freedom and choice. Whether development is viewed in terms of freedom or human capacity or poverty alleviation or human rights, "[i]ndividuals should be ultimately autonomous and free to set up structures that govern their actions."[455] Individuals

---

[450] *See supra* notes 446–449.

[451] Amy Chua is uncomfortable with this inquiry and with the very notion of culture change—first, whether it is possible, and second, whether it is normatively desirable. AMY CHUA, WORLD ON FIRE: HOW EXPORTING FREE MARKET DEMOCRACY BREEDS ETHNIC HATRED AND GLOBAL INSTABILITY 266 (2003).

[452] Huntington, *supra* note 12, at 285.

[453] Yousfi, *supra* note 13, at 30.

[454] *Id.*

[455] *Id.*

should be empowered to free themselves from traditional hierarchies that are culturally maintained and perpetuated. As Sen aptly observed, "[t]he pointer to any real conflict between the preservation of tradition and the advantages of modernity calls for participatory resolution, not for a unilateral rejection of modernity in favour of tradition by political rulers, or religious authorities, or anthropological admirers of the legacy of the past."[456] But again, where "participatory resolution" results in the diminishment of individual capacity and the diminishment of freedom, such a result should not be validated by law and development.

That law and development has failed in many ways is not disputed even by those who support the project. It is not enough to minimize one's disillusionment about law and development by insisting that success is discernible because laws have in fact been enacted and legal development is in fact taking place.[457] This insistence rests on the tacit premise that law and development should shrink its ambition and scope and that it would do well to focus on that which is do-able—fostering legal development and being satisfied with that (more limited) objective. Such assertion is premised on the notion that legal development is not and should not be understood to be the same as law and development. The fact that legal development has taken place (in a formalistic way) and has resulted in (not surprisingly) the proliferation of laws is not a cause to celebrate.[458]

In sum, there is a glaring gap in law and development studies—a blind spot to culture, norms, and customs and how they influence a country's laws and its development. The gap may be derived from a general reluctance to touch culture because of a history of cultural imperialism and current sensitivities associated with it; or from the sense that culture is hard to quantify, cannot be legislated into being, and takes a long time to change; or from the tradition in economics that economic laws transcend cultural particularities; or from the tradition in public and private international law to sidestep culture. These questions are addressed throughout the book. In the next chapter, I examine the extent to which the culture gap in law and development is due to its shared history with international law—public and private—and the latter's preoccupations with first-order principles: state and sovereignty in the case of public international law, and market, in the case of private international law.

---

456 SEN, *supra* note 322, at 32.

457 Tamanaha, *supra* note 111, at 216.

458 *Id.* ("Underneath the gloomy pessimism that pervades law and development, legal development is taking place. A central theme of this Article is that it is crucial to mark the distinction between 'law and development' activities—the modernization project—and 'legal development'—the ongoing construction of legal institutions that occurs in all societies.").

2

Culture and International Law

THE PURPOSE OF Chapter 2 is to demonstrate why and how international law as a discipline has been neglectful of culture. The acultural tradition of international law is deeply embedded in the discipline itself, and this acultural tradition has also been passed down to law and development. This is because law and development as a discipline is closely related to, if not an intellectual child of, international law. To understand the exclusion of culture from law and development, one needs to understand the exclusion of culture from international law.

There are two gravitational centers of power in the international order today, the state and the market, both of which have demonstrated a commitment to sidestep culture. Both have spawned a complex configuration of ancillary and dualistic rivalries: nationalism versus internationalism, political versus economic, sovereignty versus interdependence.[1] The state and the market have been imbued with different conceptual attributes, and nationalism and internationalism have struck different postures toward each. For some, primarily nationalists, the state is thought to be the sole or primary institutional entity that is capable of defending the political ideals of nationalism and sovereignty and national cultures.[2] For others, primarily internationalists, the state's continued insistence on archaic categories, such as nationalism and territorial frontiers, merely stands in the

---

[1] *See generally* Tom Nairn, *Internationalism and the Second Coming*, DAEDALUS, Summer 1993, at 155, 159 ("Since the fall of Napoleon's empire, these two world views have existed in a permanent, uneasy tension with one another, the Siamese twin brothers of a single world-historical process.").

[2] *See* Chapter 1, text accompanying notes 295–311 for a discussion of the many varied understandings of culture. The term "culture" carries many meanings and is subject to many definitions. Two influential anthropologists have documented more than 164 formal definitions of culture. *See* ALFRED LOUIS KROEBER & CLYDE KLUCKHOLN, CULTURE: A CRITICAL REVIEW OF CONCEPTS AND DEFINITIONS 56 (1952). For example, they define culture

way of international borders, international markets, and a general cosmopolitan spirit that transcends the particularism of national cultures. These recurrent disciplinary rivalries between the state and the market—the "politics of identity" versus the "economics of profit"[3]—are all the more pronounced because of the increasing globalization of production and the increasing mobility of goods, services, and capital across and without regard for national borders.

In this chapter, I set forth the nationalist and internationalist positions with respect to the state and the market, using polarities between nationalism and internationalism to (1) highlight the intellectual traditions, characteristic sensibilities, and biases in these two intellectual disciplines as they stand in relation to the cultural; (2) and demonstrate how international relations and international law (public and private and international human rights) have exhibited this acultural internationalist tradition as contrasted against the more culturally steeped nationalist orientation. A thorough study of nationalism and internationalism, and of each discipline's history and development, is beyond the scope of this chapter. Instead, my aim is merely to highlight the competing sets of ideas that give each discipline its respective zeitgeist or characteristics and show how each discipline navigates the cultural terrain. However, as Chapter 4 will reveal, although this acultural tradition is deep, there has been considerable pressure from within the field to expand its traditional lens to accommodate change. This development, I argue, provides the opening needed to overcome traditional reluctance to address culture in international law, which in turn should encourage similar openings and development in law and development.

In this chapter, my focus is on how international law, public and private, has coalesced around different animating principles and in the process ignored culture. Nationalism and internationalism, each with its own distinctive posture toward culture, have long vied for intellectual dominance.[4] Generally speaking, nationalism and internationalism can be understood "as ideologies, as sets of mental attitudes. Understood thus, nationalism often connotes particularism and parochialism, while internationalism connotes universalism and cosmopolitan sophistication."[5] From that premise, the nationalist posture

---

as "the total life way of a people"; "the social legacy the individual acquires from his group"; "the fund of accumulated knowledge and customs"; "the individual's or group's acquired response systems." *Id.* at 91–92.

[3] Benjamin R. Barber, Jihad vs. McWorld 8 (1996).

[4] Thomas M. Franck, *Clan and Superclan: Loyalty, Identity and Community in Law and Practice*, 90 Am. J. Int'l L. 359, 359 (1996) ("In historical terms, both nationalism and transnational regimes have long bid (sometimes competitively) for the adherence of persons."); S. R. Insanally, *Nationalism: No Longer a Domestic Dispute*, 26 N.Y.U. J. Int'l L. & Pol. 439, 440 (1994) ("There is nothing new about the tension . . . between internationalism, which the United Nations above all personifies, and nationalism."); Nathaniel Berman, Passion and Ambivalence: Colonialism, Nationalism, and International Law 244 (2011) (describing the "international legal preoccupation with nationalism"); Wolfgang Friedmann, The Changing Structure of International Law 297 (1964) (identifying in this landmark book two categorical imperatives termed modern state-nationalism and modern internationalism).

[5] Anne-Marie Slaughter Burley, *Nationalism Versus Internationalism: Another Look*, 26 N.Y.U. J. Int'l L. & Pol. 585, 585 (1993).

toward culture is quite obviously to protect the particularities of national cultures while the internationalist posture is to be skeptical about cultural glorification on nationalist grounds. Nationalism is closely related to cultural issues identified with the nation and represents "the vitality and originality of a deep-rooted and well[-]defined cultural and historical tradition, the unique contribution of one people to a global melange."[6] "Asserting a shared culture has been and still is a basic strategy of nation building."[7] Internationalism, by contrast, transcends national cultures and to the extent it has a culture at all, its cultural core is one of universalism. It doesn't favor any one particular national culture and aims to reflect heterogeneous elements that are deemed to be basic and universal. Internationalism, critics charge, is "synonymous with the bland homogenization of universal culture, of lowest-common-denominator ideas and a sterile harmony."[8]

International law's relationship to nationalism has been fraught with ambivalence, characterized by complicity with and accommodation of nationalist desires on the one hand and rivalry and containment on the other hand. Before examining this complex relationship between internationalism and nationalism and their respective stance on culture, it is important to note first that constructions of nationalism have been highly contingent and contested. Nationalism is subject to multiple meanings and interpretations.[9] Many scholars understand "nation" to be something different from "state." Between nation versus state, "[t]he term *nation* or *tribe* suggests an affinity group that has placed certain values high on its agenda: shared genealogical origins, language and historic myths, as well as cultural and, perhaps, religious compatibility."[10] States refer to a more politically based form of association than one based on commonalities from past history. In this sense, many states are not nation-states in the sense that they are multinational, for example, India, Canada, Nigeria, Switzerland.[11]

---

[6] *Id.*

[7] Sally Engle Merry, *Human Rights Law and the Demonization of Culture (And Anthropology Along the Way)*, POL. & LEGAL ANTHROPOLOGY REV., May 2003, at 55, 66.

[8] Burley, *supra* note 5.

[9] *See* John A. Hall, *Nationalisms: Classified and Explained*, DAEDALUS, Summer 1993, at 1 ("[N]o single, universal theory of nationalism is possible."); Lea Brilmayer, *The Moral Significance of Nationalism*, 71 NOTRE DAME L. REV. 7, 7 (1995) (Nationalism "means such different things to different people. There are many areas of disagreement.").

For historical accounts of nationalism, *see generally* BENEDICT ANDERSON, IMAGINED COMMUNITIES: REFLECTIONS ON THE ORIGIN AND SPREAD OF NATIONALISM (1991); ERIC HOBSBAWM, NATIONS AND NATIONALISM SINCE 1780: PROGRAMME, MYTH, REALITY (1990).

[10] Franck, *supra* note 4, at 362.

[11] When the "nations" within the state wish to free themselves from the state, for example, "nation" is not interchangeable with "state" but rather, conflicts with "state." Before the World War I peace and minorities treaties, *see infra* notes 34–43 and accompanying text, international law, with its statist foundation, was reluctant to recognize "nations." *See, e.g.*, *Nationality in International Law*, 28 TRANSACTIONS OF THE GROTIUS SOC'Y 151, 151–52 (1943) ("The word 'Nationality' does not mean what it says, nor does it say what it means. Etymologically it would mean the condition of belonging to a nation, of being a national. In International Law

For some, nationalism lies in the realm of inventions: "[N]ationalism is not the awakening of nations to self-consciousness; it invents nations where they do not exist."[12] Under that view, nations themselves are not natural entities endowed with a predestined physical existence.[13] Hans Kohn, the noted historian, defined nationalism as a "state of mind, permeating the large majority of a people and claiming to permeate all its members; it recognizes the nation-state as the ideal form of political organization and the nationality as the source of all creative cultural energy and of economic well-being."[14] Carlton Hayes saw nationalism too as an artificial construct whose "cultural bases" are "a common language" and "a community of historical traditions."[15] Nationhood may be understood by reference to subjective and objective factors. Objective factors include "religion, race, language, a common history, and a national territory, while subjective factors refer to manifestations of the political will of the people."[16] At the same time, the notion of the "nation" or the principle of nationalities remains obscure because, as some have noted, "'primitive' sources of cultural vitality intrinsically resist representation."[17] Indeed, the warning about the slippery nature of nationalism goes something like this: "One must not delude oneself with the hope that one will be able to cast a fully clarifying light on this crater filled with flames and smoke."[18]

There has been much intellectual debate over the origins of nationalism and the many historical meanings the term has been associated with.[19] Some scholars saw nationalism as dating back as early as the Reformation and the breakup of the Holy Roman Empire. "The reformation quite naturally led the peoples to rally around a *new idea* of solidarity. It was *the nation* that reaped the moral and emotional forces liberated by the dismemberment of universal values; it was the nation that enthroned itself as the inheritor of the overthrown empires."[20] In the early nineteenth century, a number of German writers also

---

'nations' are an unknown quantity. . . . The word 'national,' if used in International Law, has a technical meaning . . . [and] means a member or a subject of such a State.").

[12] Hall, *supra* note 9, at 4 (quoting Ernest Geller, Thought and Change 169 (1964)).

[13] *See* generally Ernest Gellner, Nations and Nationalism (1983). For Gellner, it is inevitably difficult to define a "nation," because the sociological attributes that make up the essence of "nation," common language, religion, ethnicity, are themselves unfixed; *see id.* at 47 ("Nations are not inscribed into the nature of things, they do not constitute a political version of the doctrine of natural kinds. Nor were national states the manifest ultimate destiny of ethnic or cultural groups."). Gellner is highly critical of Hegel's assertion that it is the destiny of nations to evolve into states. *See also id.* at 48 (stating that we must not accept the myth expressed by Hegel that "[n]ations may have had a long history before they finally reach their destination—that of forming themselves into states.").

[14] Hans Kohn, The Idea of Nationalism: A Study of Its Origins and Background 16 (1948).

[15] Carlton H. Hayes, Nationalism: A Religion 5 (1960).

[16] Nathaniel Berman, *"But the Alternative Is Despair": European Nationalism and the Modernist Renewal of International Law*, 106 Harv. L. Rev. 1792, 1812 (1993).

[17] *Id.* at 1813.

[18] *Id.*

[19] *See* Hobsbawm, *supra* note 9 at 14–17 (describing how the term "nation" has been used in reference to non-state identifications, such as guilds, corporations, feudal estates).

[20] Berman, *supra* note 16, at 1810 (quoting Robert Redslob, Le Principe Des Nationalites 11 (1931)).

emphasized the common bonds of culture and language and their importance in determining identity. Johann Gottfried Von Herder promoted the idea of the "volk," translated into English as the "people" or "nation" to describe a community with common language, culture and religion.[21]

The "volk" was seen as a "natural unit" possessing the right to develop its own political presence and status—the right to become a state. The state was the political unit and the nation a cultural one,[22] and boundaries of the former should coincide with those of the latter. "The most natural state was a community with its own national character."[23] By contrast, multinational states were "artificial contrivances—'patched-up fragile contractions . . . devoid of inner life.' "[24] Under this view, the function of the state was to protect and promote the nation.[25]

This notion of "culture as *Volksgeist,* as a set of values and beliefs that makes a people or nation distinctive, is still powerful"[26] today. It is manifested in nationalist claims for indigenous sovereignty and self-determination, for example.[27] Indeed, "[t]his conception of culture is fundamental to contemporary nationalism."[28]

As a result, nationalism generally refers to that which is associated with claims surrounding the international system of nation-states or the rights of cultural, historical or ethnic "nations" aspiring for statehood.[29] The nation as an entity is constructed around some common mooring, whether of language, ethnicity, religion, culture, or some other essential characteristic[30] upon which the state's "homogenizing project"[31] can be

---

21 *See* C. A. Macartney, National States and National Minorities 97 (1934).

22 Alfred Cobban, The Nation State and National Self-Determination 35 (1969).

23 K. R. Minogue, Nationalism: Culture & Discovery 62 (1967).

24 *Id.*

25 Boyd C. Shafer, Faces of Nationalism: New Realities and Old Myths 126 (1972) ("[The state's] purpose was 'to preserve the consciousness of the unity of the whole people . . . and to express this idea in all forms of life' ").

26 Merry, *supra* note 7.

27 *See id.* ("It is the basis for the argument that human rights are a distinctly Western concept that ignores a country's distinctive spirit or system of values.").

28 *Id.*

29 Friedmann, *supra* note 4, at 21 ("More and more, from the sixteenth to the early twentieth century, the national state, in many cases coalescing from the older and smaller entities of dukedoms, principalities, and city republics, became the sole source of legal power and the exclusive focus of political allegiance."). Nationalism in its current modern incarnation can be traced to the Wilsonian post–World War I world composed of "people" who have a right to self-determination and by implication their own nation-state. *See* Lori Fisler Damrosch, *Nationalism and Internationalism: The Wilsonian Legacy*, 26 N.Y.U. J. Int'l L. & Pol. 493, 493 (1994). Woodrow Wilson, *The Fourteen Points Address* (1918), *reprinted in* 45 The Papers of Woodrow Wilson 534, 539 (Arthur S. Link ed., 1984).

30 Brilmayer, *supra* note 9, at 10 ("There is also controversy about what exactly the defining characteristic of a nation is. A nation is an entity that is fairly homogeneous with respect to some particular variable—it is a community that shares some attribute—but it is difficult to say precisely which attribute that should be. The usual candidates are language, religion, ethnicity, culture, and race; but for every potential defining characteristic, counterexamples can be found.").

31 Katherine Verdery, *Whither "Nation" and "Nationalism"?*, Daedalus, Summer 1993, at 43.

established. Nationalism in its simplest and most general meaning may mean "simply that one identifies with the claims of one's nations and one's conationals, and takes them as one's own."[32]

The idea that the state should not be simply a juristic or territorial unit but rather a national one[33] spread throughout Central and Eastern Europe, and nationalist agitation was particularly fervent after World War I. The collapse of the Hapsburg, Ottoman, Russian, and German Empires was marked by "nationalistic claims. . . . clamoring for recognition," and the international community faced with the "discovery of 'nations crowding to be born' "[34] and the rise of "an as yet vaguely defined right to self-determination."[35]

At issue was whether disintegrating empires would be "replaced by rational and democratic forms—'peoples and nationalities' "[36] or by traditional states. The statist positivism that characterized international law meant that the state was the entity deemed to be the foundational unit in the discipline. But a form of liberal nationalism derived from Enlightenment and Romantic ideals and founded on the principle that the "nation" or "people" should provide the foundation of international law rose to challenge the conception that only states should be endowed with formal international legal status.[37] Thus, nationhood would be viewed as a legitimate factor in the drawing of political maps, through the principle of nationalities or the plebiscite principle.

Nation thus is not necessarily synonymous with state,[38] and indeed, the breakup of empires opened the door for nations to fill the void and vie with states for political primacy. The outbreak of national demands following World War I and the surge in claims by various identity groups resulted in a dramatic transformation in international law. During this cataclysmic period, nationalism was viewed as a force of dual potentials. It can be negative, for example, as Hayes described. "[I]nternational rivalries and wars have become progressively more frequent, more general and more destructive, in measure as nationalism has evolved from its humanitarian prototype, through Jacobin, traditionalist and liberal phases, into its . . . integral form."[39] Others warned that "nationality has caused more destruction than powder and gas."[40] Nationalism was "viewed as seething cauldrons of unpredictable forces and passions, rather than as sources of simple and rational first

---

[32] Brilmayer, *supra* note 9, at 8.

[33] *See* Cobban, *supra* note 22.

[34] Berman, *supra* note 16, at 1795 (citing Philip M. Brown, *Editorial Comment: Jewish Nationalism*, 13 Am. J. Int'l L. 755, 755, 758 (1919)).

[35] *Id.*

[36] *Id.* at 1800.

[37] *Id.* at 1801–03. *See also* Carlton J.H. Hayes, The Historical Evolution of Modern Nationalism 159 (1931) (liberal nationalism "assumed that each nationality should be a political unit under an independent constitutional government. . . .").

[38] *See supra* notes 20–32 and accompanying text.

[39] Hayes, *supra* note 37 at 203, 305.

[40] Berman, *supra* note 16, 1802 (quoting René Johannet, *Préface* to Louis Le Fur, Races, Nationalités, États at iii (1922)).

principles."[41] Part "fantasy," part "caprice," nationalism or "national will" "must always be understood in relation to such irrational factors as collective passion and the seemingly contingent, so-called 'objective' factors of language, history, ethnicity, etc."[42] Rooted in a "smoking crater," nationalist passion is inevitably unstable and primitive.[43]

At the same time, nationalism was also viewed as potentially revitalizing—a "turbulent source of passion that was crucial to the revitalization of European public order."[44] These emotional, primitive forces of nationalism, it was said, constituted "the true source of the state's vitality and distinguish it from a 'joint-stock company.'"[45] Founded on the Enlightenment principle of freedom and given life and force by "transformations in popular consciousness,"[46] "people and nationalities," bounded by national solidarity, called for movements of national liberation. Indeed, some scholars during the interwar years urged the international order to recognize "the *creative, emotional, passionate movement* of people who are carried forward by feeling towards a new constellation of their collective life."[47]

Whether destructive or potentially liberating, the "nation" constituted a significant force that pushed against and challenged "the constraints of the stable legal order grounded in sovereignty...."[48] These nationalist movements were guided by the view that nationalities, not state, is elemental and that "in a case of disparity between the nation and the State, a reorganization is legitimate, a reorganization which will be realized—by forceful or peaceful means—either by the foundation of a new State or by incorporation into an existing State with the same ethnic character."[49]

As was evidently clear in the post–World War I world, a "nation," even if girded by a strong national will and national identity, cannot automatically become a state because existing states defending the statist status quo are impediments to national aspirations. Due to this blockage and repression, the high nationalist dramas of the time, fanned by the then blossoming principle of national self-determination, could not find full political expression.

Faced with such challenges to the nature of the state, international law responded by engaging in a series of formulations and reconfigurations of basic international law principles. Each formulation and reconfiguration was meant to address the problems posed to the international order by nationalist assertions of, for example, culture, identity, ethnicity. The international cannot simply snuff out nationalist passion because the nation is elemental, dynamic, and potentially invigorating. On the other hand, nationalist impulses must also be regulated, contained, and disciplined through legal reason.

---

[41] Berman, *supra* note 16, at 1803.
[42] *Id.* at 1813–14.
[43] *Id.* at 1816.
[44] *Id.* at 1805.
[45] *Id.* at 1810 (quoting Robert Redslob, Le Principe Des Nationalites 12 (1931)).
[46] Berman, *supra* note 16, at 1810.
[47] *Id.* at 1803, 1810.
[48] *Id.* at 1805.
[49] *Id.* at 1810 (quoting Robert Redslob, Le Principe Des Nationalites 12 (1931)).

Nationalist tendencies and such "sources of cultural energy"[50] must be harnessed by international discipline because presumably states are better guardians of international peace than nations.[51] The reconfiguration of international law to recognize, tame, appease, and control nationalist passion can be seen in such legal techniques such as minority protections,[52] self-determination,[53] internationalization through international administration,[54] supranational legal integration,[55] mandates,[56] and universal human rights.[57]

---

[50] Berman, *supra* note 16, at 1819.

[51] *See id.* at 1818 ("[T]he conservation of the existing State sometimes provides a better guarantee for general peace than the advent of the nationality, an advent which can not always take place without the unleashing of *elemental passions*, difficult to master.") (quoting ROBERT REDSLOB, LE PRINCIPE DES NATIONALITES 12 (1931)).

[52] The redrawing of the political map of Europe after World War I inevitably created minority groups within the territorial borders of the new states. These new states were compelled to sign minority protection treaties or to make declarations guaranteeing rights for their minority groups, including civil rights for all, and specific cultural, educational, and linguistic autonomy rights for minority group members. *See generally* INIS L. CLAUDE, JR., NATIONAL MINORITIES: AN INTERNATIONAL PROBLEM 16–17 (1955).

[53] WILSON, *supra* note 29, at 538 (one solution to address the collapse of the European empires was to create "national" states. The creation of a Polish state from areas with Polish populations was addressed in Wilson's Thirteenth Point); Damrosch, *supra* note 29 ("[Woodrow] Wilson gave expression to the nationalist aspirations of peoples around the world, through his endorsement of the principle of self-determination. He also initiated the first institution that had as its objective the organization of the international community to apply concerted power in support of universal values.").

[54] When Britain relinquished its mandate over Palestine in 1947, the UN General Assembly adopted Resolution 181, which provided for the partition of the territory and the internationalization of Jerusalem. Jerusalem was to be placed under the administration of the UN Trusteeship Council, with the following plans for the implementation of an international solution: the creation of two states, one Arab, one Jewish, with self-determination rights; guarantees of minority protection for Jewish and Arab minorities in the new states; supranational integration through the "Economic Union of Palestine," overseen by Arab, Jewish, and UN representatives; and internationalization subject to plebiscite review by the residents after ten years. *See* Berman, *supra* note 16, at 1795–96.

[55] Between 1919 and 1921, the area known as Upper Silesia, the territory divided between Poland and Germany, was placed under international tutelage providing for temporary unity of the region under a fifteen-year complex legal regime, which includes the following arrangements: the imposition of a plebiscite, with an International Commission conducting the vote and a Committee of Experts and the Conference of Allied Ambassadors interpreting the results; the establishment of a supranational regime that reflected parts of the two sovereigns' legal systems; extensive provisions for minority rights; the creation of a quasi-international legal personality to residents of Upper Silesia; and the establishment of mixed local/international tribunals. *See generally* GEORGES KAECKENBEECK, THE INTERNATIONAL EXPERIMENT OF UPPER SILESIA: A STUDY OF THE WORKING OF THE UPPER SILESIAN SETTLEMENT, 1922–1937 (1942).

The formation of the European Economic Community and the European Union might constitute another example. *See* Michael Mann, *Nation-States in Europe and Other Continents: Diversifying, Developing, Not Dying*, DAEDALUS, Summer 1993, at 120–28.

[56] International law responded to the collapse of European empires by formal recognition of national states and minority rights protections. The non-European possessions of the collapsed empires, deemed not yet ready for statehood, were subjected to the mandate system. Treaty of Versailles. Art. 22, 225 C.T.S. 188, 203 (1919). The German colonies in Africa and the Pacific were placed under indefinite mandates. But the former territories of the Ottoman Empires "have reached a stage of development where their existence as independent nations can be provisionally recognized subject to the rendering of administrative advice and assistance by a Mandatory until such time as they are able to stand alone." *Id.* at 203–04.

[57] The Versailles system had aimed toward the preservation of sovereignty, national identities, individual, and minority rights. The system eventually collapsed and the international minority protection system was replaced

What the above discussion shows is the existence and persistence of two polarities that have dominated the political and economic landscape—nationalism and internationalism. Historically, the international project has been to contain nationalism and by implication cultural assertions to the extent that they are an expression of nationalist prerogatives. In other words, nation and nationalism are bound up with a general notion of common culture.[58]

By contrast, internationalism is generally built around a different set of preoccupations. In the United Sates especially, internationalism has been linked to a liberal framework of cosmopolitanism.[59] Unlike the nationalist whose identification is with the nation, the cosmopolitan's "allegiance is to the worldwide community of human beings."[60] Between the two, internationalism, rather than nationalism, is generally more friendly to the spirit of cosmopolitanism. Writing about a universal international order composed of a cosmopolitan and republican federation of liberal states governed by law, Kant, for example, rejoiced in the coming of a Weltburger (citizens of the world) and denounced "the demand of fools in Germany for national pride."[61] "The ethical cosmopolitan view, in its classical form, rejects particularist loyalties . . . ; it is a perspective committed to the well-being of humanity at large, rather than any particular community of persons. . . . In such a view, therefore, grounding one's solidarity in the nation-state is unacceptably narrow and parochial."[62] The political cosmopolitanism that underlies the international project has meant an overall preference not just for international or multilateral over bilateral or unilateral approaches to problem solving[63] but also for universal norms over national cultures.[64]

---

with the notion of universal individual human rights. Josef L. Kunz, *The Present Status of the International Law for the Protection of Minorities*, 48 AM. J. INT'L L. 282, 284 (1954).

58 *See* Akhil Gupta, *The Song of the Nonaligned World: Transnational Identities and the Reinscription of Space in Late Capitalism, in* CULTURE, POWER, PLACE: EXPLORATIONS IN CRITICAL ANTHROPOLOGY 179, 179 (Akhil Gupta & James Ferguson eds., 1997) ("The nation is . . . deeply implicated in the texture of everyday life and . . . thoroughly presupposed in academic discourses on 'culture' and 'society'. . . .").

59 *See* Burley, *supra* note 5; David Kennedy, *The Disciplines of International Law and Policy*, 12 LEIDEN J. INT'L L. 9, 22–25 (1999). As Professor Kennedy notes, "one generally does not find in the United States . . . international lawyers who are also nationalists. International law in the United States after 1945 provided a congenial intellectual home for a large number of immigrants, among them European and Jewish refugees, whose American patriotism was cosmopolitan rather than jingoistic and who have been among the field's strongest intellectual leaders." *Id.* at 23.

60 Martha C. Nussbaum, *Patriotism and Cosmopolitanism, in* FOR LOVE OF COUNTRY 4 (Joshua Cohen & Martha C. Nussbaum eds., 1996). In *Minority Cultures and the Cosmopolitan Alternative*, 25 U. MICH. J.L. REFORM 751, 754 (1992), Jeremy Waldron characterized a cosmopolitan as someone who does not secure his or her sense of identity by deeply entrenched moorings to any particular or bounded subset of place, culture, or tradition. For a classic denunciation of the notion of world citizenship, *see* HANNAH ARENDT, MEN IN DARK TIMES 89 (1968) ("A world citizen, living under the tyranny of a world empire, and speaking and thinking in a kind of glorified Esperanto, would be no less a monster than a hermaphrodite.").

61 *See* KOHN, *supra* note 14, at 395–402 (citing IMMANUEL KANT, HANDSCHRIFTLICHER NACHLASS, No. 1099, at 489).

62 Linda Bosniak, *Citizenship Denationalized*, 7 IND. J. GLOBAL LEG. STUD. 447, 494–95 (2000).

63 Kennedy, *supra* note 59, at 23; Burley, *supra* note 5, at 586.

64 *See* Emmanuelle Jouannet, *Universalism and Imperialism: The True-False Paradox of International Law?*, 18 EUR. J. INT'L L. 379, 379 (2007) (describing the "inherent paradox" in international law). Jouannet stated,

The historical contrasts between nationalism and internationalism have perhaps become even more stark as a result of globalization—indeed precisely because one might characterize globalization as a hyperstate of internationalization.[65] Thus it is not surprising that nationalism and globalization might be viewed as each other's antithesis,[66] with international law being viewed as the facilitator for ever-increasing forms of globalization and hence even more at odds with nationalism. Because "almost every factor of production—money, technology, factories, and equipment—moves effortlessly across borders . . . ,"[67] the market (as opposed to the nation or the state) is more global than territorially bounded. The modern world is increasingly flat.[68] "Many see a lag between the bold new world of international commerce, communications, regulation, and policy which *has* adapted to life in a global village and the international political institutions which have not."[69] For nationalists, globalization is associated with an inevitable "move from public to private. The state will be weaker and commerce will be strengthened"[70] in ways that will result in the increasing homogenization of social and economic relations[71] and accordingly, the dilution of cultural distinctiveness and control.

"[t]his paradox stems from the fact that international law, past and present, is the reflection of a particular—Western—culture, whilst at the same time claiming not only to internationalize but also to almost universalize the values that it conveys." *Id.*

65 Or, as antiglobalization critics may characterize it, "globalisation is merely capitalism writ large." *Profits over People*, ECONOMIST, Sept. 27, 2001, *available at* http://www.economist.com/node/796021,

66 Franck, *supra* note 4, at 362 (discussing the "thesis of nationalism and antithesis of globalization"). Some have noted the dangers should nationalism feel itself diminished by the dominance of globalization. *See* Lawrence M. Friedman, *Borders: On the Emerging Sociology of Transnational Law*, 32 STAN. J. INT'L L. 65, 88–89 (1996) ("Modern nationalism and ethnocentrism may be particularly virulent and dangerous, precisely because group identity is constantly threatened by the forces released by modernity. These powerful forces of globalization include mass communications, mobility, and tourism, and the rapid spread of fashions and tastes."); Edith Brown Weiss, *The Rise or Fall of International Law?*, 69 FORDHAM L. REV. 345, 348 ("As integration and globalization increase, there is simultaneously a growing fragmentation within States and strong pressures for decentralization of decision-making. Ethnicity, nationalism, and the need for personal affiliations and satisfaction push toward fragmentation and decentralization.").

67 ROBERT B. REICH, THE WORK OF NATIONS: PREPARING OURSELVES FOR 21ST-CENTURY CAPITALISM 8 (1992).

68 *See generally* THOMAS L. FRIEDMAN, THE WORLD IS FLAT: A BRIEF HISTORY OF THE TWENTY-FIRST CENTURY (2005).

69 Kennedy, *supra* note 59, at 39.

70 *Id.* at 40; Elizabeth Lasch-Quinn, *Democracy Should Not Have Losers*, 9 MINN. J. GLOBAL TRADE 589, 592 (2000) (describing pro-globalization internationalism as being devoid of "any conception of a world beyond the market—the political or civic or cultural world in which ideas, beliefs, traditions, even innovations have meaning beyond their salability. . .").

71 Suzanne Berger, *Introduction*, *in* NATIONAL DIVERSITY AND GLOBAL CAPITALISM 1 (Suzanne Berger & Ronald Dore eds., 1996) (criticizing the "convergence across nations in the structures of production and in the relations among economy, society, and state"); Robert Wolf, *The Regionalist Answer*, 9 MINN. J. GLOBAL TRADE 610, 621 (2000) (criticizing "the globalization of world trade and culture [as] a process of homogenization which an increasing number of people perceive as soulless and dehumanizing . . ." and "the world-wide monoculture now being created by the corporations.").

The nationalist agenda thus includes a vigorous defense of "a basic reality—that a major value of human life is a rootedness in place."[72] Vehement assertions of sovereignty at the nation-state level become all the more necessary to defend against the global economic system and the "Golden Straitjacket"[73] states must increasingly accept as a precondition to attracting capital. For many countries, wearing the Golden Straitjacket has meant, as nationalists bemoan, "your economy grows and your politics shrinks"[74]—a narrowing of politics and further erosion of national sovereignty.[75] Increasingly, nationalists defend the national project as a populist movement that speaks not an abstract, universal language but rather, the people's language—"the emotionalism, the vulgar populism, the highly-coloured romanticism of most nationalist ideology (all the things intellectuals have always held their noses at)."[76] Nationalism stakes its claims on everything territorial or national—national sovereignty, national markets, and national cultures.

To further complicate matters, for nationalists, the "marketization of international law"[77] has created an international domain that is not only global and antinational but also culturally American and therefore, by that very fact, additionally problematic.[78] As

---

[72] John Miller, *Globalization and Its Metaphors*, 9 MINN. J. GLOBAL TRADE, 594, 598 (2000); *see also* HERMAN E. DALY & JOHN B. COBB, JR., FOR THE COMMON GOOD, 233–35 (1989) (arguing that global trade erodes local communities and promotes an imagined and nonexistent "world community").

[73] *See* THOMAS FRIEDMAN, THE LEXUS AND THE OLIVE TREE 102 (1999) ("The Cold War had the Mao suit, the Nehru jacket, the Russian fur. Globalization has only the Golden Straitjacket."). This means that for countries to generate the growth necessary to embark on a program of economic development, they have to link with and engage the global market and its rules. *Id.* at 103.

[74] *Id.* at 87, 88–89. Once plugged into and linked with the global market, in other words, states are expected to manage their economies according to the rules of the international market—to wear the global straitjacket. Those who do not, have to deal with the consequences of capital flight. South Korea's prime minister in the mid-1990s, Lee Hong Koo, said, "The big decisions today are whether you have a democracy or not and whether you have an open economy or not. Those are the big choices. But once you've made those big choices, politics becomes just political engineering to implement decisions in the narrow space allowed you within this system." *Id.* at 88–89.

[75] The global market in general and the WTO in particular are viewed as a stealthy, antidemocratic, sovereignty-eroding body with "unprecedented powers that include the right to rule on whether laws of nations—concerning public health, food safety, small business, labor standards, culture, human rights, or *anything*—are 'barriers to trade' by WTO standards." Turning Point Project, *Globalization vs. Nature*, N.Y. TIMES, Nov. 22, 1999, at A15 (advertisement by coalition of nonprofit organizations ranging from the Sierra Club to Greenpeace).

[76] TOM NAIRN, THE BREAK-UP OF BRITAIN: CRISIS AND NEO-NATIONALISM 341–42 (2003).

[77] Kennedy, *supra* note 59 at 34.

[78] Prominent neo-Marxists like Tom Nairn now associate cosmopolitanism and internationalism with the self-serving elitist ideology of "big battalion" states that hide their particularistic agenda of infinite capital accumulation behind a facade of universalistic norms—and more specifically, behind the agenda of the American empire. *See* Nairn, *supra* note 1, at 151, 157, 161. According to Nairn, the recent unrestrained movements of production and capital transnationally result, for poor countries, in cultural domination, "Anglicisation or Frenchification . . . [or] more globally . . . 'Westernisation' or 'Americanisation.'" NAIRN, *supra* note 76, at 326. *Cf.* Tyler Cowen & Eric Crampton, *Uncommon Culture*, FOREIGN POL'Y, July–Aug. 2001, at 28 (describing how local culture remains popular and unstifled by American culture or by international trade in cultural

globalization spreads, the nationalist opposition to globalization on not just political but also economic grounds has taken on an additional cultural element: "We have our own culture, our own values, and we will do it our own way at our own pace."[79] Nationalism thus proclaims itself to be "against civilization being disseminated out and downwards from the appropriate centers."[80] Nationalism is a movement not just to liberate peoples imperial powers had forced to live together in empires but also to oppose the self-serving ideology of "big battalion" states that employ universalistic norms against local cultures.[81] Fearing that globalization is now the vehicle for cultural imperialism, the nationalist struggle adds local culture to the long list of ideals to be defended.[82] Nationalists claim to be speaking "from somewhere; the internationalist speaks (or claims to speak) from nowhere in particular."[83] Nationalists are "protagonists of medieval particularism"[84] against the abstractions of universality, favoring "[n]ot the implacably prescribed common sense of internationalism, but the nonlogical, untidy, refractory, disintegrative, particularistic truth of nation-states,"[85] precisely because of the "thinness of cosmopolitanism and the crucial humanizing role played by identity politics in a deracinating world of contracts, markets, and legal personhood."[86]

products); Mario Vargas Llosa, *The Culture of Liberty*, Foreign Pol'y, Jan.–Feb. 2001, at 66 (claiming that globalization does not harm local cultures but liberates them from the stifling boundaries of nationalism).

79 Friedman, *supra* note 73, at 90; *see also* Frank E. Manning, *Reversible Resistance: Canadian Popular Culture and the American Other*, *in* The Beaver Bites Back? American Popular Culture in Canada 4 (David H. Flaherty & Frank E. Manning eds., 1993) (quoting Margaret Atwood in the following: "Canada as a separate but dominated country has done about as well under the U.S. as women, worldwide, have done under men; about the only position they've ever adopted towards us, country to country, has been the missionary position, and we were not on top. I guess that's why the national wisdom vis-a-vis Them has so often taken the form of lying still, keeping your mouth shut, and pretending you like it.").

80 Nairn, *supra* note 1, at 160.

81 *Id.* at 161. Nationalists are "protagonists of medieval particularism" against the abstractions of universality, favoring "[n]ot the implacably prescribed common sense of internationalism, but the nonlogical, untidy, refractory, disintegrative, particularistic truth of nation-states," *Id.* at 155, 157–158, precisely because of the "thinness of cosmopolitanism and the crucial humanizing role played by identity politics in a deracinating world of contracts, markets, and legal personhood." Benjamin R. Barber, *Constitutional Faith*, *in* For Love of Country? 30, 31 (Martha C. Nussbaum & Joshua Cohen eds., 1996).

82 *See* Richard Falk, *Culture, Modernism, Postmodernism: A Challenge to International Relations*, *in* Culture and International Relations 268 (Jongsuk Chay ed., 1990) (arguing that the rhetoric of globalization tends to "disguise patterns of interstate hegemony, especially as between Europe and the rest of the world."); L. Amede Obiora, *Feminism, Globalization, and Culture: After Beijing*, 4 Ind. J. Global Legal Stud. 355, 381 (1997) ("[C]hanges emanating from globalization are suspiciously perceived as Trojan horses in service of cultural imperialism. As such, they are countered with fervent expressions of nationalism. . . ."); Lasch-Quinn, *supra* note 70, at 590, 593 (decrying support by "global marketers" for "globalization, 'the American steamroller,' which decimates languages, traditions, and the environment at whim").

83 Nairn, *supra* note 1, at 156.

84 *Id.* at 157.

85 *Id.* at 158.

86 Barber, *supra* note 81, at 30. In repudiating the notion of a cosmopolitan ethics, Hannah Arendt proclaimed that a citizen "is by definition a citizen among citizens of a country among countries. His rights and duties

Internationalists, on the other hand, do not condemn globalization,[87] transnationalization,[88] denationalization,[89] or postnationalization[90] but rather defend internationalization and the international order in various ways and at various levels.[91] Whatever its failings, for internationalists, the internationalist order is absolutely necessary to counter and discipline nationalist excesses. Nationalism remains somewhat of a deep, dark mystery for internationalists. In a celebrated work, Professor Hans Kohn described nationalism thus: "Its roots seemed to reach into the dark soil of primitive times and to have grown through thousands of hidden channels of unconscious development, not in the bright light of rational political ends, but in the mysterious womb of the people, deemed to be so much nearer to the forces of nature."[92] Nationalism is not just primitive and irrational but also explosive. Thus, as one commentator described, nationalism "begins as Sleeping Beauty and ends as Frankenstein's monster,"[93] as evidenced by virulent conflicts in recent years between ethnic groups in, for example, the former Yugoslavia, Rwanda, and Iraq.

---

must be defined and limited, not only by those of his fellow citizens, but also by the boundaries of a territory." ARENDT, *supra* note 60, at 81.

[87] The term "globalization" is generally associated with various forms of linkages among businesses and markets across and without regard to national borders and usually connotes some erosion of the national, provoking questions about the meaning of democracy, participation, sovereignty.

[88] "Internationalization" or "transnationalization" may simply mean "cooperative activities of national actors," bilaterally or multilaterally so that the national is not necessarily diminished. *See* Gordon R. Walker & Mark A. Fox, 3 IND. J. GLOBAL LEGAL STUD. 375, 380 (1996) (emphasis omitted). *See also* Anne Marie Slaughter, *The Real New World Order*, 76 FOREIGN AFF. 183, 184 (1997) (describing how the state is disaggregating into different parts, such as courts, agencies, legislatures, and forming ties with their counterparts abroad, creating a "transgovernmental order.").

[89] "Denationalization" is less often used, but refers to the phenomenon, economic, primarily, in which the national is diminished. *See* SASKIA SASSEN, LOSING CONTROL?: SOVEREIGNTY IN AN AGE OF GLOBALIZATION 31 (1996) ("[E]conomic globalization has contributed to a denationalizing of national territory.").

[90] "Postnationalization" implies a shift, conceptually and paradigmatically, from the national to something beyond the national, although the term does not necessarily implicate a shift in the relationship between the state and the market, as in "globalization," but rather a shift in the relationship between the state and other non-market, non-state entities, such as nongovernmental organizations in the fields of human rights and the environment. *See,* e.g., Richard Falk, *The Making of Global Citizenship*, in GLOBAL VISIONS: BEYOND THE NEW WORLD ORDER 39, 47–48 (Jeremy Brecher et al. eds., 1993); RICHARD J. BARNET & JOHN CAVANAUGH, GLOBAL DREAMS: IMPERIAL CORPORATIONS AND THE NEW WORLD ORDER 427 (1993); Paul Wapner, *Politics Beyond the State: Environmental Activism and World Civic Politics*, 47 WORLD POL., Apr. 1995, at 311, 312–13.

[91] *See supra*, notes 87–90 and accompanying text. Terms such as globalization, internationalization, transnationalization, postnationalization, and even denationalization are used to describe the process by which activities which were once taking place within national borders are now taking place beyond national borders. *See* R. J. BARRY JONES, GLOBALISATION AND INTERDEPENDENCE IN THE INTERNATIONAL POLICY ECONOMY: RHETORIC AND REALITY 3 (1995).

[92] KOHN, *supra* note 14, at 331.

[93] MINOGUE, *supra* note 23, at 7.

By contrast, for internationalists, the international represents the realm of law and reason and the national the realm of culture, passion, and irrationality. Indeed, "if faced with a choice between reason and belief, law and politics, the secular and the sacred, to choose the first term is to build the international, to choose the second is to reinforce the national."[94] The internationalist agenda thus is inclined to view the particular, the national, as something to be overcome or transcended by a more international and cosmopolitan order. Presumably, "Brussels is better than Bonn and Bonn is better than Bremen."[95]

International law is also cosmopolitan in orientation, which means it favors universality of norms rather than particularity of cultures because a focus on culture usually tends to highlight differences that are problematic to the international objective: "to empower an international public order above the nation, an international private order below or outside the state, or a complex regime of transnational order."[96] The inclination of international law is to insist on the universality of the discipline, in other words, "that a body of doctrine, a common history, a common cosmopolitan 'college' of international legal colleagues, a common language, bind international lawyers to one another across different national cultures or legal traditions. . . ."[97] International law scholars often believe "it should be possible to wring a body of legal techniques and commitments from the idea that as people everywhere share basic humanist values and face rather similar technical problems, a rational or functional inquiry will generate convergence on a set of governmental best practices."[98]

In some ways, international law treats culture the way it treats nationalism, as something that is somewhat alien to the internationalist sensibility. For international law, "culture [is] a set of local or particularist commitments, a different language altogether from the communicative methods of cosmopolitan governance."[99] Such particularist

---

[94] Kennedy, *supra* note 59, at 93.

[95] *Id.* at 98.

[96] For a discussion of international law's marginalization of culture, *see id.* at 62–69 (describing how international law's approach to dealing with culture is to cabin culture within the sovereign state and relegate it as a local, not international matter); *id.* at 85 (stating that "governance is international while culture is local."); 86 ("service of the disciplinary desire carries with it an erasure of particularist projects, sands them down, harnesses them to a universal project"); *id.* at 98 (international law considers itself a cosmopolitan project, "more universal, rational, pragmatic, and expert than what goes on nationally or locally."). "The International Monetary Fund is better than the Russian Central Bank as that Bank is better than the government budgetary process in Uzbekistan. . . . [T]he international is agnostic about how one conducts oneself at home—international law bridges between states by providing a space above cultural differences." *Id.* at 98.

The point is not that public international law never entangles itself with culture, but rather that its general sensibility, preferences, or gestalt is to highlight its universalist normative order.

[97] *Id.* at 17.

[98] *Id.*; Louis Henkin, How Nations Behave: Law and Foreign Policy 29 (2d ed. 1979) (stating that international law "establishes common standards where they seem desirable"); *id.* at 20 (stating that international law facilitates state pursuit of common interests).

[99] Kennedy, *supra* note 59, at 126.

commitments—whether expressed as culture, religion, ethnicity, or some other similar attendant category—do not inhabit the realm of law or rationality but rather are viewed by law as "natural, irrational, incontestable, and imposed. . . ."[100]

As a result, international law has devised various strategies for dealing with cultural differences. Either international law has to defend the international order against irrational cultural eruptions or tolerate cultural differences to the extent they are palatable and not too disruptive. Hence this observation: "Contemporary internationalist commentary has reacted in two quite different ways to the challenges posed to cosmopolitan commitments by culture. . . . [C]osmopolitanism . . . needs to be defended against outbreaks of more primitive sensibilities when those sensibilities challenge the possibility of a universal pragmatism, and to be more tolerant of diverse cultural differences when they do not threaten that hegemony. . . . Where this line should be drawn remains . . . a matter of controversy, but the frame is stable: culture can be managed by exclusion or assimilation."[101]

International law, in other words, sees itself as something that has progressed "beyond" culture toward a more robust universality that, transcending cultural differences, arrives at a place that engages the cosmopolitan sensibility. A UN report on human rights and cultural diversity noted that the post–Cold War world is "an increasingly global, multicultural world brimming with tension, confusion and conflict in the process of its adjustment to pluralism."[102] It warned, however, that the United Nations must come out on the side of universal human rights, characterizing human rights as "a modern achievement, new to all cultures" in stark contrast to culture itself, which it identifies with "old conventions, traditional cultures, fundamental values, and the familiar, seemingly secure, sense of one's identity."[103] Indeed, international law, reflecting a spirit of "cosmopolitanism[,] is not itself a culture, but comes after culture, emerges from the defeat of the particularism of culture, and must be 'tolerant' of cultural differences . . . precisely to retain distance from the cultural."[104] For example, international law scholars such as Myres McDougal and Harold Lasswell sought to redefine international law, steer it away from nationalist preoccupations with "the importance of naked power,"[105] and toward a view of law as an authoritative and effective decision-making process designed to create a *world* public order that would advance human dignity.[106] World public order consists of "those features of the whole social process . . . including both the identity and preferred distribution

---

[100] Madhavi Sunder, *Piercing the Veil*, 112 YALE L.J. 1399, 1402 (2003).

[101] Kennedy, *supra* note 59, at 127.

[102] Diana Ayton-Shenker, *The Challenge of Human Rights and Cultural Diversity*, UN DEP'T OF PUB. INFO. (1995), http://www.un.org/rights/dpi1627e.htm.

[103] *Id.*

[104] Kennedy, *supra* note 59, at 127.

[105] Myres S. McDougal, *International Law, Power and Policy: A Contemporary Conception*, 82 RECUEIL DES COURS 137, 157 (1953).

[106] *Id. See also* Myres S. McDougal & Harold D. Lasswell, *The Identification and Appraisal of Diverse Systems of Public Order*, 55 AM. J. INT'L L. 1, 14–15 (1959).

pattern of basic goal values, and the implementing institutions ... that are accorded protection by the legal process."[107] Indeed, viewing international law along the lines of McDougal and Lasswell, Richard Falk conceived of international law as rules or process designed to "advance the values and interests of the overall world community rather than to promote the more special and diverse interests and values of national actors who are components of that system."[108] Note here the recurring emphasis on universal rules unifying a world public order that transcends national cultural variables.

There are other reasons why international law relegates particularistic or national culture to the margin. These reasons are embedded in the conventions of both international law and international relations. Despite internecine wrangling between international law and international relations, both occupy a common intellectual territory which has had the effect of relegating culture to the margin.[109]

International law, especially public international law, shares some basic analytical assumptions with the dominant international relations school of realism, such as who are the principal actors on the international stage and what are the motivating forces that drive and constrain those actors. Realism's dominant position in international relations theory has deep historical roots that can be traced from Thucydides to Machiavelli to Morgenthau.[110] Its key organizing principles rest on the following assumptions: (1) that states are the primary actors in the international system; (2) that the international system is an anarchical one ungoverned by any central authority; and (3) that as a result, states must pursue power and rely on self-help for self-preservation.[111]

Although there was an initial period of optimism after World War I about the possibility of cooperation and world government, this optimism quickly dissipated with the onset of World War II. International and international relations scholars "reacted against Wilsonian liberal internationalism, which presumed that the combination of democracy and international organization could vanquish war and power politics. They believed instead in the polarity of law and power. . . ."[112] As a result, international relations as a discipline became further entrenched in realist preoccupations with state security and state interest.

To better understand this dangerous new world, international relations scholars sought to find patterns of state behavior and worked to come up with systemic theories about such

---

[107] McDougal & Lasswell, *supra* note 106, at 6, 10.

[108] Richard A. Falk, The Status of Law in International Society 18 (1970).

[109] "[I]nternational lawyers and international relations scholars study and ... conceptualize the same phenomenon—the behavior of the principal actors in the international system. . . . At some point, ... their understanding of what they are observing must overlap." Anne-Marie Slaughter, *Liberal International Relations Theory and International Economic Law*, 10 Am. U. J. Int'l L. & Pol'y 717, 718 (1995); *see also id.* at 721–22 ("[I]nternational relations theory is an important part of any international lawyer's toolkit.").

[110] *Id.; see generally* Michael C. Williams, The Realist Tradition and the Limits of International Relations (2005).

[111] A more comprehensive discussion of international relations follows, *see* Chapter 4.

[112] Anne-Marie Slaughter Burley, *International Law and International Relations Theory: A Dual Agenda*, 87 Am. J. Int'l L. 205, 207 (1993).

behavior.[113] Consequently, international relations, as a general matter, has adopted a theoretical model that presents theories as being universally applicable and proposes rules that are to be universally appropriate, transcending local or cultural differences.[114] For example, states are presumed to act in a certain culture-neutral way—in pursuit of power and security.[115] Some have suggested that international relations' exclusion of culture from its disciplinary lens might have to do with the perception that culture is too imprecise a concept for analysis.[116] This bias against culture was further reinforced by international relations' view of itself as an empirical science grounded in facts, not values[117] and its roots in the positivist tradition.[118]

Public international law, likewise, is statist in orientation[119] and like realism, prefers to deal with states, governments, and other sovereignty-related issues, relegating culture to the side, or more precisely, cabining culture as something to be dealt with by the state itself as part of the state's sovereign right, that is, something beyond the legitimate reach of international law.[120] "It is precisely by eschewing involvement with matters of culture, which can be kept below the line of sovereignty, and forswearing any particular culture of their own, that international lawyers have sought to persuade sovereigns to submit to their rule. The international legal order presents itself as nothing more than the normative restatement of the wills, claims, and commitments of sovereigns, confirming, enshrining, recognizing sovereigns as sovereign and registering their prerogatives."[121]

---

[113] *See, e.g.*, Kenneth Waltz, Theory of International Politics 1 (1979) (discussing a wide range of theories designed to understand the puzzle of state behavior).

[114] *See* Robert Cox, *Social Forces, States and World Orders: Beyond International Relations Theory*, 10 Millennium 126, 132 (1981); *see generally* Richard Ashley, *The Poverty of Neo-Realism*, 38 Int'l Org. 225 (1984); Barry Buzan, *The Timeless Wisdom of Realism*, *in* International Theory: Positivism and Beyond (Smith et al. eds., 1996).

[115] Waltz, *supra* note 113, at 80 (1979). For the view that international relations is not culture neutral but instead rooted in Western culture, *see* Richard Falk, *supra* note 82; Kennedy, *supra* note 59, at 118 (1999) ("The insistence on the universality of international law often denied the roots of international law in Western projects of conquest and understated the obvious density of legal and political relations within cultural, economic, or ideological blocs.").

[116] *See* Philip Darby & Albert Paolini, *Bridging International Relations and Post-Colonialism*, 19 Alternatives 371, 382 (1994); R. B. J. Walker, *The Concept of Culture in the Theory of International Relations*, *in* Culture and International Relations 8 (Jongsuk Chay ed., 1990).

[117] *See* Hans Morgenthau, Politics Among Nations: The Struggle for Power and Peace 3 (3d ed. 1964); Stanley Hoffmann, *An American Social Science: International Relations*, 106 Daedalus, Summer 1977, 41–60.

[118] *See generally* Robert Keohane, *International Institutions: Two Approaches*, 32 Int'l Stud. Q. 379 (1988); Dominique Jacquin et al., *Culture in International Relations: An Introduction to the Special Issue*, 22 Millennium 375 (1993).

[119] I am making a general claim about the tradition of public international law, mindful of the fact that public international law is attempting to move beyond its statist foundation. *See* Kennedy, *supra* note 59, at, 44 ("Whatever its various qualifications, public international law still begins with sovereign states . . . [t]he job of public international law is to bring governance to sovereigns. . . .").

[120] "The conventional view of state power assumes that culture is pre-political, in the sense that culture precedes and constitutes the state, and the state exists to protect national culture from foreign influence." Joel Richard Paul, *Cultural Resistance to Global Governance*, 22 Mich. J. Int'l L. 1, 4 (2000).

[121] *See* Kennedy, *supra* note 59, at 81.

As already noted, "[a]lthough Realism is probably best known among international lawyers for rejecting any role for international legal norms in the international system, other than the short-term service of state interests, much of both the structure and substance of traditional international law appears to be built on a Realist foundation."[122] Although international lawyers have sought to "blunt or alter the implications of a pure Realist analysis,"[123] public international law remains nonetheless tied to realist assumptions. It accepts states as the basic and foundational units of the international system. It also views "states as monolithic units identifiable only by the functional characteristics that constitute them as states."[124] Hence we have the classic realist image of states as billiard balls—states as "closed, impermeable, and sovereign unit[s], completely separated from all other states," like balls rolling about on a billiard table.[125] From this perspective, international rules governing state behaviors are applicable to all states qua states and a state's domestic or internal identity is opaque to external observers. International rules apply to all states regardless of their internal makeup (because internal matters are beyond international concern). And conversely, for the most part, states' internal relations are within the domestic jurisdiction of the states.

Consider certain tenets that are foundational in public international law. States have territorial boundaries.[126] State control over their territory is part and parcel of the exercise of their sovereignty.[127] States are sovereign.[128] In the *Island of Palmas* case, the arbitration

---

[122] Slaughter, *supra* note 109, at 722.

[123] *Id.* at 722–23.

[124] *Id.* at 723.

[125] Arold Wolfers, Discord and Collaboration: Essays on International Politics 19 (1962).

[126] Slaughter, *supra* note 109, at 723 ("[T]erritorial boundaries define the area from which resources necessary for military and economic power can be extracted, thereby circumscribing the extent of state power."); Harold G. Maier, *Jurisdictional Rules in Customary International Law, in* Extraterritorial Jurisdiction in Theory and Practice 64, 67 (Karl M. Meessen ed., 1996) (stating that the territoriality principle "is the most universally recognised [principle] because control over defined territory is not only a legal prerequisite for statehood but is also essential to permit a state's government to be responsible to other nations for internal compliance with its external community commitments.").

[127] In *The Schooner Exchange v. M'Faddon*, 11 U.S. 116, 136 (1812), the Court states:

> The jurisdiction of the nation within its own territory is necessarily exclusive and absolute. It is susceptible of no limitation not imposed by itself. Any restriction upon it, deriving validity from an external source, would imply a diminution of its sovereignty to the extent of the restriction, and an investment of that sovereignty to the same extent in that power which could impose such restriction.

See also Compania Naviera Vascongada v. Steamship Cristina, [1938] A.C. 485 (H.L.) 496–97 (appeal taken from Eng.) ("It is an essential attribute of the sovereignty of this realm, as it is of all sovereign independent states, that it should possess jurisdiction over all persons and things within its territorial limits, and in all causes, civil and criminal, arising within these limits."); *see also* Peter J. Smith, *States as Nations: Dignity in Cross-Doctrinal Perspective*, 89 Va. L. Rev. 1, 86–87 (2003) (discussing the concept of sovereignty as elucidated in *The Schooner Exchange*).

[128] *Black's Law Dictionary* describes sovereignty in absolutist terms: as "supreme, absolute, and uncontrollable power . . . supreme political authority; the supreme will . . . the self-sufficient source of political power from which all specific political powers are derived . . . [the] power of regulating . . . internal affairs without foreign

tribunal considered sovereignty central to its analysis and posited that "[t]he development of the national organisation of States during the last few centuries and, as a corollary, the development of international law, have established this principle of the exclusive competence of the State in regard to its own territory in such a way as to make it the point of departure in settling most questions that concern international relations."[129] For example, in 1876, when a US citizen asserted a claim in a New York state court against Buenaventura Baez, the former president of the Dominican Republic, for injuries caused by Baez when he was president, the court refused to hear the case although Baez was physically present in New York at the time.[130] Baez's immunity from jurisdiction was deemed "essential to preserve the peace and harmony of nations."[131] Of course this is not to suggest that a similar set of facts would yield the same result today, as international law now does impose limits on sovereign autonomy.[132] Nonetheless, public international law remains rooted in a tripartite foundation of sovereignty, territoriality, and domestic jurisdiction.

From the basic fact that states occupy and control a defined territory flows "[t]he first-order international legal principles of sovereign equality and exclusive domestic jurisdiction [that] are safeguards of the identity and opacity of the sovereign sphere."[133] Indeed,

---

dictation. . . ." BLACK'S LAW DICTIONARY 1396 (6th ed. 1990); *see* Leila Nadya Sadat & S. Richard Carden, *The New International Criminal Court: An Uneasy Revolution*, 88 GEO. L.J. 381, 458 (2000) (referring to absolute sovereignty as "the most sacred of international law principles").

US courts continue to refer to *Black Law's Dictionary*'s definition of sovereignty when confronted with this concept. *See,* e.g., Gherebi v. Bush, 352 F.3d 1278, 1296 n.21 (9th Cir. 2003) (addressing US sovereignty over the Guantanamo Naval Station in Cuba); *The Supreme Court, 2004 Term—Leading Cases*, 118 HARV. L. REV. 248, 396 (2004) (discussing the *Guantanamo* cases); Kal Raustiala, *The Geography of Justice*, 73 FORDHAM L. REV. 2501, 2535–2542 (2005) (discussing the sovereignty of the Guantanamo Naval Station in the *Gherebi* case).

129 Island of Palmas Case (US v. Neth.), 2 R. Int'l Arb. Awards 829, 838 (Perm. Ct. Arb. 1928); *see also* Steven R. Ratner, *Land Feuds and Their Solutions: Finding International Law Beyond the Tribunal Chamber*, 100 AM. J. INT'L L. 808, 810 (2006) ("the guiding principle remains that set nearly eighty years ago in the *Island of Palmas* case.").

130 Hatch v. Baez, 14 N.Y. Sup. Ct. 596, 599–600 (N.Y. Gen. Term 1876).

131 *Id.* at 600.

132 *See* Michael Byers, *The Law and Politics of the Pinochet Case*, 10 DUKE J. COMP. & INT'L L. 415, 440–41 (2000); Peter J. Spiro, *Globalization, International Law, and the Academy*, 32 N.Y.U. J. INT'L L. & POL. 567, 567 (2000); Philippe Sands, *Turtles and Torturers: The Transformation of International Law*, 33 N.Y.U. J. INT'L L. & POL. 527, 530 (2001); Harold Hongju Koh, *The Globalization of Freedom*, 26 YALE J. INT'L L. 305, 305–306 (2001); Phillip R. Trimble, *Globalization, International Institutions, and the Erosion of National Sovereignty and Democracy*, 95 MICH. L. REV. 1944, 1946 (1997). The principle of universal jurisdiction, for example, is a challenge to traditional notions of state sovereignty. Mary Robinson, Foreword to THE PRINCETON PRINCIPLES ON UNIVERSAL JURISDICTION 15–16 (2001). So is the spectacular rise in international human rights litigation in US courts, *see* BETH STEPHENS & MICHAEL RATNER, INTERNATIONAL HUMAN RIGHTS LITIGATION IN U.S. COURTS 2–3 (1996), and the establishment of the International Criminal Court. Rome Statute of the International Criminal Court art. 5, ¶ 1, July 17, 1998, U.N. Doc. A/CONF. 183/9, *available at* http://www.un.org/icc.

133 Slaughter, *supra* note 109, at 723; *see also* The Schooner Exchange v. M'Faddon, *supra* note 127, at 137 (making references to the "perfect equality and absolute independence of sovereigns . . .").

"control over a defined territory is the first criterion of statehood. . . . It thus appears that the ante for participation in the international game is the capacity to wield power."[134] In this way we return to the basic premises of realism—states as sovereign unitary actors "identified with a particular national culture"[135] wielding power within a defined territory.

This means that culture and other norm-based theories are set aside so that interest-based issues can predominate. In other words, although "[r]ealists can admit the possibility of a wide range of state preferences, conditioned by factors such as geography, culture, and ideology,"[136] states must first and foremost defend their territorial boundaries, their sovereignty and domestic jurisdiction and pursue power to ensure their own survival.[137]

As a result, public international law is reluctant to foreground *internal* matters such as culture because doing so "may break the internationalist frame in two related ways: by generating solidarities which cross the neat boundaries of nation-states or by empowering smaller entities within states to erupt into international consciousness."[138] Witness, for example, the brutal disassembling of Yugoslavia into different culturally cohesive ethnically based nation states. Thus, in order to preserve the state and its established territorial boundaries, public international law "render[s] cultural differences internal to the sovereign form, outside the arena of international governance, as local matters of politics or culture."[139]

Consequently, public international law does not make it easy for culturally distinctive minority groups within a state to break out of the sovereign form and do damage to established territorial boundaries of existing states. Divisive cultural matters are "internalized" and become "domesticated" within the state's borders. Thus, whatever rights public international law might grant to culturally distinctive minority groups within a state, for example, the right of self determination,[140] this right is heavily tempered by the desire for the preservation of national unity and the established territorial boundaries of existing states.[141] As

[134] Slaughter, *supra* note 109, at 723–24 (1995).

[135] Paul, *supra* note 120.

[136] Slaughter, *supra* note 109, at 722.

[137] *Id.* at 723 (1995). Critics like Kennedy attribute internationalism's hesitation to engage culture as a result of internationalism's focus on actions between states, such as war, refugees, and grave human rights violations. David Kennedy, The Dark Sides of Virtue: Reassessing International Humanitarianism 133–34 (2004).

[138] Kennedy, *supra* note 59, at 63.

[139] *Id.* at 66, 62–69 (describing how international law manages differences by marginalizing culture).

[140] Public international law does grant certain rights to culturally distinctive minority groups within a state, such as the right of self-determination, which requires that states allow people to "freely determine their political status and freely pursue their economic, social and cultural development." International Covenant on Civil and Political Rights (ICCPR), art. 1, Dec. 16 1966, 999 U.N.T.S. 171 [hereinafter ICCPR]. The International Covenant on Economic, Social and Cultural Rights (ICESCR) has an identical Article 1. International Covenant on Economic, Social and Cultural Rights, art. 1, Dec. 16 1966, 993 U.N.T.S. 3 [hereinafter ICESCR].

[141] The international community has consistently opposed action that would violate national unity or territorial integrity. Malcolm N. Shaw, International Law 522 (6th ed. 2008). For example, Resolution 1514

a result, public international law generally does not recognize a general right of unilateral secession[142] or a right to autonomy by groups within independent states.[143]

At the same time that public international law tries to remove itself from intervening in member states' domestic cultural realm, it is also pulled in an opposite direction—that of basic universal rights. Traditional deference to states through the principles of sovereignty and territorial integrity has not prevented the adoption of international instruments designed to protect the rights of people within a state. Various multilateral conventions for human rights[144] contain both positive and negative obligations owed by the states.[145] Obligations specific to culture include the following: states shall not deny minorities the right to enjoy their own culture[146] or to use their own language,[147] and states shall take steps necessary to conserve and develop culture.[148]

Put another way, public international law's strategy is either to exclude or assimilate cultural differences into the sovereign form.[149] In the first scenario, exclusion of cultural differences from the international agenda would mean deferring to sovereignty and

---

(XV), Declaration on the Granting of Independence to Colonial Countries and Peoples, declares the right to self-determination but clearly states that "[a]ny attempt aimed at the partial or total disruption of the national unity and the territorial integrity of a country is incompatible with the purposes and principles of the Charter of the United Nations." G.A. Res. 1514 (XV) U.N. Doc. A/66 (Dec. 14, 1960).

[142] Shaw, *supra* note 141, at 523. In 1998, the Canadian Supreme Court refused to extend the right of self-determination to unilateral secession, thus halting an attempt by Quebec to secede from Canada. *Id.* The Court cited international law as supporting the preservation of territorial integrity except "in the most extreme of cases and, even then, under carefully defined circumstances." *Id.* (quoting Court in the *Reference Re Secession of Quebec*, [1998] 161 D.L.R. (4th) 385, 438). For a discussion of circumstances when unilateral secession may be acceptable, *see* David Raic, Statehood and the Law of Self-Determination 308–97 (2002).

[143] *See* Raic, *supra* note 142, at 283. Autonomy is not forbidden as it stems from the notion of participation in the decision-making process that is inherent in the right of self-determination. *Id.* at 237.

[144] Ian Brownlie, Principles of Public International Law 562 (7th ed. 2008) (identifying four categories of binding human rights conventions: the comprehensive International Covenants (the 1966 ICESCR and ICCPR), the comprehensive regional conventions, the conventions dealing with specific wrongs (e.g., the 1965 International Convention on the Elimination of All Forms of Racial Discrimination), and the conventions related to the protection of particular categories of peoples (e.g., the 1979 Convention on the Elimination of All Forms of Discrimination Against Women)).

[145] Shaw noted an increase in the evolution of a positive obligation of states and international organizations to protect human rights. Shaw, *supra* note 141, at 276.

[146] *Id.* at 294. For example, Article 27 of the ICCPR states: "[i]n those States in which ethnic, religious or linguistic minorities exist, persons belonging to such minorities shall not be denied the right, in community with the other members of their group, to enjoy their own culture, to profess and practise their own religion, or to use their own language." ICCPR, *supra* note 140, at art. 27, Dec. 16 1966, 999 U.N.T.S. 171. The International Labour Organization (ILO) Convention No. 143, 1975, on migrant workers (supplementary provisions) calls on the States to encourage the efforts of migrant workers to preserve their national and ethnic identity and their cultural ties with their country of origin. *See* ILO Convention No. 143, Migrant Workers (Supplementary Provisions), art. 12, ¶ f. (June 24, 1975).

[147] Shaw, *supra* note 141, at 294.

[148] *See* ICESCR, *supra* note 140, at art. 15, Dec. 16 1966, 993 U.N.T.S. 3.

[149] *See supra* notes 101–109 and accompanying text.

hence leaving cultural matters for the sovereign state to address, as a matter of that sovereign state's domestic jurisdiction.[150] In practical terms, this means that international law opts to abdicate from taking a stance on cultural issues and defer to states to treat culture because culture is considered an internal matter. The state and its subunits are generally considered legitimate guardians of cultural traditions (as the international is generally transcendent of culture). Authorities *within* the state are given the power to protect and preserve authentic cultures from external encroachment and contamination.[151] In the case of gender equity in particular, national authorities often succeed in subverting equality by describing the concept of women's rights as inherently alien to national culture itself.[152] For example, although the Beijing Declaration that emerged from the Fourth World Conference on Women stated in its preamble that "[w]omen's rights are human rights,"[153] the Beijing Platform for Action suggested that women's human rights were culturally contingent.[154] In this way, the Beijing agenda is eerily similar to the posture of Convention on the Elimination of All Forms of Discrimination Against Women, as I observed in the Introduction, in that it declares the existence of rights on the one hand and allows such rights to be whittled away on the other.

In the second scenario, international law's strategy of assimilating cultural differences means that states are encouraged, as a matter of international law, to recognize the distinctiveness of a cultural or ethnic group within their territories.[155] Cultural differences are recognized and assimilated within the state's territory and international law obligates

---

[150] Public international law or international human rights law does not obligate states to grant full self-determination rights for ethnic groups within its territory, whether by allowing the groups to secede or by establishing an autonomous region within its territory for the group at issue. *See* RAIC, *supra* note 142, at 282–83.

[151] *See, e.g.*, Cornel West, *The New Politics of Cultural Difference*, *in* THE IDENTITY IN QUESTION 149, 161 (John Rajchman ed., 1995) ("[M]ost Third World, authoritarian, bureaucratic elites deploy essentialist rhetoric about 'homogeneous national communities' . . . in order to repress and regiment their diverse and heterogeneous internal forces.").

[152] Kimberley Crenshaw, *Were the Critics Right About Rights? Reassessing the American Debate About Rights in the Post-Reform Era*, *in* BEYOND RIGHTS TALK AND CULTURE TALK: COMPARATIVE ESSAYS ON THE POLITICS OF RIGHTS AND CULTURE 61, 73 (Mahmood Mamdani ed., 2000) (describing the need to "mount a human rights-based discourse that resists the almost effortless stigmatization of gender equity as alien").

[153] Report of the Fourth World Conference on Women, Annex 1, ¶ 14, U.N. Doc. A/CONF. 177/20 (1995).

[154] The Platform cautions that implementation of such rights was subject to "the significance of and full respect for various religious and ethical values, cultural backgrounds and philosophical convictions of individuals and their communities." *Id.* at ¶ 9. Of course one could also spin this position to mean that international law refuses to use international human rights as an imperialist tool, Makau-wa Mutua, *The Ideology of Human Rights*, 36 VA. J. INT'L L. 589, 589–91 (1996) (criticizing human rights discourse as imposing Western ideology on the Third World), or respects the "diversity" of cultures among its member states. Karen Engle, *Culture and Human Rights: The Asian Values Debate in Context*, 32 N.Y.U. J. INT'L L. & POL. 291 (2000).

[155] States do not have to grant affirmative rights to ethnic or culturally based groups within their territory but cannot oppress or discriminate against them. So states may not be obligated under public international law to use public resources to construct a public school curriculum centered around the ethnic group's history or identity, nor to build places of worship for the group. But states may not prohibit members from speaking

states to provide cultural groups with certain basic rights because international human rights are universal.[156]

International law vacillates between the first and the second scenario. International law can defer to national sovereignty and leave culture out of the international law framework, claiming it is doing so out of deference to each individual state's cultural diversity. Or it can exercise minimal management of cultural issues and insist that states, for example, respect minority cultures and provide basic universal rights to minority groups within its borders. In other words, there exists a built-in "tension between the universalistic principles of the founders and the practical realities of a club of members with diverse cultures. Attempts to resolve the tension have taken the form of declaring a set of universal rights and principles (some of which seem inconsistent with the 'cultures' of its members) and, at the same time, declaring the equal claim of every diverse culture to be respected."[157]

In the latter case, this has meant insulating cultures from international scrutiny. In the same way that states were once granted absolute sovereignty over "private" matters deemed within their domestic jurisdiction, culture has been elevated into a new form of sovereignty with its own quasi domestic jurisdiction, insulating it from scrutiny.[158] Although public international law has deconstructed the nation state and has weakened traditional state claims of national sovereignty,[159] for the most part it has not done so with culture. Culture is not deconstructed but remains on the pedestal of sovereignty—and practices that perpetuate poverty and even those that constitute outrageous abuses

---

their own language or learning their own history. *See* ICCPR, *supra* note 140, at art. 27; ILO Convention No. 169, Indigenous and Tribal Peoples, art. 2 (June 27, 1989).

156 *See supra* notes 101–08 and accompanying text; *see also* Guyora Binder, *Cultural Relativism and Cultural Imperialism in Human Rights Law*, 5 BUFF. HUM. RTS. L. REV. 211 (1999) (rejecting the charge that international human rights represent cultural imperialism); Jack Donnelly, *Cultural Relativism and Universal Human Rights*, 6 HUM. RTS. Q. 400 (1984) (defending the universality of certain rights).

157 Vijayendra Rao & Michael Walton, *Culture and Public Action: Relationality, Equality of Agency, and Development*, *in* CULTURE AND PUBLIC ACTION 17, 18 (Vijayendra Rao & Michael Walton eds., 2004); *see also* Thomas M. Franck, *The Legal Culture and the Culture Culture*, 93 AM. SOC'Y INT'L L. PROC. 271, 273 (1999) ("[W]e value the new global law of individual rights but also acknowledge the role of cultural diversity."); Fernando R. Tesón, *International Human Rights and Cultural Relativism*, 25 VA. J. INT'L L. 869 (1985) (arguing that international human rights must be universal, but international law requires respect for national cultures).

158 Sunder, *supra* note 100, at 1401.

159 *See, e.g.*, Charles Norchi, *Human Rights: A Global Human Interest*, *in* THE UNITED NATIONS: CONFRONTING THE CHALLENGES OF A GLOBAL SOCIETY 86 (Jean. E. Krasno ed., 2004); DAVID P. FORSYTHE, HUMAN RIGHTS AND WORLD POLITICS 4 (1983) ("The most fundamental point about human rights law is that it establishes a set of rules for all states and all people. It thus seeks to increase world unity and to counteract national separateness (but not necessarily national distinctions). In this sense, the international law of human rights is revolutionary because it contradicts the notion of national sovereignty—that is, that a state can do as it pleases in its own jurisdiction."); BRIAN HEHIR, INTERVENTION: FROM THEORIES TO CASES 6 (1995) (noting that "[i]n the Westphalian order both state sovereignty and the rule of nonintervention are treated as absolute norms" but that this order is being increasingly challenged).

of human rights are tolerated when justified as cultural—precisely because culture is deemed to be a "private"[160] or "domestic jurisdiction" matter beyond the reach of international law, human rights or otherwise.

Thus, international human rights, which has ironically pierced the veil of sovereignty where states are concerned in order to criticize human rights abuses by states, has failed to pierce the veil of sovereignty where culture is concerned. By focusing on sovereignty, potential public interveners (such as law and development actors) envision themselves as acting in a global space above sovereignty and local culture.[161] In doing so, international human rights law marginalizes efforts by groups and individuals within a culture that seeks to change the worst of practices within that culture as if—to make the parallel with state sovereignty one more time—anything that happens "within" a culture is within the "domestic jurisdiction" of that culture. International human rights sees culture as a messy, irrational, mysterious "thing" that is monolithic rather than "contested and subject to change. . . ."[162] By enshrining " 'the right to culture,' and the guarantee of 'self-determination,' "[163] international human rights "defer to the claims of patriarchal, religious elites, buttressing their power over the claims of modernizers."[164] Even international human rights law, which is premised on a fundamental skepticism of state sovereignty, has abandoned those seeking culture change to fend for themselves.[165]

In other words, despite its antisovereignty language, the international human rights movement is as stuck in the norms of sovereignty as public international law. This focus has limited the ways international human rights law is able to respond to human rights violation. As noted, public international law generally allows sovereigns to act as they like within their territory as long as they meet certain standards.[166] This turns international

---

160 The same analogy has been made with respect to religion. Madhavi Sunder paired religion with culture, *see* Sunder, *supra* note 100, at 1401 ("[R]eligion—and its attendant category, culture—represent the New Sovereignty . . ."), and subsequently showed that religion becomes "an 'extralegal field,' banished from the public and reserved to the private sphere." *Id.* at 1417. The famed anthropologist Clifford Geertz too noted parallels between religion and culture and described religion as a cultural system consisting of meanings, signs, and symbols. Clifford Geertz, *Religion as a Cultural System*, *in* THE INTERPRETATION OF CULTURES 87, 89 (1973).

161 KENNEDY, *supra* note 137, at 134.

162 Sunder, *supra* note 100, at 1403.

163 *Id.* In other words, while "self-determination" means accepting the right of the culture to determine its own meaning and identity, it has also meant deferring to the traditional elites to proclaim what is the "correct" meaning and identity of the culture and excluding as illegitimate those dissenters within the culture who seek to change the culture's traditional biases.

164 *Id.* The modernizers Sunder described are those cultural dissenters or "individuals within a community [who seek] to modernize, or broaden, the traditional terms of cultural membership." Madhavi Sunder, *Cultural Dissent*, 54 STAN. L. REV. 495, 498 (2001).

165 *See* David Kennedy, *The International Human Rights Movement: Part of the Problem?*, 15 HARV. HUM. RTS. J. 101, 118 (2002) ("The legal regime of 'human rights,' taken as a whole, does more to produce and excuse violations than to prevent and remedy them."); Sunder, *supra* note 100, at 1409 (describing how international law defers to the sovereignty claims of culture, resulting in "the increasing use of law to protect and preserve cultural stasis and hierarchy against the challenges to cultural and religious authority emerging on the ground").

166 KENNEDY, *supra* note 137, at 134.

intervention into an exception "which requires justification,"[167] which in turn creates a burden for "every humanitarian initiative."[168] The intervener must provide good reason for intervening, which tends to result in hesitation to intervene, especially when local culture may be disturbed.[169] This tempts potential interveners to focus on the defensibility rather than the possible results of international humanitarian intervention.[170] It seems easier for public international law to give preference to economic and technical interventions (such as rule of law), as humanitarians mistakenly view such intervention as acultural and apolitical.[171] "Innumerable humanitarian policy initiatives have crashed on the rocks of hesitation to engage in 'cultural imperialism.' A willingness to intervene to achieve economic development or political peace, but not to affect 'culture,' often skews international humanitarian policy making."[172]

Unlike public international law and international human rights law, private international law, or international economic law,[173] is not about states or sovereignty but rather, non-state—specifically market—actors. However, private international law, like public international law, also marginalizes culture and separates it from what it considers normal, rational market activities. Indeed, "[t]he whole legal structure of the free trade norm rests on a rational economic model. . . . Cultural claims threaten that rationality argument. Cultural claims derive from sentiment, nostalgia, insecurity; they are rooted in non-rationality. To protect the rationality of the market from the non-rationality of nationalism and culture, the international community rejects cultural exceptions."[174]

The tug of war between nationalism and internationalism can also be seen in the ways that private international law has sought to protect the international market from nationalistic assertions. Private international law, for example, depicts the international market as cosmopolitan or territorially unbound. Karl Marx was highly critical of this and denounced the international capitalistic market as follows: "The bourgeoisie has through its exploitation of the world-market given a cosmopolitan character to production and consumption in every country . . . it has drawn from under the feet of industry the national ground on which it stood. All old-established national industries have been

---

[167] *Id.* at 135.

[168] *Id.* at 136.

[169] *Id.*

[170] *Id.* at 138.

[171] *Id.* at 137.

[172] *Id.*

[173] As used in the United States, "private international law" is concerned with international business transactions and related commercial and trade matters. Joel Paul, *The Isolation of Private International Law*, 7 WIS. INT'L L.J. 149, 151 n.4; Kennedy, *supra* note 59, at 38–39.

[174] *See, e.g.*, Paul, *supra* note 120, at 80. Kerry Rittich argued against this exclusion of culture and politics from the international framework, claiming instead that politics and culture and ideology are not absent from law and development but are merely suppressed or denied by proponents despite the pervasiveness in both design and adjudication of legal regimes. Kerry Rittich, *Who's Afraid of the Critique of Adjudication?: Tracing the Discourse of Law in Development*, 22 CARDOZO L. REV. 929 (2001).

destroyed or are daily being destroyed. . . . In place of the old local and national seclusion and self-sufficiency, we have intercourse in every direction, universal inter-dependence of nations."[175]

Private international law, however, is quite comfortable with an international system that extends beyond the national and protects the market and its cosmopolitan order against the political interference of the state. The market is viewed as a technocratic domain which should be subject to economics and insulated from the irrationality of national politics. As an EU scholar bemoaned, the European common market has been de-politicized, supposedly sheltered from politics. "In a technocratic private market, the locus for political choice is less opened up than it is rendered invisible. Take the European Union, whose political decision-making always seems to take place 'elsewhere'. . . . The idea of a 'government' promoting a 'program' has been replaced by the enlightened management of prosperity. . . . EU policy managers [for example,] treat the transitional economies of Central and Eastern Europe less as a set of political exclusions and choices than as the technical management of different natural stages of development."[176]

Indeed, until most recently, private international law was quite unsympathetic to states that seek to promote and impose their particular national preferences onto the international economic system. For example, when the US government tried to prevent British fur traders from trapping seals as far back as 1893 on the grounds that seals were in danger of becoming extinct, an international arbitral tribunal overwhelmingly rejected the claim because it found that there was no basis in international law for the United States to apply its national standards of conservation to measures taking place outside its territory.[177] National preferences should be restricted to national territory and not be given extraterritorial application by the international economic system. Similarly, for years General Agreement on Tariffs and Trade (GATT) panels found that the United States could not, in its pursuit of its own environmental policies, "impose trade embargoes to secure changes in the policies which other contracting parties pursued within their own jurisdiction."[178]

---

[175] Karl Marx, *Communist Manifesto*, *in* The Marx-Engels Reader 338 (Robert C. Tucker ed., 1972). Similarly, today's critics argue that the supposed cosmopolitanism of market-driven globalization entails "a perspective of the whole [world] that is totally oblivious to the ethical imperatives of human solidarity," Richard Falk, *Revisioning Cosmopolitanism*, *in* For Love of Country? 53, 57 (Martha C. Nussbaum & Joshua Cohen eds., 1996), and is no way related to the cosmopolitanism espoused by those like Martha Nussbaum. *See also* Falk, *supra* note 90.

[176] David Kennedy, *Background Note? The Underlying Politics of Global Governance*, Harv. Int'l Rev., Summer 1999, at 52, 53.

[177] Sands, *supra* note 132, at 529; *see* Fur Seal Arbitration (United States v. Great Britain), *reprinted in* 1 John Bassett Moore, International Arbitrations To Which The United States Has Been a Party 919–20 (Washington, Government Printing Office 1898).

[178] *See* GATT Dispute Settlement Panel Report on United States Restrictions on Imports of Tuna, 33 I.L.M. 839, 898 (1994); *see also United States Restrictions on Imports of Tuna* (Sept. 3, 1991), GATT B.I.S.D. (39th

Globalization of trade and investment, the free movement of goods and services, and increasingly, of capital across national borders—free from national, political, or culturally based restrictions—are entirely compatible for private international law. Indeed, a global economic order, or at least a regional economic order such as the European Union, represents the achievement of international consensus. By contrast, cultural particularities represent potential impediments to the laudable goal of harmonization.[179] Even though some internationalists would like to see a super international regulatory structure, a globalized New Deal, so to speak, instituted to manage these changes, internationalists are not opposed per se to the rise of transnational activities and indeed seek to facilitate them.[180] Presumably, an international liberal regime of World Trade Organization (WTO) rules are "better" than a national system that reflects exotic, cultural particularities or a protectionist regime of local rules[181] that are more susceptible to capture by parochial political interests and organized interest groups.[182] Private international law is designed to manage

---

Supp.), at 155–205 (1993) (holding that a state may adopt its own national conservation policies but rejecting the state's application of such conservation policies in a way that injures other state parties to the GATT).

In a different but related subsequent case, the United States banned the import of shrimp caught in the waters of India, Malaysia, the Philippines, and Thailand, on the grounds that the shrimp had been harvested in a way that caused the incidental killing of sea turtles. The Appellate Body of the WTO found that US measures were provisionally justified (provided other requirements were met). Appellate Body Report, *United States–Import Prohibition of Certain Shrimp and Shrimp Products*, ¶ 187, WT/DS58/AB/R (Oct. 12, 1998). The different result could be explained by reference to many factors. *See* Sands, *supra* note 132, at 536–43 (2001). Of course in today's world, national borders are more permeable. But another reason why WTO recognizes the legitimacy of US preference in this case is because its preference is backed by international consensus. For example, sea turtles are internationally recognized as endangered and that they are a highly migratory species.

179 *See, e.g.*, José A. Laínez & Mar Gasca, *Obstacles to the Harmonisation Process in the European Union: The Influence of Culture*, 3 INT'L J. ACCT. AUDITING & PERFORMANCE VALUATION 68 (2006), *available at* http://inderscience.metapress.com/media/mftkvluwmj1d367rvvtk/contributions/3/1/a/t/31at8fuht2tja3xt.pdf.

180 *See generally* Anne-Marie Burley, *Regulating the World: Multilateralism, International Law, and the Projection of the New Deal Regulatory State*, *in* MULTILATERALISM MATTERS: THE THEORY AND PRAXIS OF AN INSTITUTIONAL FORM 125 (John G. Ruggie ed., 1993); G. Richard Shell, *Trade Legalism and International Relations Theory: An Analysis of the World Trade Organization*, 44 DUKE L.J. 829 (1995) (arguing for a "trade stakeholders" model which would allow individual and NGO participation in the WTO).

181 International trade legalism allows governments to resist domestic resistance to free trade. For the argument that free trade internationalism is more democratic than domestic protectionism, *see generally* John O. McGinnis & Mark L. Movsesian, *The World Trade* Constitution, 114 HARV. L. REV. 511 (2000) (discussing how internationalism of the type manifested in the WTO provides the correct antidote to naked interest-group politics and domestic rent-seeking at the national level); Jan Tumlir, *Need for an Open Multilateral Trading System*, 6 WORLD ECON. 393, 406 (1983) (the trade system and its "international rules represent a truer expression of the national interest of all the countries concerned than the mass of national [economic] legislation . . ."); Robert E. Hudec, *"Circumventing" Democracy: The Political Morality of Trade Negotiations*, 25 N.Y.U. J. INT'L L. & POL. 311 (1992).

182 For a discussion of how interest groups, particularly industries with significant political strength, press for protectionist measures that further their own rather than the national interest, *see* ROBERT Z. LAWRENCE & ROBERT E. LITAN, SAVING FREE TRADE: A PRAGMATIC APPROACH 23–24 (1986). The state is too entangled in the push and pull of "local politics (of protectionism, exchange controls, redistribution, corruption, etc.). . . ." Kennedy, *supra* note 59, at 86.

a global market freed from the failed politics of nationalism. "Globalization offers a realistic vehicle for escaping from failed nationalism to an expanded concept of global rights and duties. . . . [Its] economic potential is what gives globalization power even against antagonistic national governments."[183] For private international law, "the need is not to discuss whether globalization is a good thing, but to ask . . . 'what would be the alternative?' It would be a world divided by economic and political nationalism—a world in which we would go down the road towards power-based relations, increased tension and violence, as history has taught us."[184]

In an effort to create a dispute settlement system that is based less on diplomacy or power and more on rules and law, the Dispute Settlement Body of the WTO is empowered to issue decisions that are binding unless the Dispute Settlement Body, including the winning party, votes unanimously to overturn it.[185] To private international lawyers especially, the idea that conflicts can be "privatized" or "economized" is appealing. That is, interstate conflicts can be cabined in a private, economic sphere so that disagreements among states can be resolved through a rational regime of "technocratic cosmopolitan governance" consisting of "technocratic means, sound management and trade deals."[186] Thus, private international law consisting, for example, of international economic rules such as those of the WTO are necessary for "bringing law *in general* to bear on politics *in particular*, order to bear on anarchy, reason on chaos, the international on the national."[187]

Of course this does not mean that private international law has completely succeeded in suppressing nationalistic expressions of cultural sovereignty. Cultural claims are asserted by states and are passionately bound up with the nationalist projects of states. States continue to exhibit nationalist propensities even as they espouse the need to be internationally minded. But because states are also rational economic actors, they commit themselves to the rules of private international law designed to restrain nationalistic impulses. Thus states may on the one hand pursue a bundle of nationalist objectives—sovereignty, economic and cultural protectionism—and also, on the other hand, subject themselves to the rules of private international law which are meant to minimize state

---

[183] Michael D. Pendleton, *A New Human Right—The Right to Globalization*, 22 FORDHAM INT'L L.J. 2052, 2052–53 (1999); *see also* Renato Ruggiero, *Reflections After Seattle*, 24 FORDHAM INT'L L.J. 9, 14 (2000) ("Without the WTO, we will go back to a world of national barriers, protectionism, economic nationalism, and conflict. History has repeatedly showed where this road can lead.").

[184] Wesley A. Cann, Jr., *Creating Standards and Accountability for the Use of the WTO Security Exception: Reducing the Role of Power-Based Relations and Establishing a New Balance Between Sovereignty and Multilateralism*, 26 YALE J. INT'L L. 413, 415 n.4 (2001).

[185] Understanding on Rules and Procedures Governing the Settlement of Disputes, art. 1, ¶ 4, Apr. 15, 1994, Marrakesh Agreement Establishing the World Trade Organization, Annex 2, 1869 U.N.T.S. 401.

[186] Kennedy, *supra* note 176, at 54. Kennedy notes that "[s]pecialists tend to overestimate the technocratic or apolitical nature of economic concerns, including the independence of economic development from background cultural, political, and institutional contexts." *Id.* at 52.

[187] Kennedy, *supra* note 59, at 86. Because the international, though not necessarily antinational, does reject fealty to the national, it is thus more compatible with cosmopolitanism than the national.

trespasses into politics, culture and other nonrational realms.[188] As aptly noted, "[t]he rules of trade function to protect the rationality of the market from the irrationality of cultural preferences."[189]

With respect to the national realm which private international law has sought to manage, there have been many cases in which state actors seek exemption from the rules of private international law on cultural grounds. Globalization has exacerbated anxieties about cultural homogenization,[190] and as a result, many states have resisted and continue to resist the norm of nondiscriminatory open trade in goods and services, particularly cultural goods and services that make up the cultural industries.[191] This position stems from the concern that free trade will result in the erosion or dilution of local cultures, presumably because some goods and services that are freely traded have both economic and cultural values.[192] As already noted, a definitive definition of the word "culture" is not possible[193] either in the abstract or for the purposes of international trade law. For example, the Universal Declaration on Cultural Diversity defines culture as "the set of distinctive spiritual, material, intellectual and emotional features of society or a social group . . . in addition to art and literature, lifestyles, ways of living together, value systems, traditions and beliefs."[194] Culture thus may refer to particular products of art and literature but also to less tangible "ways of life." Conceivably then, "almost any form of international trade or trade policy could reasonably be interpreted as having a cultural

---

[188] States understand that even as they pursue cultural protectionism, the "desire to protect local culture . . . could undermine the wisdom of trade liberalisation in the first place." Tania Voon, Cultural Products and the World Trade Organization 11 (2007).

[189] Paul, *supra* note 120, at 43.

[190] *See,* e.g., Harry Redner, Conserving Cultures: Technology, Globalization, and the Future of Local Cultures 2 (2004).

[191] Cultural industries include "printing, publishing and multimedia, audiovisual, phonographic and cinematographic productions, as well as crafts and design." They may also include "architecture, visual and performing arts, sports, manufacturing of musical instruments, advertising and cultural tourism." UN Educational, Scientific, and Cultural Organization (UNESCO), Culture, Trade and Globalization: Questions and Answers 12 (2000). For a critique of the cultural industry, *see generally* Theodor Adorno & Max Horkheimer, Dialectic of Enlightenment: Philosophical Fragments (Gunzelin Schmid Noerr ed., 2002); Theodor Adorno, The Culture Industry: Selected Essays on Mass Culture 8 (J. M. Bernstein ed., 1st ed. 1991).

[192] *See* David Throsby, Economics and Culture 28–29 (2001). Economic value is rooted in marginal utility, and according to Throsby, it can be measured by the price a person is willing to pay for a good. Cultural value can be understood broadly as "a set of attitudes, beliefs, mores, customs, values, and practices which are common to or shared by any group," or more narrowly as "certain activities . . . and the products . . . which have to do with the intellectual, moral and artistic aspects of human life," *id.* at 4, such as works of the visual, performing, and literary arts. The nature of a product, who produces it, how it is produced and consumed, and how it affects local identity together make up the cultural value of a given product. Tomer Broude, *Taking "Trade and Culture" Seriously: Geographical Indications and Cultural Protection in WTO Law*, 26 U. Pa. J. Int'l Econ. L. 623, 638–42 (2005).

[193] *See* Chapter 1, notes 296–312; *see also supra* note 2.

[194] UNESCO, *Universal Declaration on Cultural Diversity*, 41 I.L.M. 57 (Nov. 2, 2001).

aspect or influence."[195] Indeed, "perceptions rooted in culture are important (and generally omitted) determinants of economic exchange . . . lower bilateral trust leads to less trade between two countries, less portfolio investment, and less direct investment, even after controlling for the characteristics of the two countries."[196] A cultural exception is likely premised on the belief that "cultural products are vehicles for symbolic messages that transcend the products' purely commercial value, such that normal market processes will not be capable of fully capturing their value to society."[197] In addition, "cultural products are essential to the expression of national identity and hence their protection is warranted in the public interest."[198] Accordingly, for countries that favor cultural exceptions, "[j]ust as quarantine laws prohibit the import of disease-bearing plants and animals, so does cultural protection seek to shield the community from infection by foreign cultural influences."[199]

For example, in 1998, Canada convened the first meeting of the International Network on Cultural Policies to forge culture-based exceptions to free trade norms. As then Canadian Culture Minister Sheila Copps declared, "[w]e can't treat culture like any other commodity in the world," presumably because culture "is at the very heart of our national identity."[200] Cultural ministers from seventeen countries declared that "cultural goods and services, including audiovisual means, deserve special treatment, since they reflect national and regional cultural identities."[201] Lionel Jospin, who served as the French prime minister from 1997 to 2002, told the French Parliament that "[w]e want to make our European partners share the simple and fundamental idea that culture cannot be treated like goods."[202] France along with other EU countries and Canada have been at the forefront in the demand for the creation of an explicit cultural exception to the GATT,[203] GATS[204] and other trade liberalization agreements.[205] Such efforts have failed but the

---

195 VOON, *supra* note 188, at 13.

196 Luigi Guiso et al., *Cultural Biases in Economic Exchange?*, 124 Q. J. OF ECON. 1095, 1131 (2009).

197 DAVID THROSBY, THE ECONOMICS OF CULTURAL POLICY 159 (2010).

198 *Id.* at 160.

199 THROSBY, *supra* note 192, at 132.

200 Paul, *supra* note 120, at 37 (internal citation and quotation marks omitted).

201 *Id.*

202 *Id.* at 38 (citing Lionel Jospin, *France Will Be "Inflexible" in Defending Culture at W.T.O.*, AGENCE FRANCE PRESSE (Oct. 12, 1999)). Referring to the doomed Multilateral Agreement on Investment which France opposed unless it contained an explicit cultural exception, Lionel Jospin declared, "I attach an absolute priority to the preservation of our cultural identity as well as that of Europe." VOON, *supra* note 188, at 32 (internal citation and quotation marks omitted). *See also* Article 128 of the European Community Treaty, which states that the European Community must "take cultural aspects into account in its action under other provisions of the Treaty." European Union, *Consolidated Versions of the Treaty on European Union*, European Union Publications Office, Mar. 2010, at 122.

203 General Agreement on Tariffs and Trade, Oct. 30, 1947, 61 Stat. A-11, 55 U.N.T.S. 194 [hereinafter GATT].

204 General Agreement on Trade in Services, Apr. 15, 1994, 1869 U.N.T.S. 183, 33 I.L.M. 1167 (1994) [hereinafter GATS].

205 Paul, *supra* note 120, at 38–39.

issue of whether private international law should contain an explicit cultural exception to free trade norms remains a heated issue.

Efforts to recognize cultural exceptions have been more successful in regional agreements. For example, although Article 87(1) of the EC Treaty prohibits the granting of aid by member States (subsidies) if such aid distorts competition, this prohibition contains an exception for aid designed to "promote culture and heritage conservation."[206] Other state actors, such as Canada and Mexico, have pressed for limits on cultural imports in bilateral and regional agreements with the United States.[207] Canada managed to assert a cultural exception to the norm of open trade in the US-Canadian Free Trade Agreement (US-Canada FTA) and the North American Free Trade Agreement (NAFTA).[208] In 1985, the Canadian Minister of Communications Benoit Bouchard said that "just as retaining our territorial sovereignty is essential if we are to remain an independent nation, so it is true that we must always retain our cultural sovereignty—the absolute right in the eyes of the world to use all the instruments at our disposal."[209]

Canadian concerns about being overwhelmed by American culture resulted in the inclusion of an article in the CFTA which excludes cultural industries from the liberalization requirements of the CFTA.[210] The significance of this exclusion should not be overstated, however, because Articles 2005 to 2007 of the CFTA, incorporated by reference into NAFTA,[211] also contain measures that "offset" the exception and recalibrate the balance in ways acceptable to the United States. For example, there are provisions that eliminate tariffs on cultural imports and mandated fair compensation for foreign investment in a cultural industry if that investment is expropriated. Other provisions require that US copyrights be respected when US television programs were rebroadcasted in Canada. The United States could also retaliate against any Canadian cultural exception by taking measures against Canadian products quantified to be of an equivalent value to the harm suffered by the US cultural industry as a result of the Canadian exception.[212]

Other examples of state actors seeking cultural exceptions to free trade norms abound. "Measures frequently adopted include direct subsidies, import restrictions, tax rebates, screen quotas, licensing restrictions, price fixing, limits on foreign investment and foreign ownership, nationality requirements, domestic content requirements and intellectual

---

[206] European Union, *supra* note 202, at 91–92.

[207] Paul, *supra* note 120, at 39; *see also Americas/NAFTA: In Brief*, 16 Int'l Trade Rep. (BNA) 338 (Feb. 24, 1999).

[208] Canada-United States Free Trade Agreement (CFTA), Can.-US, art. 2005(1), Jan. 2, 1988, 27 I.L.M. 281 [hereinafter CFTA]; *see* North American Free Trade Agreement (NAFTA), US-Can.-Mex., Annex 2106, Dec. 8, 1992, 32 I.L.M. 605 [hereinafter NAFTA].

[209] Paul, *supra* note 120, at 43–44.

[210] CFTA, *supra* note 208, at arts. 2005(1), 2012. Article 2012 defines cultural industries to include the production and distribution of books, periodicals, film, video and audio recordings, radio, television, and cable television.

[211] NAFTA, *supra* note 208.

[212] Voon, *supra* note 188, at 31.

property protection measures."[213] Many subsidize their cultural industry[214] and use tax credits to support it. Canada grants tax credits for Canadian video and film production in Canada. The United Kingdom does the same for investment in UK television and film production. France has a tax on every cinema ticket sold in order to aid French and European filmmaking. Other forms of protection include minimum content quotas. Canada imposes a requirement that "each broadcasting undertaking shall make maximum use, and in no case less than predominant use, of Canadian creative and other resources in the creation and presentation of programming."[215] France has had quotas on film screenings since the 1920s, and its quotas for European and French television programming exceed the requirements of the European Community's Television Without Frontiers Directive.[216] South Korea has imposed restrictions on the import of foreign films, especially Japanese films.[217] Although it has eased up on those controls, South Korea maintains a right to a cultural exception.[218] Although rice is not usually deemed cultural, Japan has protected domestic rice from competition from imports, claiming that rice farming is an ancient cultural tradition.[219] The United States too defends its agricultural subsidies on the grounds that they are necessary to preserve the family farm as an American way of life.[220]

The above is but a sampling of the type of protectionism used by states to support their domestic cultural industry. The former US chair of the Federal Reserve, Alan Greenspan, famously "criticized protectionist proposals as 'leading to an atrophy of our competitive ability, arguing that 'if the protectionist route is followed, newer, more efficient industries will have less scope to expand, and overall output and economic welfare will doubtless suffer.' "[221] What these examples demonstrate, however, is that states pursue objectives that are both protectionist and liberalizing. In the former case, as an exercise in national sovereignty, states declare that certain economic sectors will be exempted

---

213 Peter Van den Bossche, *Free Trade and Culture: A Study of Relevant WTO Rules and Constraints on National Cultural Policy Measures* 6 (Maastricht Faculty of Law Working Paper, No. 2007-4, Apr. 2007), http://papers.ssrn.com/sol3/papers.cfm?abstract_id=979530.

214 Voon, *supra* note 188, at 21.

215 Broadcasting Act 1991 (Canada), s. 3.1(f). Canada requires that "for Canadian conventional, over-the-air broadcasters, Canadian programming make up 60% of television broadcast time, and 50% during the evening hours ... [and] that 35% of 'popular' musical selections broadcast on radio should qualify as 'Canadian' under a government-determined point system." Voon, *supra* note 188, at 20 (internal quotation marks omitted).

216 Voon, *supra* note 188, at 21.

217 *See* Joongi Kim, *The Viability of Screen Quotas in Korea: The Cultural Exception under The International Trade Regime*, 26 Korean J. Int'l & Comp. L. 199, 206 (1998); Karsie Kish, *Protectionism to Promote Culture: South Korea and Japan, A Case Study*, 22 U. Pa. J. Int'l Econ. L. 153, 177–80 (2001).

218 Paul, *supra* note 120, at 39.

219 *See* Chandler H. Udo, *Japanese Rice Protectionism: A Challenge for the Development of Agricultural Trade Laws*, 31 B.C. Int'l & Comp. L. Rev. 169, 173 (2008) ("Domestically produced rice has occupied a central place in Japanese culture for centuries.").

220 Paul, *supra* note 120, at 40.

221 Imad A. Moosa, The US-China Trade Dispute: Facts, Figures and Myths 60 (2012).

from free trade commitments on cultural protectionist grounds. But in the latter case, the private international law system that most states are members of is also one that subscribes to free trade norms. As a result, multilateral trade agreements such as the WTO are against cultural exceptions. As I discuss further below, two points can be made about how private international law manages the nationalist demands for cultural protection. First, in certain instances where member states insist on claiming an exception for cultural *services* (as opposed to products), the WTO accommodates them by allowing them to exercise the option of not placing certain services on a liberalization schedule. But the WTO does not itself contain a cultural exception.[222] In other words, the WTO rejects cultural claims, tries to limit their assertions by states but in deference to member states' sovereignty, allows those states a limited "out" in the area of trade in services. And second, in cases where a state's protectionist measure resting on a claim of cultural exception has been challenged by another state before a GATT panel or a WTO dispute settlement procedure, the latter has ruled against the protectionist state.

To begin with my first point, the Uruguay Round of negotiations struggled between the claim of GATT contracting parties for a cultural exception and the counterclaim exerted by international trade law against such an exception.[223] Take as an example two of the agreements within the WTO, the GATT and the GATS, which establish certain baseline rules reflecting a commitment to nondiscriminatory norms governing the international trade of goods and services. GATT 1947 was only concerned with goods, and the inclusion of services pursuant to the Uruguay Rounds represented a significant expansion of the pre-WTO 1947 GATT regime. Neither the GATT nor GATS explicitly provides for any cultural exception[224] to the norm of nondiscrimination. One can conceivably argue that GATT XX(a) contains an implied cultural exception to GATT free trade requirements because it allows contracting parties to adopt measures to protect "public morals" or to ban imports that offend standards of decency and morality.[225] Article XX (f) provides another general exception to the GATT nondiscrimination principle for measures "imposed for the protection of national treasures of artistic, historic or archaeological value."[226] Although this provision was intended to protect national treasures from the predation of foreign art collectors, one could conceivably interpret the provision to allow states to adopt measures to protect the domestic cultural industries.

---

[222] In addition, as noted, *supra* notes 190–212 and accompanying text, though some bilateral or regional trade agreements (such as the CFTA and NAFTA) might contain cultural exceptions, those exceptions themselves contain clauses that water down their effectiveness.

[223] *See* John Croome, Reshaping the World Trading System: A History of the Uruguay Round 212–15, 243–44, 310–12, 324–27 (2nd rev. ed. 1999).

[224] Cultural goods include tangible products such as videos, books, and sound recordings. Cultural services include intangible products such as broadcasts, film and video distribution rights, and contracts for live artistic performances.

[225] *See* GATT, *supra* note 203, at art. XX(a).

[226] *Id.* at art. XX(f).

However, many commentators believe that Article XX must not be broadly construed because terms like "public morals" and "national treasures" are vague and ambiguous;[227] an expansive reading of Article XX would result in the exceptions swallowing up the rule of nondiscrimination.

The decision to include trade in services reflected international recognition of the high proportion of global trade that involves services[228] but at the same time, GATS liberalization is difficult and complex because barriers to trade in services "relate to fundamental domestic regulatory choices."[229] "The very fact that barriers to trade in services are so heterogeneous and difficult to quantify makes a comprehensive approach to their discipline extremely difficult to conceptualize."[230] Consequently, GATS disciplines are less robust than those for GATT, and accordingly, there is more protectionism in services than in goods, especially in cultural services.[231]

The GATS example illustrates nicely the vacillating tensions between state cultural protectionism and international liberalization. On the one hand, countries such as Austria, Peru, Romania, Canada, Brazil, and the Nordic countries insisted during the Uruguay Rounds on an exception under GATS for the protection of national or cultural values.[232] The European Community saw audiovisual services in particular as needing exemption, and this approach was supported by an array of countries such as Australia, Canada, Chile, Cuba, India, and Sweden, while Brazil, Egypt, and Finland expressed the need for "flexibility" when dealing with audiovisual services.[233] The United States, however, vociferously opposed a general exception for culture as well as a cultural exception for audiovisual services. In the end, no cultural exception was allowed, but "a way out was found through . . . GATS . . . which allows for flexibility in regard to the audio-visual sector."[234]

The European Community and the United States, as the main players during the Uruguay Rounds, settled on a compromise in which the GATS would not recognize audiovisual services as culturally special. "Specifically, members can decide whether or

---

[227] John Jackson, The World Trading System: Law and Policy of International Economic Relations 106–07 (1989); Christoph T. Feddersen, *Focusing on Substantive Law in International Economic Relations: The Public Morals of GATT's Article XX(a) and "Conventional" Rules of Interpretation*, 7 Minn. J. Global Trade 75, 112–14 (1998); John David Donaldson, 20 Fordham J. Int'l L. 90, 156–57 (1996); *cf.* Steve Charnovitz, *The Moral Exception in Trade Policy*, 38 Va. J. Int'l L. 689 (1998).

[228] On the history of GATS, *see* Mary Footer, *The International Regulation of Trade in Services Following Completion of the Uruguay Round*, 29 Int'l Lawyer 453, 460–61 (1995).

[229] Michael J. Trebilcock & Robert Howse, The Regulation of International Trade 476 (2nd ed. 1999).

[230] *Id.*

[231] Voon, *supra* note 188, at 23.

[232] *Id.* at 24.

[233] *Id.*

[234] Throsby, *supra* note 197. Although many countries have not made such commitments to liberalize in order to protect their cultural industries, the restrictions were intended to be temporary.

not to accept commitments with respect to market access, MFN [Most Favored Nation] and national treatment provisions in relation to particular services traded."[235] Member states can choose to not commit to extend GATS discipline to audiovisual services. This means audiovisual services do not have to be included in the schedule of GATS commitments to liberalize.[236] As a result, in stark contrast to the GATT framework, which imposes national treatment discipline and eliminates quantitative restrictions across the board, subject to specified exceptions,[237] the "GATS framework primarily involves a 'bottom up' or 'positive list' approach, with Members choosing the service sectors in which they are willing to make national treatment or market access commitments."[238] Thus, states can refuse to liberalize but private international law (the GATS) would not acknowledge the special cultural character of audiovisual services either nor does it create a cultural exception. In essence, "cultural services have neither been expressly excluded nor included under the national treatment provisions of GATS."[239] States thus retain the right to not commit to liberalize for cultural grounds or for any other grounds.[240]

At the same time, however, it is understood that liberalization remains a stated goal of member states. Article XIX:1 of GATS states that members are to enter into rounds of negotiations to achieve higher levels of liberalization.[241] Established to monitor GATS compliance, the Special Session of the Council for Trade in Services adopted guidelines for successive rounds of services negotiations, including an agreement which stated that "[t]here shall be no a priori exclusion of any service sector,"[242] and consequently, "the audiovisual sector is open to negotiation like any other."[243] Such negotiations have in fact been incorporated into the Doha Development Agenda.[244] The main point is that despite concessions to state demands for cultural protectionism, private international law

---

[235] *Id.; see also* VOON, *supra* note 188, at 25 (describing how member states exempted audiovisual services from MFN treatment and how few states scheduled commitments to grant national treatment or market access in the audiovisual sector).

[236] GATS applies MFN and national treatment to international trade in services. *See* GATS, *supra* note 204, at arts. II, XVI XVII, and XIX. GATS' MFN obligation applies to services generally but the national treatment obligation applies only where members have agreed to be bound by making specific commitments in the Schedules. *See also* TREBILCOCK & HOWSE, *supra* note 229, at 286–89.

[237] VOON, *supra* note 188, at 225. Under the GATT agreement, "national treatment and quantitative restrictions apply across the board, subject to specified exceptions. This is more of a 'top-down' or 'negative list' approach." *Id.*

[238] *Id.*

[239] Paul, *supra* note 120, at 36; *see also* THROSBY, *supra* note 197.

[240] For the general obligations such as MFN that apply even to unscheduled sectors, the GATS allows states to file reservations. TREBILCOCK & HOWSE, *supra* note 229, at 290.

[241] VOON, *supra* note 188, at 28. Although many countries have not subjected their audiovisual sectors to national treatment, it is understood that restrictions were intended to be temporary. Paul, *supra* note 120, at 32.

[242] VOON, *supra* note 188, at 28 (internal citation and quotation marks omitted).

[243] *Id.*

[244] Doha negotiations have revealed differences among states as well, with Australia, Brazil, and Switzerland favoring special treatment of services on cultural grounds and the United States and Japan favoring increasing GATS discipline in the area. Chinese Taipei, Hong Kong, Japan, Mexico, and the United States formally

remains committed in the long run to what it deems to be free trade undistorted by cultural claims.

With respect to my second point, in cases where challenges have been made by one or more states against another state protection of its cultural industry, the GATT (as opposed to GATS) and the WTO have held in favor of the challenging states. In *Japan-Leather II* (US),[245] a case brought under GATT 1947, Japan defended a law that restricted the importation of certain leather products into Japan by a system of import quotas and import licenses. Japan sought to retain its system against US complaint[246] of an Article XI prohibition against quantitative restrictions on the grounds that import restrictions were needed to defend a cultural minority community, the Dowa, deemed to be the lowest social class in Japan since the early seventeenth century. The Dowa were segregated and restricted to work in "traditional Dowa industries such as the tanning industry,"[247] which is inefficient and uncompetitive and thus needed state protection.[248] Japanese argument rested on cultural grounds—as noted, "Japan contended that without import quotas, the Dowa leather industry would collapse causing severe social and economic dislocation to this oppressed minority community and destroying traditional Dowa culture."[249] Japan framed its protectionism as follows: "This was a most serious and important social problem deriving from the fact that a segment of the Japanese people, owing to discrimination based on a class system formed in the process of the historical development of Japanese society, was placed in an inferior position economically, socially and culturally."[250] Indeed, scholars have observed that Japan's defense of import quotas "could be framed more specifically as measures designed to preserve a threatened culture or way of life."[251]

The GATT Panel concluded, however, that the "special historical, cultural and socio-economic circumstances referred to by Japan could not be taken into account by [the Panel] ... since its terms of reference were to examine the matter 'in the light of the

---

declared in June 2005 "concern over efforts by some key participants in the negotiations to create an a priori exclusion for such an important sector." *Id.* at 28–29.

[245] Panel Report, *Panel on Japanese Measures on Imports of Leather*, L/5623–31S/94 (Mar. 2, 1984) [hereinafter Panel Report—*Japanese Leather*]; *see also* VOON, *supra* note 188, at 13; Paul, *supra* note 120, at 52–53.

[246] The United States was joined by Australia, the European Communities, India, New Zealand, and Pakistan as exporters of leather to Japan. *Id.* at ¶¶ 2–4.

[247] VOON, *supra* note 188, at 13.

[248] Japan described the problem as follows. The Dowa minority resided in segregated districts characterized by persistent problems "relating to subsistence and survival. The Japanese tanning industry, which was a traditional and symbolic industry for the population in question, consisted of approximately 1,300 enterprises employing directly about 12,000 workers, with over 80 per cent of the concerns employing not more than nine workers. Its technological level was low, and it mostly depended on overseas raw hides. As a result its international competitiveness was considerably inferior to United States' companies." Panel Report—*Japanese Leather, supra* note 245, at ¶ 22.

[249] Paul, *supra* note 120, at 52.

[250] Panel Report—*Japanese Leather, supra* note 245, at ¶ 21(i).

[251] VOON, *supra* note 188, at 13.

relevant GATT provisions' and these provisions did not provide such a justification for import restrictions."[252]

The Panel thus ruled that Japan should end its import quotas.

Japan made another culture-based argument in a similar dispute concerning the labeling and taxing of imported wines and spirits.[253] Japan divided distilled liquors into different classifications—shochu, whiskey, or spirits (including vodka, gin, and rum) and applied different excise tax rates for different classifications. The different excise categories resulted in lower taxes on traditional Japanese drinks like sake, mirin, and shochu, despite the fact that the Japanese drinks were similar to European spirits in content and production.[254] The European Community argued that European distilled spirits were "like" or "directly competitive" with traditional Japanese alcoholic beverages and should be granted national treatment as required by GATT Article III.[255] Japan, however, claimed that Japanese consumers regard shochu as different from spirits, and thus shochu was not a "like product" when compared against imported spirits. Japan's argument rested on the claim that in determining whether a product is like or directly competitive with another, the Panel should consider not just price or physical properties, such as alcoholic content, but also image and patterns of consumption.[256]

The Panel concluded that there was likeness between Japanese shochu and imported spirits, based on the product's end uses, the product's properties, nature, and quality, objective criteria such as manufacturing and composition processes of the products, and recognition of such likeness by governments for purposes of tariff and statistical nomenclature.[257] Although consumer perspectives and preferences can be relevant for determining likeness between two products, the Panel cautioned that "'like' products do not become 'unlike' merely because of differences in local consumer traditions within a country. . . ."[258] As a result, it found that "consumer habits are variable in time and space and the aim of Article III:2 of ensuring neutrality of internal taxation as regards competition between imported and domestic like products could not be achieved if differential taxes could be used to crystallize consumer preferences for traditional domestic

---

[252] Panel Report—*Japanese Leather, supra* note 245, at ¶ 44; *see also* Paul, *supra* note 120, at 53.

[253] Panel Report, *Japan—Customs Duties, Taxes and Labeling Practices on Imported Wines and Alcoholic Beverages*, ¶¶ 1.1–1.3, L/6216–34S/83 (Nov. 10, 1987) [hereinafter Panel Report—*JAPAN*]. The Panel's conclusions were affirmed by the WTO Appellate Body. Appellate Body Report, *Japan—Taxes on Alcoholic Beverages*, WT/DS8/AB/R (Sept. 25, 1996) [hereinafter Appellate Report—*Japan*].

[254] Panel Report—*Japan, supra* note 253, at¶ 3.2.

[255] *Id* at ¶ 3.2(a)—(g) (The complaint stated that the Japanese liquor tax system violated the first sentence of Article III:2 because it taxed imports at higher tax rates than "like" domestic products; and the second sentence of Article III:2 by affording protection to "directly competitive or substitutable [domestic] products").

[256] *Id.* at ¶ 3.12.

[257] *Id.* at ¶ 5.7 (also finding that even if imported spirits such as vodka were considered to be not "like" Japanese alcoholic beverages, such as shochu, there was direct competition or substitutability between imported and Japan-made distilled liquors).

[258] *Id.* at ¶ 5.9(b).

products...."[259] Thus, "the traditional Japanese consumer habits with regard to shochu provided no reason for not considering vodka to be a 'like' product."[260]

Indeed, in a related report in which the WTO was called upon to make a product determination also involving alcoholic beverages, it found that "[f]actors such as differences in prices between the products or differences in local consumer traditions within a country have been found irrelevant for a 'like product' determination. The notion of 'like products' is an objective one, exclusively related to the characteristics of the products." Citing with approval the 1987 GATT Panel's findings discussed above, the WTO observed that the "numerous categories and sub-categories created by Japan's scheme for taxing alcoholic beverages were based on a distinction between 'traditional' and 'Western-style' beverages."[261] "Japanese products had been differentiated for tax purposes as carefully defined separate product categories on the pretext of their traditional character. As a result, 'traditional' had become virtually synonymous for 'domestic.'"[262] In essence, then, this case can be understood as one where Japan's tax differentials were struck down as GATT inconsistent because the Panel refused to recognize Japan's culture or tradition-based claim.

As I have already observed, besides the GATT and GATS, states may also claim a cultural exception to the norm of nondiscrimination in trade under other trade agreements, such as the US-Canada FTA and NAFTA. For years, the Canadian government has worried that the inundation of US news and magazines threatens Canadian sense of national identity.[263] Canada responded by restricting the publication of "split-run magazines" marketed in Canada, that is, imposing an 80 percent excise tax on advertising in split-run editions of a periodical.[264] The United States asserted that the differential tax treatment violated the National Treatment obligation of Article III:2 of the GATT because it discriminated between two "like" products—domestic non-split-run periodicals and imported split-run periodicals. The United States additionally argued that imported split-run magazines were also, at the very least, "directly competitive or substitutable" goods and that Article III(2), second sentence, prohibited states from applying internal taxes to imported products in a way as to afford protection to domestic production.

Canada, on the other hand, argued that the distinguishing feature of magazines was their intellectual content, and as such, intellectual content should be the most important characteristic for determining "like products." For Canada, the end use of a magazine was the

---

259 *Id.* at ¶ 5.7.

260 *Id.*

261 Appellate Report—*Japan, supra* note 253, at ¶¶ 4.21, 4.29.

262 *Id.* at ¶ 4.29.

263 Canadian data shows that in 1998, foreign magazines, especially US magazines, represented 81.4 percent of all newsstand circulation. Panel Report, *Canada--Certain Measures Concerning Periodicals*, ¶ 3.29, WT/DS 31/R (Mar. 14, 1997) [hereinafter Panel Report—*Canada*]; Appellate Body Report, *Canada—Certain Measures Concerning Periodicals*, WT/DS31/AB/R (June 30, 1997) [hereinafter Appellate Report—*Canada*].

264 A split-run magazine has essentially the same content as the foreign publication, but also has advertisements aimed at the Canadian market. Panel Report—*Canada, supra* note 263, at ¶ 3.30.

transmission of ideas and culture,[265] and consequently, magazines were not like any other commodities. The United States disagreed, arguing that end use, consumer tastes, and physical properties were also relevant. According to the United States, the end use of a magazine lay in its market appeal, which encompassed more than intellectual content and included a magazine's style, frequency, appearance, paper, size, texture, type, thickness, even scent.[266]

As scholars have noted, "this disagreement mirrored an underlying value difference between the United States and Canada; in the view of the United States, there was no essential difference between cultural commodities like magazines or books and other commodities. . . ."[267] Canada favored special treatment for cultural goods, specifically, exclusion of culture from free trade norms. "By insisting that cultural goods have no equivalent import, Canada denied that culture could be commodified."[268] The US response was that the GATT allowed only quantitative restrictions on foreign film, pursuant to GATT Article IV.[269] It is generally understood that "[i]n GATT, there is no exception for cultural policy as such."[270]

From the US point of view, if the Canadian position had been accepted by the Panel, that is, that a product's character should be assessed by reference to its cultural or intellectual content, "then no two cultural products could ever be truly 'like products,' and correspondingly, GATT Article III national treatment would never apply to cultural goods. Canada's argument in principle would exempt all cultural imports from the GATT,"[271] in essence creating an implied cultural exception to the GATT.

Despite its assertion that "the ability of any Member to take measures to protect its cultural identity was not at issue in the present case,"[272] the Panel held that imported split-run periodicals and domestic non-split-run periodicals were "like products,"[273] and as a result, the Canadian excise tax on the imported product violated the national treatment principle. On appeal, the Appellate Body upheld the US complaint but voided the Panel's findings that the two products at issue were like products, finding instead that split-run and domestic periodicals were directly competitive or substitutable products for purposes of the second sentence of GATT Article III(2).[274]

---

265 *Id.* at ¶¶ 3.61, 3.68.

266 *Id.* at ¶¶ 3.64–3.70, 3.78.

267 Paul, *supra* note 120, at 48; Panel Report—*Canada, supra* note 263, at ¶¶ 3.66–3.85.

268 Paul, *supra* note 120, at 48.

269 Trebilcock & Howse, *supra* note 229, at 697 (noting that GATT Article IV "specifically allows for 'screen quotas', thereby exempting from GATT discipline a practice (typical in Europe at the time) of requiring that screen time be shared between domestic and imported films.").

270 *Id.*

271 Paul, *supra* note 120, at 48.

272 Panel Report—*Canada, supra* note 263, at ¶ 5.45.

273 *Id.* at ¶ 5.26.

274 Appellate Report—*Canada, supra* note 263, at 32. The Appellate Body also concluded that the intent behind the Canadian excise tax was to "afford protection to the production of Canadian periodicals" because of the magnitude of dissimilar taxation. *Id.*

Although both the Panel and the Appellate Body addressed the controversy through a technocratic framework of "like product" and "competitive or substitutable" product analysis, the underlying significance of the case lies in the fact that both bodies rejected the Canadian claim that cultural goods should be exempt from GATT national treatment requirements. Embedded in and intertwined with the technocratic rhetoric of the likeness or nonlikeness of two products is a claim of cultural sovereignty on Canada's part and a rejection of such claim by the GATT system. As one scholar has observed, "[i]n rejecting Canada's defense to restraints on cultural imports, the [WTO] implied that Canada's true motivation was economic protectionism masquerading as cultural. . . . [C]ultural exceptions to trade fail in part because they are tainted by economic interests."[275] Private international law establishes rules that facilitate globalization. "[T]he international community distinguishes between rationality arguments and non-rationality arguments. The community does not tolerate interference in the rationality of the market by non-rationality considerations like culture."[276]

As I have explained elsewhere, the international economic system assumes a "normal" framework of rational economic activities.[277] The norms of free trade, for example, Most Favored Nation (now termed Normal Trade Relations) and national treatment, "seem perfectly neutral and have been instrumental in the establishment of a relatively predictable rule-oriented economic order."[278] "The whole legal structure of the free trade norm rests on a rational economic model. When governments grant concessions to foreign imports, they defend the cost to domestic import-competitors by invoking the rationality of free trade. Cultural claims threaten that rationality argument. Cultural claims derive from sentiment, nostalgia, insecurity; they are rooted in non-rationality. To protect the rationality of the market from the non-rationality of nationalism and culture, the international community rejects cultural exceptions."[279]

As a result, because the unstated but implicit objective of private international law is to govern, so to speak, "from a space beyond culture,"[280] it has either (1) opposed cultural

---

[275] Paul, *supra* note 120, at 43.

[276] *Id.* at 78.

[277] "According to the classical liberal model, once a market is birthed, its progression is marked by a tendency toward autonomy and normality and away from the irrational constraints of nonmarket structures. The assumption is that even though economic activities in premarket societies are heavily influenced by and embedded in social relations, with modernization, the market has the capacity to be an autonomous sphere defined less by social and political relations than by the self-interested calculations of rational economic behaviors." Lan Cao, *Towards a New Sensibility for International Economic Development*, 32 TEXAS J. INT'L. L. 209, 252 (1997); *see* Daniel K. Tarullo, *Beyond Normalcy in the Regulation of International Trade*, 100 HARV. L. REV. 546, 549 (1987); Joel R. Paul, *Free Trade, Regulatory Competition and the Autonomous Market Fallacy*, 1 COLUM. J. EUR. L. 29, 33–38 (1994).

[278] Cao, *supra* note 277, at 253.

[279] Paul, *supra* note 120, at 80.

[280] Kennedy, *supra* note 59, at 82; *see also* KENNEDY, *supra* note 137, at 126 ("[C]ommon but mistaken ideas—like the idea that international governance is separate from both the global market and from local culture, or is

exceptions that water down international trade rules (whether in the GATS and the GATT) as my discussion above reveals, or (2) affirmatively created rules to allow commercial actors to opt out of the parochialism of national systems. In the preceding sections, I have described the first instance in which states may assert a claim of cultural sovereignty but private international law may refuse to recognize such claims, revealing an ongoing tug of war between nationalism and internationalism in the economic sphere. In the second instance, to be described below, private international law goes even further to avoid nationalist assertions by establishing rules that allow global economic actors to opt out of national rules in favor of international commercial rules instead. Indeed, both instances can be understood as an attempt by private international law to establish a baseline of—from the point of view of private international law—rational rules that should not be hijacked by nationalistic and cultural exemptions.

In the rest of this section, I explore how private international law has crafted mechanisms to allow market players to sidestep the national and avoid what it deems to be the prejudices of national rules. Indeed, opting out of national systems can be viewed as opting out of the peculiarities of the local—and the whole bundle of what the local encompasses—state rules, national norms, cultures.[281] Unlike public international law, whose sensibility is centered around state actors, private international law is centered around "economic and social actors operating across borders . . ."[282] whose interests transcend national boundaries.

There are many reasons why private commercial actors may desire an opt-out option. As I have discussed elsewhere,[283] the free trade model, for example, is founded on the notion that lower barriers to economic transactions enhance national and international welfare. However, entrenched domestic interests such as inefficient domestic producers threatened by free trade will mobilize themselves and other affected constituencies to oppose, "through 'misdirection and obfuscation,'"[284] the lowering of such barriers. Political leaders are more likely to be captured by producer interests than consumer interests because producers "tend to mobilize for elections."[285] "The frequent xenophobia ('we' versus 'they'), mercantilist thinking ('exports are good, imports are bad') and other double standards in foreign policy-making (e.g., liberalization of domestic trade, protectionism vis-à-vis foreign trade) make it easy for politicians to present foreign policy measures as being in the 'national interest,' even if they reduce national consumer welfare."[286] Under these

---

more a matter of public than of private law—sharply narrow the sense among foreign policy professionals of what is possible and appropriate for foreign policy.").

281 Gary Born, International Commercial Arbitration 72 (2009).

282 Anne-Marie Slaughter, *International Law in a World of Liberal States*, 6 Eur. J. Int'l L. 503, 518 (1995).

283 Cao, *supra* note 277, at 263.

284 Shell, *supra* note 180, at 880–81.

285 *Id.* at 880.

286 Ernst-Ulrich Petersmann, *Constitutionalism and International Organizations*, 17 NW. J. Int'l L. & Bus. 398, 410–11 (1997).

circumstances, private international law has come up with various ways to accommodate commercial actors' need to bypass national systems likely to be captured by entrenched protectionist interests.

Without doubt, the trend in private international law has been to create a system that is separate from "positive law in state-based jurisdictions."[287] This preference for "private law-making is also evidence of a growing autonomous global legal culture that is truly independent of any national sovereign. . . . The implications for transnational law and global governance is that, in the absence of a supranational legislator, the participants themselves, the international merchants and bankers, are needed—indeed, required—to determine their own legal norms."[288]

Indeed, one way of opting out of troublesome national systems is to turn to voluntary norms of governance—characterized by Robert Cooter as the "new law merchant"—which can be understood as a set of rules promulgated by self-regulating economic associations[289] to regulate member behavior. Whereas public international law is preoccupied with sovereignty and territoriality, private international law can, where mandatory laws are not at issue, choose "a decentralized network of self-selected and customized rules,"[290] allowing private actors to opt out of state law and opt into private law.

Another way private international law accommodates economic actors' anxieties about the messiness of national culture and politics is through trade rules, or what one scholar termed "trade legalism" established to "overcome . . . political failure . . . ."[291] The private international law system "views international trade laws and tribunals as devices by which governments and businesses that favor free trade may circumvent domestic protectionist groups and increase the world's wealth. The mechanisms used to accomplish these goals are efficiency-enhancing international legal rules capable of trumping municipal laws and international trade tribunals that can supplant meddlesome domestic courts and

---

287 Peter J. Mazzacano, *Force Majeure, Impossibility, Frustration & the Like: Excuses for Non-Performance; the Historical Origins and Development of an Autonomous Commercial Norm in the CISG*, Nordic J. Commercial L., Issue 2011, Number 2, at 1.

288 *Id.*

289 Robert Cooter, *Structural Adjudication and the New Law Merchant: A Model of Decentralized Law*, 14 Int'l. Rev. L. & Econ. 215, 216 (1994) ("The modern economy creates many specialized business communities. . . . Self-regulating professions, like law and accounting, and formal networks, like Visa, promulgate their own rules. Voluntary associations, like the Association of Home Appliance Manufacturers, issue guidelines. Informal networks, such as the computer software manufacturers, have inchoate ethical standards. I refer to all such norms of business communities as the *new law merchant*." (internal citations omitted)); Paul Schiff Berman, *The Globalization of Jurisdiction*, 151 U. Pa. L. Rev. 311, 505–06 (2002) (describing the proliferation of nongovernmental standard-setting bodies, from the Motion Picture Association of America (which rates the content of films) to trade associations such as the National Association of Securities Dealers with the power to establish "detailed normative systems with the effect of law.").

Moreover, as others have also noted, "the norms [private actors] articulate often seep into the decisions of state legal institutions. The most obvious example of state law's recognition of non-state lawmaking is in the common law's ongoing incorporation of social custom and practice." *Id.* at 506.

290 Slaughter, *supra* note 282, at 518.

291 Shell, *supra* note 180, at 880.

agencies."[292] Indeed, commercial actors would favor "internationally developed free trade norms becoming the 'rule of law' for individual states by giving these norms direct legal effect in domestic courts and by making the awards of international tribunals convertible into domestic court judgments with only minimal substantive scrutiny."[293]

Take international dispute resolution, for example. Private international law establishes an array of commercial dispute resolution mechanisms "to reduce the legal transaction costs imposed on global businesses by nation-states. . . ."[294] Article 19 of NAFTA[295] establishes a binding arbitration system "accessible directly by private business parties through which businesses may overturn final anti-dumping and countervailing duty decisions of domestic trade regulators."[296] The World Bank's International Center for the Settlement of Investment Disputes[297] (ICSID) allows private parties to force states into arbitration whereby states must agree to "recognize an award rendered pursuant to [the] Convention as binding and enforce the pecuniary obligations imposed by that award within its territories as if it were a final judgment of a court in that State"[298]—without regard even to "public policy" exceptions available in other international arbitration systems. "In essence, ICSID permits private business creditors to obtain virtually automatic collection of awards against state debtors using debtor nations' own courts . . ."[299]

Similarly, under the Convention on the Recognition and Enforcement of Foreign Arbitral Award (the New York Convention), businesses can obtain recognition and enforcement of foreign arbitral awards subject only to minimal standards of judicial review by state domestic courts. Consequently, "[t]he international commercial arbitration system has become increasingly free of state regulation. . . ."[300] In the United States, such opting out of national systems and opting into private arbitration is allowed even in cases that are governed by the antitrust and securities laws of the United States.[301] "Such jurisdiction effectively 'privatizes' these public regulatory schemes by taking them out

---

292 *Id.* at 885.

293 *Id.; see also* Ernst-Ulrich Petersmann, *Strengthening the Domestic Legal Framework of the GATT Multilateral Trade System: Possibilities and Problems of Making GATT Rules Effective in Domestic Legal Systems*, *in* E. U. Peterstmann & M. Hilf (eds.), The New Gatt Round of Multilateral Trade Negotiations: Legal and Economic Relations 33–113 (urging national courts to interpret laws in a way that are GATT-conforming).

294 Shell, *supra* note 180, at 886.

295 NAFTA, *supra* note 208, at art. 1904(5).

296 Shell, *supra* note 180, at 887.

297 Convention on the Settlement of Investment Disputes Between States and Nationals of Other States, Aug. 27, 1965, 17 U.S.T. 1270, 575 U.N.T.S. 159.

298 *Id.* at art. 54(1).

299 Shell, *supra* note 180, at 889–90.

300 *Id.* at 888.

301 Mitsubishi Motors Corp. v. Soler Chrysler-Plymouth, Inc., 473 U.S. 614, 638–40 (1985) (holding that federal antitrust claims are arbitrable by international arbitrators); Scherk v. Alberto-Culver Co., 417 U.S. 506, 513, 519–20 (1974) (holding that claims under the 1934 Securities Exchange Act are arbitrable by international arbitrators).

of the hands of domestic judges and placing them in the hands of ad hoc international adjudicators."[302]

For business actors, the benefits of international commercial arbitration are striking. "Three out of four top lawyers at multinational companies would prefer to settle cross-border commercial disputes by arbitration rather than litigation, because of the vagaries of local courts. Key reasons put forward in favour of international arbitration . . . include more flexible procedures; the lack of publicity surrounding hearings; and the better chances of enforcing any awards made by an arbitration panel."[303] Furthermore, arbitration "affords the parties autonomy to tailor the proceedings to meet their needs. From a pragmatic standpoint, arbitral awards are easier to enforce than judgments from foreign state courts. In practice, businesses will be more likely to invest when there are reliable means available to recover losses for improper conduct."[304]

Perhaps most importantly, the need for a neutral forum in case of dispute is often an important precursor to doing business at all. "The real or imagined bias of host country judges can create an anxiety that inhibits wealth-creating transactions and discourages cross-border economic cooperation, and will inevitably either thwart cross-border economic cooperation or add to its cost."[305] Indeed, one of the primary benefits and "central objectives of international arbitration agreements is to provide a neutral forum for dispute resolution, detached from either of the parties or their respective home state governments.[306] Often, "[t]he government that hosts an international transaction or is a party to it, is ordinarily, unwilling to subject itself to the jurisdiction of the national courts of the foreign investor. Hence the need for a neutral forum, which modern international commercial arbitration provides."[307]

This neutrality is achieved in a number of ways, but primarily through the mutual selection of the arbitrators. "An essential aspect of . . . international arbitration is the composition of the arbitral tribunal. International arbitration permits the parties to play a substantial role in selecting the members of the tribunal, including the right to choose a sole or presiding arbitrator whose nationality is almost always different from that of the parties involved (thus reducing the risks of partiality or parochial prejudice)."[308]

There are many reasons why states would opt to facilitate (rather than hinder) individual choice (such as choice of forum and choice of law) in international business

---

[302] Shell, *supra* note 180, at 889.

[303] Nikki Tait, *Arbitration Preferred in Cross-border Disputes*, FINANCIAL TIMES (May 16, 2006), http://www.ft.com/intl/cms/s/0/5c00802c-e4f9-11da-8ode-0000779e2340.html.

[304] Jeffrey T. Cook, *The Evolution of Investment-State Dispute Resolution in NAFTA and CAFTA: Wild West to World Order*, 34 PEPP. L. REV. 1085, 1095 (2007).

[305] Guillermo Aguilar Alvarez & William W. Park, *The New Face of Investment Arbitration: NAFTA Chapter 11*, 28 YALE J. INT'L L. 365 (2003).

[306] BORN, *supra* note 281.

[307] W. Michael Reisman, *Reflections on Economic Development, National Sovereignty and International Arbitration*, Apr. 13, 2006, at 14.

[308] BORN, *supra* note 281, at 73.

transactions, but it is clear that those states "wishing to promote and facilitate commercial arbitration authorize their domestic courts both to compel arbitration at the request of one of the parties to the arbitral agreement and to enforce the ensuing award."[309] Indeed, the US Supreme Court has recognized that "[m]uch uncertainty and possibly great inconvenience to both parties could arise if a suit could be maintained in any jurisdiction [where personal jurisdiction could be established] . . . The elimination of all such uncertainties by agreeing in advance on a forum acceptable to both parties is an indispensable element in international trade, commerce, and contracting."[310]

What the NAFTA, ICSID, and New York Convention examples demonstrate is that private international law allows parties their own choice of law and choice of forum clauses in commercial disputes[311] precisely so they do not have to deal with national courts. Although it is true that commercial actors can choose either judicial or arbitral fora, the disadvantages of national courts are well known. As one scholar observed, "the quality of justice in local courts differs dramatically."[312]

Equally, the litigation procedures used in national courts are often ill-suited for both the resolution of international commercial disputes and the tailoring of procedures to particular parties and disputes.[313] For example, "[t]he domestic judicial system of the United Kingdom obviously has highly dissimilar competencies and capacities than the domestic institutions of Afghanistan or Liberia."[314] Private international law has expressed considerable dissatisfaction with the many inadequacies of national or local systems, "creat[ing] pressure for international law to offer a 'complete' system of rights rather than a set of interstitial supplements to domestic norms. What we need is a way to enable international law to continue its civilizing project in areas where domestic law fails to offer adequate protections. . . ."[315]

As a result, international commercial arbitration is especially appealing because it essentially allows commercial actors to "write their own rules of procedure governing the dispute resolution process."[316] Under such circumstances, "official legal actors . . . delegate lawmaking authority to non-state entities or recognize the efficacy of non-state norms. For

---

[309] Slaughter, *supra* note 282, at 519.

[310] M/S Bremen v. Zapata Off-Shore Co., 407 U.S. 1, 13–14 (1972).

[311] "Participants are free to choose the product of one legislature and the procedures and competence of another tribunal. A contract might thus specify that disputes will be tried in London under New York law. The resulting freedom and flexibility is particularly important for the efficient functioning of market economies." Slaughter, *supra* note 282, at 518.

[312] Ernest A. Young, *Institutional Settlement in a Globalizing Judicial System*, 54 Duke L.J. 1143, 1213 (2005) (citation omitted).

[313] Born, *supra* note 281, at 2–3.

[314] Young, *supra* note 312 (citation omitted); *see id.* ("As William Burke-White has observed, 'the quality of justice in local courts differs dramatically.'" (quoting William W. Burke-White, *A Community of Courts: Toward a System of International Criminal Law Enforcement*, 24 Mich. J. Int'l. L. 1, 16 (2002)).

[315] *Id.* at 1205.

[316] Slaughter, *supra* note 282, at 519.

example, commercial litigation, particularly in the international arena, increasingly takes place before non-state arbitral panels"[317] using "an independent body of law developed by international commercial arbitrators on the basis of customary transnational business practice."[318] Commentators have described the rise of international economic arbitration as the attempt by private international law to develop "in appropriate cases, a *jus gentium* or *lex mercatoria* of a new type, *free of the contingencies and prejudices* which dominate the scene in the various States."[319] The rise in reliance on arbitration by transnational economic actors and the willing accommodation, indeed, promotion, in private international law of this phenomenon has been bluntly explained this way: "[W]hen parties request that arbitrators adjudicate their dispute in accordance with international law or with the general principles of law, their intention is to escape from the national systems of law."[320]

Although the body of law created by this network of arbitrators "has no more status than voluntary norms developed and adopted by professional associations,"[321] together, both form a sort of new business custom that are significant for commercial actors who might be concerned about subjecting their transnational transaction to what they fear might be a morass of idiosyncratic national laws. Indeed, as Anne-Marie Slaughter aptly described the state of private international law, "the law of transnational society has been presented as essentially stateless."[322] Of course it is important not to overstate the case, for the law of transnational society is stateless only because states themselves allow it. As Professor Slaughter herself observed, "the availability of judicial enforcement—the coercive apparatus of the State—undergirds the entire system of international commercial arbitration."[323] Indeed, states themselves are complicit in the privatization of private international law because states agree to facilitate individual choice, even if that choice is one that bypasses state law. Again, the important subtext is that states are both pulled by nationalism and internationalism, exhibiting nationalist propensities that they themselves wish to be disciplined through the rules of private international law.

"In sum, the advantages of arbitration are a level litigation playing field where rules of an impartial institution can be applied by a relatively neutral tribunal convened in a mutually accessible country . . . in a common language according to rules that give neither side an undue advantage."[324] This framework "enables private and public actors from diverse jurisdictions to cooperatively resolve deep-seated and complex international disputes in a neutral, durable, and satisfactory manner."[325]

---

317 Berman, *supra* note 289, at 505.
318 Slaughter, *supra* note 282, at 519.
319 Rene David, Arbitration in International Trade 3 (1985) (emphasis added).
320 *Id.* at 350–51.
321 Slaughter, *supra* note 282, at 519.
322 *Id.*
323 *Id.*
324 Cook, *supra* note 304.
325 Born, *supra* note 281, at 2.

In the immediate sections below, I focus on several examples drawn from NAFTA arbitration to demonstrate how private commercial actors have used NAFTA arbitration to challenge acts of national governments or decisions of national courts that the private actors believe violate NAFTA, demonstrating again that private international law views national systems as culturally and politically bound and hence potentially problematic. Chapter 11 of NAFTA allows individuals and corporations to institute claims with arbitration tribunals (rather than national courts) if a state party is alleged to have expropriated the complainant's property.[326] Even more startling is the fact that the complainant need not first seek authorization from a NAFTA Commission or the Canadian, Mexican, or US governments; indeed, because there is no appeals mechanism, the complainant can force state parties into binding arbitration.[327] Arbitration panels are permitted to award the complainant monetary damages if they find that the state party was in violation of NAFTA's investment provisions.

Undoubtedly, there is a strong, built-in preference for vigorous enforcement of NAFTA's trade investment provisions.[328] Through Chapter 11 arbitration, private commercial actors have won large monetary settlements against host governments over regulatory takings challenges to government land use and environmental regulations.[329] This has led some to fear that NAFTA expropriation provisions are being interpreted by private arbitrators to nullify standard exercises of state power to protect public health, welfare, and the environment. Indeed, as one commentator observed, NAFTA's Chapter 11 "hamstrings traditional state police power actions by providing foreign investors with a secret forum where significant monetary relief can be sought under a theory that state action indirectly 'expropriated' their investment"[330] and as such "might be the most significant evisceration of state police power since the Supreme Court freed the states from Lochner's shackles in 1937."[331] From the perspective of private international law, however, the very arbitration mechanism that some bemoan because it empowers private arbitrators to strike down public regulation is in fact the very feature that makes

---

[326] NAFTA, *supra* note 208.

[327] Investor claims against a host-country government under Chapter 11's investor-state dispute mechanism "require neither the participation nor acquiescence of the investor's home-country government. By giving standing to individual foreign investors, the [procedure] bypasses the traditional requirement under international law that the grievances of foreign investors be brought on their behalf by their home-country governments." Vicki Been & Joel C. Beauvais, *The Global Fifth Amendment? NAFTA's Investment Protections and the Misguided Quest for the International "Regulatory Takings" Doctrine*, 78 N.Y.U. L. Rev. 30, 44–45 (2003).

[328] Paul S. Kibel, *Awkward Evolution: Citizen Enforcement at the North American Environmental Commission*, 32 Envtl. L. Rep. (Envtl. L. Inst.) 10769, 10775 (2002) (noting that enforcement mechanism under NAFTA's trade-investment provisions is more stringent than enforcement mechanism under NAFTA's environmental law provisions).

[329] *Id.*

[330] Steve Louthan, *A Brave New* Lochner *Era? The Constitutionality of NAFTA Chapter 11*, 34 Vand. J. Transnat'l L. 1443, 1446 (2001) (footnote omitted).

[331] *Id.* at 1445.

private arbitration valuable, precisely because it allows private parties to escape the perceived irrationality, overregulation, and prejudices of the national.

Concern about the judicial system of Mexico in particular is one reason for the establishment of NAFTA's robust dispute resolution. Chapter 11 contains "a powerful cause of action and an exact compensation structure because of fears arising from the perceived instability of Mexican politics and the 'Calvo clause' of the Mexican Constitution."[332] Given past invocation by the Mexican government of the Calvo clause to expropriate foreign holdings, "Chapter 11 and its contentious compensation structure was necessary if American investors were to invest significantly in Mexico."[333]

Additionally, Chapter 11 challenges may be viewed as international safeguards against the domestic excesses not just of the host country's policy or regulation but also of its judiciary—that is, as a form of "appellate review of domestic state court decisions by arbitral panels constituted under NAFTA."[334] For example, NAFTA arbitration panels have held that domestic courts' decisions on domestic law may be so wrong that it may constitute a NAFTA Chapter 11 violation.[335] One case involved a Canadian corporation with an investment in Massachusetts. In that case, the Canadian corporation sued and prevailed in Massachusetts court on contract and tort claims against the City of Boston and the Boston Redevelopment Authority. Judgment was entered by the court in the Canadian corporation's favor, despite the trial court's finding that the Authority was immune from suit under the Massachusetts Torts Claim Act. On appeal to the Massachusetts Supreme Judicial Court, the court affirmed the lower court on the immunity question, reversed it on the contract claim, and entered judgment for the American defendant. The Canadian party invoked its right to arbitration under NAFTA under the theory that the Massachusetts court's rejection of its claims was itself a NAFTA violation. Thus, as the NAFTA tribunal framed the issue, the question was whether "by the decisions of its courts, the United States effectively expropriated the value of the rights to redress arising from the failure of the project."[336] Although the tribunal ultimately held against the Canadian complainant, it "accepted this theory as pleading a 'denial of the principle justice' under Art. 1105(1)," which codifies NAFTA's "minimum standard of

---

[332] *Id.* at 1449; *see also* Richard D. English, *Energy in the NAFTA: Free Trade Confronts the Mexican Constitution*, 1 Tulsa J. Comp. & Int'l L. 1 (1993). A Calvo Clause refers to an agreement between a private actor and a foreign state in which aliens are only entitled to rights and privileges accorded to nationals. In disputes with the state, aliens can seek redress only before local authorities because the clause obligates the foreign claimant to waive the right to apply to his or her government for protection if the claim is denied by local authorities.

[333] Louthan, *supra* note 330, at 1449; *see also* Young, *supra* note 312, at 1237–38 ("[T]he expropriation provisions of NAFTA and many bilateral investment treaties seem to have been designed with a view toward preventing nationalization of investments by countries without a sufficiently protective (in the eyes of potential investors) notion of property rights.").

[334] Young, *supra* note 312, at 1171.

[335] *Id.* at 1173. Discussion of this section is drawn from this article.

[336] Mondev Int'l Ltd. v. United States (Can. v. US), ICSID Case No. ARB(AF)/99/2 42 I.L.M. 85 (NAFTA Ch. 11 Arb. Trib. 2002).

treatment provision" referencing both claims of "improper procedures and unjust decisions."[337] As noted, "[t]he principle 'recognizes that not only flagrant procedural irregularities and deficiencies may justify diplomatic complaint, but also gross defects in the substance of the judgment itself.'"[338] The underlying concern is a fear that local prejudice may be couched in neutral-sounding terms. "The rationale for this principle . . . , is to use 'the substantive injustice as indirect evidence of partiality . . . in the tribunal.'"[339] As one scholar concluded, despite protestations to the contrary, the tribunal in fact performed an appellate function and was engaged in a quite "searching review" of the Massachusetts supreme court's reasoning and decision.[340]

Other NAFTA arbitrations have also addressed the question of prejudice in the local judicial system.[341] In *Loewen Group, Inc. v. United States*, a Canadian company in the funeral home business sought to expand into the Gulf Coast region of the United States, where it came into conflict with a family-owned network of funeral homes. The O'Keefe family brought suit in state court against Loewen for breach of contract, common law fraud, and violations of Mississippi antitrust law. During the seven-week trial, before an African American judge and largely African American jury, O'Keefe's lawyers repeatedly referred to Mr. O'Keefe's military service and to Loewen's Canadian origin in an attempt to exploit local antiforeign sentiments. The O'Keefe family had requested only $5 million in compensatory damages but was awarded $500 million, with $75 million for emotional distress and $400 for punitive. To stay execution pending appeal, Loewen would have had to post a bond equal to 125 percent of the judgment and when its request to reduce the appeal bond was denied, Loewen opted to settle the case for $175 million and then turned to NAFTA arbitration.

Interestingly, Loewen did not argue that Mississippi, whether by executive or legislative action, expropriated its investment, but rather contended that the state court proceeding itself constituted a NAFTA violation. Loewen claimed that the trial court's allowance of anti-Canadian testimony violated Article 1102's "prohibition of discrimination" and Article 1105's "duty of full protection and security" for foreign investors; that the imposition of excessive damages and bonding requirement likewise violated Article 1105; and that together those acts amounted to an Article 1110 expropriation. Loewen claimed $725 million in damages from the United States.[342]

Although the United States ultimately avoided liability on technical grounds, it is noteworthy that the NAFTA panel, which included Judge Abner Mikva, formerly of

---

337 Young, *supra* note 312, at 1172.

338 Renée Lettow Lerner, *International Pressure to Harmonize: The U.S. Civil Justice System in an Era of Global Trade*, 2001 BYU L. Rev. 229, 251 (2001).

339 *Id.* at 262.

340 Young, *supra* note 312, at 1173.

341 Loewen Group, Inc. v. United States, ICSID Case No. ARB(AF)/98/3, 42 I.L.M. 811 (NAFTA Ch. 11 Arb. Trib. 2003).

342 *Id.*

the US Court of Appeals for the District of Columbia Circuit, reprimanded the trial court for allowing xenophobia, class, and race prejudice to infect the trial proceedings and essentially accepted Loewen's arguments on the merits: "Having read the transcript and having considered the submissions of the parties with respect to the conduct of the trial . . . we have reached the firm conclusion that the conduct of the trial by the trial judge was so flawed that it constituted a miscarriage of justice amounting to a manifest injustice as that expression is understood in international law."[343]

The discussion above demonstrates the main point of this section: Private international law has separated itself from cultural matters. Neither the GATT nor the GATS or any other agreement within the WTO contains a cultural exception. And other features of private international law—such as choice of law and choice of forum clauses—also reinforce the notion that international commerce should be free from national systems that are embedded in political and cultural peculiarities.

However, the proliferation of such "customary transnational business practice"[344] has also provoked waves of backlash. As I have documented, the often-vehement opposition to globalization[345] may be understood in part as a reaction against the universalist claims of internationalism and a nationalistic defense of local cultures and traditions.[346] Moreover, in recent years, culture has also been injected into the national and international mainstream because of historical changes and developments in the international system. With the end of the Cold War and the fragmentation of ideological blocs so that identity politics[347] occupy center stage in world politics, it has been increasingly difficult to ignore culture or rank it behind ideological or geopolitical considerations.[348] The

---

343 Young, *supra* note 312, at 1175 (internal quotation marks and citation omitted).

344 Slaughter, *supra* note 282, at 519.

345 I elsewhere characterize globalization as a "hyper state of internationalization." Lan Cao, *Corporate and Product Identity in the Postnational Economy: Rethinking U.S. Trade Laws*, 90 CAL. L. REV. 402, 415 (2002).

346 Nationalists opposed to the universalist and homogenizing inclinations of international law stake their claims on national and local projects that speak the people's language. NAIRN, *supra* note 76, at 354; *see also* Nairn, *supra* note 1, at 157–58.

347 Culture is necessarily implicated in identity politics. There are many definitions of culture, each emphasizing a different aspect of culture. One definition focuses on relationship and identity—"[c]ulture is about relationality—the relationships among individuals within groups, among groups, and between ideas and perspectives. Culture is concerned with identity, aspiration, symbolic exchange, coordination, and structures and practices that serve relational ends, such as ethnicity ritual, heritage, norms, meanings, and beliefs." Rao and Walton, *supra* note 157, at 4.

348 Kennedy, *supra* note 59, at 111 (referring to the end of the Cold War as unleashing "outbreaks of primitive or pre-ideological cultural passions frozen by the Cold War."). Culture and identity politics were also featured in the post–World War I Wilsonian regime, which declared that "people" have a right to self-determination, possibly meaning a right also to their own nation-state. WOODROW WILSON, *The Fourteen Points Address* (1918), *in* 1 WAR AND PEACE 155, 162 (1970). One solution adopted by the international regime to address the collapse of the European empires after World War I was to create "national" states—a Polish state, for example, from areas with Polish populations. WILSON, *supra*, at 159. In this way, one could characterize the Wilsonian position as an instance in which "the local or national or the periphery"—in other words, culture—"must be 'let in' to the international." Kennedy, *supra* note 59, at 64.

breakup of states meant a surge in identity consciousness which may be subnational as well as transnational[349]—subnational in the sense that some groups of common national identity within a state might wish to free themselves from the state, and transnational in the sense that such groups may share diaspora bonds that transcend the physical boundaries of the state.[350]

An intellectual interest in identity and culture issues has accompanied this political shift as well. For example, even in a most state-centered discipline such as international relations, there has been "greater intellectual and sociological flexibility in IR [international relations] scholarship,"[351] resulting in greater interest in exploring the ways that culture and identity influence the perceptions of actors, negotiation styles, and strategies.[352] For some scholars, this cultural world order will lead to increased cohesion within and clashes among civilizational groups,[353] and for others, modernization and convergence along a Western, liberal model.[354] In the first case, cultural or civilizational conflicts are treated as flowing from cultural differences whereas in the latter case, they are viewed as a symptom of discord produced by the processes of economic development.

Culture has figured prominently in other ways as well in the post–Cold War world—politicians and scholars from a variety of disciplines have focused on culture as a factor in economic development. For example, Lee Kuan Yew of Singapore attributed Singapore's economic success in large part to Confucian culture.[355] Scholars specializing in political economy, political science, business, public policy, and of course, sociology and anthropology have begun a concerted effort to explore whether and how culture facilitates or obstructs economic development.[356]

---

349 Franck, *supra* note 4, at 362 ("The term *nation* or *tribe* suggests an affinity group that has placed certain values high on its agenda: shared genealogical origins, language and historic myths, as well as cultural and, perhaps, religious compatibility.").

350 Samuel P. Huntington, The Clash of Civilizations and the Remaking of World Order 125–27 (1996); Anupam Chander, *Diaspora Bonds*, 76 N.Y.U. L. Rev. 1005 (2001). Huntington, for example, argued that civilizational identity, community, and alliances become a central mode of group identification after the end of the Cold War and the demise of East/West ideological divide. States are still important actors, but their interests are increasingly aligned along a cultural fault line. Huntington, *supra*, at 125.

351 Yosef Lapid, *Culture's Shipo: Returns and Departures in International Relations Theory*, *in* The Return of Culture and Identity in IR Theory 3, 4 (Yosef Lapid & Freidrich Kratochwill eds., 1996).

352 *See*, e.g., Alastair Iain Johnston, Cultural Realism: Strategic Culture and Grand Strategy in Chinese History (1995).

353 Huntington, *supra* note 350, at 125–27. In a similar vein, in contemporary, post–Cold War world politics, culture is often associated with turbulence—ethnic nationalism in Kosovo, Bosnia, or Chechnya, expressed not just in terms of national ethnic identity but also civilizational identity—Slavic, Orthodox, Islamic.

354 Francis Fukuyama, The End of History and the Last Man xiv–xv, 276–77 (1992).

355 Fareed Zakaria, *Culture Is Destiny: A Conversation with Lee Kuan Yew*, Foreign Aff., Mar.–Apr. 1994, at 109.

356 *See generally* Culture Matters: How Values Shape Human Progress (Lawrence E. Harrison & Samuel P. Huntington eds., 2000). Economists have also begun looking at how social and cultural factors influence human behavior. *See generally* Paul Sillitoe, *What, Know Natives? Local Knowledge in Development*, 6 Social Anthropology 203 (1998).

Despite this cultural ferment in related fields, generally speaking, however, international law remains ambivalent about engaging culture directly. International law has for years been in the strange position of having to defend itself as worthy of being considered "real law,"[357] wrestling with the perpetual question of "is international law law,"[358] and thus is interested, even if claiming not to be, in proving to other disciplines that it too has all the usual attributes of law. Although international lawyers have emphasized that centralized enforcement mechanisms should not be the only attribute used to decide whether something is or is not law, pointing to international law's compliance features instead,[359] they have also worked to make international law more like domestic law by strengthening international law's enforcement features.[360] In that respect, international law has shored up its positive law aspects and neglected to consider seriously the "soft" law attributes of the discipline—norms and custom (the ingredients of culture in the sense used in this book)—even while, ironically, scholars in the domestic law area are increasingly exploring their significance.[361] International law's need to prove that it is law, along with an overall reluctance to engage cultural norms, has meant that international law as a discipline remains disengaged from the culture question.

Similarly, the issue of culture remains a nonissue in law and development. Having absorbed the dichotomies and polarities staked out by nationalism and internationalism,

---

357 H. L. A. Hart, The Concept of Law 214 (2d ed. 1994) (stating that international law is not real law because of the absence of a "unifying rule of recognition" and "secondary rules of change and adjudication which provide for legislatures and courts. . . .").

358 *See,* e.g., Ruth Okediji, *Public Welfare and the Role of the WTO: Reconsidering the Trips Agreement,* 17 Emory Int'l L. Rev. 819, 837 n.43 (2003) ("The organizing inquiry of international law is 'is international law law?' "); Ruti Teitel, *The Future of Human Rights Discourse,* 46 St. Louis U. L.J. 449, 459 n.47 (2002) (addressing the positive/natural law debate in international law, "namely framing the question: to what extent is international law, law?"). The question endures because critics are not convinced that international law, without strong enforcement mechanisms, can qualify as law. International lawyers have thus spent considerable time and energy defending the field. *See,* e.g., Louis Henkin, How Nations Behave: Law and Foreign Policy 13–27 (2d ed. 1979); J. L. Brierly, The Outlook for International Law 5 (1944). One of the leading casebooks on international law addresses in Chapter 1 that very question itself—"International Law as Law—Is it Law?" Louis Henkin, Richard Crawford Pugh, Oscar Schacter, & Hans Smit, International Law: Cases and Materials 10 (1980).

359 Lori F. Damrosch, *Enforcing International Law Through Non-Forcible Measures,* 269 Rec. Des Cours 9, 19–24 (1997) (discussing how international law is in fact enforced in different ways); Detlev F. Vagts, *The United States and Its Treaties: Observance and Breach,* 95 Am. J. Int'l L. 313, 323–29 (exploring five possible grounds for compliance by countries with their treaty obligations).

360 The desire to be more like domestic law has meant crafting strong enforcement mechanisms, such as creating ad hoc international criminal tribunals, the International Criminal Courts, the Dispute Settlement Body of the World Trade Organization.

361 Elsewhere I discuss the powerful impact community norms play in facilitating the production of social capital and the conversion of such social capital into economic capital. *See* Lan Cao, *Looking at Communities and Markets,* 74 Notre Dame L. Rev. 841, 864–74 (1999). For a discussion of norms and their interaction with law, see *id.*

"as ideologies, as sets of mental attitudes,"[362] law and development has remained skeptical of cultural claims. The discipline is intransigently law-centered[363] and seems unwilling or unable to address the relationship between culture and law, culture and economic development, and even more critically, the possibility of culture change if necessary to promote development. In the next chapter, I examine those issues and argue in favor of a more robust relationship between culture and law and development, including the active and deliberate promotion of culture change where needed.

---

[362] Burley, *supra* note 5.

[363] David M. Trubek & Marc Galanter, *Scholars in Self-Estrangement: Some Reflections on the Crisis in Law and Development Studies in the United States*, 1974 WIS. L. REV. 1062, 1071–72 (1974) (describing the core attributes of legal liberalism in highly law-centered ways, as follows:

> (1) society is made up of individuals who consent to the state for their own welfare; (2) the state exercises control over individuals through law, and it is constrained by law; (3) laws are designed to achieve social purposes and do not offer a special advantage to any individuals or groups within the society; (4) laws are applied equally to all citizens; (5) courts are the primary legal institutions with the responsibility for defining and applying the law; (6) adjudication is based upon a comprehensive body of authoritative rules and doctrines, and judicial decisions are not subject to outside influence; and (7) legal actors follow the restraining rules and most of the population has internalized the laws, and where there are violations of the rules enforcement action will guarantee conformity.)

3

Law and Development, Culture and Development

THIS CHAPTER BUILDS on the premises established in Chapter 2—which focused on international law's relationship with culture—and extends them to law and development. In Part A of this chapter, I put forth the reasons why law and development has eschewed critical appraisal of cultural norms.

Part B makes the case for a culturally informed law and development framework, arguing that law and development must part ways with the acultural roots of international law. In the first section of Part B, I discuss works in a variety of scholarly disciplines, economics, and sociology that establish a link between cultural norms and economic development. Part B looks at how social capital and cultural resources may be used to facilitate economic development through mechanisms such as rotating credit associations and through ethnic economies created by ethnic minorities to advance economically. Thus Part B focuses on instances in which cultural and ethnic resources have been deployed in a positive way to facilitate positive market development.

Market development is important. As Amartya Sen persuasively explained, the relationship between markets and freedom is a vital one. Markets should be praised for both their efficiency and freedom-enhancing capacities. Although economists have emphasized market efficiency in terms of "utilities, incomes and wealth,"[1] the market's merit lies in "the central value of freedom"[2] because "a denial of opportunities of transaction, through arbitrary controls, can be a source of unfreedom in itself. . . ." Freedom of employment and "market-based freedom" (versus bonded labor, for example) are crucial

---

[1] Amartya Sen, Development as Freedom 27 (1999).

[2] *Id.* at 28.

to development in general and women's equality in particular. [3] Cass Sunstein noted that "free markets are indeed an ally of sex equality."[4] There is no doubt, for example, that denying women the right to participate in economic affairs contributes to the exclusion of women from economic resources. "The economic participation of women is, thus, both a reward on its own (with associated reduction of gender bias in the treatment of women in family decisions), and a major influence for social change in general."[5]

In terms of culture change, however, as explained in the Introduction, cultural norms and practices that constrict freedom and capability are first-order issues that need to be scrutinized and changed. This should be a resolutely nonnegotiable issue for law and development. Existing law and development work which currently focuses on rule of law should be expanded to include an explicit culture change component (as described in Chapter 6) where freedom and human capability are involved. By contrast, norms and practices that are "only" economically inefficient but that are freely chosen and truly valued by people for cultural heritage or preservation purposes are second-order issues. Here, the law and development field may embrace some form of cultural relativism.

In addition to exploring the relationship between culture and markets, Part B also explores the relationship between culture and human rights, specifically, women's rights. The second section of Part B canvasses various international human rights and feminist approaches to culture in order to demonstrate that culture cannot be severed from issues related to women's equality. Indeed, as Part B argues, if law and development is to address human rights, particularly women's rights, it cannot shy from cultural issues. Legal and institutional reform is inadequate to spawn the requisite cultural transformation that would support development, particularly women's development. In this area, my argument relies on scholars such as Sen and Nussbaum, in particular, on the latter's defense of universalism for first-order issues that harm human freedom and capability. Cultural relativism would not be acceptable here.

Part C further illustrates the link between culture and law and development, providing an array of negative examples as well concrete case studies. Part C includes an in-depth look at cultural norms underlying rural economies of sub-Saharan Africa and Islamic norms that governed Middle Eastern businesses, as well as miscellaneous examples drawn from different parts of the world to support the ideas examined in Part B. While the studies selected in Part B show how cultural norms can be employed for economic advantage, the many examples used in Part C show how cultural norms have in some cases impeded market development and in other cases impeded human rights. Again, law and development can be open to cultural accommodation of market-inefficient norms and practices. It cannot do so in the case of cultural norms and practices that

---

[3] *Id.* at 25, 29.

[4] Cass R. Sunstein, *Gender, Caste, and the Law*, *in* WOMEN, CULTURE AND DEVELOPMENT: A STUDY OF HUMAN CAPABILITIES 332, 353 (Martha Nussbaum & Jonathan Glover eds., 1995).

[5] SEN, *supra* note 1, at 201.

impede human rights, reinforce entrenched power structures, and perpetuate traditional inequalities. Through concrete examples, Part C supports the main argument developed in the book, that is, neglecting culture is a flaw and a significant cause of law and development's well-trumpeted failures. A thick conception of development requires that a cultural lens be adopted, especially when hierarchical structures are culturally supported and perpetuated.

A. A Cautionary Tale: Why Law and Development Has Ignored Culture

At the risk of over generalizing, most law and development scholars come from an international law tradition that, in the United States at least, is part of a liberal framework of cosmopolitanism.[6] In common parlance, cosmopolitanism suggests a posture of worldliness different from the more narrow and, for internationalists, parochial outlooks of nationalism. The international cosmopolitan rejects borders and "refuses to think of himself as *defined* by his location or his ancestry or his citizenship or his language."[7] This cosmopolitan sensibility has meant concerns about global justice and "positive actions aimed at protecting the vital interests of everyone, regardless of their location, nationality, or citizenship."[8] It rejects, for example, nationalist conceptions which hold that the principles of distributive justice can be applied only to bounded or cohesive groups that share a common history or culture or language.

However, the cosmopolitan also tends to "hold to a vision that accepts, even celebrates, the diversity of social and political systems in the world, taking pleasure in the existence and the products of peoples and places other than our own homes. Thus, what is distinctive about cosmopolitans is that we display our concern for our fellow humans without demanding of them that they become like ourselves."[9] Because "[c]osmopolitans are among the greatest champions of multiculturalism and diversity, finding value in cultures throughout the world,"[10] the cosmopolitan sensibility also eschews anything that smacks of nationalistic chest-thumping or suggestive of an imperialist enterprise, given the sense that it is wrong to favor one's own national customs at the expense of those of others.[11] Thus, law and development scholars steeped in the international cosmopolitan

---

[6] *See* Chapter 2, note 59.

[7] Jeremy Waldron, *Minority Cultures and the Cosmopolitan Alternative*, 25 U. MICH. J. L. REFORM 751, 754 (1992).

[8] CHARLES JONES, GLOBAL JUSTICE: DEFENDING COSMOPOLITANISM 2 (1999).

[9] Kwame Anthony Appiah, *The University in an Age of Globalization*, Lecture at the Princeton-Oxford Conference on Globalization at Oxford University (June 2002), *quoted in* Anne Marie Slaughter, *The International Dimension of Law School Curriculum*, 22 PENN. ST. INT'L L. REV. 417, 419 (2004).

[10] Anupam Chander, *Diaspora Bonds*, 76 N.Y.U. L. REV. 1005, 1045 (2001).

[11] The cosmopolitan subscribes to "[t]he belief in, and pursuit of, a style of life which . . . [reveals] acquaintance with, and an ability to incorporate, the manners, habits, languages, and social customs of cities throughout the world." ROGER SCRUTON, A DICTIONARY OF POLITICAL THOUGHT 100 (1982).

tradition are passionate about alleviating dire poverty in poor countries, but at the same time they would be reluctant to tinker with or condemn cultural norms or attributes even if they impede a country's development. Indeed, it is perhaps more accurate to say that the idea of engaging in such an ideologically thorny endeavor is unlikely to even enter their consciousness.

This is markedly so after the appearance of a seminal law and development article by two prominent scholars in which they condemn the movement for being "ethnocentric and naive"[12] and characterize the liberal legal paradigm they had favored as "inherently problematic."[13] I mention this article because of its continuing prominence among the law and development academic literature[14] and note, as others have, that one of its authors, Professor Trubek, then went on to become a figure in the critical legal studies movement (CLS).[15] Law and development academics thus tend to come from either a liberal, cosmopolitan tradition or a CLS tradition. In both instances, this tradition has resulted, especially after Vietnam, in skepticism about American power and American motives, and in a reluctance to be, or appear, ethnocentric. CLS scholars are especially prone to pronouncements of crisis,[16] despair, and self-estrangement—understandable in light of the many law and development failures. However, their solution is not to remedy the many flaws in the liberal law and development model but instead to denounce efforts to export this model based on a number of factors, many of which flowed from their own disillusionment with American society,[17] for example, "loss of faith in liberal legalism as a picture of United States society" or "doubts about the universality or desirability of the American experience."[18] Thus, law and development has been, peculiarly enough, inhabited by scholars who have doubts about the propriety and efficacy of their very endeavor.

As a result, there are two strands in law and development—first, an international cosmopolitanism that celebrates cultural diversity and thus loathe to criticize or be perceived as criticizing anybody's culture, and second, a CLS inclination that is both appropriately critical of the failed promises of legal liberalism but also devoid of viable alternatives, resulting in a bleak discourse characterized by despair, crisis, and disillusionment about

---

12 David M. Trubek & Marc Galanter, *Scholars in Self-Estrangement: Some Reflections on the Crisis in Law and Development Studies in the United States*, 1974 Wis. L. Rev. 1062, 1080 (1974).

13 *Id.* at 1100.

14 Brian Z. Tamanaha, *The Lessons of Law-and-Development Studies*, 89 Am. J. Int'l L. 470, 474 (1995) (book review) (characterizing it as "the single most influential piece in law-and-development studies").

15 *Id.*

16 Sammy Adelman & Abdul Paliwala, *Law and Development in Crisis*, *in* Law and Crisis in the Third World 10 (Sammy Adelman & Abdul Paliwala eds., 1993). Almost twenty years after Trubek and Galanter declared a crisis in the law and development movement, these authors have made a similar declaration.

17 Tamanaha, *supra* note 14, at 474–75. Professor Tamanaha observed that "[e]clectic critique may be essential to the proper functioning of already established rule-of-law systems in the West. Matters are altogether different, however, when this same relentlessly negative technique is applied to countries that have yet to establish the rule of law." *Id.* at 475.

18 Trubek & Galanter, *supra* note 12, at 1090–91.

the very objectives of the project itself—law and development. In addition to the CLS inclination in law and development, there are other schools of development that are sympathetic to the CLS approach—dependency theory and cultural critics of development. Unlike modernization theory which focuses on law, both CLS and dependency theory are skeptical of law. "CLS tends to see law as an extension of politics, and is accordingly skeptical of concepts like 'efficiency' and 'neutrality' that mask or rationalize existing political arrangements," which, to CLS scholars, reek of neocolonialism.[19] Cultural critics of development such as Arturo Escobar, for example, see development as a cultural system and focus on how the modernization perspectives of development have constructed a development discourse that perpetuates inequalities between poor and rich countries.[20]

These critiques of law and development are essentially critiques of modernization theory. "The main criticism was that modernization theory had seriously neglected factors external to societies, such as colonialism and imperialism, as well as newer forms of economic and political domination."[21] Against a critical backdrop that highlights structural inequities, "[c]ulture is seen as a diversion from the supposedly real processes of 'domination' in the contemporary world; or even worse, it is simply a deliberate obfuscation of these processes."[22],

Postcolonial theorists in particular are scathingly critical of modernization theory. Modernization theory, it is charged, is more than flawed. It "serves colonial domination, rather than merely being a theoretical mistake. Defining culture as 'a system of control', post-colonial theory revealed the ways in which a politics of representation, formed within European/Western thought in the era of colonialism and empire, continues to inform contemporary Western writing and thinking about the Third World, replicating the stereotypes and power relations of colonialism."[23]

Postcolonial theorists, CLS and other critics of the legal liberalism that inform the law and development project are also heavily influenced by a popular theory termed "Orientalism" in a landmark book, *Orientalism*, by Edward Said. As shown below, CLS scholars and others situated in the postcolonial debate are aware of and influenced by the Orientalist critique Said offered, which lobbed scathing accusations against Western cultural studies and Western interpretations of the non-West. Orientalism charges that Western knowledge of the Orient, founded on a Eurocentric and flawed cultural view

---

[19] Michael A. Livingston, *Reinventing Tax Scholarship: Lawyers, Economists, and the Role of the Legal Academy*, 83 CORNELL L. REV. 365, 384 (1998). Dependency theory, inspired by Marxism, is highly critical of the international capitalist system and true to its Marxists roots, "paid little attention to law," viewing law as merely a superstructure to the economic base. Tamanaha, *supra* note 14, at 479 (citations omitted).

[20] Vijayendra Rao & Michael Walton, *Culture and Public Action: Relationality, Equality of Agency, and Development*, *in* CULTURE AND PUBLIC ACTION 3, 10 (Vijayendra Rao & Michael Walton eds., 2004).

[21] Hela Yousfi, *Culture and Development: The Continuing Tension Between Modern Standards and Local Contexts*, *in* CULTURE, INSTITUTIONS, AND DEVELOPMENT: NEW INSIGHTS INTO AN OLD DEBATE 20, 24 (Jean-Philippe Platteau & Robert Peccoud eds., 2011).

[22] *Id.* at 25.

[23] *Id.*

of the Orient, has served as an instrument of empire. Whether wittingly or unwittingly, this charge has made culture even more of a taboo area in law and development circles. Certainly exporting Western law, as CLS has come to regret, is a flawed and Eurocentric enterprise; but anything that smacks of exporting Western culture, as Orientalism charges, is an even more normatively troubling enterprise.

As Said put it, the colonizing West is the privileged "self" against which the colonized Orient (or Third World), as "other," is to be contrasted against and improved upon.[24] In other words, the West created the idea of the Orient by its imagination and in so doing, made it fundamentally antithetical to the West. Orientalism is a process by which the Orient is cast in pervasively negative terms against the West's more positive archetype. Thus, the Orient is not a geographical or physical locale but a European creation and Orientalism the "enormously systematic discipline by which European culture was able to manage—even produce—the Orient politically, sociologically, militarily, ideologically, scientifically, and imaginatively during the post-Enlightenment period."[25] For Said, "Orientalism is fundamentally a political doctrine willed over the Orient because the Orient was weaker than the West, which elided the Orient's difference with its weakness. . . . As a cultural apparatus Orientalism is all aggression, activity, judgment, will-to-truth, and knowledge."[26]

According to Said, this production and reproduction of the Orient as a cultural negative supports a hegemonic system of imperialist ideology in which the West maintains its position of power and the Orient its position of powerlessness. For Said, the West invented the Orient and the Orient itself is but a Western mode of representation framed by the West to create an "Other" it could deem alien and inferior. Orientalism is not simply about one culture having an inaccurate but innocuous view of another culture. Indeed, Orientalism is a particularly "Western style for dominating, restructuring, and having authority over the Orient."[27] Said's provocative work has led to critical questions about cultural discourse. For example, "[h]ow does one represent other cultures? What is another culture? Is the notion of a distinct culture (or race, or religion, or civilization) a useful one, or does it always get involved either in self-congratulation (when one discusses one's own) or hostility and aggression (when one discusses the 'other')?"[28]

---

[24] EDWARD SAID, ORIENTALISM (1978); *see also* Makau Mutua, *Savages, Victims, and Saviors: The Metaphor of Human Rights*, 42 HARV. INT'L L. J. 201, 210 (2001) (describing the "impulse to universalize Eurocentric norms and values by repudiating, demonizing, and 'othering' that which is different and non-European."). Note that Orientalism is not limited to the "Orient" but extends to other locales as well. DIPESH CHAKRABARTY, PROVINCIALIZING EUROPE: POSTCOLONIAL THOUGHT AND HISTORICAL DIFFERENCE 27 (2000).

[25] SAID, *supra* note 24, at 3. Note that although the United States usually equates East Asia (China and Japan, for example) with the "Orient," Said's use of the word "Orient" is derived from a European understanding of the word and thus focuses on the Middle East.

[26] *Id.* at 204.

[27] *Id.* at 3.

[28] *Id.* at 325; *cf.* BERNARD LEWIS, ISLAM AND THE WEST 126 (1993) (arguing that what Said calls Orientalism is rooted in humanism, not imperialism).

Although there are numerous critics of Orientalism,[29] the book and its ideas remain highly influential especially in postcolonial studies. Orientalism continues to provide a powerful framework in which works by Western authors purporting to describe the non-West are critically appraised. Indeed, there is a succession of historically notable Western writers whose works fit squarely within the Orientalist frame Said depicted. For example, it is commonplace, indeed almost predictable, for the West to depict and caricaturize the Orient (and its equivalent) as frozen in time and hence incapable of progress or change. Hegel, for example, declared that "[e]arly do we see China advancing to the condition in which it is found at this day; for as the contrast between objective existence and subjective freedom of movement in it, is still wanting, every change is excluded, and the fixedness of a character which recurs perpetually, takes the place of what we should call the truly historical."[30] Weber wrote that "Chinese intellectual life remained completely static, and despite seemingly favorable conditions modern capitalist developments simply did not appear."[31] Marx made a similar observation about China: Its "isolation having come to a violent end by the medium of England, dissolution must follow as surely as that of any mummy carefully preserved in a hermetically sealed coffin, whenever it is brought into contact with the open air."[32]

Once a place is described as fixed, static, and frozen in time, it is not surprising that it would also be viewed as incapable of or unlikely to change. Henry Maine depicted "the East" as static: [I]n "those great and unexplored regions which we vaguely term the East ... the distinction between the Present and the Past disappears."[33] Friedrich Nietzsche described China as a "country in which large-scale dissatisfaction and the capacity for change have become extinct centuries ago."[34] And the English Chinese scholar Edward Parker blithely dismissed China's many thousand years as mere "monotonous history."[35] To study Chinese law, Parker stated, is to study "a living past, and converse with fossil men."[36]

If the East is passive and unchanging, the implication is that the West is by contrast dynamic and progressive. For change to occur in the East, it must be imparted and driven by the West. Even Marx, who denounced colonialism as a form of Western capitalist exploitation nonetheless concluded that it was only via the colonial encounter that much needed change could come to the East. Thus Marx understood that colonial rule was

---

29 Robert Irwin, For Lust of Knowing: The Orientalists and Their Enemies (2006); Daniel Martin Varisco, Reading Orientalism: Said and the Unsaid (2007).

30 Georg Wilhelm Friedrich Hegel, The Philosophy of History 116 (1956).

31 Max Weber, The Religion of China 55 (1951).

32 Karl Marx, Marx on China, 1853–1860: Articles from the New York Daily Tribune 4 (Dona Torr ed., 1951).

33 Henry Sumner Maine, Village Communities in the East and West 7 (1872).

34 Friedrich Nietzsche, The Gay Science 99 (1974).

35 Edward H. Parker, *The Principles of Chinese Law and Equity*, 22 L. Q. Rev. 190, 209 (1906).

36 Edward Harper Parker, *Comparative Chinese Family Law*, 8 China Rev. 67, 69 (1879), *reprinted in* Edward Harper Parker, Comparative Chinese Family Law 69 (1879).

necessary and served at least two functions—"one destructive, the other generating—the annihilation of old Asiatic society, and the laying of the material foundations of Western society in Asia."[37] For Hegel, change can only follow the path carved by Europe: "The history of the world travels from East to West, for Europe is absolutely the end of History, Asia the beginning."[38]

Similar denunciations include the charge that the "Orient," specifically China, is incomprehensible or inscrutable,[39] illogical, and developmentally stunted.[40] Western scholars even questioned whether Chinese laws could truly be considered "law."[41] For example, the chief commissioner of the United States to China in 1844 defended American application of American laws to American citizens in China because Chinese law was not deemed law by the United States. "The nations of Europe and America form a family of states, associated together by community of civilization and religion. . . . In the intercourse between Christian states on the one hand and Mohammedan on the other, a different principle is assumed, namely the exemption of the Christian foreigner from the jurisdiction of the local authorities."[42]

Given this history, it is no wonder cosmopolitan internationalists would shy away from examining the cultural dimensions of the law and development project. It is no wonder that for the Western-educated experts ("privileged subjects"), a law and development agenda aimed at bringing development to the (primitive) Third World would provoke a measure of discomfort, disillusionment, and skepticism. Indeed, with or without the proposed culture component, there may very well be, from a cosmopolitan perspective, already a whiff of Orientalism in the very objectives and assumptions of law and development itself. Referring to Europe's relationship with China specifically, although his observations are equally applicable to other developing countries, the historian Paul Cohen noted European tendency to "play[] Beauty to China's Beast, transforming by its kiss the torpor of centuries, releasing with its magical power the potential for 'development' that must otherwise remain forever locked up."[43] And as noted in Chapter 1,

---

37 Karl Marx, *The Future Results of British Rule in India*, *in* The Marx-Engels Reader 659 (Robert C. Tucker ed., 1978).

38 Hegel, *supra* note 30, at 103.

39 Foucault wrote the following of China: "[A]t the other extremity of the earth we inhabit, a culture entirely devoted to the ordering of space, but one that does not distribute the multiplicity of existing things into any of the categories that make it possible for us to name, speak, and think." Michel Foucault, The Order of Things: An Archeology of the Human Sciences xix (1994). Hegel described China as "a dull half-conscious brooding of spirit." Hegel, *supra* note 30, at 175.

40 Weber, *supra* note 31, at 125 (charging that the Chinese writing system, by ideographic or pictorial representation, has led to unfortunate results—"The power of logos, of defining and reasoning, has not been accessible to the Chinese," so that "[t]he very concept of logic remained absolutely alien" to them.) *Id.* at 125, 127.

41 For a superb examination of how the West has characterized Chinese law as "not law," *see* Teemu Ruskola, *Legal Orientalism*, 101 Mich. L. Rev. 179 (2002).

42 Wayne Sandholtz & Kendall Stiles, International Norms and Cycles of Change 149 (2009).

43 Paul A. Cohen, Discovering History in China: American Historical Writing on the Recent Chinese Past 151–52 (1984).

first wave law and development scholars had also worried about the discipline's apparent Eurocentric core.

Thus, the proposed move—to go from modernization of law, transforming legal culture, and establishing institutions on the one hand to culture and culture change on the other hand may be particularly uncomfortable and problematic. After all, if even legal liberalism—instituting laws to support a liberal market society—is suspect, then certainly "cultural liberalism"—promoting cultural attributes that would facilitate development—would be even more so, given the perception that advocating for change of another's culture is more problematic than advocating for the establishment of "mere" laws.[44]

Moreover, cosmopolitans have, rightly so, distanced themselves from a Western tendency to present Western values as universal ideas and non-Western values as parochial and particularistic. Cosmopolitans would be uncomfortable with the idea that "universalism is fine as long as it is Western ideals that are being universalized."[45] Thus to the extent that the law and development agenda has been filtered through the cosmopolitan sensibility that pervades international law, it will, not surprisingly, be hostile to any proposal that smacks of exporting Western culture under the guise of promoting universalism.[46]

Indeed, until recently, even in disciplines other than international law, culture is either irrelevant or alternatively, it can be studied—described, compared, and appreciated—but not critically appraised. For example, culture is a nonissue in economics because economists generally believe that the right economic policy will produce the desired economic result without regard to culture. Amartya Sen observed that "some economists have been tempted by the idea that all human beings behave in much the same way (for example, relentlessly maximize their self-interest defined in a thoroughly insulated way)."[47] Moreover, culture is an uncomfortable realm for economists to operate in, perhaps because "it presents definitional problems, is difficult to quantify, and operates in a highly complex context with psychological, institutional, political, geographic, and other factors."[48] As Gary Becker, who received the Nobel Prize in Economics in 1992 observed, "Individuals have less control over their culture than over other social capital.

[44] Promoting culture change may even be viewed as forcing Western culture on others while simultaneously denying that this is in fact the agenda. *See* RUTH BENEDICT, PATTERNS OF CULTURE 6 (1952) (noting that "world-wide . . . diffusion of [Western culture] has protected us as man had never been protected before from having to take seriously the civilizations of other peoples; it has given to our culture a massive universality that we have long ceased to account for historically, and which we read off rather as necessary and inevitable.").

[45] RUMUR SARKAR, DEVELOPMENT LAW AND INTERNATIONAL FINANCE 19 (2002).

[46] The CLS strand of law and development also struggled with Western tendency toward universalism as it "failed to resolve the tension between legal universalists, who believed that the Western mode for development was the most logical and, ultimately, the only acceptable mode for development, and cultural relativists who believed that imperialism was the 'necessary logical consequence of universalism.'" *Id.* at 31.

[47] Amartya Sen, *How Does Culture Matter?*, *in* CULTURE AND PUBLIC ACTION 37, 40 (Vijayendra Rao & Michael Walton eds., 2004).

[48] Lawrence E. Harrison, *Introduction: Why Culture Matters*, *in* CULTURE MATTERS: HOW VALUES SHAPE HUMAN PROGRESS xvii, xxv (Lawrence E. Harrison & Samuel P. Huntington eds., 2000).

They cannot alter their ethnicity, race or family history, and only with difficulty can they change their country or religion. Because of the difficulty of changing culture and its low depreciation rate, culture is largely a 'given' to individuals throughout their lifetimes."[49] If it is taken as a "given," it is unlikely, from a purely pragmatic standpoint, to be viewed as something that can be acted upon or altered.

Other scholarly disciplines that are related to and influence the trajectory of law and development are also disinclined to critically assess culture. Unlike economists who tend to sidestep culture, anthropologists study cultures but are generally unwilling to evaluate cultural norms and practices of another society. In 1947, the Executive Board of the American Anthropological Association declined to endorse the UN Universal Declaration of Human Rights because it viewed the Declaration as ethnocentric.[50] The prepared statement from the Association questioned if "the proposed Declaration [can] be applicable to all human beings, and not be a statement of rights conceived only in terms of the values prevalent in the countries of Western Europe and America."[51] It was additionally concerned that "ideas such as the 'white man's burden' have justified controlling the affairs of millions of people all over the world and that 'the history of the expansion of the western world has been marked by demoralization of human personality and the disintegration of human rights among the peoples over whom hegemony has been established.'"[52] According to the anthropologist Sally Engle Merry, who defended the 1947 position of the Anthropological Association against condemnation by a law professor who characterized this 1947 position as a continuing embarrassment to anthropologists, "the statement was very much a defense of small, beleaguered communities made in the name of freedom, raised to the level of a universal value. It argued that 'man is free only when he lives as his society defines freedom.'"[53] Thus, the position epitomizes "tolerance for difference and a critique of ethnocentrism."[54] And anthropologists of that era, she wrote, understandably "saw in the human rights approach a replay of earlier imperial efforts at transformation."[55] According to Merry, this was a legitimate concern then, as it is now. As Merry explained, contemporary anthropology remains appropriately anxious "about the desire of external reform movements, whether generated by colonialism, globalization, or human rights reformers, to change cultural practices without sufficient respect for difference. This was a reasonable worry in 1947, still a deeply colonial era, as

---

[49] Gary Becker, Accounting for Tastes 16 (1996).

[50] Harrison, *supra* note 48, at xxvi.

[51] Sally Engle Merry, *Human Rights Law and the Demonization of Culture (And Anthropology Along the Way)*, Pol & Legal Anthropology Rev., May 2003, at 55, 56.

[52] *Id.*

[53] *Id.*

[54] *Id.* Merry further observed as follows: "[T]he anthropological position was not the defense of all cultural practices but a more nuanced recognition that tolerance of difference was one of several important ethical considerations, as well as one under siege at that historical moment." *Id.* at 57.

[55] *Id.* at 57.

it is today under the pressures of globalizing capitalism."[56] Reform efforts are troubling to Merry because the very act of reforming others, through the rationale that they need to be saved from their own culture, carries colonial overtones. It also rests implicitly on the assumption that the victims either are governed by false consciousness or lack choice while the saviors are empowered and fully capable of exercising choice.[57]

For Merry, tolerance for cultural difference is an important value and the preoccupation in international human rights law with practices such as female genital mutilation is based on "old and well-established tropes of traditional culture, as well as on conceptions of African savagery and Islamic anti-woman ideology."[58] Indeed, her critique of the international human rights critique of culture is implicitly framed in the anti-Orientalist tradition popularized by Edward Said's Orientalism. In essence, anthropologists such as Merry object to the notion that culture is an obstacle to women's human rights and to such portrayal of culture in human rights documents such as Convention on the Elimination of all Forms of Discrimination Against Women (CEDAW), the Declaration on the Elimination of Violence Against Women, and other declarations from the Beijing Fourth World Conference on Women.[59] For Merry, it is objectionable that "human rights lawyers and activists are ideologically committed to implementing universal standards rather than appreciating local differences. This is part of the rationality of law that shapes their practice."[60] Aside from the issues of tolerance, reform, and universalism versus particularism, Merry also finds troubling the tendency in the human rights circle to equate culture as something in opposition to modernity and civilization itself.[61]

The cultural anthropologist Richard Shweder refused to pronounce even that culture matters because "the assertion that 'culture matters' is a way of saying that some cultures are impoverished or backward, whereas others are enriched or advanced. It means there are good things in life (e.g., health, domestic tranquility, justice, material prosperity, hedonic self-stimulation, and small families) that all human beings ought to want and have but that their culture keeps them from wanting and/or having."[62] For Shweder, culture is an intrinsic good and as he puts it, "I have never put much stock in the view that holds that a good reason for becoming interested in other cultures is that they are

---

56 *Id.* at 56.

57 Saba Mahmood, *Feminist Theory, Embodiment, and the Docile Agent: Some Reflections on the Egyptian Islamic Revival*, 16 CULTURAL ANTHROPOLOGY 202 (2001).

58 Merry, *supra* note 51, at 58.

59 *Id.* at 60–61. "Thus, it reinforces the idea that it is culture that is subordinating women and modernity that frees them. That modernity is also a cultural system seems lost in this formulation." *Id.* at 62. Even if a description of the objectionable cultural belief and value is accurate, this is nonetheless problematic for Merry because it is done to the exclusion of economic, social, and political factors. *Id.* at 63.

60 *Id.* at 68.

61 *Id.* at 69.

62 *See, e.g.*, Richard A. Shweder, *Moral Maps, "First World" Conceits, and the New Evangelists*, *in* CULTURE MATTERS: HOW VALUES SHAPE HUMAN PROGRESS 158, 160–61 (Lawrence E. Harrison & Samuel P. Huntington eds., 2000).

impediments to the realization of some imagined universal aspiration of all people to be more like northern Europeans."[63]

Given this long and sordid pedigree of imperialism and neocolonialism, it is hardly surprising that, as a noted sociologist observed, "[i]n the humanities and liberal circles generally, a rigid orthodoxy now prevails that can be summarized as follows: Culture is a symbolic system to be interpreted, understood, discussed, delineated, respected, and celebrated as the distinctive product of a particular group of people, of equal worth with all other such products. But it should never be used to explain anything about the people who produced it."[64]

Other reasons why cultural explanations are disfavored in certain intellectual circles include concerns about cultural determinism,[65] that is, "the tendency to culturalize problems"[66] and to see culture as an "over-determining"[67] factor to the exclusion of possibly more serious structural problems in the economic and political spheres. Thus, part of the issue for anthropologists is the possible misuse of culture "by reactionary analysts and public figures" as a way to "blame the victim"[68] or to avoid examining structural causes of poverty.[69] Relatedly, critics are also concerned that culture will be used inappropriately, so to speak, not just to overexplain Third World failures but to underexplain similar flaws in the West. For example, some critics may object to the tendency to blame non-Western cultures for the oppression of non-Western women while failing to see that

---

[63] *Id.* at 161.

[64] Orlando Patterson, *Taking Culture Seriously: A Framework and an Afro-American Illustration, in* CULTURE MATTERS: HOW VALUES SHAPE HUMAN PROGRESS 202, 202 (Lawrence E. Harrison & Samuel P. Huntington eds., 2000). This position is a reversal of the position that prevailed during the earlier times, "when the Parsonian theory of values as ends and normative regulators of action was predominant." *Id.* at 203.

[65] Sen, *supra* note 47, at 46–50 (criticizing cultural comparisons between Ghana and South Korea as an example of cultural determinism because such comparisons often ignore other differences—class, politics, the educational system, the relationship Korea had with Japan and the United States, etc.); *id.* at 38 (criticizing the belief by some that "the fates of countries are effectively *sealed* by the nature of their respective cultures.").

[66] Merry, *supra* note 51, at 63–64 ("Blaming culture for the disadvantages faced by women, minorities, and other vulnerable groups is an appealing ideology for proponents of contemporary neoliberal globalization. It blames the havoc wreaked by expansive capitalism and global conflicts on the culture of the 'other.' This absolves the rich countries of responsibility for the suffering caused by these processes and blames local people, such as battering husbands, oppressive men who veil their wives, and knife-wielding fans of FGM, for the suffering.").

[67] Patterson, *supra* note 64, at 203. This means relying on a "simplistic or untenable conception of culture" and using it "in a crudely deterministic way" to explain certain group's problems, so that culture is viewed as "a fixed, explanatory black box invoked to explain anything and everything about the group." *Id.* In contrast, Professor Sen favors a different approach, "[c]ultural interrelations within a broad framework," in which "culture, seen in a dynamic and interactive way, is one important influence among many others." Sen, *supra* note 47, at 52, 55.

[68] Patterson, *supra* note 64, at 204. Professor Patterson rejects the argument that cultural explanations amount to blaming the victim. If a person who has low self-esteem and behaves in self-defeating ways as a result of having been abused is told by someone to go to a psychologist to seek therapy, "[i]t would be absurd to accuse that person of blaming the victim. Yet this is exactly what happens when a sympathetic analyst is condemned for even hinting that some Afro-American problems may be the tragic consequences of their cultural adaptation to an abusive past." *Id.* at 204.

[69] *Id.; see also* Rao & Walton, *supra* note 20, at 10.

problematic practices, cosmetic surgery, overemphasis on beauty, for example, favored by Western women are less a product of Western women's choice and more a product of Western culture.[70] Moreover, anthropologists may also worry that culture is used in an unfairly generalized way that overcondemns. As Merry charged, "this cultural theory also relegates societies that oppress women to an inferior status. When corporate executives in the U.S. steal millions of dollars through accounting fraud, we do not critique American culture as a whole.... Similarly, the actions of a single tribal council in Pakistan should not indict the entire country. Although many communities do have practices and laws that subordinate women, these are neither homogeneous nor ancient."[71] In this way, critical examination of culture may also thwart the cosmopolitan quest to promote cultural diversity and ethnic pride.[72] Evaluating culture makes many well-meaning and considerate people uncomfortable because "criticisms of culture cut close to the ego and injure identity and self-esteem. Coming from outsiders, such animadversions . . . stink of condescension."[73]

Thus the following statement is an accurate description of the ambiguous role ascribed to culture: "We all realize that before we resort to culture today to explain the differences in economic progress or political attitudes among nations and ethnic groups, we prefer to find other explanations."[74] It is not only the cosmopolitan sensibility of international law and its law and development counterpart that has kept culture outside the analytic frame. As I have shown, a cluster of related fields, such as economics and anthropology have also sidestepped culture.

In Part B below, I argue that law and development should resist the acultural inclination of other disciplines and chart its own course, paying appropriate attention to not just laws and institutions but also culture. I focus on two concrete examples involving ethnic minorities and the marshaling of cultural resources in order to show the link between culture, markets, and development. These examples are offered to show *why* this link should be integrated into law and development studies. Other relevant questions, such as *how* culture should be incorporated into law and development, including thorny issues of changing cultural norms that are at odds with development objectives, will be addressed

---

70 *See, e.g.*, UMA NARAYAN, DISLOCATING CULTURES: IDENTITIES, TRADITIONS, AND THIRD WORLD FEMINISM (1997); Isabelle Gunning, *Arrogant Perception, World-Travelling and Multicultural Feminism: The Case of Female Genital Surgeries*, 23 COLUM. HUM. RTS. L. REV. 189 (1991–92).

71 Merry, *supra* note 51, at 64.

72 Patterson, *supra* note 64, at 204.

73 David Landes, *Culture Makes Almost All the Difference*, *in* CULTURE MATTERS: HOW VALUES SHAPE HUMAN PROGRESS 2, 2 (Lawrence E. Harrison & Samuel P. Huntington eds., 2000). Some scholars are even worried that "[t]he rhetoric of 'norms' has served a . . .—dare one say more overtly political?—function . . . . Norms help to assure the conservative or anti-collectivists that the limited laissez-faire approach of an austere common law regime can achieve the proverbial best of both worlds." David Charny, *Illusions of a Spontaneous Order: "Norms" in Contractual Relationships*, 144 U. PA. L. REV. 1841, 1844 (1996).

74 Nathan Glazer, *Disaggregating Culture*, *in* CULTURE MATTERS: HOW VALUES SHAPE HUMAN PROGRESS 219, 220 (Lawrence E. Harrison & Samuel P. Huntington eds., 2000).

in Chapter 5. The question of *whether* a culture change project should be pursued and on what normative grounds will be explored in Chapter 6.[75]

B. A Brief Look at Culture, Markets, and Development

In a provocative article, Daniel Etounga-Manguelle, a Cameroonian scholar, made the connection between beliefs, attitudes, and values on the one hand and development (economic and otherwise) on the other. The article questioned more than cultural practices. It also questioned what the author himself called (rather generally) the African mindset. Despite the immense "diversity—the vast number of subcultures" in Africa, the author believed that it is possible to generalize about African culture because "there is a foundation of shared values, attitudes, and institutions that binds together the nations south of the Sahara, and in many respects those to the north as well."[76] Etounga-Manguelle listed an array of values that he deemed to be nonconducive to economic progress. Exalting the past rather than the future means an absence of a "dynamic perception of the future"[77] which is necessary for progress. Associating authority and dominance with birth status rather than merit means that "[i]n Africa, you must be born dominant; otherwise you have no right to power except by coup d'etat."[78] Subordinating the individual to the community stifles initiative and creates a situation where, as Etounga-Manguelle puts it, "[t]he concept of individual responsibility does not exist in our hyper-centralized traditional structures. In Cameroon, the word 'responsible' translates as 'chief.' "[79] Excessively celebrating conviviality and rejecting open conflict mean "[f]riendship comes before business" and differences, even legitimate ones, are suppressed in order to maintain social harmony.[80] This social harmony norm is so strong that "[i]n some African societies, the avoidance of conflict means that justice cannot be rendered in the daytime."[81] Because there is a propensity to "attribute very little importance . . . to the financial and economic aspects of life,"[82] "[o]ther than some social groups like the well-known Bamileke of Cameroon or the Kamba of Kenya, the African is a bad *H. economicus.*"[83]

---

[75] Timur Kuran, *Cultural Obstacles to Economic Development: Often Overstated, Usually Transitory, in* CULTURE AND PUBLIC ACTION 115, 120 (Vijayendra Rao & Michael Walton eds., 2004).

[76] Daniel Etounga-Manguelle, *Does Africa Need a Cultural Adjustment Program?, in* CULTURE MATTERS: HOW VALUES SHAPE HUMAN PROGRESS 65, 67 (Lawrence E. Harrison & Samuel P. Huntington, eds. 2000).

[77] *Id.* at 69.

[78] *Id.* at 70.

[79] *Id.* at 71. Another byproduct is that without the notion of individual responsibility, "those that occupy an intermediate position in the hierarchy" are held in contempt, as it is understood that the one to solve a problem is only the minister himself. *Id.*

[80] *Id.* at 72.

[81] *Id.*

[82] *Id.*

[83] *Id.*

Although African culture, according to Etounga-Manguelle, is "one of the most—if not *the* most—humanistic cultures in existence,"[84] "peaceful cultural revolutions"[85] must be undertaken "to change Africa's destiny"[86] by "asserting the absolute preeminence of education, by suppressing the construction of religious structures and other palaces to the detriment of schools, and by modifying the content of the curricula, accenting not only science but especially the necessary changes of the African society."[87] The educational system in Africa must promote critical thinking, dissent, the importance of creating "businesspeople, and therefore job creators,"[88] and changes in the role of women in African society.[89] To transform the economic culture, "[w]e must accept profit as the engine of development."[90]

This neglect of culture in law and development is especially unfortunate because scholars in other fields have long identified certain cultural traits that appear to correlate with positive (and negative) economic performance.[91] Indeed, even economists have become more comfortable with including culture in their tool box because "thanks to the progress of game theory, economists acquired an analytic framework within which to conceptualize culture in a way understandable by them . . . they had reached a better grasp of why culture is an indispensable component of modern market economies and obtained a more precise idea of what economics can or cannot teach them about the role of culture."[92] Economists may study individual behavior but also evaluate it in the context of social groups. In so doing, they work from "specific models within a contextualized framework. As a consequence, they do not work with a general definition of culture in their minds, but instead use specific concepts of culture that are appropriate

---

[84] *Id.* at 75. African humanistic values include "the solidarity beyond age classification and social status; social interaction; the love of neighbor, whatever the color of his skin; the defense of the environment, and so many others." *Id.*

[85] *Id.* at 76.

[86] *Id.* at 75.

[87] *Id.* at 76.

[88] *Id.*

[89] *Id.*

[90] *Id.* at 77.

[91] Max Weber identified certain attributes associated with the "Protestant ethic," individualism, a desire to compete, overcome nature, and achieve chosen goals. MAX WEBER, THE PROTESTANT ETHIC AND THE SPIRIT OF CAPITALISM (1930). Others have focused on group cooperation and trust, *see* FRANCIS FUKUYAMA, TRUST: THE SOCIAL VIRTUES AND THE CREATION OF PROSPERITY (1995), and preference for investment in education and work over consumption and leisure. *See* LAWRENCE E. HARRISON, WHO PROSPERS? HOW CULTURAL VALUES SHAPE ECONOMIC AND POLITICAL SUCCESS 16–23 (1992); Edna Bonacich, *A Theory of Middlemen Minorities*, 38 AM. SOC. REV. 583, 585 (1973); THOMAS SOWELL, MIGRATIONS AND CULTURES: A WORLD VIEW 17 (1996).

[92] Jean-Philippe Platteau, *The Role of Culture in Development: An Overview*, *in* CULTURE, INSTITUTIONS, AND DEVELOPMENT: NEW INSIGHTS INTO AN OLD DEBATE 3, 7 (Jean-Philippe Platteau & Robert Peccoud eds., 2011). "Equally worth stressing is the following characteristic of the economists' approach to culture: there are typically multiple institutional solutions to a coordination problem arising in societies. . . . Culture then fulfills the function of a selecting device that causes one possible equilibrium to arise and be established." *Id.* at 8.

to the problem at hand."[93] For example, when studying the conditions or cultural factors that encourage honest dealings in market transactions, economists do not necessarily use the term culture but rather "introduce culture under the form of values that influence preferences. For example, they assume that agents are reciprocators rather than purely self-interested, opportunistic individuals."[94]

When economists have studied ethnic-based exchanges and culture is thus implicated, "culture takes on the form of group-based identity feelings that influence individual behavior in addition to standard determinants of utility such as material gain or leisure."[95] Examples include studies that look at the effect of social prestige or shame on individual behavior in groups, whereby group sanctions serve to lower the costs of enforcement. Economists have also turned to social norms, understood as a proxy for culture, to address the problem of coordination among players operating under conditions of information asymmetry. "Such norms perform the necessary function of causing expectations and actions to converge so that an equilibrium position, known as a social convention, can be established."[96]

Still, for many economists, culture may remain a difficult subject to study. "In the framework of economics, social norms, values and conventions are considered to be subject to inertia, . . . because they do not change as rapidly as the other variables of concern to economists (prices, quantities of goods and services bought and sold, etc.).... Nonetheless, economists, like sociologists and cultural anthropologists, are deeply interested in the question as to how a [sic] social practices change when an established convention is disrupted, say as a consequence of a change in the economic or technological environment."[97]

As this section shows, it is now generally accepted that norms have economic implications and thus development implications because they have the potential of correcting information asymmetries and lower transaction costs. "Since they thus constrain people's behavior and coordinate their beliefs once they are established, they are genuine institutions generated by a particular culture."[98]

1. THE CULTURE EFFECT: CULTURE AND MARKETS

Some scholars have asserted that culture plays a primary role—"culture makes almost all the difference. Witness the enterprise of expatriate minorities—the Chinese in East and Southeast Asia, Indians in East Africa, Lebanese in West Africa, Jews and Calvinists

---

[93] *Id.* at 7.
[94] *Id.*
[95] *Id.*
[96] *Id.* at 8.
[97] *Id.* at 8–9.
[98] *Id.* at 8.

throughout much of Europe, and on and on."[99] As Alan Greenspan, the chairman of the Federal Reserve Board from 1987 to 2006 conceded, post-Communist Russia did not, as he assumed, "automatically establish a free-market entrepreneurial system"[100] merely because, as he also assumed, capitalism was "human nature."[101] Instead, Greenspan acknowledged that it was "not nature at all, but culture."[102] Referring to capitalism and property rights, Robert Samuelson aptly stated, "[p]roperty rights are not the be all and end all of progress but a simple reflection of the larger culture."[103] Senator Daniel Patrick Moynihan aptly observed as follows: "The central conservative truth is that it is culture, not politics, that determines the success of a society. The central liberal truth is that politics can change a culture and save it from itself."[104] Amartya Sen correctly acknowledged the link between cultural influences and economic success[105] but cautioned that a cultural exploration must be balanced and examined "within a broad framework,"[106] so that we neither neglect culture nor privilege it "in stationary and isolated terms."[107]

Indeed, culture should not be viewed as stationary and unchanging nor should it be studied in isolation. For example, culture affects economics and economics may have cultural roots. The link between institutions and culture and its impact on development was noted by Jamaican-born sociologist Orlando Patterson, whose works show that culture has economic implications and economics in turn has cultural implications. According to Patterson, Afro American cultural models of "compensatory sexuality" and "unsecured paternity"[108] celebrating early marriage and high fertility had roots in

---

99 Landes, *supra* note 73, at 2; *see generally* DAVID S. LANDES, THE WEALTH AND POVERTY OF NATIONS: WHY SOME ARE SO RICH AND SOME SO POOR (1999). I elsewhere examine the market dominance of certain ethnic groups, some recent immigrants in the United States and other countries, and other historical "middlemen minorities" throughout the world. *See* Lan Cao, *The Diaspora of Ethnic Economies: Beyond the Pale?*, 44 WM & MARY L. REV. 1521 (2003) [hereinafter Cao, *The Diaspora*]; *see also* AMY CHUA, WORLD ON FIRE: HOW EXPORTING FREE MARKET DEMOCRACY BREEDS ETHNIC HATRED AND GLOBAL INSTABILITY (2003) (describing the market dominance of ethnic minorities such as the Chinese in Southeast Asia, the Jews in Russia, the Ibos in Africa). For a review of Chua's book, *see* Lan Cao, *The Ethnic Question in Law and Development*, 102 MICH. L. REV. 1044 (2004) (book review) [hereinafter Cao, *The Ethnic Question*].

100 William Pfaff, *Western Economic Theories Have Left Soviet Bloc Economies in Shambles*, CHI. TRIB., Aug. 31, 1999, at 15, *available at* http://articles.chicagotribune.com/1999-08-31/news/9908310187_1_eastern-europe-soviet-union-bloc.

101 *Id.*

102 *Id.*

103 Robert J. Samuelson, *The Spirit of Capitalism*, FOREIGN AFF., Jan.–Feb. 2001, at 211, *available at* http://www.foreignaffairs.com/articles/56674/robert-j-samuelson/the-spirit-of-capitalism.

104 Samuel P. Huntington, *Foreword: Cultures Count*, *in* CULTURE MATTERS: HOW VALUES SHAPE HUMAN PROGRESS xiii, xiv (Lawrence E. Harrison & Samuel P. Huntington eds., 2000).

105 Sen, *supra* note 47, at 40.

106 *Id.* at 52.

107 *Id.* Professor Sen warned against seeing culture as all-determining, cautioning that Max Weber had claimed that Confucianism did not promote rational instrumentalism and was unsuitable for an industrial economy. *Id.* at 48.

108 Patterson, *supra* note 64, at 212.

the economic institutions of slavery and sharecropping. But changing those economic institutions alone isn't sufficient if the economic institutions themselves are culturally rooted. "Although formal rules may change overnight as the result of political or judicial decisions, informal constraints embodied in customs, traditions, and codes of conduct are much more impervious to deliberate policies. These cultural constraints not only connect the past with the present and future, but provide us with a key to explaining the path of historical change."[109]

Current problems that seem endemic and entrenched and not easily changed through policy prescriptions may also need a culturally oriented push. For decades now, the Japanese economy has been struck by deflation which has been exacerbated by a skewed demography due to the country's rapidly aging population.[110] Many of the solutions bandied about—getting women to re-enter the workforce although 62 percent of working women quit after having their first child, for example—involve not just economic policy but also "overcoming cultural taboos."[111]

And overcoming cultural taboos means engaging culture and changing those aspects that need changing. For example, what might be characterized as an inextricable part of a country's cultural fabric may in fact be a recent development prompted by economic circumstances and thus potentially more susceptible to change. The Japanese, for example, insist that eating whale meat has cultural significance and therefore are unwilling to be bound by the international ban on whaling, despite considerable international pressure.[112] Yet, it was only during the postwar period, when non-whale protein sources were scarce that the Japanese relied on whale meat for school lunches.[113] In a similar vein, Japan's lifetime employment system and its high savings rate, generally deemed to be an essential component of the country's cultural characteristics, came out of the post–World War II experience; lifetime employment was instituted to control labor strife and high savings was adopted by those with direct wartime experience of deprivation and shortages.[114] "Thus it is difficult to disentangle culturally derived behaviors from behaviors that have been enhanced or encouraged by the economic system."[115] As I argue more fully

---

[109] Douglass C. North, Institutions, Institutional Change, and Economic Performance 6 (1990).

[110] *The Future of Japan: The Japan Syndrome*, Economist (Nov. 18, 2010), http://www.economist.com/node/17522568.

[111] *Id.* Don Lee, *Japan Plans to Lift Economy by Getting New Moms Back to Work*, L.A. Times (Aug. 21, 2013), http://articles.latimes.com/2013/aug/21/business/la-fi-japan-women-jobs-20130821.

[112] In 1982, the International Whaling Commission adopted a moratorium on whaling. Japan was one of the few countries that opposed the ban. *See* International Whaling Commission, Thirty-Fourth Report of the International Whaling Commission, 34th mtg. (1982); *see also* Joel Paul, *Cultural Resistance to Global Governance*, 22 Mich. J. Int'l L. 1, 58 (2000).

[113] Suvendrini Kakuchi, *Tokyo Persists with Bid to Lift Whaling Ban*, Inter Press Service (Nov. 13, 1997), http://www.ipsnews.net/1997/11/japan-tokyo-persists-with-bid-to-lift-whaling-ban/.

[114] Michael Porter, *Attitudes, Values, Beliefs, and the Microeconomics of Prosperity*, *in* Culture Matters: How Values Shape Human Progress 14, 24 (Lawrence E. Harrison & Samuel P. Huntington eds., 2000).

[115] *Id.*

in this book, these examples suggest that culture, whether norms or practices, is not static but fluid, and can be, whether purposefully or not, changed.

The purpose of this section is to probe the link between culture and development, particularly market development, and to lay the foundation for my central argument—that a culturally informed lens is vital to the success of the law and development enterprise and that cultural norms that negatively affect development should be changed. With this in mind, I explore a large body of scholarship that establishes how cultural cohesion and group solidarity promote cooperation, minimize defection, and solve collective action problems.[116] A recent study tested the culture/economics linkage using cross-country data, focusing on a country's social capital and its relationship to growth (in per capita income), and found that there is indeed a correlation between the level of trust and a group's social capital base and economic growth.[117]

Early works by Emile Durkheim studied how humans, embedded in social institutions such as the family, clan, ethnic, tribal, religious, and other groups, internalized the norms of their respective groups.[118] Later theories rely on law-and-economics studies on externalities and transaction costs to explain how norms arise and how they affect group social and economic exchanges. According to James Coleman, "norms arise as attempts to limit negative external effects or encourage positive ones. But, in many social structures where these conditions exist, norms do not come into existence" because the social structures at issue lack what Coleman called closure. According to Coleman, the members of the group must be interconnected; otherwise, punishment and sanctions are not available to penalize a member's wrongdoing. Without closure in the social structure, a broken obligation can only be enforced, if at all, by the individual to whom the obligation was owed. Collective sanctions from a community cannot be effectively applied.[119]

---

[116] *See* Jon Elster, Nuts and Bolts for the Social Sciences 126 (1989). A collective action problem exists thus: "Suppose that each member of a group has the choice between engaging in a certain activity and not engaging in it. The group has a collective action problem if it is better for all if some do it than if nobody does it, but better for each not to do it." For scholarly sources that study how decentralized groups utilize group norms to produce efficiency and order, *see* Lan Cao, *Looking at Communities and Markets*, 74 Notre Dame L. Rev. 841, 863–74 (1999).

[117] Stephen Knack & Philip Keefer, *Does Social Capital Have an Economic Payoff? A Cross-Country Investigation*, 112 Q. J. Econ. 1251 (1997). The authors used data gathered from interviews of thousands of respondents in industrialized and developing countries, in which the respondents were asked their attitudes about family life, work, religion, and other values. In seeking to measure a country's social capital, the authors asked, "Generally speaking, would you say that most people can be trusted, or that you can't be too careful in dealing with people?" For the twenty-nine market economies included in the study, they found that, controlling for income, education, and private investment, the measure of trust is correlated with growth in per capita income.

[118] *See generally* Emile Durkheim, The Division of Labor in Society (1893); Emile Durkheim, Elementary Forms of Religious Life (1912); Talcott Parsons, The Structure of Social Action (1937).

[119] James S. Coleman, *Social Capital in the Creation of Human Capital*, 94 Am. J. Soc. S95, S105–S108 (Supp. 1988).

Increasingly, research has focused on the relationship between group size and group conduct, and has found that "there are opposing behavioral implications involved in any extension in the membership of a community."[120] A person's moral-ethical principles and constraints against self-aggrandizement and interests are stronger in a small, bounded community than a large, diffuse one. On the one hand, if the group expands, members may have the advantage of being part of a larger internal market, allowing greater possibilities of trade, sponsorship activities, and preferential purchases among group members. On the other hand, the larger the group becomes, the greater the probability of breach even as the ability of the group collectively to sanction violators is itself proportionately weakened.[121]

Once "an individual recognizes himself to be a member of a group of others more or less like himself," he is more likely to be subject, not just to the *external* constraints—"economic, geological, legal, political, social, technological"—on possible behavior but also to *internal* limits.[122] While one cannot draw broad categorical boundaries to distinguish those a person considers to be "members of the tribe," and those deemed "outsiders," the point is that "there is a difference in an individual's behavior toward members and nonmembers, and that the membership lists are drawn up in his own psyche."[123] For most individuals, there are moral-ethical boundaries and limits, and they may be reached at any of these levels—the nation-state, the provincial or regional states, the local community, extended family, clan, race, ethnicity, church, and so forth. The tension between individual self-interests and community may be kept within tolerable limits only if "there is some proximate correspondence between the external institutional and the internal moral constraints on behavior."[124]

Groups characterized by common bonds such as cultural and ethnic ties then are typically the sort of groups that are likely to produce social capital [125] and promote intragroup exchanges. Generally speaking, social capital refers to "norms, and networks, that can

---

[120] James M. Buchanan, *Markets, States, and the Extent of Morals*, 68 AM. ECON. REV. 364, 364 (1978).

[121] Group sanctions of norm violators include withholding future business from the violator, disseminating the violator's negative reputation groupwide, ostracizing the violator, or banishing the violator from the group. Cao, *supra* note 116, at 872. A group that is too large and not close-knit is less likely to succeed in meting out effective sanctions against violators.

[122] Buchanan, *supra* note 120, at 366.

[123] *Id.* at 366. This phenomenon explains why in many instances, as nonexclusion or nondiscrimination rules are introduced to override an individual's personal selectivity and to increase the size of the sharing group beyond the individual's own narrow universe of preferences (opening up the club to everyone, for example), the new rules have had unintended effects, for example, spurring "the formation of smaller clubs." Robert D. Tollison, *Consumption Sharing and Non-Exclusion Rules*, 39 ECONOMICA 276, 283 (1972). When nondiscrimination rules were applied to public facilities in the United States, for example, in public schools, this led to a "movement out of public schools to the formation of more exclusive . . . private educational facilities." *Id.*, at 289.

[124] Buchanan, *supra* note 120, at 367.

[125] For a discussion of the distinction between human capital and social capital, *see* FUKUYAMA, *supra* note 91, at 26–27. Social capital consists of group-based factors that enhance group members to work together in groups and organizations, and is usually created and transmitted through cultural mechanisms like religion, tradition, or historical habits. Human capital consists of knowledge and skills, and may be acquired through education or training.

improve the efficiency of society by facilitating coordinated actions. . . ."[126] Because social capital exists in the relations among persons, not in the individuals themselves or in the physical elements of production, group members must be interconnected for the group's social capital to function in three crucial areas: obligations and expectations, information channels, and norms accompanied by effective sanctions.[127]

As discussed further below, groups with a social capital foundation of "networks, norms, and social trust that facilitate coordination and cooperation for mutual benefit"[128] are well-equipped to achieve a certain level of economic productivity. Communities characterized by a "repository of trust . . . reduces the probability of breach on a contract between insiders."[129] Trust therefore is integral to these interactions, and without the members' common ethnic ties, "elaborate and expensive bonding and insurance devices would be necessary—or else the transaction could not take place."[130] Indeed, the level of trust, which is based on a commonality of external and internal circumstances, such as labor force disadvantage or outsider status[131] and a shared cultural foundation of values and beliefs, "are not easily duplicated in any artificial community, and indeed, are rarely found in communities united by geographic proximity or other demographic characteristics."[132] Trust tends to be strongest among transactors of the same household, lineage, village, subtribe, tribe, and decreases as the circle of social distance expands, so that at the edge of the ethnic or tribal boundary, transactions might even be "consummated by force and guile."[133]

In sum then, economic behavior in many instances can be explained not by reference to individualistic behaviors but by reference to embedded relationships—"value introjection, reciprocity transactions, bounded solidarity, and enforceable trust."[134] Robert

---

126 Robert D. Putnam, Making Democracy Work: Civic Traditions in Modern Italy 167 (1993).

127 Coleman, *supra* note 119, at S95; James S. Coleman, Foundations of Social Theory 300–21 (1990).

128 Robert Putnam, *Bowling Alone: America's Declining Social Capital*, 6 J. Democracy 65, 67 (1995).

129 Robert Cooter & Janet T. Landa, *Personal Versus Impersonal Trade: The Size of Trading Groups and Contract Law*, 4 Int'l Rev. L. & Econ. 15, 15 (1984). Trust may also backfire, as may be seen in cases involving affinity fraud. *See,* e.g., Lisa M. Fairfax, *"With Friends Like These . . .": Toward a More Efficacious Response to Affinity-Based Securities and Investment Fraud*, 36 Ga. L. Rev. 63 (2001). Sarah Maslin Nir, *Latinos Who Invested Savings Claim Betrayal in Ponzi Scheme*, N.Y. Times, Aug. 23, 2012, at A18, *avalaible at* http://www.nytimes.com/2012/08/24/nyregion/latino-investors-in-queens-claim-betrayal-in-ponzi-scheme.html?_r=0.

130 Coleman, *supra* note 119, at S99.

131 "[O]utsider status, vulnerability, and disadvantage" are factors that have propelled certain groups to turn inward, promoting solidarity and cooperation among group members which in turn facilitate intra group transactions. Cao, *The Ethnic Question, supra* note 99, at 1061.

132 Patricia G. Greene, *A Resource-Based Approach to Ethnic Business Sponsorship: A Consideration of Ismaili-Pakistani Immigrants*, 35 J. Small Bus. Mgmt. 58, 67 (1997).

133 Marshall D. Sahlins, *On the Sociology of Primitive Exchange*, *in* The Relevance of Models for Social Anthropology 139, 154 (Michael Banton ed., 1965); *see also* Elizabeth Colson, Tradition and Contract: The Problem of Order 25 (1974) ("if you know a person's clan, you have a good chance of being able to find an appropriate kinship term to signal the etiquette to be used between the two of you and to define the moral imperatives that ought to govern your relationships.").

134 Greene, *supra* note 132, at 60; *see* Mark Granovetter, *Economic Action and Social Structure: The Problem of Embeddedness*, 91 Am. J. Soc. 481 (1985).

Putnam believed that the vast cultural differences between the Italian north and south are a significant contributing factor to the economic discrepancy between the two regions.[135] The civic culture in northern Italy, with its networks of associations and norms of trust helped overcome collective action problems and made individuals and groups more productive.[136]

In his study of northern and southern Italy, Putnam concluded that "success in overcoming dilemmas of collective action and the self-defeating opportunism that they spawn depends on the broader social context within which any particular game is played. Voluntary co-operation is easier in a community that has inherited a substantial stock of social capital, in the form of norms of reciprocity and networks of civic engagement."[137] In a similar vein, "[w]here people know one another, interact with one another each week at choir practice or sports matches, and trust one another to behave honorably, they have a model and a moral foundation upon which to base further cooperative enterprises. Light-touch government works more efficiently in the presence of social capital."[138]

As I discuss below, rotating credit associations illustrate the link between cultural norms and social capital on the one hand and economic capital on the other. By providing an in-depth examination of a culture-based institution with positive developmental impact, I aim to illustrate in concrete terms many of the ideas in this section about how culture guides the behaviors and expectations of group members by providing an ordered framework in which community institutions can regulate member activities in economically beneficial ways.[139] Indeed, rotating credit associations constitute an instance whereby cultural norms combine with market behaviors to marshal ethnic affinities in ways that both preserve their moral bases and further transactions that improve community economic efficiency.

A rotating credit association is a mechanism or arrangement devised to provide credit for those who need it. For example, rotating credit associations such as the Korean *kye*, the Chinese and Vietnamese *hui*, the Japanese *tanamoshi*, the Cambodian *thong thing*, the Mexican *cundina*, the Ethiopian *ekub*, and West Indian *esusu* have provided a form of ethnic community market to members of ethnic groups who would have difficulty borrowing from banks.[140] Rotating credit associations have thrived in many cultures and

---

[135] *See,* e.g., *supra* note 126, at 182.

[136] *Id.* at 167.

[137] *Id.*

[138] Robert D. Putnam, Bowling Alone: The Collapse and Revival of American Community 346 (2000).

[139] Because rotating credit associations were first observed in less developed countries, it was assumed they were inefficient precursors to full-fledged banks and would be supplanted by formal financial institutions. Christine Gorman, *Do-It-Yourself Financing*, Time, July 25, 1988, at 62; Clifford Geertz, *The Rotating Credit Association: A "Middle Rung" in Development*, 10 Econ. Dev. & Cultural Change 241, 260 (1962). This has not occurred and rotating credit associations remain viable alternatives for certain borrowers in developing countries as well as developed countries, suggesting that they continue to act as a substitute for conventional banks.

[140] Discussion on rotating credit association in this section is drawn from Cao, *supra* note 116.

originated many years ago to enable members to pool cash to finance business, burials, marriages, and other obligations. The Korean *kye*, for example, dates back to the Korean farming villages in the sixteenth century.[141] The Chinese *hui* originated in southern China and is founded on kinship, that is, on commonalities characterized by village, lineage, or clan.[142] The West African *esusu* also has historical roots—English references to it were made as early as 1794.[143] Studies showed that the *esusu* was practiced by descendants of West African slaves in the Bahamas in 1910 and operated outside the realm of formal laws. "These 'Asu' have no written statutes or regulations, no regular officers, but carry on their affairs without fraud or miscalculation."[144]

In many countries, immigrants have resorted to ethnic institutions and resources such as the rotating credit association to finance their businesses. Often newcomers lack the credit history and collateral required by banks for loans. Because a typical credit relationship is marked by transaction costs that lenders have to incur, loans will not be made if lenders believe the transaction costs of screening, monitoring, and enforcing the loans are too high to justify the loan. Information asymmetry inherently exists between borrower and lender because the borrower has more accurate information about his or her own creditworthiness. Thus, banks need to incur costs to gather information about potential borrowers[145] to distinguish between honest and dishonest borrowers.[146] To lower their screening costs, banks use various techniques. They draw inferences about the creditworthiness of an applicant by analyzing information accumulated from similar past loans and relying on information about applicant age, occupation, or neighborhood to make their determination. "In recent times . . . the most important factor responsible for discrimination probably has been information costs."[147]

In addition to screening costs, banks also face monitoring costs, especially in marginal loan transactions. Principal-agent literature is replete with observations about the costs

---

[141] Pauline Yoshihashi & Sarah Lubman, *American Dreams: How the Kims of LA and Other Koreans Made It in the U.S.*, Wall St. J., June 16, 1992, at A1; Ivan Light & Edna Bonacich, Immigrant Entrepreneurs: Koreans in Los Angeles 1965–1982, 244–45 (1988).

[142] Fukuyama, *supra* note 91, at 300.

[143] Ivan H. Light, Ethnic Enterprise in America: Business and Welfare Among Chinese, Japanese, and Blacks 30 (1972). Anthropological accounts of the *esusu* describe it in this way: "There is a society called Esusu. This society deals with monetary matters only, and it helps its members to save and raise money thus: Every member shall pay a certain fixed sum of money regularly at a fixed time. . . . And one of the subscribing members shall take the total amount thus subscribed for his or her own personal use. The next subscription shall be taken by another member; this shall so continue rotationally until every member has taken." *Id.* at 31 (quoting A. K. Ajisafe, Laws and Customs of the Yoruba People 48–49 (1924)).

[144] *Id.* at 32 (quoting Harry H. Johnson, The Negro in the New World 303 (1910)).

[145] Dwight M. Jaffee & Thomas Russell, *Imperfect Information, Uncertainty, and Credit Rationing*, 90 Q. J. Econ. 651, 664 (1976).

[146] *Id.* at 651–52.

[147] Richard A. Posner, The Economics of Justice 362 (1981); *see also* Neil K. Komesar, Imperfect Alternatives: Choosing Institutions in Law, Economics, and Public Policy 101–03, 115–21 (1994) (singling out information costs as a particularly significant cause of problems in decision making).

that principals must assume in order to monitor their agents.[148] Finally, there are the enforcement costs. Creditors may demand security to contain the high risks of default.[149] Lenders engaged in a rational cost-benefit calculus may decide against lending to certain borrowers who lack certain indicators of creditworthiness or collateral.

As a result, it is not uncommon for ethnic borrowers to sidestep the formal credit market, turn inward and create community rotating credit associations for financing purposes. Each group determines its own rules, such as how much and how often each member contributes to the pool and on what basis money may be drawn, whether by lottery, need, or rotation. By participating in a rotating credit association, every member, except the last member to draw from the pool, can access a lump sum of capital that they would not have been able to access or borrow but for the credit association. Assume that a rotating credit pool consists of $50,000 and ten members, each of whom needs $50,000 to start a business and that each member is able to save $5,000 a year. At that rate, unless a bank loan is available, it would take ten years for each member to save enough to start the business. But it would only take one year for the members together, through a rotating credit association, to raise $50,000 for one loan, resulting in an efficiency gain and a decrease in opportunity costs.

Rotating credit associations function smoothly because they are embedded in the ethnic community of the members themselves and as a result are able to avoid the high transaction costs—screening, monitoring, and enforcement—that banks face. They are efficient because they can "propagate information on job opportunities, relative prices and a host of other economic matters."[150] As noted, social capital helps lower transaction costs. Unlike the relationship between banks and borrowers, the relationship between and among the borrowers that make up a rotating credit association is not marked by information asymmetry. Hence screening costs are low because information about group members is freely available. Indeed, it is incontrovertible that the dissemination of information "has important public goods attributes"[151] and "reduces the transaction costs attributable to asymmetric information."[152] In the context of rotating credit associations, information is widely disseminated because it is embedded in the group's very structure. Members are part of a community and share a common understanding of the group's

---

[148] According to Jensen and Meckling, agency costs are the totality of "1) the monitoring expenditures by the principal, 2) the bonding expenditures by the agent, and 3) the residual loss." Michael C. Jensen & William H. Meckling, *Theory of the Firm: Managerial Behavior, Agency Costs, and Ownership Structure*, 3 J. FIN. ECON., 305, 308 (1976).

[149] JAMES C. VAN HORNE, FINANCIAL MANAGEMENT AND POLICY 536 (1974). Indeed, secured financing may be used as a means of reducing not just enforcement but also monitoring costs. Thomas H. Jackson & Anthony T. Kronman, *Secured Financing and Priorities Among Creditors*, 88 YALE L. J. 1143, 1158–61 (1979).

[150] Yousfi, *supra* note 21, at 37.

[151] Stephen Craig Pirrong, *The Efficient Scope of Private Transactions-Cost-Reducing Institutions: The Successes and Failures of Commodity Exchanges*, 24 J. LEGAL STUD. 229, 241 (1995).

[152] *Id.* at 242.

social meanings. Rotating credit associations rely on the group's cultural norms and personalistic transactions as a built-in information-gathering device. Rotating credit associations thus are a form of peer lending and peer monitoring and the typical principal/agency problems are minimized.[153] This bottom-up, decentralized approach to lending is particularly effective for small loans, especially uncollateralized ones that banks find inefficient to lend and administer.

Moreover, the same social and cultural factors allow the association to monitor members effectively. As noted, group members have ample information about the identity, history, and background of other members in order to assess their identity and trustworthiness. In this case, more perfect information can effectively serve as a substitute for traditional security devices required by banks and other formal lenders. As noted, the costs that principals must assume to monitor their agents are considerable, but other monitoring mechanisms allow agents to monitor themselves at comparatively lower costs.[154] Bottom-up peer monitoring, one of the key features of rotating credit associations, allows those in the best position to monitor the borrower to do the monitoring themselves.

Bottom-up monitoring in a rotating credit association is premised on the concept of joint liability. There are two layers of monitoring that are available, first from the organizer and second from the members themselves. The organizer screens members and monitors their performance. If a member defaults or fails to deposit her share in the next round of contribution, the organizer is liable.[155] The joint liability rule of the association induces the organizer to use community knowledge to ascertain the members' social assets such as their trustworthiness. Identity and trust, in this case, function as low-cost signals for minimizing risks in exchange relations. "Trust is an important lubricant of a social system"[156] and has "real, practical, economic value."[157]

The second layer of monitoring comes from the group itself. By its selection and approval of members, the group functions on the basis of mutual accountability and acts as an internal monitoring mechanism of itself and its members. That the group is composed of members from the same close-knit community means that the group can rely on "group incentive mechanisms"[158] for mutual monitoring. It is assumed that members would agree to form a rotating credit association with another only if they are satisfied with the other's social standing. That one who has drawn from the pool could stop her contribution—appropriate and defect rather than continue to cooperate—means that one will only join with others if one is convinced that the other's internalization of

---

[153] *See* Joseph Stiglitz, *Peer Monitoring and Credit Markets*, 4 World Bank Econ. Rev. 351 (1990).

[154] Hal R. Varian, *Monitoring Agents with Other Agents*, 146 J. Institutional and Theoretical Econ. 153, 153 (1990).

[155] Mark Arax, *Pooled Cash of Loan Clubs Key to Asian Immigrant Entrepreneurs*, L.A. Times, Oct. 30, 1988, at 1; Gorman, *supra* note 139, at 62.

[156] Kenneth J. Arrow, The Limits of Organization 23 (1974).

[157] *Id.*

[158] Varian, *supra* note 154, at 155.

community norms and constraints are sufficient to minimize opportunistic behavior. In other words, each person agrees to participate only if she trusts that the other person, as each other's and the group's agent, will act as good agents.

Enforcement costs are also markedly lower for rotating credit associations. Rotating credit associations rely on internal compliance and group-based, self-enforcement schemes to ensure continued cooperation and repayment by borrowers. Group members have internalized the group's norms and are likely to comply with group rules. That the lender is the group of which the borrower is a member also increases the likelihood of that member's compliance, thus decreasing the need for external enforcement. In other words, even those who have drawn from the pool must honor their commitment to continue contributing so others who have not drawn have the chance to draw. In this way, unlike conventional banks which face high transaction costs when making loans to marginal borrowers, rotating credit associations function efficiently for its members because norms of trust and reciprocity maximize cooperation and minimize defection. Indeed, the association can only function if every member knows that others "will continue to show up and pay their share every month, long after they have received their own payoff. . . ."[159]

Transaction costs are lowered only because rotating credit associations operate not in the open market but rather in a community market embedded in closely knit, geographically concentrated ethnic boundaries. In such communities, each member has a reputation that is known to other members of the community. This so-called "reputation bond"[160] maximizes the individual's compliance with established community norms and the community's ability to enforce its shared norms against rule breakers. An actor who acts contrary to the community's norms "creates a stigma [and] that stigma [has] a social meaning,"[161] which then sullies the violator's reputation. Other community members may sanction the norm violator by withholding their esteem for him or her, which may result in reputational injury, ostracism, and banishment from the community.[162] This type of sanction is popular among ethnic groups, for example, and is often relied upon by Orthodox Jewish dealers in the diamond industry of New York City.[163]

Avoiding default is important to members not only because of community sanctions but also because of an internalized sense of obligation to the group.[164] Norms "are expectations about action—one's own action, that of others, or both—which express what

---

[159] Joel Garreau, *For Koreans, "Keh" Is Key to Success*, WASH POST, Nov. 3, 1991, at B1.

[160] Lisa Bernstein, *Opting Out of the Legal System: Extralegal Contractual Relations in the Diamond Industry*, 21 J. LEGAL STUD. 115, 116 (1992).

[161] Lawrence Lessig, *The Regulation of Social Meaning*, 62 U. CHI. L. REV. 943, 951 (1995).

[162] Richard H. McAdams, *The Origin, Development, and Regulation of Norms*, 96 MICH. L. REV. 338, 377 (1997).

[163] For example, the Diamond Dealers Club bylaws provide that "[a]ll decisions of arbitration panels . . . which are not complied with within 10 working days, together with the picture of the non-complying member, shall be posted in a conspicuous place in the Club rooms." Bernstein, *supra* note 160, at 128.

[164] Robert D. Cooter, *Decentralized Law for a Complex Economy: The Structural Approach to Adjudicating the New Law Merchant*, 144 U. PA. L. REV. 1643, 1656 (1996); BECKER, *supra* note 49, at 225 ("Norms are

action is right or what action is wrong"[165] and as such, "internalization . . . can tip the individual's motivational balance. . . . From this perspective, internalization attaches a 'guilty penalty' to violating a norm, which can change the sign of the net psychological benefits."[166]

In essence, then, trust lies at the heart of rotating credit associations. "This literature draws attention to the communities in which enterprises are embedded and to the sociocultural ties that facilitate trust. . . . The question is, to what extent does culture influence the functioning of social networks and their ability to produce trustworthy relationships?"[167]

Members trust that others will adhere to group norms, including its implicit "no law" commitment. As noted, each rotating credit association makes up its own rules about the amount of the pool, the order of the rotation, and priority of collection, for example. There is no contract and no loan agreement. The association functions on "an unwritten honor code."[168] The association's pool is not backed by deposit insurance. There are no processing, accounting, or legal fees associated with conventional bank loans, and there are no collateral or credit checks.[169]

This level of trust exists and can be leveraged for social and economic purposes because of "preexisting social ties based on kinship or geographic residence in the native country."[170] Again, trust is crucial because absent trust, "elaborate and expensive bonding and insurance devices would be necessary—or else the transactions could not take place."[171] This form of trust, founded on external and internal factors such as societal hostility and shared cultural values, is "not easily duplicated in any artificial community, and indeed, [is] rarely found in communities united by geographic proximity or other demographic characteristics."[172]

---

those common values of a group which influence an individual's behavior through being internalized as preferences.").

[165] James S. Coleman, *Norms as Social Capital*, *in* ECONOMIC IMPERIALISM: THE ECONOMIC APPROACH APPLIED OUTSIDE THE FIELD OF ECONOMICS 133, 135 (Gerard Radnitzky & Peter Bernholz eds., 1987).

[166] Cooter, *supra* note 164, at 1662–63.

[167] Yousfi, *supra* note 21, at 37.

[168] Jim Szymanski & Jaymes Song, *Trust Is the Key to "Kye" Investment*, NEWS TRIB. (Tacoma, Wa.), June 16, 1996, at D1.

[169] Garreau, *supra* note 159.

[170] FUKUYAMA, *supra* note 91, at 301.

[171] Coleman, *supra* note 119, at S99. Social capital is especially relevant when studying the phenomenon of market-dominant ethnic minorities. Some have remarked upon the low level of social capital among certain groups, the Malays, for example, who are less likely to engage in intra-cooperative economic activities and who lag far behind the ethnic Chinese in Malaysia. Kevin Davis et al., *Ethnically Homogeneous Commercial Elites in Developing Countries*, 32 LAW & POL'Y INT'L BUS. 331, 348 (2001). "Human capital levels among indigenous Burmans are . . . abysmal" as well. Although they are the majority, they are nonetheless economically behind the market-dominant ethnic minorities such as the Chinese. CHUA, *supra* note 99, at 29.

[172] Greene, *supra* note 132, at 67.

Thus, through an overarching cultural regime of norms that promote social capital and enhance community trust, the very borrowers deemed not creditworthy by banks gain access to credit by reliance on community custom and usage to facilitate loans, ensure repayment, and resolve disputes among community members. "Norms and expectations are themselves embedded within a social structure consisting of associations and overlapping networks. . . . This is true anywhere, even in the most developed economies. But it is particularly true when formal market institutions are weak or nonexistent and the enforcement of contracts relies almost exclusively on informal enforcement mechanisms. . . ."[173]

Although cultural norms can undoubtedly lower transaction costs and enhance opportunities for economic development, at the same time, it is important to note that that there is no monocausal factor for development or nondevelopment. As culture scholars have observed, "culture is not an independent variable. It is influenced by numerous other factors, for example, geography and climate, politics, the vagaries of history."[174] Thus, given continuous interaction between the various factors, "a cultural explanation does not preclude social causes. Often what's most interesting and useful in any analysis is to identify and disentangle the complex explanatory interplay between cultural and noncultural factors, an interplay in which both sets of factors can be both independent and dependent in one's causal model."[175] A cultural model does not have to be static because "although cultural continuities certainly exist, people are not slaves to them. They use them and they can change them if they really want to."[176] Note the emphasis on the possibility of culture change.

The relationship between culture and local institutions, as broadly defined below, is an interactive one and becomes highly significant. Indeed, cultural norms are "acquired through experience that is 'local' to a particular environment and which therefore also varies widely across environments. . . . This diversity of experiences and learning has produced increasingly differentiated societies and civilizations with very different degrees of success in solving fundamental economic problems and 'efficient' institutions."[177] Consequently, the relationship between culture and other relevant factors should be seen not as a one-way relationship, but rather as a two-way relationship.[178] For example,

---

[173] Marcel Fafchamps, *Markets and the Diffusion of Institutional Innovations*, *in* CULTURE, INSTITUTIONS, AND DEVELOPMENT: NEW INSIGHTS INTO AN OLD DEBATE 143, 147 (Jean-Philippe Platteau & Robert Peccoud eds., 2011).

[174] Harrison, *supra* note 48, at xxviii; *see also* JARED DIAMOND, GUNS, GERMS, AND STEEL: THE FATES OF HUMAN SOCIETIES 417–19 (1997) ("Cultural factors and influences . . . loom large. . . . Some of that cultural variation is no doubt a product of environmental variation. . . . A minor cultural factor may arise for trivial, temporary local reasons, become fixed, and then predispose a society toward more important cultural choices. . . .").

[175] Patterson, *supra* note 64, at 208.

[176] *Id.* at 218 (referencing a cultural model in the black community that does not condemn early marriage or high birth rates).

[177] Yousfi, *supra* note 21, at 33.

[178] Patterson, *supra* note 64, at 208.

culture influences institutions—"culture is the mother and . . . institutions are the children"[179]—and vice versa. In explaining the different developments that have taken root in the former colonies of Britain and Spain in the Americas, Douglass North noted that "[i]n the former, an institutional framework has evolved that permits the complex impersonal exchange necessary to political stability and to capture the potential economic gains of modern technology. In the latter, personalistic relationships are still the key to much of the political and economic exchange."[180]

"An institution is a social generated regularity of behaviour. The institutions that affect a certain class of behaviours form an institutional system."[181] Development policy has almost uniformly emphasized formal laws and institutions. However, our understanding of institutions has been expanded to include more than just those in the formal realm, for example, customary laws, beliefs, or culture. Timur Kuran emphasized the broad elements that together make up an institution: "Thus, the laws of a country form an institutional system whose elements include customary legal procedures, rules of promotion within the judiciary, attitudes regarding the role that religion should play in adjudication, and a hierarchy of courts. By itself, none of these elements captures the social function of a legal system, which is much more than the sum of its parts. Both attitudes and behaviours may enter into the nexus of factors forming a particular institutional system. The latter concept thus subsumes what I am treating as culture."[182]

Douglass North's work too has radically changed and expanded our understanding of institutions, defining institutions broadly, as the "rules of a game in a society or, more formally, the humanly devised constraints that shape human interaction."[183] North suggested that informal constraints derived "from socially transmitted information [that is] a part of the heritage that we call culture" exert a significant impact on institutional development.[184] Such informal constraints are part of the "governing structure"—"codes of conduct, norms of behavior, and conventions" that shape our "daily interaction with others, whether within the family, in external social relations, or in business activities."[185]

For North, constraints include both what are prohibited and what are permitted, providing the "incentive framework" that guides human behavior.[186] And institutions

---

179 Etounga-Manguelle, *supra* note 76, at 75.

180 North, *supra* note 109, at 117.

181 Timur Kuran, *Economic Underdevelopment in the Middle East*, *in* Culture, Institutions, and Development: New Insights into an Old Debate 87, 88 (Jean-Philippe Platteau & Robert Peccoud eds., 2011).

182 *Id.* at 88–89.

183 North, *supra* note 109, at 3.

184 *Id.* at 37. For a discussion of new institutional economics and how different types of institutional arrangements or governance structure will play a part in determining the cost and benefit associated with the transaction, *see* Cao, *supra* note 116, at 865 n.86.

185 North, *supra* note 109, at 36.

186 Indra de Soysa & Johannes Jütting, *Informal Institutions and Development: Think Local, Act Global?*, OECD Dev. Centre & Dev. Assistance Committee–Network on Governance 3 (Dec. 11–12, 2006), http://instruct.uwo.ca/economics/317b-570/Institutions_worldbank.pdf.

can be formal or informal,[187] consisting of both "formal written rules as well as typically unwritten codes of conduct and regularized behavior that underlie and supplement formal rules."[188] The former is enforced by formal entities such as courts, judges, police, and officials, whereas the latter are "largely self-enforcing through mechanisms of obligation, such as in patron-client relationships or clan networks, or simply because following the rules is in the best interests of individuals who may find themselves in a 'Nash equilibrium' where everyone is better off from cooperation."[189]

One can argue thus that North's work embraces an understanding of institutions that is appropriately expanded to include informal but regularized codes of behavior—culture, for example. Many scholars have noted and appreciated North's special contribution which is "to map the whole social system and focus on the informal constraints imposed on the choices made by individuals. . . . North defines culture as 'communities of common ideologies and a common set of rules that all believe in'. . . . He treats culture as a robustly practical way of life that responds to changes in prices and costs, drawing the economic system along with it. . . . Culture mobilizes individuals and turns them into a community with shared norms and values."[190]

This expanded understanding of institutions is by no means uniformly accepted. Indeed, the phrase "informal institutions" has had varied and contested uses.[191] Although some scholars caution that "all informal institutions (rules governing behavior outside official channels) should not be confused with culture,"[192] they nevertheless concede that there is "a close association between . . . the 'constitutive' and 'regulatory' effects of culture and informal institutions."[193] Even if informal institutions are not synonymous with culture, informal institutions are reflected in and encompass a cultural regime. In other words, the constitutive dimensions of informal institutions "relate to aspects of culture that shape economic behavior by guiding relative valuation, categorizations and understandings of economic processes and outcomes, which are passed on through the

---

187 *Id.* at 2; *see also* Hans-Joachim Lauth, *Informal Institutions and Democracy*, 7 DEMOCRATIZATION 21 (Winter 2000); Guillermo O'Donnell, *Another Institutionalization: Latin America and Elsewhere* (Kellogg Inst. for Int'l Stud., Working Paper No. 222, 1996), *available at* http://kellogg.nd.edu/publications/workingpapers/WPS/222.pdf. One way of distinguishing an informal from formal institution is by reference to the state-societal dichotomy. "Formal institution" refers to state bodies such as courts, legislatures, and bureaucracies or state-enforced rules such as constitutions, laws, regulations, and court decisions. "Informal institution" refers to "civic, religious, kinship, and other 'societal' rules and organizations." Gretchen Helmke & Steven Levitsky, *Informal Institutions and Comparative Politics: A Research Agenda* (Kellogg Inst. for Int'l Stud., Working Paper No. 307, 2003), *available at* https://www3.nd.edu/~kellogg/publications/workingpapers/WPS/307.pdf.

188 De Soysa & Jütting, *supra* note 186, at 3.

189 *Id.*

190 Yousfi, *supra* note 21, at 33.

191 The phrase "informal institution" may refer to aspects of traditional culture, personal networks, clientelism, corruption, clan and mafia organizations, civil society, and a wide variety of norms. Helmke & Levitsky, *supra* note 187.

192 De Soysa & Jütting, *supra* note 186, at 2; *see also* Helmke & Levitsky, *supra* note 187.

193 De Soysa & Jütting, *supra* note 186, at 2.

generations of parents, schools, peers. The regulatory effects refer to the way in which the values and beliefs of a society are manifested through social norms and attitudes in ways that regulate behavior: promises must be kept, contracts must be honored."[194]

As De Soysa and Jutting observed, Nobel Prize winner Elinor Ostrom called such informal rules "rules in force" to reflect the notion that although they are generally not codified they are deemed legitimate and hence "rules in operation."[195] They are, in other words, "socially sanctioned norms of behavior (attitudes, customs, taboos, conventions, and traditions)."[196] In this respect, "[c]ultural norms and beliefs can be seen as the deepest level of institution . . . and thus the same framework can illuminate the role of cultural differences in economic performance."[197]

Rather than study only formal institutions and laws, North and others have aptly focused on informal institutions, cultural norms and practices and how they interact with formal institutions. This is especially important in developing countries which are the focus of law and development. Cultural norms may interact with formal institutions in four ways—complementary, accommodating, competing, and substituting.[198] Generally speaking, cultural norms may coexist with and complement or accommodate formal institutions, or they may converge with or operate in lieu of state law. However, it is often the case that "complementary and accommodating informal institutions exist in stable institutional settings, which are generally found in advanced industrialized countries . . . and substitutive and competing informal institutions exist in context of formal institutional weakness and instability, which are more likely found in developing and post-communist countries."[199] Moreover, it is not just that informal institutions dominate the landscape in developing countries. It is also that often, in developing countries where law and development projects operate, competing cultural norms create incentives and exert pressure on actors in ways that may be incompatible with the objectives of law and development.

---

[194] *Id.*

[195] *Id.* at 3.

[196] *Id.*

[197] Christopher Clague & Shoshana Grossbard-Shechtman, *Preface*, 573 ANNALS AM. ACAD. POL. & SOC. SCI. 8, 10 (Jan. 2001). For an example of the relationship between culture and informal institutions, information transmission, and economic development, *see* Clifford Geertz, *The Bazaar Economy: Information and Search in Peasant Marketing*, 68 AM. ECON. REV. 28 (1978). Others have studied how informal institutions, including cultural norms and practices, may be adapted to cope with problems of coordination and information asymmetry. Karla Hoff & Joseph E. Stiglitz, *Introduction: Imperfect Information and Rural Credit Markets—Puzzles and Policy Perspectives*, 4 WORLD BANK ECON. REV. 235, 243 (1990) (discussing an indigenous solution to an imperfect legal system, the "usufruct loan" allowing the lender to occupy and use the borrower's land during the term of the loan); Karla Hoff & Joseph Stiglitz, *Modern Economic Theory and Development*, *in* FRONTIERS IN DEVELOPMENT ECONOMICS: THE FUTURE IN PERSPECTIVE 389 (G. M. Meier & J. Stiglitz eds., 2001); Cao, *supra* note 116.

[198] Helmke & Levitsky, *supra* note 187.

[199] *Id.*

For example, studies show that civil servants in Ghana's public administration believe they would lose their social standing if they adhere to administrative rules rather than kinship norms that oblige them to provide jobs to family and clan members.[200] Similarly, laws against insider trading may encounter resistance from Jordanians who may find it astonishing that they would be prohibited from sharing inside information with friends and family about initial public offerings and mergers that may enrich their relatives. "Prohibiting insider trading was not seen as market transparency, but as a betrayal of their friends and family! Thus, it may be a pat assumption to believe that conforming legal principles, codes, standards, and practices to international standards is a relatively easy task where business law is concerned."[201]

It is fair to say that the two examples above involve informal institutions that compete or are in tension with the mandate of law. Alternatively, informal institutions have also thrived where formal institutions are flawed.[202] They don't necessarily compete with, undermine, or oppose formal institutions but instead act as an alternative gap filler. Market activities of ethnic minorities, as described in the following pages, fit this example. They can be understood as a compensatory mechanism used by those who are peripheral to mainstream markets and institutions.

As some have already observed, various ethnic groups throughout the world have successfully leveraged the group's cultural norms to advance economically.[203]An international perspective will show that market-dominant ethnic minorities have thrived economically despite hostile institutional environments.[204] The discussion below suggests that where formal institutions are nonfunctional or discriminatory and hostile, informal institutions, used in the Douglass North sense to include culture, are relied upon by groups in the developing and developed world, particularly ethnic minorities, to advance economically. Take as examples the ethnic Chinese in Burma, the Philippines, Thailand, Malaysia, Vietnam, and Indonesia;[205] the Kikuyu tribe in Kenya, the Ibo in Nigeria, Indians and Lebanese in Kenya and West Africa.[206] Certainly some of the market-dominant ethnic minorities come from the white colonial elite. And in some cases, their wealth may be derived from corrupt or predatory practices. But for many ethnic minorities, their economic advancement comes from the ability to create ethnic economies to sidestep societal hostility and discrimination. Many may be classic middleman minorities

[200] *Id.*

[201] SARKAR, *supra* note 45, at 256.

[202] The underground economy may be an example. *See* Richard A. Epstein, *The Moral and Practical Dilemmas of an Underground Economy*, 103 YALE L. J. 2157 (1994).

[203] *See*, e.g., SOWELL, *supra* note 91.

[204] The discussion of market-dominant ethnic minorities and the cultural and social bases for their market dominance is drawn from Cao, *The Ethnic Question*, *supra* note 99 (reviewing AMY CHUA, WORLD ON FIRE: HOW EXPORTING FREE MARKET DEMOCRACY BREEDS ETHNIC HATRED AND GLOBAL INSTABILITY (2003)); Cao, *The Diaspora*, *supra* note 99.

[205] CHUA, *supra* note 99, at 23–48, 265.

[206] *Id.* at 105, 108, 113, 114, 119.

whose commercial astuteness helped them achieve economic dominance long before the colonial age.[207] Indeed, "middleman minority" refers originally to ethnic minorities who were market traders in precapitalist societies, specializing in trading as part of global diasporas.[208] Others are immigrants at the bottom of the economic ladder who then worked themselves upward to achieve economic dominance, such as the Indians who were brought to Fiji and East Africa by the British as coolies or indentured servants.

Sociologists have long noted the existence of market-dominant minorities and explored the reasons for their economic success. A key factor is the ability to form their own ethnic economies,[209] that is, economies owned by ethnic members predominantly hiring other coethnics, or as W. E. B. Dubois called it, the "group economy: 'a cooperative arrangement of industries and services within the Negro group such that the group tends to be a closed economic circle largely independent of the surrounding white world.' "[210] An ethnic economy is a general concept used to include any ethnic group's self-employed, its employers, coethnic employees, if any, and their unpaid family workers.[211] The ethnic economy is created by ethnic minorities themselves, as distinct from the jobs generated by the mainstream labor market, and does not include coethnics who work for wages in the mainstream economy.[212] As I later discuss, it may also be supplemented and supported by the ethnic enclave and the ethnic niche, creating additional synergies that further benefit the group's market position.

Indeed, ethnic economies create, perpetuate, and capture jobs for coethnics. They operate on two principles—ethnic loyalty and economic efficiency. As in the case with rotating credit associations,[213] the cost of screening coethnic workers may be lower than screening outsiders "either because of specific knowledge of the individual or his family available within the group or because of a greater facility in reading cultural cues peculiar to the group."[214] The ethnic workforce can be replicated cheaply in the ethnic economy because both employers and employees rely on "networks for finding work, for obtaining a cheap and cohesive work force, for financial support, and for market transactions."[215]

---

[207] Clifford Geertz, Peddlers and Princes: Social Change and Economic Modernization in Two Indonesian Towns 25–26 (1963).

[208] Robin Cohen, Global Diasporas: An Introduction 101–04 (1997).

[209] Ivan Light & Steven J. Gold, Ethnic Economies 4 (2000).

[210] Roger Waldinger & Howard Aldrich, *Trends in Ethnic Business in the United States*, *in* Ethnic Entrepreneurs: Immigrant Business in Industrial Societies 49, 59 (Roger Waldinger et al. eds., 1990) (emphasis omitted) (quoting W. E. B. Du Bois, Economic Cooperation Among Negro Americans 179 (1907)).

[211] Light & Gold, *supra* note 209, at 9. Ethnic entrepreneurship may be viewed as "a set of connections and regular patterns of interaction among people sharing common national background or migration experiences." Roger Waldinger et al., *Opportunities, Group Characteristics and Strategies*, *in* Ethnic Entrepreneurs: Immigrant Business in Industrial Societies 13, 33 (Roger Waldinger et al. eds., 1990).

[212] Light & Gold, *supra* note 209, at 9, 19.

[213] *See supra* text accompanying notes 154–160.

[214] Thomas Sowell, Race and Culture: A World View 90 (1994).

[215] Mirjana Moroksavic, *Immigrants in Garment Production in Paris and in Berlin*, *in* Immigration and Entrepreneurship: Culture, Capital, and Ethnic Networks 75, 87 (Ivan Light & Parminder Bhachu eds., 1993).

To overcome market impediments, ethnic workers rely on informal networks for a competitive edge over other workers, such as connections made through word of mouth or ethnic and immigrant newspapers[216] with an established "information system that channel[s] them into those industrial niches already dominated by coethnics."[217]

Ethnic economies function on the basis of other preferences that also have economic efficiency implications. In nonretail transactions, for example, in the sale and purchase of liquor licenses, coethnics tend to buy and sell to one another. For example, Korean sellers, relying on information provided by Korean newspapers, found Korean buyers in 80.4 percent of license transfer transactions.[218] A similar degree of homogeneity characterizes business sales among Indians and Pakistanis in Britain[219] and in business co-ownership among Cubans in Puerto Rico.[220]

Ethnic economies also leverage ethnic linkages that exist between ethnic diasporas of the adopted country and the homeland institutions. The supply and distribution line, especially in the import business, is virtually all-ethnic. For example, in the import businesses established by Koreans who deal in Korean exports, Korean importers distribute Korean-made products to coethnic wholesalers who in turn distribute them to coethnic retailers for sale,[221] most likely to non-Korean customers. Korean owners in Los Angeles indicated that between 66 and 100 percent of their suppliers were Koreans and that a large portion of the Korean owners were part of "a vertical distribution network that might originate in South Korea."[222] Korean immigrants starting new businesses in sectors with an already strong Korean presence, such as wigs, handbags, and other Korean imports often "have easy access to information and can very often purchase merchandise on a credit basis. In operating such businesses, they receive preferential treatments from Korean wholesalers in item selections, prices, speed of delivery and credits."[223] Indian hotel and motel owners also deal with each other on a preferential basis, providing each other with loans without charging interest or demanding collateral.[224] Other groups such as black merchants who have vertical links to African American suppliers also used such

[216] *Id.*; Chris Spolar, *New Working Class in the Making*, WASH. POST, Dec. 15, 1987, at A1 (describing the informal recruitment methods used by immigrants).

[217] LIGHT & BONACICH, *supra* note 141, at 187.

[218] *Id.* at 239. In fact, liquor stores, grocery stores, restaurants, and bars, representing businesses with a strong Korean presence, constituted 21.2 percent of firms advertised for sale in *Korea Times* but only 11.9 percent of those for sale in the *Los Angeles Times*. *Id.* at 240.

[219] Catherine Zimmer & Howard Aldrich, *Resource Mobilization Through Ethnic Networks: Kinship and Friendship Ties of Shopkeepers in England*, 30 SOC. PERSP. 422, 439–41 (1987).

[220] Jose A. Cobas, *Ethnic Enclaves and Middleman Minorities: Alternative Strategies of Immigrant Adaptation?*, 30 SOC. PERSP. 143, 150 (1987). Although Cubans were less than 1 percent of Puerto Rico's population, Cuban entrepreneurs had other Cuban entrepreneurs as partners in 70 percent of co-owned businesses. *Id.* at 148, 150.

[221] LIGHT & GOLD, *supra* note 209, at 121.

[222] LIGHT & BONACICH, *supra* note 141, at 151.

[223] Waldinger & Aldrich, *supra* note 210, at 71.

[224] Edwin McDowell, *Hospitality Is Their Business*, N.Y. TIMES, Mar. 21, 1996, at D1.

linkages to their advantage—hence the success of black-owned barber shops and beauty parlors with connections to the large black-owned beauty products firm of Johnson Products, Inc. of Chicago.[225] Indeed, Johnson Products, the first black-owned firm to be listed on the American Stock Exchange, has had a tradition of promoting black businesses by hiring black models and other black enterprises, such as advertising agencies, and by advertising in black venues such as Soul Train.[226]

Groups with a thick social-capital base are able to "convert social characteristics of their group into economic resources, thus creating employment and income independent of class resources."[227] Ethnic resources that promote ethnic economies include "entrepreneurial heritages, entrepreneurial values and attitudes, low transaction costs, rotating credit associations, relative satisfaction arising from nonacculturation to prevailing labor standards, social capital, reactive solidarities, multiplex social networks, and a generous pool of underemployed and disadvantaged coethnic workers."[228] The abundance of ethnic resources, combined with other factors discussed below, has resulted in multiple variations of the ethnic economy—the ethnic enclave and ethnic niche.

The ethnic enclave is the spatial or locational clustering of firms and neighborhoods with a strong ethnic concentration—Germantowns, Little Italys, Chinatowns, and so on. For example, in the late nineteenth and early twentieth centuries, the Jewish quarter of Manhattan was served by ethnic trade on the Jewish East Side as New York City's clothing industry developed alongside the Jewish immigrant workers and owners clustered there. South Asians in Britain occupy certain geographical clusters. Migrants from northwest Africa and southern Europe are concentrated in the older quarters of cities such as Berlin, Frankfurt, Rotterdam, Brussels, and Paris.[229] Linkages between work and residence eventually developed, resulting in economic synergies between the ethnic economy and the ethnic enclave.[230]

Ethnic enclaves had their origin in and were reinforced by residential segregation.[231] For some ethnic groups such as the Chinese in the United States, the existence of Chinatown was reinforced by repressive laws mandating segregation of the Chinese.[232]

---

225 R. C. Longworth, *On One Street, Two Different Paths of Success*, Chi. Trib., Sept. 17, 1992, at C1 *available at* http://articles.chicagotribune.com/1992-09-17/news/9203240849_1_korean-owned-stores-blacks-shops.

226 Karen Springen, *So Much for Family Ties*, Newsweek, Mar. 23, 1992, at 49, *available at* http://www.newsweek.com/so-much-family-ties-196110.

227 Ivan Light & Carolyn Rosenstein, Race, Ethnicity, and Entrepreneurship in Urban America 24 (1995).

228 *Id.* at 22.

229 Sowell, *supra* note 214, at 103–04.

230 Roger Waldinger et al., *Spatial Dimensions of Opportunity Structures*, *in* Ethnic Entrepreneurs: Immigrant Business in Industrial Societies 106, 108, 115 (Roger Waldinger et al. eds., 1990).

231 Richard Thompson Ford, *The Boundaries of Race: Political Geography in Legal Analysis*, 107 Harv. L. Rev. 1843, 1845 (1994).

232 California enacted a law in 1879 requiring towns and cities to remove the Chinese from city limits. Bill Ong Hing, Making and Remaking Asian America Through Immigration Policy, 1850–1990, 49–50 (1993).

But the existence of ethnic enclaves, it turned out, served as a spatial anchor for the community. Segregation, in other words, facilitated the formation of ethnic economies which benefited from the presence of and proximity with ethnic enclaves. Chinatowns across the United States became residential and economic enclaves where the Chinese established homes, businesses, associations, and schools based on common geographic origins and clans.[233] By contrast, it has been suggested that West Indian business activities in Britain were not as numerous as those in the United States because the West Indian in Britain was not segregated.[234]

Indeed, the existence of an ethnic enclave, reinforced by segregation, has resulted in two scenarios, both of which further spurred the formation of ethnic economies. First, segregation imposed by society and by law created in the ethnic minorities themselves a sense of "us" versus "them," which, as sociologists have pointed out, is conducive to the creation of ethnic economies. Second, ethnic economies are further strengthened when in proximity to ethnic enclaves because proximity allowed group members who are lesser-skilled, less educated, and lacking in job-seeking connections to gain access to group resources to achieve upward mobility within the ethnic economy. This is because the agglomeration of economies is likely to encourage the proliferation of ethnic businesses and attract more customers drawn to the size and diversity of the enclave. An ethnic enclave also may further the cultural presence of the area and promote its visibility as an ethnic market. Additionally, the ethnic enclave facilitates vertical and horizontal integration of businesses along ethnic lines, allowing such firms to "suck value out of each stage of a product's movement toward the market, losing little or no value to noncoethnic firms."[235] Horizontal integration occurs when ethnic business owners cooperate "to choose store location, avoid competitive pricing, pool information, and engage in collective buying. Vertical integration occurs when a whole package of business services—ranging from credit, wholesale goods, and maintenance to parking, transportation, real estate, manufacturing, and import-export concessions—are provided by coethnics."[236] Both forms of linkages facilitate the maximization of ethnically based transactions because when an ethnic firm buys from other neighborhood coethnic firms, the flow of money recirculates within the ethnic enclave economy to the benefit of the ethnic community.

Another rather common incident of ethnic economies is the ethnic niche, also known as ethnic hegemonization,[237] industrial clustering,[238] or entrepreneurial niches,[239] where

---

[233] *Id.* at 50, 77, 84; Joyce Kuo, *Excluded, Segregated and Forgotten: A Historical View of the Discrimination of Chinese Americans in Public School*, 5 ASIAN L. J. 181, 191 (1998).

[234] Waldinger et al., *supra* note 230, at 110.

[235] LIGHT & GOLD, *supra* note 209, at 12–13.

[236] *Id.* at 122.

[237] ROBERT M. JIOBU, ETHNICITY AND ASSIMILATION 223 (1988).

[238] LIGHT & BONACICH, *supra* note 141, at 183–84.

[239] *See* Eran Razin & Ivan Light, *Ethnic Entrepreneurs in America's Largest Metropolitan Areas*, 33 URB. AFF. REV. 332 (1998).

"a certain ethnic group becomes entrenched in a clearly identifiable economic sector, working at jobs for which it has no evident cultural, geographical or even racial affinity."[240] Often, certain ethnic "groups become prominent or predominant in particular occupations in countries all over the planet,"[241] creating in essence economic niches—clustering of ethnic entrepreneurs in the same occupations and industries. In the United States, Indians and Pakistanis own a significant portion of the budget motels and gas stations in New York City.[242] Koreans own greengroceries in New York City and wig stores all over the United States.[243] Arabs and Muslims own grocery stores in Chicago and Detroit, respectively.[244] Ethnic Chinese in Malaysia, Thailand, the Philippines, and other Southeast Asian countries dominate commerce as middleman minorities, due to their "go-between" positions between producer and consumer, owner and renter, employer and employee.[245]

Take the example of the Vietnamese presence in the nail salon business in the United States.[246] In California, Vietnamese Americans constitute approximately 80 percent of nail technicians. The establishment of this niche was initially accidental. It happened when twenty Vietnamese women refugees who fled to the United States in 1975 after the fall of Saigon landed in Hope Village, a refugee tent city set up near Sacramento. Actress Tippi Hedren, who visited the refugee center, wanted to help the women and flew in her manicurist once a week to teach them how to trim cuticles, smooth out calluses, and do nail wraps. Hedren also helped the women enroll in a nearby beauty school and secure jobs.

The nail industry was relatively easy for newcomers with limited English to enter; it needed little training, and once it was established by one Vietnamese, other Vietnamese newcomers were given jobs at salons owned by friends and relatives. Like owners of other ethnic businesses, the Vietnamese owners of nail salons across the United States advertise for workers in Vietnamese-language newspapers, replicating and perpetuating the ethnic presence of the Vietnamese in the nail business.

The niche, once occupied by an ethnic group, tends to perpetuate itself due to path dependency—a type of "chain migration"[247] involving those who pioneered an economic path and those coethnics who followed, whether they are Indian motel owners, Korean

---

240 Tunku Varadarajan, *A Patel Motel Cartel?*, N.Y. TIMES MAG., July 4, 1999, at 177.

241 SOWELL, *supra* note 214, at 2.

242 Jonathan Foreman, *Bombay on the Hudson*, 7 MANHATTAN INST. CITY J., Summer 1997, at 14; McDowell, *supra* note 224; Robert Reinhold, *Flow of 3d World Immigrants Alters Weave of U.S. Society*, N.Y. TIMES, June 30, 1986, at A1.

243 LIGHT & BONACICH, *supra* note 141, at 37, 151; Richard Levine, *Young Immigrant Wave Lifts New York Economy*, N.Y. TIMES, July 30, 1990, at A1.

244 LIGHT & BONACICH, *supra* note 141, at 439 n.4.

245 HOWARD PAUL BECKER, MAN IN RECIPROCITY 225–37 (1956).

246 My-Thuan Tran, *The American Dream, One Nail at a Time*, SEATTLE TIMES, May 8, 2008, at A7. The discussion of the Vietnamese nail business is drawn from this source.

247 LIGHT & BONACICH, *supra* note 141, at 153–54.

greengrocers, Chinese laundromat operators,[248] or historically, German beer makers and Jewish tailors.[249] In other words, ethnic niches provide an "insider's edge on the profession" so that "once a niche is found, it creates a snowball effect, gathering in labor from that ethnic group and expanding exponentially."[250] Additionally, access to businesses in a particular niche "depended upon ethnic homogeneity in business transfers, which tended to advantage coethnics while excluding outsiders."[251]

As noted, "[c]apital and labor are often organized along ethnic lines. Fukienese entrepreneurs in Hong Kong, Malayalee clerks in Bombay, and Ibo plantation laborers in Equatorial Guinea were all mobilized into their economic activity on the basis of ethnic affinity."[252] Jews, for example, have been dominant in New York's garment industry. Although one may ascribe this dominance narrowly to the influx of Jewish immigrants into the city, a broader, international perspective reveals that "Jews have been prominent, if not predominant, in the apparel industry over a period longer than the entire history of the United States, and in countries ranging from medieval Spain to modern Australia, from the Ottoman Empire to the Russian Empire, as well as in Argentina, Brazil, Germany, and Chile."[253]

One way of understanding ethnic economies (and their variants, the ethnic enclave and the ethnic niche) is to see them as a form of traditional capitalism, that is, capitalism based on personal relationships and ethnic ties. According to Max Weber, outcast groups such as Jews are ethnically insular and segregated from the mainstream by their observance of "taboos, [and] hereditary religious obligations in the conduct of life."[254] Many are pariah minorities with "caste-like attributes"[255] who are politically vulnerable. They are at the mercy of the politically dominant ethnic majority, often uncomfortably "lodged between . . . two ethnic groups that stand in a classlike relation of superordination and subordination. The dominant elite of the dominant group uses the middleman minority to foster economic development, but turns it into a scapegoat when things go wrong."[256]

Max Weber observed that it was not just the Protestant ethic in Northern Europe but also Catholic discrimination against Protestants, including exclusion of Protestants from the armed forces and the civil service, which contributed to the high incidence of Protestant entrepreneurship.[257] Werner Sombart attributed Jewish dominance in

---

248 Varadarajan, *supra* note 240.

249 John Greenwald, *Finding Niches in a New Land*, TIME, July 8, 1985, at 72.

250 Donatella Lorch, *An Ethnic Road to Riches: The Immigrant Job Specialty*, N.Y. TIMES, Jan. 12, 1992, at 1.

251 LIGHT & BONACICH, *supra* note 141, at 242.

252 DONALD L. HOROWITZ, ETHNIC GROUPS IN CONFLICT 8 (2000).

253 SOWELL, *supra* note 214, at 2.

254 MAX WEBER, THE SOCIOLOGY OF RELIGION 109 (1963).

255 COHEN, *supra* note 208, at 101.

256 *Id.* at 103.

257 WEBER, *supra* note 91, at 5–7.

commerce similarly to the exclusion of Jews from medieval trade guilds.[258] Following the works of Weber and Sombart, scholars have subsequently understood that disadvantage was a major reason for the high rates of entrepreneurship and concomitant creation of ethnic economies among ethnic minorities faced with hostility and discrimination in the open market place[259] and denied "access to majority-controlled paths of economic advancement."[260]

Although Weber disdainfully called Jewish capitalism "speculative pariah-capitalism," ethnic economies, which are supported by ethnic ties and social norms of trust and cooperation, have been crucial for the economic advancement of Jews and other market dominant ethnic minorities. Because of outsider status, vulnerability, and disadvantage, boundaries are created between the ethnic group and society which in turn produce in the ethnic group intragroup cooperation and solidarity. This outsider status has forced ethnic minorities to develop an "aptitude for economic specialization" because their "psychological self-isolation would prove impossible if those who practiced it did not, at the same time, develop on the economic plane a special efficiency in the exploitation of such economic opportunities as had been left open to them."[261]

As Weber noted in the case of Jews, this experience instilled in them a "dual ethic"—one set of ethic for dealing with Jews and another with non-Jews.[262] Outsider status and ethnic boundaries caused ethnic minorities to turn inward, embrace intragroup solidarity and rely all the more on ethnic resources. As sociologists have similarly observed:

> [T]he ethnic boundary canalizes social life—it entails a frequently quite complex organization of behavior and social relations. The identification of another person as a fellow member of an ethnic group implies a sharing of criteria for evaluation and judgement . . . . On the other hand, a dichotomization of others as strangers, as members of another ethnic group, implies a recognition of limitations on shared understandings, differences in criteria for judgement of value and performance, and a restriction of interaction to sectors of assumed common understanding and mutual interest.[263]

---

[258] Werner Sombart, The Jews and Modern Capitalism 300–01 (1913).

[259] Howard Aldrich et al., *From Periphery to Peripheral: The South Asian Petit Bourgeoisie in England*, *in* 2 Research in the Sociology of Work: Peripheral Workers 1, 8 (Ida Harper Simpson & Richard L. Simpson eds., 1983) (stating that "because of native whites' prejudice and hostility," Asians in England must "seek employment below their skill level or else create their own employment opportunity by forming a small business"); Light & Rosenstein, *supra* note 227, at 161 (discussing how labor market barriers made middleman minorities turn to "defensive self-employment"); Chua Lee Hoong, *The Business of Race in the Race for Business*, Straits Times (Sing.), June 29, 1996, at 34, (describing how ethnic Chinese networks were a reaction against discrimination when banks refused to lend to "Chinamen").

[260] Greene, *supra* note 132, at 59.

[261] Cohen, *supra* note 208, at 103.

[262] Max Weber, Economy and Society 614 (Guenther Roth & Claus Wittich eds., 1968).

[263] Fredrik Barth, Introduction to Ethnic Groups and Boundaries 15 (Fredrik Barth ed., 1969).

In his efforts to promote African American ethnic economies, Fred Moore, one of the organizers of Booker T. Washington's Negro Business League, remarked, "[W]e must . . . require every person who joins a local league to pledge himself to support all worthy enterprises managed by men and women of the race . . . . How can we otherwise succeed? Some would say that this was drawing the color line. I do not believe it. Jews support Jews; Germans support Germans; Italians support Italians until they get strong enough to compete with their brother in the professions and trades; Negroes should now begin to support Negroes."[264]

Although ethnic economies can be seen as a form of "compensatory entrepreneurship"[265] that arises in response to external hostility, this response is possible only because of internal factors, for example, group characteristics consisting of cultural resources and ethnic social capital. Sociologists have observed the tendency of ethnic minorities living in hostile environments to identify members of one's ethnic group as "near or distant kinsmen whom one knows as intimates and whom therefore one can trust. One intuitively expects fellow ethnics to behave at least somewhat benevolently toward one because of kin selection, reinforced by reciprocity. . . . Fellow ethnics are, in the deepest sense, 'our people.' "[266] Ethnic economies thus are marked by a sense of "clannishness,"[267] adherence to group norms, and maintaining the ethnic boundary separating insiders from outsiders. This insular proclivity, again, often a reaction to external hostility, can be seen among different ethnic groups in different countries all over the world: the Hasidic Jews in New York City's diamond industry, Lebanese traders in Sierra Leone, the Chinese in Southeast Asia, the Indians in Uganda, the Koreans and Indians in the United States, the Turks in the garment industry in Paris and Berlin,[268] the Algerians, Moroccans, and Tunisians in the retail trade in France.[269]

As the discussion above shows, both formal and informal institutions are relevant to the establishment of ethnic economies. Ethnic minorities who face barriers to entry in the formal market turn inward, relying on the community's informal institutions to create ethnic economies instead. In this way, informal institutions created by the ethnic group serve as a bulwark against formal institutions that are hostile or discriminatory. A word of caution is also in order, however. Ethnic-based arrangements may have positive development implications, but there is also the potential for abuse, particularly if preferences for "one's own" transmogrify into entrenched discrimination against others. Moreover, ethnically conscious practices may serve economic efficiency purposes at one stage of economic development but may be economically damaging at a later stage. In

---

[264] John Sibley Butler, Entrepreneurship and Self-Help Among Black Americans 70 (1991).

[265] Light & Rosenstein, *supra* note 227, at 160.

[266] Pierre L. Van Den Berghe, The Ethnic Phenomenon 25 (1981).

[267] Sowell, *supra* note 214, at 49.

[268] Morokvasic, *supra* note 215, at 76–82.

[269] Gildas Simon, *Immigrant Entrepreneurs in France*, *in* Immigration and Entrepreneurship 125, 132–34 (Ivan Light & Parminder Bhachu eds., 1993).

that case, a parochial and ethnically particularistic inclination will impede transactions with outsiders and hence create economic inefficiencies.

Because law and development is embedded in an existing institutional regime, which includes formal and informal institutions, it must address both the formal and informal, both law and culture. Yet as Chapter 1 showed, law and development has historically dwelled primarily in the world of formal institutions. It should be no surprise then, as those who have studied the discipline's emphasis on formal institutions have remarked, "not everyone finds strong effects from formal institutions, such as the rule of law to development outcomes."[270] An almost exclusive emphasis on formal institutions and laws has resulted in the field's systematic exclusion of culture from its lens. Passing laws without regard to their interaction with existing cultural norms has meant ineffective laws.

As I noted in the Introduction,[271] in the context of developing countries especially, where the rule of law is weak and formal institutions are inefficient or dysfunctional or irrelevant to people's daily lives, informal rules exert an especially powerful pull. "People in both rich and poor countries rely on informal institutions to varying degrees to facilitate transactions, but these institutions are relatively more important in poor countries and small, traditional communities where formal institutions are less developed and the reach of formal law and state power relatively weak."[272] It is all the more imperative that a field so directly linked to the landscape of developing countries understands this reality and proceeds accordingly. "[C]hanging formal (macro- and micro-level) institutions that might be compatible with particular structural forms might yet not fit very well with informal institutions given underlying cultural factors that remain resistant to change, factors that have a more proximate bearing on the outcomes we are interested in, such as corruption, education, governance, or questions of gender equality."[273]

In this section, I have shown that culture exerts a significant influence on markets and development and must be a vital component of the law and development inquiry. Groups bound by trust and often a common culture may generate group norms that enhance the group's social capital, promoting cooperation and minimizing transaction costs. From that standpoint, there is a correlative relationship between culture and development, including but not limited to market development. Law and development has stressed formal institutions and neglected informal institutions, yet the works of Douglass North and others have shown that the latter cannot be ignored.

---

270 De Soysa & Jütting, *supra* note 186, at 5.

271 Hernando De Soto, The Mystery of Capital: Why Capitalism Triumphs in the West and Fails Everywhere Else 113 (2000) (arguing that informal arrangements such as squatting be legally formalized so that the poor can become stakeholders with property rights); *see generally* Donald Clarke, *Economic Development and the Rights Hypothesis: The China Problem*, 51 Am. J. Comp. L. 89 (2003) (arguing that in China, informal mechanisms serve as effective substitutes for formal contract enforcement).

272 De Soysa & Jütting, *supra* note 186, at 8.

273 *Id.* at 5.

Undoubtedly, "the question of institutions and development may depend greatly on how informal institutions moderate formal ones as they affect outcomes."[274] As I have shown, this issue is important in the area of economic development but perhaps even more, I would argue, in the area of human rights. How informal institutions such as culture moderate formal ones is particularly relevant for women's rights and equality in developing countries, especially because it is precisely in this area that culture has been used as a legitimate opt-out option. In the section below, I examine the relationship between culture and international human rights, particularly women's rights.

2. CULTURE AND WOMEN'S RIGHTS

Quantitative data show that there is undoubtedly a positive relationship between women's empowerment and economic development. That is, "gender equality improves when poverty declines"[275] even in the absence of gender-specific measures targeted at improving women's rights. In poverty-stricken areas, girls and women are particularly vulnerable in times of crises. For example, in India, girls' mortality rate shoots up when there is a drought, suggesting that girls' health is sacrificed when families face shortages. When families have greater resources, they are not faced with subsistence-level choices that are customarily and tragically biased against girls. "Empirically, there is a strong correlation between economic development and women's legal rights, in areas as diverse as property rights, access to land, access to bank loans, violence against women, abortion policy, etc."[276] Economic development results in women's empowerment, or at least, a decline in women's inequality.

Another approach focuses on the notion that women's empowerment is a prerequisite of development and emphasizes gender-specific policies to "address gender imbalance in 'rights, resources, and voice. . . .' "[277] This is necessary because development per se is not enough. "There is evidence that growth will not be enough to overcome discrimination in the home and in a number of domains. Sex ratios remain skewed in favor of boys"[278] as sex-selective abortions become available and affordable even in countries with rapid economic growth, for example. A gender gap persists in many areas such as the labor market, property rights, and political participation. Under this view, gender equality is

---

[274] *Id.* For example, an emerging body of research suggests that informal rules do in fact influence formal institutional outcomes in a variety of settings. In some African and Latin American countries, patrimonialist norms of unregulated executive control over state institutions have resulted in executive power assertions over legislative and judicial branches in ways unanticipated by the constitution. Guillermo O'Donnell, *Delegative Democracy*, 5 J. DEMOCRACY 55 (Jan. 1994).

[275] Esther Duflo, *Women Empowerment and Economic Development*, 50 J. ECON. LIT 1051, 1053 (2012), *available at* http://economics.mit.edu/files/7417.

[276] *Id.* at 1059.

[277] *Id.* at 1053 (citation omitted). Research in rural Tanzania showed that the murder of "witches" increases when food is scarce, as in times of drought or flood. *Id.* at 1055.

[278] *Id.* at 1060.

a good in its own right and should not simply be something that is the indirect result of economic development.

Gender equality cannot be achieved by law alone. In many countries, cultural norms limit women's rights and women's agency and negatively affect women's well-being.[279] While women's agency may lead to well-being and vice versa, as Amartya Sen has noted, one cannot exist without the other.[280] In addition, basic physical security and healthcare are both essential to advancing women's rights. At a prima facie level these needs may seem simple and easy to implement, but in reality human rights advocates and development projects face momentous obstacles in fostering women's well-being in many developing societies. In many of these countries, a propensity to commit violence against women and to subordinate women inhibits further development of the entire society. Many of the factors that perpetuate the subordination of women, and to make the point more forcefully, that perpetuate violence against women, must be understood not just within an economic or political framework but also a cultural one.

The first part of this section examines the thorny issue of women's rights juxtaposed against a cultural framework that subordinates those rights. The second part demonstrates women's agency and well-being to development, both for women's issues and for larger societal effects such as the overall health of the population and the economy.

a. Culture, Women's Rights, and Gender Violence

A law and development framework that has appropriately expanded to embrace substantive human rights norms cannot ignore culture. Just as feminists have long struggled with cultural norms and practices that perpetuate gender inequality and have argued about the appropriate responses, so should law and development. Studies that rely on empirical data have shown that there is no correlation between the rule of law and gender equality in low-income countries; the status of women in society is correlated instead with cultural norms about gender equality and those norms are essentially unaffected by legal institutions.[281] Cultural norms must be addressed on their own terms, not only through rule of law.

This part looks at women's rights and violence against women through a cultural lens, paying particular attention to how feminist scholars have struggled with questions of culture, cultural conditioning, and women's equality. Indeed, where development intersects with issues of women's equality or inequality, it is likely to implicate the culture question, so much so that feminism has been described as "becoming prone to paralysis by cultural difference . . . [and] anxieties about cultural imperialism. . . ."[282] The tension between the

---

279 The World Bank, *Gender*, http://data.worldbank.org/topic/gender (last visited Apr. 20, 2015).

280 Sen, *supra* note 1, at 190–92.

281 Katharina Pistor et al., *Social Norms, Rule of Law and Gender Reality: An Essay on the Limits of the Dominant Rule of Law Paradigm*, *in* Global Perspectives on the Rule of Law 241 (James Heckman et al. eds., 2010).

282 Anne Phillips, Multiculturalism Without Culture 1 (2007).

declaration that women's rights are part of a universal system of human rights and the international law recognition of group rights and minority cultural rights can be seen in a variety of international settings. On the one hand, there is the widely hailed statement "Women's rights are human rights,"[283] unanimously adopted by the Fourth World Conference on Women held in Beijing, China, in 1995. Or "women's progress is human progress," declared by then Secretary of State Hillary Rodham Clinton.[284] If women's rights are to be understood as inextricably linked to human rights and if development encompasses women's rights, then women's rights are legitimately a normative part of the human rights and development agenda. And if women's rights are systematically diluted not because women's equality is not protected by law but rather by cultural claims, then development would need to wrestle with the culture question. And yet, on the other hand, wrestling with the culture question is not easy because it implicates other thorny issues such as identity, group rights, and protection and preservation of minority cultures, which are themselves bound up with human rights.

Take the issue of violence against women. "The definition of violence against women as a human rights violation, framed in universalist terms and applicable everywhere around the world, raises difficult questions of culture and rights."[285] Violence against women is not simply a personal issue involving violence committed by one individual against another but rather, has cultural underpinnings. It is true violence may be "everywhere," yet it is also true that "gender-based violence is embedded in cultural understandings of gender and sexuality as well as in the institutions of marriage, community, and state legal regulations of marriage, divorce, inheritance, and child custody."[286] Although many practices of gender-based violence are not accepted in the community and indeed may be highly contested, "religious and political leaders resist this change, invoking the need to protect culture. Since defenses of culture become the basis for defending male control over women, feminist activists often lose patience with cultural defenses despite their commitment to cultural diversity."[287]

When one thinks of gender violence, the most blatant examples that often come to mind are physical atrocities, such as honor killings and female genital mutilation (FGM). Gender violence, however, takes many forms, and some of the more silent forms are the most destructive because they are invisible to outsiders. Emotional and social violence are used to suppress women from engaging with society, and violence based upon jealous feelings and notions of control over female sexuality are voiced as justification for subordinating and silencing women.[288] Perhaps the most detrimental type of violence that inhibits development is violence that leads to "political disenfranchisement and

---

283 *Women's Rights Are Human Rights*, VOICE OF AMERICA, July 14, 2012, http://www.voanews.com/policy/editorials/Womens-Rights-Are-Human-Rights-96893544.html.

284 *Id.*

285 SALLY ENGLE MERRY, GENDER VIOLENCE: A CULTURAL PERSPECTIVE 88 (2008).

286 *Id.* at 88–89.

287 *Id.* at 89.

288 *Id.* at 4.

familial disinheritance, denial of asylum and refusal of reproductive health care."[289] As Sally Engle Merry noted, "[w]omen's vulnerability to violence depends on entrenched sociocultural practices involving marriage, work, and religious and secular ideologies of masculinity and femininity."[290] Similarly "men's violence is both an effort to assert honor by controlling their women and a response to their own vulnerability in economic and social terms."[291]

One way of approaching the cultural dimension of gender violence is to ask a threshold question. Is violence truly culturally sanctioned, or is culture being manipulated and distorted to provide justification for violence? An inherent tension may exist when one attempts to separate genuine cultural practices from the ones used to manipulate. Human rights activists have long feared their efforts to eradicate oppressive and violent gender norms in cultures may be viewed as imperialistic. And yet, the same charge could be used against the entire international human rights regime (and not just the slice involving women's rights). "Indeed, the whole human rights process is based on the assumption that local features of culture, history, and context should not override universal principles."[292] It is often difficult to determine whether the practice that induces violence against women is truly traditional, or whether it is a government's "excuse for their failure to promote gender equality and the values of autonomy and choice."[293]

Feminists have adopted different approaches to culture. It is not the aim of this section to fully explicate these different and complex positions, nor is it to articulate and defend a particular approach to resolving the potential conflict between women's rights and culture. Rather, this part only lays out some of the varying approaches and shows that when it comes to women's equality, one cannot turn a blind eye to cultural claims and tackle only the legal question because the status of women in developing countries is embedded in the cultural, not legal realm.

However viewed, some feminists have categorically argued that culture cannot be used as a shield to excuse inequality or violence. Nor can it be used as a weapon to perpetuate subordination of a group, in this case, women. In an influential article entitled "Is Multiculturalism Bad for Women?,"[294] Susan Moller Okin explored two sometimes competing principles—culture versus equality or multiculturalism which favors protecting minority cultures by recognizing the special rights of the groups at issue versus

---

289 Barbara Harlow, *"What Was She Doing There?": Women as "Legitimate Targets," in* Women, Gender, and Human Rights: A Global Perspective 267, 269 (Marjorie Agosín, ed., 2001).

290 Merry, *supra* note 285, at 89 ("gender-based violence is embedded in cultural understandings of gender and sexuality as well as in the institutions of marriage, community, and state legal regulations of marriage, divorce, inheritance, and child custody."). *Id.* at 88–89.

291 *Id.* at 18.

292 Sally Engle Merry, Human Rights & Gender Violence: Translating International Law into Local Justice 131 (2006).

293 *Id.*

294 Susan Moller Okin, *Is Multiculturalism Bad for Women?, in* Is Multiculturalism Bad for Women? 7 (Joshua Cohen et al. eds., 1999).

women's equality. International human rights documents also address, unsuccessfully and unsatisfactorily, the culture versus equality question. For example, the 1966 International Covenant on Civil and Political Rights provides that "[i]n those States in which ethnic, religious or linguistic minorities exist, persons belonging to such minorities shall not be denied the right, in community with the other members of their group, to enjoy their own culture, to profess and practice their own religion, or to use their own language."[295] Subsequent UN documents have interpreted this right as a right granted to groups.[296] At the same time, while recognizing group rights, the Covenant also enshrines the principle of gender nondiscrimination that requires states "to ensure the equal right of men and women to the enjoyment of all civil and political rights set forth in the present Covenant."[297] These international documents, however, simply assert protection for both—group rights and gender equality—but do not speak directly to the issue of what should happen when one conflicts with the other.

There are many approaches to addressing this conflict. One approach, advocated by Okin, is for equality to trump culture. Okin's argument rests on the notion that Western liberal culture has evolved to become more egalitarian than other traditionally patriarchal cultures. Protecting traditional group rights of minority groups who live in the West may undermine equality objectives if those groups are suffused with practices that endanger women's rights.[298] Thus, under this approach, multiculturalism cannot be allowed to undermine the equality principle.

This is the approach favored not just by feminists such as Okin but also by international conventions and declarations on the rights of women, which typically require or exhort states to change cultural practices that perpetuate women's subordination. CEDAW, as noted in the Introduction, obligates ratifying states to work to change cultural norms and practices that discriminate against women.[299] The general recommendations issued by CEDAW in 1992, were adopted by the UN General Assembly in the Declaration on the Elimination of Violence Against Women, which cautions as follows: "States should condemn violence against women, and should not invoke any custom, tradition, or religious consideration to avoid their obligations with respect to its elimination."[300] The 1993 Vienna Declaration calls for "the eradication of any conflicts which may arise between

---

[295] International Covenant on Civil and Political Rights (ICCPR), art. 27, *opened for signature* Dec. 19, 1966, 999 U.N.T.S. 171 [hereinafter ICCPR].

[296] *See,* e.g., UN Human Rights Comm., General Comment No. 23, Art. 27, Para. 4, ¶¶ 6.1, 6.2, 7, International Covenant on Civil and Political Rights, UN Doc. CCPR/C/21/Rev.1/Add.5 (Apr. 26, 1994).

[297] ICCPR, *supra* note 295, at art. 3.

[298] For example, the French government permitted immigrant men to bring multiple wives into France in the 1980s although polygamy is illegal in France. Okin, *supra* note 294, at 9–10.

[299] *See* Convention on the Elimination of All Forms of Discrimination Against Women (CEDAW), Dec. 18, 1979, pmbl., *opened for signature* Mar. 1, 1980, 1259 U.N.T.S. 13.

[300] UN General Assembly, Declaration on the Elimination of Violence against Women, art. 4, Dec. 20, 1993, A/RES/48/104, *available at* http://www.un.org/documents/ga/res/48/a48r104.htm.

the rights of women and the harmful effects of certain traditional or customary practices, cultural prejudices and religious extremism."[301] And the 1995 Platform for Action from the Beijing Fourth World Conference on Women further states: "Violence against women throughout the life cycle derives essentially from cultural patterns, in particular the harmful effects of certain traditional or customary practices and all acts of extremism linked to race, sex, language or religion that perpetuate the lower status accorded to women in the family, the workplace, the community and society."[302] The Beijing Platform urges that governments should "[c]ondemn violence against women and refrain from invoking any custom, tradition or religious consideration to avoid their obligations with respect to its elimination as set out in the Declaration on the Elimination of Violence Against Women."[303] Similarly, in 2002 the Special Rapporteur on Violence Against Women, Radhika Coomaraswamy, canvassed cultural practices in the family that are violent to women and in a significant and provocative move, characterized such violence as "an important issue that would define the international human rights debate over the next decade."[304] The statement is significant and provocative because violence in the family is not violence perpetrated by the state and thus would not normally come under the umbrella of public international law. Still, although remarks by the Special Rapporteur are not binding on states in international law, women's rights and violence against women are both increasingly viewed as part of international human rights and states are urged not to use cultural defenses to defend human rights violations.[305]

A nongovernmental organization (NGO) based in Asia, International Women's Rights Action Watch, Asia/Pacific, similarly rejects the notion that culturally based practices that harm women should be deemed legitimate on cultural grounds. "In the view of IWRAW Asia Pacific, . . . any belief, practice or policy that results in harm cannot be seen as violating the cultural right of any community/society. Thus, even if there are women within a community/society who accept cultural practices that result in the violation of fundamental human rights, we should speak out against this. . . . This is especially

---

301 World Conference on Human Rights, June 14–25, 1993, *Vienna Declaration and Programme of Action*, ¶ 38, UN Doc. A/CONF.157/24 (Oct. 13, 1993).

302 World Conference on Women, Sept. 4–15, 1995, *Beijing Declaration and Platform for Action*, ¶ 118, UN Doc. A/Conf. 177/20 (Oct. 17, 1995).

303 *Id.* at ¶ 124.

304 UN Press Release (Apr. 10, 2002), http://www.ohchr.org/EN/NewsEvents/Pages/DisplayNews.aspx?NewsID=5487&LangID=E. In 2001, Amnesty International defined violence against women as a form of torture and began a global campaign against it. *See* http://www.amnestyusa.org/violence-against-women/stop-violence-against-women-svaw/page.do?id=1108417&n1=3&n2=39&n3=1101 (last visited May 10, 2015).

305 Note that CEDAW is an international convention and CEDAW obligations are binding on ratifying states, but many states have opted out by making culturally based reservations. Other international instruments, such as the General Assembly resolutions, the Vienna Declaration, and the Beijing Platform, which use strong language to urge states to change cultural practices that are discriminatory against women, are only aspirational.

necessary when persons who are being violated may not necessarily have the power to object. . . ."[306]

Undoubtedly then, conceptualizing women's rights and "violence against women as a human rights violation typically means demanding changes in local cultural practices concerning sexuality, marriage, and the family."[307] However, feminists have proposed other approaches as well. Rather than adopt the position that rights should trump culture, others have called for compromise, balancing cultural claims on the one hand with equality claims on the other.[308] Those favoring this approach take a cultural relativist position appropriately termed "culturally sensitive universalism."[309] They are uncomfortable with the equality trumping culture approach, which they see as being too rigid and uncompromising. Moreover, some cultural practices may already be outlawed or receive less than full support within the community and thus the problem should not be framed as culture versus rights per se. For those staking out this position, the issue, with reference to gender-based violence, for example, is "to find a space that respects cultural differences and at the same time protects women from violence. . . . Human rights activists, social service reformers, and government-policy makers constantly tack between the goals of respecting cultural difference and protecting women's safety. They use pragmatic compromise and situationally determined decision-making."[310]

From a different perspective altogether, cultural relativists object to the denunciation of culture generally, particularly to the notion that culture, in all its wild, irrational forms, oppresses women in the developing world whereas in the Western, developed world, culture is separate from elevated principles such as freedom or equality. Sally Engle Merry criticized the assumption of international human rights lawyers that backward villages are governed by culture, which is a product of tradition, and international human rights is governed by law which is a product of modernity.[311] As Wendy Brown explained, in language reminiscent of the Orientalist critique offered by Edward Said and other postcolonial scholars, "'culture' is what nonliberal peoples are . . . ruled and ordered by. . . . [W]e *have* culture while they *are* a culture. Or, we are a democracy while they are a culture."[312] For these cultural relativists, the point is that it is not only the developing world that has cultures the West finds wanting; it is also that principles and institutions in the West are themselves culturally situated. Human rights law is part of a Western cultural

---

306 MERRY, *supra* note 285, at 91.

307 *Id.* at 89.

308 *See, e.g.*, Karima Bennoune, *Secularism and Human Rights: A Contextual Analysis of Headscarves, Religious Expression, and Women's Equality Under International Law*, 45 COLUM. J. TRANSNAT'L L. 367, 396–97 (2007).

309 Karen Engle, *International Human Rights and Feminisms: When Discourses Keep Meeting*, *in* INTERNATIONAL LAW: MODERN FEMINIST APPROACHES 47, 63–64, 64 n.57 (Doris Buss & Ambreena Manji eds., 2005).

310 MERRY, *supra* note 285, at 90.

311 Merry, *supra* note 51, at 70.

312 WENDY BROWN, REGULATING AVERSION: TOLERANCE IN THE AGE OF IDENTITY AND EMPIRE 150–51 (2006).

system. So is the judicial system itself.[313] The West, in other words, is just as culturally situated as the non-West.[314] For these critics, the issue becomes one of one culture versus another culture, as opposed to culture versus reason or culture versus equality. This insight is considered important because it exposes rather than exempts the West to the kind of cultural critiques the West itself has directed against the non-Western world. As noted in the Introduction, the positions staked in this book in no way insulate Western culture from a cultural critique nor from culture change described here.[315]

According to Merry, one way of extricating the debate from the equality versus culture logjam is to reconceptualize the framework altogether. As the previous discussion shows, some women's rights proponents posited that "women's rights to protection from violence seem diametrically opposed to the protection of culture."[316] Sally Engle Merry, however, asserted that "[t]o regard violence against women as an opposition between culture and rights is to fail to acknowledge the contested and variable cultural support these acts receive in different social groups."[317] Cultural practices are open to change over time; forms of violence can be viewed as disciplinary, and they can be viewed as excessive.[318] In each culture, a sliding scale exists to determine what is "acceptable."[319] Universal systems miss how this sliding scale operates based upon the "nuances and the specific ways power is allocated in each situation."[320] Merry argued that rights groups need to "focus [their] attention on the strengths of local social arrangements in promoting human rights ideals and the importance of framing universalistic reforms in local cultural terms."[321]

Attention to current conditions in a society can make a vast amount of difference in understanding how one might go about addressing a harmful cultural practice without offending the population. Instead of viewing violence-based practices as deeply rooted in the traditions of the society, advocates wishing to enhance women's rights should "regard [gender-based violence practices] as reflecting contemporary concerns about women's sexuality and child-bearing."[322] In this regard, Merry examined "layered understandings" of cultural practices in order to separate elements that are sacred and traditional to the society from the practices that are reflective of contemporary concerns and current power struggles within the society.[323]

---

313 Leti Volpp, *(Mis)Identifying Culture: Asian Women and the "Cultural Defense,"* 17 HARV. WOMEN'S L. J. 57, 78 (1994).

314 BROWN, *supra* note 312, at 150–51; Leti Volpp, *Feminism Versus Multiculturalism*, 101 COLUM. L. REV. 1181, 1186–89, 1212–14, 1217 (2001).

315 *See* Introduction, at note 10 and accompanying text.

316 MERRY, *supra* note 285, at 89.

317 *Id.*

318 *Id.* at 22.

319 *Id.*

320 *Id.* at 92.

321 *Id.* The issue of framing is taken up in Chapter 6.

322 *Id.* at 128.

323 *Id.* at 144.

For example, Merry's analysis of FGM is designed to avoid a confrontational approach and to sidestep the culture versus equality dichotomy. It aims to recognize that the ceremony "is both a painful public ordeal that reveals strength and fortitude, thus developing self-confidence and public respect as adults, but it comes at the price of women's decreased pleasure and containment of their sexuality."[324] Girls may face harassment and a loss of respect in their communities if they do not participate because the implicit understanding is that those who do not undergo the cutting do not pass the rite of adulthood.[325] Instead of eradicating the practice altogether, it has been suggested that the negative elements, such as the cutting, be removed but that the ceremony must be maintained and provide a less invasive means of establishing adult femininity.[326] Similarly, in the realm of honor killing, "[s]ome activists argue for the assertion of women's rights as individuals and condemn religious and kinship-based control, while others advocate working through kinship and community structures."[327] These strategies seek to provide the elements necessary for women's well-being, such as bodily security and health care, without taking away core values and beliefs that are integral to the culture and that deserve respect.

For these feminists and scholars, to insist that culture is an "obstacle to progress" too often "ignore[s] cultural practices and beliefs that seek to empower women, while stigmatizing others . . . that are often central to rites of passage or ritual transformations."[328] In nongendered human rights contexts, there is not "such a stark opposition between an emancipatory rights discourse and an oppressive culture."[329] Human rights efforts to end torture generally, or to provide basic health care and bodily security to the population as a whole, do not as regularly admonish elements of the culture as the root cause of the human rights violation. Too often in the discourse of gender rights, cosmopolitans who advocate for women view a culture that supports gender violence as "other" and seek to impose a Westernized cultural system in place of that "other."[330] Levitt and Merry argued that this confrontational approach unnecessarily views culture as the enemy of women's rights and is (wrongly) "premised on a particular set of images of culture opposed to rights, even though rights are a cultural phenomenon."[331] They describe this understanding as the "imperial narrative," and note that, while at times it may be true that certain aspects of the culture may advocate the abuse of women, wholesale rejection of the

---

324 *Id.* at 141.

325 *Id.*

326 *Id.* at 144.

327 *Id.* at 133.

328 Dorothy L. Hodgson, *"These Are Not Our Priorities": Maasai Women, Human Rights, and the Problem of Culture*, *in* GENDER AND CULTURE AT THE LIMIT OF RIGHTS 138, 140 (Dorothy L. Hodgson ed., 2011).

329 Peggy Levitt & Sally Engle Merry, *Making Women's Human Rights in the Vernacular: Navigating the Culture/Rights Divide*, *in* GENDER AND CULTURE AT THE LIMIT OF RIGHTS 81, 82 (Dorothy L. Hodgson, ed., 2011).

330 *Id.* at 83.

331 *Id.*

culture leads to a reciprocal rejection of the movement—not just among those in power but among the women themselves as well.

Those concerned that a blaming-the-culture approach perpetuates an imperial narrative make an additional argument as follows. Often human rights advocates assume that women wish to have certain rights and wish to abolish certain cultural practices, when in fact the advocates themselves have not given women the proper channels for agency to explain their desires. For example, in the case of a remote tribal village in Tanzania aided by a group called the Maasai Women Development Organization, women were not as concerned with eradicating the issues of polygyny (having multiple wives) and FGM. Rather, they saw "land rights, livestock, hunger, poverty, and education as the more important issues to be addressed."[332] Women may believe that the problems they face are not "inherent to their 'cultures' and 'traditions' but the product of broader political and economic forces such as colonialism, missionary evangelization, capitalist industry, the privatization of land and other natural resources, population pressures and HIV/AIDs."[333] Certain women in the Maasai tribe indicated that they did not want to be forced to take on men's roles, desiring instead a complementarity of gender roles and the ability to exercise newfound rights within their traditional roles. These women made the poignant statement that they were "hardly the ignorant 'beasts of burden' shackled to tradition or the docile embodiment or exhibitors of culture that some have assumed."[334]

Sally Engle Merry tried to navigate this complicated terrain by starting with what she considered the foundational question of women's agency. According to Merry, failure to listen to the local population will hinder "collaboration with grassroots activists despite the desire of the CEDAW Committee to promote this collaboration and the shared commitment of both transnational and local activists to improving the situation of women."[335] From this standpoint, deference to women's agency means that women can make their own decisions, including decisions about their own culture, instead of advocates making these decisions for them. First, however, women's well-being must be addressed to ensure that women are in a safe and secure environment to exercise their agency. But of course, to achieve these objectives, culture needs to be examined, analyzed, and internalized. Merry's point is that while culture can be examined and evaluated, it cannot be wholly rejected as the problem, but rather, should be mined for a solution. To attain a solution, movements must work from within: "This is at heart a process of translation across boundaries of class, ethnicity, mobility, and education."[336]

Merry's position is not irreconcilable to the position I adopt in this book. Of course, Merry is correct that problematic practices that are supported by cultural arguments can

[332] Hodgson, *supra* note 328, at 153 (analyzing a study conducted with women of the Maasai tribe in Tanzania).

[333] *Id.* at 155–56.

[334] *Id.* at 157.

[335] MERRY, *supra* note 292, at 104.

[336] *Id.* at 134.

be condemned without condemning the culture wholesale. And of course to the extent that doing so makes women and men more receptive to changing those practices, such an approach may also make strategic sense. Merry is also correct that the modernization project, the rule of law project, the international human rights project—as I have stated throughout, is not just a law project but is itself a project that is and has been, inextricably intertwined with culture. Universalism is itself a culturally based agenda. To the extent that women may adopt certain choices that restrict their capabilities, further defined in Chapter 6, however, I would not be in agreement with Merry's position that respecting women's agency means respecting their choices, regardless of other competing values, such as freedom and capability. To that extent, my position departs from Merry's and is grounded in the work of other scholars such as Sen, Nussbaum, and Appadurai. See Chapter 6 for details.

b. Women's Agency and Women's Well-being

From the time of Mary Wollstonecraft's seminal work, *A Vindication of the Rights of Woman*, female agency has been identified in the Western world as an important factor to both women's rights and to larger societal well-being.[337] As Amartya Sen observed, the rights Wollstonecraft wrote about "included not only some that particularly related to the well-being of women (and the entitlements that were directly geared to promote that well-being), but also rights that were aimed mainly at the free agency of women."[338] Sen noted that although the women's movement has focused on well-being aspects of women's rights, in recent years, "the agency aspects are beginning to receive some attention at last. . . ."[339] When women have the freedom to make choices and decisions, they "are increasingly seen, by men as well as women, as active agents of change: the dynamic promoters of social transformations that can alter the lives of both women and men."[340]

Sen argued that there is a cyclical nature between the two concepts of well-being and agency: "[T]he limited role of women's active agency seriously afflicts the lives of all people—men as well as women, children as well as adults."[341] Logically then, when women's well-being is limited, agency will also be limited as agency is a driving force in creating well-being not just for women, but for society as a whole. Empirical research has shown that women's well-being is strongly correlated with the "ability to earn an independent income, to find employment outside the home, to have ownership rights and to have literacy and be educated participants in decisions within and outside the family."[342]

---

[337] Sen, *supra* note 1, at 189; *see generally* Mary Wollstonecraft, A Vindication of the Rights of Woman (1792).

[338] Sen, *supra* note 1, at 189.

[339] *Id.*

[340] *Id.*

[341] *Id.* at 191.

[342] *Id.*

These variables—independent work outside the home, income, property rights, literacy, and education—may seem disparate and unrelated but in fact, "what they all have in common is their positive contribution in adding force to women's voice and agency—through independence and empowerment."[343] To have agency, one must be empowered. An uneducated, isolated, economically dependent person with limited options can only have limited agency. Women's empowerment and independence enhance their well-being both outside and inside the home. The way in which women are situated within the family can have wide, "far-reaching impacts on the forces and organizing principles that govern divisions within the family and in society as a whole, and can, in particular, influence what are implicitly accepted as women's 'entitlements.' "[344]

Conflict in the family is a form of "cooperative conflict" and is often resolved based on who is entitled to make decisions for the family. Resolution is not necessarily guided by egalitarian principles and is often resolved through "implicitly agreed patterns of behavior. . . ."[345] Who is entitled to make decisions is dependent upon what contributions one makes. "[T]he freedom to seek and hold outside jobs can contribute to the reduction of women's relative—and absolute—deprivation," as she is contributing to the family income and therefore given a right to make decisions for the family.[346] If women have the opportunity to develop their own agency, they become more able to assert themselves in cooperative conflict and therefore protect themselves from violence and subordination.

Beyond women's well-being, gender rights in general have a positive effect on multiple *other* societal factors: "[W]omen's agency and voice . . . can in turn influence the nature of the public discussion on a variety of social subjects, including acceptable fertility rates . . . and environmental priorities."[347] This argument rests not just on the notion that women's rights are indispensable to the development process but rather that women's rights and empowerment have positive societal consequences.[348] "Increasing women's control over resources, even in the short run, will improve their say within the household, which will not only increase their welfare, but as research seems to have shown repeatedly, child nutrition and health as well."[349] In particular, education for women leads to a decrease in mortality rates for children and promotes the general health of the population.[350] Educated women are "more likely to understand disease prevention measures . . .

---

343 *Id.*

344 *Id.* at 192.

345 *Id.*

346 *Id.* at 194.

347 *Id.* at 193.

348 It is important not to overstate the positive catalytic effect of women's empowerment. Many studies show that "women's empowerment leads to improvement in some aspects of children's welfare (health and nutrition, in particular), but at the expense of some others (education)." Duflo, *supra* note 275, at 1076.

349 *Id.* at 1074.

350 David Brown, *A Mother's Education Has a Huge Effect on a Child's Health*, WASH. POST (Sept. 16, 2010), http://www.washingtonpost.com/wpdyn/content/article/2010/09/16/AR2010091606384.html.

and to use them."[351] Further, expansion and availability of education tend to increase a nation's wealth, thus fostering development.[352] As Sen has remarked: "The changing agency of women is one of the major mediators of economic and social change, and its determination as well as consequences closely relate to many of the central features of the development process."[353]

Given these positive statistics and the generalized knowledge generated from studies lauding the provision of education and agency to women, one may wonder why more women do not fight for well-being and agency. It is not just men who attach traditional or preconceived notions to gender; many women also believe that their proper place in society is exactly where they are. "One of the reasons that so many women and girls are kidnapped, trafficked, raped and otherwise abused is that they grin and bear it."[354] Sheryl WuDunn and Nicholas Kristof stressed that providing education to women can demonstrate to them that tradition does not dictate a lack of agency and well-being for women, and that "femininity does not entail docility."[355] Further, education "can [help] nurture assertiveness so that girls and women stand up for themselves."[356] While this assertiveness is essential to cultivating women's agency, WuDunn and Kristof emphasized the difficulty that fighting for this agency may pose to the actors.[357] Asserting themselves in this manner undoubtedly puts many women in harm's way, and multiple avenues must be possible so that women may achieve agency and well-being without risking everything.

The purpose of this section is only to show that there is a vital link between women's rights and development and that cultural issues are embedded in and intertwined with both development generally and particularly its gendered aspects. As I have argued, if development is thickly understood to encompass human rights or as Sen and Appadurai propose, freedom, capability, and voice, and if human rights, freedom, and voice all have cultural components,[358] then law and development cannot omit culture from its framework.

Again, as Sen has correctly and wisely understood, "the empowerment of women is one of the central issues in the process of development for many countries in the world today.... The changing agency of women is one of the major mediators of economic and social change, and its determination as well as consequences closely relate to many of the

---

351 *Id.*

352 *Id.*

353 SEN, *supra* note 1, at 202. In the arena of politics, women's participation—when permitted—has also had a positive effect on society. A study conducted in India revealed that women's involvement in politics resulted in far fewer violent crimes than when the social and political sphere consisted solely of men. *Id.* at 200.

354 NICHOLAS D. KRISTOF & SHERYL WUDUNN, HALF THE SKY: TURNING OPPRESSION INTO OPPORTUNITY FOR WOMEN WORLDWIDE 47 (2010).

355 *Id.*

356 *Id.*

357 *Id.* at 53.

358 *See* Introduction, text accompanying notes 152–53.

central features of the development process."[359] What I have shown in this section is that women's rights, increasingly understood in well-being and agency terms, are in turn tied to questions of culture, showing again that culture must be addressed, not sidestepped by law and development. As noted, feminist suggestions for navigating the impasse between culture and equality are complex and have varied over time. What is noteworthy is the fact that feminists have always understood that culture has to be engaged one way or another, even if it is to argue that a culturally centered inquiry is wrong or that a particular interpretation of culture is inaccurate or misplaced. Indeed, much of the issues concerning women's equality and rights revolve around culture and so when one addresses the former, the latter needs to be addressed as well.

The purpose of Part C below is to illustrate in concrete terms the mirror image, so to speak, of the arguments made in Part B. Part C contains two in-depth case studies, one drawn from African tribes to show how community imperfections have negative developmental implications, both from a market and a human rights perspective; the other drawn from Islamic cultural norms to show how adherence to such norms have slowed the market development of the Middle East. Unlike Part B, which discusses positive community norms and their ability to minimize coordination problems and reduce transaction costs, Part C's examples highlight negative norms, for example, how particularism and clan politics can lead to a degradation of markets, democracy, and other institutions, the very institutions that law and development work to establish. Examples also include cultural norms and practices that undermine women's human rights and that have proved resistant to change.

C. Negative Cultural Norms

1. LINEAGE-BASED COMMUNITIES

Some group norms do not have a positive effect on economic development. Research by Anita Abraham and Jean-Philippe Plateau on the role of institutions in economic development shows that there are three elements of lineage-based culture that pose a barrier to development: (1) unanimous decision making; (2) egalitarian and sharing norms; and (3) segregation. As discussed in Section 1 of Part B, communities that are tightly knit and bound by common bonds enforce community expectations through intense social pressure. For reasons discussed below, in the case of tribal economies, although these traditions and norms maintain social stability and preserve collective arrangements that ensure against environmental risks, they are also no longer economically viable.[360]

---

[359] SEN, *supra* note 1, at 202.

[360] The section on tribal economies is drawn from Anita Abraham & Jean-Philippe Platteau, *Participatory Development in the Presence of Endogenous Community Imperfections*, 39 J. DEV. STUD. 104 (2002).

A comprehensive study demonstrates how "lineage-based societies that inhabit the African continent are plagued by a number of community imperfections . . ."[361] detrimental to economic development. In the words of the two researchers, "traditional village societies" studied in sub-Saharan Africa are characterized by both norms of redistribution and authoritarianism. Interestingly, such tribal societies are governed by economic forces and incentives that in some ways are similar to those that govern rotating credit associations. As in the case of rotating credit associations, the issue of transaction costs, particularly agency cost, looms large. Tribal societies, like other small homogeneous groups, operate in ways that minimize the possibility of defection and lower transactions costs. For example, in such groups, there is a greater likelihood of perfect information and repeated encounters which means that would-be cheaters need to worry about their reputation and will refrain from cheating. Both parties are acutely aware of, at a minimum, each other's reputation, if not the details of one another's personal lives. Community actors that lie, cheat, or steal develop a reputation for the same within their communities, and, consequently, the community excludes them from the tribal economy.

In this way, the threat of exclusion by way of bad reputation, otherwise known as "reputation effects," incentivizes community actors to deal with each other in fair and honest terms. Reputation effects are an informal and decentralized process of sanctioning misconduct. No formal punishment is meted out against offenders. Rather, offending members suffer community displeasure through informal boycotts and social exclusion. Nor does a central authoritative body administer sanctions. Instead, community members, informed by word of mouth, respond collectively in accordance with both a community ethic and their self-interest, ultimately, refusing to deal with the offending liars, cheaters, and thieves.

These principles, which Abraham and Platteau term the Folk Theorem, only function under specific circumstances. The community must exhibit: (1) perfect information, (2) continuous interaction, and (3) trust. As such, their research confirms that such economic benefits properly accrue only in small groups with shared experiences or beliefs and inherited patterns of behavior (i.e., common culture).[362]

The absence of any of these elements inhibits the efficient communication of reputation within a community necessary to ensure the proper sanctioning of the offending actor. As groups increase in population and geographic dispersal, maintaining perfect information and continuous interaction becomes increasingly difficult. As Abraham and Platteau asserted, "disappointing results observed in some remarkable cases force us to question the optimistic view of communities operating in poor rural regions."[363] They argued that the informal reputation mechanism used by African tribal communities as well as the supporting power structure and traditions, are "unreliable in protecting the

[361] *Id.* at 106.

[362] *Id.* at 109.

[363] *Id.*

poorest households, and susceptible to retarding capital accumulation, economic growth and mobility."[364]

For example, the very norms that facilitate the operation of reputational sanctions may also, under certain scenarios, impede development. Unanimous decision making, egalitarian sharing norms and segregation may facilitate fair and honest dealing. Unfortunately, these traditions and norms simultaneously impose barriers to development, especially as tribal communities grow and the effectiveness of reputation effects decreases. Note that these redistributive or egalitarian norms are not norms that attach to the positive examples discussed in Section 1 of Part B—ethnic economies created by ethnic minorities or rotating credit associations, which use social capital to facilitate economic transactions without imposing additional constraints on group members.[365]

As discussed below, several problems which have an impact on intragroup equality and economic development arise out of the intensely personalized and embedded nature of these societies. A comprehensive study of fifty nations by Licht, Goldsmith, and Schwartz, supported by empirical evidence, shows that governance norms of any society are heavily influenced by the prevailing cultural makeup of that society. "Particularly prominent is a cultural dimension addressing the place of individuals in the group as autonomous, bounded entities (autonomy) versus entities embedded in the social fabric (embeddedness)." [366] The study found that cultural norms that emphasize autonomy and deemphasize embeddedness tend to have a positive effect on rule of law, noncorruption and democracy.[367] By contrast, "societies whose cultures view the individual as an embedded part of hierarchically organized groups will discourage [individual] independent moves as inconsistent with socially approved values. These societies are more likely to accommodate exercise of power from above as a means for social coordination"[368] and are more likely to be nontransparent.

Applying this predictive framework to lineage-based societies, it is clear that individuals in small groups, such as tribal societies, tend to be embedded in their societies, which in turn promote norms designed to ensure group harmony and cohesion. As predicted by the study, those individuals have little autonomy and the societies themselves are characterized by little transparency. Tribal norms are maintained and enforced by tribal leaders.

---

[364] *Id.* at 110.

[365] Ethnic economies are formed by an ethnic individual who then uses commonalities with other coethnics to grow their business. Rotating credit associations are devices used simply for one purpose—to help members gain access to credit. In both cases, there is no additional obligation to share wealth with other group members. Neither ethnic economies nor rotating credit associations are meant to be a permanent, enclosed community in which members interact in economic as well as in their private spheres. Nor is there any obligation owed by one member to another's welfare member beyond that which undergirds the particularized transaction at issue.

[366] Amir Licht et al., *Culture Rules: The Foundations of the Rule of Law and Other Norms of Governance*, 35 J. Comp. Econ. 659, 661 (2007).

[367] *Id.* at 661.

[368] *Id.* at 663.

To project an appearance of group harmony and cohesion, disagreements among tribal elders need to be masked and contained because disagreements in the public sphere tend to spill into the "sphere of private relations and . . . generate personal antagonisms."[369] Moreover, because tribal leaders supposedly "embod[y] the will of supernatural agencies . . . [and] disagreement among the elite is bound to cause serious suspicion about its ability to represent or act on behalf of these powers,"[370] avoidance of public disagreement dominates the social concerns of tribal leaders for fear that "interpersonal conflicts . . . threaten to undermine the social fabric" of the community.[371]

Norms that are meant to ensure group harmony also tend to mask legitimate discontent among members, resulting in group muffling of individual voice. Tribal groups suppress public disagreement through a rule of unanimous decision making supported by a laborious process of arbitration and settlement. Unanimous decision making among chiefs and elders avoids personal antagonism and creates for group consumption the appearance of spiritual authority. The community enforces unanimity through intense social pressure, constant harassment, and ideological intimidation.[372] Unfortunately, the economic and social costs incurred in achieving unanimous consent hinders economic development, and because it also involves intimidation and coercion, muffles the voice of tribal members as well. These observations are in accord with those included in the Licht, Goldsmith, and Schwartz empirical study which concluded that "[c]ountries with high scores for the prevalence of the rule of law and non-corruption are . . . low on embeddedness and hierarchy."[373]

Unanimous decision making also exacts a social cost in terms of marginalizing those members of the community not among the sociopolitical elite. If, as Appadurai defines it,[374] development is about increasing the capacity and voice of the poor, then a practice that constricts voice should be addressed and remedied. First, nonelites have no voice within the tribal political establishment. In fact, chiefs and tribal elders discourage democracy because it "officialize[s] the existence of disagreements" and is "perceived as a potential threat both to the effective enforcement of rules and decisions, and to the continuation of amicable relations."[375] The sociopolitical elite also restrain the voice of nonelites. As Abraham and Platteau described, "the elite provides an authority structure which imposes its rule or its interpretation of the tradition on the lower people who have no choice but to comply. The latter do not dare speak out their possible disagreement and, out of fear of retribution, they may just pay lip service to decisions or rules which they do not like."[376] Unanimous decision making, therefore, appears less a vehicle

---

[369] Abraham & Platteau, *supra* note 360, at 112.

[370] *Id.*

[371] *Id.*

[372] *Id.* at 113, 116.

[373] Licht et al., *supra* note 366, at 669.

[374] *See* Introduction, text accompanying notes 130–35.

[375] Abraham & Platteau, *supra* note 360, at 112.

[376] *Id.* at 113–14.

of social stability and more a means of entrenching the sociopolitical status of the tribal elite. The following description about Japanese village communities of the old Tokugawa era applies to other peasant or tribal societies today: "Tensions were more quickly and intimately felt, but overt expression of them was more resolutely suppressed in favor of an appearance for community harmony."[377]

Besides the unanimity norm, other tribal norms that appear beneficial in fact are detrimental because they entrench existing power relations. For example, in an effort to bolster social amicability, tribal communities promote egalitarian sharing norms that reduce economic differentiation. Traditional sharing norms exist not just in tribal societies but also in other societies characterized by kinship such as countries in sub-Saharan Africa, the Philippines, and Vietnam.[378] Close-knit village communities characterized by strong kinship and other personalistic ties tend to be "group-focused" societies, which nurture a presumption against individualistic pursuits that may elevate an individual above his or her group or threaten the traditional pattern of authority.[379]Abraham and Platteau stated that "generosity and hospitality are highly praised behaviors in traditional rural communities and successful individuals therefore gain social prestige and esteem when they redistribute their surplus."[380] Similar to unanimous decision making, tribal communities enforce these egalitarian norms through intense social pressure and intimidation.

The purpose underlying egalitarian sharing norms derives, on the one hand, from a desire to avoid economic differentiation which fuels the kind of jealousy and envy that can cause a small group to implode. Sharing norms also provide insurance against crop failures and the like as well as ensure against adverse selection problems. For instance, "if a prosperous individual were allowed to stop making gifts to fellow villagers, the size of the informal insurance network formed by the community would be reduced and the group's ability to spread risks would be correspondingly diminished."[381] Clearly, one can understand that kinship norms of solidarity are useful as they ensure the survival of all; in such

---

[377] Anita Abraham & Jean-Philippe Platteau, *Participatory Development: Where Culture Creeps In*, *in* CULTURE AND PUBLIC ACTION 210, 214 (Vijavendra Rao & Michael Walton eds. 2004).

[378] Salvatore di Falco & Erwin Bulte, *A Dark Side of Social Capital? Kinship, Consumption, and Savings* (2009), *available at* http://www.uni-heidelberg.de/md/awi/forschung/paper_e.bulte_kinship_jds_final.pdf. Empirical data from KwaZulu-Natal (Republic of South Africa) support other research which demonstrates that traditional sharing rules of compulsory reciprocity discourage savings and investment and perpetuate individual poverty.

[379] Abraham & Platteau, *supra* note 377, at 212–13. Though personalistic and kinship ties can facilitate economic growth, at some point they can also be a drag on economic development, dampening individual incentives to invest and accumulate wealth. Max Weber, of course, argued that the spread of Calvinism, which emphasized "individualistic motives of rational legal acquisition by virtue of one's own ability and initiative . . . had the psychological effect of freeing the acquisition of goods from the inhibitions of traditionalistic ethics." WEBER, *supra* note 91, at 179, *quoted in* ALAN MACFARLANE, THE ORIGINS OF ENGLISH INDIVIDUALISM 47 (1979).

[380] Abraham & Platteau, *supra* note 360, at 115.

[381] *Id.*

societies, "[p]rivate wealth accumulation is perceived as an antisocial behavior because it is an attempt to break away from traditional solidarity networks."[382]

However, egalitarian norms also perpetuate power relations and entrench the elites. Such norms operate as a tax on wealth aimed at curbing socioeconomic mobility. Tribal leaders do not permit individual enrichment because it supplants the authority of the sociopolitical elites—chiefs, elders, priests, typically "old men belonging to the dominant lineages"[383]—who "do not accept that commoners rise above them by acquiring old or new symbols of wealth and status."[384] Individual, nonelite efforts to move economically upward "are unavoidably viewed as conscious attempts to compete with traditional leaders and to overturn the existing social order."[385] Consequently, wealth accumulation is "strongly condemned and the prosperous commoner is immediately coerced into handing over to the chief his newly acquired riches."[386] In some circumstances, communities charge wealth accumulators with witchcraft, alleging that "economic success . . . is the result of some hidden and treacherous exploitation" rather than efficiency and entrepreneurship.[387] "Tribal communities . . . appear as societies prone to resist any differentiation process . . . [modifying] relative status positions."[388]

Development agencies and NGOs that have introduced projects that could disturb the status of traditional elites have met with strong resistance.[389] For example, in Guinea Bissau, when an NGO instituted a program to train professional fishermen and designated certain village youths to receiving training and fishing assets, the local traditional king objected to young members receiving assets when he did not. In a northeastern region of Burkina Faso, an NGO helped a women's group acquire a mill, which was confiscated by the local chief who viewed it as a status symbol that should be bestowed upon him instead—after confiscation it lay unused in his yard. In the same general area, a local chief who engaged in various mischiefs nonetheless was systematically chosen to be the chairman of each village-wide association created by an NGO to improve irrigation. When the chief, as chairman, awarded preferential dealings to his brother and pursued other dubious activities, the members did not remove him as chairman because of his identity and status as their chief.

Significant costs result from egalitarian norms—not just economic costs but also, ironically, true egalitarian costs. In other words, egalitarian norms themselves keep the rich elevated and prevent the marginalized from ever being able to achieve a level of wealth and independence that would truly "equalize" society. First, "entrepreneurial talent is

---

382 Abraham & Platteau, *supra* note 377, at 215–16.

383 *Id.* at 217.

384 *Id.* at 216.

385 Abraham & Platteau, *supra* note 360, at 116.

386 *Id.*

387 *Id.*

388 *Id.*

389 Examples in this paragraph are drawn from Abraham & Platteau, *supra* note 377, at 220–23.

wasted owing to the pervasive presence of sharing norms and the consequent[ial] loss of opportunities for accumulation and growth."[390] There are also substantial losses incurred as tribal leaders "systematically appropriate, deflect or misuse resources that have been accumulated by or accrued to deserving members of their community."[391] These costs, in turn, perpetuate the cycle of slow to nonexistent economic development. In other words, community members lack incentive to grow their capital as any surplus will be summarily taken by tribal leaders. Entrepreneurs lack incentive to create new ventures as there is no reward for their risk. And, even if entrepreneurs succeed in a venture, the venture itself is choked as capital necessary for reinvestment is confiscated by community elites.

In sum, there is a connection between informal institutions such as culture and formal institutions. As the study on lineage-based societies above shows, cultural norms have developmental implications. Other examples of negative norms abound. Understanding how a culture interacts with development is important in rule of law initiatives. The organization of a society, especially its economic, legal, social, and moral enforcement institutions, greatly affects its economic performance and financial evolution.[392] Cultural analysts and scholars suggest that different cultural factors lead to distinct trajectories of institutional structure,[393] as Section 2 below illustrates.

2. ISLAMIC NORMS AND THE MIDDLE EAST

One of the unanticipated long-term consequences of the institutionalization of Islamic law is the stagnation of the economy in the Middle East. Note that references in this section to "Islamic laws," "Islamic finance," or "Islamic economics" are drawn from works of scholars in the field who themselves use such terms, notwithstanding the existence of Islamic business practices that in fact vary by region and sect.[394]

Culture can have a dramatic impact on the economic development of an area or group as illustrated by the history of the Middle East. As of 1000 AD, the economy of the Middle East eclipsed that of Western Europe.[395] By the sixteenth century, however, Western Europe had eclipsed the Middle East as a commercial power.[396] In a provocative work that

---

390 Abraham & Platteau, *supra* note 360, at 116.

391 *Id.*

392 Avner Greif, *Cultural Beliefs and the Organization of Society: A Historical and Theoretical Reflection on Collectivist and Individualist Societies*, 102 J. POL. ECON. 912, 913 (1994).

393 *Id.*

394 *See,* e.g., ANGELO M. VENARDOS, ISLAMIC BANKING AND FINANCE IN SOUTH-EAST ASIA: ITS DEVELOPMENT AND FUTURE (2006); FARHAD NOMANI & ALI RAHNEMA, ISLAMIC ECONOMIC SYSTEMS (1994); MUHAMMAD UMER CHAPRA, ISLAM AND THE ECONOMIC CHALLENGE (1992).

395 *See* ANGUS MADDISON, THE WORLD ECONOMY: A MILLENNIAL PROSPECTIVE 49 (2001) (cited in TIMUR KURAN, THE LONG DIVERGENCE: HOW ISLAMIC LAW HELD BACK THE MIDDLE EAST 3 (2011)); *see also* JAN LUITEN VAN ZANDEN, THE LONG ROAD TO THE INDUSTRIAL REVOLUTION: THE EUROPEAN ECONOMY IN A GLOBAL PERSPECTIVE, 1000–1800, 269 (2009).

396 ZANDEN, *supra* note 395, at 271.

has also been subjected to much criticism for its indictment of Islamic law,[397] Professor Timur Kuran, a Turkish American economist, has studied this divergence between the economies of the Middle East and the West.[398] He has posited that "social mechanisms" in the Middle East worked to produce institutional stagnation. Due to the inhibiting effect of these mechanisms, the Middle East did not develop institutions that facilitated economic growth driven by larger, more complex businesses with multiple investors.[399]

Avner Greif has long noted "the historical importance of distinct cultures in economic development."[400] During the period that the Middle East declined, the economy of the West strengthened. Institutional development, especially the business corporation, served as the engine of growth in the West. Neither this entity nor any analog developed in the Middle East, and Muslims did not adopt the corporation until the twentieth century.[401] In contrast, European towns as well as the Roman Catholic Church embraced incorporation as early as the first millennium.[402] Western Europe had a history of multiple, coexisting legal systems with limited jurisdictions, that is, Roman law and canon law, which laid the intellectual foundation for accepting the corporation with its own governing structure. Under the Islamic experience and its "ideal of communal unity," however, the idea of "subcommunal self-governance" embodied in the corporation was rejected. More complex business forms, such as the corporation, never developed because certain "social mechanisms" of the Islamic system precluded the need for innovation along organizational lines. Instead, these mechanisms motivated interested parties to promote the status quo. Further, the system not only failed to reward larger ventures, it incentivized wealthy individuals to avoid pooling assets and seek out wealth shelters.

At the initial emergence of Islam in the eighth century CE, the Middle East was bubbling with commercial activity. Multiple trade centers existed south and east of the Mediterranean, and Islam, as well as the Quran, were business friendly. "Arabia was an economic society. Its leader, Muhammad, was a successful Merchant who understood the creation of commercial wealth."[403] Middle Eastern wealth and influence stretched as far

---

[397] *See, e.g.*, Arshad Zaman, *Timur Kuran, The Long Divergence: How Islamic Law Held Back the Middle East* (Review Article), 49 ISLAMIC STUDIES 277 (2010); Adeel Malik, *Was the Middle East's Economic Decline a Legal or Political Failure?: A Review of Timur Kuran's "The Long Divergence: How Islamic Law Held Back the Middle East"* (8th Int'l Conf. on Islamic Econ. & Fin.), http://conference.qfis.edu.qa/app/media/303 (last visited Apr. 20, 2015).

[398] Unless otherwise stated, all information in this section is drawn from TIMUR KURAN, THE LONG DIVERGENCE: HOW ISLAMIC LAW HELD BACK THE MIDDLE EAST (2011).

[399] *Id.* at 5–6 (defining an institution as a "system of socially produced regularities that shape, and are in turn shaped by, individual behaviors") *Id.* at 6.

[400] Greif, *supra* note 392, at 913.

[401] A Muslim-owned joint-stock company had been formed in the nineteenth century, but this was an unincorporated entity. Its largest shareholder was the Ottoman sultan. KURAN, *supra* note 398, at 97.

[402] HAROLD J. BERMAN, LAW AND REVOLUTION: THE FORMATION OF THE WESTERN LEGAL TRADITION (1983).

[403] KURAN, *supra* note 398, at 36.

as that of the Roman Empire and later, Continental Europe. Trade was central to groups of eleventh-century traders from the Muslim world. Maghribi traders were involved in large-scale long-distance trade all over the Muslim Mediterranean.[404] Similar groups of traders existed all around Europe in the Middle Ages, specifically, around modern-day Italy in the Italian city-states.

Despite these similarities between Europe and the Middle East, commercial and canon law developed in Europe, resulting in the formation of complex institutions—corporations, foundations, and trusts.[405] In the Middle East, no such organizations were formed or were recognized by Islamic law.

The crucial question is why. Indeed, in terms of wealth and influence, the commercial networks of the Islamic world achieved nothing comparable to the business conglomerates formed in Western Europe.[406] It is only in the last two hundred years that the Middle East began to catch up with the West in economic and financial institutions. Prior to its reforms of the nineteenth century, the Middle East did not produce even one indigenous joint stock company.[407] All the major banks in the Middle East in the middle of the twentieth century were Western banks, for example, the Imperial Ottoman Bank, the Imperial Bank of Persia, and the Anglo-Egyptian Bank.[408] In addition, "on the eve of World War I, very few Muslim-owned firms existed in commercial finance or manufacturing."[409]

Greif suggested that the societal and cultural difference responsible for the divergent paths of developed and undeveloped countries is "collectivism."[410] "[M]ost of the developing countries are 'collectivist,' whereas the developed West is 'individualist.' "[411] What distinguishes collectivist societies from individualist societies is surprisingly the exact feature that limits development. Collectivist societies are " 'segregated' in the sense that each individual, socially and economically, interacts mainly with members of a specific religious, ethnic, or familial group in which contract enforcement is achieved through 'informal' economic and social institutions."[412] While this cuts costs in the short term,

---

404 Greif, *supra* note 392, at 917.

405 Harold J. Berman, *Law and Revolution: The Formation of the Western Legal Tradition*, *in* JOHN HENRY MERRYMAN ET AL., THE CIVIL LAW TRADITION: EUROPE, LATIN AMERICA, AND EAST ASIA, CASES AND MATERIALS, 303 (1994).

406 Timur Kuran, *The Islamic Commercial Crisis: Institutional Roots of Economic Underdevelopment in the Middle East*, 16 (USC Center for Law, Economics and Organization Research Paper Series, Research Paper No. C01–12, 2002), available at http://papers.ssrn.com/sol3/papers.cfm?abstract_id=276377, *reprinted in* 63 J. ECON. HIST. 414 (June 2003).

407 *Id.* at 17.

408 *Id.*

409 *Id.*

410 Greif, *supra* note 392, at 913.

411 *Id.*

412 *Id.* Note that some of the arrangements discussed in Part B would follow under this category. The point is that certain arrangements have positive economic implications at one stage of development but could become an economic drag at a later stage. For example, rotating credit associations may be economically beneficial for certain groups at a certain point in time but not at later stages of development.

and makes trade efficient among group members, members of different groups do not cooperate with each other.[413] By contrast, individualist societies are characterized by economic transactions occurring between individual members of very diverse groups. Because levels of trust may not necessarily be as high as those in collectivist societies, contractual obligations are enforced through "specialized organizations such as the court" and the contracts themselves are formalized.[414] Within the passage of time that occurred simultaneously in the Middle East and the Italian city-states, city-states set the stage for corporate law while the Middle East remained stagnant, with single-generation partnerships remaining the self-reinforcing norm until the eighteenth century.

A necessary condition for organizational change, according to Greif's study, is that those who are able to initiate it expect to gain from it. "Their expectations depend on their cultural beliefs, and hence diverse cultural beliefs lead to a distinct trajectory of organizational development."[415] Whereas commercial law of the West expanded Roman law, and canon law was used to reform commercial norms to fit the need of the growing class of merchants, Islamic law has been severely tied to the text of the Quran, and challenging the authority of the Quran was considered risky.[416] The Italian city-states were far removed from the feudalism that was prevalent in the countryside. In addition, the scholars of law in Bologna University as well as those in other universities that spontaneously cropped up around Italy were often commoners and laymen, as opposed to the nobility who wished to keep the law at status quo in their favor. The Italian universities, based on their location in independent Italian city-states, facilitated legal development in a way that made law accessible to those classes in society that stood to benefit from such development. It was not uncommon for commoners and merchants to turn academic; while studying at the universities, they would often learn and analyze Roman law and later bring their knowledge back to the jurisdiction where they were from. Therefore, their contemporary and expanding knowledge of the law permeated across boundaries and affected change across Europe. The commercial nature of cities was reflected in academic institutions, and the laws that emerged protected the merchant class.[417] Islamic law was only studied in religious institutions; church (or in this case mosque) and state were not separated.

Indeed, in Europe, the law that university academics studied was a combination of Roman law, canon law, and customary law. Roman law was subject to interpretation; canon law was constantly evolving with new edicts issued by various priests and clergymen. In Europe, the concept of separation of church and state emerged as early as the

[413] *Id.*

[414] *Id.*

[415] *Id.* at 916.

[416] Kuran, *supra* note 406, at 26–27.

[417] David S. Clark, *The Medieval Origins on Modern Legal Education: Between Church and State*, *in* JOHN HENRY MERRYMAN ET AL., THE CIVIL LAW TRADITION: EUROPE, LATIN AMERICA, AND EAST ASIA, CASES AND MATERIALS 295 (1994).

third century CE with Pope Gelasius I addressing Emperor Anastasius I.[418] Thus, Roman law and canon law evolved separately and both greatly influenced the civil law tradition as well as commercial law. Priests supported the evolution of the law separate from the reign of the emperor. The emperors wanted the law to evolve separately from the church. As a result, European law propelled a separation of church and state and was greatly prone to change. Evolution of the law contributed to a sense of dynamic progress in Europe. On the other hand, in the Muslim world of the Middle East, Islamic law was the rule of the land and separation of the spiritual and temporal world did not occur.

Kuran noted that legal changes did occur in the Middle East in areas such as taxation and statecraft, but the rules of commerce remained mostly unchanged.[419] The rules of forming Islamic partnerships, developed by jurists from the seventh to tenth centuries, were inspired by customs under Islamic rule. While Islamic law favored merchants and investors in rules regarding partnerships, it was inflexible in other ways: mainly currency, interest, and inheritance.[420]

Perhaps this rigidity could be explained by analyzing the philosophy behind Islamic law of finance and economics. The two most important objectives of Islamic law of economics and finance are socioeconomic justice and the well-being of the human being. This requires balance of both the material and the spiritual needs of the human and neglecting either of them would frustrate the realization of true well-being.[421] Therefore, it is impossible to unlink the physical realm from the spiritual realm. The Islamic financial system is based on concepts of Islamic morality and ethics, not commercial success and profit.[422] There are three principles ruling Islamic economics and finance which likely retarded the formation of corporations and consequently economic and institutional growth of the kind that occurred in Europe. The prohibition on *ribah*—interest, *gharar*—gambling and gambling-like transactions, and mandatory mutual cooperation and solidarity[423] were all at play. The "persistence of Islam's formal commitments to the eradication of interest" was responsible for the delay in Middle Eastern development.[424] Whereas between individuals it is easy to conceal dealings in interest, a bank would have a harder time disguising operations in interest. As such when "the interest ban was enforced even partially, a reluctance to publicize dealings in interest would have weakened the incentive to form large financial intermediaries."[425]

---

[418] *Gelasius I on Spiritual and Temporal Power, 494*, http://www.fordham.edu/halsall/source/gelasius1.asp (last visited May 1, 2015).

[419] Kuran, *supra* note 406, at 7.

[420] *Id.* at 8.

[421] Abdul-Rahim Al-Saati, *The Permissible Gharar (Risk) in Classical Islamic Jurisprudence*, 16 J. KAU: ISLAMIC ECON. 3, 3–19 (2003); *see also* KURAN, *supra* note 398.

[422] Al-Saati, *supra* note 421; *see also* KURAN, *supra* note 398.

[423] Al-Saati, *supra* note 421; *see also* KURAN, *supra* note 398.

[424] Kuran, *supra* note 406, at 16 n.38.

[425] *Id.*

Other factors also limited economic development in the Middle East. One of the distinguishing features of the Islamic legal system, which was fully in place by the tenth century, is the absence of the business corporation.[426] A corporation has its own legal identity: It can incur debt, possess property, sign contracts, sue, and be represented in court. "Precisely because it has a legal status of its own, it can live on after its initial members die or otherwise relinquish their rights and responsibilities."[427] In the Islamic world, economic ventures requiring the cooperation of two or more individuals were carried out by family enterprises or partnerships rather than by corporations.[428] "The institution of partnership was one of the chief means in the medieval Islamic world enabling merchants and others to combine their resources and skills for investment in commercial undertakings."[429] Under Islamic law, there are rules that govern partnerships,[430] many of which, according to Timur Kuran, made partnerships inefficient and discouraged capital formation. "Because an Islamic partnership lacks legal personhood, obligations arising from its dealings fell on its members as individuals,"[431] increasing individual risk and discouraging capital investment. If a person suffered harms from the activities of the partnership, he can only make claims against the partners, not the partnership itself. Similarly, the same concept applied to the partnership's claims against third parties. "Partners could demand compensation as individuals, never as a collective enterprise."[432] It is interesting to see that changes in Islamic law did occur in areas such as taxation and statecraft but "the rules of commerce remained more or less unchanged" despite the prevalence of such changes occurring in Europe.[433]

Greif suggested that differing cultural factors between Europe and the Middle East are responsible for the prevalence of complex enterprises and corporations, versus simple partnerships, respectively. Strict interpretation of rules against *ribah* and *gharar* prevented the development of new complex corporate enterprise in the Middle East. "In an Islamic partnership, obligations arising from dealings almost always fell on the individual partners rather than on that enterprise as a whole."[434] Whereas new organizational forms were popping up all across Europe to limit the liability of individuals, Islamic law only allowed for restrictive partnerships, where liability lay with the partner making the decisions. Due to the Islamic finance principle of mandatory coordination and the Islamic law on partnerships, only traditional partnerships or sole owners conducted trade, leaving

[426] *Id.* at 5.

[427] *Id.*

[428] *Id*

[429] Abraham L. Udovitch, *Labor Partnerships in Early Islamic Law*, 10 J. ECON. & SOC. HIST. OF THE ORIENT 64, 64 (1967).

[430] Kuran, *supra* note 406, at 5–6.

[431] KURAN, *supra* note 398, at 61.

[432] *Id.*

[433] Kuran, *supra* note 406, at 7.

[434] *Id.* at 43.

very little room for institutional change. In addition, any partner who wished to exit the partnership with no legal consequences was in his right to do so.

As a result, enterprises were not lasting, having no perpetuity. In the medieval Islamic world after the formative period of Islamic law ended, the number of careers in commerce remained the same between the eleventh and fifteenth centuries, whereas bureaucratic, military, educational, legal, and religious careers multiplied significantly.[435] In the Middle East, then, commercial law did not evolve in a direction that was conducive to the formation of bigger organizations or limited liability corporations, thus hampering economic development. The state had an additional, larger concern regarding the potential rise of entities designed for the large-scale maximization of wealth of private investors. "States do not benefit automatically from organizational innovations useful to private groups. . . . Wherever organizational advances occurred, the process involved bargaining among constituencies with conflicting interests."[436] The state, fearful of a potential political threat emerging from wealthy businessmen, had a strong incentive to ensure that centralized economic and political power remained in its own hands. The Middle East example shows that "[s]ome cultural beliefs can render efficient intersociety relations unprofitable, leading to an economically inefficient social structure."[437]

By contrast, Europe has a long tradition of established corporations as a profit-oriented business. Corporations have existed since the medieval era.[438] "Enjoying an existence independent of its individual shareholders and employees, the business corporation did not have to undergo a reorganization at each change in its ranks."[439] Because the corporation was its own legal entity, it did not have to incur the debts of each individual shareholder. The development of the corporation, its root in canon law,[440] provided a secure solution to the "problem of establishing durable enterprises able to exploit economies of scale and scope."[441] This environment was friendly to business activities. Around Florence, the Medici enterprise was formed, fostering and inspiring the birth of the Italian Renaissance.[442] The Netherlands, France, and England also saw the beginnings of joint stock companies.[443]

These vastly different experiences between Europe and the Middle East are further reflected in the way Genoese traders and the Maghribi traders conducted trade. Maghribi traders of the Middle East and the Genoese traders were both "involved in large-scale, long-distance trade all over the Muslim Mediterranean."[444] Whereas the two

---

435 *Id.* at 18.

436 KURAN, *supra* note 398, at 132.

437 Greif, *supra* note 392, at 916.

438 Berman, *supra* note 405, at 302.

439 Kuran, *supra* note 406, at 21.

440 Berman, *supra* note 405, at 302.

441 Kuran, *supra* note 406, at 21.

442 *Id.* at 19.

443 *Id.* at 20.

444 Greif, *supra* note 392, at 917.

groups had similar backgrounds, formations, and beginnings, they took wildly different developmental paths because of the different cultural norms that shaped the development of European versus Middle Eastern cities. Greif suggested that it is a difference between communal versus integrated societies. In the Maghribi communal society, there were initially lower costs because they traded abroad only with people who belonged to similar cultural groups. They relied highly on reputation and on letters of communication regarding whether to trust an agent abroad. While this arrangement resulted in, at least in the short run, low cost and low risk, reliance on and coordination within a homogenous, small community was not beneficial in the development of higher organizations.[445] "In contrast, Christianity during that period placed the individual rather than his social group at the center of its theology."[446] The rise of large European enterprises meant European cities witnessed a strong change in wealth distribution, resulting in the interests of the new wealthy being represented in the political organization of the society. "Indeed, the *popoli* of Genoa revolted during the thirteenth century against the nobility and changed the political organization of Genoa to reflect and protect their growing wealth."[447] No such organizational development or representation within the governmental institutions occurred in the Muslim world.

Moreover, European societies "modified partnerships to give them greater permanence and fine-tuned corporations to give minority shareholders protections against the decisions of the majority."[448] Genoese formed agency relationships with non-Genoese,[449] thus setting the stage of an "integrated" society that requires multitudes of institutions to profit and expand, such as commercial courts, contractual obligations, corporations, and a commercial and canon law that protect merchants and recognize business entities as their own legal personalities. Canon law in the eleventh and twelfth centuries introduced modern concepts of corporate ownership, trust, and foundations. "The canonists also developed modern concepts of possessory remedies."[450] Contrary to the Middle East, in the West, many partnerships that "started as family associations . . . metamorphosed into enterprises whose family members contributed only a minority of the capital and are consistently outnumbered by outside shareholders."[451] In this, among many other ways, Western organizations found an efficient way to pool resources and bring about great commercial opportunities without the financial liability on the shareholders. As such,

---

[445] *Id.* at 922–23. Greif noted that the Maghribis were a non-Muslim group who adopted the values of the Muslim society in which they were immersed. The value that is most relevant in this discussion is *umma*, which is the concept of mutual responsibility among members of the society. This is one of the principles discussed earlier as one of the tenets of Islamic finance. Maghribis retained strong social ties and supported a collectivist equilibrium.

[446] *Id.* at 923.

[447] *Id.* at 930.

[448] Kuran, *supra* note 406, at 21–22.

[449] Greif, *supra* note 392, at 931.

[450] Berman, *supra* note 405, at 303.

[451] Kuran, *supra* note 406, at 19.

third-party creditors were also able to invest in such organizations or lend money to them without bearing the risks themselves. These kinds of corporations also allowed for third-party traders to get involved in the corporation from abroad with lower costs and lower risks. The Maghribis, on the other hand, expanded their trade in a segregated manner, by only employing other Maghribis as agents.[452] Greif suggested that because partnerships were not able to last past a person's lifetime, there was no opportunity for third parties to take a risk with the partnership beyond one trade trip or the lifespan of a partner.

Another impediment to economic development in the Middle East is the Islamic inheritance system. The Islamic inheritance system stems from Western Arabia where most wealth belonged to traders and nomads whose possessions were easy to divide, because they consisted of goods such as animals and cash.[453] Islam's inheritance rules prevented property from remaining intact across generations because of mandatory sharing.[454] The Quran restricts an individual's testamentary privileges to one-third of his or her estate. The rest of the estate goes to various sons, daughters, spouses, parents, grandparents, brothers, sisters, and even distant relatives.[455] Research on prosperous Ottoman families of the sixteenth century show that their descendants rarely remained wealthy beyond one or two generations. Because of wealth fragmentation, aristocratic families did not form in Turkey or the Arab world. They could not serve as a countervailing force for change within the government or within Islamic law.

Closely related to the effect of inheritance practices is the practice of polygyny, or having multiple wives, further resulting in the fragmentation of assets of wealthy merchants with many wives and children. While historically only a few—the very rich and powerful—engaged in the practice,[456] it resulted in the further division of the wealthiest estates.[457] Such inheritance laws discouraged the accumulation of wealth by dividing it among family members. In terms of commercial ventures to which the testator had been a partner, they would cease upon the death of the testator, and his share had to be divided among his heirs according to Islamic rules. As every heir would receive a fraction of each asset, a single heir could lead to the premature and inconvenient dissolution of a partnership by demanding his share.[458] The inheritance and polygyny practices not only fragmented wealth through the presence of and mandatory provision for multiple heirs; these practices also provided further incentive for the use of small ventures to mitigate risk of loss.

---

[452] Greif, *supra* note 392, at 930.

[453] Kuran, *supra* note 406, at 35.

[454] *Id.* at 23.

[455] *Id.* at 22.

[456] KURAN, *supra* note 398, at 84.

[457] *Id.* at 281.

[458] *Id.* at 86.

By contrast, the canon law of inheritance in Europe "increased the share and included the wife within the protection, but not the grandchildren or the parents of the decedent."[459] In Europe, wealth remained in the family, and even if a person died intestate, the children and the wife had a right of inheritance.[460] Wealth remained intact from generation to generation and prominent merchant families emerged as leaders of societies. From the Middle Ages, multiple European countries took on the practice of giving preference of inheritance to the oldest son. "This continent-wide trend allowed huge numbers of wealthy families to keep their assets intact without resorting to such costly methods as establishing a *waqf*," a specific type of trust deemed permissible under Islamic law which is very costly to create.[461] The *waqf* provided a way to shelter wealth from Islamic inheritance laws.[462] The founder, or a successor named by the founder, could control the *waqf*, hire employees, and receive a salary.[463] More importantly, it existed beyond the life of the founder who contributed the property, allowing a designated person to receive a future benefit in the form of salary. Once formed, however, the individual's contribution to the *waqf* was irrevocable.[464] *Waqf* formation, while economically rational for an individual attempting to prevent the mandated division of his wealth, resulted in resource misallocations.[465] Although in the premodern era, the *waqf* was a key instrument for delivering social services, over time, it became inflexible and prevented the emergence of alternative organizational forms. Personal savings and bequests were directed to the *waqf* rather than commerce and capital investment. This, coupled with the fragmentation of personal estates for equity reasons rather than accumulation and investment, also contributed to economic stagnation.

Significantly the explicitness of the provisions in the Quran regarding inheritance ensured that they would not be openly questioned or resisted except in a grave crisis. "Attempts at reform were unlikely to be resisted as sacrilegious."[466] In the Middle East it was risky to challenge the authority of the Quran.[467] According to Kuran, inheritance rights in the Middle East were derived from the text of the Quran. Although certain European inheritance practices were just as rigid as Islamic ones, they were not deemed to be mandated by the Bible.[468] The practice of modifying laws and codifying them in canon law to affect reform was common practice developed in the early twelfth century.[469] In

---

459 Berman, *supra* note 405, at 301.
460 *Id.* at 302.
461 Kuran, *supra* note 406, at 27. A *waqf* is a form of an Islamic trust set up to keep property intact after the owner dies.
462 KURAN, *supra* note 398, at 112.
463 *Id.* at 112–13.
464 *Id.* at 110–11.
465 *Id.* at 282, 33.
466 Kuran, *supra* note 406, at 26.
467 *Id.* at 26–27.
468 *Id.* at 26.
469 Clark, *supra* note 417, at 296.

fact, this was how the church aligned itself with the growing merchant class and resisted the power of the emperor.[470]

And so the Middle East slowly began to fall behind Europe. While European institutions met the needs of the wealthy elite by creating corporations and courts to settle corporate disputes, the Middle East remained economically stagnant. Its elementary forms of commerce were self-reinforcing. True, the partnerships were sufficiently successful in trade with Southeast Asia and East Africa such that "emulating Western business practices did not become a pressing need until the eighteenth century."[471]

Nonetheless, economic arrangements governed by Islamic norms continue to this day. For example, regimes committed to Islamization, or Islamic economics, continue to ban interest because they believe devout Muslims must resist Mammon—the evils flowing from immoral economic gain.[472] However, Islamic economics as an organized movement did not have ancient roots nor did it arise to advance an economic agenda. Rather, it only emerged near the end of India's colonial period to defend the religious identity of India's Muslim minority, partly by updating Islamic norms that prevailed during Islam's Golden Age.[473] More than sixty countries have Islamic banks that do not offer or charge interest and some, among them Pakistan and Iran, outlaw interest, requiring even foreign subsidiaries to adopt Islamic methods of deposit taking and lending.[474]

Yet, it is widely accepted that banning interest has economic consequences. Although equity-based and interest-free financial instruments may serve a useful economic purpose,[475] it does not follow that from an economic standpoint, interest should be banned. The ban is now unnecessary because of vastly different conditions that exist in today's economy. For example, instead of enslavement for nonpayment of debt, we have bankruptcy laws. The ban is not only anachronistic but may also be economically detrimental. Given the fact that interest plays a central role in the modern economy, shunning interest is likely to mean nonparticipation in the global economic system[476] and prohibitions

---

[470] *Id.* at 294, 296.

[471] Kuran, *supra* note 406, at 34.

[472] Timur Kuran, Islam and Mammon: The Economic Predicaments of Islamism ix (2004). This ban was imposed fourteen centuries ago on an agrarian and nomadic economy, perhaps due to Islam's prohibition of an ancient Arabian practice whereby defaulting debtors were penalized by having their debt doubled and redoubled, resulting in the enslavement of many poor people. Kuran, *supra* note 75, at 133.

[473] Timur Kuran, *The Genesis of Islamic Economics: A Chapter in the Politics of Muslim Identity*, 64 Soc. Res. (Summer 1997), at 1–2, 10–12, available at http://www.mtholyoke.edu/acad/intrel/kuran.htm.

[474] *Id.* at 1.

[475] Kuran, *supra* note 75, at 123. Proponents of Islamic banking argue that by forcing financiers to invest directly in a venture, rather than merely charge interest for the capital loaned, the system encourages more prudent lending and prevents "future Enrons and Argentina," presumably because everyone would have to spend within his or her means. Jerry Useem, *Banking on Allah: Devout Muslims Don't Pay or Receive Interest. So How Can Their Financial System Work?*, Fortune, June 10, 2002, *available at* http://archive.fortune.com/magazines/fortune/fortune_archive/2002/06/10/324525/index.htm (the downside of profit-and-loss sharing is that it tends to attract high-risk ventures from entrepreneurs). *Id.*

[476] Kuran, *supra* note 472, at ix.

on economic arrangements such as mortgages, credit cards, currency hedging, or futures contracts.[477] The ban prohibits people from making choices about the degree of risks they are willing to take, forcing people to engage in "time-consuming stratagems to disguise interest charges . . . , [raising] the costs of negotiating and monitoring financial agreements."[478] Despite the inefficiencies involved, clerics have generally endorsed the ban, partly because "the elevation of religious values would enhance their own authority. Weak governments . . . have had their own reasons to support Islamist efforts to define, articulate, and, where necessary, invent an Islamic way of life" to stay in power.[479] When viewed within an overall context of economic development in the Middle East, Kuran has argued that this and other practices have contributed to the "commercial crisis" in the Middle East, as "the West developed commercial institutions more efficient than those of Islam."[480]

According to Kuran, when evaluating a custom that is harmful to economic productivity, there generally exists "no simple way to modify or eradicate it."[481] Although this issue is part of the overall question of how and whether to engage in culture change, addressed in Chapter 6, I will briefly touch upon it here. For Kuran, in order to assess the value of a custom, one needs to determine, among other factors, the extent to which the population would like to preserve the custom at issue. This point is reminiscent of Sen's emphasis on open discussion and "participatory resolution"[482] when there is conflict between tradition and modernity. Kuran noted: "If it turns out that most people cherish the custom

---

[477] Useem, *supra* note 475. Other financial arrangements such as derivatives and stock options may also be prohibited. Currency hedging would not be allowed because of *gharar*, a principle that prohibits one from profiting off another's uncertainty. Nor would futures contracts be allowed. Of course given the problems associated with these forms of trading in the United States, such prohibition may be a good idea. There is disagreement about whether Islam allows the issuance of bonds. Stocks are allowed. *Id.*

[478] Kuran, *supra* note 75, at 124; Virginia Postrel, *Islamic Economic Principles May Sound Like Just What the Middle East Needs*, N.Y. TIMES, Aug. 12, 2004, at C2. Through the *murabaha*, parties may get around the interest ban. For example, a bank may buy a computer for a client who agrees to buy it back with a markup as a form of interest. For a discussion of economic arrangements that can be put together to comply with the interest ban, *see Islamic Banking Comes of Age: But What Next?* (Mar. 10, 2004), *available at* http://knowledge.wharton.upenn.edu/article.cfm?articleid=944.

[479] Timur Kuran, *The Religious Undercurrents of Muslim Economic Grievances*, *available at* http://www.ssrc.org/sept11/essays/kuran.htm (last visited Mar. 31, 2015).

[480] Kuran, *supra* note 406, at 39; *see also* Timur Kuran, *Why the Middle East Is Economically Underdeveloped: Historical Mechanisms of Institutional Stagnation* 26 (Department of Economics, University of Southern California, Nov. 30, 2003) (describing Islamist opposition to interest and insurance); Jack A. Goldstone, *Islam, Development, and the Middle East: A Comment on Timur Kuran's Analysis* (Mercatus Center, George Mason University, June 24, 2003) (generally agreeing with Kuran but arguing that his thesis is incomplete). For a positive assessment of Islamic banking especially its compatibility with microfinance, *see* Rahul Dhumale & Amela Sapcanin, *An Application of Islamic Banking Principles to Microfinance* 1 (Regional Bureau for Arab States, UN Development Programme, in Cooperation with the Middle East and North Africa Region, World Bank, Dec., 1999).

[481] Kuran, *supra* note 75, at 120.

[482] SEN, *supra* note 1, at 32.

and consider it integral to the local culture, we will have discovered that the material gains from destroying the productivity-reducing custom would be accompanied, at least initially, by a loss in cultural satisfaction."[483] On the other hand, Kuran argued that despite surface enthusiasm, "genuine support" for the economically dysfunctional custom may prove to be "narrowly based," wherein urgency to protect the custom lies with a "politically well-placed minority," and in fact lacks support from the underrepresented majority.[484]

Note that Kuran's observations were limited to evaluating the custom's harmful effect to economic productivity, as opposed to practices which reduce human freedom and capability. In the latter case, a different set of calculus may be presented and the question of whether there was genuine support for a cultural practice that constitutes a first-order human rights violation would be presumably much less appropriate. As I have posited throughout, cultural norms and practices that consign women to lives of limited freedom and capability cannot be accepted by reference to majority preference or even private preference of the women themselves.[485]

With respect to culture and economics, Kuran has also framed the issue as one between true versus false preference. Distinguishing one from the other is not easy, as the task of ascertaining public opinion on a cultural matter presents several obstacles.[486] For example, in nondemocratic countries where many people are not accustomed to honest public expression, assessing genuine public support for a customary practice may prove futile.[487] Kuran suggested that one may have to resort to the *market test* when evaluating support for practices such as the Islamic ban on charging interest. Kuran reasoned that the market test, "which relies on personal choices exercised through essentially competitive markets," gives individuals some anonymity and thus allows them to pursue their "individualistic objectives rather than communal goals."[488]

Although the Islamic ban on charging interest is justified on the grounds that it violates a sacred Islamic command and aims to preserve the "Islamic way of life,"[489] Kuran observed that in countries with both Islamic banks, which prohibit interest, and conventional banks, only a minority of the Muslim population maintains accounts at Islamic banks.[490] Furthermore, in some majority-Muslim countries that promote both Islamic and commonplace banks, Islamic banks represent only 1 percent of the market share.[491] Kuran concluded that "the market test thus indicates that the drive to prohibit interest

---

[483] Kuran, *supra* note 75, at 120.
[484] *Id.* at 121.
[485] *See* Introduction, text accompanying notes 256–62.
[486] Kuran, *supra* note 75, at 121.
[487] *Id.*
[488] *Id.* at 121–23.
[489] *Id.* at 123.
[490] *Id.*
[491] *Id.*

and Islamicize all banks lacks mass support."[492] It thus follows that a movement to eliminate this "traditional" practice would not result in a genuine "loss in cultural satisfaction." Thus attempts to reform this practice should not be met with conservative criticism and blanket resistance to modifying customs.

3. OTHER EXAMPLES

Sections 1 and 2 of this Part C zoomed in on two case studies that illustrated a negative relationship between certain cultural norms and development. This section zooms out to cast a wide net, surveying a range of culturally sanctioned practices that are detrimental to development. Such practices include, for example, ethnic or caste segregation and schooling restrictions for girls. Again, to the extent that any practice supported by culture constricts the capacity and freedom of any individual, that practice should be subject to change by changing the cultural norms that sanctify it.

Admittedly, these practices may enjoy widespread public support, including support from members of the negatively affected group,[493] even though they are antithetical to the objectives of development as discussed by Sen, Nussbaum, and Appdurai. Many of these practices have both human rights and economic implications. India's caste system is viewed as a human rights issue[494] but increasingly, also as a hurdle to the country's socioeconomic development.[495] By perpetuating the notion of deserved and inherited inequality, the system extinguishes the aspirational capacity of the lower caste members,[496] limits their occupational choice, closing off possibilities for upward mobility, and "hinders efforts to escape from poverty. . . . It thus causes economic harm through mechanisms that shape Indian beliefs, preferences, and behaviors."[497] Hoff and Pandey have shown that social identity in a discriminatory regime can influence behavior negatively so as to hinder a group's economic ability even after the end of the regime.[498] Their work demonstrated the negative effect of stereotype threat, whereby the expectations

---

492 *Id.*

493 *Id.* at 130. False consciousness is the term for acceptance of a negative stereotype about one's group. Jennifer Crocker et al., *Social Stigma*, *in* THE HANDBOOK OF SOCIAL PSYCHOLOGY 504, 510 (Daniel T. Gilbert et al. eds., 1998). In such instances, the group may view their negative position as fair.

494 The Draft UN Principles and Guidelines to Eliminate Caste Discrimination were presented in 2009 with the support of the Office of the High Commissioner for Human Rights. Rikke Nohrlind, *Caste Discrimination Against India's "Untouchables" is an International Issue*, TELEGRAPH (Apr. 16, 2010), http://www.telegraph.co.uk/news/worldnews/asia/india/7597109/Caste-discrimination-against-Indias-untouchables-is-an-international-issue.html (India has lobbied heavily against such action, insisting that caste discrimination is not a matter of international human rights law but, rather, an internal matter.).

495 B. S. Sule, *Illiteracy in India*, CHI. TRIB., Aug. 17, 1996, at 21, *available at* http://articles.chicagotribune.com/1996-08-17/news/9608170055_1_india-economic-reforms-caste-system.

496 Kuran, *supra* note 75, at 118.

497 *Id.*

498 Karla Hoff & Priyanka Pandey, *Economic Consequences of Social Identity: Discrimination, Social Identity and Durable Inequalities*, 96 AM. ECON. REV. 206 (2006).

associated with a certain stereotype affect individual performance when the stereotype is invoked.[499] Additionally, an important study by the noted economists George Akerlof and Rachel Kranton showed how an individual's understanding of his or her own self, which is in turn tied to his or her socially constructed being—a "Hindu," an "untouchable"—determined access to education, trading group, and social network and was critically connected to his or her economic performance and success.[500]

Both studies illustrate a situational threat—one relevant in the context of the particular stereotype regarding identity.[501] With identity assigned by the caste system, people have no choice in membership. Therefore, the threat stemming from a lower caste identity is always present—perhaps even after leaving the country.[502] The pervasive nature of the caste system continues "to limit economic efficiency by distorting educational and occupational choices"[503] and devaluing caste members' potential abilities within a market society. Stereotypes can be utilized to perpetuate the caste ideology, helping to explain intergroup differences.[504] While some point to sporadic signs of easing, economic growth has not weakened the rigidity of the caste system.[505] It has remained remarkably durable partly due to geographic and religious reasons. Geographically, the majority of India's population lives in rural villages, whereas most of the recent growth has taken place in urban areas.[506] Social customs remain strong in these rural areas including the contested Hindu religious belief that the lower castes are simply where they are because of past

---

[499] *Id.* Hoff and Pandey administered tests to young boys in India belonging to either high or low castes. When the caste of the participants was publicly revealed, the performance of the lower caste boys dropped noticeably relative to their performance when caste was not revealed.

[500] Kuran, *supra* note 75, at 119; George Akerlof & Rachel Kranton, *Economics and Identity*, 115 Q. J. ECON. 715, 725 (2000).

[501] Crocker et al., *supra* note 493 at 519.

[502] *Caste Prejudice "May Exist" in British Workplaces*, BBC NEWS, Mar. 3, 2010, http://news.bbc.co.uk/2/hi/uk_news/politics/8546661.stm (citing concerns by the British government that people from lower castes may receive unfair treatment in the workplace in the United Kingdom).

[503] Kuran, *supra* note 75, at 134; Sukhadeo Thorat & Paul Attewell, *The Legacy of Social Exclusion: A Correspondence Study of Job Discrimination in India*, ECON. & POL. WKLY., Oct. 13, 2007, *available at* http://web.iitd.ac.in/~sbpaul/HUL736/Caste/thorat%20and%20attewell,%20epw.pdf. Research by Thorat and Attewell showed that job applicants with high caste names were statistically more likely to succeed in private sector job applications than equally qualified applicants with lower caste or with Muslim names.

[504] Crocker et al., *supra* note 493, at 509.

[505] Somini Sengupta, *Even Untouchables Get a Taste of the New India: Economic Growth Shatters Caste Order*, INT'L HERALD TRIB., Sept. 1, 2008, at 2. Experts debate whether any signs of progress can be tied to economic growth as the growth period coincided with the rise of politicians from the ranks of the untouchables. In addition, India's economic boom stems from a knowledge-based economy requiring job seekers to be well educated—an achievement long reserved for the higher castes.

[506] Amitabh Kant, *India Must Modernise Its Cities or See Them Implode Due to Rising Population Pressure*, TIMES OF INDIA (Sept. 27, 2012), http://articles.timesofindia.indiatimes.com/2012-09-27/edit-page/34103311_1_urbanisation-people-per-sq-km-cities.

sins.[507] To change entrenched social categories would potentially devalue the identity of other members, thus leading to vociferous resistance to any such change.[508]

Similarly, schooling restrictions for girls, often founded on cultural preferences favoring boys, have significant implication for development.[509] From an economic standpoint, studies have shown, for example, that "when a society denies girls an education it loses economic competitiveness, if only by condemning all children, including boys, to be raised by ignorant mothers in households deficient in intellectual stimulation."[510] A World Bank study reported that as the Middle East and North Africa are embarking on an export-oriented, market-based development that would necessarily rely less on natural resources and more on human resources, women's participation would be crucial to economic development there, as it was in East Asia, particularly in the textiles and electronics industries. Yet, women are currently "an untapped reservoir of human potential for countries in the region."[511] Although girls' school enrollment rates and literacy rates in the Middle East and North Africa have increased, the completion rates for girls remain significantly low due in large part to "social norms requiring women to prefer domestic duties over schooling."[512]

Other studies show that gender inequality in education has a direct, negative impact on economic growth by lowering the quality of human capital; interestingly, the data also suggest that this difference of women in the work force accounts for differences in growth rates among East Asian and sub-Saharan Africa, South Asia and the Middle East.[513] Although the World Bank study acknowledged that "gender and family values are likely to be treated as the ultimate test of cultural authenticity"[514] and hence must presumably be protected on cultural grounds, it stressed that "gender is ultimately also an economic issue."[515] As such, addressing the "gender agenda" is not only a cultural, social,

---

507 Lan Cao, *Culture Change*, 47 VA. J. INT'L L. 357, 387 (2007). For the view that the caste system is not rooted in Hinduism but is, in fact, contrary to the religion, *see* M. V. Nadkarni, *Is Caste System Intrinsic to Hinduism? Demolishing a Myth*, 38 ECON. & POL. WKLY. 4783 (2003). Social dominance theory posits that ideologies such as that of the caste system exist to control social conflict by legitimating inequalities between groups. Crocker et al., *supra* note 493, at 509.

508 Akerlof & Kranton, *supra* note 500, at 725.

509 Sen, *supra* note 47, at 52 ("India today may be immensely more advanced technologically and even economically . . . and yet India is paying a very heavy price for ignoring the cultural lessons on the critical role of basic education.").

510 Kuran, *supra* note 75, at 132.

511 THE WORLD BANK MENA DEVELOPMENT REPORT, GENDER AND DEVELOPMENT IN THE MIDDLE EAST AND NORTH AFRICA: WOMEN IN THE PUBLIC SPHERE xiii (2004) [hereinafter WORLD BANK, MENA DEVELOPMENT REPORT].

512 *Id.* at 34.

513 Stephan Klasen, *Does Gender Inequality Reduce Growth and Development? Evidence from Cross-County Regressions* 17–20 (World Bank Policy Research Report on Gender and Development, Working Paper No. 7, 1999).

514 WORLD BANK, MENA DEVELOPMENT REPORT, *supra* note 511, at xiv; *see also id.* at 20 (discussing how gender-related reforms "became an important symbol of resistance to modernization—and westernization. . . .").

515 *Id.* at xiv.

or anthropological issue,[516] but also an economic development issue[517] with significant implications for economic growth, productive employment, and poverty reduction.[518] Therefore, it is in the self-interest of poor countries to improve the education of girls if they wish to move up the global economic ladder.

It is also increasingly clear that "[g]ender equality is not only a goal in its own right, but an essential ingredient for achieving all other Millennium Development Goals"—to eradicate extreme poverty and hunger, reduce child mortality, combat AIDS, malaria, and other diseases, and so forth, as declared by the United Nations in 2002.[519] Then Secretary of State Hillary Rodham Clinton observed as follows: "[W]e are focusing more of our investment on women and girls, who are critical to advancing social, economic, and political progress. Women and girls are one of the world's greatest untapped resources. Investing in the potential of women to lift and lead their societies is one of the best investments we can make." If women receive just a year of education, their "children are less likely to die in infancy or suffer from illness or hunger, and more likely to go to school themselves."[520] A comprehensive study on India demonstrates "that girl and mother's education i.e. female education, is the single most important determinant of any improvement (change) in living standards in health and education."[521] For example, there is a consistent and strong correlation between higher levels of educational achievement among adult females and lower infant mortality rates.[522] By contrast, there is no such positive correlation between increased state expenditures and improvements in living standard—in fact, it is the opposite, that state spending has "a statistically significant and negative effect on improvement in living standards."[523] The results of this study have been replicated in empirical studies from different countries and confirm that education

---

[516] *Id.* at 1.

[517] *Id.* at xiv; *see also id.* at 1–4 (discussing the costs of low participation of women in the economy and the benefits of enhanced participation).

[518] *Id.* at 14; *see also id.* at 18 (discussing how discrimination against women impedes economic efficiency). *See also* World Bank Gender and Development Group, Gender Equality & the Millennium Development Goals, 6 (2003) [hereinafter World Bank Gender and Development Group] ("Investment in human capital, especially girls' and women's education and health, raises productivity.").

[519] World Bank Gender and Development Group, *supra* note 518, at 21.

[520] Hillary Rodham Clinton, *Remarks to the Center for Global Development*, Washington, D.C., Jan. 6, 2010, *available at* http://www.state.gov/secretary/20092013clinton/rm/2010/01/134838.htm. The United States is designing development programs that focus on employing women for agricultural and health education as well as collecting data to measure how the work is improving women's health, income, and access to education and food. Local women are then trained to carry on the development work. *Id.*

[521] Surjit S. Bhalla et al., *Girls' Education Is It—Nothing Else Matters (Much)* 2 (World Development Report 2003/04); *id.* at 40; *see also* Monica Das Gupta et al., *State Policies and Women's Agency in China, the Republic of Korea, and India, 1950–2000: Lessons from Contrasting Experiences, in* Culture and Public Action 234, 251 (citing Census of India 2001 and noting that as of 2001, only 54 percent of girls and women in India were literate).

[522] Bhalla, et al., *supra* note 521, at 40.

[523] *Id.* at 57.

for girls produces positive rippling effects, such as "improved birth spacing, lower infant and child mortality and morbidity, and enhanced educational attainment of children."[524]

The World Bank study noted that most of the efforts on schooling girls have focused on overcoming external constraints, such as lack of schools, teachers, and textbooks, and thus "on *supplying* education for girls."[525] As I argue in this book, more needs to be done to address internal or cultural constraints, or as the World Bank puts it, on increasing "girls' *demand* for education."[526] This will necessarily involve efforts at culture change, that is, to change the widespread perception especially among rural and poor urban families that boys have a right to education that girls do not have because girls should prepare themselves for marriage, not jobs.[527] The decision to educate boys and not girls is a cultural decision, not an economic one, although it has severe economic consequences. As the authors of a study that covered one hundred countries concluded, underinvestment in girls and their education "is not efficient for growth but reflects cultural preferences."[528] Undertaking to change such preferences in order to promote girls' education "may raise a country's income but reduce the welfare of those who have a preference for gender inequality."[529]

The link between culture and economics can be seen in the credit market as well. It has long been well established that capital accumulation is a critical issue in economic development. In his classic and highly influential work *Economic Development with Unlimited Supplies of Labour*, Sir Arthur Lewis discussed the causes of and solution to underdevelopment.[530] At the heart of Lewis's theory is his observation that subsistence economies with unlimited supplies of labor are characteristically low-productivity, low-income economies. Low wages caused by unlimited labor present the most significant obstacle to economic development because, according to Lewis, they impede the very process which stimulates economic growth-capital accumulation; low wages mean no savings and no capital accumulation.[531] The solution, according to Lewis, lies in the ability of

---

[524] WORLD BANK, MENA DEVELOPMENT REPORT, *supra* note 511, at 28; SEN, *supra* note 1, at 129 ("[A] general expansion of education and literacy in a region can facilitate social change (even the reduction of fertility and mortality . . .) and also help to enhance economic progress from which others too benefit.").

[525] WORLD BANK, MENA DEVELOPMENT REPORT, *supra* note 511, at 38.

[526] *Id.*

[527] *Id.* at 39.

[528] David Dollar & Roberta Gatti, *Gender Inequality, Income, and Growth: Are Goods Times Good for Women?* 2 (World Bank Policy Research Report on Gender and Development, Working Paper No. 1, 1999).

[529] *Id.* "[S]ome societies have a preference for inequality and are willing to pay for it," or rather, more accurately, "those who control resources in the society have a preference for gender inequality that they are willing to pay for."). *Id* at 3.

[530] W. Arthur Lewis, *Economic Development with Unlimited Supplies of Labour*, *in* PARADIGMS IN ECONOMIC DEVELOPMENT: CLASSIC PERSPECTIVES, CRITIQUES, AND REFLECTIONS 59 (Rajani Kanth ed., 1994).

[531] As Lewis states: "The central problem in the theory of economic development is to understand the process by which a community which was previously saving and investing 4 or 5 per cent. of its national income or less, converts itself into an economy where voluntary saving is running at about 12 to 15 per cent. of national income or more." *Id.* at 72.

such economies to accumulate capital and invest it productively.[532] Research has shown that credit is crucial to economic development and that the credit market is as important as the equity market.[533]

Yet, capital and credit are often deliberately denied to women. In a region in India, microlending, which has emerged to lend to the poor, has been systematically denied to Muslims. However, this denial is not motivated by extreme Hindu nationalism. It is, rather, organized by Muslim *anjumans* (community organizations) in order to deny credit to Muslim women in Karnataka. The *anjumans* are centers of patriarchal power authority and the borrowers are mostly poor women. Although a microbank in the area has had virtually 100 percent repayment rate from its Muslim borrowers, in recent years, repayment has been almost zero because of "non-payment directives by anjumans. . . ."[534] Despite the *anjumans'* claims that loans do not have to be repaid because the interest on them is un-Islamic, they have not targeted loans made to Muslim businessmen. "In contravention of basic freedoms under the law and Constitution, the anjumans claim the right to control the behaviour of any Muslim woman, and the authority to punish all Muslim female borrowers ignoring their illegal directives."[535]

Commitment and deference to authoritarian pattern, status, and personal relationships are likely to conflict with the values of equality and opportunity, whether it be in terms of participation or economic opportunities. Since the currency crisis in Asia in 1997, for example, there has been a similar effort to change "the traditionally particularistic personal relationships that have dominated the East Asian economies. . . ."[536] because of the possibility that such relationships can impede individual initiatives[537] or even foster corruption.[538] Other cultural traits, the tradition of taking a "long view," for example,

---

[532] *Id.* at 95–97.

[533] Kenneth Dam, *Credit Markets, Creditors' Rights and Economic Development* (Brookings Institute, John M. Olin Law & Economics Working Paper No. 281, Feb. 1, 2006) (arguing that the credit market is just as important as the equity market); Rajeev Dehejia & Roberta Gatti, *Credit Access Cuts Child Labor in Developing Countries* (National Bureau of Economic Research Working Paper No. 9018, June 2002) (showing that in the absence of developed financial markets, households appear to resort substantially to child labor to compensate for income variability. Access to credit could be highly effective in reducing child labor).

[534] S. A. Aiyar, *Anjumans Deprive Muslim Women of Microcredit*, TIMES OF INDIA (Nov. 8, 2009), *available at* http://blogs.timesofindia.indiatimes.com/Swaminomics/entry/anjumans-deprive-muslim-women-of/.

[535] *Id.*

[536] Harrison, *supra* note 48, at xxiii.

[537] Subsequent scholars have echoed Weber's warnings of the fetters of kinship. *See,* e.g., PETER T. BAUER & BASIL S. YARNEY, THE ECONOMICS OF UNDER-DEVELOPED COUNTRIES 64 (1957) ("The extended family . . . is an example of an institution which has many advantages in one stage of economic achievement, but which may later become a drag on economic development."); ARTHUR LEWIS, THE THEORY OF ECONOMIC GROWTH 114 (1955) ("The extended family system has tremendous advantages in societies living at a subsistence level, but it seems not to be appropriate to societies where economic growth is occurring. In such societies it is almost certainly a drag on effort.").

[538] LEWIS, *supra* note 537, at 114 (noting that strong group ties may facilitate bureaucratic corruption and nepotism because bureaucrats may be bound first by obligations to traditional networks rather than to outsiders with superior credentials).

has meant that many East Asian businesses neglected periodically to monitor the profitability of enterprises. "The supposed virtue of such long-term perspectives was reinforced by the cultural propensity to see great virtue in delayed gratification and the willingness to suffer in the short run in the expectation that in time there would be greater rewards for steadfastness."[539] Such values and behaviors were useful at the initial stages of development but were conducive to problems at the later stages.

There are efforts currently underway in many countries around the world to transform traditional cultural norms and practices that are deemed to be detrimental to development objectives. How this transformation can and should be undertaken will be taken up in Chapters 5 and 6.

This chapter has demonstrated that regardless of the pervasive acultural orientation of international law, and despite law and development's close relationship to international law, law and development must reject international law's acultural framework. Culture is too interwoven with the issues central to law and development for it to be sidestepped or ignored. In Chapter 4 I look at how developments and dynamics within international law and international relations can provide support—from a disciplinary standpoint—for a culture change project in law and development. Chapter 4's discussion of customary international law and norm change cycles in international relations shows that international norm change is an established fact within these two related fields. Chapter 4 thus lays the foundation for Chapter 5's discussion of changing cultural norms.

Chapter 4 is important to the arguments and proposals set forth in the book for the following reasons. First, it shows that international law norms, as reflected in the rules of customary international law, are not fixed but rather evolving, similar to cultural norms that are also not fixed and also evolving. In this way, customary international law norms and the process of change embedded in international law provide a parallel pathway for understanding culture change. Similarly, a strand of international relations, constructivism, provides an account of norm change and norm creation in ways that are again, similar to the process of culture change studied in Chaptert Five. An argument can be made that law and development can credibly look to international law and international relations for support for its admittedly controversial culture change proposal. Thus, despite the apparent statism of international law and international relations, there is room for custom, norms, and values to play a part in the understanding of the discipline. Using the language of international law, which is a familiar language to law and development, I show that law and development too can be comfortable with engaging culture and facilitating culture change.

Second, Chapter 4 also demonstrates that the state-entrenched focus of the field has been loosened in recent years by developments within international law and international relations. Both disciplines have been nudged by tensions within to take into account of

---

[539] Lucian W. Pye, *"Asian Values" From Dynamos to Dominoes?*, *in* CULTURE MATTERS: HOW VALUES SHAPE HUMAN PROGRESS 244, 253 (Lawrence E. Harrison & Samuel P. Huntington, eds. 2000).

and accommodate other actors, particularly non-state. As a result, relevant players now include non-state actors, nongovernmental organizations, and other civil society groups that may be part of a transnational network of domestic and international activists acting as norm entrepreneurs to alter or modify international norms. As Friedrich Kratochwil remarked, "Actors are not only programmed by rules and norms, but they reproduce and change by their practice the normative structures by which they are able to act, share meanings, communicate intentions, criticize claims, and justify choices."[540] Traditionally, such actors could only be state actors, but this state-dominant paradigm has been expanded. This expansion opens up the debate to arguments of the kind proposed in this book, that non-state actors be engaged, that values and norms be embraced, and that norm change or culture change be considered. These developments show that to the extent that law and development has been influenced by international law, it should not be skittish about embracing culture nor embracing cultural change at the subnational level.

Finally, as Chapter 4 will make clear, the formulation and evolution of international customary law provide lessons about how custom might change at the subnational level. It is not my claim that adopting a theory that explains this development in international law will by itself replicate this development in the field of law and development. Rather, it is worth noting that the process of culture change is similar, whether in international law or in law and development. There is preexisting custom. There is dissent. State and non-state actors can trigger this dissent and in the process activate custom change at both the international and domestic levels, especially because the boundaries delineating one from the other are not always impermeable. Moreover, that this phenomenon has occurred at the international level is highly salient for law and development. For example, that the International Committee of the Red Cross was able to change the norms of how non-combatants should be treated by states is salient to our objective of culture change in law and development. That an array of NGOs were able to persuade states to limit their own sovereignty in order to create the International Criminal Court by marshaling norms against international atrocities and criminal violations of international law and converting them into international policy consensus is highly significant. This is not a case where powerful states manage to change existing state norms. Rather, it is a case involving non-state actors who succeeded in becoming relevant players. It is also a case where "norms are transformed from radical ideas into conventional wisdom."[541] If such norm change can be accomplished in international law and bind states in the hard-core universe of state interest and power, norm change can certainly be accomplished in law and development.

---

[540] Friedrich Kratochwil, Rules, Norms and Decisions: On the Conditions of Practical and Legal Reasoning in International Relations and Domestic Affairs 61 (1989).

[541] Michael J. Struett, The Politics of Constructing the International Criminal Court: NGOs, Discourse and Agency 27 (2008).

4

International Law Norms

THIS CHAPTER STUDIES the evolution of international law and international relations and argues that relatively new developments in these state-centric disciplines support a more culturally oriented approach to law and development. Thus, although international law has resisted embracing culture, these developments should make the incorporation of a cultural lens more palatable to the discipline. This is essentially an argument about the nature of the relevant disciplines—as international law and international relations as state dominated, acultural disciplines have changed, so too should law and development.

I make two primary points in this chapter. First, because international law has wrestled with the long and complex process of evolving custom at the international level, it should not be reluctant to embrace culture change at the domestic or subnational level. Likewise, law and development should be cognizant of these changes in international law and be willing to use these openings to grapple with culture and pursue a robust culture change agenda in its development work.

To support this first point, I show that international law is replete with instances in which once entrenched norms have changed and been replaced by new norms. Studying customary international law, constructivist theory, and other norm cycle theories reveals that the creation of international norm and customary international law has been a vehemently contested and ongoing process. It also provides a framework for understanding how international norms are transformed. That custom in international law is contested and evolves as a result of such contestation is especially relevant for the culture change project of this book.

Second, in recent years, even as custom and norms continue to change and be changed, international law and international relations have also changed, becoming a much more pluralistic, value-laden discipline. I examine the ways heterodox international law and international relations scholars, for example from the New Haven School of international law and the constructivist school of international relations, have expanded the international framework. Both the New Haven School and constructivism have, in different ways, pushed against the entrenched conventions of public international law, inserting values and norms into what has traditionally been a discipline almost exclusively devoted to state power and interest. The New Haven School has opened international law up to non-state interests, inviting non-state actors onto the international stage and thus contributing to the development of a more pluralist construction of international law. Similarly, constructivist study of how non-state norm-generating communities produce norms and create norm change is particularly important for this book project because it creates a platform for the study of culture change by non-state and state actors.

These two observations—the inherently contested nature of custom and norms coupled with pluralistic developments in the international sphere—provide relevant lessons about how culture can be changed. Indeed, in international law, norms have always been contested, subject to the push and pull of different states. In a similar way, as I discuss in Chapter 5 and Chapter 6, culture too has always been contested, subject to the push and pull of different individuals and groups in a society. A difference that is worth highlighting, however, is that in the latter case, culture has often been misleadingly viewed as static and monolithic (Hindu culture and Confucian culture, for example), and the internal fluidity within a culture's many layers has been masked. Once culture is viewed as dynamic and changeable, more like customary international law, its hybridity and heterogeneity will be more conspicuous. Different actors striving to shape and change it will be viewed as a normal part of the social fabric, as commonplace as state actors and non-state actors vying for influence in the formation and evolution of international custom.

Some critics may balk at the notion that norm change in the international sphere provides relevant lessons for culture change in the domestic sphere. But the overlap between the national and international is more pronounced in recent years because of the pluralistic tilt in previously state-centric international law and international relations. The route some nongovernmental organizations (NGOs) choose to forge international policy consensus among sovereign nations, to influence the development of international custom on armed conflicts or international criminal matters, or the route some NGOs choose to change the cultural practice of footbinding have similarities that are worth noting.

This is so because the two spheres—national and international—are no longer clearly demarcated or distinctly differentiated. In fact, many "activist NGOs [are] simultaneously domestic and international actors."[1] In many instances, the norm change movement

[1] Margaret E. Keck & Kathryn Sikkink, *Transnational Advocacy Networks in International and Regional Politics*, 159 Int'l Soc. Sci. J. 89, 92 (1999) (emphasis omitted), *available at* http://isites.harvard.edu/fs/docs/icb.topic446176.files/Week_7/Keck_and_Sikkink_Transnational_Advocacy.pdf.

is situated within "transnational networks"[2] of non-state actors engaging with each other, with states, and with international organizations, which "multiply the voices that are heard in *international and domestic* policies."[3] The point is that network actors may operate in national, regional, and international spheres; their interests may have both international and domestic implications.[4] Indeed, two of the foremost scholars on transnational advocacy networks concluded as follows: "Although we had initially expected that transnational networks would function in quite different ways from domestic social movements, we found that many of the characteristic strategies, tactics and patterns of influence resembled those outlined in the literature on social movements."[5]

Such advocacy networks are "blurring the boundaries between a state's relations with its own nationals and the recourse both citizens and states have to the international system."[6] Many of these networks "participate simultaneously in domestic and international politics, drawing upon a variety of resources, *as if they were part of an international society*."[7] Network activists recognize that whether in the national or international sphere, there are certain "contested understandings as well as stable and shared ones. Network activists can operate strategically within the more stable universe of shared understandings at the same time as they try to reshape certain contested meanings."[8]

Undoubtedly different actors may have different motivations at different points in time, but the different motivations arise more from differences in the subject matter at issue (footbinding versus treatment of prisoners of war) than in the fact that one occurs in the international sphere and one in the domestic sphere (international versus domestic). As Keck and Sikkink emphasized, "[a]dvocacy networks are significant transnationally, regionally and domestically."[9] For example, in changing the cultural norm of footbinding, which was a practice that was wholly domestic, that is, it occurred wholly within China's domestic territory or within Chinese communities, there is nonetheless much interaction between domestic interests, China's governmental interests and international interests. How the norm change actor, which may be an NGO or a state actor, frame an issue is often the key. How this actor interacts with others, whether domestic or national, is another important factor in the determination of whether consensus can emerge to create a tipping point in favor of a new norm. Norms may percolate upward into the

---

[2] Margaret E. Keck & Kathryn Sikkink, Activists beyond Borders: Advocacy Networks in International Politics 2–4 (1998). "Networks are forms of organization characterized by voluntary, reciprocal and horizontal patterns of communication and exchange." Keck & Sikkink, *supra* note 1, at 91.

[3] Keck & Sikkink, *supra* note 2, at x (emphasis added).

[4] *Id.* at 1 ("Advocacy networks are significant transnationally and domestically. By building new links among actors in civil societies, states, and international organizations, they multiply the channels of access to the international system.").

[5] Keck & Sikkink, *supra* note 1, at 91.

[6] *Id.* at 89.

[7] *Id.* at 90.

[8] *Id.* at 91.

[9] *Id.* at 89.

international level or downward from the international level into the state and substate level. Again, the notion that norm change and norm change actors in the international sphere are wholly a separate and distinct phenomenon from that process in the national (or subnational) sphere is wholly inaccurate. The two spheres are not separate but interactive. "Network theory can thus provide an explanation for transnational change, a model that is not just one of 'diffusion' of liberal institutions and practices, but one through which the preferences and identities of actors engaged in transnational society are sometimes mutually transformed through their interactions with each other."[10]

Examples of norm change discussed in this chapter have certain common dynamics worth pointing out at the outset. Again, the pertinent issue is less whether the desired change is located in the international or the national setting. Norm change actors might be part of the many transnational advocacy networks that transcend the national versus international dichotomy. Transnational activism "within and between issue areas are similar to those . . . of domestic activism. Individuals and foundation funding have moved back and forth among them."[11] Their target might be governments, international organizations such as the World Bank, or private actors such as corporations.[12] Other norm change actors might be governments themselves, targeting cultural norms and practices that the governments work to change, such as footbinding and honor killing. Norm change actors rely on a common range of tactics that Keck and Sikkink categorize as follows: information politics—gathering and disseminating information in a sociocultural context that is effective and appropriate; symbolic politics—identifying issues that are symbolically powerful to catalyze action; leverage politics—identifying points of leverage, for example, persuading policy makers to link the desired change with "something else of value: money, trade or prestige";[13] and accountability politics—holding governments and other actors accountable to positions they have publicly committed to.[14]

The defense of culture change in this chapter is a defense that is rooted in the discipline of international law, using the new vocabulary and tools developed *within* international law and international relations. A different defense of culture change—from a normative standpoint—will be undertaken in Chapter 6.

Part A briefly explores how international relations and international law have moved beyond a strictly state-centric universe, expanding in a direction that is more open to the study of values and norms. Part B looks at how other disciplines have moved in a similar direction, that is, one that welcomes the examination of how law intersects with norms. Part C explores how and why norms have changed in international law, relying on insights from norm change theories and customary international law to understand the

[10] *Id.* at 100.
[11] *Id.* at 92.
[12] *Id.* at 97.
[13] *Id.*
[14] *Id.* at 95–98.

norm change process. Part D provides concrete examples to illustrate the norm change cycle that has occurred in international law.

A. Developments in International Relations and International Law

In international law and international relations, states have traditionally occupied a unique and central role. For example, only states can make law. States make treaties with other states. Only states can participate in the process of making customary international law. Thus, international law is highly state-centric. In the two primary sources of law in international law, treaties and custom, states are the only actors whose acts and practices have lawmaking capacity.

One may ask why states are the sole legal actors in international law. One answer lies in the state-centric framework that flows out of certain beliefs and assumptions about the nature of the international order. For years international law has been defined or heavily influenced by the realism bent that has dominated international relations theory in the United States and Britain. The subject of international relations was but a nascent field of academic study before World War I. The destruction caused by World War I spurred new thinking, especially in Britain and the United States, and produced a new sense of "liberal internationalism" deemed necessary to manage the international system. Liberal internationalism included a firm belief in democratic systems reflecting the sense that democracies do not wage wars because "people" do not want war. Constitutional government and the rule of law were deemed to be appropriate animating principles for both the domestic and international spheres.[15]

However, World War II, the rise of Nazism, and the popular support Hitler received, shattered liberal thinking. After 1945, realism became the dominant international relations model.[16] For international relations realists, international law is the product of state power and state sovereignty,[17] and states are moved by self-interest, not rule of law. One of the leading realist scholars, Hans Morgenthau, saw power as intrinsically embedded in politics and especially international politics: "Politics is a struggle for power over men, and whatever its ultimate aim may be, power is its immediate goal and the modes of acquiring, maintaining, and demonstrating it determine the technique of political action."[18] More accurately, Morgenthau attributed the aggressive, power-maximizing actions of states to human nature: "Political realism believes that politics, like society in general, is

---

[15] Chris Brown, Understanding International Relations 22–23 (2d ed. 2001).

[16] *Id.* at 29–31; *see also* Wayne Sandholtz, *Explaining International Norm Change*, *in* International Norms and Cycles of Change 1, 1–2 (Wayne Sandholtz & Kendall Stiles eds., 2009).

[17] Hans. J. Morgenthau, Politics Among Nations: The Struggle for Power and Peace 5 (5th ed. rev. 1978) (stating that the "main signpost that helps political realism to find its way through the landscape of international politics is the concept of interest defined in terms of power.").

[18] Hans. J. Morgenthau, Scientific Man vs. Power Politics 195 (1946).

governed by objective laws that have their roots in human nature."[19] International relations is, to put it bluntly, about states pursuing their interests to maximize their power. Even if non-state actors exert influence and pursue their own interests independently, the state remains the key actor because the state provides the regulatory vehicle through which other actors operate. As a result, the "realist bent of much post-War scholarship had no truck for a purported 'rule of law' in international relations,"[20] as "legalities can never constrain power."[21] States vie for power, authority, and influence through a variety of spheres, military, political, economic, and legal. In the latter case, states shape international law through participation in treaties, which only bind states if they consent, and customs, which constantly evolve and may be deemed binding on states even if they object.[22] If rules matter less than power, then norms can hardly matter, as it is the power of states that determine international outcomes.[23] "For realists, culture and identity are, at best, derivative of the distribution of capabilities and have no independent explanatory power. For rationalists, actors deploy culture and identity strategically, like any other resource, simply to further their own self-interests."[24]

The normative core of realism is state survival in a world characterized by power politics—rivalry, conflicts, and war. The international system is anarchic. People create states with governments infused with power and authority to protect them from domestic and foreign disorders—in essence to shield them from the Hobbesian state of nature.[25] "Anarchy has two principal consequences. First, there is little room for trust among states. . . . Second, each state must guarantee its own survival since no other actor will provide its security."[26] Because the normative core of realism is state survival and because realists believe that states first and foremost pursue their own national interests, it follows that other states cannot be relied upon completely and even international conventions are only provisional.

---

[19] MORGENTHAU, *supra* note 17, at 4.

[20] David J. Bederman, *Constructivism, Positivism, and Empiricism in International Law: Legal Rules and International Society*, 89 GEO. L.J. 469, 469 (2001).

[21] *Id.* at 473.

[22] Statute of the International Court of Justice art. 38(1), June 26, 1945, 59 Stat. 1055, 33 U.N.T.S. 993 (stating that the primary sources of international law are treaties and conventions, customary practices of states deemed as law, general principles of law common to most legal systems, casuistic decisions, and opinions of respected publicists, respectively).

[23] Sandholtz, *supra* note 16, at 2.

[24] Peter J. Katzenstein, *Introduction: Alternative Perspectives on National Security*, *in* THE CULTURE OF NATIONAL SECURITY: NORMS AND IDENTITY IN WORLD POLITICS 1, 17 (Peter J. Katzenstein ed., 1996).

[25] THOMAS HOBBES, LEVIATHAN 78 (Michael Oakeshott ed., Basil Blackwell Oxford 1955) (1652) (referring to the state of nature: "In such condition, there is no place for industry; because the fruit thereof is uncertain: and consequently no culture of the earth; no navigation, nor use of the commodities that may be imported by sea; no commodious building; . . . no arts; no letters; no society; and which is worst of all, continual fear, and danger of violent death; and the life of man, solitary, poor, nasty, brutish, and short.").

[26] John J. Mearsheimer, *Back to the Future: Instability in Europe After the Cold War*, *in* THE COLD WAR AND AFTER: PROSPECTS FOR PEACE 141, 148 (Sean M. Lynn-Jones & Steven E. Miller eds., 1993).

Other international relations theories that follow have adopted a similar statist orientation. Neorealism focuses on the structure of the international system and the relative distribution of power within it. As a result, actors, states or otherwise, are less important because the analytic focus is structural. Nonetheless, states still feature prominently because the structures studied are those that flow from the state-centric system. Kenneth Waltz, for example, viewed the international system as one that is determined by each state's sense of its own national interests: "[E]ach state plots the course it thinks will best serve its interests."[27] The international system, in other words, is essentially a decentralized structure of anarchy, a self-help system in which states must look after their own interests and respond to the competitive pressure exerted by others. At the time of his writing, Waltz saw the system as bipolar, as only the United States and the Soviet Union had the power to threaten the other's survival. Waltz's balance of power theory does not lead to the conclusion that there is always a balance. In fact, states may wish to create imbalances by eliminating the other poles of power. As other states do not want this to occur, they will respond to potential cues about possible imbalances and act accordingly.[28]

Furthermore, Waltz advocated in favor of a theory of the international system which aimed toward a systemic understanding of international relations, arguing against theories that give but a general accounting of different aspects of international relations (such as pluralism). According to Waltz, because there are patterns of the international systems that recur over time, these patterns are derived from the structure of the system itself, not from the subunits that make up the system because these subunits are mutable components of the system. The basic structure of the system remains an anarchic one and states act and react in ways that best maximize their security. States act within this state structure and are bound by the structure's deterministic constraints. "Structural constraints explain why the methods are repeatedly used despite differences in the persons and states who use them."[29]

Other neorealists operate out of the same structural framework but leave more room for statecraft and diplomacy. For example, although Thomas Schelling conceded that the structure of the international system confines states to act in certain ways, he believed that states are faced with an array of choices, even if they might be confined by circumstances. Schelling's works leave room for bargaining and strategic behavior even if within a constrained framework of situated choices.[30]

However, other traditions in international relations have arisen to challenge realism and have progressively pushed against the boundaries erected by state centrism. While realists and neorealists see international relations as the study of relations between sovereign states, liberals, for example, seek to expand that scope to include relations among

---

[27] Kenneth N. Waltz, Theory of International Politics 113 (1979).

[28] *Id.* at 118.

[29] *Id.* at 117.

[30] *See generally* Thomas C. Schelling, The Strategy of Conflict (1960).

people, NGOs, and groups across different countries. The liberalism strand of international relations, thus, works from an initial starting point defined by pluralism and transnationalism. As one of the prominent liberal theorists, James Rosenau, explained, transnationalism is "the processes whereby international relations conducted by governments have been supplemented by relations among private individuals, groups, and societies that can and do have important consequences for the course of events."[31] Liberals want to show that even in an anarchic international system, cooperative relations and transnational ties exist. A more integrated global society of common bonds promotes a sense of community that is crucial to the maintenance of peace. This has occurred in the North Atlantic region, for example, because certain conditions that promote the emergence of a sense of community came together: a general increase across the board in communication, mobility, economic ties, and interactions and transactions.[32]

Liberalism also views international institutions as playing a crucial role in promoting cooperation among states and in restraining the unbridled powers of powerful states. International institutions that have emerged and achieved international prominence do not seem to be merely tools of the powerful states that created them, further calling into question realist assumptions that states are the sole key actors in international relations.[33] Although the international system is indeed anarchic, institutions ameliorate the problem of international anarchy because they lower transaction costs associated with monitoring and coordination, increase the level of interstate cooperation, and enhance political transparency. Organizations such as NATO or the European Union establish "regimes" that set rules that govern state action in particular areas. In certain geographic regions, such as Europe or certain economic areas such as trade and investment, the scope and depth of institutionalization can be quite pronounced. Many studies demonstrate, for example, that the countries of the EU countries cooperate extensively, having established a regulatory framework for cooperation in agricultural and industrial policies. Institutional liberals have argued that institutions in Western Europe function as effective shock absorbers to lessen the shock caused by the end of the Cold War and promote the reunification of Germany. Institutions facilitate the flow of information between states, increasing communication and providing a forum for negotiation and compromise. Institutions also provide a fora in which governments can mutually monitor each other's compliance with and implementation of agreed

---

[31] James N. Rosenau, The Study of Global Interdependence: Essays on the Transnationalization of World Affairs 1 (1980).

[32] Karl W. Deutsch et al., Political Community and the North Atlantic Area: International Organization in the Light of Historical Experience 5 (1957).

[33] *See generally* Robert O. Keohane, International Institutions and State Power: Essays in International Relations Theory (1989); Marc. A. Levy et al., *The Study of International Regimes*, 1 Eur. J. Int'l Rel. 267, 267–330 (1995); Richard Falk, Predatory Globalization: A Critique 4 (1999) ("These institutional ingredients of global governance are needed to encourage cooperative approaches to conflict and complexity.").

upon commitments.[34] Instability that could have followed the demise of the bipolar world dominated by two superpowers, the United States and the Soviet Union, was cushioned by the high level of institutionalization existing in Europe. International relations, in other words, is not only about the relationship between monolithic states but also the study of regimes and institutions aimed at advancing a world of more cooperative arrangements.

In addition, for liberalism, international relations is moving broadly toward a more pluralistic, cobweb-like model of transnational relationship.[35] In his cobweb model, John Burton dissected the state and identified the various constituent groups within each state, showing how groups within one state, for example, labor, religious, business groups, and so forth, have various external ties with their corresponding constituent groups within another state. Under this view, the state is hardly a self-contained unit dealing with another state but rather a porous entity with a multiplicity of groups that cross-pollinate with their counterparts across the artificial boundaries of states.

Social movements around the world have formed alliances with each other to challenge the state-dominated international order, a phenomenon Richard Falk called "globalization from below."[36] States, international institutions and networks of nongovernmental groups organized around various social movements[37] have engaged and interacted with each other, pushing against and altering preexisting norms. The importance of non-state actors has grown to a large extent and some international law scholars have responded by pushing international law to recognize non-state actors as "international actors."[38] In this globalized new world order, "a statist future will be modified by market forces of various kinds and by the democratizing struggles of peoples and their associations and movements in many local, national, regional, and global settings."[39]

The liberal, pluralistic model starts with the notion that the anarchic, state-centric system has been supplemented by an array of competing nonsovereign collectivities that exist apart from the dominant state actors and that overlap with their counterparts in

---

[34] Robert O. Keohane & Joseph S. Nye, *Introduction: The End of the Cold War in Europe*, *in* AFTER THE COLD WAR: INTERNATIONAL INSTITUTIONS AND STATE STRATEGIES IN EUROPE, 1989–1991, at 1, 1–19 (Robert O. Keohane, Joseph S. Nye, & Stanley Hoffman eds., 1993).

[35] *See* JOHN W. BURTON, WORLD SOCIETY 35–44 (1972).

[36] RICHARD FALK, LAW IN AN EMERGING GLOBAL VILLAGE: A POST-WESTPHALIAN PERSPECTIVE 218 (1998).

[37] *See generally* Symposium, *Passing Through the Door: Social Movement Literature and Legal Scholarship*, 150 U. PA. L. REV. 1 (2001); JOEL F. HANDLER, SOCIAL MOVEMENTS AND THE LEGAL SYSTEM: A THEORY OF LAW REFORM AND SOCIAL CHANGE 14–16 (1978); Alan Hunt, *Rights and Social Movements: Counter-Hegemonic Strategies*, 17 J.L. & SOC'Y 309, 320–21 (1990); Julie Mertus, *From Legal Transplants to Transformative Justice: Human Rights and the Promise of Transnational Civil Society*, 14 AM. U. INT'L. L. REV. 1335, 1336–1338 (1999).

[38] *See, e.g.*, FALK, *supra* note 36, at 55–58; Steve Charnovitz, *Two Centuries of Participation: NGOs and International Governance*, 18 MICH. J. INT'L L. 183, 183–85 (1997); Louis B. Sohn, *The New International Law: Protection of the Rights of Individuals Rather than States*, 32 AM. U. L. REV. 1, 13–17 (1982).

[39] FALK, *supra* note 33, at 12.

other states. A significant implication flows from this model. This transnational cross-cutting of interests where individuals in one state are members of different groups should mean a lessening of conflict because these individuals tend to be less tied to "their states" and have significant connections with individuals in other states,[40] resulting in not just an increase in transnational relations among peoples of different states but also increased interdependence.

Equally significant is the fact that interdependence exists not only between non-state actors but also between states. The European Union is an example of economic interdependence and political integration—a process whereby "political actors . . . are persuaded to shift their loyalties . . . toward a new centre, whose institutions possess or demand jurisdiction over the pre-existing national states."[41] Robert Keohane and Joseph Nye called this a condition of "complex interdependence"[42] which greatly undermines the unitary state assumptions of realism. Even state-state relationships are disaggregated into different issue areas—security, trade, or finance—and each of these issues produces its own politics of complex interdependence. Under such conditions, international relations is no longer a study of states dealing with states or state leaders dealing with state leaders in the singular area of "high politics" such as security and survival. Instead, for scholars like Keohane and Nye, international relations has expanded to encompass first, relations at many different levels and branches of governments of one state with parallel counterparts in other states in areas once considered "low politics" such as economics and social affairs; and second, relations between individuals and groups outside the states.

Rosenau's observation that individuals and non-state entities have exerted influence and grown in importance also supports Keohane and Nye's claim that what were once merely the "low politics" of economics and social relations have also become important global matters. Rosenau noted, for example, that certain interdependence issues, such as environmental pollution, currency crises, AIDS, and the global drug trade have become part of the global agenda. The state, in other words, is no longer the sole salient entity in international relations.[43] There are multiple channels of access between societies. In this new setting, military force is less useful and salient, and international relations come to resemble domestic politics.

These transnational cross-dealings and cross-alliances between states, government branches and departments, individuals, and NGOs are important for my purposes because the overlapping occurrence of such activities in the national and international

---

[40] David Nicholls, Three Varieties of Pluralism 22 (1974); James N. Rosenau, *Citizenship in a Changing Global Order*, *in* Governance Without Government: Order and Change in World Politics 272, 282 (James N. Rosenau & Ernst-Otto Czempiel eds., 1992).

[41] Ernst B. Haas, The Uniting of Europe: Political, Social, and Economic Forces 1950–1957, at 16 (2004) (emphasis omitted).

[42] Robert O. Keohane & Joseph S. Nye, Power and Interdependence: World Politics in Transition 23 (1977).

[43] *Id.* at 24–26.

sphere means the distinctions we draw between "different realms" are no longer that distinct. On the one hand, we may have an NGO in country A working with its counterpart in country B (with or without the active support of the government of country B) to change an objectionable cultural norm in country B. On the other hand, we may have an NGO in country A working with its counterpart in country B to change the policy consensus of country B's government. These are similar players operating in slightly different circumstances. A set of actors may pressure states to enact a law and enforce that law by changing the cultural meaning of that law via culture change. These actors may push for states themselves to adopt emerging international custom in international criminal law or international human rights law. These same actors may also pressure states to take steps to translate those norms into their domestic territory, or these actors may work with their counterparts in civil society to ensure the acceptance of such norms into the local cultural fabric. This process involves a pattern of challenging, pushing, contesting existing meaning in order to create new meaning and bring into reality a desired practice. Strategies may be different because of the different norms that may be at issue. In essence, however, the nature of the norm change project in today's globalized, pluralistic world is sufficiently similar that the phenomenon of norm change in international law is worth studying in culture change projects in law and development.

This is because "[d]ifferent issues generate different coalitions, both within governments and across them, and involve different degrees of conflict. Politics does not stop at the water's edge."[44] States and transnational actors such as corporations and NGOs and other groups may pursue different or similar goals. States are not insular and coherent units but instead are subject to the tug and pull of different institutions and branches within the government and different objectives of nonsovereign entities and individuals within and across their borders. Given the multiplicity of crisscrossing actors, there is no hierarchy of issues because both "high" and "low" politics issues might rise to the top of the international agenda at any one point in time. This contrasts with realism, which operates under the assumption that security is here, there, and everywhere.[45]

Of course it is premature to declare the demise of the state or of state actors. In fact, even liberals such as Keohane and Nye who observed that the international system has grown into a state of "complex interdependence" conceded that realist insights remain relevant. Even among the Western democracies conflicts may trigger issues that are "a matter of life and death,"[46] and "realist assumptions would again be a reliable guide to events."[47] It is nonetheless fair to say that state power and authority have been supplemented by new and significant actors on the global stage. The state, for example, is now pressed by supranational norms and structures (such as international human rights and

---

[44] *Id.* at 25.
[45] *Id.* at 24.
[46] *Id.* at 29.
[47] *Id.* at 28.

international trade), subnational, cultural groups demanding distinct minority rights (distinct from universal human rights), and transnational groups within the state but exerting and responding to cross-border ties.[48]

As discussed, realist assumptions about the state system have been questioned by different approaches in international relations which have studied nongovernmental organizations, international institutions, and other players active in transnational networks and movements. But even liberalism assumes that state "[i]nterests across the states system [are] . . . both stable and roughly identical."[49] Even liberalism, which has been critical of realist assumptions, reproduces those assumptions—liberalism too assumes states want power, security, and wealth but allow room for cooperation. As Keohane wrote, "much of my own work has deliberately adopted Realist assumptions of egoism, as well as rationality, in order to demonstrate that there are possibilities for cooperation even on Realist premises."[50] Thus even critics of the dominant international relations models accept certain basic assumptions of the very system they criticize. They may study the different ways "states play the game of being rational egoists in an anarchic world, but they take for granted that states *are* rational egoists and that the identification of the world as anarchic is unproblematic, in other words that the game is preordained."[51] For example, pluralism and liberalism may take into account the rise of national and transnational non-state actors engaged in a crisscrossing network of ties that are not controlled by the state nor bound by national boundaries. And pluralism and liberalism may look at how state behavior might be influenced or altered by those non-state actors. But neither asks underlying questions about subjects such as the goals and values that shape state pursuit of power, security, and wealth.

Perhaps the strand of international relations that has been most critical of the major international relations paradigms is "constructivism," a term which originated in Nicholas Onuf's work.[52] Unlike other critical theories, this one questions the very construct of the statist structure. Constructivism treats "social structures as causal variables and derive actors and interests from them."[53] Indeed, there is a debate in social science which centers on "whether, analytically, one treats actors (i.e., agents), capabilities, and preferences as given and derives social structures from their interaction, or whether one takes the social structures as given and treats actors, their preferences and powers, as defined by the social system(s) in which they are embedded."[54] As an example, studies of capitalism

---

[48] T. Alexander Aleinikoff, *Sovereignty Studies in Constitutional Law: A Comment*, 17 Const. Comment. 197, 201–02 (2000).

[49] Martha Finnemore, National Interests in International Society 1 (1996).

[50] Robert O. Keohane, *Empathy and International Regimes*, *in* Beyond Self-Interest 227, 227 (Jane J. Mansbridge ed., 1990).

[51] Brown, *supra* note 15, at 51.

[52] The term "constructivism" originated in Nicholas Onuf's work. *See* Nicholas Greenwood Onuf, World of Our Making: Rules and Rule in Social Theory and International Relations 35 (1989).

[53] Finnemore, *supra* note 49, at 14.

[54] *Id.*

that focus on the structure of capitalism first and ask how capitalism creates actors (such as firms and states) that act in accordance with capitalist preferences for expansion and profit would fit into this category. Structures are the starting point of analysis,[55] whether they be material or economic structures or structures of "shared knowledge and intersubjective understandings . . . [that] shape and motivate actors."[56] Constructivism seeks to "develop a systemic approach to understanding state interests and state behavior by investigating an international structure, not of power, but of meaning and social value."[57]

> Socially constructed rules, principles, norms of behavior, and shared beliefs may provide states, individuals, and other actors with understandings of what is important or valuable and what are effective and/or legitimate means of obtaining those valued goods. These social structures may supply states with both preferences and strategies for pursuing those preferences.[58]

The very term "constructivism" suggests that those engaged in this vein of international relations are interested in the process of social construction and the "impact of cultural practices, norms of behavior, and social values on political life."[59]

Constructivism is particularly helpful to my core ideas about culture change because its inquiry centers on goals, values, and perceptions, which are also inquiries into culture and culture change. For example, constructivists believe that state interests, which other theories take as a given, "are not just 'out there' waiting to be discovered; they are constructed through social interaction."[60] Constructivism postulates that human relations, including international relations among states, are influenced by ideas and thoughts, not just material conditions. For constructivists, ideas, conceptions, assumptions, thoughts, and so forth are a focal point of inquiry because those intersubjective beliefs form the basis of human identities and shape the way humans see themselves in relations to others. Social institutions and structures in turn reflect such collective beliefs. As Alexander Wendt, a prominent constructivist remarked, "[s]ocial structures have three elements: shared knowledge, material resources, and practices. First, social structures are defined, in part, by shared understandings, expectations, or knowledge. These constitute the actors in a situation and the nature of their relationships, whether cooperative or

---

[55] *Id.* at 14–15.

[56] *Id.* at 15.

[57] *Id.* at 2.

[58] *Id.* at 15.

[59] *Id.*

[60] *Id.* at 2. But some liberals such as Keohane are receptive to the insertion of values into the debate. "A complete analysis of regimes would have to show how international regimes could change as a result not of shifts in the allegedly objective interests of states, or in the power distributions and institutional conditions facing governments, but of changes in how people think about their interests, including the possibility that they may be interested in the welfare of others, both from empathy and from principle." Keohane, *supra* note 50, at 236.

conflictual."[61] As Wendt observed, "neorealists think [the social structure] is made only of a distribution of material capabilities, whereas constructivists think it is also made of social relationships."[62] For the former, material capabilities and resources—military might, economic and natural resources—are crucial for understanding a state's social structure in the international system. How big is its army and navy? Does it have important natural resources such as oil or scarce minerals? What is its gross national product?

For constructivists, however, social structures are not simply taken for granted but rather infused by shared expectations and knowledge. Consequently, constructivists make a distinction between "brute facts" about the world, which are independent of human understanding, and "social facts" that are embedded in social conventions.[63] Conventional international relations theories mix up the two, ascribing natural status to conditions that have been socially produced and thus subject to change. For example, even a core issue such as anarchy does not by itself dictate any particular course of state action. Anarchy does not by itself create an international system of mistrust and self-help. Much will depend on how states understand that anarchy. Indeed, anarchy is what states make of it.[64] Wendt noted that "500 British nuclear weapons are less threatening to the US than 5 North Korean nuclear weapons, because the British are friends of the US and the North Koreans are not, and amity or enmity is a function of shared understandings."[65]

Evolution is a central theme for constructivists.[66] Most approaches to international relations assume that state preferences are a given fact and are inherent to the actors at issue.[67] But because constructivists see norms and values as centrally relevant to state interests, and because norms and values are hardly fixed and immutable, constructivists question how preferences are socially constructed and how they evolve. They study how states are socialized to adopt new norms, values, and perceptions, which in turn trigger a change in state actions. Constructivists who use sociological organizational theory, particularly the institutionalist strand, look at how international organizations change states.

The key point is *not*, as liberalism posits, that international organizations provide stability and equilibrium to the state system, or cushion international shock that may accompany major events such as the end of the Cold War or the unification of Germany,[68] or

---

[61] Alexander Wendt, *Constructing International Politics*, 20 INT'L SECURITY 71, 73 (1995).

[62] *Id.*; FINNEMORE, *supra* note 49, at 6 (making claims "about the importance of norms and values also shift attention from the largely material conceptions of international politics espoused by neorealists and neoliberals to a more social and ideational conception.").

[63] JOHN R. SEARLE, THE CONSTRUCTION OF SOCIAL REALITY 26–27 (1995).

[64] Alexander Wendt, *Anarchy Is What States Make of It: The Social Construction of Power Politics*, 46 INT'L ORG. 391, 394–95 (1992).

[65] Wendt, *supra* note 61, at 73.

[66] In that narrow but nonetheless significant way, it is similar to customary international law, which also sees evolution as an essential feature of international law.

[67] FINNEMORE, *supra* note 49, at 7–8.

[68] *See supra* text accompanying notes 33 and 34.

constrain states from acting in certain inappropriate ways. Although liberalism accords significant status to international organizations, viewing them as important mediators of state interests because they further transparency and serve as effective monitors of state behaviors, in the end, liberalism does not invest international organizations with "autonomous and causal status."[69] The unique contribution of constructivism is that the international system of international organizations "can change what states *want*. It is constitutive and generative, creating new interests and values for actors. It changes state action, not by constraining states with a given set of preferences from acting, but by changing their preferences."[70] By contrast, the two major international relations paradigms, realism and liberalism, presuppose that states are "pre-specified actors pursuing pre-specified preferences."[71]

Another key insight provided by constructivism is that changes in state preferences may be located outside the state, not just inside. Realism and liberalism, for example, tend to assume that state preferences are rooted in internal, domestic sources although even these two schools see the relevant roles played by actors in one domestic sphere interacting with their counterparts in the international sphere.[72] Still, to the extent that realism and liberalism observe changes in state interests, they are inclined to see the reconfiguration of state interests as a reflection of changes in the functional needs and material conditions of states.[73] Constructivists, on the other hand, assert that "state preferences are malleable"[74] as they are not "inherent in states and may not be wedded to material conditions."[75] This opens up the international law and international relations fields of inquiry dramatically. State preferences and policy shifts are not understood to be a result only of internal pressure by domestic groups or state reaction to internal crises, though of course that is an eminently plausible explanation for constructivists because they are open to studying the role and influence of non-state actors in the international system.[76] Thus, as discussed later in this chapter, an NGO such as the International Committee of the Red Cross (ICRC) may successfully pressure states to perceive their interests differently, to warrant state willingness to adopt new norms governing state obligation toward noncombatants. How that is accomplished can provide useful parallels for NGOs that work to change cultural perception—in a way that pushes state commitment to girls' education but also societal internationalization of such commitment.

---

[69] Finnemore, *supra* note 49, at 13.

[70] *Id.* at 5–6; *see also id.* at 15 ("Preferences are strongly influenced and often constituted by social norms, culturally determined roles and rules, and historically contingent discourse.").

[71] *Id.* at 9 n.10.

[72] *See supra* text accompanying notes 39–50.

[73] Finnemore, *supra* note 49, at 8–10.

[74] *Id.* at 11.

[75] *Id.*

[76] *Id.* at 15 ("Socially constructed rules, principles, norms of behavior, and shared beliefs may provide states, individuals, and other actors with understandings of what is important or valuable. . . ."); *see also id.* at 4 n.4.

More markedly, for constructivists, the impetus for shifts in state policy and preferences might also lie *outside* the state, in international organizations, and might not be only a reaction to crises or pressing demands but a response to changing international norms. Because, as liberalism espouses, states are part of a dense network of transnational and international relations, states' views of their interests are influenced by internationally held norms. Decision makers are influenced by the values embedded in this normative context. This normative context also evolves over time so that internationally held norms and values will change accordingly, triggering in turn "coordinated shifts in state interests and behavior across the system."[77] This means that state preferences are not always properties of states nor are they always generated by internal demands and internal power struggles. Rather, they are also a result of "[i]nternational norms, shared beliefs, discourse, culture" which "may shape and define the preferences of actors in ways not related to internal conditions, characteristics, or functional need."[78]

Outside international relations, other disciplines such as sociology, through institutionalism, see social structures as constituted not by an international society of states but by the expansion of a world culture. Many features of nation-states are derived from and highly influenced by "worldwide models constructed and propagated through global cultural and associational processes. These models and the purposes they reflect (e.g., equality, socioeconomic progress, human development) are highly rationalized, articulated, and often surprisingly consensual."[79] These culturally based rules shape state action by infusing them with goals such as the pursuit of modernity, economic progress, and development. This strand of sociology "builds on contemporary sociological institutionalism" and views "the nation-state as culturally constructed and embedded rather than as the unanalyzed rational actor depicted by realists."[80] The key point is that there is a worldwide culture, not just local or national culture, which has had a significant impact on the institutional development of the nation-state. New, emerging states in today's times would be embedded in a certain cultural logic (not simply the logic of objective, material forces) that favors a set of rationalizing rules about progress and modernity.[81]

For example, Peter Katzenstein advanced a sociological perspective on national security and put forth the idea that even "security interests are defined by actors who respond

---

[77] *Id.* at 2.

[78] *Id.* at 22.

[79] John W. Meyer, John Boli, George M. Thomas, & Francisco O. Ramirez, *World Society and the Nation-State*, 103 AM. J. TECH. 144, 144–45 (1997) (emphasis omitted).

[80] *Id.* at 147.

[81] *Id.* at 147–48; *see also* Martha Finnemore, *Norms, Culture, and World Politics: Insights from Sociology's Institutionalism*, 50 INT'L ORG. 325, 330–31 (1996); John W. Meyer, *Self and Life Course: Institutionalization and Its Effects*, *in* INSTITUTIONAL STRUCTURE: CONSTITUTING STATE, SOCIETY, AND THE INDIVIDUAL 242, 242–60 (George M. Thomas et al. eds., 1987) (describing how Western world culture has defined states and individuals, so that international politics should be understood not as a process resulting from state interactions but rather an outgrowth of the worldwide expansion of Western culture).

to cultural factors."[82] Even in the "high politics" area of national security, norms, and identities (not just power) play a significant role in issues such as weapons acquisitions, humanitarian interventions, and military alliances and postures in specific countries. Realist accounts of deterrence rely on the notion of fear of retaliation to explain why states refrain from using weapons of mass destruction. For example, international norms of what constitutes "responsible" or "civilized" behavior, not only rationalist calculations or fear of retaliation,[83] have served to deter the use of nuclear weapons. Constructivists, however, observe that states have refrained from such use even when there was no threat of retaliation, as in the cases of the Spanish Civil War, the Korean War, the French wars in Indochina and Algeria, the United States in the post–World War II world, or the Soviets in Afghanistan. The widespread nonuse of these weapons, according to constructivists, can be fully understood only if one takes into account the "development of prohibitionary norms that shaped these weapons as unacceptable 'weapons of mass destruction.'"[84] These norms normalize or marginalize certain behaviors and at the same time constitute both the identities and interests of the actors involved. In other words, these prohibitionary norms not only restrain behaviors but also influence how states view themselves—as actors who engage or not in certain types of behavior.[85]

Conventional deterrence theory is relevant to the understanding of how nuclear weapons acquired the status of taboo weapons. The United States became vulnerable to Soviet nuclear attack and it was in the United States' interest to make nuclear use unacceptable. Constructivism, however, looks at how "normative considerations, identities, and interests regarding nuclear use mutually shaped each other and hence influenced outcomes." American leaders defined nuclear use in the post–World War II world as contrary to America's place and identity in the moral fabric[86] and sought to diffuse this norm more broadly *upward* into the international level.[87]

Other scholars have looked at how international organizations have marshaled certain norms and diffused them *downward* into the state level. For example, Martha Finnemore investigated the transformation of war, from a historically "anything goes" phenomenon to a highly regulated institution constrained by rules that were created and imparted to states by a transnational, nongovernment group, the ICRC. The humanitarian claims of the ICRC, subsequently codified in the Geneva Conventions, assume the existence of a

---

[82] Katzenstein, *supra* note 24, at 2.

[83] Richard Price & Nina Tannenwald, *Norms and Deterrence: The Nuclear and Chemical Weapons Taboo, in* The Culture of National Security: Norms and Identity in World Politics 114, 117 (Peter J. Katzenstein ed., 1996).

[84] *Id.* at 115.

[85] *Id.* at 125 ("Actors conform to norms in order to validate social identities, and it is in the process of validating identities that interests are constituted.").

[86] *Id.* at 138.

[87] *Id.* at 144–45 (arguing that, to avoid moral opprobrium, "[n]ational leaders are forced to seek or develop alternative technologies for use in war or defense. . . . 'Society,' not anarchy, is the source of constraining and permissive effects.").

framework that is not easily compatible with a conventional state-dominated framework associated with state sovereignty. An assertion that humans have rights that are derived from their humanity, rather than by their relationship to any particular state, produces certain normative claims that vie with claims asserted by states because those humanitarian claims seek to circumscribe and constrain state power.[88] Nonetheless, the ICRC insists on the protection of individuals from state violence even in wartime, when state interests are presumably at their most vital.

Interestingly, Finnemore's thesis makes clear that the usual explanations for the origin of the ICRC and the Geneva Convention are insufficient. For realists, state acceptance of humanitarian norms was founded partly on reciprocity—hoping that repatriating enemy wounded would increase the likelihood of reciprocal treatment for their own wounded.[89] Yet, initial applications of the Geneva Convention were unilateral and equally important, the "discussions surrounding the adoption of the Geneva Conventions and subsequent compliance were not about interests and advantage. They were discussions about duties, responsibility, and identity. They were discussions about appropriateness,"[90] which are normative, not strategic considerations.

And most importantly for constructivists, the main impetus for the Convention was not states but "a few morally committed private individuals—individuals without government positions or political power—and the elite networks they were able to use to build an international organization."[91] Indeed, one individual, Henry Dunant, a Genevese-Swiss banker, was the catalyst for the founding of the ICRC and for the dissemination of its message, which was premised on humanitarian values that are at odds with an absolutist view of state sovereignty and power. As a result, the "international community is said to have a 'duty' and 'responsibility' to prevent [humanitarian] disasters. But responsibilities and duties are created by normative understandings and social structures,"[92] as evidenced, for example, by the increase in humanitarian interventions to save civilian populations in places with little geopolitical significance.[93]

More recently, NGOs, particularly international human rights organizations, played a vital role in persuading states to become parties to the Rome Statute of the International Criminal Court (ICC), creating an independent court that conferred considerable power, independence, and authority to its chief prosecutor.[94] They were able to "delegitimize dominant understandings of international politics"[95] and pressed states to embrace norms

---

88 FINNEMORE, *supra* note 49, at 71–72.

89 *Id.* at 72.

90 *Id.* at 87.

91 *Id.* at 86.

92 *Id.* at 87–88.

93 Martha Finnemore, *Constructing Norms of Humanitarian Intervention*, *in* THE CULTURE OF NATIONAL SECURITY: NORMS AND IDENTITY IN WORLD POLITICS 153, 153 (Peter J. Katzenstein ed., 1996).

94 MICHAEL J. STRUETT, THE POLITICS OF CONSTRUCTING THE INTERNATIONAL CRIMINAL COURT: NGOS, DISCOURSE, AND AGENCY 23 (2008).

95 *Id.* at 27.

of universal justice although "norm change in the world political system is indeterminate because it depends on the interlocking choices of thousands (or more) individual human beings."[96] The Coalition for the ICC (CICC), an umbrella group of pro-ICC organizations that numbered in the hundreds, played a prominent role in effectively framing the issue (with the support of pro-ICC states), engaging in both advocacy directed at the elites as well as "mass mobilization strategies."[97] The CICC was particularly successful at getting states to relinquish a not insignificant degree of national sovereignty because it was able to frame the issue in ways that resonate transnationally. As Keck and Sikkink observed:

> New ideas are more likely to be influential if they fit well with existing ideas and ideologies in a particular historical setting. Since networks are carriers of new ideas, they must find ways to frame them to resonate or fit with the larger belief systems and real life contexts within which the debates occur. The ability of transnational advocacy networks to frame issues successfully is especially problematic because, unlike domestic social movements, different parts of advocacy networks need to fit with belief systems, life experiences, and stories, myths, and folk tales in many different countries and cultures.... [T]he two types of issues most characteristic of these networks—issues involving bodily harm to vulnerable individuals, and legal equality of opportunity—speak to aspects of belief systems or life experiences that transcend a specific cultural or political context.[98]

Tapping into the universal principle against bodily harm, the CICC succeeded in "enhancing communication with victims, individuals, and groups in war-torn or otherwise marginalized parts of the world community."[99] Of critical importance was the ability of the CICC "to translate the emotional appeals of victims of war crimes into the formal legalistic reasoning that characterized the ICC debate."[100] The CICC was thus able to defend and promote the "morally resonant" universal principle of equal justice.[101] Research on the formation of the ICC showed that NGOs played a vital role in persuading states to ratify the treaty. Although "causation is an elusive phenomenon in the social sciences,"[102] Michael Struett was able to rely on policy reports and interviews with NGOs and state actors to assess NGO influence on state decision making, using what has been referred to as "process tracing" to essentially retrace the steps involved.[103] The conclusion: NGO influence "can be logically related to the choices that were made in the final

---

[96] *Id.* at 28.

[97] *Id.* at 29.

[98] Keck & Sikkink, *supra* note 2, at 204.

[99] Struett, *supra* note 94, at 34.

[100] *Id.* at 42.

[101] *Id.* at 23.

[102] *Id.* at 25.

[103] *Id.* at 34.

drafting of the Rome Statute,"[104] and as a result, the final statute bore a close resemblance to the early proposals advanced by the NGOs.

Another constructivist case study involving the norms of development and the World Bank reveals a similarly transformative shift in international norms, in this case, development norms. This transformative shift resulted in a new understanding of development that goes beyond conventional economic indicators and takes into account explicit humanitarian objectives. An early understanding of development focused on increasing wealth measured in terms of raising the GNP[105] but left open the questions of means as well as ends. For example, development by what means? Toward what ends—wealth to do what, for whom? In the early 1950s and 1960s, states generally understood development to mean increasing wealth. Projects that captured the attention of most governments were capital-intensive, such as the construction of large, industrial plants.[106]

By the mid-1970s, however, the understanding of development itself had changed. Poverty alleviation became a key goal and most importantly, was understood as a condition not just of "poor countries" but of people. This shift is significant in at least two ways. First, "the poor" came to mean not just weak or poor states but individual human beings. Second, "[s]tates were disaggregated in these new development policies and the poor were targeted *within* states."[107] Such a view essentially pierced the veil of sovereignty and created the intellectual space needed to examine how an international organization, the World Bank, promulgated a new norm and transported it to the nation-state.

Finnemore found, for example, that of the three interested actors involved in development—states, whether industrialized or developing, development experts, and international organizations—it was the international organization, the World Bank, that played the crucial part needed to shift development goals and strategies. The World Bank example thus illustrates how nongovernmental organizations can play a significant role in producing norm change that alters the international norms of development. In essence, Robert McNamara, the head of the World Bank during the critical years of the norm shift, made the bank "an effective proselytizer for poverty concerns."[108] Although states are deemed to be the main actors in the international system, in this case, the role they played was negligible for two reasons. First, developing countries had little interest and saw little political advantage in shifting resources to poverty alleviation. Second, developed countries too had little stake in helping the poor in developing countries as most

---

[104] *Id.* at 116.
[105] FINNEMORE, *supra* note 49, at 89.
[106] *Id.*
[107] *Id.* at 90.
[108] *Id.*

aid was government to government. The development community, scholars and practitioners, was divided over the issue.

Ultimately, the World Bank under Robert McNamara was able to institutionalize already-existing concerns about global poverty into the mainstream development conversation, turning it into "an inextricable part of what development was all about."[109] By injecting a discussion of poverty into a dialogue that had theretofore been focused on economic and infrastructural growth, McNamara was able to foster a sea change in the global view of what it meant to participate in "development."[110] While there had been something of a shift toward thinking that poverty alleviation had a significant role to play in development efforts,[111] theorists who advanced such claims critiqued existing paradigms without necessarily advancing "clear, consensual blueprint[s] for alternative policies."[112]

Finnemore argued that McNamara achieved this feat by taking advantage of changes within the organizational structure of the World Bank, rather than by altering how poverty norms were viewed.[113] These organizational changes had begun under the aegis of George Woods, who was McNamara's immediate predecessor. Woods significantly increased the connections between the World Bank and the International Development Association (IDA), which was chartered in 1961 with the explicit intention of "promot[ing] economic development . . . in the less-developed areas of the world."[114] In addition, Woods began to expand the World Bank's lending practices into education and agriculture.

McNamara built on this framework on two fronts. Driven by an ideological belief that "aid was a moral obligation of rich nations,"[115] he first successfully doubled the Bank's lending in his first five years in office,[116] and second, began to take a more active interest in directing how developing countries were to use Bank funds.[117] Having accomplished the first task, McNamara was better able to make certain structural changes within the Bank itself. For example, he used his strong executive power within the World Bank to fill staff positions with people who believed that development should be retooled to better address poverty concerns and those with extensive technical and managerial (rather than formal banking) backgrounds, and he commissioned reports on possible poverty-reduction initiatives.

---

[109] *Id.* at 92.

[110] *Id.*

[111] *See generally*, e.g., GUNNAR MYRDAL, THE CHALLENGE OF WORLD POVERTY: A WORLD ANTI-POVERTY PROGRAM IN OUTLINE (1970); DEVELOPMENT IN A DIVIDED WORLD (Dudley Seers & Leonard Joy eds., 1971).

[112] FINNEMORE, *supra* note 49, at 103.

[113] *Id.* at 91.

[114] Int'l Dev. Ass'n, *Articles of Agreement*, art. I (Sept. 24, 1960).

[115] FINNEMORE, *supra* note 49, at 104.

[116] ROBERT S. MCNAMARA, THE MCNAMARA YEARS AT THE WORLD BANK: MAJOR POLICY ADDRESSES OF ROBERT S. MCNAMARA, 1968–1981, at 6 (1981).

[117] FINNEMORE, *supra* note 49, at 107.

In addition to altering the organizational structure in ways that would allow him to further his policy agenda, McNamara also capitalized on the relative strengths and weaknesses of the World Bank when it came to finding a niche in which the poverty-alleviation agenda could be most effective. Finnemore illustrated how resistance to "mak[ing] . . . value judgments"[118] prevented the institution from focusing on population control measures; equally, the field of health and nutrition was deemed subject to the domain of other international organizations (including the World Health Organization).[119] Ultimately, the World Bank focused its attentions on rural development and agricultural aid—this was an area of development in which the Bank already had expertise. Furthermore, this approach allowed the Bank to target the world's poorest, without necessarily alienating the governments of (particularly developing) borrower countries.[120]

While the paradigm shift within the development field may have begun with the work of poverty-focused theorists such as Gunnar Myrdal, the World Bank played a key role in drawing such critiques into the field, thereby causing a change in the paradigm. Peter Katzenstein's work suggested that a state, for example Turkey, may alter its cultural views of women and its own views of power if it begins to see itself as a (potential) EU member state, in accordance with those cultural norms and values espoused by the European Union. Similarly, Finnemore argued that the leaders in developing countries—who could reap great material benefits from large infrastructure projects—acceded to less personally useful World Bank poverty projects "more as the price of continued funding for other, more desired projects and as the price for the continued good will of the Bank than out of concern about poverty."[121]

Humanitarian norms, antiwar crime norms, and antipoverty norms, championed and transmitted by the ICRC, the CICC, and the World Bank, respectively, displaced older, more state-centric norms that saw state interests as paramount in both war and development. Constructivist accounts of norm change reveal a process of pulling and tugging at once-dominant norms until the balance tips and a new norm somehow gels into place.

Because norms play such a central role in the constructivist understanding of the international order, constructivists have tended to draw on sociological insights to explain the influence of norms on state behavior. This means, for example, drawing on sociological approaches to explaining the role of organizations in "institutionalizing and propagating cultural norms—norms that define identities, interests, and social realities for the people who inhabit those organizations."[122] Constructivists study the "socially constructed nature of international politics."[123] Because the central insight of my book rests on the idea that cultural beliefs, habits, and interests are socially constructed and subject to constant change and evolution, much of constructivist explanations will be a useful

---

118 *Id.* at 111.
119 *Id.* at 111–12.
120 *Id.* at 112.
121 *Id.* at 118.
122 *Id.* at 3.
123 *Id.*

complement to the thesis set forth in this book. The constructivist project, which brings norms and values into international politics, coincides with my aims in this book—which is to bring culture front and center into the law and development framework.

International law, like international relations, has also made sweeping progress from a state-based orientation to a more pluralistic view that legitimizes the role of non-state actors in the creation of international legal norms. Breakthrough from this dominant state-centric, coercive-force, and coercive-command perspective came from the so-called New Haven School of international law, which understands law to be a process of authoritative decision making[124] among various institutional actors, not merely a reflection of sovereign commands or the pursuit of naked power or state unitary interests. The New Haven School finds fault with the then dominant paradigm in international relations, which "underestimates the role of rules, and of legal processes in general, and over-emphasizes the importance of naked power."[125] For the New Haven School, rules are part of the process of decision making in the same way that law is itself an interactive social process which transcends the idea that law is law only if it is a sovereign command backed by the state's coercive powers. Professor Michael Reisman, for example, sees law in "brief encounters" and sees all of us as sovereigns engaged in "microlegal processes."[126]

By taking seriously the ongoing interactions among institutional actors who participate in this dynamic constitutive process of decision making, the New Haven School has undoubtedly pushed the boundaries of international law by expanding the lens through which it views the subject. Still, because its emphasis remains on "authoritative decision [making]" whereby various institutional actors create "reciprocal demands, expectations, identities and operational patterns" and "specialized institutional practices,"[127] the locus of the New Haven School resides in "authoritative" communities (as opposed to, by implication, nonauthoritative, nongovernmental communities). It has been noted, for example, that although the New Haven School looks at policy and process and hence departs from the naked power perspective that had dominated international relations, it still "equates law with fundamental goals or values of the dominant states. Normativity disappears, as rules *per se* have no genuine independent role."[128]

---

124 Symposium, *McDougal's Jurisprudence: Utility, Influence, Controversy*, 79 Am. Soc'y Int'l L. Proc. 266, 272–77 (1985); Harold D. Lasswell & Myres S. McDougal, Jurisprudence for a Free Society: Studies in Law, Science and Policy 31–32 (1992).

125 Myres S. McDougal, *International Law, Power and Policy: A Contemporary Conception*, 82 Recueil Des Cours 137, 157 (1953).

126 W. Michael Reisman, Law in Brief Encounters 2 (1999); Michael Reisman, *A Jurisprudence from the Perspective of the "Political Superior*,*"* 23 N. Ky. L. Rev. 605, 605–08 (1996).

127 Myres S. McDougal et al., *The World Constitutive Process of Authoritative Decision*, 19 J. Legal Educ. 253, 254–55 (1967).

128 Sandholtz, *supra* note 16, at 7.

Nonetheless, this framework, which embraces "the interactions and interdeterminations of peoples across state lines,"[129] has been further expanded as international law scholars identify an expanding universe of normative communities each struggling to assert their normative visions and commitments.[130] The New Haven School provides the foundation for international law scholars to embrace yet a more robust, pluralist view of the discipline in which the prerogatives of the states are challenged.[131] As Michael Reisman remarked, "since the Second World War, an increasing number of international norms of both customary and conventional provenance . . . now restrict or displace specific law-making and applying competences of states."[132] A "transnational legal process" model, articulated by its primary proponent, Harold Hongju Koh, looks at the ways in which nation-states internalize transnational norm and whether or not those norms are issued by the state or enforced by state power.[133] More recently, scholars in a range of academic fields have studied the effect of norms on a multiplicity of issues ranging from security to war, apartheid, and human rights.[134] The conventional boundaries of international law are undoubtedly being challenged—starting from the naked-power view of a realist-based international law to the New Haven School's model of a policy-oriented decision-making process, and now to a more multivalent, pluralistic understanding of processes of international norm development.

---

129 Myres S. McDougal et al., Studies in World Public Order, at x (1960).

130 *See,* e.g., Carol Weisbrod, Emblems of Pluralism: Cultural Differences and the State 7–8 (2002); Boaventura de Sousa Santos, Toward a New Legal Common Sense: Law, Globalization, and Emancipation 2 (2d ed. 2002); Marc Galanter, *Justice in Many Rooms: Courts, Private Ordering, and Indigenous Law,* 19 J. Legal Pluralism 1, 18–23 (1981); Sally Engle Merry, *International Law and Sociolegal Scholarship: Toward a Spatial Global Legal Pluralism,* 41 Stud. L. Pol. & Soc'y 149, 149–50 (2008).

131 John Griffiths, *What Is Legal Pluralism?,* 24 J. Legal Pluralism 1, 2–4 (1986); Sally Engle Merry, *Legal Pluralism,* 22 Law & Soc'y Rev. 869, 870 (1988); William W. Burke-White, *International Legal Pluralism,* 25 Mich. J. Int'l L. 963, 967–69 (2004); Benedict Kingsbury, *Confronting Difference: The Puzzling Durability of Gentili's Combination of Pragmatic Pluralism and Normative Judgment,* 92 Am. J. Int'l L. 713, 713 (1998).

132 W. Michael Reisman, *Introduction, in* Jurisdiction in International Law, at xi, xii (W. Michael Reisman ed., 1999).

133 Harold Hongju Koh, *Transnational Legal Process,* 75 Neb. L. Rev. 181, 183–84 (1996); Harold Hongju Koh, *How Is International Human Rights Law Enforced?,* 74 Ind. L.J. 1397, 1399 (1999); Harold Hongju Koh, *Why Do Nations Obey International Law?,* 106 Yale L.J. 2599, 2604 (1997).

134 *See,* e.g., Martha Finnemore, The Purpose of Intervention: Changing Beliefs About the Use of Force 84 (2003); Gary Goertz & Paul F. Diehl, *Toward a Theory of International Norms: Some Conceptual and Measurement Issues,* 36 J. Conflict Resol. 634, 634 (1992) ; Robert H. Jackson, *The Weight of Ideas in Decolonization: Normative Change in International Relations, in* Ideas and Foreign Policy: Beliefs, Institutions, and Political Change 111, 111–38 (Judith Goldstein & Robert O. Keohane eds., 1993); Katzenstein, *supra* note 24, at 2; Audie Klotz, Norms in International Relations: The Struggle against Apartheid 13 (1995); John Mueller, *Changing Attitudes Towards War: The Impact of the First World War,* 21 Brit. J. Pol. Sci. 1, 1–28 (1991); Ethan A. Nadelmann, *Global Prohibition Regimes: The Evolution of Norms in International Society,* 44 Int'l Org. 479, 479–80 (1990); James Lee Ray, *The Abolition of Slavery and the End of International War,* 43 Int'l Org. 405, 405–07 (1989); Janice E. Thomson, *State Practices, International Norms, and the Decline of Mercenarism,* 34 Int'l Stud. Q. 23, 23 (1990).

Koh's emphasis on multiple norm-generating communities echoes the works of Robert Cover, known for his celebration of multiple and pluralistic normative centers.[135] Cover refused to elevate lawmaking by the state above lawmaking by non-state entities, arguing that "*all* collective behavior entailing systematic understandings of our commitments to future worlds [are entitled to] equal claim to the word 'law.'"[136] Cover's normative vision, though claimed in reference to the domestic context generally and US federalism particularly, nonetheless stands in sharp contrast to that of international law, which has traditionally elevated the role of states and views states as having monopoly power over the articulation of law and norms. But Cover equated official law with its nonofficial counterparts, allowing interpretive communities the space and the right to "create law and . . . give meaning to law through their narratives and precepts."[137] Official law "must share the dignity with thousands of other social understandings. In each case the question of what is law and for whom is a question of fact about what certain communities believe and with what commitments to those beliefs,"[138] leaving open the possibility of contestation, engagement, and adaption of competing normative visions.

It is thus quite telling that Koh, for example, described the transnational legal process as a "jurisgenerative" process,[139] using the very terminology Cover used to describe how law's essential jurisgenerative capacity can project, through soft law and persuasion, an "alternity"—defined by Cover as "the 'other than the case', the counter-factual propositions, images, shapes of will and evasion with which we charge our mental being and by means of which we build the changing, largely fictive milieu for our somatic and our social existence."[140] For Cover, law is "a bridge in normative space" connecting the world as it is with the world as it can be imagined to be. By incorporating Cover's vision of competing legal conceptions and pluralistic normative communities,[141] Koh is similarly incorporating such a vision into the transnational universe. Summoning Cover's jurisgenerative concept, Koh noted and applied it to describe the participation of non-state transnational actors in the formation and progress of transnational norms, describing this interactive process as one that:

> [N]ot only generated law—the domestic private law of letters of credit, the domestic public law of executive power, the international private law of dispute-resolution,

---

[135] *See, e.g.*, Robert M. Cover, *The Uses of Jurisdictional Redundancy: Interest, Ideology, and Innovation*, 22 Wm. & Mary L. Rev. 639, 643 (1981).

[136] Robert M. Cover, *The Folktales of Justice: Tales of Jurisdiction*, 14 Cap. U. L. Rev. 179, 181 (1985).

[137] Robert M. Cover, *The Supreme Court, 1982 Term, Foreword: Nomos and Narrative*, 97 Harv. L. Rev. 4, 40 (1983). *Cf.* Brian Z. Tamanaha, *The Folly of the "Social Scientific" Concept of Legal Pluralism*, 20 J.L. & Soc'y 192, 193 (1993) (critiquing that this broad view of law dilutes the very concept of law that makes law distinctive).

[138] Cover, *supra* note 136, at 182.

[139] Harold Hongju Koh, *Transnational Legal Process*, 75 Neb. L. Rev. 181, 186 (1996).

[140] Cover, *supra* note 137, at 9.

[141] Cover, *supra* note 136, at 181.

> and the public international law of diplomatic relations law—but generated new interpretations of those rules and internalized them into domestic law that now guides and channels those actors' future conduct.[142]

In turn, nation states may respond to certain transnational norms by internalizing them, whether or not they are backed by the state's coercive powers and even if they are articulated by nontraditional legal actors such as NGOs.[143] As described previously, the ICRC and the World Bank's articulation of new transnational norms and transmission of such norms to the international system and to the domestic system of nation states can be seen as examples of this process. From a law and development perspective, NGOs, whether at the international or domestic level, can play a vital role in pushing states to adopt new norms and to diffuse such norms into the cultural fabric of the country at issue.

Increasingly then, international law scholars drawn to the New Haven School and to Koh's transnational legal process model have been studying the ways by which non-state communities generate norms that may be internalized by states and transformed into state practices. They have pushed further against the model as well, however. The focus is not just on how non-state-generated norms are internalized by state actors but also on how transnational webs of norm entrepreneurs manage their collection of discrete and disparate interests by contesting certain norms, invoking new norms, whether local or nonlocal, in an effort to subvert or change current norms. The process is neither solely top-down or bottom-up but a constantly evolving crisscrossing of efforts among the local, the national, and the international. As a result, the line between NGOs challenging states to adopt new custom in international law and one in which NGOs push for the diffusion of international norms into the local in law and development is not a clearly demarcated one. For example, in the law and development context, the following questions would be particularly relevant. How do local actors ally themselves with or oppose NGOs? How are international norms transferred into local communities? How do local communities deploy their own local norms to absorb and support or contest and reject the nonlocal norms?

---

[142] Koh, *supra* note 139, at 186.

[143] *Id.*; Harold Hongju Koh, *Why Do Nations Obey International Law?*, 106 Yale L.J. 2599, 2648 (1997) (describing how an "epistemic community" gelled around and supported a particular interpretation of the Antiballistic Missile Treaty and how this community succeeded in pushing the US government to adopt its interpretation) (quoting Peter M. Haas, *Introduction: Epistemic Communities and International Policy Coordination*, 46 Int'l Org. 1, 3 (1992)); Joel R. Paul, *Holding Multinational Corporations Responsible Under International Law*, 24 Hastings Int'l & Comp. L. Rev. 285, 285–86 (2001) (noting that "private individuals and non-governmental organizations acting both internationally and domestically are contributing to the emergence of new international norms. These new international norms confer greater rights and obligations on private individuals and firms, shifting the focus of international law.").

B. Non-State Law and Norms

My proposal that law and development incorporates a cultural lens to supplement its legal development can be supported not just by developments in international law, as discussed in Part A, but also by developments in fields other than international law. Indeed, for many years, scholars in other disciplines have been studying the process of private lawmaking and thus have been drawn to the realm of non-state-generated values and norms. Before the rise of the nation-state system, much lawmaking occurred within autonomous institutions and subunits such as cities and guilds.[144] Even since the establishment of modern nation-states, there is much lawmaking that takes place outside the official realm of the state, and scholars in a variety of academic fields have studied a wide range of non-state lawmaking.[145] The works of Sally Falk Moore, a legal anthropologist, demonstrate, for example, that neither law nor culture can be reduced to a system of rules. There exists, instead, a plurality of legal and customary rules, and it is through the interaction of such rules with the social world that determines how these legal and customary rules operate in practice. Her works can be essentially characterized by the idea that "not all that are lawlike have their source in government."[146] Others have drawn on empirical studies to examine how cattle ranchers rely on nonlegal norms as a source of social control[147] or how the manufacturing industry use nonlegal mechanisms to settle disputes[148] or how various social organizations ranging from the insurance market to the Jockey Club opt for self-regulation among their own members.[149] Even in the complex legal, trading, and financial universe, industry-wide rules that bind banks, credit, and industry-wide agencies can have the effect of law even absent governmental involvement.[150]

---

[144] Eugen Ehrlich, Fundamental Principles of the Sociology of Law 14–38 (Walter L. Moll trans., Russell & Russell 1962) (1936).

[145] *See, e.g.*, Walter Otto Weyrauch & Maureen Anne Bell, *Autonomous Lawmaking: The Case of the "Gypsies,"* 103 Yale L.J. 323, 323 (1993) (describing autonomous lawmaking in ethnic enclaves and interactions between the norms of the Romani people and the laws of their host countries); Carol Weisbrod, The Boundaries of Utopia, at xi (1980) (examining contractual lawmaking in four nineteenth-century religious communities—the Shakers, the Harmony Society, Oneida, and Zoar); Lan Cao, *Looking at Communities and Markets*, 74 Notre Dame L. Rev. 841, 846 (1999) (describing lawmaking among immigrants using rotating credit associations to secure credit); Marc Galanter, *Justice in Many Rooms: Courts, Private Ordering, and Indigenous Law*, 19 J.L. Pluralism 1, 28 (1981) (observing that the field of church and state is the "locus classicus of thinking about the multiplicity of normative orders") (emphasis omitted); Lon L. Fuller, Anatomy of the Law 43–48 (1968) (stating that everything from rules governing a camping trip among friends to merchant law qualifies as "implicit law").

[146] Sally Falk Moore, *Legal Systems of the World*, *in* Law and the Social Sciences 11, 15 (Leon Lipson & Stanton Wheeler eds., 1986).

[147] Robert C. Ellickson, Order without Law: How Neighbors Settle Disputes 53 (1991).

[148] Stewart Macaulay, *Non-Contractual Relations in Business: A Preliminary Study*, 28 Am. Soc. Rev. 55, 60–62 (1963).

[149] F. W. Maitland, *Trust and Corporation*, *in* Maitland: Selected Essays 141, 191–95 (H. D. Hazeltine et al. eds., 1936).

[150] Janet Koven Levit, *A Bottom-Up Approach to International Lawmaking: The Tale of Three Trade Finance Instruments*, 30 Yale J. Int'l L. 125, 126 (2005); Amitai Aviram, *A Paradox of Spontaneous Formation: The*

Increasingly, litigants prefer to submit themselves to the jurisdiction of non-state arbitral panels. Much financial market regulation is left to non-state, standard-setting bodies such as the National Association of Securities Dealers. Individual industry groups, such as the chemical industry, are governed by industry associations, for example, the Canadian Chemical Manufacturers Association and the International Counsel of Chemical Associations, which set industry standards in consultation with NGOs such as Greenpeace.[151] And as governments at different levels of economic development find it difficult to come up with international labor standards, private companies in the apparel industry have adopted codes of conduct and participated in the UN Global Compact.[152] States have even consented to share norm-making power with private parties, especially in the commercial and trade area, by permitting private parties acting as plaintiffs to challenge domestic governmental regulations; under NAFTA's Chapter 11, private investors have standing to challenge a NAFTA government's decisions,[153] and the Convention on the Settlement of Investment Disputes between States and Nationals of Other States permits private creditors to sue debtor states in an international forum.[154] Similarly, the Convention on the International Sale of Goods (CISG) allows buyers or sellers from contracting states to opt out of a state law and opt into international merchant law.[155]

In sum, norms and how they change or can be made to change are crucial questions for this book. Part A of this chapter explored how change is endemic to international law itself, as evidenced by the evolution of international relations and international law from their state-centric foundations to create room for non-state actors and norms. Part B examined how other disciplines have similarly embraced non-state lawmaking. What Parts A and B demonstrated is that even in the international system where states remain the principal actors, there is now space for the study, within international law and international relations, of not just interests and power but values and norms. Part C below

---

Evolution of Private Legal Systems, 22 YALE L. & POL'Y REV. 1, 3 (2004) (describing the ability of private legal systems to enforce norms); Lisa Bernstein, *Private Commercial Law in the Cotton Industry: Creating Cooperation Through Rules, Norms, and Institutions*, 99 MICH. L. REV. 1724, 1724–25 (2001).

[151] Lee A. Tavis, *Corporate Governance and the Global Social Void*, 35 VAND. J. TRANSNAT'L L. 487, 508–09 (2002) (describing the interrelationship among private sector associations, NGOs, and governmental institutions).

[152] Marisa Anne Pagnattaro, *Enforcing International Labor Standards: The Potential of the Alien Tort Claims Act*, 37 VAND. J. TRANSNAT'L L. 203, 208 (2004).

[153] Greg Block, *Trade and Environment in the Western Hemisphere: Expanding the North American Agreement on Environmental Cooperation into the Americas*, 33 ENVTL. L. 501, 507 (2003) (describing how NAFTA allows private investors to sue NAFTA governments for breach of investment provisions).

[154] IGNAZ SEIDL-HOHENVELDERN, COLLECTED ESSAYS ON INTERNATIONAL INVESTMENTS AND ON INTERNATIONAL ORGANIZATIONS 374 (1998) (describing how "Convention attempts to encourage foreign investors to invest in developing countries by granting to them, in case of a dispute with the host country, a status equal to that enjoyed by that State.").

[155] Clayton P. Gillette, *The Law Merchant in the Modern Age: Institutional Design and International Usages Under the CISG*, 5 CHI. J. INT'L L. 157, 159 (2004) (describing how the CISG "explicitly incorporates trade usages into contracts that it governs, permits usages to trump conflicting CISG provisions, and authorizes courts to interpret and complete contracts by reference to usages.").

asks how norm change has occurred internationally and explores the theories proposed to explain how norms change and why. Part D provides an in-depth study of two norm change scenarios. One, the transformation of the norm of conquest, was driven primarily by changing state practice, and the other, the transformation of the norm of slavery, was driven by a combination of state practice and newly emerging Enlightenment norms espoused by non-state actors.

C. How and Why International Rules and Norms Change

How have rules and norms changed internationally? How did international law norms, for example, of slavery, conquest, colonization, once commonplace and acceptable, become verboten, supplanted by entirely new sets of norms?

International law has a well-developed theory about how norms change. Indeed, international law scholars have long grappled with the question of how custom is formed and how established custom changes in response to new state practice. It is important at the outset to distinguish a custom in customary international law from an international norm. Once something is deemed a custom in international law, it is legally binding. By contrast, a norm does not necessarily have legal ramification, although it can certainly serve as a guide for behavior.

Whether something is a custom in customary international law is wholly dependent on whether it accords with a legal understanding of custom, as explained below. How customary international law is legally formed is often unclear and ambiguous. Thus although it is relatively simple to define customary international law, it is difficult to understand its formation and evolution. In essence then, custom in international law is as subject to change and evolution, as difficult to define, as riddled with ambiguity, and as contested by opposing forces as culture and culture change is. How a cultural norm, as it exists at a moment in time, is understood and viewed by members of a group and how this norm may be contested and changed, has interesting parallels to how custom changes in international law.

Customary international law is one of several sources of international law, along with conventions or treaties, general principles of law recognized by civilized nations, judicial decisions, and the most qualified juristic writings.[156] Customary international law is commonly understood to be a set of rules derived from a consistent pattern of conduct by states acting from a sense of legal obligation. In other words, custom is constituted by two elements—practice and law. Although "[n]o definition of customary law has

---

[156] Statute of the International Court of Justice art. 38(1), June 26, 1945, 59 Stat. 1055, 33 U.N.T.S. 993 (requiring the ICJ to apply the sources of international law as enunciated therein: "The Court, whose function is to decide in accordance with international law such disputes as are submitted to it, shall apply: . . . international custom, as evidence of a general practice accepted as law.").

received universal agreement,"[157] it is generally accepted that "[c]ustomary international law results from a general and consistent practice of states flowing from a sense of legal obligation."[158]

The Restatement comments state: "Thus, for customary law the 'best evidence' is proof of state practice, ordinarily by reference to official documents and other indications of governmental action."[159] There is no uniform understanding or agreement about which types of behaviors by states count as state practice for purposes of determining customary international law. Official policy pronouncements, national legislation, diplomatic statements are usually considered reliable evidence of state practice, along with UN General Assembly Resolutions and other soft, nonbinding statements.[160]

Customary international law may change and evolve over time because of changing state practice. It is possible that the practice of one state that deviates from existing custom can spark a chain of events that leads to a change in that custom.[161] Although it is a process of lawmaking, it is unwritten (like cultural norms), and as such how it is formed and how it changes over time has become a source of debate among international law scholars. Because custom is generated by a decentralized and spontaneous process of lawmaking, the very process by which change occurs is riddled with ambiguity and is thus subjected to contestations by different states. Whereas treaties specify a textually-bound set of formalized rules in a relatively structured process, for example, negotiation, signature, and entry into force, customary international law manifests little structure and contains no clearly demarcated phases and no specified temporal dimensions. "The determination of customary international law is more an art than a scientific method."[162]

---

[157] Restatement (Third) of Foreign Relations Law of the United States § 102 Reporters' Notes 2 (1987).

[158] *Id.* at § 102(2). This traditional understanding of customary international law has been challenged by Jack Goldsmith and Eric Posner. Their argument rests on the claim that customary international law (and international law generally) is a result of states acting out of self-interest, not a result of states acting out of a sense of legal obligation. Jack L. Goldsmith & Eric A. Posner, The Limits of International Law 39 (2005).

[159] Restatement (Third) of Foreign Relations Law of the United States § 103 cmt. a (1987).

[160] H. W. A. Thirlway, International Customary Law and Codification 80–94 (1972); Stephen M. Schwebel, *The Effect of Resolutions of the U.N. General Assembly on Customary International Law*, 73 Proc. Soc. Int'l L. 301, 302 (1979).

[161] But as Justice Story observed with reference to the customary norm of the law of the sea, "no single nation can change the law of the sea. That law is of universal obligation, and no statute of one or two nations can create obligations for the world. Like all the laws of nations, it rests upon the common consent of civilized communities. It is of force, not because it was prescribed by any superior power, but because it has been generally accepted as a rule of conduct." The Scotia, 81 U.S. (14 Wall.) 170, 187 (1871).

[162] Mark W. Janis, An Introduction to International Law 44 (4th ed. 2003); *see* G. J. H. van Hoof, Rethinking the Sources of International Law 85 (1983) ("confusion and divergence of opinion . . . reign supreme as far as customary international law is concerned") (footnote omitted); David P. Fidler, *Challenging the Classical Concept of Custom: Perspectives on the Future of Customary International Law*, 39 German Yearbook Int'l L.198, 198 (1996) ("CIL [customary international law] stands at the heart of modern international law while generating frustration and frictions in its identification and application. CIL appears indispensable and incomprehensible.").

Note then that a key point about customary international law is its unfixed, nontextual, and porous nature. Thus the mechanisms for determining whether a customary international law rule has been formed or whether a nation has consented to a customary rule are often unclear. It is true that a nation can show unambiguous consent to a rule of customary international law by conforming its actions to the rule at issue, supplemented by official declarations that its compliance derives from legal obligation. It is also true that a nation can show unambiguous opposition to a rule of customary international law by persistently defying the rule, supplemented by official declarations that its behavior is meant to show disagreement with the rule.

This regime to signal consent or objection to a rule is relatively clear if the rule at issue is already recognized as custom. But ambiguity is heightened when the dispute concerns whether a new custom has displaced an old custom. Thus another key point about customary international law is its highly contestable nature because custom, unlike treaty, is vague and ambiguous.

As one of the main components of custom is state practice, the question of whether custom has changed or is in the process of changing can only be determined if state practice is considered and evaluated. The potentially new rule of customary international law challenging the old rule emerges when enough states shed the old practice in favor of the new practice, coupled with declarations that adherence to the new practice derived from legal compulsion. The flouting state can be viewed as one that innovated a new rule or one that broke a traditional rule. There will be a period in which the flouting state's status—as rogue or as innovator—will be unknown and will be in flux because it is how other states react that will determine the flouting state's status. The legality of the flouter's act will often be known not at the time of the act but only in retrospect, based on other states' reactions. At some point, the process consisting of various acts by states reaches a tipping point in which these acts of state practice "ripen" into a rule of international law and become legally binding.[163] In other words, at some point, state practice here, there, and everywhere somehow becomes law once "international behavioral regularities emerge from disorder."[164]

Once a pattern of state practice emerges, it must then be determined whether such state practice follows from a state's sense of legal obligation. This is the opinio juris element of custom, defined as the psychological component underlying custom's formation.[165] But

[163] *See,* e.g., The Paquete Habana, 175 U.S. 677, 686 (1900) ("By an ancient usage among civilized nations, beginning centuries ago, and gradually ripening into a rule of international law, coast fishing vessels . . . have been recognized as exempt . . . from capture as prize of war.").

[164] Eric A. Posner & Jack L. Goldsmith, *A Theory of Customary International Law* 9 (John M. Olin Program in Law and Economics Working Paper No. 63, 1998).

[165] Thirlway, *supra* note 160, at 47 ("The precise definition of the opinio juris, the psychological element in the formation of custom, the philosophers' stone which transmutes the inert mass of accumulated usage into the gold of binding legal rules, has probably caused more academic controversy than all the actual contested claims made by States on the basis of alleged custom, put together.") (emphasis omitted); *see also supra* text accompanying note 158.

because customary international law is constantly changing and evolving, at some point, some state practice that deviates from standards of customary international law at the time must be capable of planting the seeds of a potentially new norm of customary international law.[166] States may themselves perceive their interests to have changed over time and may behave in a way that deviates from established custom, for example.[167]

For international law scholars, how custom changes in customary international law remains something of a conundrum. It is both static and evolutionary. A custom might seem fixed at a moment in time but might be nudged and challenged at another moment in time. As discussed later, this is quite similar to cultural norms which are similarly static and evolutionary, likely fixed at a moment in time but also subject to being nudged and challenged at other times.

International relations scholars have also studied norm change.[168] Some explain norm change as a result of actions taken by utility-driven actors or as the result of a transnational process of pluralistic politics.[169] As noted, theorists use the idea of "transnational advocacy networks"[170] to describe the diffusion of norms. They suggest that international human rights norms can be proliferated amongst states by a process of "socialization"[171] in which domestic and transnational actors form networks with international regimes and create norm change by applying "top-down" and "bottom-up" pressure to repressive regimes. By placing norm-violating states on the international agenda in a way that creates moral awareness, and by helping to empower domestic opposition groups in target states, these transnational networks manage to reduce the number of options available to norm-violating governments in such a way as to institutionalize change.[172]

Finnemore and Sikkink described the following three-part norm change process. In the first stage, "norm entrepreneurs" attempt to convince a critical mass of world leaders to adopt a certain norm.[173] In the second, for various reasons, the norms "cascade through the rest of the population,"[174] and in the third stage, norms lose their controversial quality and cease to become a matter for public debate.[175] The motivations for states to engage in norm change or to respond to norm change persuasion vary. Some suggest that "a combination of pressure for conformity, desire to enhance international legitimation,

---

166 Posner & Goldsmith, *supra* note 164, at 41–42.

167 *Id.* at 28.

168 *See generally* Sandholtz, *supra* note 16.

169 *Id.* at 5.

170 Thomas Risse & Kathryn Sikkink, *The Socialization of International Human Rights Norms into Domestic Practices: Introduction*, *in* THE POWER OF HUMAN RIGHTS: INTERNATIONAL NORMS AND DOMESTIC CHANGE 1, 4 (Thomas Risse et al. eds., 1999). *See also supra* text accompanying notes 5–11.

171 Risse & Sikkink, *supra* note 170, at 5.

172 *Id.*

173 Martha Finnemore & Kathryn Sikkink, *International Norm Dynamics and Political Change*, 52 INT'L ORG. 887, 895 (1998).

174 *Id.*

175 *Id.*

and the desire of state leaders to enhance their self-esteem facilitate norm cascades";[176] similarly, others describe the reasons for which repressive governments adapt to normative pressures as playing both on "instrumental"[177] necessity as well as "communicative rationality."[178]

Under these constructivist accounts of norm change, non-state groups ally themselves with others similarly minded, whether local or abroad, and together form a transnational alliance to pressure governments.[179] Whether in the international or domestic sphere relevant to international law or law and development, an array of actors are engaged in pressuring, persuading, and framing new norms to supplant old ones. If successful, the process will reach a tipping point (where old norms are supplanted by new norms) and will accomplish what has been referred to as a "spiral"[180] or a "cascade"[181] of norm transformation. This bargaining process differs both from the processes outlined in traditional international relations theory and many legalization models, which focus very much on the role that states play in changing and proliferating norms. These constructivist accounts lend a lot of credence to the ability of non-state actors to actively participate in norm change processes, even as simply as using the phrase "norm entrepreneurs," which could be—but are not always necessarily—state actors.

Another account of norm change can be explained by the legalization model which views norms as the outcome of institutional design in international relations.[182] States vie for a particular set of rules that best promote their interests and best order their interactions. "The content of those rules, as well as their degree of obligation, precision, and delegation, are the outcome of bargaining among interested actors."[183] For example, the New Haven School understands international law to be the product of a decision-making process, in which the "most powerful states dominate international decision making."[184] As such, according to academics from this school, international law essentially reflects the goals and values of the most dominant states in the global political system. On the other hand, the International Legal Process school takes the converse approach, arguing that law actually shapes decision making and the structure of institutions, and that the implementation of a legal regime can help to shape, clarify, and elaborate on already-existing norms.[185] A third framework that has already been discussed here, that of Harold Koh's Transnational Legal Process, provides that transnational actors provoke interactions that

---

[176] *Id.*

[177] Risse & Sikkink, *supra* note 170, at 15.

[178] *Id.*

[179] Keck & Sikkink, *supra* note 2, at 214.

[180] Risse & Sikkink, *supra* note 170, at 3.

[181] Finnemore & Sikkink, *supra* note 173, at 895–96.

[182] Sandholtz, *supra* note 16, at 4.

[183] *Id.*

[184] *Id.* at 7.

[185] *Id.* at 8.

then help to "enunciat[e]"[186] and modify norms. Koh's approach has the most similarity to the processes described by the constructivist theorists above, because the Transnational Legal Process does leave room to integrate non-state participants into the norm change conversation.

Under these models, then, norms are seen as the natural outcome of either pluralistic or legalistic bargaining among various state and non-state groups. "[N]orms emerge when they acquire sufficient support in the relevant political arena, whether that is an interstate negotiation (legalization) or an international process of pressure and persuasion (transnational networks)."[187] Both models, in other words, are limited by their focus on international rules as outcomes: In particular, legalization models tend to focus on "the development of international rules, both hard and soft, as a matter of regime choice or institutional design."[188] This view of international rule development as the result of "bargaining among interested actors"[189] allows for an adequate description of the process by which rules are made; however, it provides no insight as to the longer-term consequences of the formed regimes.[190] Similarly, the transnational networks analysis, according to Sandholtz, shows how norms can be formed (namely, via pluralistic political processes);[191] but it sees a norm only as a result, rather than a further input into a set of changes.

Wayne Sandholtz has proposed a cycle theory of norm change that in some ways can be analogized to the process of evolution that characterizes customary international law (except that a norm is not a source of international law and norm change does not necessarily have legal significance). Indeed, Sandholtz's account sees norm change as continual, cyclical, or dialectical, a product of the constant interplay among rules, behavior, and disputes. In this way, it can be likened to the process of custom formation—how customary international law is formed, challenged, and changed. Across the stretch of time and diverse substantive domains, ranging from piracy and conquest to terrorism and slavery, genocide and humanitarian intervention to the right to democracy, Sandholtz's key finding is that norm change occurs via the cycle dynamic. Every normative system, according to Sandholtz, begins with a web of existing norms that guide actors on how to act and how to evaluate the behavior of others. [192] Before acting, a state, or as is increasingly more common, a non-state actor, will most likely focus on how its behavior will be received by others; how others will react, whether they will consider the action compatible or incompatible with current rules and norms. In making this calculation, the actor must

[186] *Id.*

[187] *Id.* at 6.

[188] *Id.* at 4.

[189] *Id.*

[190] *Id.* at 4–5.

[191] *Id.* at 5.

[192] Wayne Sandholtz, Prohibiting Plunder: How Norms Change 9–10 (2007).

also comprehend the applicable rules as well as current modes of interpreting those rules, and to the extent necessary, the similarities and differences between the present scenario and precedents.

At the same time, regardless of how skilled the actor is at assessing his or her action against a background context of governing rules and norms, his or her choice of action is likely to trigger disputes. Even a complex rule system will be characterized by certain features: vagueness and incompleteness,[193] as well as by internal contradictions.[194] For example, because any given society is likely to have multiple frameworks of rules for different scenarios, tensions and contradictions are likely to arise as certain actions are deemed by different actors to evoke different requirements and rules.[195] In international law, many rules within the UN framework, for example, seemingly are in tension with each other—nonintervention versus human rights protection, for instance. Interested parties operating within this framework of rules with corresponding gaps and tension will likely find themselves adopting different interpretations of the rules and taking opposite positions on what is appropriate. Indeed, a dialectical relationship marks the interaction between rules and actors—norms might guide the behaviors of actors, but actors might also modify norms through behaviors and disputes. Again, in the law and development context, there are similar fractures within a seemingly homogeneous cultural fabric. Interested actors seeking to introduce norms of women's equality are likely to find a social framework marked by internal disputes, tensions, and contradictions that can be interpreted in accordance with a pro-development rather than an anti-development objective.

This dynamic has been noted by other scholars as well, notably by Harold Koh, who described a similar set of events: "One or more transnational actors provokes an interaction (or series of interactions) with another, which forces an interpretation or enunciation of the global norm applicable to the situation."[196] Such disputed acts themselves cause the affected parties to offer normative arguments that may result in a modification of existing norms and possibly the internalization of such norms by applicable parties. As a result, actions, whether by state or non-state actors, regularly trigger disagreements among actors who argue about the meaning or legitimacy of a norm and its applicability to the underlying action.

Both sides will engage in rhetorical persuasion, marshal the power of rules, and interpret precedents to justify their positions. The norms at issue will likely change,

---

[193] H. L. A. Hart, The Concept of Law 119–20 (1961) ("Nothing can eliminate this duality of a core of certainty and a penumbra of doubt when we are engaged in bringing particular situations under general rules. This imparts to all rules a fringe of vagueness or 'open texture'"); *see also* Neil MacCormick, Legal Reasoning and Legal Theory 65–66 (1978) ("Almost any rule can prove to be ambiguous or unclear in relation to some disputed or disputable context of litigation.").

[194] Sandholtz, *supra* note 16, at 10.

[195] Friedrich V. Kratochwil, *How Do Norms Matter?*, *in* The Role of Law in International Politics: Essays in International Relations and International Law 35, 43 (Michael Byers ed., 2000).

[196] Koh, *supra* note 143, at 2646 (emphasis omitted).

strengthened or weakened, broadened or narrowed. "Actors are not only programmed by rules and norms, but they reproduce and change by their practice the normative structures by which they are able to act, share meanings, communicate intentions, criticize claims, and justify choices."[197] If a consensus cannot be forged, its absence might very well indicate that the norm at issue is becoming weak or vague and will likely be subject to continuing contestation. "The process of disputing reveals the extent to which states and other actors agree on the international rules in question. The crucial point, however, is that the cycle of normative change has completed a turn and modified the norms underlying the dispute."[198] An actor acting in accordance with a line of precedents is likely to find that his or her action is likely to be unopposed by other actors; one acting contrary to a line of precedents will likely find that his or her action will be deemed by others to be unjustified.

Which normative vision will turn out to be the winning one? Sandholtz and Stiles observed that certain factors will have an impact on which of the rivaling norms will prevail.[199] First, power. While those with economic and military powers might be able to violate norms without suffering much punishment, it does not follow that they will be able to change the rules by their power alone. Indeed, rule change will occur only if an economically powerful actor is able to persuade others to accept a new norm or modify an existing norm. Second, foundational norms. Certain norms are so foundational that it is likely they will carry persuasive weight: Norms of equality and individual dignity, for example, would prohibit slavery and sexual exploitation, torture and cruel treatment. Third, precedents. Precedents are valued because they allow the system to exhibit a sense of consistency and stability. The number of precedents supporting a particular norm is important, and recent precedents will likely be more persuasive than those distant in time.

Norm change is most likely to occur when a set of international conditions exist that will most likely result in a challenge of existing international rules. Wars, for example, will have an effect on many norm universes, with implications for legal rules dealing with a range of subject matters: use of force, human rights, refugees, asylum; political change likewise triggers international disputes, with multiple ripple effects through multiple norm domains.

This model also incorporates the foundations established by the New Haven School and by the transnational legal process. The cycle identified can be described in this way: normative context, triggering events, arguments about relevant rules, and norm shift. State actors along with transnational NGOs, activists, and norm entrepreneur are all part of "longer, cyclic dynamics of norm change."[200] Different episodes of action,

---

[197] Friedrich V. Kratochwil, Rules, Norms, and Decisions: On the Conditions of Practical and Legal Reasoning in International Relations and Domestic Affairs 61 (1989) (footnote omitted).

[198] Sandholtz, *supra* note 16, at 7; *see also* Sandholtz, *supra* note 192, at 20.

[199] Sandholtz, *supra* note 16, at 15–19.

[200] *Id.* at 18.

reaction, norm revision, and modification cannot be seen simply as "free standing cases" but rather as part of a "larger, longer process of norm change. The cycle theory enables us to see that specific cases or episodes are linked forward and backward: each takes place in a context shaped by previous disputes, and each modifies the normative context for subsequent controversies."[201]

This model of norm change is to be examined within a modern context defined by two foundational principles in the international system: sovereignty norms and liberal norms. While it is undoubtedly the case that the UN Charter, for example, has as a foundational principle "the sovereign equality of all its Members" enshrined in Article 2(1), it is also the case that the Charter contains a stream of norms tied to the notion of individual human rights. Similarly, law and development is also guided essentially by two normative currents—sovereignty norms and liberal norms. Liberal individualism is foundational for politically democratic systems. Market economies leave economic decision making to individual choice and individual freedom of exchange. As previously noted, the shift from seeing development in terms of poverty alleviation rather than industrial growth represented a significant cultural shift spearheaded by non-state actors like the World Bank. Other examples of paradigm shifts in international norms are further explored in Part D below. Part D demonstrates, through various examples, that norms are highly relevant even in a statist discipline such as international law; and that even norms that appear deeply entrenched can be challenged and transformed.

D. Norm Change Scenarios: Two Examples

Conquest as a means of expanding empire was seen, for the majority of recorded history, as a relatively uncontroversial prospect—at least for victorious and expanding states. Figures such as Alexander the Great, Henry II of England, and the Mughal emperor Akbar of India were internationally acclaimed for their successes. Yet, revolutions and wars starting from the eighteenth century produced norms of self-determination and territorial integrity that eventually superseded the norm of conquest.

Sharon Korman described the right of conquest as "the right of the victor, in virtue of military victory or conquest, to sovereignty over the conquered territory and its inhabitants."[202] The notion that conquest was perceived as a "right" is telling; to suggest that a conqueror invaded a sovereign territory by right rather than by show of power, suggests in turn that there existed some societal permission to conquer as well as its opposite—the "possibility of restriction."[203] In general, classical international law acknowledged that

---

[201] *Id.* at 19.

[202] Sharon Korman, The Right of Conquest: The Acquisition of Territory by Force in International Law and Practice 8 (1996).

[203] *Id.* at 95 (emphasis omitted).

aggressive warfare was a method by which legal title over territory could be acquired.[204] Indeed, even as late as 1928 it was generally accepted that "[t]itles of acquisition of territorial sovereignty in present-day international law [is] . . . based on an act of effective apprehension, such as occupation or conquest."[205]

In general, the international norm was that conquest, recognized by a third party, could confer legal control over a given territory. When Spain raised a legal objection to the United Kingdom's control over Gibraltar before the UN Special Committee on Decolonization in 1964 (control which Spain had ceded to the United Kingdom at the Treaty of Utrecht, following the War of Spanish Succession), it did not allege that sovereignty could not transfer via the process of conquest and succession; rather, it argued that the *elements* of conquest had not been properly fulfilled.[206] This example suggests that the rules and norms surrounding the right of conquest were so deeply entrenched that they can form the basis for coherent legal arguments even in modern time. That conquest is no longer seen as an acceptable norm for territorial acquisition is a very recent development.

Conquest was perceived, in the medieval era as a divinely judged way to determine sovereignty disputes.[207] Through the eighteenth century, when colonization became a more generally accepted scheme, conquest of far-flung territories was justified by those "bearers of a spark from the sacred fire."[208] Colonizers often used the notion of the "civilizing" mission to justify their right of conquest.

However, the wars and revolutions of the eighteenth and nineteenth centuries almost certainly laid the foundations for the shift away from conquest norms. The revolutions in the Americas as well as in France sowed the intellectual seeds for the latter-day notion of "self-determination," which itself is tied up deeply with the principles of conquest, colonization, and territorial integrity. Revolutionaries of the French Revolution were inspired by the philosophy of Jean Jacques Rousseau, who boldly declared that "[t]he right of conquest has no foundation other than the right of the strongest,"[209] thus laying the foundation for the principle of self-determination; indeed, consent of the people had to be obtained before sovereignty over them could be secured. The French Constitution of 1791 embodied anticonquest principles: "The French nation renounces the undertaking of any war with a view of making conquests, and it will never use its forces against the liberty of any people."[210] Despite this aspirational statement, Napoleon's military

[204] Brook Gotberg, *The End of Conquest: Consolidating Sovereign Equality*, *in* International Norms and Cycles of Change 55, 56 (Wayne Sandholtz & Kendall Stiles eds., 2009).

[205] Matthew M. McMahon, Conquest and Modern International Law: The Legal Limitations on the Acquisition of Territory by Conquest 67 (Kraus Reprint 1975) (1940); Korman, *supra* note 202, at 96.

[206] Korman, *supra* note 202, at 96–98.

[207] *Id.* at 96.

[208] Joseph Conrad, Heart of Darkness 2 (Dover 1990) (1902).

[209] Korman, *supra* note 202, at 121.

[210] Gotberg, *supra* note 204, at 57; 1791 Const. tit. VI (Fr.).

might during the period of 1803–15 was renowned, and by and large the concept was not espoused by other Western leaders. In 1858, the British Crown took over the administration of the Indian subcontinent from the British East India Company; France, Germany, England, and Belgium were all active in what is known today as the "Scramble for Africa"; even the United States, which had fought its own war of independence in the 1700s, was embroiled in the Philippine-American War by the end of the century. While it may be argued that European leaders were aware of the limitations of the wider colonial project as early as the mid-1800s, it appears that the solidification of the principles of self-determination and territorial integrity gained prominence and traction in international thought only in response to German actions prior to the First World War.

European inter-state alliances were in constant flux during the nineteenth century. However, Otto von Bismarck's desire to unify a German state comprising Prussia, Austria, and Alsace-Lorraine drove deep divisions between (what would later become) Germany and its neighboring states. The French territory of Alsace-Lorraine had certain historical and cultural ties to Germany and Prussia, although the German "liberation" claim was tenuous.[211] Historians argue that the cultural claims were at best secondary to Bismarck's goals, suggesting alternately that he sought merely to strengthen the strategic position of a larger German state relative to France, and that he sought a buffer against further possible French aggression.[212]

While Prussia was not the primary aggressor of the Franco-Prussian engagement, it is generally acknowledged that Bismarck engineered the circumstances surrounding France's declaration of war. This provided him with a legal justification for the annexation of Alsace and Lorraine. In short, France had declared war on a "guileless Prussia,"[213] and, in losing the subsequent military engagement, had lost territorial control over Alsace and Lorraine. Additionally, as some have suggested, public opinion may have weighed slightly more in Germany's favor on account of the still-recent memory of Napoleonic aggression.[214]

Despite continued acknowledgment of the norm of conquest and the weight of popular public opinion against French aggression, by 1871 the concept of national self-determination had started to gain more traction. As such, critics (including Karl Marx) took exception to Germany's violations not only of French territorial integrity but also took note of Alsatian and Lorrainian rights to determine their own nationalities. Indeed,

---

[211] Gotberg, *supra* note 204, at 60.

[212] *Id.* (citing DAN P. SILVERMAN, RELUCTANT UNION: ALSACE-LORRAINE AND IMPERIAL GERMANY 1871–1918, at 29 (1972)); KORMAN, *supra* note 202, at 90 (citing RUTH PUTNAM, ALSACE AND LORRAINE: FROM CAESAR TO KAISER, 58 B.C.–1871 A.D., at 184–85 (1915)).

[213] SARAH WAMBAUGH, A MONOGRAPH ON PLEBISCITES 21 (1920).

[214] *Id.* ("To the righteous anger of many of these liberals it appeared to be mere justice that France should herself suffer those pains of conquest which she had meant to inflict."); *see also* Gotberg, *supra* note 204, at 62; ("Prussia's annexation of Alsace-Lorraine was justified not in terms of a right to conquest, but as punishment for France having initiated hostilities.").

"moral disapproval of the German annexation"[215] constitutes an important first step in the shift away from the general acceptance of right by conquest. That there was *any* view at all that Germany had violated Alsatian and Lorrainian sovereign rights indicates a step away from classical thought and toward more liberal values.

As stated, wars are a very obvious means through which norm changes can be accelerated. In the case of the norm of conquest, twentieth-century history seems to indicate that the German exercise of the right to conquest was one of the precipitating causes for the movement away from the conquest norm. Kaiser Wilhelm II's desire to attain colonial assets in Africa and Asia has been well documented,[216] and much has been made by historians of the impact that his desire for European primacy had on inter-state relations. For example, German attempts to take advantage of Moroccan commercial interests led to the Tangier and Agadir Crises in 1905–06 and 1911, respectively; and the Anglo-German naval race undoubtedly contributed to the formation of the anti-German Triple Entente in 1907.

German aggression leading up to 1914 existed in contrast to an increasingly vocal movement (particularly on the parts of newer states) in support of territorial sovereignty and in opposition to conquest norms. In 1907, at the Second Hague Peace Conference, Brazil suggested that the right of conquest be denied; however, the Conference did not prohibit conquest.[217] Additionally, and prior to these movements in international politics, Karl Marx had been a particularly vocal critic of the colonial project, and in 1917, Lenin adopted the anticonquest principle into the rules and standards of the Revolution. In April 1917, the Provisional Government stated that "Free Russia does not aim at . . . occupying by force foreign territories; . . . its object is to establish a durable peace on the basis of the rights of nations to decide their own destiny."[218] President Woodrow Wilson's Fourteen Points and their underlying ideological emphasis on national self-determination further weakened the legitimacy of the then dominant norm—the right of the victorious states to annex territory of the defeated, aggressor state.[219]

Some scholars, such as Brook Gotberg, observed that the First World War resulted in a general European aversion to all forms of aggression, and that as a result of the violence nations began espousing a policy of "peace at all costs."[220] This view may have been at least partially influenced by the fact that squabbles over territorial possession (with regards

---

[215] KORMAN, *supra* note 202, at 92.

[216] David E. Kaiser, *Germany and the Origins of the First World War*, 55 J. MOD. HIST. 442, 443 (1983) ("[I]t is fair to say that a far-reaching consensus of German, British, and American historians now agrees that German foreign policy after 1897 must be understood as a response to the internal threat of socialism and democracy. . . . the [German] government decided to deal with domestic discontent by pursuing an aggressive foreign policy. . . .").

[217] Gotberg, *supra* note 204, at 62.

[218] KORMAN, *supra* note 202, at 136.

[219] Gotberg, *supra* note 204, at 63.

[220] *Id.* at 62.

to Alsace-Lorraine and Morocco) had certainly contributed to the outbreak of the First World War. However, Gotberg's assessment—that limits on aggression necessarily led to a view that conquest itself is a problematic paradigm—is not borne out by the historical record. Indeed, even during the war, England and France partitioned the Middle East into colonial mandates, and while states in Europe *may* have come to "a tacit agreement to respect one another's territorial integrity,"[221] this agreement—to the extent that it existed at all—was limited to those states that won the war.

State action during this period did not reflect uniform acceptance of the principle of self-determination nor of the right of conquest. Indeed, because the norm of conquest was being weakened but not yet fully rejected, and a new norm of self-determination was emerging but not yet fully recognized, states operated in essentially a norm void riddled with contradictions and ambiguities. For example, anti-German "revanchist" sentiments, grounded in French fantasies of avenging and reversing German annexation of French territory, were eerily similar to the very sentiments that provided justification for German annexation of Alsace-Lorraine—annexation as revenge for French aggression.

The Rhineland demilitarization by the Allies following World War I and the use of mandates by European states reflect a new intellectual compromise. As noted, the old norm of annexation and conquest was eroding but not yet fully replaced by the new norm favoring self-determination. Despite French claims (as Germany had in 1871) that possession of territory was integral to security interests, President Wilson and British Prime Minister Lloyd George felt that detaching the Rhineland and granting it to France "ran counter to the principle of national self-determination."[222] Thus, instead of taking it away from Germany and giving it to France, the Allies chose to demilitarize it instead.

The reorganization of what remained of the Ottoman Empire similarly reflected this new twilight reality. Although Ottoman Empire territory was divided between France and England into various colonial possessions, the usage of "mandates" as opposed to outright annexation of those Middle Eastern territories is significant. This shift—from colonies to mandates—demonstrates that the norm of conquest was indeed eroding, albeit slowly. Although they were certainly imperialist in tone and practice, mandates were not colonial possessions per se. The usage of a "mandate" structure in the Middle East did limit the degree of sovereignty that a European power was able to impose on a foreign people.

In general, while World War I did not result in the complete erosion of the conquest norm, it did seriously call such norm into question.[223] The demilitarization (rather than the annexation) of the Rhineland suggests wider acceptance of the belief that "security should *not* be sought through expansion,"[224] and indeed, the 1923 French annexation of

---

[221] *Id.*

[222] KORMAN, *supra* note 202, at 145.

[223] *Id.* at 150.

[224] *Id.* at 151.

the zone can fairly be considered one of the triggering long-term causes of the Second World War.

While liberal principles concerning the right to self-determination on the parts of conquered peoples contributed to the dissolution of the conquest norm, the Second World War added a more "pragmatic"[225] consideration to this emerging right. Not only did Fascist expansionism espoused by Germany in Europe, Italy in Abyssinia, and Japan in South-East Asia violate the principle of territorial integrity, it also presented a threat to the global order. Although the Anschluss and the annexation of the Sudetenland could be justified under a German self-determination argument,[226] the invasion of Poland and the repeated threats against France and England—both strong advocates of liberal anti-conquest norms—precipitated the Second World War.

Equally, the events of the war certainly contributed to a departure from the previous norm that conquest and loss of territory was an acceptable punishment for a state that had initiated a war of aggression. As such, German and Japanese territory "was not annexed by the victors."[227] The liberal principles espoused in documents like the Fourteen Points and the Atlantic Charter of 1941 "meant that conquest was no longer regarded as granting entitlement to territory, or as a legitimate claim to rule."[228]

In the last half of the nineteenth and the first half of the twentieth centuries, wars of aggression that almost inevitably resulted in the shifting of state borders and the conquest of territory were the triggering events for serious discussions regarding the validity and even practicality of conquest norms. French and German revanchist sentiments negatively affected inter-European relations, and the destruction wreaked by the First and Second World Wars demonstrated the impact that title conferred by conquest could have on the global order. The establishment first of the League of Nations, and subsequently the United Nations, solidified the concepts of self-determination and sovereign independence in the national dialogue.

It is not just in the realm of state sovereignty that liberal norms have managed to supersede traditional and classical worldviews. In the past three hundred years, the institution of slavery—which had been prevalent since antiquity—has become a taboo tradition. While liberal values of human dignity have long held sway in discussions regarding the morality of the slave trade, many state and non-state factors (including religious moralism and humanistic values) have contributed to the demise of the slavery norm. The discussion below of antislavery norms is significant because unlike anticonquest norms, which were altered primarily by state actors, antislavery norms were eroded by both state

[225] Gotberg, *supra* note 204, at 70.
[226] *Id.* at 71–73.
[227] KORMAN, *supra* note 202, at 177.
[228] *Id.*

and non-state actors. It can thus be viewed as an example of what Koh called the transnational legal process or what Sandholz referred to as norm-cycle theory.

Texts dating as far back as 2000 BCE address the issue of slavery;[229] laws from early periods of human history all deal with the basic issues of "who could be enslaved, under what conditions, and whether it was a status that was inherited generally."[230] Aristotelian theory suggested that slavery was just as well as necessary to the maintenance of social order; indeed, Aristotle's natural slave theory proposed that certain people, who are "deficient in reason . . . need to be subordinated to their intellectual and moral superiors in a master/slave relationship."[231] Although this view of natural slavery was utilized by European colonizers as late as 1838,[232] ancient Christian theologians did take exception to the notion. For example, St. Augustine argued in *De civitate Dei* that: "By nature, in the condition in which God created man, no man is the slave either of man or of sin."[233] Clearly, the debate regarding the legitimacy of the slave trade is nearly as old as the institution itself. Yet, the relevant question is: What triggered the erosion of such an ancient and well-established custom in a relatively short time frame?

"[A] combination of international and domestic factors in the major slave trading states. . . . [which] have their own sources in deeper political-economic trends, including the emergence of free-market capitalism, the rise of the middle class, [and] the advent of industrialization" [234] were all contributing factors to this rapid norm change.[235] But all through different periods of history, various expressions of antislavery norms could be found. Medieval Christian and Muslim leaders were inclined to discourage followers from enslaving members of their own religious communities.[236] While slavery was a generally accepted norm, it appears that religious leaders even during the early periods were sufficiently aware of the negative impact of slavery that they desired to avoid subjecting their own people to it. Indeed, such moral qualms were not necessarily limited to religious leaders. Elizabeth I of England supposedly "had expressed deep reservations

---

229 Kendall Stiles, *Slavery: Liberal Norms and Human Rights, in* INTERNATIONAL NORMS AND CYCLES OF CHANGE 169, 170 (Wayne Sandholtz & Kendall Stiles eds., 2009).

230 SLAVERY 92 (Stanley Engerman, Seymour Drescher, & Robert Paquette eds., 2001); PETER GARNSEY, IDEAS OF SLAVERY FROM ARISTOTLE TO AUGUSTINE 7 (1996) ("while the juridical status of chattel slaves was more or less invariable from one society to another, there was plenty of scope for the differential treatment of slaves.").

231 GARNSEY, *supra* note 230, at 13.

232 *Id.* at 15–16 ("William Harper . . . recommended Aristotle's *Politics* to his fellow slaveowners in the deep South.").

233 *Id.* at 14.

234 Stiles, *supra* note 229, at 176.

235 *See* Donald A. Yerxa, *Introduction: Historians, Moral Progress, and the Limits of History, in* BRITISH ABOLITIONISM AND THE QUESTION OF MORAL PROGRESS IN HISTORY 1, 5 (Donald A. Yerxa ed., 2012) ("A great deal of ink has been spilled assessing the relationship of antislavery to capitalism and free market ideology. . . . [but] we must recognize the significance of a moral vision that 'could transcend narrow self-interest and achieve genuine reform.'").

236 Stiles, *supra* note 229, at 172–73.

about the slave trade—fearing God's punishment for participating in it."[237] Additionally, the British abolitionist movement was driven by figures like William Wilberforce, who tended to use religious as well as humanitarian arguments (rather than economic ones) to advance their antislavery arguments.[238]

Both political and economic factors on the one hand and "cultural-ideological factors"[239] on the other contributed to the rise of antislavery norms. Political and economic factors include the rise of free-market capitalism and concern that continuation of the slave trade would benefit plantation productivity and profit in, for example, the West Indies.[240] Cultural factors include moral concern and misgivings about the slave trade expressed by the nineteenth-century transatlantic abolitionist movement. If the movement from conquest to anticonquest norms was generally directed by state actors, the liberal principles underlying the shift toward the antislavery norm were accelerated by non-state intellectuals and activists. Those principles also affected the norm shift in two "separate, though linked, cycles of norm change."[241] The first change resulted in the abolition of the slave *trade*; the second resulted eventually in the abolition of slavery itself. Driven by the secular, Enlightenment belief that people enjoy a set of basic and inalienable rights (including the right to be free from ownership by another human),[242] and the Christian, evangelistic belief that all men are equal in the eyes of God, activists including British Member of Parliament William Wilberforce successfully won the abolitionist vote in both of the English parliamentary houses. As a result, in January 1808, Britain outlawed the slave-trading business.[243]

Given the economic benefits that the slave trade conferred on Spanish and Portuguese colonial economies, Great Britain met considerable resistance in its initial international efforts to implement bans on the slave trade. However, Britain had already established its naval primacy by the turn of the nineteenth century, and its successful defeat of Napoleonic aggression in 1815 led to a rise in its ability to influence other states and change custom.[244] Portugal, for example, had been protected by British forces during the Peninsular campaign against Napoleon, and as such was a "dependent ally."[245] Portugal had colonies in Angola (Portugal's foremost source of slaves) and Brazil (one of the larger slave economies), and British leaders were able to capitalize on this diplomatic advantage

---

[237] *Id.* at 174.

[238] Yerxa, *supra* note 235.

[239] Jeremy Black, *Suppressing the Slave Trade*, *in* BRITISH ABOLITIONISM AND THE QUESTION OF MORAL PROGRESS IN HISTORY 27, 28 (Donald A. Yerxa ed., 2012).

[240] *Id.* at 33–34; DAVID BRION DAVIS, INHUMAN BONDAGE: THE RISE AND FALL OF SLAVERY IN THE NEW WORLD 231–33 (2006).

[241] Stiles, *supra* note 229, at 191.

[242] *Id.* at 176.

[243] *Id.* at 180.

[244] Black, *supra* note 239, at 29.

[245] *Id.* at 35.

in order to mitigate the trade and use of slaves within those Portuguese economies.[246] Britain used bilateral treaties promising "hundreds of thousands of pounds of indemnity"[247] in exchange for mutual search-and-seizure tribunals that would allow the British to board foreign ships in search of evidence of the slave trade. Although the mutual search-and-seizure tribunals in Rio di Janeiro and Havana were unpopular,[248] they were able to put over five hundred slavers out of commission between 1819 and 1845.[249] The British capitalized on their similar power dynamic with Spain in order to achieve similar results in curtailing the Spanish slave trade. Britain was able to advance the antislavery ideological agenda in international politics to some degree by trading on its power relations, despite the relative unpopularity of the abolitionist movement in Spain and Portugal.[250]

The United States and France, the other two significant players in the international slave trade, were less subject to British pressure. The necessity of the slave trade to the economy of the American South undoubtedly influenced US resistance.[251] At any rate, the abolition of the slave *trade* was not sufficient to dismantle the institution of slavery, let alone the slavery norm. For the latter event to occur, Britain was generally dependent on the wider proliferation of antislavery norms in foreign states. Nevertheless, British naval power (and the continuing public popularity of abolitionism in Britain) allowed the Royal Navy to successfully challenge "established maritime law."[252] The combined use of military and diplomatic pressure did *eventually* result in a shift, in international customary law, toward a ban on the slave trade.

The ban on slavery *itself* was rooted less in state action by Britain and more in the emerging norms that provided intellectual support for the French Revolution. Indeed, the slave revolt in Haiti could be viewed as a response to the Revolution itself.[253] As Robin Blackburn observed, "[p]olitical crisis did . . . strongly correlate with the rise of anti-slavery."[254] So, in one sense, while forms of top-down white activism appear to provide support for the antislave trade narrative,[255] it can be argued that the story of black resistance is what drives the *emancipation* narrative. "Black resistance and revolt . . . and the latent antagonism of free blacks to slavery"[256] are part of the driving forces behind the

---

246 *Id.* at 35–36; Stiles, *supra* note 229, at 183.

247 Stiles, *supra* note 229, at 184.

248 *Id.*

249 *Id.*

250 *Id.* at 183. ("Abolitionist sentiment in Portugal was very muted, and even the more enthusiastic abolitionists still opposed a sudden end to the traffic. Abolitionist sentiment in Spain . . . did not emerge until the 1850s.") (citation omitted).

251 *Id.* at 185.

252 Black, *supra* note 239, at 42.

253 Stiles, *supra* note 229, at 191–92.

254 Robin Blackburn, The Overthrow of Colonial Slavery 1776–1848, at 522 (1988).

255 Black, *supra* note 239, at 52.

256 Blackburn, *supra* note 254, at 528.

wider antislavery movement. According to Blackburn, it was not solely a moral ideology that drove emancipation, but rather the power discrepancies between master and slave, particularly in the Caribbean—where white plantation owners were far outnumbered by their black slaves.[257] By contrast, in North America—where the power dynamic between black and white was drastically different—emancipation was granted *to* black slaves; in the Caribbean, it was taken *by* them. As such, American emancipation was dependent on a slightly different moral ideology—one that was based on Christian theology, and as such was more similar to that espoused by British abolitionists.

A comprehensive survey of the American abolition debate is outside the scope of this analysis; but in general, the abolitionist critique was based essentially on both Christian evangelistic arguments, as well as secular Enlightenment ideology. While there likely is a complex interrelationship between these liberal values and increasingly industrial market forces, as suggested by Blackburn,[258] what becomes clear from the entire case study is that it *is* possible for a set of moral, liberal norms to gain enough traction as to affect a global sea change.

Today, the definition of slavery extends "beyond chattel to encompass. . . . a wide range of practices . . . [including]: debt bondage, traffic in persons, sale of organs, the exploitation of prostitutes, the sale of children, child prostitution, child pornography, trafficking in children, exploitation of child labor, sexual mutilation of female children, and use of children in war."[259] This reality seems to reflect the extension of the fundamental Enlightenment principle that people should be free from ownership by other people, to a view that people should be free from forms of coercion that could result in what can be seen as constructive ownership.

While state institutions like the US Department of State do take certain actions to mitigate these modern forms of chattel slavery (for example, the publication of the annual Trafficking in Persons Report), contemporary international rules tend to focus more on expanding the definition of "modern forms of slavery" than on actually prohibiting them. That forms of indentured servitude still exist highlights the existence of a not-insignificant discrepancy between international ideology and international action.[260] Nonetheless, just as early abolitionist thinkers, influenced by religious and secular principles, were able to translate ideology to action, the definitional expansion at least provides room for action that could very well turn an ideological norm change into a legal one.

The purpose of this chapter is to lay a foundation for culture change examination described in Chapter 5. I have shown that public international law has had ample

[257] *Id.* ("The defeats inflicted on British and French colonial slavery in the Caribbean reflected the special vulnerability of a slaveholding order dependent on a distant metropolitan state.").

[258] *See generally id.*

[259] Stiles, *supra* note 229, at 195, 198.

[260] *Id.* at 201–02 ("[A]lthough the United States as hegemon is making moves in the direction of tougher enforcement . . . its commitment to codifying free trade law. . . . is a juggernaut capable of rolling over any barriers intended to protect the weakest.").

experience with custom evolution and that both it and international relations have also become more open to participation and even lawmaking by non-state actors. Many of these actors are states, but many are also non-state actors who are part of what some scholars call transnational advocacy networks with transnational ties and interests. In the latter case, their objectives transcend the conventional dichotomy of national versus international—often they seek, through information, symbolic and political leverage, for example, to change norms and behaviors of states as well as those of international organizations. Thus, one can conclude that such developments should have significant implications for law and development and its traditional reluctance to incorporate culture. First, to the extent that the parent disciplines of international law and international relations have accepted and accommodated value-oriented inquiries, so should law and development. And second, the process of norm change and the actors involved in international law are sufficiently similar that useful lessons can be drawn for culture change actions in law and development.

The following chapter, Chapter 5, studies actual examples of culture change scenarios at different points in time and in different settings. These examples demonstrate first and foremost that culture change can be done. Second, culture change has been done in widely different societies—some of the examples are drawn from postconflict societies that had to be rebuilt and redeveloped, and this endeavor included both rule of law development as well as culture change development.[261] Other examples studied include more conventional projects customarily associated with law and development. Despite difficulties and complexities, these concrete case studies do show that there are many successful examples of culture change historically and currently. The question is not whether it is possible to do culture change. Rather, the question is bringing this normative framework into the discipline of law and development.

---

[261] Some may object to the inclusion of these examples on the theory that culture change is "easy" when a society has to be rebuilt from scratch. Yet history shows that this is not the case. It is difficult to do rule of law as well as to change culture in collapsed states, as experiences in the Republic of Sierra Leone and the Democratic Republic of the Congo have shown.

5

To Change a Culture

IN THIS CHAPTER, I leave the public international law and international relations framework and return to the law and development model. I continue the critique of culture and demonstrate how a thick conception of development, as discussed primarily in the Introduction and Chapter 1 (but also throughout the book), necessitates an examination of not just law but also culture. Certain cultural attributes deemed authentic or traditional by some may increase economic inefficiency or constrict human freedom and capability. In the section below, I situate my critique of culture and place it in the context of law and development, focusing on historical and current efforts to effectuate culture change.

The first third of the chapter deals with historical culture change in Turkey, Japan, and Germany. These countries underwent both conventional law and development and postconflict development experiences. The examples chosen to illustrate the workings of the proposal are varied and eclectic for several reasons. First, I do not intend the book to have a singular regional focus, whether it be Asia or Europe or Africa or Latin America. Second, I wish to show, through many different examples, how different societies have grappled with this issue and how culture change may be applicable to law and development in a broad way. In other words, a cultural analysis is applicable to a wide range of problematic scenarios—implicating practices that have a negative impact on markets, human rights, and at times, both.

Turkey provides an example of cultural change effectuated solely by the local regime. Turkish modernization provides examples of social, governmental, and educational modification, both successful and unsuccessful for the reasons discussed below. In many cases, there is little consultation with the local communities, and there is in turn minimal, if any, local participation. On the contrary, development goals were defined at the top, in Turkey's case, by a visionary leader, and implemented using cultural strategies. Clearly, this does not accord with Sen's emphasis on giving voice and power to those affected by development decisions. Nonetheless, I include Turkey only to show that culture change is not just normatively appropriate in many cases but also pragmatically feasible.[1]

Much of this chapter also centers on Japan's experience, particularly its modernization in the Meiji era. Here, Japan's drive to modernize was (like Turkey's) internally driven, but unlike Turkey's experience, involved the active participation of many civic organizations and not just the result of directives issued by a ruler. It involved the push and pull of elites, civic organizations, and the masses, and encompassed a core cultural component. Following World War II, however, Japan's modernization was influenced by both foreign intervention and introspective culture change. I argue that it was this mix of introspective cultural examination, the Japanese view of American occupation as liberation, and the American view of the occupation as a divine intervention that made the change in Japan successful. Further, I explore a similar demilitarization and democratization campaign in postwar Germany, and the ways in which these efforts were both successful and unsuccessful, depending upon the method of cultural modification. In many cases, even when change was directed from above or even externally imposed, it was nonetheless a complex process characterized not just by top-down commands blindly accepted by or forced upon a passive local population. Rather, reform and change also included a significant degree of active interaction between and among the different groups involved.

The second third of the chapter includes efforts taken by different countries as well as nongovernmental organizations (NGOs) to effect culture change. Examples are drawn from cases where culture change was successful as well as unsuccessful. As demonstrated in the examples given, a significant portion of the unsuccessful law and development projects have occurred when governments only attempted change through the enactment of laws, and these newly enacted laws were at odds with traditional cultural norms. This portion of the discussion is separated into three categories: (1) instances where laws have been enacted in tandem with culture change projects—state actors play a prominent and often persuasive role here; (2) instances in which only laws have been enacted to change practices—state actors also play a prominent role, but their role is less persuasive in the absence of cultural support; and (3) instances in which NGOs have become involved in communities to bring about change. In the NGO examples, culture change projects are characterized, not surprisingly, by much discussion and interaction with the local communities at issue in an attempt to persuade them to abandon certain culturally

[1] Change is sometimes a result of internal pressure and/or external pressure, and sometimes mysterious. For example, after years of indifference to foreign sanctions and pressure, under the startling leadership of General Thein Sein, Myanmar opened up economically and politically, even instituting changes that defied China, its primary sponsor. Why General Thein Sein decided in favor of openness at this moment in time remains unknown. Joshua Kurlantzick, Op-Ed., *Myanmar's Opening Gambit*, Bos. Globe, Dec. 4, 2011.

based practices. Given the degree of local discussion and participation in these projects, the NGO examples would count as those that most closely approximate Sen's vision of informed, participatory development. All the examples chosen, however, demonstrate that cultural dynamics are an important part of development work. Sidestepping culture will likely result in ineffective reform. Moreover, even in instances where culture change was pursued by visionary leaders and involved essentially top-down commands, they are worthy of examination because they demonstrate that culture change is indeed possible, contrary to assertions that culture cannot be changed.

The final third of the chapter explores efforts taken in Kosovo, East Timor, Iraq, and Afghanistan. These high visibility case studies show how actors, mainly the United Nations and United States, have tried to establish legal systems in countries that have recently been embroiled in conflict and unrest. An important element to consider in all of these case studies is the effect of security, or rather a lack of security, on forces attempting to implement law and development. Further, Iraq and Afghanistan provide a comparison between implementing a system of law within the constraints of indigenous culture, as with Afghanistan, and implementing a system of law with little consideration given to the existing culture, as in Iraq. In both cases, neither system has been effective at developing rule of law within the society or changing culture practices that go against norms of international human rights.

Given the primacy of culture change in this section, it is important to clarify what it is I am *not* arguing. I am not claiming "that cultural managers could construct any culture they wish" or that "given the right social context, any social activity can be turned into a ritual at the whim of ritual specialists."[2] Rather, "[r]ituals, and the reality they construct, depend upon the values of the parties to that ritual."[3] I am also not arguing that "backward" cultures are the universal cause of economic underdevelopment. But I am suggesting that there is some relationship between culture and economic productivity—the degree to which a relationship exists will depend on the particularities of history, economics, and politics. Acknowledging that such a link exists, however, does not mean that culture is used to "deflect[] attention from other factors which might provide an equally compelling explanation of underdevelopment."[4] The World Trade Organization (WTO) and other institutions of the international economic system may in fact be structurally problematic, as evidenced by the exclusion from WTO rules, until recently, of textiles and agriculture, two areas where developing countries have a comparative advantage. Exploring the relationship between culture and markets should in no way detract from efforts to expose the structural biases against poor countries or promote

---

[2] Lawrence Lessig, *The Regulation of Social Meaning*, 62 U. Chi. L. Rev. 943, 986 (1995) (citation omitted).

[3] *Id.*

[4] Chantal Thomas, *Causes of Inequality in the International Economic Order: Critical Race Theory and Postcolonial Development*, 9 Transnat'l L. & Contemp. Probs. 1, 8 (1999).

a "colonialist ideology that views the North as rightly and naturally dominant over the South"[5] or the South as a justly colonized . . . Other[6] to the North. The point is not that some cultures are intrinsically better than others; it is rather simply that there are certain attitudes, inclinations, norms, and behaviors that impede or promote a particular objective—economic growth—and if a group or nation, through inclusive debate and conscious choice, so determines, it could, if it chooses, take steps toward promoting culture change.

Where cultural norms are at odds with the development of human freedom and human capability, however, they should be deemed antithetical to universal principles and subject to culture change. Cultural relativism should have little place in this category of antidevelopment norms.

A. Historical Examples

1. TURKEY

The events surrounding the birth of the Turkish Republic can be seen as an example of culture change in the modern era instituted largely from within. In the first part of the twentieth century, the Ottoman Empire, known as the "sick man of Europe," crumbled.[7] The empire had gone from an autocracy to a constitutional monarchy, only to be occupied by the victors of World War I and relieved of its territories.[8] These events and the aftermath of World War I allowed Mustafa Kemal, later called Atatürk,[9] to rise to power and to institute sweeping reforms in the residual Ottoman apparatus in the hopes of securing Turkey's place among the European powers.[10] Like others before him, he believed modernization was necessary for the Europeans to recognize Turkey as a fellow power.[11] Failure would likely result in exploitation by the European powers whose presence had loomed large since the nineteenth century;[12] Turkey could become a target for European

[5] *Id.* at 6.

[6] *Id.*

[7] Carter Vaughn Findley, Turkey, Islam, Nationalism, and Modernity 192–98 (2010). In 1922, the struggle for independence ended with the beginning of negotiations with Europeans to withdraw. *Id.* at 223–26.

[8] *Id.* at 215–19.

[9] Mustafa Kemal was known as Atatürk after 1934. Niyazi Berkes, The Development of Secularism in Turkey 502 (1964).

[10] *See* Emre Kongar, *Turkey's Cultural Transformation*, *in* The Transformation of Turkish Culture: The Atatürk Legacy 19, 29 (Günsel Renda & C. Max Kortepeter eds., 1986). The foundation for Atatürk's reforms had been laid by a series of events dating back to the French Revolution. *Id.* at 46.

[11] Paul Dumont, *The Origins of Kemalist Ideology*, *in* Atatürk and the Modernization of Turkey 25, 34–35 (Jacob M. Landau ed., 1984); *see also* Osman Okyar, *Atatürk's Quest for Modernism*, *in* Atatürk and the Modernization of Turkey 45, 51 (Jacob M. Landau ed., 1984).

[12] Berkes, *supra* note 9, at 137–44. European power had played a role previously in Ottoman history when it contributed to the period known as the Tanzimat, a time of reforms beginning in 1839. *Id.* at 137–200. "Tanzimat" translates as "reforms." *Id.* at 144–45. Berkes traced the origins of secularization and modernization efforts to

colonial tendencies.[13] As one scholar opined: "An underdeveloped nation had to strive to make itself equal to the developed nations if it did not want to continue to be exploited by them."[14]

Atatürk believed that the only way to escape exploitation by the West was for Turkey to become a wholly Western society.[15] This view differed from earlier proponents of modernization who urged that Turkey should remain an Islamic civilization, adopting only certain elements of Western society.[16] Meiji Japan, for example, had retained its traditional symbols, such as the emperor, and harnessed them to implement modernization.[17] The reform discussions of nineteenth-century Turkey frequently mentioned the experience of Meiji Japan, which some suggested as an alternative to the Western model.[18] Like Turkey, Japan also felt a sense of urgency to eliminate any semblance of backwardness to avoid colonial threat.[19] Proponents of the Japan model believed that the Ottoman Empire could maintain its Eastern identity and still be accepted by the powers of Europe.[20] Earlier efforts at modernization, ironically, proved unsuccessful as they failed to legitimate the changes in the existing system.[21] Legitimacy was predicated on being a part of established tradition; change was seen as antithetical to tradition.[22] Earlier changes succeeded to the extent that proponents understood this need for legitimacy and couched the desired changes accordingly. During the late nineteenth century, a tactic for trying to legitimate borrowed elements from Europe had been to claim that the element—be it the constitutional system, math, or science—was actually Arab, and not European, in origin.[23]

Unlike these earlier attempts, Atatürk's vision for Turkish modernization necessitated nothing less than a social transformation of the Turkish people, a complete shift in the ideological foundation of the system.[24] Atatürk, under the banner of nationalism,

---

the period prior to the Tanzimat, the rule of Mahmud II, who discarded the medieval notion of order in favor of a state with a concept of justice based on equality of religious communities. *Id.* at 90–97.

[13] *Id.* at 333–35, 432–33. The need for "defensive modernization" was not a new development according to Findley, who described the motivating forces of the earlier Tanzimat reforms as "[t]he drive for centralization and defensive modernization" as well as "the sense of backwardness and the need to catch up." FINDLEY, *supra* note 7, at 88.

[14] BERKES, *supra* note 9, at 463.

[15] Kongar, *supra* note 10. Kongar identified Atatürk's desire for Turkey to become a Western society as an important break from earlier modernization efforts that looked only to imitate the West. *Id.*

[16] BERKES, *supra* note 9, at 296, 359–66 (1964).

[17] S. N. Eisenstadt, *The Kemalist Regime and Modernization: Some Comparative and Analytical Remarks*, *in* ATATÜRK AND THE MODERNIZATION OF TURKEY 3, 6 (Jacob M. Landau ed., 1984).

[18] *See* Renee Worringer, *"Sick Man of Europe" or "Japan of the Near East"?: Constructing Ottoman Modernity in the Hamidian and Young Turk Eras*, 36 INT'L J. MIDDLE EAST STUD. 207, 208 (2004).

[19] *See* discussion *infra* text accompanying notes 69–281 for the experience of Japan.

[20] *See* Worringer, *supra* note 18, at 207.

[21] Frank Tachau, *The Political Culture of Kemalist Turkey*, *in* ATATÜRK AND THE MODERNIZATION OF TURKEY 57, 59–60 (Jacob M. Landau ed., 1984).

[22] *Id.*

[23] BERKES, *supra* note 9, at 263–64 (1964).

[24] *Id.* at 463–466. Under Atatürk, Turkey faced its third and, ultimately, most successful attempt at secularism. *Id.* at 467.

embarked on an all-encompassing quest to change the culture of Turkey and its inhabitants[25] through a campaign of "induced acculturation" focused on "introducing a contemporary western culture into a traditional Islamic Turkish society."[26] For this process to succeed, the ideological foundation of the new system had to change from that of the Ottoman Empire.[27] Secularism, not tradition, would serve as the basis to legitimate and to achieve the envisioned reforms in the system.[28]

Existing institutions and symbols of authority were considered vestiges of the Empire[29] and therefore, incompatible with the new secular foundation.[30] The sultan was the traditional Ottoman ruler.[31] He also held the Islamic title of caliphate, the successor to Muhammad, which served to combine worldly and religious authority in a single figure.[32] The *ulema* were the educated, religious class, who interpreted both religious policy and state matters according to religious law.[33] Their position as the keepers of tradition and law allowed them to block innovation and even to depose the ruler.[34] The old system and its shareholders stood in the way, but neither could simply be removed and replaced to make way for the new secular state. Before the new state could emerge, the allegiance of the people also had to shift from the Ottoman system and the sultan.[35]

To defeat those who opposed the new, secular Turkish state, Atatürk harnessed the power of nationalism.[36] The opportunity to link reform to popular sentiment presented itself when a European plan to grant parts of Turkey to Greece and Armenia gave rise to

---

[25] Kongar, *supra* note 10, at 27 ("[R]evolutionary cadres used cultural and ideological factors to give impetus to political change toward new socio-economic and cultural frontiers."). *Id.*

[26] *Id.* at 38.

[27] *See* Sabri M. Akural, *Kemalist Views on Social Change*, *in* ATATÜRK AND THE MODERNIZATION OF TURKEY 125, 125–26 (Jacob M. Landau ed., 1984); *see also* Eisenstadt, *supra* note 17, at 9 ("The Turkish revolution completely rejected the religious basis of legitimation and attempted instead to develop a secular national one as the major ideological parameter. . . .").

[28] Akural, *supra* note 27, at 126 ("Secularism was the foundation stone on which all the other Kemalist reforms were built."); *see also* Eisenstadt, *supra* note 17, at 9 (describing the "revolution" as a "redefinition of the political community" and a withdrawal "from the Islamic framework into that of the newly defined Turkish nation").

[29] BERKES, *supra* note 9, at 465. In a 1922 speech, Atatürk declared: "Ideas full of irrational superstition are morbid. Social life dominated by irrational, useless, and harmful beliefs is doomed to paralysis. We must begin by purging minds and society of their very springs. . . ." *Id.* at 465–66.

[30] *Id.* Berkes noted that Turkish secularism was not a separation of church and state along the lines of Western Europe, but placing all of life, including religion, under the secular authority of the new state. *Id.* at 480–81.

[31] *Id.* at 10.

[32] *Id.* at 9–10.

[33] *Id.* at 14–16. "If the Turkish people were to be liberated from the restrictive and introspective Ottoman value system, if they were to be set free to turn their attention to the worldly problems of dominating the physical and natural environment, and if they were to think and act for themselves, for their own benefit, radical change in the psychological climate was imperative." Okyar, *supra* note 11, at 45, 51.

[34] BERKES, *supra* note 9, at 16; *see also* Eisenstadt, *supra* note 17, at 13.

[35] Okyar, *supra* note 11, at 48–51.

[36] *Id.* at 46–48; BERKES, *supra* note 9, at 450–60. The debate between reform and tradition had been, and remained, an intra-elite conflict. *See* Ilter Turan, *Continuity and Change in Turkish Bureaucracy: The Kemalist Period and After*, *in* ATATÜRK AND THE MODERNIZATION OF TURKEY 99, 102 (Jacob M. Landau ed., 1984).

a nationalist reaction.[37] While the plan was part of the larger, postwar dismantlement of the Ottoman Empire, the removal of these territories constituted an attack on the Turk homeland, giving rise to a Turkish opposition and the Turkish War of Independence.[38] This opposition transcended the differences between modernists and traditionalists and gave power to the nationalist movement.[39] The traditionalists who joined the nationalist independence effort hoped to reinstate the Ottoman system.[40] When the nationalists finally succeeded in independence, however, they were faced with the question of what Turkey would become, stoking the tensions between religion and reform once again.[41]

The actions of both the sultan and the Europeans aided Atatürk's European and secular vision of Turkey.[42] The sultan believed he had a better chance to remain in power if he allied himself with the Europeans.[43] He miscalculated; his actions outraged the relatively conservative National Assembly, setting the stage for the abolition of the sultanate.[44] The sultan, however, traditionally held a second title—caliph, the leader of the greater Islamic community.[45] This title remained after the abolition of the sultanate only to be quickly co-opted by those who sought to use the position as a power base.[46] Of the old system, the caliphate remained as a major potential hindrance to change. It too would fall, and its fall rooted in an ironic source. The title became linked with the fear of foreign intervention—a pressing concern for the Turks who were now under European occupation—when two Indian dignitaries requested the elevation of the caliphate due to its importance to all Muslim countries, including some who were at the time European colonies.[47] The overriding concern of future foreign intervention trumped the religious

---

It should be noted that it is difficult to measure the real effect of Atatürk's reforms on the masses. *See* Akural, *supra* note 27, at 128.

37 Berkes, *supra* note 9, at 432–33; Sİna Akşİn, Turkey from Empire to Revolutionary Republic: The Emergence of the Turkish Nation from 1789 to the Present 156–60 (2007) (discussing the Treaty of Sèvres).

38 Berkes, *supra* note 9, at 432–33; Akşİn, *supra* note 37, at 159–69. It has been suggested that the Turkish experience was not a real revolution. *See* Findley *supra* note 7, at 192–94 ("Scholars debate whether the Ottoman polity really experienced revolution in this period."); *see also* Eisenstadt, *supra* note 17, at 9–15 (comparing the Turkish experience with the English and Russian revolutions).

39 Berkes, *supra* note 9, at 433. The National Assembly in Ankara, founded by the nationalist movement in 1920 did not look initially to social change but had a surprisingly religious orientation. *Id.* at 436, 448. The pro-religion faction supported popular sovereignty as long as the people chose an authority based on religion. *Id.* at 455.

40 Turan, *supra* note 36, at 103.

41 *Id.* at 102 ("The ability of the nationalist leadership under Mustafa Kemal to create a political organization that could conduct a successful war of independence did not indicate, however, the presence of either intra-elite or elite-mass consensus of what was to be done after the war.").

42 Okyar, *supra* note 11, at 48–50; Berkes, *supra* note 9, at 449–50.

43 Berkes, *supra* note 9, at 433–34.

44 *Id.* at 449–50; Akşİn, *supra* note 37, at 179–81.

45 Berkes, *supra* note 9, at 9. The caliph was the religious complement to the temporal sultan. *Id.*

46 *Id.* at 450–56; Akşİn, *supra* note 37, at 179.

47 Berkes, *supra* note 9, at 458–59; Akşİn, *supra* note 37, at 191–92.

opposition and convinced the National Assembly that vestiges of the old system were dangerous to nationalism and Turkish sovereignty.[48] Like the sultanate, the caliphate was abolished.[49] This sequence of events, culminating in the removal of the final remnants of Ottoman rule, illustrates an important point: "[I]deas themselves are not sufficient to arouse a nationalist movement, even when they have been imported . . . ideas begin to mean something only when certain sociological conditions come into existence; even then, the imported ideas serve only as raw material for a nationalistic doctrine."[50]

Once modernization prevailed under the banner of nationalism, institutional transformation proceeded. In the government realm, all schools were placed under the jurisdiction of the Ministry of Education.[51] The Ministry of Religious Affairs and the Ministry of the General Staff were abolished and replaced with the Directorate of Religious Affairs, effectively limiting the influence of the clergy on government policy.[52] The religious courts were disbanded, and the government adopted a new civil code adapted from the Swiss model along with new commercial and penal codes.[53]

Beyond government, Atatürk sought to transform Turkey at a basic, societal level.[54] The Turkish people were to be marked as equals, not as a target for colonization.[55] The Hat Law, for example, required government officials to replace the *fez* with the headgear of the so-called civilized world, a hat with a brim.[56] The *fez*, ironically, had itself been imposed in the previous century.[57] Headgear had long been a marker of social identity in the Ottoman system; The hat traditionally signified a non-Muslim.[58] In addition to Western-style hats, officials had to wear Western-style suits.[59] The change in dress provided visible notice to the world of Turkey's modernization.[60] Another change came in the form of language reform, which began with the introduction of a new alphabet.[61] A Turkish alphabet, using Latin script, replaced the Arabic script traditionally used to

48 Berkes, *supra* note 9, at 457–60.

49 Akşİn, *supra* note 37, at 192.

50 Berkes, *supra* note 9, at 313.

51 Akşİn, *supra* note 37, at 192.

52 *Id.* at 193.

53 *Id.* at 194.

54 *See,* e.g., Mary Lou O'Neil, *You Are What You Wear: Clothing/Appearance Laws and the Construction of the Public Citizen in Turkey*, 14 Fashion Theory 65, 68 (2010).

55 Akşİn, *supra* note 37, at 202–03.

56 O'Neil, *supra* note 54, at 69.

57 Berkes, *supra* note 9, at 124–25. Under Mahmud II, the *fez* replaced the turban, the traditional headgear worn by the *ulema*, the learned of Islam. *Id.*

58 Akşİn, *supra* note 37, at 202–03.

59 O'Neil, *supra* note 54, at 69.

60 *Id.* at 69; *see also* Akşİn, *supra* note 37, at 203.

61 *See* G. L. Lewis, *Atatürk's Language Reform as an Aspect of Modernization in the Republic of Turkey, in* Atatürk and the Modernization of Turkey 195, 195 (Jacob M. Landau ed., 1984). The second part of language reform involved purifying the Turkish vocabulary. *See generally* Yilmaz Çolak, *Language Policy and Official Ideology in Early Republican Turkey*, 40 Middle E. Stud. 67 (2004).

write Turkish.[62] Atatürk insisted on a truncated transition period of three months, much shorter than the minimum of five years recommended by those who would create the new alphabet.[63] Classes in the new script were held for officials, professors, and even the public.[64] Use of the new official alphabet was mandated in government documents and schoolbooks.[65]

One scholar has suggested that the source of success lay in the nationalism of the period, noting that "the language served both as an instrument for propagating nationalism and also as a symbol of that nationalism."[66] Like the experience of Japan in the previous century, discussed below, becoming "modern" was equated with nationalism and the need to gain the respect of the Europeans so as to avoid future domination by them. It should be noted that, despite the apparent success of such changes, modern-day Turkey is not without tension between the traditional and the new.[67] Turkey remains, however, unique among its neighbors in the region due in large part to this program of cultural change.[68]

2. JAPAN

a. The Pre–World War II Cultural Change

Japan is an obvious example of a country that has successfully launched culture change campaigns, in the late 1800s and after World War II. When it realized it was militarily and economically inferior to Europe, it committed itself to change[69]—not just by adopting new legal codes but also by adopting an intensive and systematic culture change project.[70] As a popular Japanese song of the 1880s so aptly put it: "There is a Law of Nations,

---

[62] Lewis, *supra* note 61, at 197. Previous attempts at modifying the existing alphabet had been viewed as incompatible with Islam. *See generally* Frank Tachau, *Language and Politics: Turkish Language Reform*, 26 REV. POL. 191 (1964).

[63] Lewis, *supra* note 61, at 199.

[64] *Id.* at 200.

[65] *Id.* at 201.

[66] Tachau, *supra* note 62, at 204. From a practical standpoint, the younger generation would have less access to the classical Ottoman literature, as the ideas embodied within these works were written in the Arabic script. *Id.* at 195.

[67] *See, e.g.*, *On Their Heads Be It; Headscarves in Turkey*, ECONOMIST, Oct. 30, 2010, at 57, *available at* http://www.economist.com/node/17363686 (discussing the debate over the ban of the Islamic-style headscarf in certain settings including universities and state institutions).

[68] *See, e.g.*, *A Hard Act to Follow; The Turkish Model*, ECONOMIST, Aug. 6, 2011, at 20, http://www.economist.com/node/21525408.

[69] Social scientists have identified exogenous shocks as a major trigger of behavior change, while some economists have suggested that it could take a crisis to alter entrenched behavior and interests. *See* Katharina Pistor et al., *Social Norms, Rule of Law, and Gender Reality: An Essay on the Limits of the Dominant Rule of Law Paradigm*, *in* GLOBAL PERSPECTIVES ON THE RULE OF LAW 241, 272–73 (James J. Heckmann et al. eds., 2010).

[70] Unless otherwise stated, the discussion of Japan's Meiji Restoration is drawn from David Landes, *Culture Makes Almost All the Difference*, *in* CULTURE MATTERS 1, 7–10 (Lawrence E. Harrison & Samuel P. Huntington eds., 2000).

it is true, / but when the moment comes, remember, / the Strong eat up the Weak."[71] During the period known as the Meiji Restoration of 1860, the Japanese saw that they were not equal to "the more progressive powers of the world"[72] and decided to modernize by bringing foreign experts to Japan and sending Japanese agents abroad to study European ways. In broad terms, the Meiji Restoration was a "revolution from above" to modernize, to "learn[] the ways of the West in order to reform virtually every aspect of national life,"[73] and through this reformation, defend the country from Western threat.[74] Again, as with Turkey, the reforms described here would not be reconcilable with Sen's framework, reflecting instead an instrumentalist conception of top-down change, albeit directed internally by the emperor.

The main impetus driving the country toward modernization was fear. Japan saw what was happening to neighboring China and feared that Japan too would be victimized by European aggrandizement. For two hundred years Japan only had extremely limited exposure to the West through the Dutch traders at Nagasaki.[75] A Russian envoy had attempted to secure a trade agreement through forceful negotiations in 1791, but was denied.[76] The shogunate regarded the Russians, and indeed all foreigners, with distrust, fearing both military aggression as well as proselytizing of the kind that led foreigners too close to Japanese borders in 1640.[77] Then in 1853, the United States sent Commodore Perry to Japan to signal American interest in trade with Japan with an added warning, personally from Perry, that Japanese failure to respond positively to American interest would provoke a different response from America.[78] Western powers pressured Japan to open its ports,[79] and treaties with unequal terms were concluded despite Japanese reluctance.[80] The Japanese found certain treaty provisions especially humiliating. For example, there were stipulations that Western residents in Japan be subjected to the laws of their own countries, administered in consular courts, rather than Japanese law or Japanese courts. The assumption was that Japanese law was backward and unenlightened.

The Japanese moved swiftly to develop a modern legal system, one that would be viewed by the powerful Western nations as developed enough to qualify as "law." "Japanese rulers

---

[71] JOHN W. DOWER, EMBRACING DEFEAT: JAPAN IN THE WAKE OF WORLD WAR II 21 (1999).

[72] Sidney D. Brown, *Ōkubo Toshimichi: His Political and Economic Policies in Early Meiji Japan*, 21 J. ASIAN STUD. 183, 190 (1962) (discussing the perceptions of Okubo Toshimichi upon his visit to Western countries such as England).

[73] Bill Ong Hing, *Nonelectoral Activism in Asian Pacific American Communities and the Implications for Community Lawyering*, 8 UCLA ASIAN PAC. AM. L.J. 246, 248 n.16 (2002).

[74] Tom Ginsburg, *Dismantling the "Developmental State"? Administrative Procedure in Japan and Korea*, 49 AM. J. COMP. L. 585, 588 (2001).

[75] Grant Goodman, *"Dutch Learning," in* 2 WM. THEODORE DE BARY ET AL., SOURCES OF JAPANESE TRADITION 1600 TO 2000, at 361, 361–62 (2d ed. 2005).

[76] George Alexander Lensen, *Early Russo-Japanese Relations*, 10 FAR E. Q. 3, 17–29 (1950).

[77] *Id.* at 22–24, 28; Goodman, *supra* note 75, at 361–62; CHITOSHI YANAGA, JAPAN SINCE PERRY 6–8 (1949).

[78] HUGH CORTAZZI, THE JAPANESE ACHIEVEMENT 176 (1990).

[79] *Id.*

[80] HIROSHI ODA, JAPANESE LAW 26 (2d ed. 1999).

considered it necessary to modernize the legal system in order to convince foreign countries that there was no problem in acknowledging Japanese jurisdiction over foreigners in Japan."[81] The Japanese government implemented what we would now consider the standard law and development menu. Reformers wrote new codes and invited overseas experts to provide legal advice.[82] Judges were trained in English and French law and before the enactment and entry into force of newly written Japanese codes, used English and French law in their judicial rulings.[83] The Five Charter Oath of 1868 set forth guiding principles to be followed by the Meiji emperor, and the modernizing state committed to a more democratic participation in government. A new council of state and legislative bodies, a new taxation system, and new administrative rules were established.[84]

In December 1871, Japan sent a diplomatic team to the United States and Europe to acquire an understanding of Western learning for the express purpose of modernizing Japan.[85] In constructing a new legal system, the Japanese were heavily drawn to the French civil law system and translated the French civil code into Japanese.[86] A French legal expert, Emile Gustave Boissanade de Fontarabie, was brought to Japan to draft both the Civil Code and Japan's first Criminal Code and Code of Criminal Procedure.[87] Japan gradually shifted toward German law in the 1800s as a way of reconciling the Meiji imperial government model with Western liberalism, though French influence remained strong.[88] A German adviser, Professor Herman Roessler, drafted the Code of Civil Procedure in the early 1880s.[89]

In 1876, the Department of Justice opened a law school with specialized courses on commercial law and the French civil law tradition taught in French or English by instructors from France, Britain, and the United States.[90] That same year Tokyo University College of Law was founded and instruction was initially centered on Anglo American

---

[81] *Id.* (explaining why the Japanese rejected the Chinese model) ("Chinese codes proved to be obsolete and unsuitable for a nation aspiring to achieve equal status with European countries in its economical and military strength. It was only natural that political leaders turned to Europe for a better model.").

[82] These include Georges Bousquet at the Paris Court of Appeal and Gustave Boissonade, a professor at the Faculty of Law in Paris, and German constitutional expert Hermann Roesler. Boissonade stayed in Japan for twenty years and worked on the penal and criminal procedure codes. Yosiyuki Noda, Introduction to Japanese Law 44–53 (Anthony H. Angelo ed., trans., 1976).

[83] Noda, *supra* note 82, at 52–53; *see also* Constance Hamilton & Michael Young, *Historical Introduction to the Japanese Legal System*, *in* Japanese Law in Context Readings in Society, the Economy, and Politics 2, 2–10 (Curtis J. Milhaupt et al. eds., 2001).

[84] Yanaga, *supra* note 77, at 48; *see also* Cortazzi, *supra* note 78, at 185–86. *See generally* Marius B. Jansen, The Making of Modern Japan (2000); Donald Keene, Emperor of Japan: Meiji and His World 1852–1912, at 137, 148 (2002).

[85] Cortazzi, *supra* note 78, at 187.

[86] Hideo Tanaka, The Japanese Legal System 163 (Hideo Tanaka ed., 1976).

[87] *Id.; see also* Oda, *supra* note 80, at 27.

[88] Oda, *supra* note 80, at 27; Irokawa Daikichi, The Culture of the Meiji Period 57 (Marius B. Jansen ed., trans., 1985).

[89] Oda, *supra* note 80, at 24.

[90] Tanaka, *supra* note 86, at 178–79.

private law with courses in contracts and torts.[91] In 1886, the Imperial University of Tokyo was formed and instruction focused on English, French, and German law.[92]

Yet, it is also clear that Japanese efforts at modernization went far beyond the standard law and development prescriptions. The Charter Oath, for example, described as "a constitution for all ages,"[93] did not call for only the establishment of assemblies or the adoption of institutional attributes deemed necessary for modernization. Article 4 of the Oath promised eradication of "absurd customs and practices of the past" and adherence to just "laws of heaven and earth."[94] Article 5 declared "wisdom and knowledge shall be sought all over the world in order to establish firmly the foundation of the Empire."[95] The Charter Oath, in other words, enunciated the basic principles of the Meiji regime, which firmly grasped the need to modernize not just through the establishment of laws and institutions but also the inculcation of values.

The Charter Oath's call, in Article 4, to change customs of the past seems unconventional from a Western perspective. Yet, it is quite familiar to the Japanese. It is true that the great push to modernize was precipitated by confrontation with the West in the late 1800s. It is also true that changing culture was elevated into one of the five principles that would govern the Meiji-era modernization effort to accelerate growth and development. But throughout its history, Japan had undertaken to reshape the mores of the people through a variety of cultural projects.[96] These projects were essentially social management projects in which the Japanese state exhorted private groups throughout society to participate in various ambitious programs to achieve certain stated objectives. The process involved continuous interaction and cooperation between Japanese private groups and an interventionist Japanese state to formulate and implement programs to manage society.[97] As I demonstrate below, throughout its history, the Japanese state did not strive merely for passive support from the people. Instead, the government mobilized people from all areas of Japanese life to participate in a direct and interactive manner in programs that had changing the nation's habits as their stated objective. Interestingly, while the British and the American governments have both resorted to their people's sense of patriotic duty to promote austerity drives, British and American mobilizations were undertaken during wartime.[98] The Japanese, by contrast, have for the most part viewed peacetime mobilization to alleviate poverty as part of an ongoing moral suasion endeavor, combining the standard institutional structures of law and development with

---

[91] YANAGA, *supra* note 77, at 78.

[92] *Id.* at 78.

[93] KEENE, *supra* note 84, at 340.

[94] YANAGA, *supra* note 77, at 48.

[95] *Id.* at 48.

[96] SHELDON GARON, MOLDING JAPANESE MINDS 6 (1997).

[97] *Id.*

[98] *Id.* at 13.

a norm change component reflecting "an ongoing, managerial process of persuading or teaching the masses to internalize appropriate values."[99]

For example, even as early as the Tokugawa period or early modern era, from the 1600s to the mid-1800s, authorities of the shogunate put into place structures to address poverty but also implemented long-term programs based on "kyoka," or "moral suasion," to exhort peasants and the poor to "work hard, pay their taxes, and avoid luxury."[100] It is critical to understand that moral suasion supplemented institutions and structures. During this period Japanese officials responded to poverty by putting into place a relief system to assist the poor—the poor should be helped first by relatives, then the village as a whole, and as a last resort, by the state following investigation by a magistrate.[101] State involvement as a last resort, however, was quite comprehensive. "[C]ommunal relief mechanisms were introduced and closely supervised by the authorities."[102] Communal institutions such as the popular village-level emergency granaries were maintained mostly through regular peasant contribution of their harvests; poor houses, relief shelters, workhouses, and job-placement shelters were constructed to assist the poor.[103] In the 1790s, a shogunal chief councilor created an endowment financed by shogunal donation and special levies to create a reserve fund administered by a newly created office to provide assistance, whether it be temporary assistance for disaster victims or ongoing assistance for those in need but devoid of relatives to aid them.[104]

In pursuit of the dual strategy of combining communal relief structures with moral suasion, reformers were dispatched to the countryside to introduce new methods to improve productivity and to teach Confucian values of filial piety and diligence.[105] State bureaucracies were created to run moral suasion campaigns and to work with local moral suasion groups to convince the populace that diligence meant self-management to restrain innate "indolence and selfishness." Moral suasion during the Tokugawa period

[99] *Id.* at 7.

[100] *Id.*

[101] *Id.* at 29; IKEDA YOSHIMASA, NIHON SHAKAI FUKUSHISHI 95 (1986). Scholars and the ruling elite cultivated a renewed interest in Confucian philosophy during the Tokugawa period and this likely had a substantial influence on social welfare theories. Confucian concepts of benevolence and ruling with virtue, in particular, along with a concern for systematization to avoid arbitrariness and to ensure only the truly needy received state help, likely led to this formulation of poor relief. *See* Willem Boot, *Confucianism in the Early Tokugawa Period*, *in* 2 WM. THEODORE DE BARY ET AL., Sources of Japanese Tradition 1600 to 2000, at 29, 29–32 (2d ed. 2005) (discussing Confucian philosophy and the influence of Confucian thought during the Edo period); *see also* Kurozumi Makoto, *The Nature of Early Tokugawa Confucianism*, 20 J. JAPANESE STUD. 337, 337 (Herman Ooms trans., 1994).

[102] GARON, *supra* note 96, at 29.

[103] *Id.* at 30; YOSHIMASA, *supra* note 101, at 102–03; JAMES L. MCCLAIN, KANAZAWA: A SEVENTEENTH-CENTURY JAPANESE CASTLE TOWN 127–29 (1982).

[104] GARON, *supra* note 96, at 30; YOSHIMASA, *supra* note 101, at 124–27.

[105] GARON, *supra* note 96, at 31.

focused on inculcating self-reliance, though by "self" reformers meant not only the individual but the entire community through mutual assistance.

This idea that poverty could be effectively addressed by adopting the right institutions and mechanisms as well as by joint enterprises "to reform the morals of the poor"[106] continued into the post-Tokugawa era. Two important points should be stressed at this juncture. First, post-Tokugawa Japan created an emperor-centered system that was both interventionist and centralized to fill in the political void that followed the collapse of the Tokugawa system in 1868.[107] Second, the government's focus on poverty alleviation was undertaken as part of a broad effort to advance the nation's developmental interest, rather than as an effort to provide charity or to help the poor. In this respect, studying these efforts makes sense from a law and development perspective.

The Meiji government framed its poverty relief drives as part of the struggle to develop economically, advance the nation, and catch up with the West. But to do this the government had to create a strong sense of nationhood. It adopted measures to create a sense of national cohesiveness and authority, which had been virtually nonexistent during the quarter millennium of Tokugawa rule; examples of these efforts include establishing a national postal service, public education for boys and girls, universal military service, and so forth. The government took such measures to create a new imperial state and to "imbue its subjects with a sense of higher duty to the emperor and country and to link this patriotism to work."[108] Again, note that these measures were aimed not only at transforming political or economic institutions but also included a significant cultural component. Fundamental government, social, and in particular, educational reform was essential to many of the leaders in the "Civilization and Enlightenment" movement.[109] Takayoshi Kido, a leading bureaucrat of the Meiji government and a member of the 1871 mission to Europe and the United States, stressed the importance of educating the masses. After touring several public schools in San Francisco he wrote, "[i]t is not enough to have a few able men make good; nothing is more important than schools."[110] Kido was one of the drafters of the Charter Oath and reportedly insisted on Article 4. He saw schools as the way to erase the "evil customs of the past" and remake Japan into a modern Westernized nation, stating:

> [n]othing is more important than schools for improving social conditions and uprooting social evils . . . A long-range program for the stability of our country

---

[106] *Id.* at 32.

[107] Under the Tokugawa shogunate, Japan was divided into two hundred and fifty semi-autonomous domains controlled by territorial barons. The demise of the shogunate in 1868 meant centralized authority had to be located and deposited elsewhere—into a more emperor-centered system. In 1871, the domains were abolished and replaced with prefectures administered by governors appointed by the central government. *Id.*

[108] Landes, *supra* note 70, at 10.

[109] Fred G. Notehelfer, *The Meiji Restoration*, *in* 2 Wm. Theodore de Bary et al., Sources of Japanese Tradition 1600 to 2000, at 669, 678 (2d ed. 2005).

[110] Daikichi, *supra* note 88, at 54.

> will never be carried out if we have only a small number of able people; we have to have universal adherence to the moral principles of loyalty, justice, humanity, and decorum.[111]

Japanese schools instilled in students notions of discipline, order, and responsibility and devoted themselves to the teaching of ethics. In an effort to transcend parochial loyalties that characterized the period prior to the Meiji restoration, schools displayed pictures of the emperor to promote national unity; on national holidays, throughout the country and at the same time, the same ritual was performed in front of the emperor's picture.[112]

Thus, in its efforts to catch up with the West, the Japanese government

> energetically disseminated an "emperor-system ideology" to the public, inculcating patriotism, loyalty to the emperor, and the virtues of diligence and thrift. The state did so by utilizing a highly centralized set of institutions: the national school system, the military, a network of State Shinto shrines, and numerous hierarchically organized associations[113]

while at the same time channeling the "Japanese people into active participants in the state's various projects."[114] Indeed, as some have put it, "[t]he cultural values underlying Japan's successful strategy in catching up with the West were nurtured and manipulated by the elites in the interest of the developmental state."[115] The government took the lead in furthering certain values but also adopted an inclusionary approach vis-à-vis the citizens.

With the emperor-centered system in place, the state took on the task of inculcating patriotism and loyalty to the emperor, and the virtues of diligence and thrift were deemed crucial to the modernization and development tasks. It is important to understand that this was not a social work campaign but rather, as I argue, a campaign more akin in spirit to that undertaken by law and development. To achieve these objectives, the government took on the task of changing its people's customs. "Civil servants worked closely with 'customs reform' groups to eliminate wasteful consumption in drinking, weddings, and funerals" and to promote savings.[116]

This approach represented a conscious choice on the part of some of the most prominent intellectual and political leaders of the Meiji, who themselves recognized the need to revolutionize not only the institutions of government but the fundamental cultural practices of the wider public as well. Yukichi Fukuzawa, for example, was a leading scholar of

---

[111] Notehelfer, *supra* note 109.

[112] David Landes, The Wealth and Poverty of Nations 376 (1998).

[113] Garon, *supra* note 96, at 5.

[114] *Id.* at 6.

[115] Charlotte G. O'Kelly, Book Review, 547 Annals Am. Acad. Pol. & Soc. Sci. 176, 177 (1996).

[116] Garon, *supra* note 96, at 9–10.

"Western studies," a prolific writer, and influential thinker of his day. He traveled extensively in Europe and the United States, and was a major proponent of Westernization, but Fukuzawa criticized a top-down-only approach as insufficient to bring about the successful modernization of Japan as a whole.[117] Writing in the mid-1870s, his assessment of the early Meiji effort echoes the woes of law and development projects today.

> The present Meiji government thinks that it is not being entirely successful because the various head officials are not able men; even with a great deal of shuffling of offices and functions the results always end up the same. Because of the dearth of personnel, foreigners are being employed as teachers or advisers, but the affairs of government still show no improvement. It would seem from the lack of improvement that the officials are all incompetent, and the foreigners hired as teachers and advisers are all fools. Yet the present government officials are among the most talented men in the country, and the foreigners selected are no fools . . . Government heads are not unaware of the failure of their policies, but what can they do about it? . . . The reason the government cannot handle its affairs is not some fault of a handful of officials, but this public opinion. When the mass of society is in error, one should not put the blame on the policies of officials . . . The most urgent national task is to rectify the ills of public opinion.[118]

In response, a newly created Meiji-era Home Ministry launched coordinated campaigns reminiscent of those from the Tokugawa period "to improve the general morals of the poor and develop their industry while establishing programs to encourage their diligence, thrift, and vigorous efforts."[119] Home Ministry officials considered themselves "shepherds of the people"[120] who saw reform of the poor's habits and poverty alleviation as a necessary component of state fiscal responsibility. Such relief work was not viewed as social work to assist individuals needing help but rather as part of an overall reformatory campaign to guide them to become "a self-reliant people who worked selflessly on national

---

[117] *The Debate over Seclusion and Restoration*, *in* 2 Wm. Theodore de Bary et al., Sources of Japanese Tradition 1600 to 2000, at 616, 657–58 (2d ed. 2005).

[118] Albert Craig, *Civilization and Enlightenment*, *in* 2 Wm. Theodore de Bary et al., Sources of Japanese Tradition 1600 to 2000, at 694, 704 (2d ed. 2005). For Fukuzawa, this assessment was based at least in part on his definition of "civilization" itself. In other passages, he downplayed the importance of elites in evaluating the developmental level of a given nation, and stated that instead, the "knowledge and virtue" of the wider public define the level of development. *Id.* at 703–05. Fukuzawa's understanding of the need to reform "public opinion" was also based on his own bewilderment at European customs during his travels abroad. In traveling, he focused his energy on learning culture rather than technology, because it was "most difficult to comprehend" and difficult to find in books, whereas technology had been extensively published. In particular he described difficulty understanding English political parties and the idea of "fighting" over political ideology and yet remaining friends and sitting down to dinner together. *Id.* at 659–60.

[119] Garon, *supra* note 96, at 43.

[120] *Id.* at 16.

prosperity while making few demands on the state."[121] In other words, the Meiji government saw poverty relief as an important component in the quest for national development and secured the participation of many sectors of what would now be considered civil society, including transnational NGOs. Beginning in 1908, under the auspices of the Home Ministry, a series of twenty-eight seminars brought together a wide array of local leaders—charity workers, civil servants, teachers, religious people—who were taught methods of moral suasion to counter socialist thought and dependency on government relief and strengthen family bonds.[122] Even though many Japanese saw Christians as foreign agents,[123] the government joined forces with "Western-educated Protestant social reformers . . . to teach the poor the virtues of hard work, savings, and self-help"—all with the aim "to improve the diet, hygiene, work habits, housing, consumption patterns, and ritual life of the Japanese people."[124]

Besides exhorting people to be diligent or pious or moral, reformers also focused on getting the poor to take certain concrete actions. At the local level, under the district commissioner system, local "people of virtue" were selected as unpaid commissioners, each of whom was responsible for two hundred households in his or her neighborhood. District commissioners gathered detailed information about poor households and their living conditions and acted as intermediaries between social services and the poor, counseling the poor on better hygiene and savings habits.[125] Those deputized as district commissioners tended to be drawn from the middle class—for example, teachers, priests, store owners—and had great incentive to work with the poor to improve living conditions in their surrounding neighborhoods.[126] Again and again, various bureaucracies, in conjunction with local groups, ran moral suasion campaigns, many of which aimed to instill changes in customary habits and through such changes and encourage the formation of capital and productive investment. The Local Improvement Campaign, launched from 1906 to 1918, persuaded villages and small towns not just to pay taxes but also to practice frugality and avoid indulgence.[127]

Through central coordination and widespread local participation of the sort that Sen would approve as inclusive, the government succeeded in inundating the country with well-honed messages about the nation's needs for frugality and savings. It used all available methods—motion pictures, handbills distributed to households, posters on public building exhorting savings and frugality—to supplement nationalistic appeals and moral suasion, promote "middle-class commitments to the modernization of popular beliefs,

---

[121] *Id.* at 45.

[122] *Id.* at 47.

[123] *Id.*

[124] *Id.* at 20; *see also* Sheldon Garon, *Rethinking Modernization and Modernity in Japanese History: A Focus on State-Society Relations*, 53 J. Asian Stud. 346, 351–52, 355 (1994).

[125] Garon, *supra* note 96, at 52.

[126] *Id.* at 54.

[127] *Id.* at 9.

daily habits, and gender relations,"[128] and "eliminate the 'evil customs of the past.' "[129] The daily life improvement campaigns publicized economic revitalization of villages through the use of visual montage. In the 1930s, widely posted photographs captured how villages worked to improve habits and reduce waste. For example, in a montage captioned "The Latest in Daily Life Improvement," photographs showed: a bride wearing an inexpensive cotton kimono; a communal clock exhorting "attention to, and respect for time"; a cooperative lending out funeral accoutrements to help reduce the costs of funerals; and a model village whose members have given up alcohol.[130] The intensity with which the campaign was conducted is evidenced by the fact that in only two months in a rural prefecture, the Moral Suasion Mobilization Campaign held more than three hundred public lectures and exhibitions and two hundred sixty meetings of local groups.[131]

Again and again in the 1920s and 1930s, daily life improvement campaigns were established under various names and under the guidance of various ministries, although it would be fair to say that most programs were under the administrative jurisdiction of the Home Ministry and the Ministry of Education. There was the Home Ministry's Campaign to Foster National Strength, an organization that urged urban consumers to return to the "beautiful customs of diligence and thrift."[132] The Ministry of Education began the first of a successive series of "daily life improvement campaigns" to introduce methods of "scientific budgeting, better nutrition and hygiene, and avoiding wasteful spending on festivals, alcohol, and tobacco."[133] Home Ministry officials actively promoted modern science and argued against "superstition and absolute nonsense."[134] Drawing from Tokugawa-era's attempts to eliminate rituals such as incantations and divination, the Meiji regime passed several ordinances against using spells and spiritual healing as medical treatment[135] and championed measures against "evil cults." In 1924, the Home Ministry formed a national Federation of Moral Suasion Groups, and by 1925, there were seven or eight hundred moral suasion groups with tens of thousands of members.[136] The Home Ministry reformed norms and habits of the poor by cultivating "in peasants and the urban poor the spirit of 'self management' . . . a commitment to diligence, thrift, and other good habits so that individuals and families would avoid relying on public assistance."[137]

---

128 *Id.* at 19.

129 *Id.* at 20; *see also* Notehelfer, *supra* note 109, at 678.

130 Garon, *supra* note 96, at 12.

131 *Id.* at 13.

132 *Id.* at 11; *see also* Kuni Nakajima, *Taishōki ni okeru "Seikatsu Kaizen Undō,"* 15 Shisō 54, 58 (1974).

133 Garon, *supra* note 96, at 11; *see also* Nakajima, *supra* note 132, at 54.

134 Garon, *supra* note 96, at 81.

135 *Id.*

136 *Id.* at 11. According to the Ministry of Education, in 1925, there were seven or eight hundred moral suasion groups. In Osaka alone, there are five thousand moral suasion commissions.

137 *Id.* at 7, 16.

To ensure spirited participation from the local district and village level, the Home Ministry would send inquiries to district chiefs and would receive reports containing detailed village-by-village information on time devoted to funerals and weddings, and in the latter case, the numbers of attendees, the ceremony type, and the food served.[138] Interestingly, whether Japanese cultural reformers were aware of it or not, such efforts to encourage frugality and promote savings are wholly in accord with the traditional aims of development economics, which identifies the elimination of wasteful spending as a necessary step toward capital formation, accumulation, and investment.[139] Given the traditional tendency in many societies to spend surplus capital on "tombs, country houses, temples," and other economically unproductive activities,[140] a key issue in development is to "tempt capital into productive channels rather than into the building of monuments,"[141] or on funerals, weddings, and other lavish ceremonies.

As the discussion above shows, the government reached out to a wide spectrum of civil society groups, for example, community leaders, youth groups, religious organizations, and other civic associations. Although various organizations or ministries within the state apparatus coordinated much of the efforts, it is also important to note that many of the activities and programs resulted from demands by nongovernmental groups which used the state's mobilization networks to further their own agenda. In those cases, the aspirations and objectives of the nongovernmental groups coincided with the state's, and the level of cooperation was very much two-way rather than top-down. This is especially evident in the case of women's groups who worked relentlessly to involve the state in managing gender relations. In this way, Japanese reforms aimed at culture change are reminiscent of norm change efforts undertaken by transnational advocacy networks described in Chapter 4. As I show below, the increased participation of Japanese women in public life, the state's response to such increased participation, and the resulting cultural transformation such participation engendered produced an interesting triangular relationship involving gender, state, and culture.

To be sure, Japanese women faced a difficult battle in their struggle for equality—the Civil Code of 1898, for example, granted men status as head of household and "reduced women, upon marriage, to legal incompetents."[142] Article 5 of the Public Order and Police Law of 1900 barred "women and minors" from attending political meetings or joining political groups.[143] In the private sphere, however, the Meiji government saw the need for the education of women and modernization of domestic practices. Meiji leaders

---

[138] *Id.* at 12–13.

[139] W. Arthur Lewis, *Economic Development with Unlimited Supplies of Labour*, *in* Paradigms in Economic Development: Classic Perspectives, Critiques, and Reflections 59, 66, 75 (Rajani Kanth ed., 1994).

[140] *Id.* at 73.

[141] *Id.*

[142] Garon, *supra* note 96, at 115.

[143] *Id.* at 119.

had feared "that women might be resistant to the new influences, infectious carriers of Japan's backwardness."[144] The 1871 mission to Western nations included five girls aged eight to sixteen for the purpose, among others, of studying abroad in America.[145]

Although women's groups such as the Japanese Women's Christian Temperance Union vehemently protested women's subordination, it was not until women's participation was needed for wartime mobilization purposes that discussions about the role of women in society rose to the forefront. At the onset of World War I, the government needed women's participation in the modernizing state but also feared activities by women that would take them outside their traditional roles as wives and mothers.[146] Women's participation in the public spheres of life increased during the Russo-Japanese War when the Patriotic Women's Association was founded to help wounded soldiers and their families. This arrangement formed the basis for an alliance between the women's group and the state and allowed the former to use it as a foundation for subsequently pressing for greater integration of women into public life.

Interestingly, women's contribution to the wartime effort did not escape the state's notice. Local and central leaders saw the value of women's service, and Home Ministry officials began to mobilize women for their savings and frugality campaigns.[147] Women's organizations proliferated at the end of World War I. Education for girls and women expanded significantly. In 1921, Article 5 of the Police Law prohibiting women's participation in politics was revised with little opposition.[148] Support for the political inclusion of women grew when the issue was linked to and equated with national development. Again, the mantra of catching up with the West was invoked, as Japanese supporters of women's political mobilization spoke of Western government's political inclusion of women and the need for Japan to do the same.[149] Women activists played up the need for women to be part of the public sphere and enthusiastically cooperated with the state in its social management programs to influence the discourse on gender. Women's groups, as well as the state, proclaimed that women's advancement would further national advancement

---

[144] Sharon H. Nolte, Liberalism in Modern Japan: Ishibashi Tanzan and His Teachers, 1905–1960, at 91 (1987).

[145] Yōichi Chino, Kindai Nihon Fujin Kyōikushi: Taiseinai Fujin Dantai no Keisei Katei o Chūshin ni 13 (1979).

[146] Garon, *supra* note 96, at 121.

[147] *Id.* at 122.

[148] *Id.* at 123.

[149] *Id.* at 125 (quoting a member of the Lower House who asserted that "today's woman must be liberated from her submissive position within the household and be encouraged to contribute socially, politically, and to the State."); *id.* at 126 (describing how the Japanese government surveyed European and North American experience and "highlighted the indispensable assistance of women's groups" during World War I); *id.* at 129 (describing increasing awareness among Japanese politicians of the status of women in the West and hence of the need to ensure that Japan "does not lag behind the trends of the world." Women's associations thus were interested in "promot[ing] awareness and activity among women for the family . . . but also for the State and society."); *id.* at 131 ("European women today [1917] fight the enemy indirectly as noncombatants.").

as it would "double our national strength."[150] Women's groups had different agendas depending on their political inclinations, but many "placed moral reform, educational work, philanthropy, and the dissemination of child-rearing techniques ahead of the quest for equal rights during the nineteenth and early twentieth centuries."[151]

The relationship between women and the state changed significantly in the interwar years. Interwar Japanese governments mounted vigorous national campaigns of moral suasion and saw women as crucial to the success of the campaigns.[152] Women's groups, in turn, saw these campaigns as providing the necessary opening to advance women's interests. Many understood that from a tactical standpoint, their causes would be most furthered by pursuing them in domains traditionally considered female, such as management of the household.[153] To this extent, the objectives of women's groups coincided with those of the state, and both embarked upon a series of collaborative actions. For example, throughout the 1920s and 1930s, the Home Ministry's Campaign to Foster National Strength, which was aimed at "boosting household savings rates, warding off socialist and democratic thought, and encouraging 'public-spiritedness' and 'the spirit of sacrifice,' "[154] identified women as a group to be mobilized. Faced with a postwar recession and high prices, the government worked to encourage savings but realized that a savings campaign's success depended greatly on the cooperation and energies of women who, due to societal changes, were increasingly in charge of household management and finances. Some women's groups considered the very fact of state mobilization as a progressive force if for no other reason than the fact that women worked outside of the household structure.[155] Officials of the Home Ministry and the Ministry of Education jointly adopted programs that relied on women as the "state's prime agents in improving 'daily life' " and disseminating "social education."[156] In concrete terms, this meant working to improve diet, hygiene, work habits, and ritual life.

Again and again, the state and women's groups denounced the tradition of committing family resources to rituals such as weddings and funerals. This effort is reminiscent of that undertaken during the Tokugawa era. The twentieth-century drives were couched in the language of modernization, and accordingly, campaigns were organized in ways that would synchronize their objectives with those of the Meiji-era Charter Oath. In language that paralleled that used in Article 4 of the Charter Oath, "the Ministry of Education called on women to 'sweep away the evil customs' of the past."[157] Ministry

---

150 *Id.* at 131. The government saw the issue in terms of advancing the national interests, not advancing women's rights.

151 *Id.* at 132; *see also* NOLTE, *supra* note 144, at 123–28.

152 *Id.* at 91.

153 GARON, *supra* note 96, at 142.

154 *Id.* at 126; *see also* Nakajima, *supra* note 132, at 57–58.

155 GARON, *supra* note 96, at 142.

156 *Id.* at 129; *see also* Nakajima, *supra* note 132, at 54.

157 GARON, *supra* note 96, at 129. Article Four of the Charter Oath called for the elimination of the "evil customs of the past." *Id.; see also id.* at 133 (describing how the organizers of the Federation of Women's Associations

officials and teachers gave lectures to women "on the need to practice 'scientific diligence and thrift,' 'rational consumption' of inexpensive and healthy foods and 'rational, budgeted living and savings.'"[158] Because women's groups, with few exceptions,[159] focused less on individual rights of women than on moral reform, they favored "modernizing the mores and habits of ordinary women."[160] A distinctly modernizing agenda was embraced. Women's groups sought the state's involvement in introducing "'scientific' methods of child rearing to rural and lower-class women."[161] Women activists initiated a drive for improvements in daily life, encouraging women to manage household account books and arguing in the process that exercising jurisdiction over household management was a sign of equality. Indeed, in spearheading the drives to improve daily life, women's groups did not follow the government but, more often than not, led the way and inspired the state's subsequent embrace of such campaigns. The Japanese experience is an illustration of how the interaction between civil society and the state can lead to "mutual transformation of participants," as described by Keck and Sikkink.[162]

Indeed, throughout the 1920s, it became clear that women's groups and the state worked in tandem to further their respective objectives especially when there was overlap. In the late 1920s the government specifically sought out the support of women's groups for its economic program. When the government decided that Japan would return to the gold standard and to peg the yen at its prewar value, it promoted a deflationary campaign, which meant encouraging citizens to exercise "restraint in consumption" and public spending.[163] Cabinet ministers sought out women to help bring "thrift in the kitchen of every home," and the intensity with which the government sought the help of women caused one leading women's activist to observe that "never before has a government or cabinet so clearly appealed to women or attempted to borrow their power."[164]

From a women's rights standpoint, women's participation to further the national interest in ways promoted by the state did not directly result in the advancement of women's rights per se.[165] From a law and development standpoint, however, state action in mobilizing

of Western Japan pledged to "devote our energies to eliminating evil customs that are not in accord with the times and to reconstruct daily life."), Nakajima, *supra* note 132, at 55.

158 Garon, *supra* note 96, at 129; *see also* Nakajima, *supra* note 132, at 65–68.

159 Some liberal feminists distrusted the government's statist agenda and favored increased liberties and rights for women as something to be promoted separately from the state's agenda of national advancement. Garon, *supra* note 96, at 131–32.

160 *Id.* at 132.

161 *Id.* at 20.

162 Margaret E. Keck & Kathryn Sikkink, *Transnational Advocacy Networks in International and Regional Politics*, 159 Int'l Soc. Sci. J. 89, 92 (1999), *available at* http://isites.harvard.edu/fs/docs/icb.topic446176.files/Week_7/Keck_and_Sikkink_Transnational_Advocacy.pdf.

163 Garon, *supra* note 96, at 136.

164 *Id.* at 136.

165 For example, ministry officials remained against granting full civic rights to women even at the municipal level because they thought such rights were "premature." *Id.* at 137. The government's civic rights bill in 1931, for example, contained a provision that required a victorious female candidate to obtain her husband's

women was markedly significant. The Japanese government, whether from the Tokugawa or Meiji era, understood that addressing women's issues and involving women were necessary for the success of their ambitious modernization campaign. The government also understood that modernization required transforming traditions. For example, inducing savings involved getting people to stop spending on economically useless activities even if these activities, weddings and funerals, for example, were age-old, traditional rituals.

It is interesting to note that many of the campaigns had a distinct law and development flavor, although scholars of law and development have not viewed the efforts in this light. Few law and development scholars have come to grips with Japan's success in marshaling the resources of diverse groups to foster certain cultural norms and practices for the purpose of economic advancement and cultural modernization. And few Japan scholars have understood these efforts in terms of law and development. Yet, these reform efforts encapsulate many of the relevant issues for law and development scholars and practitioners today.

At the heart of the debate is the role of capital in economic development. There are many intellectual strands within the field of economic development,[166] and proponents of each have wrestled with many questions; for example, promoting structural change[167] or minimizing constraints[168] faced by poor countries in order to spur economic growth

---

consent before she could hold office. Nonetheless, it would be fair to note that women's groups succeeded in using their collaboration with the state to fashion more authoritative roles for women within the household and within the public sphere. *Id.*

[166] One intellectual strand of economic development posits that different countries typically go through historically similar stages of economic development. To put it simply, one implication of this view is that developing countries are at an early stage of development while developed countries are at a later stage. *See generally* ALEXANDER GERSCHENKRON, ECONOMIC BACKWARDNESS IN HISTORICAL PERSPECTIVE (1962) (propounding the "linear stages" theory of economic development but at the same time acknowledging that countries such as Meiji Japan and Soviet Russia might skip several stages); WALT W. ROSTOW, THE STAGES OF ECONOMIC GROWTH: A NON-COMMUNIST MANIFESTO (1960) (positing that from an economic standpoint, all societies fall within one of five categories: the traditional society, the preconditions for takeoff, the takeoff, the drive to maturity, and the age of high mass-consumption).

[167] Some development economists subscribe to the view that the appropriate structural changes for developing countries include transforming the more backward subsistence agricultural sector and encouraging the growth of a modern, industrial economy. *See* Lewis, *supra* note 139, at 68–72. Lewis's theory as elucidated in his two-sector surplus model is that agrarian societies are saddled with large surplus labor but that this initial disadvantage can be remedied if surplus labor can be used to spur the development of an industrial sector. A similar approach is presented in Hollis Chenery's "patterns of development" analysis, which views sectoral shifts as crucial to economic growth. *See generally* HOLLIS CHENERY, STRUCTURAL CHANGE AND DEVELOPMENT POLICY (1979); HOLLIS CHENERY & MOISES SYRQUIN, PATTERNS OF DEVELOPMENT, 1950–1970 (1975); HOLLIS CHENERY ET AL., INDUSTRIALIZATION AND GROWTH: A COMPARATIVE STUDY (1986).

[168] There are domestic and international constraints on development. Domestic constraints include institutional constraints such as government policies that are detrimental to economic growth or a country's resource endowment or low access to domestic capital. International constraints include lack of access to international capital or impediments that hinder international trade. This understanding of constraints and their impact on development should be distinguished from the understanding of constraints that are reflected in the dependency theory of development. Dependency theory sees the poverty of poor countries as being deeply and inherently rooted in the constraints of the international capitalist system, which mires poor countries in a

or improving the lives of the poor measured in terms of infant mortality rate, health, education, and other indicators.[169] Development economists from many different schools of thought identify capital formation as necessary (though not necessarily sufficient) for economic growth and development.[170] Central to the quest for economic growth is this riddle: How can poor countries with no capital effectively engage in the process of capital formation? Or in other words, if you have no money, how do you get money? One of the principal strategies of development is to mobilize domestic savings in order to accelerate growth. Throughout its history, Japan has strived for the support and participation of its people in its myriad savings and frugality campaigns.

From today's law and development perspective, these projects might be viewed as reflecting a high level of state and civil society interaction and cooperation. For Japan and the issues it faced, reform centered on three interrelated issues: (1) inducing capital formation, which in turn required the government to get people to change their long-standing tradition of spending the family fortune on nonproductive endeavors such as weddings and funerals; (2) exhorting in direct and less direct ways the population to reject "backward or evil custom" and internalize appropriate values necessary to catch up with the more economically advanced European countries; and (3) creating a sense of nationhood by rallying the country, after the Tokugawa collapse, around the emperor.

b. Post–World War II Japan

Japan's emergence as a modern, democratic nation following the ashes of World War II was accomplished as part of a law and development effort that included a thick, substantive notion of the rule of law as espoused in this book. An intense culture change campaign began following the arrival of Commodore Matthew Perry and continued with similar intensity post–World War II, when Japan engaged in a deeply introspective examination of its culture. The Allied occupation of Japan began in August 1945 and ended in April 1952 after Japan's defeat following the atomic bombings of Hiroshima and Nagasaki. During this period, Japan was completely deprived of sovereignty;

---

perpetually dependent relationship with rich ones. For a discussion of dependency theory, *see* Chapter 3, notes 19–22 and accompanying text.

[169] Clive Bell, *Development Economics*, *in* THE NEW PALGRAVE: A DICTIONARY OF ECONOMICS 818, 825 (John Eatwell et al. eds., 1987).

[170] RAGNAR NURKSE, PROBLEMS OF CAPITAL FORMATION IN UNDERDEVELOPED COUNTRIES (1953) (generally emphasizing the role of savings and capital formation in economic development and in proposing his theory of balanced growth, viewing development as a process that entails an expansion of market and production, both requiring capital and capital investment); *see also* PAUL N. ROSENSTEIN-RODAN, CAPITAL FORMATION AND ECONOMIC DEVELOPMENT (1964); W. ARTHUR LEWIS, THE PRINCIPLES OF ECONOMIC PLANNING 52 (reprint 2003) (1949) (stressing that "[i]nvestment must be matched by savings, either voluntary domestic savings, or foreign savings . . ."); AKHTAR HOSSAIN & ANIS CHOWDHURY, MONETARY AND FINANCIAL POLICIES IN DEVELOPING COUNTRIES 26 (1996) (discussing Kaldor and Robinson's model of economic growth, which "rejects the classical notion that savings determine investment" and arguing instead that "investment determines savings.").

no Japanese could travel abroad and no major decisions—whether in the political, economic, or social sphere—could be undertaken without American approval. The American vision of a postwar Japan was fueled by two primary objectives: demilitarization and democratization, described by some as "in every sense a remarkable display of arrogant idealism—both self-righteous and genuinely visionary."[171] The American agenda reflected a desire for the transplantation of American labor reform and a full bill of rights panoply. Of course there was an odious colonial era whiff about the process[172]—it is largely undisputed that General Douglas MacArthur ruled in a bold, neocolonial style not open to challenge or criticism—but by the time the Americans departed, "the ideals of peace and democracy took root in Japan—not as a borrowed ideology or imposed vision, but as a lived experience and a seized opportunity."[173] It is a main argument in this section that law and development in postwar Japan succeeded because it was accompanied by a sweeping cultural change that accompanied the project.

How did militarist Japan become a new democratic, peaceful nation? What was the set of preexisting cultural norms that defined Japan when the American occupiers arrived? While the Allied powers also occupied postwar Germany, it is undisputed that it was Japan and not Germany that seemingly exhibited, at least to Western eyes, an exoticism that evoked in the allies an almost messianic fervor to remake the country. Indeed, when the Americans arrived, they were in the midst of a "cross-cultural moment [that was hardly] more intense, unpredictable, ambiguous, confusing, and *electric* than this one."[174] Whatever their deeply held notions of Japan's rightful place in the world or its innate cultural superiority, the Japanese dealt with defeat by exploring this phenomenon from every possible perspective, including through books, magazines, and articles.[175] Their ultimate conclusion after the soul-searching that accompanied defeat could be boiled down to this: a commitment to peace and democracy.

The cultural moment that defined Japan after World War II, when Japan encountered General MacArthur, can be traced back to the 1800s when Japan encountered Commodore Perry. It was with that interaction that the obsession with becoming an *itto koku* (first-rate country) began coupled with the fear that it would be relegated to a *yonto koku* (fourth-rate country), a term General MacArthur used at a press conference to describe postwar Japan,[176] thereby triggering the resurgence of a cultural and historical

---

[171] Dower, *supra* note 71, at 23.

[172] *See, e.g.*, James C. Thompson, Jr. et al., Sentimental Imperialists: the American Experience in East Asia (1981).

[173] Dower, *supra* note 71, at 23.

[174] *Id.*

[175] *Id.* at 28.

[176] *Id.* at 43–44. This sentiment was also expressed by Fleet Admiral William Halsey, who regretted that the war "ended too soon because there are too many Nips left" and who believed that if MacArthur's policies were implemented, "Japan will never rise above a fifth or sixth place power." *Still "Too Many Nips Left," Halsey Quoted as Saying*, N.Y. Times, Sept. 25, 1945, at 2.

obsession of national magnitude. A national mantra in the early postsurrender period was one that exhorted Japan to become "a nation of culture."[177]

Culture thus was at the heart of the matter for the Japanese as they pondered reconstruction. Japanese writers wrestled with this notion. Others explored how Japan should deal with defeat and with American occupation. A famous cartoonist, Kato Etsuro, depicted a drawing of an exuberant crowd of Japanese stretching their arms heavenward as parachutes dropped canisters labeled "Democratic Revolution." The heading was "A Gift from Heaven." Kato provoked a national discussion with this question "Well, we Japanese, who lost in war, who were exhausted by war, how did we receive this gift? How *are* we receiving it . . .?"[178]

This cartoon, and its evocative title, captures a dominant Japanese sentiment in the postwar years. It was time to view the enemy, now victorious, as liberators—"the agents of a revolution from above."[179] In fact, "democratic revolution from above" was a common mantra used by both the vanquished Japanese and MacArthur, who regularly invoked the idea that he was putting into place a spiritual revolution in Japan.[180] Various political parties in Japan rallied behind the need to move beyond defeat. Tokuda Kyuichi, a Communist Party leader imprisoned for eighteen years, recited an "Appeal to the People" upon his release in October 1945, which read: "We express our deepest gratitude that the occupation of Japan by the Allied forces, dedicated to liberating the world from fascism and militarism, has opened the way for the democratic revolution in Japan."[181] In addition to Kato's "received revolution," in which Japan was to receive a gift of democracy from heaven, leftists and liberals also saw the American occupation force as an army of liberation bestowing "reform from on high" or a "Potsdam revolution."[182]

Indeed, there was no objection expressed against the American "Initial Postsurrender Policy," framed to carry out the American dual objectives in Japan—demilitarization and democratization. The document stated that the aim of the occupation was as follows:

a. To insure that Japan will not again become a menace to the United States or to the peace and security of the world;
b. To bring about the eventual establishment of a peaceful and responsible government which will respect the rights of other states and will support the objectives of the United States as reflected in the ideals and principles of the Charter of the United Nations. The United States desires that this government should conform

---

[177] DOWER, *supra* note 71, at 63.

[178] *Id.* at 67.

[179] *Id.* at 66.

[180] Harry Emerson Wildes, *Revolution from Above*, *in* TYPHOON IN TOKYO: THE OCCUPATION AND ITS AFTERMATH 38 (1954); JOHN W. DOWER, JAPAN IN WAR AND PEACE: SELECTED ESSAYS 288–89 (1993); JUSTIN WILLIAMS, SR., JAPAN'S POLITICAL REVOLUTION UNDER MACARTHUR: A PARTICIPANT'S ACCOUNT (1979).

[181] DOWER, *supra* note 71, at 69 (quoting Tokuda Kyuichi).

[182] *Id.* at 69–70.

> as closely as may be to principles of democratic self-government but it is not the responsibility of the Allied Powers to impose upon Japan any form of government not supported by the freely expressed will of the people.
>
> These objectives will be achieved by the following principal means:
>
> . . .
>
> (b) Japan will be completely disarmed and demilitarized. The authority of the militarists and the influence of militarism will be totally eliminated from her political, economic, and social life. Institutions expressive of the spirit of militarism and aggression will be vigorously suppressed.
>
> (c) The Japanese people shall be encouraged to develop a desire for individual liberties and respect for fundamental human rights, particularly the freedoms of religion, assembly, speech, and the press. They shall also be encouraged to form democratic and representative organizations.[183]

As discussed below, the Japanese public generally supported these aims. Kato expressed Japanese sentiments about American military prowess and Japanese military defeat in another cartoon in which he depicted an exhausted Japanese couple lying among water pails and bamboo spears as the remnants of atomic ruins surrounded them. This absurdity was not lost to the general Japanese public, who saw the ludicrousness of Japan initiating war against the United States.[184] Indeed, this sentiment against militarism and military solution was so strong that the "no war" clause in the 1947 Japanese constitution, drafted by the Americans, found great support among the Japanese public itself.[185]

Of course there were counterstrains as well. Conservatives feared Communist manipulation, and there were other more cynical observers who saw great irony and contradiction in the notion of democracy by conquest or fiat. But for the most part, this counter notion did not hold sway. Instead, the concern was more that the revolution from above was not being sufficiently internalized. One of Kato's drawings depicted a figure lazing about in a house filled with gifts, followed by the following commentary:

> Chains were cut—but we must not forget that we did not shed a drop of blood, or raise a sweat, to cut these chains . . . We Japanese seem to have gotten accustomed to

---

[183] *U.S. Initial Post-Surrender Policy for Japan*, 13 DEP'T ST. BULL. 423, 423 (1945).

[184] Kato's depiction "captured a widespread and politically explosive sentiment. In sum, it amounted to this: Japan's ideologues and military spokesmen had deceived the people and led the country into a hopeless war against a vastly superior United States." John W. Dower, *The Bombed*, *in* AMERICA'S WARS IN ASIA: A CULTURAL APPROACH TO HISTORY AND MEMORY 27, 29–30 (Philip West et al. eds., 1998).

[185] *Id.* at 31.

> the sweetness of the revolution we have received . . . and to have become extremely sparing in our efforts to turn this valuable gift into our flesh and blood.[186]

The president of Tokyo University, Nanbara Shigeru, declared that World War II had exposed the failings of Japan, and that Japan should now embrace the principles of European Renaissance—individual search for truth. He observed that the Meiji era reform had only resulted in an "external appearance" of modernity, so that national wealth and state power had been emphasized while humanistic values had been subordinated. His concern was that the mere veneer of democracy and modernity might result in the re-establishment of reactionary forces.[187]

The Americans, with the support of the defeated Japanese, "set about doing what no other occupation force had done before: remaking the political, social, cultural, and economic fabric of a defeated nation, and in the process changing the very way of thinking of its populace."[188] Indeed, as I suggested above, Japan became a domain in which the United States was able to carry out its law and development project with almost messianic, ethnocentric, and missionary zeal. Unlike vanquished Germany, which was viewed simply as an essentially modern, Western country temporarily cursed with the evil of Nazism, Japan instead was exotic, alien, non-Western, non-Christian; indeed in his groundbreaking work, *Orientalism*, Edward Said described Western view of it as a pagan "other."[189] Japan's backwardness was viewed as reflecting its very feudalistic, Orientalist essence. Hence, for the American occupiers, "much of the almost sensual excitement involved in promoting their democratic revolution from above derived from the feeling that this involved *denaturing* an Oriental adversary and turning it into at least an approximation of an acceptable, healthy, westernized nation."[190] This missionary crusade was called upon to not just write new laws or put into place new institutions but rather "to *create* new norms that might eradicate forever the 'will to war.'"[191]

And so this project involved a revolution, thoroughly from above by external occupiers, yet also essentially supported by an eager Japanese populace more than willing to rectify its country's failings.[192] Although the American reconstruction was the catalyst, it was a reconstruction that was supported for the most part by a fully participatory Japanese public. This revolution from above included, in quick succession, the following

---

[186] Dower, *supra* note 71, at 71. Other commentators also saw the irony in the notion of democracy from above, noting that if democracy were to be easily exported, it would fail to take root and could, ironically, reinforce the "logic of irresponsibility" in which citizens were trained to take orders from above. *Id.*

[187] *Id.* at 71–72.

[188] *Id.* at 78.

[189] *See generally* Edward Said, Orientalism (1979).

[190] Dower, *supra* note 71, at 80.

[191] *Id.*

[192] Contrast this with the observation that "[e]nduring political and social revolutions generally emanate from below." *Id.*

reforms: Japan was ordered to extend the franchise to women, allow labor unionization, adopt a more liberal education in its schools, eradicate the *zaibatsu* (a Japanese conglomerate of family-controlled monopolies) by revising "monopolistic industrial controls," and generally eliminate all feudalistic, despotic vestiges from society.[193]

The defeat of Japan by Allied forces left the unmistakable impression on the Japanese people that the West and, more specifically, the United States, was powerful, while Japan was vulnerable and weak.[194] The people of Japan were acutely aware of the magnitude of their defeat, with approximately 2.6 million Japanese troops surrendering in China, in addition to five hundred thousand in Taiwan and nine hundred thousand in Korea.[195] Although the postwar period was referred to as an Allied occupation, the United States acted alone to determine "basic policy and exercised decisive command over all aspects of the occupation."[196] The US War Department framed broad ideological terms to begin its great campaign to set loose the civil liberties of the Japanese people in a democratic "revolution from above."[197] This revolution would include not only the reform of civil and criminal law but also a sea change in the political, social, cultural, and economic fabric of Japan, changing the fundamental way of thinking of the Japanese populace.[198] In a departure from the normal development of democracies from popular movements within an indigenous society, the Allied forces set out to create this revolution through military means, requiring the restructuring of the entire legal and political machine and the promotion of the democratic ideal through media, along with regulation and censorship of the press, radio, film, and private communications.[199] Under these ironically authoritarian strictures, the Japanese people were eager to rebuild Japan into a "nation of culture"[200] and embraced the new regime's focus on civil liberties, individual freedom, and popular expression.[201]

i. Changes to Japanese Rule of Law

The Potsdam Proclamation, which outlined the terms of the Japanese surrender to Allied forces, required the complete dissolution of military forces and the establishment of "[f]reedom of speech, of religion and of thought as well as respect for the fundamental human rights."[202] Despite the fact that the more conservative State Department and many

---

193 *Id.* at 81.
194 *Id.* at 43.
195 *Id.* at 49.
196 *Id.* at 73.
197 *Id.* at 69, 74.
198 *Id.* at 78.
199 *Id.* at 75.
200 *Id.* at 63.
201 *Id.* at 84.
202 Terms for Japanese Surrender, U.S.-China-U.K., July 26, 1945, 3 Bevans 1204, *available at* http://www.ndl.go.jp/constitution/e/etc/c06.html [hereinafter The Potsdam Proclamation].

Japanese officials were explicit in their disbelief that the Japanese people would ever be capable of self-government,[203] the goal of a democratic Japan was motivated by the need to permanently demilitarize and block the spread of communism.[204] Allied forces passed laws designed to break down features of Japanese society they believed led to Japan's willingness to engage in warfare, replacing them with rules that would support democratic ideals. The feudalistic family system that rendered women legally inferior was eliminated, while laws improving working conditions, labor organization, school curriculum, and the electoral system were introduced.[205] Additional changes included antimonopoly, deconcentration, and land reform laws, which were designed to dispossess the landowning class and create a large constituency of small owners.[206] While crimes of resisting the former regime were granted amnesty, the arrest of Class A war criminals increased.[207]

General MacArthur determined that to avoid any weakness in the face of communism, the emperor must be kept on as a uniting figurehead in the new Japanese government, although he was required to renounce his claims to divine descent.[208] Some officials expressed concern that trying the emperor as a war criminal would be blasphemous to the Japanese people and, thus, a denial of religious freedom.[209] Despite dissent in the State Department[210] and a general lack of concern for the emperor among Japanese people,[211] the Allied powers chose not to prosecute Emperor Hirohito for war crimes out of fear that abdication would lead to a total breakdown of Japanese civility.[212] Allied publications made it clear that, while they were in charge, they were hospitable to the emperor[213] and had absolutely no interest in investigating his actual role in the war.[214] MacArthur believed that the emperor could be a powerful tool for the Allied mission by recharacterizing him as having been duped and betrayed by the Japanese military, and so not responsible for their crimes.[215] This also played into MacArthur's belief that the Japanese needed to be led by dominant authority figures, such as the emperor, and would find themselves in chaos without clear leadership.[216] By separating the emperor from the mistakes of the recent past, Allied forces could redefine the true spirit of Japan as respectful of human rights and freedoms.[217]

---

[203] DOWER, *supra* note 71, at 65, 74.
[204] *Id.* at 75.
[205] *Id.* at 82.
[206] *Id.*
[207] *Id.*
[208] *Id.* at 3, 14–15, 324.
[209] *Id.* at 299.
[210] *Id.* at 327.
[211] *Id.* at 305.
[212] *Id.* at 324.
[213] *Id.* at 293.
[214] *Id.* at 324.
[215] *Id.* at 281.
[216] *Id.* at 282.
[217] *Id.* at 288.

The terms of the Potsdam Proclamation were implemented by the mandated adoption of an entirely new constitution, which retained the imperial system while simultaneously establishing the principles of popular sovereignty and guaranteeing a wide assortment of human rights.[218] Although originally planned to be a collaboration between the imperial establishment and the Allied occupiers, communication between the two camps failed to create any reasonable compromise toward a new constitution.[219] Once MacArthur determined that the Japanese government was incapable of proposing revisions that would satisfy the Potsdam requirements, he resolved that the Allied Forces would take the lead.[220] The occupiers prepared a model constitution based on several foreign constitutions but which carried a distinctively American imprint.[221] MacArthur then demanded that the document be approved within a week.[222] When the Japanese government objected to the dramatic terms of the draft, they were told that if the cabinet did not act within forty-eight hours, the constitution would be taken directly to the people.[223]

In the face of the Allies' drafted constitution, Emperor Hirohito's rescript read:

> Consequent upon our acceptance of the Potsdam Declaration the ultimate form of Japanese government is to be determined by the freely expressed will of the Japanese people. I am fully aware of our nation's strong consciousness of justice, its aspirations to live a peaceful life and promote cultural enlightenment and its firm resolve to renounce war and to foster friendship with all the countries of the world. It is, therefore, my desire that the constitution of our empire be revised drastically upon the basis of the general will of the people and the principle of respect for the fundamental human rights. I command hereby the competent authorities of my government to put forth in conformity with my wish their best efforts toward the accomplishment of this end.[224]

The prime minister also voiced support for the new democratic order, speaking of "the passage of mankind from war to peace, cruelty to mercy, slavery to liberty, tyranny and confusion to order."[225]

The new constitution embodied an imperial democracy, "premised on a responsible electorate" with a simple amendment procedure, while still being reasonably permanent.[226] The section enumerating the "rights and duties of the people" was, and still is,

---

[218] Nihonkoku Kenpō (1946) [Kenpō] [Constitution] (Japan), *available at* http://www.ndl.go.jp/constitution/e/etc/c01.html.

[219] Dower, *supra* note 71, at 354.

[220] *Id.* at 360.

[221] *Id.* at 370.

[222] *Id.* at 371.

[223] *Id.* at 377.

[224] *Id.* at 384–85.

[225] *Id.* at 384.

[226] *Id.* at 372.

one of the most generous grants of human rights in the world, including guarantees of gender equality.[227] The Japanese constitution codified the prohibition of war as a means of resolving international dispute, even as a means of self-defense.[228] This remains the most striking example of an occupier-drafted constitution, but it received tremendous support by the Japanese people as it tapped into the "popular aspirations for peace and democracy."[229] While the Japanese constitution granted its citizens many civil liberties they had been denied,[230] its view of the Japanese people as needing to be led by authority illustrates the difficulties of legitimizing such a revolution from above.[231] To legitimize this top-down reform, it would be necessary to gain the support of the Japanese people.[232] Thus, on the same day the constitution came into effect, the government issued twenty million copies of a booklet entitled "Atarashii Kempo, Akarui Seikatsu" or "New Constitution, Bright Life."[233]

ii. Changes to Japanese Culture

The people of Japan had been socialized to anticipate and accommodate radical change since the Meiji Restoration in the 1860s.[234] In addition to the acknowledged traditions of reverence for the past and submission to leadership, Japanese culture was deeply imbedded with strains of renovation and iconoclasm.[235] Wartime propaganda had called for " 'A New Culture Tied to a Radiant Past,'" emphasizing the importance of newness in the imperial regime.[236] This history of dynamism provided an ideal basis for the revolution from above to take hold because it was a traditional and accepted function of pundits to discuss how they would effect change, only altering the goal of what their new world should look like.[237]

A primary example of Japanese democratic principles prior to the war included the Meiji-era Charter Oath of 1868, which emphasized equality and mandated the seeking of knowledge by all people.[238] Parliamentary government was practiced under a constitutional monarchy as early as 1890, with a political pluralist movement emerging in the 1910s and 1920s.[239] This populist foundation would provide material for postwar

[227] *Id.* at 369.

[228] Nihonkoku Kenpō (1946) [Kenpō] [Constitution], art. 9 (Japan), *available at* http://www.ndl.go.jp/constitution/e/etc/c01.html#s2.

[229] Dower, *supra* note 71, at 347.

[230] *Id.* at 68.

[231] *Id.* at 72.

[232] *Id.* at 77.

[233] *Id.* at 402.

[234] *Id.* at 178.

[235] *Id.* at 179.

[236] *Id.* at 178.

[237] *Id.* at 179.

[238] Notehelfer, *supra* note 109, at 672.

[239] Dower, *supra* note 71, at 180.

commentators to link the imposed democracy to the history of passionate desire for democracy manifested by the Japanese people's rights movements of the Meiji period and the early-twentieth-century proletarian movements.[240]

It is important to stress that the Allied occupation rested on the ideals of respect for individuality, freedoms of speech and religion, and world peace, based on a foundation of the requirements of humanity and universal justice, rather than the mere desires of the occupiers themselves.[241] Power was concentrated among Americans not only in central areas but also in civilian and military personnel stationed throughout the country, along with "hands-on manipulation of the educational system and everyday culture."[242] The difficulties of imposed democracy were apparent at every level, easily abused by functionaries that suddenly possessed far more power than they could have exerted within their own country.[243] Indeed, ordinary officers and civilian officials, who would have been firmly grounded in the middle class at home, lived in requisitioned upper-class houses in Japan.[244] Thus, the contradiction between the equality and principled democracy espoused by the Allied powers and the reality of their privileged positions was clear.[245]

(1) MEDIA. Americans who had publicized Japanese as identical, monkey-men, who were subject to incarceration in the United States merely based on nationality, were re-educated to perceive the Japanese as allies in the East.[246] Many of the materials distributed to the American public following the war were focused on "the notion that the 'little Japanese' were almost humans like themselves."[247] Americans were told that the Japanese brain was like a sponge that had been taught terrible things by warlords and military gangs.[248] According to American materials, the Japanese people had been indoctrinated to believe that "The Sun Goddess Created the Japanese to Rule all Other Peoples of the Earth" and that the job of the Allied forces was to fix their brains.[249] The GIs were told that they could prove to the Japanese people the superiority of the American way, simply by being themselves.[250] By construing the Japanese urge to engage in warfare as a result of recent socialization and indoctrination, rather than an innate characteristic, the prospect of re-education did not seem so impossible.[251]

---

[240] *Id.* at 185.
[241] *Id.* at 187.
[242] *Id.* at 205.
[243] *Id.* at 206.
[244] *Id.* at 207.
[245] *Id.* at 211.
[246] *Id.* at 213.
[247] *Id.* at 214.
[248] *Id.* at 215 (citing the film "Our Job in Japan").
[249] *Id.* at 216.
[250] *Id.*
[251] *Id.* at 217.

By focusing on changing the social and economic factors believed to be contributors to Japan's willingness to engage in warfare, the Allied forces set out to fundamentally change Japanese culture into a democratic and demilitarized society.[252] To ensure the single-minded message of democratization, the Allied powers chose to continue the total monopolization of the radio airwaves by a national broadcasting agency.[253] The first Allied directive on freedom of speech and the press granted only an "'absolute minimum of restrictions on freedom of speech,'" which was based on requirements that the expression be truthful and not disturb the "public tranquility."[254] But the media was not allowed to disagree with Allied policy or to speak negatively of any of the Allied powers;[255] indeed, early key logs included approximately sixty prohibited subjects.[256] The Allies created a Civil Censorship Detachment that was closely supported by the propaganda issued through the Civil Intelligence and Education Section.[257] Even the existence of the censorship was not disclosed to the public, presenting an even less transparent apparatus as compared to the prewar Japanese style, which had at least marked deletions with X's and O's.[258]

The censorship of the Japanese media's coverage of the trials of war criminals was especially disturbing, since it impeded the public's ability to engage in reasonable and therapeutic discussions of the proceedings.[259] Although the defendants themselves were entitled to a vigorous defense, the Japanese media was required to support the prosecution without question.[260] This censorship led to the inescapable conclusion that the defendants were to be presumed guilty until proven innocent—hardly a democratic ideal.[261] Nor were media outlets allowed to question either the composition of the court or the decision to prosecute only a portion of the highest wartime leaders.[262]

In the place of such censored material, Allied Forces provided extensive pro-democracy propaganda to reinforce the message of democracy. Much of the postsurrender propaganda centered on information about systematic depredations abroad that had been suppressed by the imperial regime.[263] By shedding light on the atrocities committed during the war, a great desire was implanted in the Japanese people to make atonement in a way that would give meaning to those who had perished.[264] Several aspects of the

---

252 *Id.* at 77.
253 *Id.* at 206.
254 *Id.* at 407.
255 *Id.* at 211.
256 *Id.* at 410.
257 *Id.* at 407.
258 *Id.* at 410.
259 *Id.* at 413.
260 *Id.*
261 *Id.*
262 *Id.*
263 *Id.* at 487.
264 *Id.*

postsurrender media campaign involved the reinterpretation of images and phrases used in imperial propaganda. Following the Japanese surrender, propaganda often called upon the very themes of construction and culture that had been used during wartime campaigns, transforming them into a rallying cry for the creation of a democratic and peaceful nation.[265]

(II) EDUCATION. The democratic revolution necessitated extensive reform of the educational situation of Japan, with both students and teachers being called upon to recast Japan as a nation of culture—again emphasis on the cultural aspects of reconstruction. Educators, who were grief stricken by the loss of their young students to the war effort and overwhelmed with guilt for encouraging them toward their deaths, embraced the ideals of peace and democracy.[266] The Allied Forces required Japanese students to go through their old textbooks, marking out any passages that were considered too nationalistic, militaristic, or undemocratic.[267] Japanese teachers were given guides describing the "Fundamental Problems in Constructing a New Japan" that addressed their tasks in promoting respect for civil rights and the pursuit of knowledge.[268] They were told that Japan had fallen behind Western civilization by borrowing the West's inventions without adopting the scientific spirit behind their development.[269] The teachers were instructed that Japan had been defeated because their people were not respectful of "human nature, personality, and individuality."[270] Because this failing belonged to the population as a whole, the only means of reparation would be the implementation of the Potsdam Proclamation and Allied orders to construct a new Japan.[271] The Allies published " 'Democracy Reader for Boys and Girls,'" and promised that the work of the Allied nations would allow Japan to quickly democratize and rejoin the world, adding that the simple history of humankind dictated that democracy was the natural and true state of all people.[272] The Minister of Education thanked schoolchildren for their wartime efforts but told them that they must now elevate the scientific and spiritual power of Japan to its highest level to elevate itself to be equal with or exceed that of the Western world.[273]

---

265 *Id.* at 177 (citing slogans such as "Construct a Nation of Peace" and "Construct a Nation of Culture").

266 *Id.* at 250.

267 *Id.* at 247.

268 *Id.* at 248 (citing chapters addressing self reflection concerning Japan's present state; eliminating militarism and ultranationalism; promoting respect for human nature, personality, and individuality; raising scientific standards and philosophical and religious refinement; carrying out thorough democracy; constructing a peaceful nation of culture and individuality, civic education, women's education, scientific knowledge, physical education, art and culture, and vocational education).

269 *Id.*

270 *Id.*

271 *Id.*

272 *Id.* at 249.

273 *Id.* at 494.

Along with youth programs, the Allies implemented programs designed to reach across all age groups. Adult education methodologies were introduced beginning in 1947 to teach adults how to "learn the consciousness, habits, and lifestyles of a democratic people."[274] The entire nature of the Japanese language was retooled through the introduction of hundreds of new words and phrases to embody the democratic principles to be promoted.[275] This led to numerous odd Japanese-English neologisms that had no natural development in either language and had to be defined for unfamiliar readers, capturing the rapidly changing form of public discourse.[276] Although the change was radical, Japan had experienced a similar revolution in everyday language twice before, adopting many Chinese texts and concepts during ancient and medieval eras and significantly borrowing from European cultures during the mid-nineteenth century.[277]

It is likely that these previous revolutions helped the Japanese to accept culture change from interveners such as the United States. In all, between Japan's introspective search for modern acceptance in the global community and the occupation of Japan after the war, the nation successfully implemented culture change among its people through the use of both framing new cultural practices within old ones as well as demanding change in areas that would advance the Japanese society. Ironically, some scholars today have suggested that the American legal system take a page from the Japanese book and model the US legal system after the more informal system of Japan. These scholars postulate that American society, "built on individualism and competition,"[278] where the only "common ground is enlightened self-interest,"[279] is an obstacle to justice. Cultural attitudes, a rigid formal system, and bureaucratic concerns are cited as challenges to developing a more informal system of law.[280] In sum, a change to the American systems of law could lead to changes in society that value community and social responsibility, areas that have recently been neglected in American society.[281]

Below, I examine how the Allied powers, specifically the American government, implemented similar institutions to those of Japan in Germany. Here, culture change resulted in different outcomes from Japan as different strategies were employed given the forces of Nazism and communism that were at play after World War II. A strong focus of the Allied strategy in Germany was rooting out remnant Nazi powers and developing a strong economy in order to ensure that another Fascist state or dictatorship would not again arise.

---

274 *Id.* at 251.

275 *Id.*

276 *Id.*

277 *Id.*

278 Frank K. Upham, Law and Social Change in Postwar Japan 223 (1987).

279 *Id.*

280 *Id.* at 224.

281 *Id.* at 227.

3. GERMANY

The reconstruction of Germany after its defeat in the Second World War is often cited as an example of effective democracy building from the ruins of a totalitarian regime. As stated, it differs from the Japanese experience in that the Allies viewed Germany as a modern, Western country that had been temporarily held captive by Nazism while Japan was foreign and exotic, malleable to modernization. The rule of law development in Germany focused heavily on the formation of a stable economy and a change in attitude toward other races and inclusion. Still, similarities exist among the methods used by the Allies in effectuating cultural and political change in both Japan and Germany, as democratization and demilitarization were goals in both spheres. Further, both efforts utilized the media to effectuate change through entertainment and re-education.

When the Allies met at Potsdam in July 1945, they agreed to divide Germany into four zones, each to be administered by one of the four powers of the United States, Great Britain, France, and the Soviet Union. The Allies recognized that the occupation of Germany provided the powers with an important opportunity to reshape the political, economic, and cultural landscape of formerly Nazi Germany. Some advocated permanently weakening the Germans so that Germany would never again be a player on the international stage. However, all the Allies eventually agreed that the traditions that had led to the success of Hitler and National Socialism needed to be eradicated, and that this would best be achieved in the long run by ensuring that Germany would abandon its militaristic leanings and become a productive member of the global community.

To this end, the Allies envisioned a four-prong reconstruction effort. They agreed on what has become known as the "4 Ds": democratization, denazification, demilitarization, and decartelization. These four goals were to be implemented by each power within its zone, allowing for widely different systems and methods between zones modeled after the zone's occupying power. The American strategy, laid out in the Joint Chiefs of Staff directive 1067, was initially punitive, focusing on the removal of former Nazis from power, preparation for a long occupation, and creation of at least a minimal standard of living for ordinary Germans. However, as American and Soviet relations began to break down and the world began to polarize around the two powers, American strategy began to shift in favor of democratization and the stabilization of the Germany economy. West Germany, under American tutelage, became the Federal Republic of Germany and underwent what came to be known as the Economic Miracle; it integrated with the rest of Western Europe through the North Atlantic Treaty Organization, the European Economic Community, and eventually the European Union. Yet, how did the Americans and the Germans manage to transform Germany from a Fascist state into a democratic nation, and what about this transformation could be repeated or implemented in other democracy-building contexts?

This section will focus on American policies in West Germany after 1945 with respect to cultural components implemented to create a democratic state. This section will explore the creation of a German democracy by examining the implementation of new political institutions and a new civil society. It will then discuss how the Americans sought to democratize the German public through film and culture, as well as how this budding democratic state interpreted issues of race and inclusion. Finally, this section examines decartelization efforts and the creation of a capitalist economy, which the Americans viewed as integral to the democratization of Germany. In each of the 4 Ds, the American occupation government sought to use and change culture in order to refashion Germany in the interests of both America and the German people. As relations between the Americans and Soviets disintegrated and the Cold War emerged, the importance of Germany, sitting at the intersection of East and West, grew exponentially. The focus of the occupying powers shifted. Now each power sought, not only to reconstruct Germany, but sought to do so in a way that would symbolize the superiority of its own system. Even though it was forced to walk a fine line between a global war of ideologies, pitting capitalist democracy against communism, West Germany was able to redefine itself not merely as dictated by an outside power, but in ways that were uniquely German.

a. Denazification and Demilitarization

The four powers agreed early on that the first major task of reconstruction was to remove Nazi influence on the German political scene. The "specter of the fall of the Weimar Republic"[282] was fresh in the minds of both the Allies and the Germans. Therefore, the goal of removing the Fascist Nazis was not only an emotional response to the atrocities of war but also a pragmatic maneuver to ensure the stability of the new German state. With the Nazis removed from power, the political vacuum could be filled with Germans who would support Allied plans for reconstruction. However, each ally went about this process in different ways, and to varying degrees of zealousness. After the establishment of over five hundred courts, staffed by more than twenty thousand officials across the four zones, it is estimated that only about 6 percent of those investigated were ever convicted for Nazi crimes, and the vast majority of these were convicted of only minor offenses.[283] In addition, many ex-Nazis were able to keep their jobs, despite an agreement at Potsdam that called for the immediate dismissal of all former Nazi officials in the German bureaucracy due to policies that differentiated between major and minor party members.

The trials at Nuremberg were viewed as a promising start to the criminalization and destruction of the Nazi regime. The Nuremberg Tribunal heard 13 trials, involving over 170 people, but it passed only 20 life sentences, 25 death sentences, and 35 acquittals.[284]

---

[282] Peter H. Merkl, *The German Response to the Challenge of Extremist Parties, 1949–1994*, *in* The Postwar Transformation of Germany: Democracy, Prosperity and Nationhood 1, 35 (John S. Brady et al. eds., 1999).

[283] Anthony Glees, Reinventing Germany: German Political Development since 1945, at 31 (1996).

[284] *Id.* at 32.

The Nuremberg trials were established to deal mainly with the major party members and those visibly responsible for the war and the government's actions. While the trials handled some of the most recognizable Nazi figures, the Allies were still concerned about the amount of influence the party maintained among lower officials in the bureaucracy and government of Germany. At first, the Americans took a harsh stance against former Nazis, removing even those with minor ties to the party and its organizations. Every German over the age of eighteen was required to fill out a questionnaire stating their previous allegiances before they could be hired for any important position, but with so many bureaucrats dismissed from office,[285] the occupation government found itself awash in paperwork.[286]

Even the issuing of blanket amnesties for those under the age of twenty-eight and earning less than 3600 DM annually were not enough to lighten the load of the program.[287] The Americans were quick to turn over the responsibility of the program to the new German administration,[288] but the procedure grew more and more lax as the realities of the emerging Cold War set in. As the Soviets and the Americans rushed to grab the best German talent, exceptions for former Nazi technicians, scientists, and artists were made.[289] The need for experts in certain fields also forced the denazification effort to make exceptions. In the legal field, for example, the early Huckepack system, which called for the appointment of ex-Nazi judges alongside judges who had clean or anti-Nazi records, was scrapped by June of 1946, leading to the unrestricted rehiring of former Nazi supporters.[290]

This practice was common throughout the civil service, and in 1951, the newly created Republic of Germany passed the 131 Law, which established a quota reserving at least 20 percent of government jobs for former Nazi-era officials who were returning to Germany from the lost provinces. In many cases, the Americans simply turned a blind eye to the rehiring, objecting only when an appointee became too controversial to ignore.[291] In the end, the Americans were more interested in their anti-Communist campaign, leaving German rehiring policies to the Germans themselves. This is not to say that the

---

[285] *Id.* at 33. Estimates range over 3.5 million, or a quarter of the adult population.

[286] *See* Konrad H. Jarausch, After Hitler: Recivilizing Germans, 1945–1995, at 52 (Brandon Hunziker trans., 2006) ("Although the military government wanted to continue its rigid policy of purging Nazis, the enormity of the task, along with growing criticism from the German population, eventually forced them to modify its implementation.").

[287] *See* John P. Teschke, Hitler's Legacy: West Germany Confronts the Aftermath of the Third Reich 22 (1999).

[288] *See* Jarausch, *supra* note 286, at 50 ("Not until the promulgation of the 'law for the liberation of National Socialism and Militarism' on March 5, 1946, was the task of denazification transferred into the hands of German review boards.").

[289] Teschke, *supra* note 287, at 26.

[290] *See id.* at 27 ("By 1948, well over half of the judges holding office in the western zones had served the Nazi regime in some fashion.").

[291] *Id.* at 62.

denazification program was entirely a failure. The Nazi organizations were gone, prominent Nazis were executed, imprisoned, or otherwise eliminated from public life, and Nazism itself was discredited as a valid political and ideological movement. These long-term successes, according to Jarausch in his book entitled *After Hitler*, allowed a "return to the values and practices of Western civilization [which] require[d] a fundamental change in 'national mentality' that would cure it once and for all from its pan-German pretensions."[292]

Although the denazification of Germany resulted in the return of many Nazis to their former government posts, it is also the case that the American occupation authorities were nonetheless committed to the eradication of the traditions and political culture that had made the atrocities of National Socialism possible. The objective was "not only to repair the short-term damages wrought by Nazism, but also to break decisively with the long-term, problematic traditions of German political culture that were, at least in part, to blame for them." [293] To this end, demilitarization was viewed as one of the most important of the Allied goals for denazification and reconstruction. In order to prevent another war of aggression, the Allies deemed it necessary to do more than simply remove Germany's weapons and weapons-making capacity; reconstruction would require the remaking of the nation's military culture and traditions.[294]

The demilitarization process began with the physical disarmament of the German populace. This process was multiphased. Over ten million men were still serving in the German military when it surrendered to the Allies, who interned these forces in improvised camps until they were released into agricultural or industrial production to relieve the shortage of manpower. As part of the process of disarmament, the Allies confiscated weapons, ammunition, and military equipment, demolished fortifications, and ended arms production in Germany proper.[295] In addition, the Allies banned the possession of weapons on the penalty of death. Military installations, such as barracks, airfields, ports, and sites for war production were taken over or destroyed.

While the German military and its related organizations such as the SS, SA, and Gestapo had been dissolved by the Allied Control Council on September 25, 1945, the Allies sought to destroy the social and cultural sources of militarism. To this end, they

---

[292] Jarausch, *supra* note 286, at 55.

[293] *Id.* at 6.

[294] *See* Jennifer Fay, Theaters of Occupation: Hollywood and the Reeducation of Postwar Germany 33 (2008) ("Germans would have to unlearn that they had evolved into a superrace 'called by destiny to be the leaders of the world and to rule all other countries in a new order'; that the individual is subordinate to the state over which its leader has supreme authority; that war is the highest, most 'holy' manifestation of the state and may thus be carried out with unbridled brutality; that 'envy and Schadenfreude [...] are legitimate and morally justifiable emotions'; and that Germans, envied the world over, should not be 'duped into friendship with others.'").

[295] *See* Jarausch, *supra* note 286, at 27 ("Some 46 million bullets, 24 million small artillery shells, 2.59 million gas masks, 709,000 hand grenades, 82,000 rifles and pistols, 148,000 landmines, 34,000 rockets, 1,842 ships, and 420 airplanes had to be taken out of service by the Americans alone.").

banned not only the possession of weapons but also the wearing of uniforms, emblems, medals, or insignia. However, this directive was sometimes unenforced due to the shortage of civilian clothing, and further exceptions were made for police officers and firemen. These policies were meant to break the German population's ties to the military, and the Allies did not stop there. They further banned all military traditions deemed to glorify war. Military schools, organizations, and clubs of any sort were banned, including veterans associations. This policy had far-reaching effects, as military pensions, benefits, and disability payments were also stopped and reintroduced as regular welfare and social security programs.[296] Even athletic associations of military character were banned, resulting in the prohibition of flying, parachuting, fencing, and target shooting. The policy was further expanded in May 1946 to include a ban on war memorials, monuments, and propaganda in public spaces. Military holidays were suspended, and all books that advocated violence were to be handed over to the Allied command. By October of 1946, the Allies finally agreed to the creation of a joint commission to oversee the demilitarization effort, to take inventory of all possible war industries, and to destroy all plants used solely for arms production.[297]

The effects of these policies were felt only years after their enactment. At first, many former soldiers refused to admit defeat, continued to believe in the greatness of Hitler, and denied the existence of the concentration camps. The trials at Nuremberg, the humiliation of defeat and occupation, and the death of their leaders forced many to come to terms with postwar reality. Those who had lived through the war were simply happy to be alive, concerned for their families, and looking for a way to adapt to civilian life.[298] Few wanted a return to the dark days of war, and though some retained positive memories of the war, "the majority of the 'burned children' of the second carnage concluded, 'that which we have lived through should never be allowed to happen again.' "[299] The success of Allied policies, coupled with a collective memory of suffering and death, can be seen in the debate against German rearmament in the 1950s.

As the Cold War intensified, the Americans began to fear the influence of Russia on a defenseless Germany. Their desire to see Germany act as a buffer zone against the Soviets

---

[296] *See* James M. Diehl, *Change and Continuity in the Treatment of German Kriegsopfer*, *in* West Germany Under Construction: Politics, Society, and Culture in the Adenauer Era 93, 100 (Robert G. Moeller ed., 1997) (noting that the Allies "believed that the generous pensions and the favored (i.e. separate or *gehoben*) treatment of the victims of war in Germany had served to encourage pro-military sentiment and to shield Germans from fully comprehending and experiencing the horrible consequences of war. In their view, the treatment of the war-disabled as a favored group only worked to perpetuate the German tradition of glorifying the military and war—including its victims—a practice that had allowed the military to retain its position as a privileged and arrogant caste."); *see also* Jarausch, *supra* note 286, at 29 ("Fearing that they might become potential refuges of revanchism, the Allies also dissolved all veterans' associations, even canceling military pensions and other benefits.").

[297] *See* Jarausch, *supra* note 286, at 30.

[298] *See id.* at 32.

[299] *Id.* at 33.

forced them to reconsider the disarmament of their western zone of influence. However, disarmament policies had, by then, already affected the German psyche,[300] and popular opinion was sharply against the idea of rearmament. In the end, the Americans got their way with the formation of the West German Bundeswehr in the mid-1950s, but the army was to be overseen by the civilian-controlled office of the commissioner of the armed forces. In addition, while mandatory military service for twelve months was instituted, conscientious objectors could fulfill the requirement through volunteer services in old-age homes or hospitals. Similar objection to the presence of weapons of mass destruction throughout the 1970s and 1980s evidences the long-term success of Allied demilitarization policies.[301]

b. Democratization

The loss of the war and the removal of former Nazis from the government left Germany with a political vacuum, and the Americans were well aware that an occupation government could not fill this vacuum indefinitely. Therefore, the reconstruction of Germany's political system became one of America's major goals. This process focused on the creation of a new constitution and the construction of new political institutions, as well as the reformation of Germany's political culture in order to support the new democratic state. While the Allies agreed that democracy had to be included among the 4 Ds, the presence of the Soviets complicated matters. After a tense and uncooperative Soviet delegation derailed talks in London in 1947, the remaining Allies decided to band together to create a common political order in the West. Joined by Belgium, the Netherlands, and Luxembourg, the Western Allies met in London in 1948. There, they created the Frankfurt Documents, which called for the convening of a national convention to draft a provisional constitution for the western portion of occupied Germany.[302] The Allies always intended for this constitution to be temporary, as they still anticipated the eventual reunification of the eastern and western halves. However, shortly after the adoption of the Basic Law and the creation of the Federal Republic of Germany in the west on May 23, 1949, the Soviets created the

---

[300] *See id.* at 35 ("Producing what was effectively a decade-long moratorium on military institutions, the rigorous disarmament and demilitarization policy did enable most Germans to recommence their civilian lives . . . the interruption of the military tradition offered a chance to reverse the centuries' old process of social militarization . . . For the political culture . . . the discrediting of the military provided a unique chance to acquire new, more peaceful values and forms of behavior.").

[301] *See* JARAUSCH, *supra* note 286, at 45 ("In the 1970s and 1980s four-fifths of the West German population rejected any deployment of weapons of mass destruction and did not want to see them introduced into the armed forces arsenal, even as a deterrent. Nevertheless, some three-fifths demanded that the Federal Republic be defended against an attack from the East, although merely a slight majority would tolerate a war on German soil. Only a third of those questioned considered duty in the Bundeswehr as a contribution to peace, while a majority of the older generation still supported military service. The attempt to implement a rigorously civilian policy that would avoid all military entanglement was a logical consequence of such public ambivalence.").

[302] FED. RES. DIV., LIBR. OF CONG., GERMANY: A COUNTRY STUDY 87 (Eric Solsten ed., 3d ed. 1996) [hereinafter Solsten].

German Democratic Republic in the east, complete with its own constitution built on Communist ideology. When the two states merged in 1990, it was decided that the new unified nation of Germany would adopt the Basic Law as its permanent constitution.

i. The Basic Law

According to the Frankfurt Documents, the creation of the Basic Law was to be a primarily German affair, but the documents also stipulated in the Occupation Statute that the Allies would maintain a strong relationship "vis-à-vis the new state."[303] The occupation powers predicated their acceptance of the Basic Law on the rejection of the idea of German superiority and the unequivocal commitment to human rights. They made it clear that they desired the new constitution to reflect German traditions while incorporating Western liberal ideals.[304] The members of the constituent assembly, or the Herrenchiemsee convention (10–23 August 1948), were appointed by the newly formed *Länder* (states) as created by the Allies in London. They created a Basic Law, which combined the German traditions of self-government, a professional bureaucracy, and federalism with Western ideals of fundamental rights and constitutional supremacy. The convention, chaired by Christian Democrat and future chancellor Konrad Adenauer, was careful to avoid the mistakes of the Weimar republic, which had allowed the Nazis to take advantage of the splintered political parties to circumvent democratic processes and seize power. To this end, the delegates decreased the powers of the president, now merely the ceremonial head of state, in favor of the chancellor and the lower house of Parliament, the Bundestag.[305] While the Weimar constitution had relegated individual rights to the category of state objectives, the Basic Law lists them as fundamental and inviolable, guaranteeing democracy, republicanism, social responsibility, federalism, and the right of resistance should they be violated.[306] Federalism was significantly strengthened under the Basic Law due to the *Länder*'s inclusion in the upper house of Parliament,[307] the Bundesrat, and the process for removing the federal chancellor was changed to require a constructive vote of no confidence.[308] In addition, a federal constitutional court was created to oversee the constitutionality of laws.[309] This court could also ban any political party that sought to destroy or obstruct German democracy.[310] In this way, the Basic

---

[303] *Id.*

[304] *See* JARAUSCH, *supra* note 286, at 114 ("The West German Basic Law that emerged in this highly charged atmosphere was thus a compromise between reviving Germany's own constitutional traditions and importing new models from the West."); *see also* GLEES, *supra* note 283, at 27 ("On the whole, German political and institutional forms were adapted, and filled with Western liberal contents.").

[305] GRUNDGESETZ FÜR DIE BUNDESREPUBLIK DEUTSCHLAND [GRUNDGESETZ][GG][BASIC LAW], May 23, 1949, BGBL. I (Ger.).

[306] *Id.*

[307] *Id.*

[308] *Id.*

[309] *Id.*

[310] *Id.; see also* Solsten, *supra* note 302, at 89 ("The activities of a number of openly antidemocratic parties during the Weimar Republic had inspired the authors of the Basic Law to include this strong provision.").

Law borrowed elements from German political tradition and infused them with a more Western liberal code to create a new democratic system from the ruins of fascism.

ii. Media, Music, and Film

The United States understood that "hard strategic power remains inextricably linked to soft 'cultural' power, in the form of tacit values, public opinion, and the osmotic sway of popular culture. . . ."[311] Hence the Americans were quick to realize the necessity of influencing and building this "soft cultural power" in supporting and maintaining the new German democracy.[312] To this end, America sought to use its own music, media, and film to transform Germany in its own image, making it more accepting of democracy, as well as American policy and products. Some Germans initially resisted American mass culture, clinging to traditional German classics.[313] However, the economic expansion of West Germany and the growing fascination of the German youth with all things American advanced a cultural synchronization that would be most clearly manifested in the late 1960s youth riots. One of the primary lessons to be learned from the American cultural policy during the period is that the success it managed to accomplish was due primarily to its ability to adapt to German tastes and the German willingness to accept it.

While the policy was dictated from the outside, the democratic liberalization of the German politic drove home the lesson that mass culture is indeed in the hands of the masses, and it can only become successful if the population is willing to buy it. Mass consumerism is not a byproduct of democratization, but one of its driving forces, and it can be used to convince a population of the merits of a system which gives them a greater voice in what they see, hear, and learn. By empowering the populace to make its own choices, American cultural policy favored German self-empowerment through the creation of a vibrant German political culture. However, some policies, most notably those regarding race, did not manage to make as much of an impact and have left Germany with challenges of inclusion and acceptance with which it continues to struggle to this day.

German television and radio broadcasting after the First World War was conceptualized as a medium for high culture and educational pursuits, not as a conduit for American-style, popular culture for the masses. Before the Nazis, the German broadcasting system was characterized by privately owned companies in which the state owned

---

[311] Michael Ermarth, *Counter-Americanism and Critical Currents in West German Reconstruction 1945–1960*, *in* AMERICANIZATION AND ANTI-AMERICANISM: THE GERMAN ENCOUNTER WITH AMERICAN CULTURE AFTER 1945, at 25, 27 (Alexander Stephan ed., 2005).

[312] *See* JARAUSCH, *supra* note 286, at 139 ("Despite the successful establishment of democratic institutions, the cultural process of adopting the spirit of democracy remained difficult, as authoritarian thought patterns and habits of behavior tended to persist.").

[313] *See* Jost Hermand, *Resisting Boogie-Woogie Culture, Abstract Expressionism, and Pop Art*, *in* AMERICANIZATION AND ANTI-AMERICANISM: THE GERMAN ENCOUNTER WITH AMERICAN CULTURE AFTER 1945, at 67, 67–68 (Alexander Stephan ed., 2005).

the majority share, with funding through fees paid by listeners.[314] Government control gradually increased, leading to increased censorship and the eventual takeover by the Nazi propaganda machine.

After World War II, the American occupation government sought to dismantle the state-controlled media outlets of the Nazis and transform them into the bastions of free speech and freedom of the press, but the Germans were used to a system and programming that prioritized education over entertainment. The Americans sought to transform this industry into a free-market medium in its own image, one that would bow to the demands of mass consumerism and popular appeal. What resulted was a dual system divided between public and commercial demands.

Although the Americans sought to create a regionalized broadcasting system free of government influence, they also recognized that in the face of European economic ruin, a purely commercialized system would inevitably fail. Instead, the Western Allies used the British Broadcasting Corporation as a model, creating a public institution with controlling bodies composed of all major social interest groups. Technical and economic independence would provide the journalistic independence and integrity necessary to soothe American concerns with freedom of the press, but the Germans nonetheless remained skeptical,[315] and the political parties sought to influence the programming by placing loyal people in the controlling bodies.[316]

In the beginning, these political actors controlled most of the programming on both radio and television, as the same broadcasting companies ran them. However, the industry was forced to change and adapt with the growing economic prosperity of West Germany. Advertisements were originally shunned as uncouth interruptions of cultural programming, and it was believed that popular tastes and trends should not be allowed to dictate programming choices. However, as listeners and viewers dwindled, the stations were forced to bend to popular demand and mix in more entertainment with their educational programming.[317] As programming got more expensive and demand grew for more varied entertainment, stations were similarly forced to incorporate more advertising,

---

[314] *See* Kaspar Maase, *From Nightmare to Model?*, *in* AMERICANIZATION AND ANTI-AMERICANISM: THE GERMAN ENCOUNTER WITH AMERICAN CULTURE AFTER 1945, at 78, 80 (Alexander Stephan ed., 2005).

[315] *See* FAY, *supra* note 294, at 99 ("The Allies would permit German democratic self-determination only when Germans were sufficiently reoriented and predetermined. Alarm bells went off when a 1948 survey indicated that more than 50% of those living in the Western zones *still* believed that Nazism 'was a good idea poorly carried out' and that 'a plurality' of Germans *still* 'appeared doubtful of their ability to carry on democratic self-government.' ").

[316] *See* Maase, *supra* note 314 at 78, 81.

[317] *See id.* at 83–84 (stating that a 1924 poll showed Operetta, daily news, and chamber/concert music as the most popular programming, but that the majority of listeners polled just two years later preferred lighter music and humorous programs. This showed that even as early as the 1920s, the media networks were attempting to balance the programming they believed the listeners should hear with the programming the listeners preferred. The Nazis had allowed entertainment to dominate during the war, catering to the whims of the masses in order to keep them happy and to transmit the party's propaganda. After the war, broadcasters used this to

mainly aimed at the working-class women who listened while doing their housework and at the youth who grew increasingly infatuated with American entertainment and products. With the growing affluence of the nation, more families could afford multiple media outlets, and this also contributed to the rising demand for varied types of entertainment. Competition from international stations drove German broadcasters to appeal to different target groups in order to draw in listeners and viewers. In this way, even though the state continued to exert influence on radio and television programming, the power of the mass market forced these media outlets to adapt themselves to a more American consumer image.

Political parties were quick to see the value in this and often leveraged the difference between programming choices and consumer taste for political gain, giving the voice of the majority a degree of legitimacy in media policy.[318] While there was no American policy accounting for the shift, more broadcasters began airing American and international shows. These shows appealed to audiences because they depicted an idealized version of reality in which familiar stars tackled familiar problems, families were happy and whole, and the happy ending reigned supreme. German broadcasters liked the fact that they did not have to spend money producing original shows, while advertisers could enjoy the free marketing for their products embedded in the shows.[319] American values were transmitted to German audience by German media sources because this was welcomed by the people. Playing American songs on the radio and American shows on television would have done little good without German audience to receive them. In the end, however, individualization and economic prosperity allowed the Germans to take control of their own information and entertainment, a democratization of its media industry reflective of German, not American, interests.

The American military government was just as quick to realize the importance of film to their re-education and democratizing mission. The Nazis had used film as a propaganda tool to culturally condition the populace to not only accept and support the war, but to radicalize race relations.[320] According to Jennifer Fay in her book *Theaters of Occupation*, "the United States counters one 'successful' use of propaganda by appropriating and reorienting it against itself. Americans share with Nazis the means of swaying public

validate their arguments that media should not bow to the people but should uphold the educative values of Western civilization and culture.).

318 *See id.* at 93.

319 *See id.*

320 *See* Jeffrey Herf, The Jewish Enemy: Nazi Propaganda During World War II and the Holocaust 2 (2006) ("During World War II, the propaganda of the Nazi regime repeatedly asserted that an actual political subject, an actor called Jewry or international Jewry, was 'guilty' of starting and prolonging the war and that a Jewish international conspiracy was intent on exterminating Germany and the Germans. These statements rested on a paranoia inherent in the Nazis' radical anti-Semitism. In the context of World War II, these beliefs transformed the centuries-old European anti-Semitism from a justification for traditional forms of persecution into what the historian Norman Cohn called a 'warrant for genocide.'").

opinion but hope that Germans recognize the different political ends."[321] Throughout her book, Fay analyzed the impact of American policy regarding film, a policy meant to teach Germans how to act like Americans through portrayals of everyday democratic life. Fay explained that "[f]or the Americans, democracy was never understood merely as a matter of voting, political self-determination, or the creation of parliamentary and judicial systems. Democracy was also a type of behavior, a public attitude, and an affective relationship to the state, independent of these other political institutions . . . Indeed, in the minds of U.S. occupation officials, American democracy was inseparable from its culture."[322] To this end, the United States not only exported its own films, but also attempted to remake the German film industry in the image of Hollywood. The American occupation government believed that Hollywood could not only transmit democratic messages, but also act as the model of a democratic cultural institution, a medium of the free market that was forced to respond to consumer tastes.[323]

To accomplish its end, the American government set up a twofold system. At first, American authorities focused on exporting American films to form the foundation of German democracy, and then they imagined the creation of a German film industry that, like Hollywood, was free of speech and trade barriers, was self-regulated, and was not supported by any subsidies or quota systems.[324] The Americans began by impounding all films within their zone, removed all German personnel in the film industry pending denazification checks, and began rebuilding theaters to showcase their own movies.[325] Film quickly became the primary form of entertainment across Germany. However, one of the most striking aspects of the American film campaign is that many of the movies the United States exported to Germany were not made for the purpose of re-education but for the purpose of entertaining American audience.[326] The Office of War Information (OWI) selected the films for export in order to emphasize specific themes, such as

---

321 Fay, *supra* note 294, at 43.

322 *Id.* at xiv–xv.

323 *See id.* at xix ("Hollywood features were the perfect 'democratic' medium for the occupation because, as the captains of industry argued, these films were produced in a market economy free from government censorship. To profit, they argued, Hollywood had to respond to (as opposed to dictate) American consumer desires. As a commodity and signifying medium, Hollywood films were presumed to be naturally imbued with the democratic sensibility of American spectators and thus could be shipped abroad as democratic products.").

324 *See* Fay, *supra* note 294, at xx.

325 *See id.* at 40 ("Just months after VE Day, film exchanges opened in Munich, Frankfurt, and Berlin to service the 16 movie theaters then in operation.").

326 *See id.* at 47 ("Importantly, Hollywood produced not a single feature film specifically for German reeducation. The military government initially selected from a list of about thirty-five features that were made during the war to entertain and, in some cases, patriotically galvanize American audiences in the United States. As the occupation progressed, the US government shipped postwar films that were still tethered to the American experience of nationhood and history. . . . Thus films made in the United States for the predominantly American market were exhibited in Germany to perform a pedagogical function far afield from the production's original intent.").

individuality, civic courage and duty, and the triumph of good, ingenuity, and kindness over the evils of ignorance.[327]

In order to more directly influence the German populace, the American military government released the newsreel *World in Film*, which directly addressed the occupation and the fall of the Nazis and was increasingly anti-Communist in tone.[328] However, these films and those selected by Hollywood were slow to be replaced and requests for new films were often ignored early in the process. This would not change until the 1948 currency reform brought more films to West German audiences. Eventually, the German film industry was re-established and converted from American military censorship into a self-regulated industry. The occupation government still wanted to control the film industry in order to ensure that it was in fact a democratic instrument, but its new regulations were quite tolerant and required only that films not negatively influence German morals, religion, or politics.[329] However, the German film producers still had to compete with American films, which continued to set the commercial standards due to higher production values, the presence of internationally recognizable stars, and a growing fascination with American products and culture in the wake of West German economic growth.[330]

The American films that were chosen shared specific themes and similar messages. Fay argued that for American audiences, " 'democracy' depends on a mimesis that erases difference" due to a "myth of immigrant assimilation" which asserts that "culture and not blood is the basis for national belonging."[331] These films depicted the United States as a multiethnic land where immigrants were transformed into democratic Americans by accepting the idea that "no group is superior or inferior to any other, [that the world] is made up of human beings with the same basic hopes, needs, strengths, and frailties, [who] before God . . . are the same."[332] Fay presented the example of Brown's 1942 film

---

[327] In order to choose these films, the OWI set out specific criteria that a film had to exhibit: "A. Wish to fix German guilt and truth of Nazi exploitation of Europe. B. Indicate unfavorable global attitudes toward Fascism and Nazism. C. Offset efforts of Nazi propaganda about the USA and correct German misconceptions of modern history. D. Demonstrate great values and strength of democratic living. E. Indicate the US as a strong democratic society striving for full realization of the 4 freedoms. F. Motion pictures should be of the best cinematographic art, with some Technicolor included." *Id.* at 50.

[328] The German response to this newsreel was fairly negative, as many believed it was simply another obvious form of state-sponsored propaganda that was not only obviously biased, but often humiliating and depressing. *See id.* at 55.

[329] *See id.* at 127–28 ("In the spirit of the Hollywood Production Code Administration, on which the [Freiwillige Selbstkontrolle der Filmwirtschaft] was modeled, producers should simply learn to offend the fewest people possible while attracting patrons to the theater with interesting content. Indeed, according to the US military government, film industry self-regulation 'modified to suit the German mentality' was 'one of the most important steps towards the democratization of the German film industry,' not least because now that Germans were presumed to be democratically reeducated they could be trusted, as American audiences were, to support democratic films.").

[330] *See id.* at 128.

[331] *Id.* at xvi.

[332] *Id.* at 26.

The Human Comedy, which detailed the efforts of a typical Irish American family to fit into a small Californian town throughout the war.[333] This film, and others like it, not only showed the American way of life but also demonstrated that "there is a cultural (often corporal) price to pay for American citizenship, as non-European newcomers especially are expected to 'shed their old skins' and disavow or erase visible signs of their foreign nativity."[334] However, Fay was quick to point out the "omission of Asian Americans, African Americans, and Native Americans in Brown's film," which "signals that American citizenship is multiple only to the point of what Carrie Tirado Bramen calls 'variegated whiteness.' "[335] According to Fay, the United States thus exported not only its films but also its ideas about nationalism and race.[336] Ironically, these ideas were also embodied in historical films depicting the Wild West and America's founding.[337]

German reactions to American film policy were not quite the simple replication that occupation officials had desired or anticipated; instead, the Germans "reinterpreted, adapted, and domesticated" American themes as portrayed through film.[338] American officials had hoped that Germans would simply reproduce the democratic spirit they saw on the screen and would undertake the immigrant transformation without the trek across the ocean. However, according to Fay, "the German movie theater became a site of protest and film criticism, a venue for political critique . . . German audiences read [American films] in rather unexpected ways that exposed the hypocrisy of the reeducation campaign and the perils of genuinely imitating America's contemporary culture or its developmental experience."[339] Movies that sparked American patriotism simply reminded Germans of the fact that they were the losers and the occupied.[340] Depictions of race in American films "revealed in its fissures, obscurities, and curious asides a darker side of American politics to those audiences open to alternative readings, as indeed the Germans were."[341] The depiction of the immigrant myth similarly left many Germans

---

[333] *See id.* at 44.

[334] *Id.* at 59.

[335] *Id.* at 47.

[336] *See id.* at 48 ("Hollywood ethnology tutored audiences to scrutinize the faces and bodies of ethnic others to discern the good immigrants from the bad foreigners. In efforts to reeducate the Germans by showing them what, according to Hollywood, American democracy looked like, Americans unwittingly exported not only their unbridled nationalism but their own racial notions of statehood and justification for exclusionary violence.").

[337] *See id.* at 75 ("These films take us to pivotal moments and romantic spaces in America's westward expansion where the pioneers clash with Native Americans in their efforts to tame the land and bring legal order. While each film pits 'savage Indians' against the white settlers so as to authorize the genocide that made possible American's democratic founding, these films also argue for the ethnographic proposition that culture and not blood determines one's access to citizenship.").

[338] *Id.* at xvii.

[339] *Id.* at xxv.

[340] *See id.* at 53 ("Rather than convince Germans that they really had been defeated by superior democratic forces (as if the air raids and subsequent occupation alone were not proof enough), these war films reignited in some filmgoers the 'flame and spirit' of militarism.").

[341] *Id.* at 58.

reluctant to conform to the requirement that they replace their German identity with an American one.[342] In the process of watching American films, Germans learned that they didn't "need to become *more* like Americans but to find new paradigms of 'ethnological correctness' and ethnographic sympathy."[343]

iii. Racial and Ethnic Relations

Genocide meant race became a sensitive and critical issue in the two reconstructed East and West Germanys. In forming a representative democracy, it is critical that all groups, including ethnic, cultural, and racial minorities, have an equal opportunity to voice their concerns. Tensions between the majority and minorities often impede this process and hinder the construction of a functioning democracy. However, after the war, American and Allied authorities did little to actually address race and ethnic relations within Germany, and often created conflicts with their own example.[344] The reconstruction period was marked by a recasting of terms for racial difference, banning the use of the word *Rasse* (race) that had been marred by Nazi ideology, in favor of the words *Andersartigkeit* (difference) and *Andersaussenhen* (looking different).[345] While the terminology of race and outward manifestations of racism became taboo,[346] the national and social dialogue remained highly racialized,[347] and questions of difference took center stage in redefining what it meant to be German.

The question of Jewish reintegration would seem to be one of the most important concerns facing the reconstruction of West Germany for the Americans and the other

---

342 *See id.* at 80 ("Most of the Hollywood films brought to Germany under the aegis of reeducation, especially those concerned with American westward expansion and the history of immigration, did little to teach Germans about democracy or assure them that assimilating to the customs of their occupiers would restore them to a more enlightened, liberal way of being. . . . Rejecting Hollywood's western formula, Germans refused identification with their occupiers and thus resisted both the Americanization of their culture during the occupation and the explicit assimilationist mandate of reeducation.").

343 *Id.* at 81.

344 *See* Anson Rabinbach, *Restoring the German Spirit: Humanism and Guilt in Post-War Germany*, *in* GERMAN IDEOLOGIES SINCE 1945: STUDIES IN THE POLITICAL THOUGHT AND CULTURE OF THE BONN REPUBLIC 23, 34 (Jan-Werner Müller ed., 2003) ("It is remarkable that given the widespread recognition of the crimes of the Nazi regime, so little attention was paid to the doctrinal sources of Nazi racial policy in volkisch thought. Instead, the regime was perceived as lacking any doctrinal or ideological commitments, as an amoralism without intellectual foundations.").

345 *See* Heide Fehrenbach, *Learning from America: Reconstructing "Race" in Postwar Germany*, *in* AMERICANIZATION AND ANTI-AMERICANISM: THE GERMAN ENCOUNTER WITH AMERICAN CULTURE AFTER 1945, at 107, 107 (Alexander Stephan ed., 2005); *see also* Rita Chin & Heide Fehrenbach, *Introduction: What's Race Got to Do with It?*, *in* RITA CHIN ET AL., AFTER THE NAZI RACIAL STATE: DIFFERENCE AND DEMOCRACY IN GERMANY AND EUROPE 1, 3 (2009).

346 *See* Chin & Fehrenbach, *supra* note 345, at 3 ("The term *Rasse* has virtually disappeared from the German lexicon and public discourse since 1945 despite the persistence of social ideologies and behaviors that look an awful lot like racism.").

347 *See id.* at 4 ("[R]acialized thinking can be found in institutional patterns, policies, social practices, and behaviors that target, stigmatize, treat as unequal, exclude, or adversely affect individuals on the basis of their perceived ethnoracial membership, 'even if *conscious* belief that they are inferior or unworthy is absent.'").

Allies. While most Germans in 1945 did not approve of the way Jews had been treated during the war, a significant portion felt it was a good thing to break their economic and political power,[348] a point of view in keeping with Nazi propaganda, which cast Germans as the innocent victims of an all-powerful Jewish international conspiracy. After the war, Jewish survivors of the concentration and death camps began returning to Germany or fleeing the Soviets in the East,[349] and soon it became apparent that at least some of them were going to become a permanent reality.[350] The American zone had the largest number of Jewish survivors, spread throughout the German towns or in camps for displaced persons. Jewish communities (*Religionsgemeinden*) were established in several cities throughout West Germany, often at the request of local Jews to the occupation government. These communities did not only establish communal and political bonds between survivors. They also helped them establish the self-government necessary to survive the difficult early weeks of reconstruction when little aid was provided due to the overwhelming and unexpected effect the Jewish re-emigration had on the occupation's already taxed bureaucracy. Most Jews were simply waiting to emigrate to Palestine or the United States and were skeptical of the possibility that Germans and Jews might ever be able to live side-by-side peacefully within Germany again. Those who did hope to stay often attempted to return to their homes only to find them filled with unwelcoming and nervous Germans, and often this journey was made with little or no assistance from the occupation government or their fellow Jews in the Allied countries.

During this period of emigration, the American government, in accordance with the directives of the Supreme Headquarters of the Allied Expeditionary Forces in Europe, did not distinguish between Jews and ordinary Germans. Special treatment was to be specifically avoided in case it perpetuated Nazi propaganda of racial difference, and as a consequence, Allied forces often treated Jews as defeated Germans rather than war victims.[351] Even in the area of film, efforts were made to sidestep or ignore questions of Jewish racial or biological difference by portraying them as no different from other white races, recasting their difference as cultural or ethnic.[352]

---

[348] *See* Frank Stern, *The Historic Triangle: Occupiers, Germans and Jews in Postwar Germany*, *in* WEST GERMANY UNDER CONSTRUCTION: POLITICS, SOCIETY, AND CULTURE IN THE ADENAUER ERA 199, 201–02 (Robert G. Moeller ed., 1997) (including a survey analysis of the Office of Military Government, US in Germany (OMGUS) in November 1945); *see also* WERNER BERGMANN ET AL., ANTI-SEMITISM IN GERMANY: THE POST-NAZI EPOCH SINCE 1945, at 1 (1997).

[349] *See* Stern, *supra* note 348, at 202.

[350] *See* Atina Grossman, *From Victims to "Homeless Foreigners": Jewish Survivors in Postwar Germany*, *in* RITA CHIN ET AL., AFTER THE NAZI RACIAL STATE: DIFFERENCE AND DEMOCRACY IN GERMANY AND EUROPE 55, 57 (2009) ("Relations between Germans and Jews became even more complicated and confused once it became clear that some, a small minority certainly, of those survivors in transit to new lives would in fact become permanent residents of an only partially renovated post-Nazi Germany.").

[351] *See* Stern, *supra* note 348, at 205.

[352] *See* Fehrenbach, *supra* note 345, at 112.

This policy did not change until the summer of 1945 when General Dwight D. Eisenhower, under Jewish lobbying pressure in Washington, mandated the establishment of Jewish displaced persons (DP) camps and the removal of General George Patton for failure to stringently enforce denazification and afford preferential treatment of the Jewish survivors. However, preferential treatment of Jewish survivors had a specific drawback: It gave Germans an excuse to revive their old prejudices.[353] Resentment over real and imagined aid, along with the denazification of the country which included the confiscation of former Nazi property for Jewish DP, led to legal disputes over questions of restitution and a development of mistrust on both sides of the racial debate.[354] Slowly, Germans came to realize that their anti-Semitic attitudes would not be punished by the occupation authorities as long as they abided by any pro-Jewish decrees and regulations, and even newspapers began focusing on the suffering of the German prisoners of war and civilians as interest flagged in the plight of the returning Jewish population.[355]

Often, it was the Jewish communities who were most active in supporting the causes and needs of the Jewish survivors, confronting the German and American occupation bureaucracy directly when no one else was willing or able to address their concerns.[356] "The fact that antisemitism was no longer official state ideology and that German officialdom thus was no longer supposed . . . to implement antisemitic policies, was a result of the abolition of antisemitic Nazi legislation by decrees of the Allied Control Council."[357] However, "OMGUS [Office of Military Government, US] reports point out that pressure had to be exerted by the occupying powers and their appointed state commissioners in the German bureaucracy to deal with the problems and needs of the persecuted and the victims of the Nazi regime."[358]

The American military government, weighed down by its other responsibilities in administering a war torn nation, was hampered in this effort by conflicting orders and its own prejudices and biases. A report was released in July 1945 detailing the conditions and sentiments within the Jewish DP camps. The Harrison Report found that many were resentful of the fact that the camps continued to be overlooked by the occupation authorities in favor of German civilians:

> the military government officers manifest the utmost reluctance or indisposition, if not timidity, about inconveniencing the German population. They even say that their

---

[353] *See* Grossman, *supra* note 350, at 64 ("Not only had there been 'no horrified outcry' about the atrocities [the Germans] had perpetrated, but the very presence of the survivors had given rise to a new antisemitism, driven by resentment of Jews as the visible but unwanted reminders of German crimes, demanding some restitution.").

[354] *See* Stern, *supra* note 348, at 207–08.

[355] *See id.* at 208–09 ("Those who had suffered were Germans: German men, German sons—there was little room for the suffering of others, for the hardships endured by 'foreigners.'").

[356] *See id.* at 210–11 (detailing specific accounts from a few small German towns).

[357] *Id.* at 213.

[358] *Id.*

> job is to get communities working properly and soundly again, that they must "live with the Germans while the DP's are a more temporary problem." . . . Actually, there have been situations where displaced persons, especially Jews, have found it difficult to obtain audiences with military government authorities because ironically they have been obliged to go through German employees who have not facilitated matters.[359]

Even though this report prompted Eisenhower to issue a directive naming the concerns of displaced Jews as the highest priority, a UN report found in the spring of 1946 that "[t]he directives of General Eisenhower have not been and are not being properly implemented in the field. The majority of officials are woefully ignorant of the problem and the few officers remaining who have knowledge of, and sympathy for it, are unable to make their influence felt at the troop level."[360]

Even the German political parties hesitated to deal with Jewish topics or anti-Semitism for fear of losing voter support, and often addressed them only when it became politically expedient. OMGUS sought to create community organizations and civil liberty leagues to help Jews promote their interests within a democratic society turning against them, but by 1947, this was too little too late. American focus had already begun to shift to the Cold War struggle and anticommunism, while Jewish demands for restitution became louder in the face of West German economic recovery. The American occupation government responded by passing the Law of Restitution in March 1947 in order to deal with the issue of the return of property, but under political pressure and the fear of a resurgence of anti-Semitism fueled by German resentment, the law covered only those Jews who had been forced to give up their land under compulsion, not due to emigration.[361] Soon, the Americans and the German political leaders gave up touching the hot-button issue of Jewish reintegration altogether. However, the American government preferred to leave the matter of dealing with the presence of anti-Semitism to the newly elected German Bundestag. As a result, the Jewish community was forced to come to terms with the fact that they had only two options: to learn to live with the new realities of a society that didn't want them and didn't want to talk about them or to leave it altogether. Some Jews continued to wait, bags packed and close at hand, for the day when they would receive their reparations or when they would get their ticket to leave, and, as they waited, they continued to live off the meager welfare support they could get from the German government. This led even more Germans to renew their resentments, as "Germans were even more likely to perceive those [Jews] still there not as victims of persecution but as 'asocial' and 'homeless' foreigners (*heimatslose Auslander*), 'parasites' on West Germany's developing economy," and familiar stereotypes reappeared.[362]

---

[359] *Id.* at 216.

[360] *Id.*

[361] *See id.* at 223–24.

[362] Grossman, *supra* note 350, at 66; *see also* BERGMANN, *supra* note 348, at 1–2.

The integration of Jews into German society was not the only racial challenge German society faced during the reconstruction period. Another racial group, categorized as the "black occupation children," suffered immensely from the recasting of racial difference in terms of physical appearance.[363] While in the aftermath of the war, there was a tendency to recast any difference between Jews and Germans as ethnic or cultural,[364] rather than physical, black occupation children were immediately identifiable as different because of their skin tone. The American occupation government had attempted to address anti-Semitism, though often ineffectually, by eliminating it from the debate, from media, and from everyday life.

However, due to its own prejudices, the United States did very little to address the developing black and white racism in postwar Germany and in fact did much to promote it. "Although the American Military Government in Germany put a good deal of emphasis on official efforts to denazify and reeducate the German public, 'race' barely figured in formal reeducation programs (beyond the legal language against discrimination that ultimately entered West Germany's *Grundgesetz* in 1949). As a result, racial reconstruction in early postwar Germany resulted primarily not from official Allied pronouncements on programs, but more spontaneously through Germans' interaction with, and observation of, the social and racial dynamics of occupation on the ground in Germany." [365]

Thus, the German public internalized much of their racial stereotypes from the occupying powers:

> Military occupation, combined with postwar Germans' observations of antiblack racism in the U.S. Army and often violent reaction to the civil rights movement, a growing market for African American rock 'n' roll, jazz, and rhythm and blues, and the political destabilization caused by decolonization created a new lens through which Germans began to interpret "race."[366]

---

[363] *See* Heide Fehrenbach, *Black Occupation Children and the Devolution of the Nazi Racial State*, *in* RITA CHIN ET AL., AFTER THE NAZI RACIAL STATE: DIFFERENCE AND DEMOCRACY IN GERMANY AND EUROPE 30, 30–31 (2009) ("After 1945 and the demise of the Third Reich, children remained a focus of racialized social policy in Germany, particularly in the decade and a half following the war. . . . It was through the articulation of social policy regarding abortion, adoption, schooling, and integration of these [black] youth into the workforce that questions of German racial redefinition after 1945 were worked out.").

[364] Fehrenbach, *supra* note 345, at 112 ("[P]ostwar West German definitions of race paralleled those of the postwar United States, where, during the 1940s, social scientists 'softened' the differences among whites of European origin (including, in particular, Jews) to a cultural one and conceived of these groups in terms of 'ethnicity.'").

[365] Fehrenbach, *supra* note 363, at 33; *see also* FAY, *supra* note 294, at 120 ("Thus, through its policies, the army in effect imported American Jim Crow laws to the 'liberated' territory, while US information preached the virtues of American ethnic difference.").

[366] Chin & Fehrenbach, *supra* note 345, at 18. However, it is important to note that the Germans did not learn antiblack racism from the American occupation forces. As Chin explains, "Germans had a long tradition of such bigotry that predated and was intensified by Germany's short stint as colonial power prior to 1918 and shorter stint as National Socialist power between 1933 and 1945. Rather, informal contacts between occupier and occupied—along with the discriminatory policies of the US military toward its minorities and the

It is often easy to forget that America was experiencing its own racial tensions, and through the presence of the American military and the infiltration of American cultural products in the German market, the United States exported its own ways of viewing racial divides to Germany. "Despite the American military's best efforts to downplay the racist practices of its own organization, the lesson that white supremacy and racial inequality could coexist with democracy came through loud and clear to occupied Germans."[367] Germans could watch as white GIs responded negatively, and sometimes violently, to interracial relationships between white German women and black GIs.[368] After the war, interracial relationships and their resulting offspring became a center of controversy within the German public sphere, yet the American occupation government hesitated to address the issue at all, leaving it to the Germans and their emerging civil society to deal with the problem.

c. Decartelization

The decartelization of the German economy is the last of the 4 Ds, and arguably the one that made the strongest impact on the transformation of the German society and culture. The Americans particularly placed a great deal of emphasis on the restructuring of the German economy because they viewed capitalism as an essential principle of democracy.[369] In particular, they emphasized the free market system in several key areas, including the film industry,[370] and opposed the idea of state ownership.[371] As the Cold War shifted the focus of the Allies from dismantling to reconstructing the German

tense relations among occupation soldiers of differing ethnicities—affected the ways Germans perceived and received American political and social values after 1945." Fehrenbach, *supra* note 363, at 33.

367 Chin & Fehrenbach, *supra* note 345, at 20; *see also* Fehrenbach, *supra* note 345, at 109.

368 *See* Fehrenbach, *supra* note 363, at 33–34; *see also* FAY, *supra* note 294, at 120.

369 *See* GLEES, *supra* note 283, at 36 ("It was America's belief that a new economic order was necessary, not only to lay the foundations for future prosperity, but also to permit a western-style democracy to flourish."); *see also* FAY, *supra* note 294, at 118 (discussing "American desire for Germans to adopt American cultural and consumptive practices (including watching Hollywood films and listening to jazz music) as a means of achieving, or perhaps even in place of a demonstrable commitment to, democracy."); Volker R. Berghahn, *West German Reconstruction and American Industrial Culture, 1945–1960*, *in* THE AMERICAN IMPACT ON POSTWAR GERMANY 65, 72 (Reiner Pommerin ed., 1995) ("In the American view, a modern industrial society needed an open economic marketplace just as much as it required a free-wheeling political 'market.' These markets were complementary, and one could not exist without the other. In this sense, there were also two reeducation jobs to be done—one political and another of economic.").

370 *See* FAY, *supra* note 294, at xx ("[F]ree trade was the economic cornerstone of free speech and trade barriers were indicators of totalitarian mind control. This was Hollywood's brand of market empire that was pointedly obscure in its description of a democratic film defined as anything the American people will pay to see. Based on the Hollywood model, the American occupation forces insisted that the German film market be open to free trade, that the film industry abide by self-regulation as opposed to government or civic censorship, and that any form of subsidies or quota systems be banned.").

371 *See* GLEES, *supra* note 283, at 42–43 (discussing the role of General Clay in refusing to accept the nationalization of the German coal and iron companies as proposed by the constituent assembly in June 1946).

economy, the Americans and the Soviets began an epic battle to model their respective German zones into reflections of their own ideologies.[372] The Americans recognized that in order to transform West Germany into a democratic state, they first needed to sell the Germans on the merits of such a system by showing them that a democracy could translate into tangible benefits.[373] American efforts to install a capitalist system in a formerly totalitarian state resulted in a "majority [that] developed unambiguously positive feelings for America, its democratic system, its dynamic economy, and its entertainment culture."[374] In order to reach this result, America convinced the German public the idea that consumer democracy could be realized "in the equality of producers and consumers as social partners towards a common goal: *Wohlstand fur alle* (Prosperity for all)."[375] They were successful because "capital was hungry for new markets, the German nation for democracy."[376]

Indeed, "[no]ting that even France and Britain were more inclined toward socialism and were increasingly critical of American designs for living, the New York Office of the Civil Affairs Division proposed a new, unabashedly propagandistic campaign that emphasized capitalism as the most distinct and least understood feature of American political life. . . . [P]ropaganda needed above all to galvanize Germans by linking their faith in capitalist consumerism to confidence in political democracy and, conversely, needed to naturalize the culture of American consumer capitalism as *the* culture of democracy."[377]

A "combination of initially tough but then more limited interventions changed the economy's basic structures in the direction of competition, while collective learning processes of entrepreneurs and consumers helped [Germans] internalize the opportunities of the market."[378] Konrad Jarausch pointed to the availability of the work force, rapid accumulation of capital by businesses through tax exemptions, and a free trade policy as

---

[372] *See* Jarausch, *supra* note 286, at 79 (discussing how the victors "placed a higher priority on confirming the legitimacy of each system and taking advantage of the potential in each part than on the joint exploitation of Germany. During the first five years of the postwar period, priorities thus shifted slowly from stripping Germany of its economic power to reviving a transformed economy within the victors' respective sphere of control.").

[373] *Id.* at 115 ("Adenauer's policy of cooperation with the Western Allies was on the whole sufficiently successful to convince a skeptical electorate that closer cooperation with the West would bring more tangible benefits."); *see also* Glees, *supra* note 283, at 99 ("Adenauer's success, then, lay not merely in executing the policies of Western integration but in giving them form through treaties, through rearmament and, above all, through economic and political integration with western Europe.").

[374] Jarausch, *supra* note 286, at 127.

[375] Erica Carter, *Alice in the Consumer Wonderland: West German Case Studies in Gender and Consumer Culture*, *in* West Germany Under Construction: Politics, Society, and Culture in the Adenauer Era 347, 353 (Robert G. Moeller ed., 1997).

[376] *Id.* at 354 ("Conflating concepts of freedom and democracy with images of a critical consumer was an indispensible mechanism in the organisation of public consensus in the emergent social market economy.").

[377] Fay, *supra* note 294, at 87–88.

[378] Jarausch, *supra* note 286, at 93.

the reasons behind the German economic miracle of the postwar period, which transformed Germany from a war-torn, defeated shell into the engine of the European economy it is today.[379] However, it was several key American policies that set the stage for this development: the decartelization of the economy, currency reform, and the Marshall Plan.[380] These policies helped change German consumer culture and planted the seeds for democracy's acceptance among the German populace.[381]

While a great deal of change took place in Germany after the war, it was the 1920s that set the stage for the "Americanization" of Germany, and the war merely interrupted the already growing consumerist trend.[382] The "economic miracle" of 1950s Germany was plagued by the reluctance of the traditional business and industrial elites to abandon their prewar concepts of industrial organization, which had been discredited by the fall of the Fascist state.[383] Nonetheless, there was also a great deal of mixing new and old ideas to create a new capitalist Germany.[384] It was the influence of outside factors, namely the American industrial society and capitalist model that spurred this change. "In the initial postwar years, the society of the Federal Republic was exposed to models of political culture and patterns of everyday life that came from other Western industrial societies, particularly the US. This took the form of the occupation forces' early attempts to bring about a 'reeducation,' then a 'reorientation' to democracy. The opening of the West German economy to the world market, which soon followed, was another part of this process."[385] This is due not only to the fact that the United States had become one of the dominant world powers after the war but also that the American capitalist model had stood as the opponent to the Fascist cartel system of Hitler's Germany.[386]

---

379 *Id.* at 89; *see also* Axel Schildt & Arnold Sywottek, *"Reconstruction" and "Modernization": West German Social History During the 1950s*, *in* WEST GERMANY UNDER CONSTRUCTION: POLITICS, SOCIETY, AND CULTURE IN THE ADENAUER ERA 413, 419–20 (Robert G. Moeller ed., 1997).

380 However, it is important to note that "[e]conomists cannot agree . . . whether Erhard's reforms, and the measures taken by the Allies (in particular the new Deutschmark), were the cause of West German economic strength (which predated 1945), or merely a useful kick-start to it." GLEES, *supra* note 283, at 81.

381 *See generally* Carter, *supra* note 375, at 347–70 (discussing the growth of the consumer culture and its impact on women's enfranchisement in the postwar period).

382 *See* Schildt & Sywottek, *supra* note 379, at 417–18 ("the social development of the 1950s emerges as the resumption of trends that were interrupted by the destruction during World War II and the changes that took place in the postwar years. . . . Under National Socialist rule, there were already elements of 'modernity' experienced in daily life—from laundry detergent to Coca-Cola—that would intensify after the war.").

383 *See* Berghahn, *supra* note 369, at 65, 71 ("Washington's industrial policies generated a good deal of resentment and resistance on the part of those West German entrepreneurs who, having reemerged in their companies and associations pretty much unscathed, continued to regard the German cartel system as fundamentally sound and worth retaining.").

384 *Id.* at 67 ("[T]here was no restoration in the strict meaning of the word; nor was there a rupture that turned German society and its economy upside down to give rise to something different. The challenge and difficult task is therefore to calibrate more precisely the mix of old and new and to identify the agents of change.").

385 Schildt & Sywottek, *supra* note 379, at 417–18. *See also* Berghahn, *supra* note 369, at 67–68.

386 Berghahn, *supra* note 369, at 69.

American insistence on the decartelization of the German economy[387] meant that cartels and syndicates were banned, and giant corporations, which had enjoyed near monopoly status during the war, were broken up as part of the American trust-busting effort.[388] While America was busy transforming the old factories of the German war machine into engines of its new capitalist system, it was exporting a new industrial and consumer culture that would ultimately leave a great mark on the German system.[389] Recognizing this fact, many German industrialists began sending executives to America and the rest of industrialized Europe to study the "fruits of low-cost, rationalized production . . . and mass consumption . . . turn[ing] it into a powerful ideology."[390] However, not all changes were rapidly accepted,[391] and it took some time before these "fruits" convinced the skeptics that "American, rather than traditional German, methods offered the best solution to the problems of modern industry."[392] Policies like the Marshall Plan and currency reform eventually allowed German industries, especially iron and steel, to compete in the global market, and the suspension of Allied trade restrictions led the Federal Republic to a trade surplus by 1952, and by 1960, its exports represented 17 percent of the net national product.[393]

The American mass production, industrial culture was not the only capitalist importation of West Germany after the war. American consumer culture also spread across the Atlantic, leading to great changes in the German way of life.[394] While Germany had been suffering from a crippling unemployment at the beginning of the 1950s, by the end of the

---

387 *Id.* at 70 (discussing how the government bodies, like the Committee on Economic Development, planned to establish a world economy with a "viable organizational and constitutional framework" built on the basis of an "Open Door capitalist order" and the rejection of cartels and syndicates, which would lead the "players in industry [to] adjust their behavior and their national structures to comply").

388 *Id.* at 71–72. However, due to the resistance of the industrial barons, the Basic Law included a proviso which allowed the Cartel Office to grant exceptions. *Id.* at 72; *see also* JARAUSCH, *supra* note 286, at 88 (discussing the efforts of Ludwig Erhard to pass a cartel law, over the objection of the League of German Industrialists (BDI), which, while weakened throughout the political passage process through the Federal Diet, solidified the American decartelization of West Germany).

389 Berghahn, *supra* note 369, at 73 ("[W]hen, during the period of reconstruction, West German companies introduced American technology, as many of them did, they imported more than machines, involving them in a complex process of interaction between the two industrial cultures.").

390 *Id.* at 75.

391 *See id.* at 75–76 ("[T]here was opposition to the introduction of American methods of management and factory organization. Even the use of the word 'manager' was frowned upon by some as unsuitable for the West German situation. Insofar as these opponents believed in any management training at all, they would send their employees to Reinhard Hoehn's Harzburg Academy, where they would be taught an authoritarian model of leadership inspired by the Prussian General Staff. So, here, too, there were obstacles, cultural and ideological 'filters' that the hegemonic power of the West had to contend with in Germany and elsewhere.").

392 *Id.* at 76.

393 *See* Schildt & Sywottek, *supra* note 379, at 420 (discussing the rise of the West German finishing and processing industries, called its "industrial miracle").

394 *See* Berghahn, *supra* note 369, at 77 ("[I]t was not just West German market organizations and management methods that became 'Americanized'; the West German consumer also fell under America's spell.").

decade it found itself facing a labor shortage.[395] Growing economic prosperity fostered a favorable view of capitalism and democracy and had a large impact on the restructuring of German culture.[396] As geographic migration slowed and families began to settle down in a replica of American suburban life, the number of commuting workers (and thus the number of automobiles) began to grow exponentially.[397]

While the German economy rapidly developed, many adopted a "culture of work," and according to a 1995 survey, "about 40 percent of West Germans felt stressed and overworked" by a schedule that included only an average of three hours a day for leisure time.[398] The introduction of women into the work force and the shrinking leisure time led many to retreat to popular media forms like radio, television, and movies; "[c]ontemporary observers who emphasized the significance of leisure and consumption also called attention to the ways in which society was increasingly dominated by the media and increasingly informal in nature."[399] This change in leisure and consumer culture led West Germans to experience " 'a change in values,' moving away from a 'heroic past and an emphasis on community and hard work' to an emphasis on 'guiding principles of behavior [that stressed] individual success and the pleasures of life.' "[400] The era of rapidly changing technology, social norms, and lifestyles led to a "climate of stability, capable of withstanding the socioeconomic, political, and cultural convulsions of the 1960s."[401]

d. Lessons Learned: The Role of the Germans

World War II and its resulting occupation had a profound impact on Germans and their culture. In half a decade, the country went from a war-torn, defeated, Fascist dictatorship to a democratic state and economic powerhouse. As Anthony Glees stated in his book *Reinventing Germany*, "the history of the Federal Republic shows us that what was constructed after 1945 was *not* the product of chance but of a conscious set of policies, deliberately pursued, and with a particular purpose in mind."[402] Glees maintained that the reinvention of Germany was partly a product of the Germans themselves, but "one to

---

395 *See* Schildt & Sywottek, *supra* note 379, at 419.

396 *Id.* at 426 (" '[T]he universal consumption of industrial mass production' was the most significant factor contributing to 'overcoming the class conditions of industrial society' and providing for a 'relative leveling of the stratified structure of social relations that once prevailed.' This was, according to Schelsky, 'perhaps the most dominant development in the present transformation of German society.' ") (quoting Helmut Schelsky, *Die Bedeutung des Schichtungsbegriffes für die Analyse der gegenwärtigen deutschen Gesellschaft* (1953), in idem, AUF DER SUCHE NACH DER WIRKLICHKEIT: GESAMMELTE AUFSÄTZE 332f. (Düsseldorf, 1965)).

397 *See* Schildt & Sywottek, *supra* note 379, at 423.

398 *Id.* at 433.

399 *Id.* at 434.

400 *Id.* at 438 (quoting Ralf Dahrendorf, *Die neue Gesellschaft: Soziale Strukturwandlungen der Nachkriegszeit, in* BESTANDSAUFNAHME: EINE DEUTSCHE BILANZ 1962, at 215 (Hans Werner Richter ed., 1962)).

401 Schildt & Sywottek, *supra* note 379, at 440.

402 GLEES, *supra* note 283, at xix.

which all Germany's victors made a strong contribution."[403] The role of the Germans in this process cannot be overlooked because "[i]n order to rebuild Germany, its occupiers had to understand what now needed to be altered and what could be retained. . . . The people had been changed and conditioned by Nazism, and anyone seeking to make a new, and above all democratic, Germany was obliged to accept this."[404] While the form of the reinvention was "ultimately the subject of inter-Allied and not German decisions,"[405] the success and failure of cultural policies depended upon their interpretation by the Germans who viewed them through the lens of defeat, occupation, and their existing cultural background. "The success of this project of a comprehensive 'reeducation of the Germans' . . . depended not only on pressure from the occupation powers but also on the willingness of the defeated people to participate in it."[406]

The 4 Ds, denazification, demilitarization, democratization, and decartelization, formed the backbone of Allied and American occupation rule, but each was achieved with varying degrees of success because of German interpretation and implementation. Denazification did not remove and punish all those associated with the defeated regime as intended;[407] it opened a door to democracy by removing those influences which had been acting as barriers to its rise before the war.[408] This denazification campaign was accompanied by a dismantling of German militarism in an effort to prevent the resurgence of Nazism.[409] The "complete 'elimination of the military and military traditions' "[410] in Germany included not only the removal of all weapons but also all emotional and symbolic references to war, aggression, and the military, destroying the positive associations which the Allies believed responsible for the rise of aggressive nationalism and Nazism.[411] This process was, however, aided by the fact that the defeat and occupation had destroyed many of these positive associations already.[412] While the broad Allied bans

---

403 *Id.* at xxvii.

404 *Id.* at 25; *see also* Peter K. Breit, *Culture as Authority: American and German Transactions*, *in* THE AMERICAN IMPACT ON POSTWAR GERMANY 125, 128 (Reiner Pommerin ed., 1995) (arguing that the American efforts to change German culture were ultimately successful because "the effort involved reclaiming and nurturing that which was peculiarly German, cleansed of its fascism, racism, nationalism, militarism, and romanticism.").

405 GLEES, *supra* note 283, at 28. *But see* Diehl, *supra* note 296, at 104 ("although the occupying powers generally imposed their will, German officials were able to wage determined (if not always successful) opposition against unpopular policies, occasionally undertook important initiatives of their own, and frequently played a not insignificant role in shaping legislation implemented during the occupation."); Robert G. Moeller, *Equality, Difference, and the Grundgesetz: Women, Families, and the Federal Republic's Basic Law*, *in* THE AMERICAN IMPACT ON POSTWAR GERMANY 149, 149–161 (Reiner Pommerin ed., 1995) (explaining that much of the German family policy was overseen by the Germans themselves).

406 JARAUSCH, *supra* note 286, at 20.

407 *See* TESCHKE, *supra* note 287, at 20.

408 *See* GLEES, *supra* note 283, at 31; *see also* TESCHKE, *supra* note 287, at 24; JARAUSCH, *supra* note 286, at 48.

409 *See* Diehl, *supra* note 296, at 100.

410 JARAUSCH, *supra* note 286, at 24.

411 *See id.* at 25, 29.

412 *Id.* at 31; *see also* Gordon A. Craig, *Konrad Adenauer and the United States*, *in* THE AMERICAN IMPACT ON POSTWAR GERMANY 1, 2–3 (Reiner Pommerin ed., 1995).

were an important part of the process of demilitarization, "[e]qually important, however, was how Germans themselves dealt with the trauma of war, because only their break with the glorification of military heroism could keep revanchism from flaring up again."[413] In fact, some are worried that this demilitarization was too successful and has "been exaggerated to the point that regardless of circumstances, peace is now viewed, like war had been before, as an absolute, incontestable, and always valid good."[414]

The democratization of Germany is perhaps the Allied goal that most clearly demonstrates the important role of the occupied population's role in the success and failure of cultural policy. This process involved not only the creation of a political system and complementing culture but also questions concerning race and gender. The Americans relied particularly on mass media as a way to educate the Germans about democracy.[415] Not only was the rebuilt German film industry to be modeled on the American vision of free market capitalism[416] but it was also used to communicate to the Germans what it meant to live in a democracy. "The U.S military government believed that Germans would develop a politically enlightened culture, in part, if they could learn to act like Americans or like Hollywood actors portraying Americans, and to this end required that Hollywood films be screened in German theaters so that audiences could study the behaviors of everyday democratic life."[417] However, the German public "did not merely imitate Hollywood examples; they reinterpreted, adapted, and domesticated"[418] what they saw on the screen. The American occupation government selected films calculated to convey to the Germans a multiethnic and democratic society,[419] but "[i]n efforts to reeducate the Germans by showing them what, according to Hollywood, American democracy looked like, Americans unwittingly exported not only their unbridled nationalism but their own racial notions of statehood and justification for exclusionary violence."[420]

Hollywood was not the only medium through which the Americans communicated to the Germans the idea that democracy was not necessarily incompatible with racism. The presence of the American military helped shift German conceptions of difference away from the now taboo ethnic definitions to racial definitions,[421] a problem most clearly

---

[413] Jarausch, *supra* note 286, at 44.

[414] *Id.* at 45.

[415] *See* Fay, *supra* note 294, at ix ("In Germany, the Americans exhibited their film culture to the defeated population to make a show of US military and moral superiority and to offer American culture as a model for imitation. The Germans in turn, and in order to regain independence, were expected to enact and make visible their rehabilitation by behaving like their wardens.").

[416] *See id.* at xix–xx.

[417] *See id.* at xiii.

[418] *Id.* at xvii.

[419] *See id.* at 47–50.

[420] *Id.* at 48.

[421] *See* Fehrenbach, *supra* note 345, at 107–08 ("Racialist thinking, however, did not disappear with the Nazi regime. The language and ideology of race underwent fundamental changes after 1945, yet the social landscape and national imagery of both postwar Germanys remained highly racialized, if in ways distinct from the interwar and wartime years. The postwar years mark a period of crucial transition, as military defeat,

articulated in the confusion over the integration of the children of black occupation soldiers and German women.[422] The Jews returning to their homeland from the concentration camps and exile faced their own reintegration problems, notably their recovery of lost or stolen property and German resentment over their perceived favorable treatment by the Allies.[423] However, very few Jews were left in Germany after the war and many chose to leave for Israel or the United States, allowing the Germans to avoid many uncomfortable questions.[424] While the Americans did try to address anti-Semitism,[425] much of the process of reintegration took place during everyday interactions between the Germans and the Jews, leading to a "strong and entirely acceptable antisemitism" that lurked underneath the surface of these relationships.[426] In the area of race relations, the Americans either unconsciously transmitted their own stereotypes and prejudices or unwittingly made things worse by not directly confronting the problem as they had in the areas of denazification and demilitarization. The Germans were therefore able to transform their culture while maintaining some of their older and most problematic traditions, updating them so as to more closely conform to their occupier's expectations and mores.

As noted, "[m]imicry may camouflage the occupied and in this way serve as a mechanism of subterfuge and resistance . . . [or] mimicry may function as a technology of 'unwitting collaboration' and perhaps even authentic ideological conversion."[427] When the Americans set out to reinforce their democratization of Germany by transforming it into a capitalist economy, some Germans, particularly in industry, were initially resistant and preferred the centralized system of old where the government played an important role in promoting and protecting national industries.[428] However, the Marshall Plan and currency reform, spearheaded by both Americans and Germans, put money in German pockets and kick-started an economic recovery that saw an influx of American products, ideas, and culture.[429] This prosperity convinced many of the German detractors that increased democracy could result in tangible benefits, and mass consumer culture

---

occupation, and the Cold War mandated a rethinking of the fit between race and nation in the emerging democratic and socialist societies of West and East Germany."); *see also* Chin & Fehrenbach, *supra* note 345, at 18.

[422] *See* Fehrenbach, *supra* note 345, at 113–14 (arguing that the black occupation children were "viewed as the physical manifestation of a humiliating defeat and occupation, displaced German masculinity and weakened German patriarchy, and the offspring of traitorous German women, who, through their fraternization with black troops, transgressed national and racial boundaries, as well as the deeply held moral values upon which these were based."); *see also* Fehrenbach, *supra* note 363, at 30–52.

[423] *See* Grossman, *supra* note 350, at 56–76.

[424] *See id.* at 68 ("[A]bout 30,000 Jewish [displaced persons] remained in Germany in late 1948.").

[425] *See id.* at 59 ("Despite the Americans' . . . considerable efforts to organize repatriation or resettlement, this was not immediately accomplished.").

[426] *Id.* at 67.

[427] Fay, *supra* note 294, at xiii.

[428] Berghahn, *supra* note 369, at 71.

[429] Jarausch, *supra* note 286, at 83–84.

began to change German political culture and society.[430] It was the Germans who took these outside influences, adapted to them, and made them an integral part of their social change.[431] However, this process can be unpredictable, and often American influence was interpreted in ways that were unexpected or unintended by the American occupation government.[432] If the German experience can teach us anything, it is the powerful but unpredictable way in which outside influences can shape culture in a developing society.

B. Miscellaneous Practices

This section addresses efforts by governments, international agencies, and organizations to deal with human rights violations and other obstacles to development. While not implementing change across society as a whole, the practices described in this section to effectuate change are similar to those discussed above in the country-specific sections. Throughout history and across nations, legal reform by itself has frequently failed to end harmful practices when those practices are embedded in the society's culture. However, antidevelopment cultural practices have been successfully changed when individuals and states specifically target them through a combination of legal and cultural change.

The section below looks at (1) how a few select countries have undertaken culture change projects with some, albeit limited, success; and (2) how certain select development issues (education, property rights, for example) have been targeted for change by different actors.

1. LAW AND CULTURE

Anthony Appiah argued that cultural revolutions have occurred throughout history and involve a sudden change in moral behavior.[433] Appiah also asserted that many cultural changes have occurred when society's perception of honor and the honor code changed.[434] An honor code is a set of social norms that determines how a person gains or loses what society determines constitutes honor.[435] This theory rests on the principle that

---

[430] *Id.* at 126–27 ("The result of these changes in values and behavior, carried out over several decades, was a reorientation of the political culture, which is sometimes celebrated as the return of a chastened apostate to a common Western civilization.").

[431] *See* Winfried Fluck, *California Blue: Americanization as Self-Americanization*, *in* AMERICANIZATION AND ANTI-AMERICANISM: THE GERMAN ENCOUNTER WITH AMERICAN CULTURE AFTER 1945, at 221, 221–232 (Alexander Stephan ed., 2005) (arguing that Americanization is the culmination and amalgamation of global influences, tastes, and cultures but that "audiences are more active and critical, their responses more complex and reflective, and their cultural values more resistant to manipulation and 'invasion' than many critical media theorists have assumed.").

[432] *See id.* at 222.

[433] KWAME ANTHONY APPIAH, THE HONOR CODE xi (2010).

[434] *Id.* at xiii.

[435] *Id.* at 175.

human beings desire respect and modify their behavior to meet the social requirements for respect.[436] Thus, when an individual's concept of morality and society's ideas about what is honorable change, dishonorable cultural practices will end.[437]

For example, in England, although the duel was outlawed as murder under the common law in the 1760s,[438] the practice did not die until the mid-1800s.[439] As an end to the practice took at least fifty years, clearly the mere fact that it was illegal was not the cause. Rather, the duel ended in Britain around the same time the aristocracy lost power and businessmen and bureaucrats came to power in both government and society.[440] The duel had been an honor ritual and a cultural practice of the aristocracy, which the new class viewed as a dishonorable "symbol of aristocratic privilege."[441] In addition, once the popular press exposed the practice and nongentry began to engage in duels, the duel lost its power to distinguish the honor of a gentleman from a regular man, and thus fell out of favor with the aristocrats as well.[442] Here, a change in class power led to a change in the definition of honor. Within this new framework, the duel was no longer viewed as honorable, and this change in perception led to its demise.[443]

a. China

i. Footbinding

In China, the government had unsuccessfully attempted to ban footbinding for years.[444] The Manchus tried to abolish the practice when they took power, but the practice in fact became more widespread.[445] In the early 1900s, the empress Cixi "issued an edict urging the end of footbinding" to no avail.[446] Footbinding continued despite its illegality precisely because it was a cultural practice associated with honor.[447] Many believe the practice originated as a method by which the emperor ensured the fidelity of his concubines.[448] Footbinding later became a symbol of upper-class status, showing that the women did not need to work.[449] Eventually, bound feet came to be regarded as beautiful.[450] Even after

---

436 *Id.* at 183.
437 *Id.* at 188.
438 *Id.* at 10.
439 *Id.* at 49.
440 *Id.* at 45.
441 *Id.* at 47.
442 *Id.* at 46.
443 *Id.* at 49.
444 *Id.* at 69.
445 *Id.*
446 *Id.* at 60.
447 *Id.* at 62.
448 *Id.* at 68.
449 *Id.* at 65–66.
450 *Id.* at 66 ("Men came to long for small-footed women . . . the conviction that their tiny feet were simply beautiful.").

the practice was recognized as unhealthy and a means of subjugation, it still continued.[451] The practice of footbinding led to complications like "ulceration, paralysis, gangrene, and mortification of the lower limbs . . . perhaps 10 percent of girls did not survive the treatment. . . ."[452] Despite opposition and medical problems, this practice "was defended even by women and was transmitted by them."[453]

As in the case of the demise of the duel in England, honor was the reason for the eventual decline of footbinding. In China, this change in the definition of honor stemmed not from class stratification but from national standing. Increasing contact with Western nations caused the Chinese to be concerned about China's national honor.[454] Industrialization in the West and the rise of Western powers diminished China's sense of superiority.[455] Britain forced China to a humiliating trade treaty, and France compelled China to open its ports to Christian missionaries.[456] These foreign victories and internal revolts caused the Chinese government to recognize its weaknesses.[457] This led China to look toward the West to adopt Western technology, and the country began to allow Chinese people to study abroad.[458] Students who returned learned that footbinding was unpopular outside of China and began to oppose the practice themselves as oppressive to women.[459] These encounters with the West led Chinese citizens to compare themselves to Westerners. Because they increasingly wanted respect from the West, they began to view footbinding as a "source of national shame."[460] Appiah claimed that by

> drawing attention to the contrast between China and the advancing industrializing world, at a time when some of the literati had lost confidence in the capacity of their own traditions to defend them from modernizing strangers, they were able to persuade some among the literati that they needed to promote reform.[461]

The expatriate elite wives formed a national anti-footbinding society.[462] These societies urged parents "to refrain from binding your daughters' feet and from marrying your sons to foot-bound women."[463] Academics began to insist that "havoc wrought in military invasions from abroad was made worse by the fact that so many women were literally

---

451 *Id.* at 71.

452 Gerry Mackie, *Ending Footbinding and Infibulation: A Convention Account*, 61 AM. SOC. REV. 999, 1000 (1996).

453 *Id.*

454 APPIAH, *supra* note 433, at 60.

455 *Id.* at 75.

456 *Id.* at 77.

457 *Id.* at 79.

458 *Id.* at 80.

459 *Id.* at 83.

460 *Id.* at 92.

461 *Id.* at 99.

462 *Id.* at 86.

463 *Id.* at 98–99.

unable to run away; and they argued that the physical vigor of women who could engage in sports because their feet were free would make them mothers of healthier children."[464] The change in perspective that viewed footbinding as a shameful rather than honorable practice eventually led men of elite classes to require wives with natural feet;[465] this contributed to the abandonment of footbinding as a practice once linked to high status and no longer was, thus causing the practice to lose its appeal.[466]

Reformation of footbinding in China was coupled with successful strides to end other cultural practices such as those that perpetuate gender inequality. The national and local anti-footbinding societies that emerged and "propagandized the disadvantages of footbinding in Chinese cultural terms, promoted pledge associations, and subtly conveyed international disapproval of the custom"[467] also "carried out a modern education campaign, which explained that the rest of the world did not bind women's feet—that China was losing face in the world and was subject to international ridicule."[468] The education campaign "explained the advantages of natural feet and the disadvantages of bound feet." [469] Perhaps most importantly, the societies required pledges from individuals not to bind their daughters' feet or allow their sons to marry a woman with bound feet.[470] Footbinding continued because it was associated with honor and often necessary for marriage, so these pledges likely helped end the practice as parents rejected footbound brides. Additionally, the education campaign "stressed that China was alone in the world in binding female feet,"[471] which perhaps at a moment of military defeat and globalization also encouraged people to reject the practice. The end of footbinding was mainly the result of exposure to the Western world and the propaganda and education programs of what would now be referred to as civil society organizations.

ii. One-Child Policy

The One-Child Policy, in effect until October 2015, has been the work of China's central government, implemented through local governments. Its methods have also been successful, as "fertility has fallen from just under 3 to 1.5–1.6 children per woman."[472] The government has tried to shift the cultural preference from many children to just one because "the excessive growth of Chinese numbers hindered the party's plans for

---

464 *Id.* at 91.

465 *Id.* at 99.

466 *Id.* at 99.

467 Mackie, *supra* note 452, at 1001.

468 *Id.* at 1011.

469 *Id.*

470 *Id.*

471 *Id.* at 1012.

472 Susan Greenhalgh, Cultivating Global Citizens 1 (2010). In October 2015, the Chinese government ended the one-child policy and allowed married couples to have two children. Chris Buckley, *China Ends One-Child Policy, Allowing Families Two Children,* N.Y. Times, Oct. 29, 2015, available at http://www.nytimes.com/2015/10/30/world/asia/china-end-one-child-policy.html?_r=0

rapid industrialization and socialist construction,"[473] and because it wished to "normalize China's society to modern, global standards."[474] The government framed the problem in international terms and hitched overpopulation to national backwardness—a Chinese people of

> backward bodies and backward minds, making them uncompetitive in the global economy and unfit for citizenship in a modern state. The solution was to foster superior (*yousheng*) persons, understood as global persons, who fit the highest international norms on health, education, and ethics. Initially the effort was primarily eugenic—preventing defective births through medical and legal means. Later, as the notion of quality (more generally rendered as *suzhi*) expanded to include health, education, and child rearing more generally, all social forces were encouraged to promote the rearing of high-caliber youngsters, who would grow into a high-quality labor force.[475]

This framing was politically effective because "it fit perfectly into the core national narrative of the People's Republic. In that narrative of nation, the Chinese Communist Party (CCP) repeatedly rescues China from disaster, putting it on the road to modernization and, for its efforts, earning the right to rule."[476] The state has used its control of the national media to popularize and promote its One-Child Policy.[477] Propaganda slogans include: "the modern earth is too tired to sustain more children,"[478] "open a small hole to close a large hole,"[479] and "have one, quality child."[480] These "slogans promoting the one-child policy have been widely propagandized—on billboards and building walls, in schools, in the mass media, in parenting books and magazines."[481] Additionally, China's government has used "mandatory parenting classes,"[482] books, magazines, and pictures of Western babies[483] to educate its populace about the importance of few children. The government has also created government agencies to coordinate One-Child Policy efforts and monitoring.[484] Another technique to change cultural preferences has been to classify the one child as the "quality child," the single-child mother as "the good mother," and the task of parenting as "nurturing the perfect child."[485] Propaganda and education efforts

---

473 GREENHALGH, *supra* note 472, at 16.
474 *Id.* at xiii.
475 *Id.* at 20.
476 *Id.* at 17.
477 *Id.* at 44.
478 *Id.* at 56.
479 *Id.* at 89.
480 *Id.* at 89–90.
481 *Id.* at 90.
482 *Id.* at 59.
483 *Id.* at 60.
484 *Id.* at 82.
485 *Id.* at 40.

have defined the proper mother as one "who would sacrifice her own interests for her youngster and follow the prescriptions of the latest science in conceiving, giving birth to, and rearing a high-quality child."[486]

Furthermore, the government provides incentives and penalties to ensure compliance. Incentives for compliance include "post-surgical and maternity leave; living allowances; old-age support, social support, and social insurance schemes such as basic pension insurance, basic medical insurance, childbirth insurance, and social welfare; and priority in receiving housing allocations, poverty relief, job and technical training, charity assistance, and subsidized loans."[487] The government even provides a " 'special assistance system for couples practicing birth planning' whose single child has been injured, disabled, or died. These programs are designed to address the concrete needs that underlie high fertility preferences . . . and to alleviate the very real risks faced by couples."[488] For those who don't comply, China imposes fines.[489]

Although the One-Child Policy proved to be fairly successful, it also overreached and has been associated with widespread governmental abuse due to overzealous enforcement. For example, to ensure that local governments enforced the policy, the central government penalized local officials by taking away

> bonuses, promotions, and other benefits, should they fail to meet their population targets. Facing possible loss of their jobs, local cadres reacted in the way the state had hoped—by overriding people's preferences and strictly enforcing the policy. The campaigns of the early 1990s produced terror and trauma in the countryside . . . [that] resulted in violent struggle that tore communities apart . . . [and] the rough methods posed threats to women's health.[490]

The government also used "physical force against the people, relying on late-term abortions, confiscation of property, demolition of houses, and other over-the-top methods that drove people in some places to violent extremes."[491] Furthermore, "in 1983 it launched a nationwide sterilization campaign, directing local officials to sterilize one member of all couples with two or more children, insert an IUD in all women with one child, and abort all unauthorized pregnancies."[492] Although these methods are used rarely now, they did play a role in the implementation of the One-Child Policy, but at the cost of trauma to society and individuals. [493]

---

[486] *Id.* at 59.
[487] *Id.* at 91.
[488] *Id.* at 54.
[489] *Id.* at 67.
[490] *Id.* at 50.
[491] *Id.* at 49.
[492] *Id.*
[493] *Id.* at 96.

China's One-Child Policy also provides an example of the need for a comprehensive approach to culture reform. Culture is the embodiment of multiple and interrelated norms and practices. The government's attempt to decrease the preference for many children has indirectly increased the cultural preference for sons and resulted in a growing sex-imbalance.[494] "The proliferation of ultrasound technology, which has facilitated an increase in sex-selective abortions, can also explain the abnormal sex ratio only as a contributing factor."[495] Of course, the root of this imbalance stems from "traditional gender attitudes holding women inferior and subordinate to men."[496] Economically, sons inherit and work the family land, and therefore are seen as more valuable.[497] Traditionally, men carry the family name, perform ancestral rites, and have higher status in patriarchal Chinese society.[498] The One-Child Policy has only further exacerbated this gender preference. But the government's failure to address gender inequality when implementing the One-Child Policy has led to its "sex ratio at birth [being] 119 boys per 100 girls, far above the global norm of 106."[499] This sex imbalance is not just a problem for women's rights, but poses other social consequences: "[p]rostitution is likely to increase as millions of young men, mostly poor, are unable to marry;"[500] "women now face increased dangers of being kidnapped, with an increase in prostitution and woman-trafficking. It is estimated that tens of thousands of women aged 13–24 are abducted each year to be sold or traded as wives or prostitutes";[501] and the "impending surplus of unattached young men could be a driving force behind increased crime, explosive epidemics of HIV and other sexually transmitted diseases, and even international threats to the security of other nations."[502]

The One-Child Policy itself has enabled this gender preference—"[t]he exceptions to the population policy from the 1980s allowing couples to have a second child if the first was a girl are an example of the possibly unwitting reinforcement of the belief that not only are sons preferable, but that daughters do not fully count as children at all."[503] Today, "sex-selective abortion appears to be the primary means of exercising control over the sex of couples' progeny."[504] But the government has since taken steps to address this gender inequality. It is still unclear if the methods will be successful, but they include education and propaganda efforts similar to those used to implement the One-Child Policy and end footbinding. The government has created slogans like "girls can also carry the family

---

[494] Liang Ying Tan, *Changing Mindsets: How China's Abnormal Sex Ratio Is Turning Its Government into a Champion of Gender Equality*, 3 Asian J. Comp. L. 1, 2 (2008).

[495] *Id.* at 1.

[496] *Id.*

[497] *Id.* at 5–6.

[498] *See id.* at 6.

[499] *Id.* at 2.

[500] *Id.* at 4.

[501] *Id.* at 3.

[502] *Id.* at 5.

[503] *Id.* at 8.

[504] *Id.* at 11.

line,"[505] " 'realise gender equality for social development progress';[506] 'son or daughter, let nature take its course';[507] 'daughters can also achieve success';[508] and 'to love today's girls is to be concerned about the future of the people.' "[509] Education efforts to promote female rights and status have been led by the government, individuals, and organizations. For example, these include:

> visiting families with daughters twice a year and giving the girls health checkups to ensure they are being treated well by their parents, empowering women economically by making small loans and teaching them income-generating farming and production technology, and raising self-awareness by giving lectures to change women's ideas about life and birth. Such localised projects are essential to the attempts at correcting the sex ratio because they directly address the birth culture and humanise the government's policy.[510]

The government organized the Care for Girls campaign, which seeks to " 'improve the environment for girls' survival and development' "[511] by equalizing the opportunities available to girls and promoting the view that girls are as valuable as boys. The campaign's stated objectives are to "eradicate sex discrimination and protect girls' legal rights, and it is promoted as a central component of the population policy."[512] The government has also created a test program in Fujian province where it provides "pensions of $180 to about 300,000 rural elderly people who have only one child or only daughters. This is an attempt to address the economic root of the preference for sons: farm families want boys for labour; daughters marry out of the family and therefore cannot provide the social security that sons should."[513] The government has also awarded free tuition to female students in Fujian.[514] Some critics such as Liang Ying Tan fear that these campaigns and incentives "may unwittingly attach a stigma on such families and perpetuate the perception that it is indeed a form of hardship to only have daughters."[515] She recommends that the government instead "support localized women's interest groups . . . rather than hand out monetary incentives to daughters-only households"[516] to promote female rights and the value of daughters.

---

[505] *Id.* at 20.

[506] *Id.*

[507] *Id.*

[508] *Id.*

[509] *Id.*

[510] *Id.* at 21.

[511] *Id.* at 18.

[512] *Id.*

[513] *Id.* at 19.

[514] *Id.* at 20.

[515] *Id.* at 26.

[516] *Id.* at 27.

b. South Korea

South Korea is another example of a society that successfully modified certain key cultural norms. South Korea has experienced rapid economic growth since the 1950s due to educational and structural reforms.[517] During the Japanese colonial occupation of South Korea (1910–45), the nation built a modern infrastructure by revolutionizing "the areas of finance, production, transportation, and commerce."[518] In the 1950s, "the country's gross national product (GNP) per capita was less than $100, and over 40% of the population lived in absolute poverty."[519] However, by 1995, the GNP per capita had risen to over $10,000 (UNDP 1998), and South Korea had become the fifteenth largest economy in the world.[520] Notably, like Japan, South Korea's economic transformation was accompanied by a revolutionary restructuring of the country's education system and a breakdown of traditional Korean power structures.[521] Sen noted that from the 1940s onward, South Korea "did not rely just on its traditional culture . . . it deliberately followed lessons from abroad to use public policy to advance its backward school education."[522] Sen attributed much of South Korea's economic success to the public policies pursued in the post–World War II period, notably the conscious effort to create a more literate and educated population.[523] Sen stated,

> [t]here is every evidence that when Korea decided to move briskly forward with school education at the end of the second world war, it was influenced not just by its cultural interest in education, but also by a new understanding of the role and significance of education, based on the experiences of Japan and the West, including the United States.[524]

Notably, efforts to educate the population included overcoming customary gender roles that restricted the education of women and girls.[525]

Furthermore, South Korea pursued a restructuring of the traditional Korean power structures that existed in the pre–World War II period.[526] Through efforts such as

---

517 Monica Das Gupta et al., *State Policies and Women's Agency in China, the Republic of Korea, and India, 1950–2000: Lessons from Contrasting Experiences*, *in* CULTURE AND PUBLIC ACTION 234, 245 (Vijayendra Rao & Michael Walton eds., 2004).

518 *Id.*

519 *Id.*

520 *Id.*

521 Amartya Sen, *How Does Culture Matter?*, *in* CULTURE AND PUBLIC ACTION 37, 46–49 (Vijayendra Rao & Michael Walton eds., 2004).

522 *Id.* at 47.

523 *Id.* at 50.

524 *Id.* at 50 (citing KI-BIKE, LEE, A NEW HISTORY OF KOREA (1984); NOEL F. MCGINN ET AL., EDUCATION AND DEVELOPMENT IN KOREA (1980)).

525 Das Gupta et al., *supra* note 517, at 245–46.

526 *Id.* at 245.

constructive land reform, the government sought to break down the country's well-rooted social organizations dominated by local clans and lineages.[527] Scholars such as Das Gupta argued that the process of breaking down these traditional structures created a more egalitarian society and in turn facilitated a "crucial basis for subsequent development."[528] By the 1990s, reform efforts, which focused on human development and economic growth, had dramatically transformed living conditions for both men and women in South Korea.[529]

Although economic and social reform in South Korea included efforts to educate women and increase women's participation in the labor force, women, however, continue to be constrained by traditional gender structures viewed as central to Korean culture.[530] Patrilineal kinship systems in Korea, a traditional practice that largely marginalizes women with respect to their role in the family, remain entrenched.[531] In patrilineal societies, "group membership is passed on through the male line."[532] "Typically, this involves passing on the main productive assets through the male line, which constrains women's ability to be economically viable without being attached to a man.... [t]he combination of rigid patrilineality and patrilocality essentially means that women have little independent social or legal personhood."[533] Notably, in the patrilineal clan system, a woman's social and legal identity is determined by "her relationship to the male head of the family."[534] Land is inherited through the male, and "[i]n the event of divorce, a woman ha[s] little chance of" receiving land or marital property without the consent of the husband.[535]

Efforts to reform customary family and marriage law in Korea have attempted to break down this system; however, in practice there has been very slow progress with regard to women's legal rights.[536] Thus, although the nation has experienced major economic growth, "[t]he social, economic, and political participation of Korean women are still among the lowest in the world (UNDP 1998)."[537] It follows that to be successful, there needs to be reform within the culture that gives value to equal rights between men and women, especially concerning property and marriage rights.[538]

---

527 *Id.*

528 *Id.*

529 *Id.*

530 *Id.* at 246.

531 *Id.* at 245.

532 *Id.* at 236.

533 *Id.*

534 *Id.* at 247–48.

535 *Id.* at 248.

536 *Id.* at 247.

537 *Id.* at 245–46.

538 *See* Emmanuelle Jouannet, *Universalism and Imperialism: The True-False Paradox of International Law?*, 18 Eur. J. Int'l L. 379, 402 (2007) (arguing that cultural issues must be dealt with on a local level) ("It demonstrates that the problems of legal culture cannot be dealt with at the international level in the same manner as any other type of conflict, and that it is essential that (internationalist) jurists look for solutions at the level of training, education and teaching.").

c. Educational Development

As the above examples of South Korea and China demonstrate, current efforts undertaken in many developing countries to effectuate culture change have appropriately targeted educational reform. Peru provides yet another example of such reform. After determining that Japanese children learned progressive values and Peruvian children did not, a Peruvian businessman established the Institute of Human Development in 1990 in Peru to promote the "[t]en Commandments of Development: order, cleanliness, punctuality, responsibility, achievement, honesty, respect for the rights of others, respect for the law, work ethic, and frugality."[539] The Institute has attracted more than two million Peruvian students in the past decade. Its works have been adopted by Nicaragua's minister of education in his own educational reform projects and by Mexico's prestigious Monterrey Institute of Technology and Higher Studies.[540] Other civic organizations in several Latin American countries have focused on curricular changes in the public education system to promote wholesale changes in certain cultural attributes.[541]

Educating girls in particular has been a specific priority of many rights organizations. Nicholas Kristof and Sheryl WuDunn noted that "[s]chooling is also often a precondition for girls and women to stand up against injustice, and for women to be integrated into the economy."[542] In turn, educating women contributes to larger issues, as scholars note that it is one of the most effective ways to combat poverty.[543] Until women have received an adequate education, however, it is difficult for them to engage and contribute to their respective economies.[544]

The main problem in many regions is not that education is not provided for both boys and girls, but rather that it is difficult to achieve mere attendance.[545] Many advocates believe that the simple provision of facilities and resources will result in an education for students, but school construction is not the end-all, be-all solution to providing education.[546] It is an expensive endeavor, and there is no guarantee that students will actually attend or that teachers will fulfill their duties.[547] Kristof and WuDunn offered the following statistics in their book: "[o]f the 115 million children who have dropped out of elementary school, 57 percent are girls. In South and West Asia, two thirds of the children who are out of school are girls."[548] In many instances, health problems, monetary need for

---

539 Lawrence E. Harrison, *Promoting Progressive Cultural Change*, *in* CULTURE MATTERS 296, 303 (Lawrence E. Harrison & Samuel P. Huntington eds., 2000).

540 *Id.*

541 *Id.* at 304–05.

542 NICHOLAS D. KRISTOF & SHERYL WUDUNN, HALF THE SKY: TURNING OPPRESSION INTO OPPORTUNITY FOR WOMEN WORLDWIDE 170 (2009).

543 *Id.* at 169.

544 *Id.* at 170.

545 *Id.* at 171.

546 *Id.*

547 *Id.*

548 *Id.*

children either to mind the household or work themselves, and the cost of school deter parents from providing education to their girl children.[549]

Kristof and WuDunn have suggested multiple health initiatives that have been deemed effective; these initiatives both place girls physically within the classroom and provide for actual learning once the girls are in attendance. Two general health issues that all students face, and which inhibit their ability both to attend school and to learn, are intestinal worms and a lack of iodine in their diet.[550] Intestinal worms are a hindrance to students' "physical and intellectual growth"; therefore the practice of deworming has been effective at increasing both school attendance and attentiveness. "[A] landmark study in Kenya found that deworming could decrease school absenteeism by a quarter."[551] Further, students were found to be more alert and attentive when their bodies weren't focused on fighting off infection from these intestinal worms.[552]

Iodization of salt has also been a popular, health-based method that is geared toward increasing mental acuity among students and hence has an impact on education. According to Kristof and WuDunn, "[s]ome 31 percent of households in the developing world do not get sufficient iodine from water or food."[553] This is a serious issue for children as "iodine deficiency typically shaves ten to fifteen points off a child's IQ."[554] In response, aid groups have provided iodized salt to poor areas, and capsules of iodized oil have been distributed to women who may become pregnant in order to provide fetuses with the proper nutrients for growth and development.[555] The positive effect of this prenatal practice was demonstrated in a study in which "daughters of those women given capsules managed to stay in school markedly longer and performed better" in comparison with daughters of women who did not receive the capsule.[556]

Specific to girls, aims at managing menstruation have also become prevalent to combat low school attendance. Because the girls at risk for receiving no education are often very poor, they lack resources to deal with menstruation and often only own one pair of underwear and use the same rag during menstruation.[557] As a result of this practice, girls often stay home during this time to avoid "embarrassing leaks and stains."[558] Aid workers have provided both sanitary pads to girls and have installed toilets in which to change the sanitary pads, as few schools have an available restroom. The implementation of these

---

549 *Id.* at 171–72.
550 *Id.* at 171 73.
551 *Id.* at 171.
552 *Id.*
553 *Id.* at 172.
554 *Id.*
555 *Id.* at 172–73.
556 *Id.* at 173.
557 *Id.* at 172.
558 *Id.*

facilities has been expensive, however, and activist groups have faced challenges in securing the funds to put the structures in place.[559]

Funds have been appropriated in a different context, resulting in improved female school attendance and participation. "Oportunidades," a program pioneered in Mexico, essentially bribed parents to send their daughters to school.[560] As food subsidies were failing amid a deep recession in the country in 1995, the deputy finance minister, Santiago Levy, decided that the best way to educate and feed the populace was to give parents food on the condition that the parents would send the children to school and take the children for annual medical check-ups.[561] It is estimated that the program has served approximately "one quarter of Mexican families."[562] According to the World Bank, "the program raised high school attendance by 10 percent for boys and 20 percent for girls."[563] The United Nations' school feeding program has used a similar system to induce more participation and attendance from girls. Food is provided to schools, parents are asked to come in and prepare the meals, and "girls with good attendance often get a take-home ration as an inducement to parents to keep educating them."[564]

Once attendance has been solidified through the provision of health services and food to families, monetary assistance has been provided to families to increase girls' class participation. Kristof and WuDunn noted a study that was conducted in Kenya by a Harvard economist in which the top 15 percent of girls taking sixth-grade tests were awarded a "$19 scholarship for seventh and eighth grade."[565] These scholarships were offered in a select number of schools; compared to control schools in which the scholarships were not offered, the girls who received scholarships performed markedly better.[566]

Though women's education is essential to empower women and advance women's rights, Kristof and WuDunn warned that cultural barriers do impede such efforts, often in unforeseeable ways.[567] They caution against "tinkering with the culture, religion, and family relations of a society that we often don't fully understand."[568] As an example, the authors describe an instance in which the United Nations set up a project in Nigeria meant to empower women through the planting and selling of cassava, a native, edible plant. Although a large harvest was yielded, the women of the village did not have time to harvest the crop on top of their other responsibilities, and the men considered the act of harvesting "women's work" and would not help to reap the crop.[569] When the aid

---

559 *Id.*

560 *Id.* at 173.

561 *Id.*

562 *Id.*

563 *Id.* at 174.

564 *Id.*

565 *Id.* at 175.

566 *Id.*

567 *Id.* at 177.

568 *Id.*

569 *Id.*

group introduced processing equipment, however, and the women began making a substantial amount of profit, the venture became attractive to the men of the village. They saw the profitable crop as rightfully theirs, as the custom of the village was that men sold profitable crops and women sold sustainable crops. Therefore, the men took over the project immediately.[570] In turn, the women were left with nothing.[571] However, it should be noted that the underlying problem is the cultural norm supporting the presumption that men control profits and women provide sustenance should be questioned. Unless that underlying norm is changed, providing women with access to profitable projects will simply backfire as it did in this case. If anything, the example illustrates, in fact, the need to change offensive cultural norms; it does not illustrate that cultural norms should not be changed. Indeed, the act of planting is not just about farming or growing crops. It is, rather, an act embedded in a cultural framework in which profits are naturally assumed to be subject to male control. Similarly, implementing a project (planting) without engaging this cultural context will, it is true, exacerbate the problem.

2. CONVENTIONAL RULE OF LAW (WITHOUT CULTURE CHANGE)

As the above examples demonstrate, governments have historically been involved in culture change as part of a national modernization campaign. In today's world, such efforts are unlikely to be controversial if the underlying cultural norm is at odds with modern notions of human rights; however, a law-only approach will not be sufficient if such cultural norm is deeply entrenched.[572] Examples of failed law-only attempts abound. At one point, Turkey, for example, had required midwife and nursing students to be virgins and that testing could be performed to ensure compliance. In an effort to be admitted to the European Union, Turkey issued a directive banning forced virginity testing in 2002.[573] As a ratifier of the Convention on the Elimination of All Forms of Discrimination Against Women (CEDAW), Turkey is obligated to abolish not only discriminatory laws but also "to promote equality by breaking down commonly held stereotypes impacting culture and tradition. . . ."[574] Although human rights groups applaud this decree, commentators rightly warn that because Turkey "faces a tension between enduring cultural norms

---

570 *Id.*

571 *Id.* at 177–78.

572 Even more counterproductive is the phenomenon of "decoupling" in which states "adopt" a law or norm in order to gain legitimacy in the eyes of the international system, but then makes no concrete implementation efforts. *See* Ryan Goodman & Derek Jinks, *How to Influence States: Socialization and International Human Rights Law*, 54 DUKE L.J. 621, 656–74 (2004) (discussing three ways to influence state behavior: coercion, persuasion, acculturation).

573 Chante Lasco, *Virginity Testing in Turkey: A Violation of Women's Human Rights*, 9 No. 3 HUM. RTS. BRIEF 10 (2002).

574 Hadar Harris, *Current Processes for Assessment of Women's Human Rights in International Law*, 9 ASIL INSIGHTS, no. 10 (Mar. 12, 2005), http://www.asil.org/insights/volume/9/issue/10/current-processes-assessment-womens-human-rights-international-law; *see also* Lasco, *supra* note 573, at 13.

and international human rights standards," legislation is likely to be inadequate unless the government follows up with a nationwide educational campaign.[575] Other CEDAW member countries, such as Nigeria, South Africa, Zimbabwe, and Indonesia, all acknowledged in their reports to the Committee on the Elimination of Discrimination Against Women that implementing CEDAW has been difficult because of "entrenched traditional attitudes regarding women."[576]

a. Honor Killing

A striking example of an entrenched, traditional practice is that of honor killing. The United Nations estimated in 2000 that approximately five thousand women and girls are the victims of honor killings every year.[577] In most cultures the practice stems from the value of honor; in Muslim culture, specifically, the male honor is called *sharaf* and represents the man's social standing as well as his moral behavior.[578] The equivalent for women in these societies is called *ardh* and is intertwined with female virginity, modesty, and chastity.[579] In fact, sex outside of marriage is illegal in most, if not all, Arab countries. Men have the opportunity to regain their honor, but for females "the loss of ardh is irreparable."[580] The loss of *ardh* of the female has a great impact on the loss of *sharaf* for a man; therefore, the consequences may prove deadly for the woman because it is through her death that the man may regain and uphold the family honor.[581]

Honor killing is a practice that is not specific to one region or geographic location. "Honor killings have been reported in Bangladesh, Great Britain, Brazil, Ecuador, Egypt, India, Israel, Italy, Jordan, Pakistan, Turkey, [the United States,] and Uganda. . . ."[582] The practice may be ingrained as a regional practice or may follow immigrants to other countries. Where the practice is illegal, many cases go unreported as family members seek to cover up the killing as an accident or suicide to evade prosecution.[583]

---

575 Lasco, *supra* note 573, at 10; *see also* Dicle Kogacioglu, *Citizenship in Context: Rethinking Women's Relationships to the Law in Turkey*, *in* CITIZENSHIP AND THE NATION-STATE IN GREECE AND TURKEY 144 (Faruk Birtek & Thalia Dragonas eds., 2005) (noting the tension between state patriarchy and state feminism in Turkey resulting in a *de facto* support for traditional male-dominated power structures due to a lack of institutional enforcement for women's legal rights).

576 Valerie A. Dormady, *Status of the Convention on the Elimination of All Forms of Discrimination Against Women (CEDAW) in 1998*, 33 INT'L L. 637, 639 (1999).

577 APPIAH, *supra* note 433, at 146 (noting also that "[t]here is widespread agreement that these official figures understate the extent of the devastation.").

578 Shira T. Shapiro, *She Can Do No Wrong: Recent Failures in America's Immigration Courts to Provide Women Asylum from "Honor Crimes" Abroad*, 18 AM. U.J. GENDER SOC. POL'Y & L. 293, 296 (2010).

579 *Id.* at 296–97.

580 *Id.* at 297.

581 *Id.*

582 John Alan Cohan, *Honor Killings and the Cultural Defense*, 40 CAL. W. INT'L L.J. 177, 192 (2010).

583 *Id.* at 192–93.

However, in many countries, honor killing is not a crime or is not considered to be as serious of a crime as murder. In Jordan, for example, the penal code which stated that "[h]e who catches his wife, or one of his female unlawfuls committing adultery with another, and . . . kills, wounds, or injures one or both of them, is exempt from any penalty,"[584] was amended to "[h]e who commits a crime in a fit of fury resulting from a wrongful and dangerous act on the part of the victim shall benefit from a reduced penalty."[585] In Iraq, although the country ratified CEDAW in the 1980s and vowed to prosecute and put an end to practices like honor killings, during the 1990s "civil courts regularly acquitted men who admitted committing honor killings."[586] Further, the Iraqi penal code reads, "if a man 'with honorable motives' kills a female relative because of adultery, he will receive a reduced sentence."[587]

Even in countries where considerable effort has been expended to outlaw the practice by statute, impediments such as judges' personal beliefs and unwillingness of the populace to follow the law have halted efforts to end honor killings. In Turkey, for example, the country has strived to become part of the European Union as a modernized, Arab nation. The Turkish government has sought to outlaw the practice of honor killings through law. As crimes of honor are dictated by a passion element where "violence against the woman is justified by a man's fury at the discovery or suspicion of a woman's sexual interaction with another man which he feels dishonors him,"[588] Turkey has tried to revise the penal code for a more definitive statement of what provocation justifies a crime of passion and what is needed to prove such a crime.[589] Further, legal reform in Turkey has also been geared toward granting more women legal rights in marriage and general equality rights.[590] However, problems still exist because honor is such a distinct part of the cultural dialogue of the country. Sections of the penal code continue to allow for reductions of sentences for infanticide and child abandonment "if members of [a] 'dishonored' family

---

584 Kathryn Christine Arnold, Note, *Are the Perpetrators of Honor Killings Getting Away with Murder? Article 340 of the Jordanian Penal Code Analyzed Under the Convention of the Elimination of All Forms of Discrimination Against Women*, 16 AM. U. INT'L L. REV. 1343, 1362 (2001) (quoting the Jordanian Penal Code, Article 340 prior to amendment).

585 Ayla M. Kremen, *Suicide in the Name of Honor: Why and How U.S. Asylum Law Should Be Modified to Allow Greater Acceptance of Honor-Violence Victims to Prevent "Honor Suicides,"* 21 WM. & MARY J. WOMEN & L. 213, 220 (2014) (quoting an amendment to the Jordanian Penal Code Article 340 to provide for punishment of honor killings and noting the establishment of a special court to prosecute them); Mohamad Fdailat, *Jordan's "Honor" Killings Persist Despite Reform Efforts*, AL-MONITOR (Aug. 10, 2012), http://www.al-monitor.com/pulse/culture/2012/08/jordans-dishonorable-honor-killings.html (discussing Article 340's mitigating reasons for penalty reduction).

586 Patricio Asfura-Heim, *Tribal Customary Law and Legal Pluralism in al Anbar, Iraq*, *in* CUSTOMARY JUSTICE AND THE RULE OF LAW IN WAR-TORN SOCIETIES *239, 255* (Deborah H. Isser ed., 2011).

587 *Id.*

588 SALLY ENGLE MERRY, GENDER VIOLENCE: A CULTURAL PERSPECTIVE 129 (2009).

589 Rebecca E. Boon, Note, *They Killed Her for Going Out with Boys: Honor Killings in Turkey in Light of Turkey's Accession to the European Union and Lessons for Iraq*, 35 HOFSTRA L. REV. 815, 829–33 (2006).

590 *Id.* at 833.

abandon an illegitimate child."[591] And although Article 29 of the Turkish penal code states that "the Turkish provocation defense should not apply to honor crimes. . . ."[592], reforming social attitudes is necessary if change is to take hold among the citizens themselves. This is evident, as even the judges and prosecutors who are expected to uphold the new laws and statutes are themselves embedded in the cultural norms of old. "Judges still systematically interpret laws in ways that privilege family honor: 'The value placed on family honor at the expense of women's welfare is evident both in legal text and legal practice; it is not the problem of just a few problematic codes.'"[593] Coupled with the above failure, law enforcement officials often praise honor killing and participate in the intimidation of female activists at a local level.[594]

Indeed Kwame Appiah noted that when the issue is seen as a conflict between "Western" culture and "traditional" culture, supporters of the latter often manage to characterize "Westerners [and Westernized activists] *bay ghairat*, lacking in a sense of honor."[595] Further, heads of countries argue Westerners attempt to ruin the country's "good name" by exposing the practice through media to the rest of the world.[596] The solution, Appiah suggested, may lie in a form of cultural shaming.[597]

With reference to Chinese footbinding and the cross-Atlantic slavery, Appiah argued it was collective cultural shaming that brought these practices to an end by "persuading people that their honor practice brought collective dishonor on them, in the face of a wider honor world."[598] In the case of honor killings, Appiah observed that collective shaming (and reinterpreting certain religious passages) should be an important component of the effort to end the practice.[599] As Appiah noted, "[i]f an Islamic republic is to recognize the human rights of its citizens, it will have to repudiate this element of Muslim tradition."[600] This repudiation should take place through the work of insiders and outsiders to the culture. From a strategic perspective, both groups should work toward changing the definition of honor within the society, but not argue against the concept of honor, which would only serve to deepen resistance among people who believe their culture is under attack.[601] In essence, Appiah stated that while we should still continue to remind these societies that "honor killing is immoral, illegal, irrational, irreligious,"[602] this alone

---

591 *Id.* at 836.
592 *Id.* at 838.
593 *Id.* at 838–39.
594 *Id.* at 840.
595 Appiah, *supra* note 433, at 152.
596 *Id.* at 160.
597 *Id.*
598 *Id.* at 163.
599 *Id.* at 164–66.
600 *Id.* at 166.
601 *Id.* at 169.
602 *Id.* at 172.

will not stop the practice.[603] Instead of mere disapproval, interveners must work from the inside, making the practice of honor a practice of dishonor and making individuals in that society "want their nation to be worthy—in their own eyes—of respect"[604] and not just in the eyes of outsiders.

b. Property Rights for African Women

Recently, rule of law efforts in Africa have also focused on creating property rights, as property rights free up capital for investment and help economic growth.[605] As discussed in the Introduction and Chapter 1, property rights is a subject that is part of any conventional law and development agenda. However, these efforts have not been successful as they have failed to address "two property rights issues that impede capital formation in Sub-Saharan Africa: the presence of customary law and the complex social status of women."[606] In many parts of Africa, customary law governs land arrangements.[607] "Customary law is recognized by the courts and exists as a second body of law (in addition to statutory law) governing citizens in the countries of Sub-Saharan Africa."[608] Men have historically used this law to assert power over women.[609] During the colonial era, land not owned by the colonizers was left to the local community, and chiefs and custom controlled its allocation.[610] Today, attempts to grant property rights have generally been focused on creating a land titling system that essentially follows customary law.[611] This has failed to free up capital because customary law itself grants women, the main agricultural producers, no property rights, and the adoption of custom into law has only further weakened a woman's control of land.[612] Existing cultural norms consider women as property and as such incapable of owning property.[613] Thus, even when the law does provide for co-ownership of land, preexisting cultural norms act in opposition to newly enacted legal property rights.[614] In many cases, even judges and law enforcement steeped

---

603 *Id.* Indeed, Merry has also noted that "simplistic efforts to point to Islam as the root cause of honor killings has generated resistance rather than reform." MERRY, *supra* note 588, at 13. This resistance likely stems from a feeling of Western judgment and superiority toward other cultures in general and not necessarily from active support for the specific practice at issue.

604 APPIAH, *supra* note 433, at 172.

605 S. F. Joireman, *The Mystery of Capital Formation in Sub-Saharan Africa: Women, Property Rights and Customary Law*, 36 WORLD DEV. 1233, 1233 (2008).

606 *Id.* at 1233.

607 *Id.* at 1235 ("In contemporary Sub-Saharan Africa, it has been estimated that up to 75% of the land is held under forms of customary tenure.").

608 *Id.*

609 *Id.*

610 *Id.* at 1236.

611 *Id.* at 1236–37.

612 *Id.* at 1238.

613 *Id.*

614 *Id.*

in customary law may disregard women's legal property rights.[615] In many cases, while tradition may grant women access rights to the land of their male relatives,[616] legal reform has not included these access rights within property titles.[617] For these reasons, legal solutions are not only inadequate to address women's property rights, but often, "formalizing existing customary property rights will effectively alienate women."[618]

There has been some success in creating women's property rights through cultural reform; "[i]n Burkina Faso, Ghana, Uganda, and Tanzania, women lawyers' associations and civil society groups have played a large role in agitating for women's property rights, educating the populace, bringing test cases regarding women's property rights to court and promoting the enforcement of laws that protect women's property."[619] Here, more carefully defining property rights within the law, and specifically including women within the definition of property holders, could also help.[620]

However, efforts at reform have also met many challenges. For many populations in sub-Saharan Africa, issues such as marriage, divorce, burial, and inheritance rights continue to be governed by customary law.[621] As noted, "[a]lthough conceptually distinct from culture, customary law is a legal expression of cultural norms and values."[622] Many African states have retained a legal structure wherein the customary law of inheritance, which generally excludes women as potential heirs, and statutory law operate simultaneously.[623] Driven by traditional notions of culture and gender relationships, customary law has excluded women from property ownership and inheritance.[624] A woman's relationship to land has traditionally been defined through her relationship to her father or husband.[625] While married, a woman gains access to use of the land; however, following the death of a husband, the woman no longer holds any rights in the land.[626] The practice of "property-grabbing" has recently developed; following the death of a father or husband, family members and elites repossess the male's property, often leaving widows and orphans "homeless and destitute."[627]

---

[615] *Id.* at 1241.

[616] *Id.* at 1238.

[617] *Id.*

[618] *Id.* at 1240.

[619] *Id.* at 1241.

[620] *Id.* at 1242.

[621] Johanna E. Bond, *Gender, Discourse, and Customary Law in Africa*, 83 S. CAL. L. REV. 509, 558–60 (2010).

[622] *Id.* at 517–18 (2010); *see also* Thandabantu Nhlapo, *Indigenous Law and Gender in South Africa: Taking Human Rights and Cultural Diversity Seriously*, THIRD WORLD LEGAL STUD., 1994–1995, at 49, 53 ("Sometimes termed customary law, indigenous law is the system of norms which governs the lives of millions of African people, particularly (but not exclusively) in the rural areas.").

[623] Bond, *supra* note 621, at 514–18.

[624] Abby Morrow Richardson, *Women's Inheritance Rights in Africa: The Need to Integrate Cultural Understanding and Legal Reform*, 11 NO. 2 HUM. RTS. BRIEF 19, 19 (2004).

[625] *Id.*

[626] *Id.*

[627] *Id.*

Where a statute has been at odds with customary law, the latter has generally prevailed when the underlying issue involves gender relations. The Supreme Court of Zimbabwe, for example, refused to interfere with tribal, customary law when the tribe of the deceased man refused to appoint his eldest daughter as heir to the estate because the man is also survived by a son.[628] The court rejected the daughter's allegation that tribal law constituted "a prima facie violation of the Zimbabwean Constitution's guarantee of equality for women," holding instead that "the Constitution exempts customary law."[629]

Thus, although there are efforts to alter gender relations, these efforts have occurred primarily at the statutory level. Given "the persistence of traditions and cultural norms that give preference to men,"[630] and that seek to preserve "religion and culture as spheres of despotism,"[631] experts in this area have recommended " 'massive awareness campaigns' at both the national and local levels."[632] Unless cultural norms are confronted and altered, through deliberate education campaigns[633] and other measures,[634] "[t]hese statutory changes generally have no practical effect on the great majority of the population."[635]

3. NONGOVERNMENTAL ORGANIZATIONS

a. Tostan, CEOSS, and Female Genital Mutilation

Approximately 100 million women in Africa are subjected to the practice of female genital mutilation (FGM)[636] despite rule of law efforts to end it.[637] In fact, the practice is

---

628 Madhavi Sunder, *Piercing the Veil*, 112 YALE L.J. 1399, 1430–31 (2003).

629 *Id.* at 1431.

630 Dormady, *supra* note 576, at 641.

631 Sunder, *supra* note 628, at 1434.

632 Dormady, *supra* note 576, at 640.

633 Richardson, *supra* note 624, at 22.

634 Japan, for example, prohibits employers from discriminating on the basis of sex in recruitment, hiring, assignment, and promotion decisions. But the law also allows the Ministry of Labor to "make a public announcement" if "an employer fails to comply with" the Ministry's directive. "Because of deep-seated cultural norms, the theory behind this sanction is that the threat of public embarrassment will be enough to prevent companies from discriminating on the basis of gender." Kelly Barrett, Student Article, *Women in the Workplace: Sexual Discrimination in Japan*, 11 No. 2 HUM. RTS. BRIEF 5, 6 (2004).

635 Richardson, *supra* note 624, at 19.

636 Female genital mutilation, also known as female circumcision or female genital cutting, refers to the cutting and removal of female genitalia. *See* ELLEN GRUENBAUM, THE FEMALE CIRCUMCISION CONTROVERSY: AN ANTHROPOLOGICAL PERSPECTIVE 2–4 (2001). The practice varies across cultures with women undergoing the procedure as early as infancy. *Id.* at 2. In Egypt, the usual age for girls is between nine and twelve years. Traditionally, midwives or health barbers performed the cutting using knives or razor blades and no anesthetic. *Female Genital Mutilation: Issues and Impact*, UNICEF EGYPT, http://www.unicef.org/egypt/protection_148.html (last visited June 14, 2015). More recently, the number of cases of physician-performed FGM, termed medicalization, have increased dramatically. FATMA EL-ZANATY & ANN WAY, EGYPT DEMOGRAPHIC AND HEALTH SURVEY 2005, at 214 (2006), *available at* http://www.measuredhs.com/pubs/pdf/FR176/FR176.pdf (showing that 75 percent of all procedures were performed by medical personnel as of 2005).

637 Mackie, *supra* note 452, at 999.

spreading.[638] For example, in Somalia today, "99 percent of women are mutilated."[639] FGM is practiced in many African nations—supported and continued by women, its victims[640]—as a means of ensuring "female chastity and fidelity."[641] Although currently illegal in many countries, many cultures still consider FGM necessary for marriage.[642] FGM can be a slight pricking of the clitoris,[643] the removal of the clitoris,[644] and even the removal of the clitoris and the sewing together of the labia into a small hole.[645] The latter procedure is often performed without painkiller and is known to result in difficult urination and menstruation.[646] FGM can cause severe health risks,[647] painful intercourse,[648] infertility,[649] problematic childbirths,[650] lack of orgasm, and depression.[651] The custom originated as a means to ensure women's fidelity and guarantee paternity.[652] Eventually, FGM became a requirement for marriage,[653] as it ensured virginity and reduced female sexual desire.[654] Mythical claims, such as the belief that FGM enhances male desire, also increase its practice—despite the fact that "reports from Nubia and the Sudan indicate that men aware of the difference prefer intact or excised women to infibulated women";[655] some believe the clitoris kills a man or the baby.[656] Referring to the practice of FGM, Kenyan President Jomo Kenyatta argued that "the moral code of the tribe is bound up with this custom and that it symbolizes the unification of the whole tribal organization."[657] As a result of these myths and FGM's deep cultural roots, outlawing it has failed to eradicate it.

---

638 *Id.*

639 *Id.* at 1004.

640 *Id.* at 999.

641 *Id.*

642 *Id.*

643 *Id.* at 1002.

644 *Id.*

645 *Id.*

646 *Id.* at 1003.

647 *Id.* (listing potential immediate consequences of FMG including "[p]ain, hemorrhage, shock, acute urinary retention, urinary infection, blood poisoning (septicemia), fever, tetanus, and death.").

648 *Id.*

649 *Id.*

650 *Id.*

651 *Id.*

652 *Id.* at 1008 ("The higher the male's rank, the greater the resource support he offers, the greater number of consorts he attracts, the greater his costs of fidelity control, and thus the greater the competition among female families to guarantee paternity confidence. Therefore, families will advertise the honor of their lines, the purity of their females, and their members' commitment to the values of chastity and fidelity, the so-called modesty code.").

653 *Id.* at 1004.

654 *Id.*

655 *Id.* at 1005.

656 *Id.* at 1009.

657 Arati Rao, *The Politics of Gender and Culture in International Human Rights Discourse*, *in* WOMEN'S RIGHTS, HUMAN RIGHTS: INTERNATIONAL FEMINIST PERSPECTIVES 167, 170 (Julie Peters & Andrea Wolper eds., 1995) (citing JOMO KENYATTA, FACING MT. KENYA: THE TRIBAL LIFE OF THE GIKUYU 133–34 (1953)).

In many African nations, individuals and organizations have attempted to combine legal measures with cultural reform to end FGM and female disenfranchisement. Some scholars, like Gerry Mackie, have argued that education of FGM's negative impact on fertility could persuade society to end FGM, as "both male and female could better afford children if the female's fertility, productivity, and longevity were not damaged by mutilation. For the purposes of reform it is important to realize that the ordinary male, when fully informed, may be motivated to support convention shift."[658] Mackie proposed that education focus on letting "people know the physiological facts, explaining to women and men the advantages of natural genitals and the disadvantages of mutilation."[659] Emphasizing international public opinion's opposition to FGM in a tactful way could also be useful, much like it was in ending Chinese footbinding.[660] Government or civil society could also create "associations of parents who pledge not to infibulate their daughters nor let their sons marry infibulated women [which] may, as in China, decisively lead to change."[661]

On-the-ground actions that supplement state efforts at culture change have proven more effective when NGOs are involved. Indeed, it was clear that many villagers across Egypt planned to continue FGM even after Egypt's health minister banned all forms of the practice.[662] Officials in charge of implementing the law acknowledged "that some social customs are too potent to be extinguished by law."[663] Nonetheless, after intensive efforts by one of Egypt's largest nonprofit development groups,[664] the practice of FGM has declined significantly in Tayeba[665] and Deir El Barsha[666], two villages in the Minya governorate. The group attacked the practice at its roots by pursuing an education campaign aimed at women, religious leaders, and unmarried men, portraying the issue as one related to the promotion of literacy, family planning, and health care.[667] The

---

658 Mackie, *supra* note 452, at 1008.

659 *Id.* at 1015.

660 *Id.*

661 *Id.*

662 Neil MacFarquhar, *Mutilation of Egyptian Girls: Despite Ban, It Goes On*, N.Y. TIMES, Aug. 8, 1996, at A3. One farmer is quoted as saying, "Am I supposed to stand around while my daughter chases men? . . . I would have circumcised my daughter even if they passed a death sentence against it." *Id.* In 1996, Egypt's health minister issued a decree prohibiting FGM by any nonphysician or by a physician in a hospital or clinic unless for medical purpose. FEMALE GENITAL MUTILATION: A GUIDE TO LAWS AND POLICIES WORLDWIDE 142 (Anika Rahman & Nahid Toubia eds., 2000). In 2008, the Egyptian Parliament officially criminalized the practice through the passage of law number 126. Mustafa Suleiman, *Egypt Makes First Arrest over Female Circumcision*, AL ALARABIYA NEWS (Aug. 13, 2009), http://www.alarabiya.net/articles/2009/08/13/81698.html (reporting the first arrest made under the law).

663 MacFarquhar, *supra* note 662, at A3.

664 *See* COPTIC EVANGELICAL ORGANIZATION FOR SOCIAL SERVICES, http://www.ceoss.org.eg (last visited June 14, 2015).

665 John Lancaster, *Village Gives up a Painful Ritual*, WASH. POST, June 21, 1998, at A19.

666 *See generally* AMAL ABDEL HADI, WE ARE DECIDED: THE STRUGGLE OF AN EGYPTIAN VILLAGE TO ERADICATE FEMALE CIRCUMCISION (Manr Wafa trans. & Nida Kirmani, rev. 1998).

667 Lancaster, *supra* note 665, at A19.

development group enters a village only with an invitation signed by community leaders, appoints a two-person team to live in the village for as long as seven years, trains local volunteers to continue the group's objectives after the team leaves, and conducts follow-up work. The group's volunteers typically begin their work by visiting local houses to give women information on family planning and health care before slowly introducing the topic of female circumcision. Despite initial hostile reactions, the group has achieved a 70 percent success rate in eight of the twenty-two participating villages, with success being determined by whether girls remain uncut past the age of twelve.[668]

While the village is 100 percent Christian, Abdel Hadi, the leader of the research team that studied the reported abandonment of FGM by the village of Deir El Barsha, did not attribute the village's decision to religion as both Christians and Muslims practice FGM.[669] In his opinion, the religious leaders did play a role in that their moral authority supported the decision of those who chose to abandon the practice.[670] Adbel Hadi determined that the village's decision to renounce the practice was significantly affected by a combination of two factors, which led to a fundamental shift in gender relations that included increased respect and autonomy for women.[671] The first factor was the community's participation in the development program provided by CEOSS (Coptic Evangelical Organization for Social Services).[672] The program encouraged community involvement in development projects including income-generating activities, health courses, and community education focused on women and girls.[673] Abdel Hadi pointed to these projects as the main factor in cultural transformation;[674] this approach "meant that it [anti-FGM effort] was seen as a wider campaign for empowering the community" and that "community engagement enabled many people to build their own capacity for fighting harmful social practices."[675] The village women did precisely this through an independent women's committee created by CEOSS.[676] Members of the committee in Deir El Barsha began a home visitation program in which they visited the families of girls at the traditional age for FGM.[677] Not only was this program effective, but it also earned

---

668 *Id.* Overall, the national rate of FGM in Egypt remains very high. The rate was 96 percent as of 2005 for women aged fifteen to forty-nine who are or have been married. *See* Fatma El-Zanaty & Ann Way, Egyptian Demographic and Health Survey 2005, at 211 (2006). While the data suggest a decline by 2015, more than half of all girls will still be affected. *Id.* at 212.

669 Hadi, *supra* note 666, at 27.

670 *Id.* at 99.

671 Amal Abdel Hadi, *A Community of Women Empowered: The Story of Deir El Barsha*, *in* Female Circumcision: Multicultural Perspectives 104, 104–05 (Rogaia Mustafa Abusharaf ed., 2006).

672 *Id.* at 112; *see also* Hadi, *supra* note 666, at 92–93 (reporting the findings of the original study).

673 Hadi, *supra* note 671, at 113.

674 *Id.*

675 *Id.* at 117.

676 *Id.* at 113.

677 *Id.* at 114.

respect for the women's committee in a setting where traditional village decision making rarely included women.[678]

The second factor was the tendency of most males to spend at least some time working abroad.[679] The money they sent back allowed their wives to set up households independent of their in-laws and to prove—to themselves and to the men—that they were capable of honorably handling responsibilities beyond their traditional roles.[680] This, in turn, suggested that FGM was not required for women to protect the family's honor as was traditionally believed.[681]

Similar success has been reported by a nonprofit organization in Senegal known as Tostan.[682] Tostan describes its educational policy as guided by positive social change:

> Social norms are clusters of expected behaviors that bind people together culturally. They are systemic, perpetuated by multiple actors within a system and acted out without critical thought as to their origin or function. Our educational approach encourages dialogue and deliberation about the assumption and beliefs that hold social norms in place within communities. Such public deliberation has led to a shift in social norms and group expectations: thousands of communities have organized to abandon harmful practices such as FGC.[683]

The organization provides nonformal education on topics including health, human rights, and problem solving for everyday situations upon receiving a request from a village.[684] The program takes steps to include locals who hold positions of influence and power such as religious and traditional leaders.[685] The participants set the goals for the program and are encouraged to incorporate their traditional culture and values into the learning process

---

678 *Id.*

679 *Id.* at 106; *see also* HADI, *supra* note 666, at 92–93 (reporting the findings of the original study).

680 Hadi, *supra* note 671, at 119–20.

681 *Id.* at 120.

682 TOSTAN, http://tostan.org (last visited June 14, 2015); *see also* Thomas Gagen, *Social Change in Senegal*, BOS. GLOBE, Dec. 28, 2001, at A26.

683 TOSTAN, TOSTAN: COMMUNITY-LED DEVELOPMENT 9–10 (2009), http://www.tostan.org/sites/default/files/resources/tostan%20brochure.pdf (encouraging participants to share what they have learned so that knowledge is disseminated through social channels and even nonparticipants may and do benefit); *see also* Paul Stanley Yoder, *Long-Term Evaluation of the Tostan Program in Senegal: Kolda, Thiès, and Fatick Regions* 25 (UNICEF, Working Paper, 2008), http://www.childinfo.org/files/fgmc_tostan_eng.pdf.

684 TOSTAN, *supra* note 683, at 10–12 (providing an overview of the Tostan program). Knowledge of Tostan and its work can be surprisingly high even among villages that have never participated. *See id.; see also* Yoder, *supra* note 683, at 20–21. In the villages studied by UNICEF, villagers indicated they had learned of Tostan primarily through the organization's radio programs and/or through word-of-mouth. *Id.* The village authorities of Malicounda Bambara, for example, requested a Tostan center after seeing the positive effects of the Tostan program in nearby communities. *Senegalese Women Remake Their Culture*, IK NOTES, Dec. 1998, at 1, *available at* http://www.worldbank.org/afr/ik/iknt3.pdf [hereinafter *Senegalese Women*].

685 TOSTAN, *supra* note 683, at 6.

to help them understand the concepts presented.[686] A community group coordinates and manages development efforts including the microcredit provided by Tostan for individual projects such as small business ventures or group projects such as building wells, schools, and health centers.[687] Information on FGM is presented in the context of an educational segment on health.[688] Tostan first provided the information in response to a request by participants in the village of Malicounda Bambara who later publicly declared the abandonment of FGM.[689] The "Oath of Malicounda" drew criticism from neighboring villages prompting a delegation from Malicounda, including a local religious leader, to visit the surrounding area to build consensus for abandoning the practice.[690]

Overall, the national rate of FGM in Senegal is very low compared to Egypt,[691] although major disparities continue to exist between regions within the country. Certain regions have had markedly elevated rates of FGM due in part to differences in ethnic composition.[692] Other regions have shown markedly lower rates of FGM. One such region is Kolda,[693] where the rate shows signs of continuous decline. In 2005, forty-four villages in the Kolda region publicly declared their abandonment of FGM.[694] In 2009, the organization reported that 4,121 communities in Senegal have abandoned the practice of FGM.[695] An evaluation of the program for UNICEF recently confirmed the

---

686 *Id.* at 5, 22. The work of Cheikh Anta Diop, under whom Tostan's founder studied, serves as the basis for the program's philosophy. *Id.* at 22. Diop believed that "to foster democracy, development must be *educational for all involved*, always rooted in and growing out of existing cultural practices and local knowledge." *Id.* at 5.

687 *Innovation in the CEP*, TOSTAN, http://www.tostan.org/program/community-development-grants (last visited June 9, 2015).

688 *Community Empowerment Program*, TOSTAN, http://www.tostan.org/community-empowerment-program (last visited June 9, 2015).

689 *Senegalese Women, supra* note 684, at 1–2.

690 *Id.*

691 As of 2005, the national rate of FGM was 28 percent. SALIF NDIAYE & MOHAMED AYAD, ENQUÊTE DÉMOGRAPHIQUE ET DE SANTÉ AU SÉNÉGAL 2005, at 239 (2006). The data indicate a decline in the rate with younger generations: 31 percent of women aged forty-five to forty-nine versus 25 percent of women aged fifteen to nineteen. *Id.* Officially, the practice of FGM was outlawed in Senegal in 1999. FEMALE GENITAL MUTILATION: A GUIDE TO LAWS AND POLICIES WORLDWIDE, *supra* note 662, at 207.

692 Kolda is 79 percent Poular and Mandingue ethnic groups, both of which practice FGM. Yoder, *supra* note 683, at 8. Other groups in Senegal that practice FGM include the Soninké and the Diola. *Id.*

693 As of 2005, the rate of FGM in Kolda region was 94 percent. NDIAYE & AYAD, *supra* note 691, at 239. When asked about the reasons for continuing the practice, survey participants in the Kolda region cited hygiene and social reasons. *Id.* at 251.

694 TOSTAN, TOSTAN ANNUAL REPORT 2005, at 6 (2006), *available at* https://jacquideelstra.files.wordpress.com/2011/09/tostan-2005-annual-report.pdf.

695 *158 Villages in the Department of Koungheul Join the Movement to Abandon Harmful Traditional Practices*, TOSTAN (Nov. 20, 2009), http://www.tostan.org/news/158-villages-department-koungheul-join-movement-abandon-harmful-traditional-practices. One alarming statistic is that girls who undergo FGM are now cut at a younger age. *See* Nafissatou J. Diop & Ian Askew, *Strategies for Encouraging the Abandonment of Female Genital Cutting: Experiences from Senegal, Burkina Faso, and Mali, in* FEMALE CIRCUMCISION: MULTICULTURAL PERSPECTIVES 125, 136 (Rogaia Mustafa Abusharaf ed., 2006). Diop and Askew state this shift could be an effort to prevent opposition by the girls themselves. *Id.*

organization's long-term success.[696] Tostan attributes its success to its respectful, collective approach, which allows the communities to make their own decisions on FGM.[697] Scholars who have studied Tostan's program have reached similar conclusions, describing the program as "an opportunity for self-determination"[698] and as a chance for participants to "assert themselves as agents of requisite social transformations."[699] All of these explanations point to the social focus of Tostan's policy and its recognition that the practice of FGM is a social convention that cannot effectively be changed at the individual level.[700]

The successful efforts in Egypt and Senegal share several characteristics. Both groups, Tostan and CEOSS, provide developmental education incorporating women's health and empowerment into a larger curriculum that provides "the full-belly quotient" of tangible development benefits.[701] One woman described how the village women utilized the management skills learned in the Tostan program:

> [b]efore, women had nothing, they only had the things that their husbands would give them. Now, when they are given some money, they buy goods to resell them. When they do well, they buy their chairs, their cabinets, sheets and curtains. They buy everything. So you see that these activities are important.[702]

These programs encourage active local participation and leadership but also ultimately relinquish control of development projects to community leaders. The focus on community participation and leadership helps to ensure that any decision—such as one to abandon FGM—is viewed as a local, internal decision.[703] One could take the position that to the extent community leaders can be convinced to support the endeavor, such

---

696 Yoder, *supra* note 683, at 73 (finding a "very clear change in perceptions relating to circumcision"). This finding echoes earlier studies that found the Tostan program has resulted in "tremendous improvements" in women's awareness and "substantial shifts in their attitudes toward FGC." Diop & Askew, *supra* note 695, at 135. The same studies, however, also found that the practice was not entirely abandoned.

697 *Female Genital Cutting*, TOSTAN, http://www.tostan.org/female-genital-cutting (last visited June 10, 2015).

698 Diop & Askew, *supra* note 695, at 139.

699 L. Amede Obiora, *A Refuge from Tradition and the Refuge of Tradition*, *in* TRANSCULTURAL BODIES: FEMALE GENITAL CUTTING IN GLOBAL CONTEXT 67, 75 (Ylva Hernlund & Bettina Shell-Duncan eds., 2007).

700 Diop & Askew, *supra* note 695, at 141 ("In order to be effective, strategies should be designed to generate social change rather than merely influence individuals. . . .").

701 Obiora, *supra* note 699, at 81, 83–85. *But see* GRUENBAUM, *supra* note 636, at 158–75 (arguing that economic development does not always have a positive impact on FGM).

702 Yoder, *supra* note 683, at 73 (finding a "very clear change in perceptions relating to circumcision").

703 Even local efforts can meet with resistance as in the case of one local NGO in Sudan whose efforts were undermined by Islamic clerics urging communities to resist Western practice and protect the traditional cultural practice of FGM. Janice Boddy, *Gender Crusades: The Female Circumcision Controversy in Cultural Perspective*, *in* TRANSCULTURAL BODIES: FEMALE GENITAL CUTTING IN GLOBAL CONTEXT 46, 66 (Ylva Hernlund & Bettina Shell-Duncan eds., 2007).

support from the local leadership is important as resistance to abandonment efforts may be based on symbolic opposition to colonialism as well as defense of traditional culture.[704] Some African scholars also take issue with the portrayal of African women and girls as victims,[705] viewing much of the Western-based dialogue as misguided and ignorant of women's situation in Africa at best, and imperialistic and arrogant at worst.[706] Under this view, the practice of FGM involves more than the physical act of cutting. For some, it is a rite of passage from girls into women. For some, it is a sign of belonging to a social group.[707] Thus, it is not a behavior that an individual may choose to change alone, as pointed out by villagers themselves.[708]

Failure to conform to the norms of behavior associated with traditional social identity may have serious consequences for the nonconformer, such as lack of access to community resources including marriage within the community.[709] Programs that build community consensus help to protect individuals who choose not to conform to traditional norms by creating a group of fellow nonconformers.[710] This is especially effective when influential members of the community, such as religious leaders, are a part of the nonconforming. The efforts of Tostan and CEOSS have been successful because their programs recognize the complex social nature of the practice and the need for organic change.

Note also, however, that FGM is not the only practice that is socially embedded. So was footbinding. One could say footbinding is not just binding the feet alone but also a practice that signaled social and economic status as well as desire. Eliminating it required taking a holistic approach which involved changing community perception, not individual action alone. None of these legitimate observations should serve to insulate the practice from scrutiny and change. The values of freedom and capability enhancement, championed by the law and development, should override local resistance—even if opposition to changing the practice were prevalent.

---

[704] GRUENBAUM, *supra* note 636, at 103.

[705] Obioma Nnaemeka, *African Women, Colonial Discourses, and Imperialist Interventions: Female Circumcision as Impetus*, *in* FEMALE CIRCUMCISION AND THE POLITICS OF KNOWLEDGE: AFRICAN WOMEN IN IMPERIALIST DISCOURSES 27, 30–32 (Obioma Nnaemeka ed., 2005).

[706] *Id.* at 37–39.

[707] Boddy, *supra* note 703, at 48.

[708] TOSTAN, *supra* note 683, at 10. In Senegal, Tostan learned from a local religious leader that a single village could not end the shared practice of FGM due to the intermarriage between villages. Changing FGM, for example, is not like changing an individual behavior, such as smoking, given the presence of multiple stakeholders. Bettina Shell-Duncan & Yiva [*sic*] Herniund [*sic*], *Are There "States of Change" in the Practice of Female Genital Cutting?: Qualitative Research Findings from Senegal and The Gambia*, AFR. J. REPROD. HEALTH, Aug. 2006, at 57, 61.

[709] Shell-Duncan & Herniund [*sic*], *supra* note 708, at 61.

[710] Diop & Askew, *supra* note 695, at 139–41.

b. WLUML

Women Living Under Muslim Laws (WLUML), a transnational organization devoted to fighting fundamentalism in Algeria, seeks to challenge restrictions imposed on women's autonomy "in the name of 'Islamic' laws and customs. . . ."[711] WLUML has worked with women from Muslim communities outside Algeria and has sought to chronicle alternative legal systems in Muslim communities that do not adopt fundamentalist views of women.[712] This opens up other options for women who do not want to leave their religion but also do not wish to submit to a particularly repressive construction of their identity.[713]

WLUML's strategy is important for two reasons. First, it is a locally driven organization actively involved in pushing against the parameters of religious custom and in pressing for culture change precisely because it recognizes that "[i]n most of the Muslim world, patriarchal customs—rather than state law—restrict women's mobility, severely limit their access to public spaces, certain occupations, and information, and deny women equal access to economic resources, health facilities, judicial processes and to educational and job opportunities."[714] WLUML aims to counter the dominant religious customs purported to reflect the truth about Islam with "information about the actual diversity of laws and customs throughout the Muslim world,"[715] thus demonstrating "the political and historical contingency of practices thought to be essential to Islam."[716] The organization serves as a clearinghouse for information, available in multiple languages, about a wide variety of Muslim laws and promotes face-to-face meetings for women from diverse Muslim societies to forge friendship and solidarity.[717] WLUML can show, for example, that female genital mutilation has varied historically and geographically, has not even been practiced in some Muslim communities, and is more popular in certain Christian communities than Muslim communities.[718]

Second, this organization is contesting traditional custom not by using secular strategies or human rights language per se but rather by working within a cultural/religious framework using traditional language familiar to those within the cultural framework. This is a deliberate strategy designed to enable "Algerian women to pursue greater freedom and equality, but without conceding their right to religion."[719] Human rights manuals such as that titled "Claiming Our Rights: A Manual for Women's Human Rights

---

[711] Sunder, *supra* note 628, at 1434.

[712] *Id.* at 1436.

[713] *Id.* at 1437.

[714] *Id.* at 1436 n.181 (quoting Women Living Under Muslim Laws, *Laws, Initiatives in the Muslim World* 9 (1998)).

[715] *Id.* at 1437.

[716] *Id.*

[717] *Id.*

[718] *Id.*

[719] *Id.* at 1435.

Education in Muslim Societies," provide the necessary cultural texts and stories to bring abstract rights into local Muslim communities.[720] Thus, the organization is in essence promoting culture change but within a particular cultural context; there is no issue of cultural homogenization because the change being pushed is one that is situated within a particular cultural and religious community. Indeed, the pursuit of that strategy is deliberate because the organization "recognizes that many women will resist rights if they are only possible outside the context of religious and cultural community."[721]

In many cases the standard criticism—that change results in Westernization—is not applicable because concepts used to anchor the desired changes are rooted in indigenous roots—myths, ideas, and idioms.[722] The work of WLUML proves this observation inapposite: "Imaginations of socially just futures for humans usually take the idea of single, homogeneous, and secular historical time for granted."[723] For example, in discussing "equality," workshop leaders refer to a hadith from the Prophet Muhammad, which stated that "[a]ll people are equal, as equal as the teeth of a comb"[724] and that "[t]here is no claim of merit of an Arab over a non-Arab, or of a white over a black person, or of a male over a female."[725] Where relevant texts from Quran verses are ambiguous, or where different verses carry conflicting messages, the texts are juxtaposed and women are encouraged to weigh and judge the textual tensions[726] and, through role playing and practical exercises, participate directly in the process of interpreting the texts and negotiating the conflicts.[727] Indigenous cultural frameworks provide the reference points—some portions of a text might support certain rights deemed part and parcel of the international human rights, but other portions might be read as not supportive at worst and ambiguous at best. In the latter case, workshop facilitators highlight the issue of women's equality and autonomy in light of the religious and international legal text and encourage women to question and judge the texts themselves.[728]

c. Microfinance Institutions

Microfinance institutions are not engaged only in finance but also in culture change. As their names suggest, their main objective is finance, but many have supplemented development in the financial sphere with development in the cultural sphere. As a result, these institutions not only provide capital to the poor but also insist on altering

---

[720] *Id.* at 1444.
[721] *Id.* at 1441.
[722] *Id.* at 1446.
[723] Dipesh Chakrabary, Provincializing Europe 15 (2000).
[724] Sunder, *supra* note 628, at 1447 (quoting passages from the Quran).
[725] *Id.* (quoting passages from the Quran).
[726] *Id.* at 1447–48.
[727] *Id.* at 1449.
[728] *Id.* at 1447.

the very cultural norms that are detrimental to their development. In other words, these microfinance organizations adopt an integrated, nonminimalist approach and thus are not merely stand-alone finance institutions. Rather, they provide "complementary support" that goes beyond the standard focus on credit and efficiency.[729] The Bangladesh Rural Advancement Committee, for example, touts its belief that "credit alone has severe limitations as a development tool."[730] Another interesting example is the Grameen Bank founded by an economist from Bangladesh. This institution encourages certain cultural change in its borrowers, and most of Grameen's loans go to women. First and foremost, empowering women economically so they have access to capital, and perhaps a degree of economic independence, is in and of itself a radical concept with deep ramifications, given the subordinate and dependent position of women throughout the world.[731] The mere act of lending to women is itself an act aimed at cultural transformation. "[T]he predominance of women in borrowing groups has raised the prospect that women, who are often the objects of oppression, might be empowered vis-à-vis men in general and their husbands in particular."[732] It is without doubt then that the very decision to focus on lending to women is itself a bold decision that in some instances goes against local cultural norms. To that extent, microfinance organizations that lend primarily to women are already engaging and challenging local cultural norms that discourage female financial independence. This is so even if, as is the case, microfinancing alone cannot transform long-standing cultural norms. "Change in gender equity and economic status takes place over the long term, and is seldom a linear process. 'Snap-shots' may be misleading."[733]

---

[729] Norman MacIsaac, Can. Int'l Dev. Agency, Asia Branch, The Role of Microcredit in Poverty Reduction and Promoting Gender Equity 20 (1997), *available at* http://gadguatemala.weebly.com/uploads/3/7/5/2/3752316/microcredit_and_gender_equity.pdf.

[730] *Id.*

[731] "Microfinance delivery techniques can develop a sense of responsibility and leadership, strengthen social capital, empower the poor, especially women, and create a building block for collective action. Combining financial and non-financial services can enhance this empowerment effect." Craig Churchill & Cheryl Frankiewicz, Making Microfinance Work, Managing for Improved Performance 22 (2006), *available at* http://www.ilo.org/public/libdoc/ilo/2006/106B09_313_engl.pdf.

[732] Brian Fikkert, Christian Microfinance: Which Way Now? 28 (Jan. 6, 2003), *available at* http://www.gordon.edu/ACE/fikkert.doc. Note, however, that studies have been conflicting about this point. A study of women in Bangladesh showed that 63 percent of women borrowers did not completely exercise control over the loans taken in their names, as husbands retained considerable influence over decision making. Yet, "even this finding does not undermine the possibility that women's bargaining power within the household was increased, and many observers believe there is considerable evidence of women's empowerment." *Id.* at 29.

Indeed, even when studies find that women only have partial control over their microloans or turn control over to male members of the family, it is not the case that there are no benefits for the women involved. "As part of a broader effort to raise awareness and mobilize women, credit could play an important role as an 'entry point' to strengthen women's networks and mobility, increase their knowledge and self-confidence, and increase their status in the family." MacIsaac, *supra* note 729, at 5.

[733] *Id.*

The Grameen Bank made the decision to lend to women because it recognizes that lending to women has positive development effects. According to Grameen's founder, Mohammed Yunus, who was awarded the Nobel Peace Prize in 2006, "[g]iven the opportunity to fight against poverty and hunger women turn out to be natural and better fighters than men."[734] Although the Grameen Bank initially pursued both men and women as clients, the Bank shifted its focus to women because they used household resources in a more altruistic fashion, with the outcome being greater health, nutrition, and income levels within the borrowing households.[735] In the Grameen Bank's own words,

> [c]onventional banks focus on men. Grameen gives high priority to women. 97 per cent of Grameen Bank's borrowers are women. Grameen Bank works to raise the status of poor women in their families by giving them ownership of assets. It makes sure that the ownership of the houses built with Grameen Bank loans remain with the borrowers, i.e., the women.[736]

In addition, by providing the poor (men or women) with an opportunity to gain access to credit, microfinance organizations such as Grameen also expand their universe in startling ways. The obvious one is economics; as Nicholas Kristof of the *New York Times* observed, microfinance creates alternatives for poor borrowers who would have to finance needed expenditures—to pay for a wedding, an illness, or grow a business—by turning to money lenders who charge high interest for loans.[737] Furthermore, microfinance organizations charge lower interest, which means that their presence by itself has the effect of "undermining whatever power these moneylenders wield over the poor."[738] The poor, who would not be able to borrow under normal economic circumstances, would be able to borrow under the different considerations used by microfinance institutions. The Grameen Bank, for example, makes microloans conditioned not on the financial creditworthiness of the borrower (most have no credit history and no collateral) but rather on the borrowers' social capital or social collateral. The bank typically lends to a

---

[734] Rashmi Dyal-Chand, *Reflection in a Distant Mirror: Why the West Has Misperceived the Grameen Bank's Vision of Microcredit*, 41 Stan. J. Int'l L. 217, 262 (2005) (citing Muhammad Yunus, Banker to the Poor: Micro-Lending and the Battle Against World Poverty 204 (New York: Public Affairs, 2003)).

[735] *Id.*; *see also* MacIsaac, *supra* note 729, at 7 ("A large number of these programs have focused on supporting women, who bear the brunt of poverty and have been left out of most poverty reduction programs in the past. In many programs, women make up as many as 90 percent of borrowers. Lending to women is also assumed to result in a greater multiplier effect because women pass on the benefits to children, through increased spending on the household, education and nutrition.").

[736] *Is Grameen Bank Different from Conventional Banks?*, Grameen Bank (Mar. 12, 2011), http://www.grameen-info.org/is-grameen-bank-different-from-conventional-banks/.

[737] Nicholas Kristof, *The Role of Microfinance*, On the Ground (Dec. 28, 2009, 2:28 PM), http://kristof.blogs.nytimes.com/2009/12/28/the-role-of-microfinance/.

[738] Fikkert, *supra* note 732, at 28.

circle of five women. It grants a loan to the first borrower. If the first borrower repays the loan, the second individual in the circle is entitled to a loan. Those who received a loan are responsible, by their repayment or nonrepayment, for whether or not others are qualified to borrow.[739] Grameen Bank boasts a high success rate because it uses peer pressure and a sense of social obligation among community members to ensure repayment.

But there are other, perhaps less obvious, benefits to microloans as well. An increase in economic standing also results in an increase in what Sen, Nussbaum, and Appadurai call capability or capacity and voice. "Bringing low-income persons—especially women—into groups for regular meetings and giving them access to a financial system clearly appears to reduce isolation from others and from 'the system.'"[740] As observed, "the creation of a regular forum at which large numbers of poor women can meet and talk represents a 'breakthrough' in the social norms of rural Bangladesh."[741] Indeed, income is but one component of a broader framework. Other factors—what Appadurai called voice and capacity—such as "enhancing women's visibility and enabling them to voice their concerns may be a key means to achieve long-term impact in raising women's status and improving gender equity. While women are occupying non-traditional roles and occupations, for example, they are challenging accepted norms and breaking the path for future generations."[742] Taking part in microfinance programs, going to the requisite weekly members' meetings, and generally participating in lending circles increase their mobility and establish or strengthen networks, especially among women who had previously not had much external contact. This is especially important in rural areas where women's mobility is limited.[743]

In addition, the Grameen Bank undertakes to introduce a social development agenda to its borrowers, as reflected in the "16 decisions" Grameen borrowers are expected to adopt.[744] The purpose of the bank is to help people in poor countries cross the poverty line economically and also to live "a life of dignity and honour."[745] The bank believes that although "credit is an efficient instrument that can quickly augment income, poverty has

---

739 *Grameen Bank Helps You to Get Small Business Unsecured Loans*, GRAMEEN BANK (Mar. 7, 2015), http://www.grameen-info.org/grameen-bank-helps-you-to-get-small-business-unsecured-loans/. For a discussion of alternatives to peer group lending, *see* MACISAAC, *supra* note 729, at 24.

740 Fikkert, *supra* note 732, at 29.

741 *Id.*

742 MACISAAC, *supra* note 729, at 5.

743 *Id.* at 7. By contrast, mobility and visibility are the norm for urban vendors who have routine contact with traders. *Id.* at 18. One downside of the participatory dimension of microfinance is the time commitment it imposes on borrowers, who must bear the opportunity costs of weekly meetings, which take time away from "important domestic tasks as well as other remunerative activities." This will tend to have the most impact on the poorest women who cannot afford to go to meetings or those with the heaviest burden or with other significant commitments, such as caring for young or sick children. *Id.* at 11.

744 *16 Decisions*, GRAMEEN BANK (Mar. 11, 2008), http://www.grameen-info.org/16-decisions/.

745 *The Value of Microenterprise Development: Hearing Before the H. Comm. on Int'l Relations*, 104th Cong. app. at 48 (1995) (statement of Professor Muhammad Yunus, Managing Director, Grameen Bank).

many dimensions,"[746] which includes social and political consciousness. Grameen Bank's "16 decisions" reflect the bank's effort to address the social and cultural elements of poverty. Hence, at weekly meetings, borrowers agree to follow and advance these principles of Grameen Bank: "discipline, unity, courage and hard work."[747] The purpose of the "16 decisions" is to encourage sound financial discipline, as well as to instill in borrowers certain social goals.[748] Borrowers are encouraged to memorize and recite the "16 decisions," some of which deal with "mundane subjects such as sanitation—'we shall build and use pit latrines'—and nutrition—'we shall grow vegetables all year round,'" as well as more sensitive topics.[749] Examples of the latter include the pledge to educate their children, not take any dowry at a son's wedding, not give any dowry at a daughter's wedding, not to practice child marriage,[750] and not overspend on weddings and funerals.[751] Dowries and child marriage are culturally significant issues that can have deleterious effect on women's capability and freedom. Overspending on weddings and funerals negatively affect capital accumulation and investment, both of which implicate core concerns of the economic development literature. The underlying principle behind the "16 decisions" is nurturing pride[752] and discipline—such as "deferral of selfish gratification . . . and educating children. . . ."[753] This effort is in fact not different from that taken by Japan, when it pursued culture change, in the 1800s, as previously described in Part A of this chapter.[754]

Although the Grameen Bank is perhaps the most well-known microfinance institution, there is an array of other organizations formed to further women's capability. These programs "provide space for women as leaders and role models, often in non-traditional occupations."[755] The Bangladesh Rural Advancement Committee, for example, trains women "paraprofessionals" who in turn train others to be " 'barefoot' vets and paralegals," carpenters and brick makers.[756] The Entrepreneurship and Career Institute focuses on "designing and implementing a very orthodox program for supporting women entrepreneurs."[757] South Africa's Intervention with Microfinance for AIDS and Gender Equity (IMAGE) is another microfinance institution that links the provision of loans with a broader campaign to empower women by combining "financial services with training and skills-building sessions on HIV prevention, gender norms, cultural beliefs,

---

[746] *Id.* at 51 (1995).

[747] *16 Decisions, supra* note 744.

[748] Irene Tinker, *Alleviating Poverty: Investing in Women's Work*, 66 J. AM. PLAN. ASS'N 229, 232 (2000).

[749] Rone Tempest, *Breaks Many Rules: Bangladesh: A Bank Just for the Poor*, L.A. TIMES, Nov. 28, 1987, at 1, *available at* http://articles.latimes.com/1987-11-28/news/mn-5966_1_grameen-bank.

[750] *16 Decisions, supra* note 744.

[751] Tinker, *supra* note 748, at 232.

[752] Tempest, *supra* note 749, at 1.

[753] William H. Simon, *The Community Economic Development Movement*, 2002 WIS. L. REV. 377, 421 (2002).

[754] *See supra* notes 69–170 and accompanying text.

[755] MACISAAC, *supra* note 729, at 17.

[756] *Id.*

[757] *Id.*

communication and intimate partner violence."[758] IMAGE reaches out to the wider community, using "education and skills-building sessions that address a variety of social issues and engage men and boys."[759] IMAGE makes a point of including men and boys in their microfinance programs and their accompanying consciousness-raising agenda in order to "change the attitudes of whole communities, making them more receptive to female empowerment. . . ."[760] Increases in female financial independence may cause conflicts. "Disagreements over the control of newly acquired assets and earnings, combined with women's changing attitudes towards traditional gender roles, improved social support and greater confidence to defend themselves against male authority, sometimes led to marital conflicts and violence against women perpetrated by their partners. Increases in violence following participation in credit programmes have also been reported . . . at least in the initial stages of membership."[761] Including men in the process of cultural change is thus important to minimize the possibility of backlash. It is also important because an underlying change in traditional gender roles may be needed to ensure that the provision of credit for women work as planned. For example, unless men shift out of their traditional paradigm and share household work, "microcredit for income generation will likely increase women's, and in some cases children's, workload, especially girls who share domestic responsibilities and are less likely to be attending school."[762] Similarly, unless girl children are as valued as boy children, increased capital garnered through microfinance does not necessarily mean that female offspring will receive equal benefits derived from increased expenditures as male offspring.[763]

Perhaps due to the inclusion of men and high rates of male participation, IMAGE can claim that two years after completing their program, "participants reported 55% fewer acts of violence by their intimate partners in the previous 12 months than did members of a control group."[764] Controlling behavior by partners also decreased, and participants reported that they were more likely after enrolling in the program than before to "disagree with statements that condone physical and sexual violence. . . ."[765]

Such results can also be attributed to changes in economic circumstances and attitudes.[766] Women's standing in the household is enhanced when they contribute to the

---

758 World Health Org., *Promoting Gender Equality to Prevent Violence Against Women*, *in* Violence Prevention: The Evidence 79, 85 (2009), *available at* http://apps.who.int/iris/bitstream/10665/77936/1/9789241500845_eng.pdf?ua=1.

759 *Id.*

760 *Id.*

761 *Id.*

762 MacIsaac, *supra* note 729, at 13.

763 *Id.*

764 World Health Org., *supra* note 758, at 85.

765 *Id.* Interviews with participants of the Bangladesh Rural Advancement Committee also revealed that they were less likely to have been beaten by their partners as those who did not participate in such programs. *Id.* at 85–86.

766 *Id.*

household in economically tangible ways. Additionally, increased interaction with the outside world also means greater visibility and exposure, including exposure of violence inside the home. Perhaps more surprisingly, however, is the finding that these programs benefit the entire community, not just those who participate. For example, intimate partner violence is 30 percent lower even for nonparticipating women living in villages with microfinance organizations than nonparticipating women in villages without microfinance programs.[767]

There are yet other microfinance organizations that provide an array of education for clients. Christian development organizations, for example, are engaged in the inculcation of values premised on the notion that "religious beliefs provide moral guidance and influence people's will to improve their lives."[768] The Fellowship of Confessing Anglicans in the United Kingdom and Ireland, which is the spiritual home for Orthodox and Mainstream Anglicans, has founded the Anglican International Development for Relief and Change (AID) fund to partner with churches around the world to improve education, health care, and job creation and to support economic development through microfinance.[769] When Southern Sudan voted for independence in 2011, after two decades of war between the Muslim majority in the north and the non-Muslim, non-Arabic speaking Sudanese in the south, AID, in conjunction with the Episcopal Church of Sudan, set up Manna Microfinance, a microfinance entity to help the poor, particularly the Anglican Christians who account for about a third of the population of southern Sudan. Manna Microfinance's focus will be on the families of the Episcopal Church of Sudan. As the deputy governor of the Bank of Sudan observed when he welcomed the launch of Manna Microfinance in March 2011, "Why do we want to be independent? . . . We want to organize our own administration, we want to develop ourselves and be part of the world of nations. But to be independent we must be able to work to feed ourselves."[770] The need for capital, as identified by Arthur Lewis,[771] thus remains paramount in today's development debate. Recipients will be small retail and agricultural businesses and individuals offering manual services such as tailoring and embroidery. Project-finance is provided in the form of a loan, plus interest.

---

[767] *Id.* at 85.

[768] Roy Mersland et al., *The Effect of Religion on Development Efforts: Evidence from the Microfinance Industry and a Research Agenda*, 41 WORLD DEV. 145, 145 (2012).

[769] The discussion that follows of AID and the microfinance institution in Sudan is drawn from *Microfinance*, ANGLICAN INTERNATIONAL DEVELOPMENT, http://interanglicanaid.org/our-work/microfinance/ (last visited June 11, 2015).

[770] *Launch of Manna Microfinance in Juba Sudan*, MICROFINANCE AFRICA (Mar. 30, 2011), http://microfinanceafrica.net/news/launch-of-manna-microfinance-in-juba-sudan/ (last visited Jan. 4, 2016).

[771] W. Arthur Lewis, *Economic Development with Unlimited Supplies of Labour*, *in* PARADIGMS IN ECONOMIC DEVELOPMENT: CLASSIC PERSPECTIVES, CRITIQUES, AND REFLECTIONS 59 (Rajani Kanth ed., 1994). *See also* Introduction, text accompanying notes 226–29; Chapter 1, text accompanying note 88; Chapter 3, text accompanying notes 530–32.

Manna Microfinance Institution is owned by the Episcopal Church of Sudan and managed by the Bridge Foundation, India, with the support and funding of AID.[772] Like the other microfinance institutions discussed in this chapter, Manna adopts a multi-pronged approach that includes finance and economics and also culture, values, and attitudes. Manna works to identify potential micro-entrepreneurs within churches and train existing ones in business and financial management, with an emphasis on how to save and how to manage loan repayments. Manna microfinance officers provide church support via self-help and intragroup mentoring in groups that meet regularly. Bishop Enoch Tombe emphasized that "what was needed was also an attitude and culture change,"[773] for example, tribal culture that looked down on market transactions. Other bishops observed, "the church would make a vital contribution in helping to change people's attitudes. 'Real and true development happens when peoples attitudes change.' "[774]

Other microfinance organizations concentrate on tying micro loans with financial education designed to help clients understand the basics of loan repayments, calculating interests, and understanding basic terms of a loan.[775] Credito Con Education Rural (CRECER), Pro Mujer in Bolivia, Taytay Sa Kauswagan, Incorporated in the Philippines, and Sarvodaya Economic Enterprise Development Services (SEEDS) in Sri Lanka, for example, provide a host of services to poor clients—credit, savings, insurance, education, and health, though each adopts its own particular mix of product and service. The Self-Employed Women's Association (SEWA) with more than fifty thousand members has worked to improve the lives of female workers in the informal sector. It also has a SEWA bank. Women who come to the bank understand the bank's motto, as articulated by its founder: "This bank is like our mother's place"—because SEWA's founder Ela Bhatt understands that "a woman's mother takes her seriously, keeps her secrets, and helps her solve her problems."[776] Borrowing money from an organization such as SEWA means having access to credit and potentially income. Perhaps more importantly, owing money to SEWA is different from owing it to others, even family members. "[B]eing part of a mutually supportive community of women was crucially different, with respect to both practical reason and affiliation, from being a poor relation getting a handout."[777] As one SEWA member explained, "When we make videos, and women like us watch them, we get confidence to try and make changes. When we see women like us who have done

---

[772] The Bridge Foundation has over twenty-five years of experience in this area, with a high repayment rate of its loans. *Microfinance, supra* note 769.

[773] *Launch of Manna Microfinance in Juba Sudan, supra* note 770.

[774] *Id.*

[775] B. Gray et al., *Can Financial Education Change Behavior? Lessons from Bolivia and Sri Lanka* 5 (Global Fin. Educ. Program, Working Paper No. 4, 2009), *available at* https://www.freedomfromhunger.org/sites/default/files/GFEP.LowIncome.Paper_.pdf.

[776] Martha C. Nussbaum, Women and Human Development: The Capabilities Approach 15 (2000).

[777] *Id.* at 107.

something brave and new, then we get the confidence that we can learn something new too."[778] It is not unusual for SEWA educators to spend an entire day working on an exercise to get SEWA women to stand up and say their names in public.[779]

Many of these organizations provide financial education to clients in various formats, some during the scheduled credit meetings, others at focused discussion groups or separately scheduled workshops, emphasizing debt management, savings, and budgeting.[780] Sometimes, radio and television are also used to provide financial information. SEEDS, for example, reported that after financial education sessions, there was an "attitude change" in their clients, resulting in a positive change from 74 to 85 percent of clients who reported that it was important to save.[781] Indeed, CRECER, Pro Mujer, and SEEDS reported that clients who took the financial education course understood the importance of saving, budgeting, and managing money, learned about savings strategies, and accordingly were able to set aside some of their earnings toward savings.[782]

A randomized study with the SEWA Bank in Gujarat, India, "revealed that the women who were randomly assigned to receive financial education took out twice as many loans as those who did not," and more importantly, were also more likely to take out loans in pursuit of sound financial objectives, such as home purchase, business expansion, or financing of their children's education.[783] This result was confirmed in other studies. A six-month midpoint study (of a full-year evaluation) by Freedom from Hunger of adolescent girls in West Bengal, India, found that girls who were randomly selected to receive financial education were more motivated to save, more confident about their ability to manage money, and in fact, saved more often when compared to the control groups who received no education. "Overall, the findings show that financial education took the intervention groups one step closer to attitude- and behavior-change."[784] The microfinance institutions described use education to instill a norm of saving into their clients precisely because, as the noted economist Arthur Lewis identified,[785] saving is a necessary step toward capital formation.

d. Gender-focused NGOs and Education

Other community programs have been founded with the specific purpose of challenging gender norms and attitudes that justify intimate partner violence. One of the most

---

778 *Id.* at 111.
779 *Id.* at 268.
780 Gray et al., *supra* note 775, at 13.
781 *Id.* at 18.
782 *Id.* at 21.
783 *Id.* at 7.
784 *Id.* at 8.
785 *See* Gustav Ranis, *Arthur Lewis' Contribution to Development Thinking and Policy* (Yale Univ. Econ. Growth Center, Discussion Paper No. 891, 2004), *available at* http://www.econ.yale.edu/growth_pdf/cdp891.pdf.

established and evaluated is the Stepping Stones program, a life-skills training program for HIV prevention in Africa and Asia. In thirteen three-hour sessions convened for single-sex groups of women and men, followed by mixed peer groups and community meetings, Stepping Stones uses role-playing and encourages participants to reflect on relationship issues, including gender-based violence and HIV communication.[786]

Programs similar to Stepping Stones have been adopted and evaluated in different countries. One of the most thorough studies was conducted in the Eastern Cape province of South Africa with participants aged fifteen to twenty-six years old.[787] The study showed that, compared to men in a control group, men who participated in the program are less likely to commit physical or sexual violence in the two years following the program.[788] Another study in Gambia comparing couples who participated in the program, and those in a control group who did not, found that the former group developed better communication skills and argued less; men who participated also were more understanding if their wives refused sex and were less likely to resort to physical violence.[789]

Raising Voices and the Center for Domestic Violence Prevention run a community initiative in Uganda for men and women to challenge preexisting gender norms and prevent violence against women and children. This program uses different methods to accomplish its stated objectives—raising community awareness of domestic violence, building support networks, using door-to-door visits, theater, public discussions, and media such as radio, television, and newspapers to promote women's rights.[790] A review of the program after two years showed positive results with a decrease in domestic violence overall in the community. However, 8 percent of women and 18 percent of men reported an increase in violence against women that can be attributed to men feeling threatened by women's empowerment.[791]

Researchers in Central America studying civil society's campaign to promote women's rights found similar results in Nicaragua, that is, the occurrence of male backlash and hence an increase in gender-based violence. The Universidad Centro Americana and the Institute for Gender Studies attribute the backlash to two factors: first, greater willingness to report abuse because women are encouraged to speak out, and second, a "growing awareness among women that cultural traditions that foster violence are no longer acceptable under international law. In turn, as Nicaraguan women have more actively opposed male hegemony, domestic conflicts have increased and more men have resorted to domestic violence."[792]

---

786 World Health Org., *supra* note 758, at 86.

787 *Id.*

788 *Id.*

789 *Id.*

790 *Id.*

791 *Id.*

792 *Id.* at 87.

As a result, many programs are aimed specifically at changing the values and attitudes of men by targeting male peer groups and redefining traditional understanding of masculinity. For example, Men as Partners operating in Africa, Asia, Latin America, and the United States works with men in a variety of ways, bundling services such as health care, consciousness-raising, educational and skills-building, encouraging men in the process "to explore their attitudes regarding sexuality and gender...."[793] Results from an informal study showed that among the men who attended a five-day workshop in South Africa and filled out surveys, there was a significant change in outlook after the workshop. In a pretraining interview, 54 percent of men disagreed with the statement that "men must make all the decisions in a relationship" compared with 75 percent three months later; and 61 percent of men disagreed with the statement "women who dress sexy want to be raped" before training compared with 82 percent three months later.[794]

Brazil's Program H also focuses on male peer groups and uses a two-prong approach to change male-female relationships and prevent sexually transmitted infections. Program H holds education workshops using video, role-playing, and discussions, lasting two hours per week for six months "to promote changes in attitude and behaviour; and a social marketing campaign to promote changes in norms of masculinity and lifestyles."[795]

Lest one too blithely disparages efforts to institute change through the educational system, it is important to note that scholars have long studied how "education constructs culture."[796] The works of Pierre Bourdieu demonstrate "the central role that schools have in both changing and in reproducing social and cultural [structures] . . . from one generation to the next."[797] As Bourdieu explained, "[i]f it be accepted . . . that culture . . . is a common code enabling all those possessing that code to attach the same meaning to the same words, the same types of behavior and the same works," then "it is clear that the school . . . is the fundamental factor in the cultural consensus in as far as it represents the sharing of a common sense which is the prerequisite for communications."[798] Cultural traditions may also be constructed—a process Eric Hobsbawm described as "invented tradition," defined as "a set of practices, normally governed by overtly or tacitly accepted rules and of a ritual or symbolic nature, which seek to inculcate certain values and norms of behaviour by repetition, which automatically implies continuity with the past."[799] Again, education would play a vital role in the construction and reshaping

---

[793] *Id.*

[794] *Id.*

[795] *Id.*

[796] Lessig, *supra* note 2, at 974.

[797] *Id.* at 973 (citation omitted).

[798] *Id.* at 973–74 (citation omitted). *See also id.* at 975 (describing how education is a vehicle for government norm management, Lessig states "[e]ducation thus proceeds (1) through a practice, (2) directed by an authority, (3) that coerces without appearing to coerce. . . .").

[799] *Id.* at 978 (quoting Eric Hobsbawm & Terence Ranger, The Invention of Tradition 1 (Cambridge 1983)).

of such cultural traditions—whether to promote frugality, trust, delaying gratification, sacrificing for the national interest, the time value of money—by adopting "a process of formalization and ritualization. . . ."[800] and "organizing cultural productions,"[801] as undertaken by Japan during the Meiji Restoration period.

Civil society groups have effectively used media—radio, the Internet, newspapers, magazines, television—"to reach a wide range of people and effect change within society. They aim to increase knowledge, challenge attitudes and modify behaviour. Media interventions can also alter social norms and values (e.g. the belief that masculinity is associated with aggression) through public discussion and social interaction."[802] Media campaigns have been aimed at not just changing gender norms generally but also at reducing violent behavior. Research shows that understanding the behavior of the target audience and including the targeted individuals in the development of the intervention contribute to the program's effectiveness. One of the best-known and most carefully evaluated media programs is Soul City in South Africa, which uses radio and television episodes, supplemented by nationally distributed information booklets, to discuss intimate partner violence, date rape, and sexual harassment.[803] A follow-up study on Soul City's effectiveness reported a link between exposure to the series and a change in attitudes toward intimate partner violence, with the percentage of people agreeing with the statement "no woman ever deserves to be beaten" increasing from 77 percent to 88 percent, and the percentage disagreeing with the assertion "women who are abused are expected to put up with it" increasing from 68 percent to 72 percent.[804]

In Nicaragua, a mass communication strategy called "Somos Diferentes, Somos Iguales" (We are different, We are equal) aimed at promoting gender equality and empowering women used a national television series (Sexto Sentido, Sixth Sense) broadcasted weekly with issue-based storylines to convey its underlying message. The organization also relied on a radio talk show aimed at youths and community training workshops and youth leadership camps.[805]

A 2001 Australian campaign known as Violence against Women—It's Against All the Rules targeted twenty-one- to twenty-nine-year-old men and relied in part on sports celebrities to convey the message that violence is not a characteristic of masculinity.[806] The Men Can Stop Rape Campaign in the United States aimed at boys and men adopted the slogan, "My strength is not for hurting," and emphasized that strong men do not need to overpower others.[807] Internationally, the White Ribbon campaign mobilizes boys and

---

800 *Id.* at 978 (citations omitted).

801 *Id.* at 982 (citations omitted).

802 World Health Org., *supra* note 758, at 89.

803 *Id.*

804 *Id.*

805 *Id.*

806 *Id.* at 89–90.

807 *Id.*

men to end violence against women by encouraging men to speak out against it and supporters to wear white ribbons symbolizing their commitment to the campaign.

Although the degree of the state's involvement may vary, in terms of "official encouragement, outright subsidies, and governmental coordination,"[808] there is currently, as discussed above, a concerted effort in some developing countries to engage in culture change—whether as a human rights matter, as in efforts to eradicate female genital mutilation, or as an economic development issue. This process includes the construction of social capital through educational reform and various forms of civic participation, which resemble, in broad strokes at least, the earlier efforts toward social management adopted by the Japanese. One could also imagine other forms of government involvement in culture change, for example, the government as a "meaning manager, or meaning architect, who has identified a social meaning that is to be transformed, and must find the techniques to achieve this transformation."[809] This could be accomplished through the technique of tying, as Lawrence Lessig puts it, by associating one act with "another social meaning that conforms to the meaning that the architect wishes the managed act to have."[810] Through education in schools and coordination with other civic organizations, these governments could promote certain virtues, such as saving and frugality necessary for capital accumulation; a future-oriented mindset that encourages individuals to stop defining themselves primarily as occupiers of inherited social status; or a norm that makes individual accumulation of wealth acceptable or even desirable.

If cultural norms carry socially constructed meaning[811] and if social meanings are collective goods, and collective action is needed (sometimes, at least) to change collective goods,[812] public education may be necessary to alter such social meanings. Rituals may be an effective way of promoting the desired form of tying[813] because "rituals serve to coordinate individuals in support of a new meaning."[814] For example, the Japanese government resorted to various emperor-centric rituals and mandated that they be performed daily in school[815] when it wished to inculcate a sense of national identity. Similar political rituals have been used in the United States, as when West Virginia required children "to stand and salute the flag in school."[816] Development could also be tied to certain attributes,

---

808 Sheldon Garon, Molding Japanese Minds: The State in Everyday Life 235 (1997).

809 Lessig, *supra* note 2, at 1008.

810 *Id.* at 1009.

811 For example, in countries that practice female genital mutilation, the practice is justified on the grounds that girls not subject to female genital mutilation will become nymphomaniacs, and therefore those who have been subject to the procedure are "good" girls. Philip Smucker, *Egyptian Women Fight Circumcision*, Pittsburgh Post-Gazette, Feb. 25, 2001, at A4, http://old.post-gazette.com/headlines/20010225mutilation4.asp.

812 Lessig, *supra* note 2, at 993.

813 *Id.* at 1013–14.

814 *Id.* at 1016.

815 *See* David Landes, The Wealth and Poverty of Nations: Why Some Are So Rich and Some So Poor 376 (1998).

816 Lessig, *supra* note 2, at 1014.

for example, frugality or a future orientation, and the citizenry of a developing country exhorted to adopt and internalize such attributes.

Certainly any effort by governments to change social and cultural meanings may be viewed pejoratively as propaganda, as a troubling form of "industrial policy for norm generation" resulting in "boundless and oppressive state efforts to manipulate social norms."[817] Some may find it all the more "chilling"[818] when undertaken by liberal states that do not as a matter of course engage in propaganda or brainwashing.[819] Yet, such efforts may already be more commonly pursued by governments, including the United States', than one may initially realize.[820] Besides Japan, the former Soviet Union is another example of a government engaging in "'consciously shaped and directed' cultures"[821] whereby "rituals served as an 'instrument of cultural management enabling political elites . . . to gain acceptance for a general system of norms . . . congruent with their interpretation of Marxism-Leninsm.' "[822] The same way Japan's Home Ministry sought to alter certain Japanese norms during the Meiji Restoration period, the Soviets too established "ritual specialists"—"local organizers and administrators of the Party, the Komsomol, the trade unions and the local soviet"[823]—to engage in social and cultural reconstruction, often through "an extensive advertising campaign."[824] "Governments trade on standing social meanings to advance state ends,"[825] which have ranged, in the United States, for example, from promoting "family values" in order to exclude homosexuals from social integration to, in the former Yugoslavia, constructing race and ethnic identities to build up nationalism.[826] And depending on the nature of the state's efforts to produce and

---

[817] Richard H. Pildes, *The Destruction of Social Capital Through Law*, 144 U. PA. L. REV. 2055, 2057–60 (1996).

[818] Lessig, *supra* note 2, at 1016.

[819] For an excellent essay on the dangerous line between government speech and government propaganda and the First Amendment of the US Constitution, *see* William W. Van Alstyne, *The "Competition of The Market": "Enter the Elephant!" [A t Reintroduction of a Most Perplexing First Amendment Conundrum], available at* http://ssrn.com/abstract=2438907.

[820] Even in the United States, for example, despite proclamations that the government does not "prescribe what shall be orthodox in politics, nationalism, religion, or other matters of opinion. . . ." Lessig, *supra* note 2, at 945 (quoting *American Booksellers Assn', Inc. v. Hudnut*, 771 F.2d 323, 327–28 (1985)), the US government, as well as governments elsewhere, regularly "act to construct the social structures, or social norms, or . . . the social meanings that surround us. For these social meanings are what is orthodox. They constitute what is authority for a particular society, or particular culture. To the extent that they are built, or remade, or managed by government, then to that extent government is 'prescribing' the orthodox. . . ." Lessig, *supra* note 2, at 947. One example of government transformation of norms for progressive purposes is the passage of the Civil Rights Act, which altered the cultural landscape by providing a cultural and legal safe harbor for businesses that served black customers; by making discrimination illegal, the law allowed a business who served blacks to be viewed as doing so in order to obey the law, not necessarily to favor blacks. Lessig, *supra* note 2, at 965–66.

[821] Lessig, *supra* note 2, at 983.

[822] *Id.*

[823] *Id.* at 984 (citation omitted).

[824] *Id.* at 985 (citation omitted).

[825] *Id.* at 957.

[826] *Id.*

reshape social and cultural norms, this effort toward norm construction and management may or may not raise the specter of "thought control."[827]

Given the above examples, a common pattern can be discerned regarding culture change. Whether the actors are governments or transnational networks of NGO activists, effectuating development through rule of law alone is likely to be ineffective. In many cases, development includes purposeful culture change, which in turns necessitates the framing of the new cultural norm in a way that resonates locally. This was and is one of the challenges faced by the United States in Iraq and Afghanistan and the United Nations in nation-building projects in countries such as Kosovo, Somalia, and East Timor. Below, I examine the efforts utilized in these countries and theorize that attempts at establishing rule of law in these regions have failed due to a lack of framing new cultural practices within the constraints of indigenous practices. I will also examine complications to culture change projects such as lack of security and the overwhelming commitment required to rebuilding and changing a culture.

C. Modern-Day Law and Development Case Studies

This section examines high-visibility, law and development projects undertaken in countries that have emerged from conflicts or wars. Because the environment in which law and development will be pursued is different from Part A's historical examples of culture change, special considerations need to be taken into account. The scenarios detailed below involve law and development projects justified by military and humanitarian interventions; these countries continue to face humanitarian and security problems that require a long-term commitment to rebuilding and reforming institutions. These postconflict projects involve an "extremely complex bundle of cultural commitments and institutional structures that support peace, human rights, democracy, and prosperity."[828] This is no easy task because Western citizens will be loath to involve their countries in the reconstruction of postconflict states when the endeavor seems open-ended, risky, and expensive. Here, a cultural-based approach will face an even steeper uphill climb. Unlike drafting laws or training judges, which can be monitored and concretely measured by reference to various indicators or yardsticks, changing a cultural tradition seems hopelessly diffuse and open-ended. Opposition to the proposal will likely be higher under such circumstances.

As the select examples below show, the law and development projects undertaken in these countries contain additional layers of difficulties and risks. The postconflict conditions in each are such that security and stability are in flux. Military missions, whether

---

[827] *Id.* at 945.

[828] Jane Stromseth et al., Can Might Make Rights? Building the Rule of Law after Military Interventions 4 (2006).

undertaken unilaterally by intervening countries or multilaterally by the United Nations, often cannot guarantee security. In some cases, as in Afghanistan and Iraq, armed conflict may continue even after interveners have secured an initial military victory. In many instances, the states where intervention took place might have been "failed states" lacking in the most basic infrastructures. Some have not completed the state-building process and their governments lack the capability and the resources to maintain order within their territory. As a result, intervention and law and development under such conditions are extremely precarious and understandably, security concerns are paramount and overwhelm other pressing issues.

Security plays a large role in the effectiveness and acceptance of law and development projects in these countries: "Absent basic security, efforts to reform political institutions, adopt new laws, promote national reconciliation, and jump-start economic growth are destined to fail."[829] Law and development projects at first may appear illegitimate to the populace as their experience with authority has previously been negative. In many cases, "pre-intervention security and police forces of the state operated primarily to impose or support the ruling elite's hold on power . . . these security forces terrorized regime opponents, persecuted minorities, and instilled lasting distrust of state authority in the general population."[830] As a result, it is often difficult to garner support from the citizenry; "after a legacy of repression, citizens may be deeply distrustful of legal institutions."[831]

Security, therefore, is difficult to maintain as "public order, at least outside of a police state, rests on a societal consensus about the legitimacy of state institutions and confidence in the capacity of such institutions to deliver basic services."[832] Public order is impossible when the citizenry is wary of or confused as to what the law and development is meant to provide for them; often, the projects "and their sponsors are largely silent as to whether the rule of law is designed to provide citizens with their right to justice and to safeguard their dignity, or merely to provide order in society."[833] This could explain why so many rule of law initiatives do not gain a strong footing within the society, especially in those societies where human rights have been previously ignored or consistently violated. "In societies that have been wracked by conflict, law and order often have completely broken down, and institutions are devastated or minimally functional. A deep and pervasive popular skepticism about government institutions may be widespread . . . ."[834] As such, when developing new rule of law practices, "public concerns about the legitimacy of these institutions need to be a major focus, and their relationship to traditional practices carefully considered."[835] If the traditional norm in a country is not fair to vulnerable segments

829 *Id.* at 134.
830 *Id.* at 135.
831 *Id.* at 187.
832 *Id.* at 135.
833 *Id.* at 76.
834 *Id.* at 185.
835 *Id.*

of the population, such as minorities or women, incorporating the norm into rule of law initiatives may bring about stability but at the expense of the perceived legitimacy of new institutions.[836] Moreover, as I have maintained throughout the book, traditional norms that constrict freedom and capability of any group or perpetuate the marginalization of the group should be addressed because they go against universal development values.

At the same time, culture change is especially delicate because ideally, the process must also meet basic standards of inclusiveness and participation. Law and development reformers will need to partner with local reformers who dissent from local cultural norms. This is important because reforms that last are those that include the "commitment of local leaders and ordinary people alike, on local involvement in decision-making, and on strengthening cultural foundations for the rule of law."[837] Otherwise, feelings of reservation and exclusion will prevail, causing the local population to "doubt law's fairness or efficacy" and "seek alternative methods of ordering their lives and settling problems, and changes in the law or in institutions will consequently have less of an effect on their behavior."[838]

Jane Stromseth suggested that "[a]nthropologists and country experts—as well as individuals with functional expertise in rule of law assistance—should participate in the effort" of assessing the useful information necessary for yielding the proper system of rule of law.[839] "Including local participation and perspectives is also critical to gaining a comprehensive understanding of the unique needs and resources of the country at issue and to designing reforms that are more likely to enjoy local support and buy-in."[840] Further, plans for rule of law development need to include "a realistic, strategic assessment of existing local *resources* for the rule of law. Such an assessment will help to identify what resources—cultural, human, material, and, indeed, legal—are available and also how best to make use of them."[841] If there are positive cultural resources and practices that exist to help resolve disputes, they can be incorporated into the new system.[842] If not, then these cultural resources need to first be created before rule of law is able to take root. "Interveners eager to foster the rule of law must thus seek ways to persuade both elites and ordinary people to value the rule of law . . . interveners must seek to create a rule of law culture."[843] More than that, I have argued that interveners must also create a pro-development culture that supports universal norms.

Strengthening rule of law immediately after a country has faced military intervention and armed conflict often proves to be quite difficult.[844] The time after successful

---

836 *Id.*
837 *Id.* at 187.
838 *Id.* at 311.
839 *Id.* at 189.
840 *Id.*
841 *Id.* at 190.
842 *Id.*
843 *Id.* at 311.
844 *Id.* at 187.

intervention is sometimes a great opportunity to create change and a system that is both trustworthy for the citizens and democratic.

> Although this window closes quickly, the opportunity to significantly alter the status quo, to provide new opportunities for previously disadvantaged and disempowered groups (such as women and minorities), and to reform institutions generally exists in a more dramatic way in the wake of an international military intervention than in more traditional reform programs in countries that have not experienced such intervention.[845]

Understanding what caused the civil conflict is necessary as "[a] comprehensive strategic assessment needs to address a series of interrelated issues, the most fundamental of which relates to the causes and consequences of the conflict—the *conflict legacy*."[846] Since the public may have no trust in state institutions or officials, "understanding what ordinary people view as urgent priorities is a critical part of a valuable strategic assessment."[847] Yet, that understanding and the desire for local buy-in are difficult and complex. Local preferences may be hard to discern and false versus true preferences may be hard to distinguish. And again, the continuing lack of stability and security often remain a persistent and urgent problem for law and development interveners.

To illustrate the gargantuan task of law and development in postconflict reconstruction and development, take Somalia as an example. Somalia never possessed an effective government capable of carrying out routine administration. The end of the Cold War meant that neither the United States nor the Soviet Union had much strategic interest in the country or in any particular regime. The country's government collapsed in the early 1990s and the country quickly deteriorated into anarchy. The United States engaged in a humanitarian mission to establish a secure environment for the distribution of food. It discovered, however, that even this narrow mission could not be accomplished in the absence of effective institutions, and establishing institutions became part of a mission toward nation building. US efforts to maintain control failed as warring clans fought each other for control, and Somalia descended into further chaos, with American casualties projected on television for the world to see. The United States fled Somalia, and soon so did the United Nations.

Afterward, Somalia, a once feudal-type system of warlord governance riddled with tribal affiliations, had no effective government for more than two decades.[848] Following

---

845 *Id.* at 188–89.

846 *Id.* at 189.

847 *Id.* at 190.

848 Marc Lacey, *In Somalia, Islamic Militias Are Fighting Culture Wars*, N.Y. TIMES, June 19, 2006, at A11, *available at* http://www.nytimes.com/2006/06/19/world/africa/19somalia.html?pagewanted=all; *Somalia Profile—Overview*, BBC NEWS (May 5, 2015), http://www.bbc.com/news/world-africa-14094503.

the US departure in 1994, a centralized Islamic government came into power, and Islamic courts and schools, enforced and protected by zealot militias, effectively supplanted a secular lifestyle similar to pre-revolution Iran with that of strict religious conservatism.[849] Roaming gangs no longer randomly killed and raped as frequently, but public viewings of soccer matches were prohibited, men were required to grow their beards, and women were required to stay covered by hijab and not leave their homes except to perform sharia-sanctioned tasks.[850] Now, extremist terrorist groups plague Somalia despite the installation in 2012 of an internationally backed government—nearly two decades after the United Nations' failed peacekeeping/nation-building mission in which over three dozen UN troops and nearly one thousand Somalis died.[851]

i. EAST TIMOR AND KOSOVO

Other experiences in postconflict law and development have been beset by similar problems. The United Nations aimed to establish rule of law institutions in East Timor[852] and international financial assistance for the nation-building mission in East Timor reached hundreds of millions of dollars per year.[853] But, after overseeing the creation of a constitution and the execution of free and fair elections, the United Nations declared the mission complete and handed the reins to Timorese leaders.[854] Within four years, East Timor had reverted to a state of violence and instability.[855] The United Nations had given East Timor the institutional "training wheels" of a functioning rule of law democracy, but as some have noted, "[a] 'democratic' society without justice is less appealing than a just society in which elections have been delayed until it is safe for them to be held"[856].

As demonstrated by the collapse of East Timor, building a functioning police force is one of the most important aspects of rebuilding the rule of law. This becomes increasingly difficult in societies where the police are distrusted by the public and have a history of human rights abuses and practice clan politics.[857] In Kosovo the existing police forces were distrusted by the public and notorious for criminal activity and abuse of human rights.[858] Aside from vetting the police force, screening out the corrupt members of the police force, and reorganizing and retraining, members of the improved police force must be

---

[849] Lacey, *supra* note 848.

[850] *Id.*

[851] *Somalia Profile—Overview*, *supra* note 848; Robert McMahon, *Seeking a Patient Path to Nationbuilding*, FOREIGN SERV. J., Nov. 2006, at 22, 27.

[852] McMahon, *supra* note 851, at 23.

[853] *Id.*

[854] *Id.*

[855] *Id.*

[856] *Id.* (quoting Ramesh Thakur & William Maley, *Commentary: The Art of Building Peace in Postconflict Societies*, DAILY YOMIURI, July 2006) (internal citations omitted).

[857] STROMSETH et al., *supra* note 828, at 208.

[858] *Id.*

instructed in the practice of service to the community and evenhandedness.[859] In Kosovo this occurred by providing 20 percent of the seats in the new police force for "former police dismissed after Kosovo's loss of autonomy in 1989, and 20 percent for women."[860] Even then, however, the cultural program to change the police force and instill an ethos of impartiality does not necessarily result in a change in public perception. "[D]espite efforts to overcome Kosovo's ethnic divide, problems persist . . . in 'Albanian-dominant areas, KPS [Kosovo Police Services] units had virtually no minorities,' whereas in Serb dominated areas, 'KPS units tended to be almost entirely Serb,' perpetuating largely separate or parallel systems."[861] It has been noted that in Kosovo, including minorities within the police force has not translated into fundamental changes in social practices.[862]

The intervention efforts in Kosovo also did not incorporate an adequate understanding of the culture of corruption and ethnic hatreds. The UN Interim Administration Mission in Kosovo (UNMIK) failed to identify this distinction: "UNMIK's policy-makers could never entirely decide whether their ultimate goal was to promote self-determination or to promote and ensure human rights."[863] In the absence of a good body of law, Western policy makers decided to use pre-March 1999 laws, which the Kosovar Albanian population viewed as the law of the oppressors. After judges and prosecutors around the country refused to apply these laws, UNMIK issued a regulation declaring (the presumably more popular) pre-1989 laws as applicable in the state.[864] These laws, however, did not comply with modern international human rights norms. To combat these and other issues, "UNMIK established a variety of consultative bodies designed to include the Kosovars in decisions about the all-important project of reestablishing the rule of law."[865] Unfortunately, when the meetings to address the rule of law concerns became gridlocked in conflict between the two ethnic sides, UNMIK dismissed the meetings and made its own choices. As a result, UNMIK's popularity with the Kosovars disintegrated.[866] One lesson from the Kosovo experience is that interveners themselves must be committed to transparency in their own actions. They must be accountable for their own actions and provide a forum for complaints when they violate their own rules. This would help foster a rule of law culture and contribute to the establishment of a system that the local population perceives to be trustworthy.[867]

---

859 *Id.*

860 *Id.* at 209.

861 *Id.* (quoting Charles Call, Conclusion: Constructing Justice and Security after War 389 (2007)).

862 *Id.*

863 *Id.* at 318.

864 *Id.* at 317 (citing UNMIK Regulation 24, *reprinted in* US Department of State: Kosovo Judicial Assessment [Mission Report] (2000)).

865 *Id.* at 319.

866 *Id.*

867 *Id.* at 326.

The obstacles described above show the difficulties endemic to law and development projects generally and postconflict development particularly. Societies emerging from conflict are mired in mistrust and remain combustible. Security continues to be an issue. Poverty and human rights violations, as well as economic collapse, are continuing problems. Rule of law, rule of law culture, *and* culture change are all important components of development projects.

Below, I provide a more in-depth examination of the two approaches taken by interveners in Iraq and Afghanistan. While the Afghanistan approach focused on working with cultural norms to establish new institutions and law and the Iraq approach focused on control and acceptance of Western institutions, neither seems to have fully appealed to the people as legitimate or trustworthy. Each effort appears to have been too one-sided, missing elements that the other approach took too far.

2. AFGHANISTAN AND IRAQ: TWO APPROACHES

The September 11 attacks showed that non-state actors in unstable, weak, or failed states could threaten the security of Western countries. After the attacks, the international community prioritized facilitating the prompt transformation of unstable states into rule of law societies.[868] Rebuilding a postconflict state, however, has proven to be a task riddled with complications and likely to result in failure. Unlike the development paths historically undertaken by Japan and Germany, rule of law development nowadays emphasizes formal laws and formal institutions. As one author explains:

> Nation-building in the years after World War II was understood by a spectrum of U.S. policymakers and international actors to be a collective activity. The nation-building energy expended during the Cold War was not solely that of state agencies. Nongovernmental, international, and, particularly, private business organizations were involved in the complex task of reconstructing and developing nations.[869]

After the 1960s, following intense criticism of the very idea of development, disillusionment set in—and grand ideas such as nation building "fell out of favor."[870] Constructing new and foreign institutions in failed or collapsed states has proven to be

[868] James A. Goldston, *Reflections on Twenty Years in Human Rights: The Rule of Law Movement in the Age of Terror*, 20 HARV. HUM. RTS. J. 15, 18 (2007) ("The September 11 attacks were a graphic demonstration of the extent to which globalization has enhanced the power of non-state actors in countries lacking the rule of law to threaten personal security in Western capitals. As a result, the importance of improving the quality of governance everywhere has become more widely appreciated. . . . [W]eak or failed states are increasingly (and properly) seen to be a universal and pressing problem.").

[869] David Ekbladh, *From Consensus to Crisis: The Postwar Career of Nation-Building in U.S. Foreign Relations, in* NATION-BUILDING: BEYOND AFGHANISTAN AND IRAQ 19, 19 (Francis Fukuyama ed., 2006).

[870] *Id.* at 20.

extraordinarily difficult. Francis Fukuyama observed that interveners most likely do not fully understand local conditions. Referring to local institutions, Fukuyama cautioned that "while we understand their importance in promoting economic development and can figure out how they work where they exist, we know relatively little about how to create or strengthen them in societies where they are nonexistent or weak."[871] The record for nation building contains "few successes and a large number of failures; and where the successes occurred, they required an extraordinary level of effort and attention."[872]

Against this backdrop, Fukuyama noted, "the rhetoric of the international community stresses 'capacity-building' while the reality has been rather a kind of 'capacity sucking out' . . . The international community, including the vast numbers of NGOs that are an intimate part of it, comes so richly endowed and full of capabilities that it tends to crowd out rather than complement the extremely weak state capacities of the targeted countries."[873] In such instances, the need for engaging with local culture is all the more important to ensure that new institutional capacities are supported by the cultural fabric and if not, taking steps to embark on the kind of culture change advocated in this book.

The World Bank noted that half of "all attempts at rebuilding after war result in renewed fighting," not a stable nation.[874] Despite the discouraging probability of success, scholars have developed a model for postconflict reconstruction. The three facets of this model are pursuing accountability against those who have committed serious crimes, creating legal/governmental framework, and establishing judicial institutions.[875] This section analyzes the general method of law and development in postconflict countries by highlighting action taken by reformers in Afghanistan and Iraq.

In both countries, international interventions had ended the reign of oppressive regimes. Both countries also have a history of decentralization and traditional/tribal Islamic orientation.[876] Despite their postconflict similarities, reformers took two vastly different approaches in each country. In Afghanistan, the international community took

---

[871] FRANCIS FUKUYAMA, AMERICA AT THE CROSSROADS: DEMOCRACY, POWER, AND THE NEOCONSERVATIVE LEGACY 123–24 (2006).

[872] *Id.* at 131.

[873] FRANCIS FUKUYAMA, STATE-BUILDING: GOVERNANCE AND WORLD ORDER IN THE 21ST CENTURY 103 (2004); STROMSETH et al., *supra* note 828, at 64 (noting the "wholesale appropriation by outsiders of key internal governance tasks.").

[874] Johanna Mendelson Forman, *Striking Out in Baghdad: How Postconflict Reconstruction Went Awry*, *in* NATION-BUILDING: BEYOND AFGHANISTAN AND IRAQ 196, 198 (Francis Fukuyama ed., 2006).

[875] *See generally* David Tolbert & Andrew Solomon, *United Nations Reform and Supporting the Rule of Law in Post-Conflict Societies*, 19 HARV. HUM. RTS. J. 29 (2006).

[876] This highlights another difference between the success of post-conflict reform in Japan and Germany and the failure of intervention in Iraq and Afghanistan. Fukuyama distinguished the former from the latter, noting that Japan and Germany "started out as highly developed countries with strong states whose cores for the most part survived the war intact. They were, moreover, thoroughly defeated societies that had turned decisively against the political forces that led them to war." FUKUYAMA, *supra* note 871, at 132. Of course, the question of *why* Japan and Germany were willing to embark on culture change against existing militaristic norms is also worth pursuing.

a light-stepping approach tailored to keep reform in line with Afghan customs. Reformers allowed Afghanistan a constitution that allowed traditionalists a religious override over international human rights standards and a two-pronged legal system that permitted the widespread survival of an informal legal system. In Iraq, a more overbearing and direct approach was taken. A US-led coalition directly occupied Iraq and transplanted Western institutions. Despite the differences in approach, substantially the same results (or lack thereof) were achieved.

a. Accountability

Establishing accountability in postconflict countries is of particular importance, symbolic and real. Rule of law societies function on the notion that no person is above the law, so extending impunity to actors who have committed mass crimes—especially actors who continue to hold official positions—would taint rule of law reform with hypocrisy.[877] The postconflict society must be sure that state institutions will protect rather than violate its rights. Promoting accountability is thus not only a core rule of law pursuit—legal practitioners, scholars, and policy makers generally agree that it is part of the very definition of what constitutes law;[878] after all, rule of law has to mean that everyone, including rulers and state officials, are subject to its purview and reach.[879] But accountability also helps to establish faith in state institutions. In places like Iraq and Afghanistan, state institutions were "tools of oppression," so building trust in these institutions is of paramount importance.[880] Accountability has a catalytic effect on society as a whole, promoting the necessary virtuous cycle, that is, by reintroducing and reinforcing trust into the cultural fabric.

Additionally, establishing accountability can prevent retaliatory conflict from emerging.[881] As an example, failure to address past atrocities in Yugoslavia resulted in renewed

---

877 Tolbert & Solomon, *supra* note 875, at 34 ("The basis of the rule of law is that no person, no matter his or her position, is above the law. There can be little hope for a society that continues to be governed by those who have committed mass crimes with impunity.").

878 William Maley, *The Rule of Law and Weight of Politics*, *in* THE RULE OF LAW IN AFGHANISTAN, MISSING IN INACTION 61, 78 (Whit Mason ed., 2011).

879 Rachel Kleinfeld Belton, *Competing Definitions of the Rule of Law*, *in* PROMOTING THE RULE OF LAW ABROAD: IN SEARCH OF KNOWLEDGE 31, 36 (Thomas Carothers ed., 2006); RULE OF LAW HANDBOOK: A PRACTITIONER'S GUIDE FOR JUDGE ADVOCATES 5 (2011) ("[T]he [s]tate is [i]tself [b]ound [b]y [l]aw and [d]oes [n]ot [a]ct [a]rbitrarily.").

880 Simon Chesterman, *Rough Justice: Establishing the Rule of Law in Post-Conflict Territories*, 20 OHIO ST. J. ON DISP. RESOL. 69, 69 (2005) ("One of the most important and difficult challenges confronting a post-conflict society is the reestablishment of faith in the institutions of the state."); *see also* Jane E. Stromseth, *Pursuing Accountability for Atrocities After Conflict: What Impact on Building the Rule of Law?*, 38 GEO. J. INT'L L. 251, 252 (2007) (Noting that establishing the rule of law depends on the society's confidence in the legal system that they will be "protected from predatory state and non-state actors . . . and that legal and political institutions will protect rather than violate basic human rights").

881 Stromseth, *supra* note 880, at 253 ("Trials can also give victims a sense of justice that helps them move forward without a need to seek personal vengeance.").

violence in the early 1990s, whereas post–World War II Germany employed heavy accountability and was able to establish a society based on the rule of law.[882] Given these results, the international community generally regards impunity as a detriment to the development process, noting "impunity is 'a very serious impediment to efforts undertaken to consolidate democracy.' "[883]

The Bonn Agreement of 2001guided most aspects of Afghan reform. Aside from establishing a transitional authority and timelines for the formation of a new government, this agreement also guided the accountability process in Afghanistan.[884] The Bonn Agreement did not include amnesty provisions for actors in Afghanistan.[885] The majority of Afghans surveyed opposed amnesties and expressed "overwhelming" support for the removal of perpetrators from power.[886] The international community deferred to these sentiments and judgment of the Afghan people in determining how justice would be served, while still advancing international standards. Deference to local wishes in this case is wholly appropriate because it also reinforces a basic rule of law tenet—accountability—which is important to rule of law establishment for the reasons discussed above.

In the wake of the Taliban's removal, the United Nations urged the transitional Afghan government to make decisions based on "international human rights standards, Afghan cultural traditions, and Islam."[887] Of course, this leaves unaddressed what happens when cultural traditions clash with international standards. The Afghan people also preferred to dispense justice on their own, as opposed to having trials conducted outside the country or with international jurists.[888] The United Nations' involvement was limited to investigating human rights violations and recommending corrective actions.[889] The United Nations also convened the National Workshop on Human Rights, which established four domestic working groups that would integrate guiding UN human rights principles into Afghan frameworks.[890] In practice, however, the reach of accountability is rather constrained in Afghanistan. Afghanistan cannot apply accountability because the central government has no reach outside of the capital—Kabul.[891] Outside

---

882 Tolbert & Solomon, *supra* note 875, at 34–35.

883 Chesterman, *supra* note 880 at 77 (quoting Rep. of the Hum. Rts. Comm., ¶ 347, U.N. Doc. A/51/40; GAOR, 51st Sess., vol. 1, Supp. No. 40 (1997)).

884 Agreement on Provisional Arrangements in Afghanistan Pending the Re-Establishment of Permanent Government Institutions, in letter dated Dec. 5, 2001 from the Secretary-General addressed to the President of the Security Council, U.N. Doc. S/2001/1154 (Dec. 5, 2001), *available at* http://www.refworld.org/docid/3f48f4754.html [hereinafter Agreement on Provisional Arrangements in Afghanistan]; Chesterman, *supra* note 880, at 91–92.

885 Stromseth, *supra* note 880, at 255.

886 *Id.* at 261.

887 Chesterman, *supra* note 880, at 92.

888 Stromseth, *supra* note 880, at 261.

889 Chesterman, *supra* note 880 at 91.

890 *Id.* at 92.

891 Stromseth, *supra* note 880, at 316–17.

of Kabul, regional warlords wield the most power, and they continue to abuse human rights with impunity, causing a loss of faith in central institutions.[892] In 2007, after about three years of unsuccessful attempts at accountability, the central government seemed to give up by creating a new amnesty law that shielded "belligerent groups" who fought during the "conflict era."[893]

In the end, despite initial commitment, the government was unable to implement measures needed to fully establish accountability in the post-Taliban period. By contrast, Iraq proved to be an example of the opposite end of the spectrum— overaccountability. The cornerstone of Iraqi accountability following the removal of Saddam Hussein was "de-Ba'athification"—the broad removal of anyone who had held a significant position in the Ba'ath Party, regardless of whether the person was directly involved in the commission of serious crimes.[894] The US occupational administration—the Coalition Provisional Authority—placed a controversial—and bitter—exile returnee in charge of this process.[895] Under this returnee, the reach of de-Ba'athification extended to "mid-level party civil servants, including doctors and teachers," excluding them from public life.[896] This process overlooked the fact that a requirement of state employment was loyalty to the Ba'ath party, and the state was the country's largest employer.[897] The result was a purge of thirty thousand employees within the first few months of US occupation, which created much hostility.[898] Additionally the Iraqi army was also disbanded in order to purge officers,[899] which amounted to the unemployment of 7 percent of the Iraqi workforce, placing 10 percent of the population in economic crisis.[900] The end result was that so many individuals were removed that it undermined existing institution's stability and the foundations for building new ones.[901]

The post-Saddam administration also set up the Iraqi Special Tribunal for Crimes Against Humanity. In this tribunal, Iraqis serve as the judges and prosecutors, with foreigners' involvement limited to assisting with evidence preparation and matters regarding due process standards.[902] As is the case with Afghanistan, Iraqi leaders viewed this process as more legitimate,[903] but it was criticized as being too limited since the subject matter

[892] *Id.* at 264 n. 25 ("Many persons who committed gross human rights violations remain in power today. This has provoked a profound disappointment in Afghans together with an almost total breakdown of trust in authority and public institutions.").

[893] *Id.* at 315–16.

[894] Larry Diamond, *What Went Wrong and Right in Iraq*, *in* Nation-Building: Beyond Afghanistan and Iraq 173, 182–83 (Francis Fukuyama ed., 2006).

[895] *Id.* at 183.

[896] Forman, *supra* note 874, at 205.

[897] *Id.*

[898] *Id.*

[899] Diamond, *supra* note 894, at 183.

[900] Forman, *supra* note 874, at 204.

[901] Stromseth, *supra* note 880, at 263.

[902] *Id.* at 312–13.

[903] *Id.* at 313.

jurisdiction was restricted to crimes against humanity that occurred during the dates of Hussein's reign. Critics highlight that while the tribunal is facially dedicated to punishing crimes against humanity, its subject matter limitations make the tribunal, in effect, an organization with the sole purpose of punishing Saddam Hussein and his agents.[904] The controversy was whether a tribunal dedicated to punishing one person and his agents can pursue justice with fairness given to all parties.

In both Afghanistan and Iraq, accountability was pursued as a primary, immediate need. Reformers in both countries sought punishment for the perpetrators of major atrocities; in Afghanistan, this accountability was not attainable, whereas in Iraq, the accountability was too easily attainable, which led to a destabilizing and overprosecution of much of the Iraqi population.

b. Creating a Legal Framework

The next step in modern postconflict law and development is the establishment of basic governance needed in order to avoid instability and chaos.[905] In most postconflict cases, the UN Security Council has established a transitional administration, with Iraq being the notable exception.[906] In Afghanistan, the international community took a lighter, less involved approach. Termed the "light footprint" approach, the United Nations' involvement saw minimal international presence, limited material resources, and no operational role in the development of a new administration in Afghanistan.[907] The Bonn Agreement provided for the creation of the transitional framework for Afghanistan. It established the 1964 constitution of Afghanistan as the transitional authority and mandated that existing laws and regulations would continue to apply as long as they were not inconsistent with the provisions of the agreement.[908] The agreement set a timeline for a new constitution and government to be created. Motivated by the fear of Afghanistan breaking into fiefdoms run by competing warlords, Western reformers advised that national sovereignty and identity needed to be established before political, economic, and social structures could be built.[909]

However, the fragmented, multiethnic country posed many obstacles to establishing a new framework. Perhaps most devastating for the law and development project, conflict

---

904 Forman, *supra* note 874, at 207.

905 *See,* e.g., Tolbert & Solomon, *supra* note 875, at 41.

906 *Id.* at 41–42.

907 Chesterman, *supra* note 880, at 89; Laurel Miller & Robert Perito, *Establishing the Rule of Law in Afghanistan*, U.S. INST. OF PEACE: SPECIAL REPORT 4 (Mar. 2004), *available at* http://www.usip.org/sites/default/files/sr117.pdf.

908 Chesterman, *supra* note 880, at 90–91.

909 S. Frederick Starr, *Sovereignty and Legitimacy in Afghan Nation-Building*, *in* NATION-BUILDING: BEYOND AFGHANISTAN AND IRAQ 107, 107–08 (Francis Fukuyama ed., 2006) ("The reestablishment of Afghanistan's sovereignty presented itself as the foundation that had to be put in place before everything else that was considered desirable in the political, economic and social spheres could be built.").

still continued. In the south, the United States was still fighting with Al Qaeda and struggling with the re-emergence of the Taliban along the Pakistan border.[910] In the north, there was "recurrent armed conflict among regional warlords" and provincial governors who refused to turn over revenue to the central government.[911] In these areas, the rule of law was replaced with the rule of the gun. The provincial warlords exercised complete control over whatever legal systems existed outside of Kabul, and did so through fear and intimidation, whether or not they held official positions.[912] A UN special representative in Afghanistan accurately captured the reality with this apt observation: "The people of Afghanistan are afraid of the guns that are held by the wrong people and used not to defend them . . . but to terrorize [them]. . . ."[913] In addition, the United States continued to finance these regional warlords as agents in the fight against Taliban remnants.[914]

Aside from the conflict occurring outside of Kabul, establishing legitimacy in the central government was also a large obstacle. Western reformers were primarily interested in establishing the sovereignty of a national government and assumed that legitimacy would flow from elections,[915] but the domestic population was more concerned with whether the government would provide necessary governmental services—such as security, reconstruction, and education—and distribute resources and official positions in a fair manner across the various ethnicities and regions of Afghanistan.[916]

Ironically, in the early transitional phases, international presence itself inadvertently whittled away at the legitimacy of the very central government that interveners were trying to establish. The Northern Alliance that aided the United States in the fight against the Taliban became the most privileged party in the post-Taliban era. This group was filled primarily with Tajiks and Uzbeks—two minority groups—who filled government positions exclusively with their own, while excluding the Pashtuns—the largest Afghan ethnic group.[917] Although an early compromise saw a Pashtun, Hamid Karzai, named interim president, Pashtuns still viewed the government as exclusive and illegitimate.[918] The excluded groups then fell back onto the local, informal systems of law which pervaded the country.[919] The regional warlords enjoyed more legitimacy than did the central

---

910 Miller & Perito, *supra* note 907, at 3.

911 *Id.*

912 *Id.* at 15.

913 *Id.* at 3.

914 *Id.* at 15.

915 Starr, *supra* note 909, at 109.

916 *Id.* at 110 (adding that legitimacy of a central government could not be achieved without ethnic and regional balance).

917 *Id.* at 111.

918 Larry P. Goodson, *The Lessons of Nation-Building in Afghanistan*, *in* NATION-BUILDING: BEYOND AFGHANISTAN AND IRAQ 145, 158 (Francis Fukuyama ed., 2006).

919 Afghanistan's legal framework is an amalgamation of different systems: "local customary practice, Islamic religious law (sharia) and the state legal code, including the formal constitutions adopted by the state. The customary system employs common cultural and ethical standards to resolve disputes. The main institution that has traditionally operated as the mechanism of dispute settlement is the jirga/maraca among the Pashtuns and its

government in Kabul, and this situation was exacerbated by continued US support for warlords who fought against Taliban remnants and Al Qaeda.[920] It was clear that the international community was primarily focused on threats to the central government, such as the Taliban and Al Qaeda, and not threats to legitimacy.[921] Indeed, legitimacy was assumed to attach to the central government. Hence reformers were concerned with disbanding groups that could stand to depose the new government, but they were not yet concerned with the domestic population's acceptance of the government and its processes in all areas of the country. As a result, the law's reach only extended to Kabul and areas where the controlling Tajiks and Uzbeks were the majority; outside of these areas warlords maintained power and refused to submit to the central government that they viewed as illegitimate.[922]

Eventually the international community saw the need to deal with legitimacy issues surrounding the government it had put into place. The United States formed the Afghan Reconstruction Group to assume the lead role in rebuilding the Afghan army and police force, and disarming regional warlords.[923] The United Nations also made disarmament attempts that successfully demobilized over one thousand fighters.[924] Afghanistan's neighbors, such as Pakistan, even mounted military operations to remove anti-Kabul militants from their border regions.[925] Also, Interim President Karzai was able to convince some warlords to abandon their local seats of power to take positions in Kabul, while convincing some Taliban groups to cease fighting and join mainstream society and government.[926] The international community also pressed the central administration for ethnic and regional balance after 2003. Half of the provincial governors, along with 75 percent of local police chiefs were removed.[927] The new wave of appointments focused more on qualifications than on ethnicity or regional origin.[928] "Several new ministers not aligned with the Northern Alliance" were also appointed in Kabul.[929]

After firmly establishing the interim government, Afghanistan was able to move onto the next phase in developing its legal framework—constitution drafting. The Bonn Agreement stated that the new constitution needed to "embody the basic principles of Islam, democracy, pluralism, social justice, rule of law, and Afghanistan's international

approximate equivalent, the *shura*, among non-Pastuns." Carol Wang, *Rule of Law in Afghanistan: Enabling a Constitutional Framework for Local Accountability*, 55 Harv. Int'l L. J. 211, 216 (2014).

920 Goodson, *supra* note 918, at 158; Starr, *supra* note 909, at 113.

921 Starr, *supra* note 909, at 112–13.

922 *Id.* at 118.

923 Marvin G. Weinbaum, *Rebuilding Afghanistan: Impediments, Lessons and Prospects*, *in* Nation-Building: Beyond Afghanistan and Iraq 125, 137 (Francis Fukuyama ed., 2006).

924 Miller & Perito, *supra* note 907, at 15.

925 Weinbaum, *supra* note 923, at 134.

926 Starr, *supra* note 909, at 122.

927 *Id.* at 121.

928 *Id.*

929 *Id.*

obligations."[930] In this same spirit, President George W. Bush added that "America will not impose our style of government on the unwilling. Our goal instead is to help others find their own voice. . . ."[931] A number of scholars noted that Islam has been a unifying force in Afghanistan, providing continuity and predictability, so development should operate from within the framework of Islam.[932] These sentiments show that reformers tried to balance international values with the dominant sentiments and traditions of local society. It would not be surprising if reformers had hoped that the rule of law project itself would produce new laws, which would in turn produce development-friendly norms within the existing cultural framework of Afghanistan.

Ethnic politics, however, re-emerged and impeded the drafting process. The majority Pashtun group wanted a strong, centrally run state, while the minority groups wanted stronger local forces.[933] Non-Pashtuns feared a strong president because he would presumably be a member of the majority group, and they were determined not to let the Pashtuns regain the political dominance that they had previously held.[934] Ethnic voting ensued.[935]

Despite the sentiments of minority groups that favored a weak central government, a strong president with a system of checks and balances was established; the fear of a dysfunctional, fragmented national assembly in combination with international support for a strong president trumped the minority position.[936] The fear of ethnic polarization led to disintegration and instability and caused stakeholders to coalesce around the principle of strong centralism.[937] Balancing both concerns, Article 137, Chapter 8, of the Afghan constitution states that "the government, in preserving the principle of centralism, shall transfer necessary powers, in accordance with the law, to local administrations in order to accelerate and improve economic, social as well as cultural matters. . . ."[938] Nonetheless, there is a central bias expressed most notably by the United States and the international

---

930 Agreement on Provisional Arrangements in Afghanistan, art. II; Jason Lawrence Reimer, *Finding Their Own Voice? The Afghanistan Constitution: Influencing the Creation of a Theocratic Democracy*, 25 PENN ST. INT'L L. REV. 343, 350 (2006).

931 Reimer, *supra* note 930, at 345.

932 Nusrat Choudhury, *Constrained Spaces for Islamic Feminism: Women's Rights and the 2004 Constitution of Afghanistan*, 19 YALE J.L. & FEMINISM 155, 166 (2007).

933 Michael Schoiswohl, *Linking the International Legal Framework to Building the Formal Foundations of a "State at Risk": Constitution-Making and International Law in Post-Conflict Afghanistan*, 39 VAND. J. TRANSNAT'L L. 819, 839–40 (2006).

934 *Id.*; Weinbaum, *supra* note 923, at 132.

935 After the permanent constitution and government were established voting was largely ethnic. Each group voted for the candidate from their ethnicity. Accordingly, Hamid Karzai, a member of the majority Pashtuns won the election, although it should be noted that Karzai was able to secure a significant number of votes outside of his ethnicity as well. *See* Goodson, *supra* note 918, at 159.

936 Schoiswohl, *supra* note 933, at 837, 839.

937 *Id.* at 840.

938 The Constitution of the Islamic Republic of Afghanistan, Jan. 3, 2004, art. 147 [hereinafter Afg. Const. 2004], *available at* http://www.embassyofafghanistan.org/sites/default/files/documents/constitution2004_english.pdf (unofficial English translation).

community who prefer to have one central entity to deal with rather than a web of decentralized coordinates.[939] "Consequently, a uniquely centralized constitution granted the executive unusually strong powers, exemplified by a presidential system without a prime minister or constitutional court and with virtually unfettered appointment authority extending to the provinces."[940] Dari and Pashto—spoken by the majority groups—were proclaimed to be the official languages, while smaller languages were recognized as the third official language in the areas where the majority spoke it.[941]

The new constitution also declared that Afghanistan is an "Islamic Republic" and "[n]o law shall contravene the tenets and provisions of the holy religion of Islam in Afghanistan."[942] The Supreme Court in Afghanistan was given the power to review compliance with the constitution and, accordingly, Islam.[943] The constitution also privileges the *Hanafi* school, a conservative school of Islamic thought to act as a filler "when there is no statute or constitutional provision on point" with the issue at hand.[944] This is in stark contrast to prior periods in Afghanistan's history when then King Amanullah in 1919 imposed a legal separation between state law and sharia law, adopting secular and civil codes derived from Egypt and Turkey.[945] The principle of secular laws and secular courts was continued under King Nadir Shah and enshrined in the new constitution of 1931.[946] This principle was further strengthened in 1933 by his son, Zahir Shah, who combined sharia courts and state courts into one system. The 1964 constitution even proclaimed that state law was supreme over sharia law—Article 69 stated that "only that when no such state law exists" would "the provisions of the Hanafi jurisprudence of the Shariaat of Islam . . . be considered as law."[947] Sharia law became the exclusive and supreme source of law only with the victory of the Taliban government in 1996.

In the area of fundamental rights, the constitution explicitly guarantees freedom of religion and prohibits gender discrimination.[948] Under the 1977 Afghan Civil Code,[949]

---

[939] *See* William Maley, *The Rule of Law and the Weight of Politics: Challenges and Trajectories*, *in* THE RULE OF LAW IN AFGHANISTAN, MISSING IN INACTION 61, 73 (Whit Mason ed., 2011); Jonathan Morrow, *Deconstituting Mesopotamia: Cutting a Deal on the Regionalization of Iraq*, *in* FRAMING THE STATE IN TIMES OF TRANSITION: CASE STUDIES IN CONSTITUTION MAKING 563, 565 (Laurel E. Miller ed., with Louis Aucoin, 2010).

[940] Wang, *supra* note 919, at 222.

[941] Schoiswohl, *supra* note 933, at 841.

[942] *Id.* at 836 (quoting Afg. Const. 2004, art. 1–3).

[943] Schoiswohl, *supra* note 933, at 837.

[944] Choudhury, *supra* note 932, at 172 (citing Constitution of the Islamic Republic of Afghanistan, Jan. 3, 2004, art. 130. ("If there is no provision in the Constitution or other laws . . . the courts shall, in pursuance of Hanafi jurisprudence . . . rule in a way that attains justice in the best manner.")).

[945] Wang, *supra* note 919, at 217.

[946] *Id.*

[947] *Id.* (quoting Afg. Const. of 1964, art. 69).

[948] Afg. Const. 2004, *supra* note 938, preamble (stating obligation to "[observe] the United Nations Charter [and to respect] the Universal Declaration of Human Rights."); *see also* Schoiswohl, *supra* note 933, at 843 (2006).

[949] CIVIL LAW OF THE REPUBLIC OF AFGHANISTAN (1977).

women have the right to inherit or own property; Articles 70 and 71 set the minimum age for marriage; Article 80 codifies the right of a woman to choose her own partner.[950] There is no shortage of national programs, such as the 2008 Afghanistan National Development Strategy, the 2008 National Action Plan for Women of Afghanistan, and the many ministerial strategies that proclaim the paramount significance of women's rights.[951] Moreover, Article 7 of the constitution specifically provides that "the state shall abide by the U.N. Charter, international treaties and international conventions that Afghanistan has ratified, and the Universal Declaration of Human Rights."[952] The government of Afghanistan has also ratified the International Covenant on Civil and Political Rights, the International Covenant on Economic, Social and Cultural Rights, the Convention on the Elimination of All Forms of Racial Discrimination, the Convention Against Torture, the Convention on the Rights of the Child, and the Convention on the Elimination of All Forms of Discrimination Against Women.[953]

Not surprisingly but rather predictably, references to international human rights norms, including women's rights, coexist with constitutional provisions that also reference Islam. Article 2 declares that Islam is the official state religion, and Article 3 states that no law shall contravene its "tenets and provisions."[954] The constitution has no provision to resolve conflicts between international human rights law and Islamic law, such as "disparities between men and women under *sharia* with regard to marriage, divorce, inheritance rights, and court testimony."[955]

There is a rigorous debate over how the interpretation of Islam can shape law. The West seems to argue that aspects of sharia are inconsistent with international human rights standards, whereas some Islamic scholars believe that "human rights lie at the heart of Islam."[956] The Islamic community can be divided into traditionalists and modernists. Traditionalists believe that there is no difference between the state and religion.[957] They also apply conservative Islamic law. To draw a parallel between traditionalist thought and conservative thought, a Taliban attorney general once said, "[t]he Constitution is the Shari'a so we don't need a constitution."[958] Practitioners of this school of thought have used extreme interpretations of Islamic law to prohibit girls' education, require women

---

[950] Anastasiya Hozyainova, *Sharia and Women's Rights in Afghanistan*, U.S. Inst. of Peace: Special Report 2 (May 2014), *available at* http://www.usip.org/sites/default/files/SR347-Sharia_and_Women%E2%80%99s_Rights_in_Afghanistan.pdf.

[951] *Id.*

[952] Afg. Const. 2004, *supra* note 938, art. 1.

[953] Wang, *supra* note 919, at 224.

[954] Afg. Const. 2004, *supra* note 938, art. 2-3.

[955] Wang, *supra* note 919, at 224. Reimer, *supra* note 930, at 362–63.

[956] Schoiswohl, *supra* note 933, at 855; Joëlle Entelis, *International Human Rights: Islam's Friend or Foe?*, 20 Fordham Int'l L.J. 1251, 1305 (1997) ("The Western notion of human rights is not inherently and irreconcilably at odds with Islamic law.").

[957] Reimer, *supra* note 930, at 361.

[958] *Id.* at 348.

to be accompanied by a male relative when traveling, and to justify the stoning of women for adultery.[959]

Conversely, modernists believe that certain interpretations of Islam can advance human rights. Much of their argument centers on how a correct interpretation would advance more women's rights in Islamic society.[960] Many contend that the Western-supported 2004 constitution is not robust enough to eradicate practices based on flawed interpretations of Islam. For example, Afghanistan acceded to the Convention on the Elimination of All Forms of Discrimination Against Women without reservation in 2003; however, leaders in rural areas still apply extreme, tribal interpretations of sharia to justify keeping women in burqas, and killing teachers and students at co-education schools.[961] At issue is a fundamental clash—over cultural norms that support the universalism of development and the narrow particularism of religious claims that are themselves internally contested. In these cases, a law and development agenda that emphasizes constitutions and statutes while leaving untouched cultural norms that support strict, conservative interpretation of sharia laws and custom is doomed.

Indeed, a significant gap remains between legal rights promised in the formal legal system and the reality of cultural norms that are at odds with those rights. As noted above, women's rights, for example, seem quite firmly established on paper. And yet, in Afghanistan, cultural norms continue to perpetuate the inequality of women, violence against women, and degradation of women. These entrenched cultural norms, not formal laws, have more practical implications on how women experience their lives. To be sure, there has been a marked improvement in women's rights in post-Taliban Afghanistan. For example, in the 2011–12 academic year, three million girls constituting 39 percent of enrolled students went to school compared to the few thousands who had access to underground schools under the Taliban.[962] Women can vote and run for office—in 2009, during the presidential and provincial council elections, two women ran for president, seven for vice president.[963] Many of the protections guaranteed by law, however, have failed to translate into practice. Although there is a ban on child marriage, for example,

---

959 Choudhury, *supra* note 932, at 157.

960 Modernists believe that a general lack of education as to Islamic law has allowed those in power to hijack sharia. They believe that Islamic law permits women to become educated and pursue professions and public service. *See id.* at 162, 165. They conclude that modern religious controls are state-made. In support of this view they highlight that the coming of Islam brought centuries of improved women's rights to Arabia. Before the Taliban, women enjoyed liberalized inheritance rights, property rights, and equal treatment and protection in marriage and divorce. Holly Taylor, *The Constitutions of Afghanistan and Iraq: The Advancement of Women's Rights*, 13 New Eng. J. Int'l & Comp. L. 137, 142–44 (2006).

961 Schoiswohl, *supra* note 933, at 857; Taylor, *supra* note 960, at 150–51 (adding that a male teacher was beheaded for teaching girls in a rural area); *see also Convention on the Elimination of All Forms of Discrimination Against Women*, UN Treaty Collection, http://treaties.un.org/Pages/ViewDetails.aspx?src=TREATY&mtdsg_no=IV-8&chapter=4&lang=en (last visited June 15, 2015) (listing CEDAW parties).

962 Hozyainova, *supra* note 950, at 2.

963 *Id.*

21 percent of all women are married by age fifteen. Female victims of sexual violence and trafficking, rather than the predators and traffickers, are persecuted and imprisoned.[964] Women's right to inheritance, property rights, land, and their control over earned income are restricted in practice "because women's economic independence is often not tolerated at the community level."[965] Often, when cases concerning women's rights are articulated by reference to formal law, they are rejected. Judges insist instead that women's rights must be argued within the context of Islamic law.[966] "In other words, despite formal guarantees, the courts and society at large still act within the framework of conservative social norms that restrict women's rights in economic and political spheres."[967]

As in Afghanistan, reconstruction and development in Iraq were also complicated by security issues since armed conflict continued after Saddam Hussein was overthrown. Instead of operating from an advisory role, the United States undertook direct occupation of the country.[968] The Coalition Provisional Authority (CPA) was created by the United States to act as the interim government over Iraq and given complete judicial, legislative, and executive power.[969] The CPA was also charged with disarming any insurgents, coordinating humanitarian assistance, and appropriating funds.[970] As a non-Iraqi agent of control, the CPA ran into serious legitimacy issues. The CPA failed to comprehend how the Iraqis perceived its presence. The US coalition thought that it would be seen as a savior who ended Hussein's tyranny;[971] however many Iraqis saw direct occupation not as an "international intervention" but as an "invasion" by the Western, Christian, Anglo American world.[972] The Coalition also underestimated the amount of support that Hussein had from the population (particularly from the Arab Sunnis, who had enjoyed a monopoly over the state and its resources during Hussein's reign).[973] Sunni

---

964 *Id.*

965 *Id.*

966 *Id.* at 4. As a result, "[t]he evidence from the field has led some women's rights groups to argue that women's empowerment strategies based on Islamic law might carry more weight with communities than Western rights-based approaches." *Id.*

967 *Id.* at 2.

968 Between 2003 and 2005 Iraq was ruled by two sets of laws: the laws issued by the first US civil administrator in Iraq, Paul Bremer, who arrived in Baghdad in May 2003; and the Transitional Administrative Law for Iraq (TAL), which was issued by the Coalition Provisional Authority (CPA) that Bremer led.

969 Forman, *supra* note 874, at 208. For a discussion of the perception if not fact of illegitimacy surrounding the CPA, *see* Saad N. Jawad, *The Iraqi Constitution: Structural Flaws and Political Implications*, LSE Middle East Centre Paper Series, Nov. 2013, at 7–8, *available at* http://www.lse.ac.uk/middleEastCentre/publications/Paper-Series/SaadJawad.pdf.

970 Forman, *supra* note 874, at 208.

971 Diamond, *supra* note 894, at 175 ("Pentagon officials assumed that Iraqis would broadly and joyously welcome American and international troops as liberators.").

972 *Id.* at 182.

973 *Id.* ("The CPA also failed to grasp that Saddam was not without a base of popular support in Iraq.... [M]uch of the Arab Sunni population either supported him ... or opposed his ouster for fear that regime change would cost them ... their historic monopoly....").

Muslims turned to terrorism because they felt they were being excluded from the occupation government, while Shiite men who lacked access to jobs joined urban insurgency movements.[974]

Because of the prevailing violence and chaos, the CPA opted for control over legitimacy.[975] In Iraq, the most effective and rapid means of development was through local and provincial coordinators. But the CPA elected to control the flow of all funds centrally.[976] However, the CPA relinquished some control to the local level when it created the Iraqi Governing Council (GC) in July 2003. The GC consisted of domestic constituents, including representatives from the two major Kurdish political parties, the two major Shiite parties and a Sunni party.[977] Nonetheless, the GC was essentially an advisory council; the CPA guided it and held veto power over its decisions.[978] The GC was also not completely representative of the Iraqi population since the CPA appointed all of the members, and more than half were embittered exile returnees.[979] The appointed representatives were extremely disconnected from their constituencies.[980] When the time came for the United States to hand control back to the Iraqis, the CPA called for a transitional parliament system that would be elected by tiered caucuses even though most Iraqis believed that this system was opaque and would give power to whomever the CPA anointed.[981]

The process of developing a constitutional framework in Iraq was mired in ethnic debate just as much as in Afghanistan. The central government, under Hussein, had brutalized the Kurds, so naturally they pushed for a decentralized system.[982] The Kurds also wanted their region to maintain a great deal of autonomy. To satisfy the Kurds, enactments by the transitional authority had to be approved by unanimous decisions from the Iraqi President Council, where the Kurds had one seat.[983] This effectively gave the Kurds a veto power, causing the majority Shiites to circulate critical materials labeling the government a "dictatorship of the minorities."[984] The majority of Sunnis chose to boycott the drafting process.[985]

---

974 *Id.* at 181.

975 *Id.* at 186 ("[T]he American administration opted for control over legitimacy whenever the trade-off presented itself.").

976 *Id.* at 182.

977 *Id.* at 184–85.

978 Forman, *supra* note 874, at 209.

979 Diamond, *supra* note 894, at 185.

980 *Id.* ("It was not uncommon for most of them to be out of the country travelling at any given time. Few Iraqis ever saw any of them in their towns and communities.").

981 *Id.* at 187.

982 *Id.* at 190.

983 *Id.*

984 *Id.* at 190–91.

985 Faleh A. Jabar, *Iraq Four Years After the U.S.-led Invasion: Assessing the Crisis and Searching for a Way Forward*, Carnegie Endowment Int'l Peace: Pol'y Outlook, July 2007, at 5, http://carnegieendowment.org/files/faleh_al_jabba_formatted.pdf.

The question of Islam's role, and in particular, sharia law, became a contentious issue in constitutional drafting. Even moderate Shiite leaders such as Grand Ayatollah Ali al-Sistani, who insisted he did not want to impose Iranian type theocracy in Iraq announced that "[t]he religious constants and the Iraqi people's moral principles and noble social values should be the main pillars of the coming Iraqi constitution."[986] Kurdish leader Jalal Talabani, shortly becoming president of Iraq, declared, "[w]e will never accept any religious government in Iraq. Never. This is a red line for us. We will never live inside an Islamic Iraq."[987] Maysoon al-Damluji, president of the Iraqi Independent Women's Group, was similarly concerned and declared that "the interpretation of sharia law will take us backward."[988]

However, when the new constitution of Iraq was passed, it proclaimed that "Islam is the official religion of the State and is a foundation source of legislation . . . [n]o law may be enacted that contradicts the established provisions of Islam. . . ."[989] This language is similar to that of the Afghan constitution, except the Afghan constitution named Islam as *the* superior source of law, whereas the Iraqi constitution only establishes Islam as *a* source of law. In addition, the constitution of Iraq also establishes human rights, such as gender equality.[990] Although Article 2 declares that "[n]o law may be enacted that contradicts the established provisions of Islam," it also states that "[n]o law may be enacted that contradicts the principles of democracy" and further, that "[n]o law may be enacted that contradicts the rights and basic freedoms stipulated in this Constitution." [991] Such constitutional ambiguities and potentially irreconcilable internal contradictions have led observers to worry that the constitution constitutes "a fundamental setback for a majority of Iraq's population—namely, its women."[992] Professor Saad N. Jawad, who taught political science at the University of Baghdad, astutely observed as follows: "[W]ith the domination of the religious parties, institutions and personalities, any liberty could be cancelled if a religious institution claimed that it contradicts Islamic beliefs, as we have seen in many Middle Eastern states."[993] Iraqi scholar Isam al-Khafaji warned that provisions

---

986 Isobel Coleman, *Women, Islam and the New Iraq*, FOREIGN AFF., Jan.–Feb. 2006, at 24, 29, 31. Iranian-style theocracy has resulted in the following actions taken after the 1979 revolution. Suspension of the country's relatively progressive family law, removal of female judges, enforcement of the hijab on women, lowering marriage age to nine, permitting polygamy and unilateral divorce for men and not women, granting fathers sole custody of their children after divorce.

987 *Id.* at 29.

988 *Id.*

989 Article 2, Doustour Joumhouriat al-Iraq [The Constitution of the Republic of Iraq] of 2005, *available at* http://www.iraqinationality.gov.iq/attach/iraqi_constitution.pdf (English translation); *see also* Taylor, *supra* note 960, at 138 (emphasis added).

990 The Constitution of the Republic of Iraq, *supra* note 989, at art. 14 ("Iraqis are equal before the law without discrimination based on gender . . . ."); *see also* Taylor, *supra* note 960, at 138, 155.

991 The Constitution of the Republic of Iraq, *supra* note 989, at art. 2.

992 Coleman, *supra* note 986, at 24.

993 Jawad, *supra* note 969, at 15.

in the constitution "could easily deprive women of their rights."[994] Yanar Muhammad who headed the Organization of Women's Freedom in Iraq expressed concern that the Islamic provisions in the constitution will transform Iraq "into an Afghanistan under the Taliban, where oppression and discrimination of women is institutionalized."[995]

At one point, Iraq was a leading country at the forefront of women's rights. It was the first Arab country to have a female minister in the 1950s and to have a law that conferred on women the right to ask for divorces.[996] Zakia Hakki was Iraq's first female judge, appointed in 1959.[997] Yet, maintaining or reinvigorating that tradition will be difficult. In 2003, US authorities appointed Nidal Nasser Hussein the first female judge in the Shiite holy city of Najaf, an appointment that provoked protest at her swearing-in ceremony and the issuance of *fatwas* (Islamic religious decrees) by senior clerics who proclaimed that under Islamic law, only men can be judges.[998] The United States responded by delaying her appointment indefinitely.

The State Department's August 2003 "Fact Sheet" indicated US commitment

> to helping the Iraqi people transition to a sovereign, representative form of government that respects human rights, rejects terrorism and maintains Iraq's territorial integrity without threatening its neighbors. We recognize that the women of Iraq have a critical role to play in the revival of their country and we strongly support their efforts.[999]

In fiscal year 2004, for example, as part of the estimated $21 billion that the United States spent on Iraqi reconstruction, substantial amounts were allocated to help Iraqi women with "democratic organization, education, advocacy, and entrepreneurship."[1000] US-sponsored Iraqi reconstruction projects that address women's issues—many of which correctly "target[] women in education, local governance, health care, and civil society,"[1001] still face an uphill struggle. Despite certain provisions in the constitution, such as Article 49.4, which is designed "to achieve a percentage of representation for women of not less than one-quarter of the members of the Council of Representatives," "elements of Iraqi civil society and culture continue to undervalue the role of women in areas such as political participation and private industry. Furthermore, issues of personal status,

---

994 Coleman, *supra* note 986, at 24.

995 *Id.*

996 Michael S. Schmidt & Yasir Ghazi, *Iraqi Women Feel Shunted Despite Election Quota*, N.Y. Times, Mar. 12, 2011, at A4.

997 Coleman, *supra* note 986, at 35.

998 *Id.*

999 Aaron D. Pina, Cong. Research Serv., RL32376, Women in Iraq: Background and Issues for U.S. Policy 6 (2005), *available at* http://fpc.state.gov/documents/organization/50258.pdf.

1000 *Id.* at CRS-1.

1001 *Id.* at CRS-14. For a description of reconstruction projects to help Iraqi women, *see id.* at CRS 14–16.

like polygamy, continue to hamper gender equality in Iraq."[1002] Again and again, the gap between formal law and actual reality that has pervaded law and development projects around the world continues to exist in Iraq.

Analysts and observers are "concerned that the growing religious conservatism within Iraqi society is threatening women who are liberal, secularist, and non-Muslim or those Muslim women who do not wish to be ruled by a religious-based law."[1003] In many areas, especially rural, that apply subscribe to conservative interpretations of Islam, women are still forced to wear burqas due to threats and harassment, and killing female family members in the name of honor can still be done with impunity because these matters are concealed and handled in customary systems.[1004] Little was done to change customary law. Interveners sought to establish a stable, federal system in Iraq not only to allow a certain level of autonomy to the various regions and sects but also to maintain the Iraqi state and prevent Kurdish or Sunni secession.[1005] With the aim of preserving Iraqi federalism, interveners and the central Iraqi government worked to keep the tribal areas under state rule, refraining from interfering in tribal affairs or meddling with customary law.[1006]

c. Building Legal Institutions

After a constitutional framework has been established, postconflict law and development theory then looks to establish legal institutions—establishing an independent judiciary, a competent legal profession, and a solid system of legal education.[1007] This step may also involve changing the attitudes of legal professionals and society toward essential legal institutions.[1008]

In Afghanistan, reformers tried to work within the preexisting legal culture. The Bonn Agreement charged the interim government with creating a judicial commission that would "rebuild the domestic justice system in accordance with Islamic principles, international standards, the rule of law [,] and Afghan legal traditions."[1009] In turn, interim president Karzai appointed an ultraconservative pre-Taliban-era chief justice who had never studied secular law, while reformers advocated for a three-pronged legal system that would mirror the preexisting reality in Afghanistan.[1010] Since the formal legal system in

---

1002 *Id.* at CRS-2. *See also id.* at CRS-10.

1003 *Id.* at CRS-12.

1004 Taylor, *supra* note 960, at 151.

1005 *See,* e.g., Marina Ottaway, *Back from the Brink: A Strategy for Iraq*, CARNEGIE ENDOWMENT POL'Y BRIEF, Nov. 2005, at 1, 6, *available at* http://www.carnegieendowment.org/files/pb43.ottaway.FINAL.pdf (suggesting that in order to maintain a federal Iraqi state, the Coalition and the Iraqis will need to convince the Sunnis to accept federalism through a viable Sunni region).

1006 Amatzia Baram, *The Iraqi Tribes and the Post-Saddam System*, BROOKINGS (July 8, 2003), http://www.brookings.edu/research/papers/2003/07/08iraq-baram.

1007 Tolbert & Solomon, *supra* note 875, at 44.

1008 *Id.* at 45.

1009 Chesterman, *supra* note 880, at 93 (quoting Agreement on Provisional Arrangements in Afghanistan, art. II).

1010 *Id.* at 95; *Rebuilding Afghanistan: A Framework for Establishing Security and the Rule of Law*, U.S. INST. OF PEACE 3 (Dec. 11, 2001) [hereinafter *Rebuilding Afghanistan*], *available at* http://usip.org/files/file/rebuild.pdf.

Kabul never penetrated into the local system that had been established for generations in Afghanistan, reformers envisioned two separate legal systems: The first sphere would be the formal legal system applicable in major cities, like Kabul; the second sphere would be the customary system that was in place outside of those cities.[1011] Legal reform in Afghanistan was not geared to changing or challenging localist culture. Instead, reformers cited the long-standing practice of adjudicating civil and criminal disputes through tribal practices and sharia law and the historical absence of a robust central government outside Kabul.[1012] Yet, relinquishing broad swaths of the country to informal rule meant further entrenching customary laws that are less likely to meet universal development norms of freedom, voice, and capacity as Sen, Appadurai, and Nussbaum advocated respectively.[1013]

To exacerbate matters, efforts to strengthen the formal system are ironically weakened by the formal system's nonrecognition of customary practices. Faced with what it considers the potential overreach of formal law, customary law hunkers down, for example, insisting on shielding disputes from formal intervention to insulate communities from exploitation by the formal system.[1014] Even though few critics stake the full force of their argument, as I do, on culture change, many still believe that the informal system of norms needs to be engaged in some way, rather than treated as separate from the formal legal track. For example, some propose that the two systems be melded in order to re-establish rule of law and alleviate the tension between customary and formal practices of law.[1015] These scholars suggest that interveners need "to build mutually beneficial linkages between the systems without threatening the integrity of either. The goal should be to harness the positive aspects of each system and mitigate the negative."[1016]

Given the current state of legal reform in Afghanistan, even if Kabul were to replace tribal law and extend its legal system outside of the major cities, structural flaws in the formal system would hinder its effectiveness. For one, a legal culture has not taken root,[1017] and the absence of a culture that supports rule of law reform is deeply problematic, as the first wave law and development reformers observed. For example, the constitution calls for nine justices on the Supreme Court, but the chief justice has appointed many more.[1018] The chief justice has also issued rulings on matters not brought before his (or

---

1011 *Rebuilding Afghanistan, supra* note 1010, at 3.

1012 *Id.*

1013 Amartya Sen, Development as Freedom (1999); Nussbaum, *supra* note 776, at 12; Arjun Appadurai, *The Capacity to Aspire: Culture and the Terms of Recognition*, *in* Culture and Public Action 59, 63 (Vijayendra Rao & Michael Walton eds., 2004).

1014 Thomas Barfield et al., *The Clash of Two Goods: State and Nonstate Dispute Resolution in Afghanistan*, *in* Customary Justice and the Rule of Law in War-Torn Societies 159, 183 (Deborah H. Isser ed., 2011).

1015 *Id.*

1016 *Id.* at 189.

1017 "The burgeoning narcotics trade presents a fundamental challenge to the future of Afghanistan, and specifically to efforts to develop a culture of rule of law." Miller & Perito, *supra* note 907, at 2.

1018 *Id.* at 5; *see also* Choudhury, *supra* note 932, at 180–81.

any) court.[1019] He has also effectively exercised legislative authority to outlaw an act by declaring it un-Islamic.

The poor quality of judicial personnel has been cited as the greatest deficit in Afghanistan's formal legal system.[1020] "Judges routinely make decisions without reference to written law; there are effectively no means of enforcing decisions; and despite a theoretical right to counsel, there are virtually no defense lawyers in the country."[1021] Many judges in Afghanistan have no secular or statutory legal education; they are educated in *madrassas* (religious schools) on Islamic law.[1022] The judges are also religious leaders who lead prayers and sermons.[1023] When they cannot access or determine current laws, they simply apply their own religious views on the law.[1024] Appointments are largely made on the basis of connections as opposed to qualifications.[1025] Corruption is also a large problem with personnel because salaries are only thirty-six dollars per month.[1026]

Another flaw is that written law is not widely known or applied. The Kabul formal legal system is based on pre-Taliban laws of the 1960s and 1970s;[1027] there is limited access to legal texts as well as lack of clarity regarding what laws still exist.[1028] Conflict and Taliban rule caused the destruction of significant legal texts, while the overlap and contradictions between different laws between different periods have caused confusion regarding which laws are still applicable.[1029] To illustrate, the 1977 family laws gave women rights against forced marriage and equal right to divorce, but a succession of regime changes has resulted in the "withering away" of these rights.[1030] "To a great extent, the written law in Afghanistan is not applied—or even widely known, including by judges and lawyers. As one senior Afghan judicial official put it, Afghanistan 'has many laws, but no implementation.'"[1031] Pervasive ignorance of the law has also meant that people have been jailed indefinitely because they do not know whether something is or is not a legal offense. For example, women have been jailed because they had supposedly violated a nonexistent law—refusing to live with their husbands or running away from home.[1032]

[1019] Chief Justice Shinwari declared the broadcast of women on TV and co-education illegal with no case being brought before him. *See* Choudhury, *supra* note 932, at 180–81.

[1020] Miller & Perito, *supra* note 907, at 7.

[1021] *See,* e.g., *id.* at 5.

[1022] *Id.* at 7.

[1023] Reimer, *supra* note 930, at 348.

[1024] Choudhury, *supra* note 932, at 190.

[1025] Miller & Perito, *supra* note 907, at 5.

[1026] *Id.* at 7.

[1027] *Rebuilding Afghanistan, supra* note 1010, at 3.

[1028] Miller & Perito, *supra* note 907, at 9.

[1029] *Id.*

[1030] Choudhury, *supra* note 932, at 189.

[1031] Miller & Perito, *supra* note 907, at 5.

[1032] Choudhury, *supra* note 932, at 188 (highlighting women jailed for the nonexistent crimes of refusing to live with their husbands or running away from home).

For the above reasons, most Afghans do not trust the formal legal system. In rural areas where 75 percent of the population live, people see the formal legal system as "remote, elitist, illegitimate, bankrupt, costly, and slow" and most avoid contact with it.[1033] The end result is that the vast majority of the population use customary law for civil and criminal matters.[1034] Rather than attack the problems that contribute to the widespread use of customary systems, reformers have deferred to the two-pronged system, allowing it to continue to exist indefinitely. Laws and institutions in the formal system remain deeply flawed. And the deeply problematic cultural norms of the informal system remain untouched and unchanged.

Surprisingly, although legal education was a core component of law and development work during the first wave, law and development essentially ignored legal education in postconflict Afghanistan. There are but a few training programs for judicial officials and legal professionals. In the early years, the largest program was sponsored by the International Development Law Organization and gave four hundred and fifty individuals three hundred hours of training over sixteen months. Participants had had "no experience in producing written opinions, no experience with defense advocates in the courtroom, and are accustomed to disposing of issues without any reference to legal texts. Working to impart the basic idea of making judicial decisions based on actual law has been an important element of the training."[1035]

The obstacles to establishing a foundation for a solid legal education system seem to have deterred any attempts to revitalize this area. After decades of conflict and turbulent reign, libraries have been destroyed, and students cannot afford books even when they are available.[1036] The Taliban, for instance, allowed the complete destruction of the University of Kabul's law library.[1037] Under the Taliban, the law faculty at the University of Kabul ceased functioning,[1038] so the law curriculum needs much updating, buildings need repair, and most of the faculty has "no more than an undergraduate degree."[1039] To date, law and development has disregarded legal education in Afghanistan.[1040] Legal education remains fragmented, divided between the Faculties of Law and Political Science and Shari'a Law. Law professors have little training, little knowledge of core subjects and little understanding of how the law works, and few have degrees in teaching.[1041] First wave reformers' observation about the formalism that characterized most Third World

---

1033 *Id.* at 185.

1034 *Id.* at 185–86.

1035 Miller & Perito, *supra* note 907, at 10.

1036 *Id.*

1037 Christopher P. M. Waters, *Reconceptualizing Legal Education After War*, 101 AM. J. INT'L L. 382, 386 (2007).

1038 *Id.* at 388.

1039 Miller & Perito, *supra* note 907, at 10.

1040 *Id.* ("Virtually no assistance has yet been provided to the law faculties in Kabul or in provincial capitals.").

1041 Geoffrey Swenson & Eli Sugerman, *Building the Rule of Law in Afghanistan: The Importance of Legal Education*, 3 HAGUE J. ON THE RULE OF L. 130, 137 (2011).

legal education in the 1960s is equally applicable to today's Afghanistan. The curriculum conveys "archaic, technical information. Pedagogy consists almost exclusively of formal lecturing and memorization. There is little student engagement and a concomitant critical lack of development of legal research, analysis, and reasoning skills."[1042] An agreement in 2008 to reform and standardize legal education by adopting a "common core" was hindered when a year later the Faculty of Shari'a Law denied the agreement existed. Ironically, as there is uneasy bifurcation between formal law on the one hand and customary and sharia law on the other, a similar acrimonious bifurcation exists between Afghanistan's two types of law schools.[1043]

Similar obstacles have hampered efforts to revitalize legal education in Iraq. Immediately after the 2003 invasion by coalition forces, law schools were looted of all possessions and books were burned.[1044] The universities of Iraq had already been understaffed due to the high amount of emigration during Hussein's reign.[1045] It is evident that, ironically, the US occupation worked against legal education. The law school libraries were not looted until after US occupation, and the occupational administration removed many of the individuals who could have helped stabilize development in Iraqi law schools.

In Iraq, the West took a much more active approach to facilitating the development of other legal institutions. Establishing a judicial system according to international standards was set as the "earliest priority for the new Iraqi government."[1046] The Central Criminal Court was established first in 2003 as the "pillar of a new democracy."[1047] To further support the nascent judicial system, the United States established a "legal Green zone" that would not only act as secure housing and accommodation for judges, their families, witnesses, investigators, and detainees but would also serve as a venue for court proceedings.[1048] American lawyers helped prosecute cases adjudicated by judges that had received Western legal training in Prague and The Hague,[1049] while FBI agents trained Iraqi investigators.[1050] Reports quickly surfaced, however, regarding the shortcomings of Iraq's new judicial system.[1051] The courts were inundated with defendants brought in by American and Iraqi forces.[1052] Iraqi judges rendered knee-jerk verdicts based on paltry

---

1042 *Id.* at 138.

1043 *Id.* at 139.

1044 Waters, *supra* note 1037, at 385.

1045 In 2003, The University of Baghdad had only thirty-one full-time faculty members to 3,000 students. *Id.* at 387.

1046 Michael A. Newton, Op-Ed, *Iraq's New Court Find Itself on Trial*, N.Y. Times, Nov. 24, 2004, at A23, http://www.nytimes.com/2004/11/24/opinion/24newton.html?ref=iraq.

1047 Michael Moss, *Iraq's Legal System Staggers Beneath the Weight of War*, N.Y. Times, Dec. 17, 2006, at 1, http://www.nytimes.com/2006/12/17/world/middleeast/17justice.html?pagewanted=1&ref=iraq.

1048 Michael R. Gordon, *Justice from Behind the Barricades in Baghdad*, N.Y. Times, July 30, 2007, at A1, *available at* http://www.nytimes.com/2007/07/30/world/middleeast/30military.html?pagewanted=1&ref=iraq.

1049 Moss, *supra* note 1047.

1050 Gordon, *supra* note 1048.

1051 Moss, *supra* note 1047.

1052 *Id.*

evidence, and the accused received little to no representation from court-appointed attorneys.[1053] Sectarian divisions and corruption permeated the court's rulings, and torture was a common tool to compel confessions.[1054]

Over two hundred Department of Justice employees descended on the courts to attempt to improve the fractured relationship between police officers and court officials, as the former routinely ignored court orders from the latter.[1055] However, plans by the State Department's rule of law coordinator to create a public defender program to train and pay defense lawyers failed due to a lack of financial support from a judicial system largely dominated by American prosecutors.[1056]

The early court system of the new Iraq reflects US attempt to implant foreign institutions on still rocky ground. The result is a system subject to opposing forces—US ideals and Iraqi norms and values that have evolved after decades of a corrupt regime. The United States took complete control over Iraq's development, forcing US institutions against Iraqi norms, but doing so without engaging in the sort of nuanced culture change and strategic cultural framing required to engage and change local norms. "Concerns about becoming embroiled in local politics are precisely why most U.S.-based rule-of-law programs are conceived in technical terms that avoid political sensitivity."[1057] Moreover, given that "donor organizations and US governmental agencies expect rule-of-law specialists to be able to demonstrate specific results,"[1058] law and development programs tend to avoid projects that are hard to measure or that are deemed too broad. Expanding law and development to encompass cultural norms "runs counter to the argument that rule-of-law work is most effective when it is politically uncontroversial and technical."[1059]

Consequently, "programs on broad issues of improving legal education, fostering social support for law, and building citizen knowledge of legal protections are only a tiny piece of the U.S. rule-of-law industry; such programs are generally quite unlikely to produce obvious or quick results."[1060] And yet, what is needed is not a narrow technocratic focus which will fail, ironically, because it is too narrow and divorced from the preexisting cultural framework. Rather, law and development needs a broader, more expansive, more contextual approach. Going beyond law into the cultural realm will not distract from law but rather strengthen rule of law. Judicial reform may benefit greatly not just from programs to

[1053] Gordon, *supra* note 1048.

[1054] *Id.*

[1055] Solomon Moore, *In Decrepit Court System, Prisoners Jam Iraq's Jails*, N.Y. TIMES, Feb. 14, 2008, at A16, *available at* http://www.nytimes.com/2008/02/14/world/middleeast/14justice.html?ref=iraq.

[1056] Moss, *supra* note 1047.

[1057] David M. Mednicoff, *Legalism* Sans Frontières*?: U.S. Rule-of-Law Aid in the Arab World* 12 (Carnegie Endowment for Int'l Peace, Carnegie Paper No. 61, 2005), *available at* http://www.carnegieendowment.org/files/CP61.Mednicoff.FINAL.pdf.

[1058] *Id.*

[1059] *Id.* at 14.

[1060] *Id.* at 12.

train judges but also from complementary efforts to encourage "broader popular support and respect for law. . . ."[1061] By contrast, "[p]rograms that are limited to a narrow stratum of judges and approved by autocratic officials may actually have the effect of further isolating the judiciary from sources of political support and, thereby, strengthening these autocrats' political control."[1062] Hence, even though a bite-sized approach may seem more doable, it is in fact less likely to achieve the desired development objectives.

Nonetheless, although it is acknowledged that narrowly construed and separately cabined programs are problematic in the long run, in the end, short-term goals tend to dominate. Again and again, the same agenda is recycled from country to country. Pass laws (commercial, corporate, contract, property); train the police and judges. Each project is isolated from the next. And there is little cultural work done to support the technocratic dimensions of law and development.

In other words, even in the relatively narrow rule of law sliver of the law and development pie, there is little attempt to inculcate a rule of law culture, much less a development-friendly culture proposed in this book. Indeed, the legal formalism and the entrenched authoritarianism that concerned first wave law and development scholars working in Latin America in the 1960s also continue to plague law and development projects in today's world. As one practitioner expressed his worries:

> If Arab citizens and lawyers are taught that their legal system has little respectability and reliability, then judges can find few allies or pressures to challenge their subordination and the subordination of law more generally to the authoritarian political systems in which they operate. Making courts function more efficiently in such a context may serve to further centralize antidemocratic governments and even increase Arabs' cynicism about what the rule of law means in practice.[1063]

Judicial reform cannot mean only efficient courts, and even judicial review if it is decoupled from cultural reform. Again, a conventional agenda that focuses on creating and improving judicial institutions in isolation from creating a rule of law culture will not yield results reformers hope, for example, judicial expertise and independence.

As I described in Chapter 1,[1064] some observers have suggested the need to incorporate a cultural lens—but not much beyond being culturally sensitive or culturally wary. For example: "One obvious first step is for reform efforts to be more specific about recognizing the common and contentious points discussed above with respect to the nature and cultural reception of the law."[1065] Or "American humility and introspection may prove to

---

1061 *Id.* at 15.

1062 *Id.*

1063 *Id.* at 13.

1064 *See* Chapter 1 text accompanying notes 438–446.

1065 Mednicoff, *supra* note 1057, at 14.

be the best strategy to foster legal reform in the long run."[1066] Some have ventured a few concrete suggestions: "[C]areful engagement with tribal customary law and community-based dispute resolution mechanisms, ultimately reconciling the roles of the customary and state justice systems by appropriately nesting aspects of the informal into the formal."[1067]

This is a start—the recognition that proposed laws must be evaluated against a pre-existing cultural context. At the same time, some worry that combining customary and formal laws may be impossible given the clash of values between the two systems.[1068] For example, from the perspective of customary law proponents, "[a]dherence to tribal customs, as opposed to dependence on the state for security and justice, shows courage and tribal solidarity."[1069] Therefore, it is "unlikely that a rule-of-law development strategy focusing solely on the state legal system will have a large effect on these informal institutions' continued popularity in the short to mid term."[1070] Engaging local culture, whether it be tribal or religious norms, is necessary. And where local culture is at odds with the universalist norms of freedom and capability, taking steps to change local culture is, under those circumstances, defensible. By contrast, as I have argued throughout the book, where local cultural practices are not at odds with universalist norms, it is up to the local people whether to continue them.

1066 *Id.* at 13.

1067 Asfura-Heim, *supra* note 586, at 240.

1068 *Id.*

1069 *Id.* at 274.

1070 *Id.* at 280.

6

A Normative Defense of Culture Change

As aptly put by Vijayendra Rao and Michael Walton, "[m]uch of the discussion on the role of culture in development has either seen it as a primordial trap, a mystical haze, or a source of hegemonic power."[1] As I have already discussed in Chapter 2, there is the view, especially in international law, that culture is mystical, mysterious, and messy and to be entangled in it is to be mired in a trap—hence better avoid confronting it head-on. Public international law and related fields such as international relations have for the most part abstained from cultural interventions and have relegated culture to the domestic jurisdiction of states. Private international law has similarly cabined culture. Indeed, as Senator Elizabeth Warren observed in an editorial,[2] the pending Trans-Pacific Partnership, a free-trade agreement with Mexico, Canada, Japan, Singapore, and seven other countries, contains a now-common feature of trade agreements called "Investor-State Dispute Settlement," which allows investors to bypass the national judicial systems of host countries (and presumably their varying cultural particularities) and escape to the more reliable, technocratic world of international arbitration instead. Culture is messy, cannot be quantified or measured, and should not get in the way of laws and efficient market norms.

Given this pervasive tendency in international law to sidestep culture, why should law and development embrace and pursue active culture change? And how can this project be normatively defended?

---

[1] Vijayendra Rao & Michael Walton, *Culture and Public Action: Relationality, Equality of Agency, and Development*, *in* Culture and Public Action 3 (Vijayendra Rao & Michael Walton eds., 2004).

[2] Elizabeth Warren, *A Trade Deal's Corporate Giveaway*, Wash. Post, Feb. 26, 2015, at A17.

The margin for error is often small, the consequences of failure potentially large, and each project arguably so region-specific that we cannot ever mount a systematic campaign or readily predict and measure success.[3] As discussed in Chapter 2, internationalists are also cosmopolitans who value diversity.[4] Moreover, with the background of exploitation, colonialism, and racism in some regions, culture change becomes an explosive endeavor.[5] There is a lot to lose and (some would argue) little to gain. Moreover is this not the same as cultural intrusion? By pursuing culture change, are we taking up the White Man's Burden once again and introducing "lesser developed" cultures to "civilization"? Are we pulling them from their true authentic cultures and giving them something more to our (Western) liking? Would it be better to focus on quantifiable developmental goals and metrics, such as economic growth, legal and institutional reform, instead of pursuing something as seemingly slippery and amorphous and explosive as culture change? Is culture change itself problematic because by its very nature, it tends to "culturalize problems"[6] that may have economic and political roots?

This chapter builds on prior discussions of culture and offers a normative defense of culture change from a law and development perspective. Indeed, in many circumstances, embarking on a culture change campaign is defensible and can be appealing to development economists because it produces measurable, just, and positive *economic* outcomes. In other words, culture change is not restricted only to change in the cultural realm. As previous chapters in this book already show,[7] a growing body of scholarship helps illustrate the positive social, political, and economic outcomes of pursuing culture change. For example, a cultural norm that supports underinvestment in women and girls is not "just" culturally problematic. It is also detrimental to economic growth. There are many studies that measure the potential economic and social gains of changing some cultural attitudes, specifically about educating girls and providing access to family planning.

---

[3] Despite gains in health care and education for girls, the status of women in Afghanistan still ranks at the bottom even of the developing world. Efforts to train and hire policewomen have collided with traditional sexual mores and cultural norms against women working outside the home, resulting in terrible backlash against the women. Alissa J. Rubin, *Dangerous Culture for Afghan Policewomen*, N.Y. TIMES, Mar. 2, 2015, at A1. Women's shelters which give women the option of leaving abusive family situations are also viewed as an assault on Afghan culture. Alissa J. Rubin, *A Thin Line of Defense Against "Honor Killings,"* N.Y. TIMES, Mar. 3, 2015, at A1, *available at* http://www.nytimes.com/2015/03/03/world/asia/afghanistan-a-thin-line-of-defense-against-honor-killings.html.

[4] Diversity is generally a good value. For example, linguistic diversity is certainly good. But as Martha Nussbaum argued, "languages, as such, do not harm people, and cultural practices frequently do." MARTHA C. NUSSBAUM, WOMEN AND HUMAN DEVELOPMENT: THE CAPABILITIES APPROACH 50 (2000). For an argument in favor of banning female genital mutilation even when practiced by uncoerced adults, *see id.* at 94–95.

[5] *Id.* at 35.

[6] Sally Engle Merry, *Human Rights Law and the Demonization of Culture (And Anthropology Along the Way)*, PoLAR, May 2003, at 55, 63.

[7] *See* Introduction, Chapter 1 and Chapter 3.

A report published in 2008 demonstrated the potential benefits of educating girls and women around the world.[8] Citing years of research, the report touted the benefits of educating women—higher wages, better family planning, intergenerational benefits, and better health.[9] The report posited that girls around the world are often denied an education for many reasons—often lumped together as "culture."[10] The report argued that a shrinking gender gap in education is tied to greater economic output and higher levels of human capital.[11] The report stopped short of recommending any specific approach toward educating women and girls, but it does recommend that cultures which generally value women less re-evaluate their positions and begin greater investment in women and girls. Put another way, cultures should consider changing their positions on women and girls in order to reap the benefits of a larger educated population and workforce needed for economic development.

Similarly, the link between culture and market, amply demonstrated in economics and sociological scholarship, has been discussed in Chapter 3. Cultural traditions can be leveraged to lower transactions costs, as the discussion on rotating credit associations relied upon by many ethnic groups and immigrant communities show. Cultural traditions that mandate egalitarianism and that oppose individual wealth accumulation tend to result in not just market inefficiency but also reduced opportunities for individual advancement. Other norms that prohibit charging interest can also result in higher costs for doing business. Clearly, some cultural norms that create barriers to economic activities and growth can be viewed as "only" being against markets. As stated throughout the book, it is appropriate to adopt a cultural relativism perspective in this case if, as Amartya Sen put it, such norms are the result of a freely chosen, fully participatory process that values inclusion and voice of all the citizens concerned. Culturally varying methods for organizing the market are not incompatible with law and development. The proper criteria for each society to determine the balance between the value of preserving local traditions and the trajectory of market growth and organization are rightly influenced by each culture's traditions.

At the same time, however, the line between which anti-market cultural traditions "cross the line" because they pose obstacles to human freedom and capability is not always a clear one. In other words, the demarcation between markets and freedom can be a blurry, problematic one. For example, Metha Bai, a widow with two children in Rajasthan, India, was prohibited from working outside the home because she was a member of a low caste, even if staying home meant starvation for herself and her children.

---

[8] Sandra Lawson, *Women Hold Up Half the Sky* (Goldman Sachs, Global Econ. Paper No. 164, 2008), http://www.goldmansachs.com/our-thinking/investing-in-women/bios-pdfs/women-half-sky-pdf.pdf.

[9] *Id.* at 6–7.

[10] *Id.* at 8.

[11] *Id.* at 6.

If she attempted to leave to go to work, her in-laws would beat her and her children.[12] According to social scientists such as Amartya Sen and Jean Dreze, the evidence shows women's involvement in outside work enhances their status even within the family and results in less anti-female bias in distribution within the family.[13] Market access or the right to work is not "just" a matter of markets; it can also be a matter of female mortality rates, women's status, and justice.[14] When one is poor and food is scarce, it is cultural tradition that dictates who gets food and health care. In the case of Metha Bai, as in many others in the world, cultural traditions may cause systemic harm to the voiceless and the poor as well as women—many of whom are voiceless and poor, which is why I have paid particular attention to the condition of women and the cultural grounds upon which women's marginalization has been justified.[15] Similarly, property rights are central to the interests of the poor and women in developing countries, not "just" as an economic matter but also as a matter of developing human capability and a sense of self.[16] As Martha Nussbaum powerfully declared, "[c]ustoms, in short, are important causes of women's misery and death."[17]

Although this chapter will affirmatively set forth a defense of culture change, "[t]he burden of justification [should be] on those who claim that inequalities of distribution are just."[18] Whatever theory of justice is used—utilitarianism, Rawlsian, Aristotelian, and so forth—it is evident that extensive inequalities and systemic disadvantages due to gender and caste,[19] for example, cannot be considered just.[20] Cass Sunstein's "anticaste principle" would "forbid social and legal practices from turning sex, a morally irrelevant

---

[12] Martha C. Nussbaum, *Introduction*, *in* WOMEN, CULTURE AND DEVELOPMENT 1, 1 (Martha Nussbaum & Jonathan Glover eds., 1995). Martha Chen, *A Matter of Survival: Women's Right to Employment in India and Bangladesh*, *in* WOMEN, CULTURE AND DEVELOPMENT 37, 37 (Martha Nussbaum & Jonathan Glover eds., 1995) (describing the predicament of poor women in poor countries "who must break with tradition and act independently because they lack the security the tradition is supposed to offer").

[13] Chen, *supra* note 12, at 52.

[14] *Id.* at 52–55.

[15] Amartya Sen, *Gender Inequality and Theories of Justice*, *in* WOMEN, CULTURE AND DEVELOPMENT 259, 259 (Martha Nussbaum & Jonathan Glover eds., 1995).

[16] NUSSBAUM, *supra* note 4, at 156–57.

[17] Nussbaum, *supra* note 12, at 3.

[18] Jonathan Glover, *The Research Programme of Development Ethics*, *in* WOMEN, CULTURE AND DEVELOPMENT 116, 122 (Martha Nussbaum & Jonathan Glover eds., 1995).

[19] *See* Chapter 3, notes 494–529 and accompanying text for a discussion of the caste system. *See also* Chen, *supra* note 12, at, 45–50 (describing the complex reality of lives mediated by caste and the restrictions of women within castes and the caste hierarchy).

[20] Sen, *supra* note 15, at 259. *See also* Cass R. Sunstein, *Gender, Caste, and Law*, *in* WOMEN, CULTURE AND DEVELOPMENT 332, 349 (Martha Nussbaum & Jonathan Glover eds., 1995) ("A systemic disadvantage is one that operates along standard and predictable lines in multiple important spheres of life . . . [which] include education, health care, freedom from private and public violence, wealth, political representation, and political influence.").

characteristic, into a systemic source of social disadvantage"[21] and equally, using culture to justify and reinforce "the caste system rooted in gender."[22]

In a developed Western society, would it be just if a government prohibited women from inhering property; if girls are given less food than their brothers; if they were denied access to education; if they are subjected to forced marriages; if wives could only eat leftovers after the husbands have finished their meals; if women were denied freedom of movement. As Jonathan Glover rightly noted, something so ludicrous and unjust yet described by women in Bangladesh as their daily reality should not suddenly become culturally acceptable just because it occurs in Bangladesh and justified as "Asian" or "Bangladeshi culture."[23]

"Depressingly many traditions have portrayed women as less important than men, less deserving of basic life support, or of fundamental rights that are strongly correlated with quality of life, such as the right to work. . . ."[24] Again, access to market activities is not only about markets. Rather, it is pivotally connected to other capability indicators—such as "self-respect and autonomy [and] . . . to full political functioning."[25] In those instances, such market restrictions are not simply economically deleterious to society but also restrain and diminish women's freedom and capability. In such cases critical judgment is proper and culture change is justifiable when cultural norms are a source of "real evil and real oppression."[26]

In other words, the point is that certain cultural norms, for example, those that marginalize the poor or subordinate women, should be changed simply because they are antithetical to development metrics such as those articulated by Amartya Sen, Martha Nussbaum, and Arjun Appadurai—*whether or not* doing so will generate economic benefits. This universalist approach that emphasizes freedom and capability is not compatible with cultural relativism.[27] It is not satisfied with a framework that says that the criteria for freedom, voice, or capability are culturally determined.[28] Rather, it is staked

---

[21] Sunstein, *supra* note 20, at 332.

[22] *Id.* at 348.

[23] Glover, *supra* note 18, at 117.

[24] Nussbaum, *supra* note 12, at 1.

[25] *Id.* at 7.

[26] *Id.* at 1.

[27] Both Sen and Nussbaum endorse a capability-oriented framework of development. But there are nuanced differences between their respective approaches, which are each founded on different theoretical assertions. Nussbaum's philosophical foundation means that she is primarily interested in developing "a universal theory of the good: it applies to all social justice issues, and to the world as a whole," with appropriate contextual and cultural modifications. *See* Ingrid Robeyns, *Sen's Capability Approach and Gender Inequality: Selecting Relevant Capabilities*, 9 FEMINIST ECON. 61, 68 (2003). Sen's approach is more abstract and focuses less on enumerated list and more on "fair and consistent democratic procedures to draw up the list." *Id.* at 69.

[28] The universalism versus cultural relativism debate has also played out in the area of international human rights. Are human rights universal as claimed by the Universal Declaration of Human Rights, or is it culturally specific? For a discussion of the similarities between the capability approach and human rights, *see* NUSSBAUM, *supra* note 4, at 97. For Nussbaum, *rights* may exist in constitutions and laws but for the right to exist, people

on a universal stand, "indeed an increasingly specific stand, on what functions of human beings are most worth the care and attention of public planning, the world over. And it has also taken a clear stand on gender equality, pointing to the unequal level of functioning of the world's women as a bad state of affairs to be altered."[29] As Cass Sunstein aptly observed, the principle of freedom and full human capability "is universal in its scope. It applies even in areas in which it would (for example) collide with religious convictions and firmly entrenched traditions."[30]

To expand on the discussion already in the Introduction, a capability approach is centered on the principle of human functioning, a principle that, as Nussbaum rightly observed, has been adopted by many political theorists, as seen, for example in the "human improvement" remarks of John Stuart Mill; Amartya Sen's "human capability;" and "human development" adopted by the United Nations.[31] This line of work, known as the capability approach, postulates that development should be about human freedom and human capability, not only utilities, resources, commodities[32]—what people are free to do and are able to do, not on what they can earn and consume. "The capability approach is a framework of thought, a normative tool, but it is *not* a fully specified theory that gives us complete answers to all our normative questions. It is not a mathematical algorithm that prescribes how to measure inequality or poverty, nor is it a complete theory of justice."[33]

This universal, essentialist position emphasizes that which is common among humans, rather than that which is different (without of course neglecting differences). The starting point of the capability approach is not local norms but rather universal, human norms.[34] "We *are* members of local communities whose values have shaped us, but at the same time we are members of the global human community."[35] As Kwame Appiah wrote, "We will only solve our problems if we see them as human problems arising out of a special

---

must have the *capability* of exercising it. "In short, thinking in terms of capability gives us a benchmark as we think about what it is to secure a right to someone." *Id.* at 98.

[29] Nussbaum, *supra* note 12, at 5.

[30] Sunstein, *supra* note 20, at 349.

[31] Martha C. Nussbaum, *Human Capabilities, Female Human Beings*, *in* WOMEN, CULTURE AND DEVELOPMENT 61, 63 (Martha Nussbaum & Jonathan Glover eds., 1995).

[32] If one were to ask questions about female capability, for example, a focus on GNP alone does not provide the answer. For example, Pakistan, Zimbabwe, and Honduras may at one point share similar GNP per capita but gender equality is drastically different in each country. Pakistan has a 23 percent female literacy rate; Zimbabwe a 60 percent, and Honduras a 71.6 percent female literacy rate. NUSSBAUM, *supra* note 4, at 61.

[33] Robeyns, *supra* note 27, at 64.

[34] Universalism is a core element of both capabilities and international human rights. However, as Martha Nussbaum explained, "the language of capabilities has one further advantage over the language of rights: it is not strongly linked to one particular cultural and historical tradition, as the language of rights is believed to be." NUSSBAUM, *supra* note 4, at 99. As such, the capabilities approach is less likely to be charged with being part of a Western and hence illegitimate agenda.

[35] Glover, *supra* note 18, at 138. "[C]ertain moral values, including some recognizable version of justice, are to be found in the part of our common humanity that crosses cultural boundaries. . . . [S]ociety is a human creation . . . we can change it when it does not fit our human needs and values." *Id.* at 139.

situation, and we shall not solve them if we see them as African problems, generated by our being somehow unlike others."[36]

In defense of her capability project, Nussbaum has compiled a tentative "first approximation"[37] of a broadly shared conception of the human being that shapes a human life, for example, mortality, hunger and thirst, sexual desire, the need for shelter, mobility, pleasure and pain, cognitive capability, infant development, practical reason, affiliation with other human beings, relatedness to other species, humor, play, separateness.[38] As Nussbaum acknowledged, the list is an underspecified working list composed of human limits and human capabilities. It consists of limits humans are cognizant of and work to overcome, as well as capabilities humans strive to realize. With respect to the latter, the list constitutes a floor, "a minimal conception of the good,"[39] so that one could say that a human life without such and such items is a life that is not a good human life. According to Nussbaum, basic human functional capabilities include being able to lead a life of normal length, to be adequately nourished, to avoid unnecessary pain, to use the senses, such as to think, reason, be informed and educated, to have attachments to things and persons, to form a conception of the good, to plan one's own life, to live one's own life, without interference in matters such as "marriage, childbearing, sexual expression, speech and employment,"[40] and with guarantees of freedom of association, freedom from unwarranted search and seizure, integrity of personal property, though it may be modified in different ways and different degrees by demands of social equality.[41]

Clearly there is ample room for disagreement and debate about complexities and ambiguities as one goes through Nussbaum's list, as general as it deliberately is.[42] My purpose in including it is to set the stage for further refinement of this capability framework, through additional adaptation, negotiation, and specification. Different scholars have studied this from different platforms. Some have combined Sen's and Nussbaum's approaches—freedom and capability—to ask the following primary question: What freedom does a person have to pursue her or his capabilities, which include a set of functioning she or he can achieve, given the availability of personal, material, and social resources available to her or him? "Capabilities measure not actually achieved functionings, but a person's

---

36 Nussbaum, *supra* note 31, at 63.

37 *Id.* at 75.

38 *Id.* at 76–79.

39 *Id.* at 80.

40 *Id.* at 85.

41 *Id.* at 85. It has been noted that Nussbaum's "list has ten dimensions: life; bodily health; bodily integrity; sense, imagination and thought; emotions; practical reason; affiliation; other species; play; and control over one's environment." Robeyns, *supra* note 27, at 73.

42 Onora O'Neill, *Justice, Capabilities, and Vulnerabilities*, *in* Women, Culture and Development 140, 145 (Martha Nussbaum & Jonathan Glover eds., 1995) (explaining why a vague but thick conception of the good is inevitable because "[a]ny moral reflection at this level is going to be relatively indeterminate." Thickness is also to be expected because "there are a lot of different matters that must be taken into account.").

freedom to achieve valued functionings."[43] In negative terms, people should be entitled to the capabilities needed to avoid oppressive relationships—this would include prohibition against female genital mutilation, for example; in positive terms, people should be entitled to capabilities to function as an equal citizen in a democratic society.[44] Others eschew at a general level, Nussbaum's working list and reject outright any definitive list of capabilities, focusing instead on a more procedural, inclusive approach to fleshing out the meaning of human capability.[45] At a more specific, more contextual level, different scholars ranging from Germain Grisez, Joseph Boyle, and John Finnis have come up with their own lists.[46] Yet others have attempted to flesh out the parameters of capabilities and functionings: "Capabilities are opportunities to function, but what are functionings?"[47] Do functionings include "physical and mental activities (running, playing piano, etc.), as well as physical and mental states (such as being adequately nourished, being in good health, being happy)"?[48] Do all functionings need to be included or only a subset? Do functionings include desirable as well as undesirable ones, states of pleasure and states of pain, respectively?[49] Should all functionings be considered? Or is justice concerned with only certain basic capabilities, and how should this criteria of basic capabilities be determined? For example, one criterion is the "species-normal adult criterion," whereby the functionings considered are those "exercised by most adults of the species on a regular basis."[50] Another criterion is the "basic needs criterion" whereby the functionings considered are "those necessary for survival and non-poverty."[51] Another is the "human flourishing criterion, according to which the relevant functionings are those that are necessary for a good human life."[52]

A law and development framework that honors human capability generally would still "leave room for plural specification and also for further negotiation"[53] consistent with the particularities of different countries. But as Nussbaum insisted, whatever version of the capability approach is chosen, it must also satisfy "specific requisites of equal female capability."[54] This book has defended the "universal notion of the human being and human functioning" against cultural relativism and has urged that traditions that oppress be altered, not only because changing them will produce economic benefits but also because changing them is necessary to maximize human capability, including women's capability. The

[43] Elizabeth S. Anderson, *What Is the Point of Equality*, 109 ETHICS 287, 316 (1999).
[44] *Id.*
[45] Robeyns, *supra* note 27, at 61.
[46] *Id.* at 71–72, 74.
[47] Peter Vallentyne, *Debate: Capabilities Versus Opportunities for Well-Being*, 13 J. POL. PHIL. 359, 361 (2005).
[48] *Id.* at 361.
[49] *Id.* at 361–62.
[50] *Id.* at 362.
[51] *Id.*
[52] *Id.*
[53] Nussbaum, *supra* note 31, at 85.
[54] *Id.*

distinctive characteristic of the capability approach is that it shifts the focus from purely economic indicators like income and resources toward human capability and functioning.

For example, the marginalization of women exists separate and apart from economic development and cannot be explained away or justified on cultural grounds. "Poverty alone does not cause women to die in greater numbers than men. When there is a scarcity, custom frequently decrees who gets to eat the little there is, and who gets taken to the doctor. And custom is always crucial in determining who gets to perform wage labour outside the home, an important determinant of general status in the family and community."[55] The normative basis for interfering with those cultural traditions is not one based on market efficiency but rather, one firmly rooted in a universalist defense of freedom, as espoused by Sen, human capability, as espoused by Nussbaum, and voice, or capacity to aspire, as espoused by Appadurai.[56] These holistic metrics also demonstrate the need for a deep and consistent culture change campaign based on the unrecognized intrinsic worth of human beings in general and women in particular, not simply because they are an untapped social and economic asset. A campaign designed to show how changing cultural attitudes about women and girls is not just right on its own terms but can also produce a net social gain would be the right course of action. By focusing on freedom and capabilities, the core development question is one tied to quality of life, that is, one's "capabilities for functioning, unlike a focus on opulence (say, GNP per capita). . . ."[57]

Similarly, certain practices, such as trafficking of women and girls as sex slaves, must be eradicated even if they are economically productive or profitable for their practitioners.[58] Nowadays, countries and agencies put resources into fighting human trafficking because it is an unjust practice, regardless of the economic implications. For example, Kwame Anthony Appiah characterized this issue in terms of honor in his discussion of the Atlantic slave trade.[59] Appiah suggested that the abolition of the slave trade was actually contrary to British economic interests, and yet strong grounds existed to support its abolition.[60] It is important thus to look beyond a purely utilitarian economic output calculation. As the British merchant class and middle class grew in size and influence, so did the value and honor of their work.[61] By highlighting the plight of slaves across the sea, the working class came to identify with slaves in the "oppression they shared" as workers.[62]

---

[55] Nussbaum, *supra* note 12, at 3.

[56] Amartya Sen, Development as Freedom (1999); Nussbaum, *supra* note 4; Arjun Appadurai, *The Capacity to Aspire: Culture and the Terms of Recognition*, *in* Culture and Public Action 59 (Vijayendra Rao & Michael Walton eds., 2004). *See also* Introduction.

[57] Nussbaum, *supra* note 12, at 5.

[58] ILO, Profits and Poverty: The Economics of Forced Labour 27 (2014), *available at* http://www.ilo.org/wcmsp5/groups/public/---ed_norm/---declaration/documents/publication/wcms_243391.pdf (estimating $99 billion in total annual global profits from forced sexual exploitation).

[59] Kwame Anthony Appiah, The Honor Code: How Moral Revolutions Happen 126–32 (2010).

[60] *Id.* at 106–07.

[61] *Id.* at 120–26.

[62] *Id.* at 126.

This implies that the honor and value of the work of serfs, slaves, and peasants counted for as much as the work of a British worker. Once the British worker gained political power, Appiah noted that "[d]iscrimination, in the sense of making distinctions in how we treat people on the basis of their social identities, began to need justification," and the rising power of the commons could find no justification for an immutable class system.[63] Appiah added that equality is key in all social institutions, implying that without equality these social institutions would be unjust.[64] The abolition of slavery, at least in the British Empire, came at the heels of this re-evaluation of class structures as inherently unjust.

In addition, focusing on easily measurable outcomes (economic efficiency, economic development, and concomitantly modernization) in order to support culture change narrows the potential impact of a culture change campaign because it risks overlooking other critical concerns. One modern assumption of culture and economic development rests on the notion that societies continually evolve in a continuum that range from primitive to modern—from less to more civilized.[65] On its face this might seem intuitively correct. It implies that human rights abuses are more stark and common in less developed countries, and moreover, once a nation or a culture is sufficiently developed, human rights, particularly women's rights will be embraced, respected, and enforced. Yet this has not been so. A cultural re-evaluation of women, not just as potential tools of economic expansion, but as actual human beings with rights needs to occur.

Consider acid attacks in Bangladesh, which are illegal, yet are simultaneously the most common form of domestic violence against women in Bangladesh.[66] Acid attacks are a capital crime in Bangladesh.[67] Yet these attacks are so common that almost everyone in Bangladesh knows what to do right after an acid attack (douse the victim in water).[68] Perpetrators of acid attacks are usually jilted lovers or jealous spouses, and they are rarely punished—a corrupt judiciary and a lack of economic alternatives for women (many of the attacks are by husbands and breadwinners) keep prosecutions down.[69] Similar attacks that occur in Cambodia are ignored by authorities as "personal matter[s]."[70]

Acid attacks point to a series of strange dilemmas that are representative of core concerns in this book. The fact that an acid attack is a capital crime in Bangladesh shows a

---

[63] *Id.* at 127–28.

[64] *Id.* at 128.

[65] SALLY ENGLE MERRY, HUMAN RIGHTS AND GENDER VIOLENCE: TRANSLATING INTERNATIONAL LAW INTO LOCAL JUSTICE 12 (2006).

[66] Marianne Scholte, *Acid Attacks in Bangladesh: A Voice for the Victims*, SPIEGEL ONLINE (Mar. 17, 2006, 3:46 PM), http://www.spiegel.de/international/acid-attacks-in-bangladesh-a-voice-for-the-victims-a-406485.html.

[67] Roland Buerk, *Bangladesh's Acid Attack Problem*, BBC NEWS (July 28, 2006), http://news.bbc.co.uk/2/hi/5133410.stm.

[68] Scholte, *supra* note 66.

[69] *Id.*

[70] Seth Mydans, *Vengeance Destroys Faces, and Souls, in Cambodia*, N.Y. TIMES, July 22, 2001, http://www.nytimes.com/2001/07/22/world/vengeance-destroys-faces-and-souls-in-cambodia.html.

strong condemnation of these attacks against women. On the other hand, about two hundred attacks occur every year—typically with no repercussions to the perpetrator.[71] Meanwhile Bangladesh is on its way to meeting its Millennium Development goals—Bangladesh has even had a female prime minister.[72] Yet domestic violence against women in Bangladesh and around the world is so prevalent that "[w]omen aged 15–44 are more at risk from rape and domestic violence than from cancer, motor accidents, war and malaria."[73] In India, even as thousands marched to protest a brutal gang rape of a young woman on a bus in December 2012, even as the Indian middle class was "jolted into action by the shocking assault that led to the young woman's death,"[74] "the same demographic group is also at the heart of an illegal practice that experts say contributes to violence and deep-seated discrimination against women in this rising economy: sex-selective abortion."[75] Indeed, India's child-gender ratio of girls to boys is more lopsided that it has been in fifty years, as couples abort female fetuses or neglect infant girls in favor of infant boys. It has been assumed that such odious preferences are held by the uneducated and rural poor. Yet "researchers say the practice is quickly growing in the urban enclaves where incomes are rising. . . ."[76]

This is yet another reason why a law and development approach should adopt a capability framework rather than one that honors private preferences. There is no denying that questioning people's preferences can be problematic. It smacks of paternalism to tell people that what they prefer is bad for them. But at the same time, many of the problematic preferences are themselves a reflection of paternalism, especially against women. The world is replete with paternalistic values that tell women that they cannot be full agents and that they lack full capacity to make their own decisions. How ironic that culture change efforts would be attacked as paternalistic when such efforts are designed to reverse the preexisting paternalism that permeates women's lives.[77]

Moreover, one can only take the paternalism charge so far. Any law, especially any bill of rights that seeks to ensure associative, religious, and other liberties can be charged with being paternalistic because it prohibits people from behaving in ways they have traditionally behaved.[78] And "[m]ore generally, any system of law is 'paternalistic,' keeping some

---

71 Scholte, *supra* note 66.

72 Nita Bhalla, *South Asia's Growing Modernity Masks Women's Plight*, REUTERS, June 14, 2011, *available at* http://www.spiegel.de/international/acid-attacks-in-bangladesh-a-voice-for-the-victims-a-406485.html.

73 UNiTE, *Fact Sheet: How Widespread Is Violence Against Women?* (Feb. 2008), http://www.un.org/en/women/endviolence/pdf/VAW.pdf.

74 Shyamantha Asokan, *India's Rising Middle Class Prefers Sons*, WASH. POST, Jan. 12, 2013, at A6, *available at* http://www.washingtonpost.com/world/asia_pacific/indias-rising-middle-class-prefers-sons/2013/01/11/2dd1b984-5b2e-11e2-88d0-c4cf65c3ad15_story.html.

75 *Id.*

76 *Id.*

77 NUSSBAUM, *supra* note 4, at 52.

78 *Id.* at 52–53.

people from doing things that they want to do."[79] Thus, even constitutions that prohibit people from treating others unequally or discriminate against people on the basis of race, sex, or caste, for example, can also be accused of paternalism because they change or at least thwart people's preferences.

How should law and development treat preferences that are antidevelopment? While Sen correctly noted that often, it is the "elite 'guardians' of tradition" who claim authority to speak about the authenticity of certain cultural traditions,[80] it is also admittedly true that many of the problematic preferences discussed in this book are held by the poor or women themselves. Thus, it is important to confront the issue of preferences head-on. Even assuming that people's stated or articulated preferences are true,[81] their preferences can be influenced by society's institutions. As John Rawls stated, "Everyone recognizes that the form of society affects its members and determines in large part the kind of persons they want to be as well as the kind of persons they are.... Thus an economic regime is not only an institutional scheme for satisfying existing desires and aspirations but a way of fashioning desires and aspirations in the future."[82] Preferences can also be distorted by law and culture, "deformed in various ways by oppression and deprivation."[83] As Nussbaum explained, "[i]f someone who has no property rights under the law, who has had no formal education, who has no legal right of divorce, who will very likely be beaten if she seeks employment outside the home, says that she endorses traditions of modesty, purity, and self-abnegation, it is not clear that we should consider this the last word on the matter...."[84] Preferences may be accepted simply because they have been internalized by the very people who have come to accept their own poverty, marginalization, and oppression. Preferences may seem natural when in fact they are a product of oppression, limited opportunities, and social prejudices.[85] The oppressed, marginalized, mistreated, or poor may also have a low threshold of what they themselves consider their desires, needs, or capabilities. "People with a truncated psychology of this kind may have nearly all their desires satisfied in a way that masks their fundamental deprivation."[86]

---

[79] *Id.* at 53.

[80] SEN, *supra* note 56, at 31.

[81] Preferences can be false because true preferences cannot be asserted due to oppression or pressure. *See* Introduction. For an examination of the distinction between "manifest preferences" and "true preferences," *see* NUSSBAUM, *supra* note 4, at 125 (according to John Harsanyi, manifest preferences may be based on "erroneous factual beliefs, or on careless rational choice," but true preferences are those a person would have if he or she had all relevant information and acted from a rational choice basis).

[82] John Rawls, *The Basic Structure as Subject*, 14 AM. PHIL. Q. 159, 160 (1977). *See also* JOHN RAWLS, POLITICAL LIBERALISM 269 (1993).

[83] Nussbaum, *supra* note 12, at 5. As preferences can be distorted, they "are not always reliable indicators of life quality...."). *Id.* NUSSBAUM, *supra* note 4, at 112–15.

[84] NUSSBAUM, *supra* note 4, at 43.

[85] The economist Gary Becker argued that the beliefs of others, especially those in position of authority or those from influential groups, that minorities are less productive can be self-fulfilling, resulting in underinvestment by those minorities in education, training, and other important traits, such as punctuality. GARY BECKER, *The Economic Way of Looking at Life*, *in* ACCOUNTING FOR TASTES 139, 142 (1996).

[86] Glover, *supra* note 18, at 123.

People adapt their preferences to their reality, for example, acquiescing in their own marginalization.[87] As Jon Elster framed the question, "why should individual want satisfaction to [sic] be the criterion of justice and social choice when individual wants themselves may be shaped by a process that preempts the choice?"[88] In many cases, human beings, like foxes, may declare they no longer prefer something out of their reach because it is sour anyway. But it is their exclusion of that something which prompts that declaration of preference. Thus, their preference is simply an "adaptive preference"[89] which is a nondeliberative, nonautonomous preference. This phenomenon of preference adaptation or nonautonomous preference was in fact illuminated by John Stuart Mill when he perceptively demonstrated women's participation in their own subjugation. While feudal lords maintained their power over vassals by force, men's perpetuation of their systemic superiority over women is maintained and enforced through something more sophisticated:

> Men do not want solely the obedience of women, they want their sentiments. All men, except the most brutish, desire to have, in the woman most nearly connected with them, not a forced slave but a willing one, not a slave merely, but a favourite. They have therefore put everything in practice to enslave their minds. . . . The masters of women wanted more than simple obedience, and they turned the whole force of education to effect their purpose. All women are brought up from the very earliest years in the belief that their ideal of character is the very opposite to that of women; not self-will, and government by self-control, but submission, and yielding to the control of others. All the moralities tell them it is the duty of women, and all the current sentimentalities that it is their nature, to live for others.[90]

For Mill, the liberty to construct one's own "individuality of power and development"[91] as proposed by Wilhelm Von Humboldt, unhampered by the constraints of other people's "traditions and customs,"[92] is itself an expression of human nature. "Human nature is not a machine to be built after a model, and set to do exactly the work prescribed for it, but a tree, which requires to grow and develop itself on all sides, according to the

[87] O'Neill, *supra* note 42, at 142 ("Where people accept that small mercies are all they deserve, when they see their oppressors as benevolent father-figures, these distorted preferences will be given undeserved weight within any fundamentally subjectivist approach to ethics and justice.").

[88] JON ELSTER, SOUR GRAPES: STUDIES IN THE SUBVERSION OF RATIONALITY 109 (1983).

[89] *Id.* at 110.

[90] JOHN STUART MILL, THE BASIC WRITINGS OF JOHN STUART MILL 137–38 (Modern Library 2002).

[91] *Id.* at 59.

[92] *Id.* at 60. Even if the customs are good customs, to conform to them merely because they are customs "does not develop in him any of the qualities which are the distinctive endowment of a human being." *Id.* Human desires devoid of "intentionality and responsiveness" and reflecting a preference to be without equal rights, without freedom, without literary, and so forth, cannot be a guide to social policy. NUSSBAUM, *supra* note 4, at 147.

tendency of the inward forces which make it a living thing."[93] Jawaharlal Nehru's condemnation of British rule included a condemnation of the psychological subordination of Indians. Referring to colonialism, Nehru said, "[t]he fact that the British Government should have imposed this arrangement upon us was not surprising; but what does seem surprising is that we, or most of us, accepted it as the natural and inevitable ordering of our lives and destiny."[94]

Habituation, culture, institutions, and laws shape preferences and many preferences thwart rather than honor individual freedom and development. Nussbaum found that many women in Bangladesh did not want education or literacy and even expressed satisfaction with their uneducated, illiterate lot.[95] For example, poor women underestimate their own health problems.[96] In 1944, the All-India Institute of Hygiene and Public Health commissioned health surveys on widows and widowers. About 48.5 percent of the widowers said they were in ill or indifferent health, compared to 2.5 percent of widows, although in reality, the widows were in worse health than the widowers.[97] "In these circumstances it would seem odd to base health policy on subjectively held views about health conditions. Such an approach would ensure that existing discrimination would be severely aggravated."[98]

In the law and development context especially, the notion that the stated preferences of those in the poorest of poor countries are in fact cramped by deprivation is hardly controversial. Therefore, it cannot be just to reference preference satisfaction as a determinant of the good life if preferences have been corrupted by bad lives. If a person is starving or unjustly imprisoned or is suffering from other capability constraints, the question cannot be whether or not that person has suitably adjusted to such injustice.[99] A better framework for development is not satisfaction of preferences, which "so readily legitimates or minimizes vulnerability and oppression,"[100] but rather, realization of human freedom and capability, which might require not just economic development but also the removal of cultural norms that are deleterious to development.[101]

---

93 MILL, *supra* note 90, at 61.

94 NUSSBAUM, *supra* note 4, at 150 (quoting from JAWAHARLAL NEHRU, AN AUTOBIOGRAPHY 417 (Bodley Head 1989) (1936)).

95 Sunstein, *supra* note 20, at 351 n.55.

96 O'Neill, *supra* note 42, at 142.

97 Sunstein, *supra* note 20, at 351.

98 *Id. See also* NUSSBAUM, *supra* note 4, at 134 (observing that Richard Posner has stated that preference-based economics is "a potential menace to basic liberties" and "could furnish economic justification for every manner of discrimination against despised minorities.").

99 AMARTYA SEN, RESOURCES, VALUES AND DEVELOPMENT 363 (1984) ("[T]here are good grounds for arguing that a person's capability failure may well be judged not on the metric of how upset he is about it, but by the *extent* of the capability failure itself.").

100 O'Neill, *supra* note 42, at 143.

101 The capabilities approach is meant to promote education, human dignity, bodily integrity, and so forth. Promoting capability means also indirectly shaping preferences and preferences formed within such framework are likely to be more informed than those formed within a framework of inequality, deprivation, poverty, illiteracy, oppression, and so forth.

Indeed, economic development alone has not resulted in a fundamental culture change in attitudes about gender. To the contrary. "Indian sociologists say upwardly mobile families are eager to protect recently acquired wealth and enterprises, and daughters are seen as expensive in a country where dowries, though officially outlawed, remain widespread. After marriage, a bride typically moves in with her in-laws, and her inheritance in effect goes to her new family."[102] This cultural norm is entrenched and unchanged. Such norm has generated a set of preferences that has in turn produced a skewed sex ratio, which in turn may be fueling other secondary but serious crimes such as sexual assault and bride trafficking. Although India has taken steps to remedy the problem—outlawing pregnant women from finding out the sex of the fetus—the middle class has the means to evade the law by bribing doctors to reveal the information. Others travel outside the country for ultrasounds. The Mumbai municipal council has also launched a pilot program to counsel pregnant women visiting public clinics about sex-selection. However, middle-class Indians visit private doctors.

If anything, modernization masks the problem faced by Bangladeshi, Indian, and other women because it is assumed that women in developing societies now face fewer and fewer obstacles.[103] Bangladesh is a telling example of why culture change, and not just socioeconomic progress, is necessary. It is not enough that an acid attack is a capital crime. Nor is it enough to hope that rule of law reform exists in tandem with or facilitates economic growth, which in turn will be accompanied by social and cultural transformation. Rather, cultural attitudes about women and their rights must be changed from within. Mona Mehta, the leader of Oxfam's "We Can" campaign against violence toward women in South Asia, contended that "[i]t's not enough to have a law. The implementation needs to be resourced well enough for it to work . . . a lot depends on the attitudes of local officials charged to implement (change). They come from the same communities, have the same patriarchal biases that the community has . . . they don't think it's important . . . [or] relevant."[104]

The notion that economic development can mask cultural attitudes finds even stronger support in the developed world. Gender violence continues to be an underreported problem.[105] The difference, however, is that in a developed nation it is often easier to marshal and deploy social, economic, and intellectual resources to begin a culture change campaign. In 2002, for example, Rutgers University's Center for Women's Global Leadership spearheaded a campaign to create "a culture that says no to violence against women."[106] The campaign used terms and methods that had previously been used to change culture in furtherance of civil rights in the past, and they could be repurposed toward ending

---

[102] Asokan, *supra* note 74.

[103] Bhalla, *supra* note 72.

[104] *Id.*

[105] *Id.*

[106] Merry, *supra* note 65, at 28.

violence against women today. Such a campaign is more easily implemented in a country with independent media and a history of cultural and social change movements to draw upon, like the United States.

To reiterate, culture change should be defensible on its own terms, not as ancillary to or a byproduct of legal development (as the first wave law reformers had hoped) and/or economic development. To defend culture change, it is important to define what culture is, and very often critics of culture change define culture in intractable terms. This chapter builds on concepts of culture already discussed throughout the book. Specifically, this chapter will attempt to answer some of the critics of culture change campaigns—particularly that culture change campaigns are simply Westernization campaigns that impose inauthentic cultural values. This chapter argues that those two positions misunderstand or misinterpret cultural campaigns and culture itself. Both of these imply that cultures exist in a pure state inside indestructible bubbles, when in fact cultures actively mingle and mix.

A. Revisiting the Culture Question in International Law: A Critical Analysis

As discussed in Chapter 2, the fact that international law has had a long history of sidestepping cultural claims means that it is highly resistant to incorporating culture into its disciplinary framework. This resistance has been passed down to other related disciplines such as international human rights and law and development. Thus, it is important for the purposes of this book to (1) show that culture has been inappropriately cabined by international law and related disciplines; (2) explain, in Chapter 4, why, despite this long history of reluctance, law and development can use openings in international law and international relations to address culture; (3) demonstrate how culture change has been accomplished historically and can be accomplished now—through concrete examples provided in Chapters 3 and 5; and (4) argue why culture change should be pursued, as I aim to do in this Chapter 6. Thus, this chapter shows that culture change is normatively defensible and provides different ways of approaching this project.

As discussed in Chapter 2, "[t]he conception of culture as Volkgeist as a set of values and beliefs that makes a people or nation distinctive, is still powerful in the domain of international human rights. It appears in claims to indigenous sovereignty, religious nationalism, ethnonationalism, and a separate status for diasporic populations. It is the basis for the argument that human rights are a distinctly Western concept that ignores a country's distinctive spirit or system of values. This conception of culture is fundamental to contemporary nationalism."[107]

---

[107] Merry, *supra* note 6, at 66.

Paradoxically, it is also fundamental to contemporary internationalism. Although the internationalist sensibility is decidedly different from the nationalist sensibility, in many instances, international law has (perhaps inadvertently) allowed itself to be co-opted by nationalism to further a generally extreme nationalist agenda. Internationalism has been "enlisted on the side of traditionalists and fundamentalists who turn to law to reinforce their traditional stronghold over a community. Seeing their power threatened by forces such as globalization and modernization, increasingly leaders of cultural groups seek to use the 'right to culture,' the 'right to religion,' the 'freedom of association' and the right to 'self-determination' to suppress internal change and preserve the status quo."[108]

Take the last right mentioned, the right to self-determination. Public international law has enshrined self-determination in a multitude of international human rights documents,[109] proclaiming it to be a universal and fundamental right. Invoking self-determination allows cultural traditionalists to suppress internal challenges to cultural traditions on the grounds that such challenges promote values that are foreign and external to the culture and thus inauthentic.[110]

In other words, international law takes a laissez faire attitude when cultural conflicts are played out, in essence, letting the cultural status quo stand and allowing fundamentalists to dictate the terms of the debate. The internationalist stance, that is, leaving national cultures outside the jurisdiction of international law, is ironically also consonant with and supported by the cosmopolitan sensibility that pervades internationalism. In international, cosmopolitan circles, the sentiment can be succinctly stated this way, as the founder of an Algerian nongovernmental organization Women Living Under Muslim Laws put it: "Well, it's their culture. Who are we? Are we racists? We can't interfere."[111]Although internationalists are political liberals who have little in common with fundamentalists, they are also concerned about repeating the nineteenth-century quest to civilize the Third World, not justified, as it was then, on the basis of superior Western morality, but rather, in a more sophisticated and acceptable language

---

[108] Madhavi Sunder, *(Un)disciplined*, Response, PoLAR, May 2003, at 77, 83.

[109] The International Covenant on Civil and Political Rights endows minority cultures with rights such as the "right . . . to enjoy their own culture, to profess and practise their own religion, or to use their own language." International Covenant on Civil and Political Rights, art. 27, Dec. 16, 1966, *adopted*, 999 U.N.T.S. 171, 179. *See also* International Covenant on Economic, Social and Cultural Rights, art. 3, Dec. 16, 1966, *adopted*, 993 U.N.T.S. 3, 5 (declaring that all state parties must ensure the social and cultural rights of their people); Universal Declaration of Human Rights, G.A. Res. 217(III)A, at 76, U.N. GAOR, 3d Sess., art. 27(1), U.N. Doc. A/810 (Dec. 10, 1948) (asserting that all persons have right to participate in the cultural life of the community); Convention Concerning Indigenous and Tribal Peoples in Independent Countries, art. 2, June 27, 1989, ILO, 28 I.L.M. 1382, 1385 (requiring state parties recognize and promote the cultural rights of indigenous peoples).

[110] Richard T. Ford, *The Repressed Community: Locating the New Communitarianism*, 65 TRANSITION 96, 99 (1995) (reviewing AMITAI ETZIONI, THE SPIRIT OF COMMUNITY: RIGHTS, RESPONSIBILITY, AND THE COMMUNITARIAN AGENDA (1993), ROBERT BELLAH, RICHARD MADSEN, ANN SWIDLER, & STEVEN TIPTON, THE GOOD SOCIETY (1992), DUNCAN KENNEDY, SEXY DRESSING: ETC. (1995)).

[111] Madhavi Sunder, *Piercing the Veil*, 112 YALE L.J. 1399, 1438 (2003).

of today—as an imperative of modernity. Similarly, they may worry that despite global trade and global diffusion of cultures, countries with greater power can overwhelm those with lesser power, not just economically but also culturally, with the latter finding itself in a position of "submissive supplication."[112] Thus, even those who are open to cultures adapting and changing, whether from the inside or prodded from the outside, may need assurances—rightly so—that change results from choice, freedom, and informed judgment, not from domination.[113]

For those reasons, internationalists may feel deeply ambivalent about supporting cultural intrusions. The doctrine of national self-determination serves then as a shield precisely to reinforce nationalist rights, warding off internationalist interventions, even if those very nationalist rights are offensive to the internationalist sensibility. This self-imposed cosmopolitanism, coupled with the public international law tradition of consigning "the private spheres of family, culture, and religion . . ."[114] to the realm of "domestic jurisdiction," means that internationalists tend to end up leaving culture alone, allowing nationalists to exercise a stranglehold on the issue. While fundamentalists defend culture, internationalists are reluctant to criticize it. While fundamentalists claim self-determination to insulate culture from change, internationalists are ambivalent and torn.

Because international law has abstained from cultural issues, it has in effect ceded the cultural terrain to the nationalist. In this way, by succumbing to the nationalist agenda and its insistence on cultural authenticity, international law is indeed behind the times.[115] It recognizes only the right of groups "to enjoy their own culture"[116] or requires state parties only to ensure the social and cultural rights of their people.[117] These rights, however, were postcolonial-era rights, designed primarily to protect colonized peoples. Group-based rights such as the right to self-determination may carry a wide range of meanings; the right to self-rule, local autonomy, democracy, or freedom from intervention and preserving culture and tradition. In the current era and under different circumstances, these rights have been anachronistically "interpreted to defend cultural groups against the forces of modernization and change. Internal cultural ferment is suppressed as law authorizes the exclusion of dissenters who threaten to dilute a culture's distinctiveness."[118]

---

112 Vijayendra Rao & Michael Walton, *Culture and Public Action: Relationality, Equality of Agency, and Development*, *in* CULTURE AND PUBLIC ACTION 20 (Vijayendra Rao & Michael Walton eds., 2004). *See also* EDWARD W. SAID, CULTURE AND IMPERIALISM xi (First Vintage Books 1994) (1993).

113 Amartya Sen, *How Does Culture Matter?*, *in* CULTURE AND PUBLIC ACTION 37, 52 (Vijayendra Rao & Michael Walton eds., 2004).

114 Sunder, *supra* note 111, at 1443.

115 Madhavi Sunder, *Cultural Dissent*, 54 STAN. L. REV. 495, 500 (2001).

116 International Covenant on Civil and Political Rights, *supra* note 109, 999 U.N.T.S. at 179.

117 International Covenant on Economic, Social and Cultural Rights, *supra* note 109, 993 U.N.T.S. at 5. *See also* Ronald Niezen, *Culture and the Judiciary: The Meaning of the Culture Concept as a Source of Aboriginal Rights in Canada*, 18 CAN. J.L. & SOC'Y, no. 2, 2003, at 1, 18.

118 Sunder, *supra* note 115, at 500.

Public international law thus has put its force and weight into preserving cultures and insulating them from change. In doing so, public international law has assumed in essence that international law must favor cultural integrity over culture change, committing itself to "the old-world view of cultural diversity as existing across cultures, but not within them."[119] This stance also allows public international law to sidestep cultural issues at odds with individual freedom, and economic and social development because culture has to be preserved and insulated from the critical eye of law under the name of cultural integrity, authenticity, and self-determination.

Cognizant of this internationalist tendency, fundamentalists and nationalists have aggressively exploited the language of internationalism (one sliver of which is the right to self-determination, for example) to promote nationalist objectives. Fundamentalists have relied on international law's deference to the cultural domain to retain their traditional power base and have used the armor of culture to eliminate any "conceptual space for internal change."[120] Wearing the mantle of nationalism, they adopt an anti-foreign, anti-Western rhetoric and strike a confrontational or hostile stance against the influence of foreign cultures. As discussed in Chapter 2, nationalists tend to fear that "cultural globalization" will itself bring about the "destruction of local cultures—a loss that may culturally impoverish nonwestern societies" based on the "constant cultural bombardment" that tends to come from the Western world through "MTV," "Kentucky Fried Chicken," and the like.[121] This concern promotes the belief that each country or society must stick to its "own culture," no matter how attractive foreign cultures may be, and reject importing McDonald's and other strikingly "Western" influences.[122] Sen argued that this misguided concern arises from the fact that culture tends to be defined by the "geographical origin of a practice, rather than by its manifest use and enjoyment."[123] Thusly, "regional labeling" facilitates a need to identify Western culture as the "other."[124]

Interestingly and paradoxically, these nationalists not only use the language of internationalism to promote nationalism or employ the language of cosmopolitanism to further particularism. But they have also, in many cases, succeeded in defending cultural homogeneity in the name of cultural diversity—again, using the language of diversity to entrench homogeneity. For example, during a human rights conference in 1993, Singapore's then foreign minister "warned that 'universal recognition of the ideal of human rights can be harmful if universalism is used to deny . . . the reality of diversity.' "[125] The Chinese

---

[119] *Id.*

[120] Sunder, *supra* note 111, at 1462.

[121] Sen, *supra* note 113, at 52–53.

[122] *Id.* at 54.

[123] *Id.*

[124] *Id.*

[125] Amartya Sen, Human Rights and Asian Values, Sixteenth Morgenthau Memorial Lecture on Ethics and Foreign Policy (May 25, 1997), *in* HUMAN RIGHTS AND ASIAN VALUES 9 (1997), *available at* http://www.carnegiecouncil.org/publications/archive/morgenthau/254.html/_res/id=sa_File1/254_sen.pdf.

delegation put forward a bolder proposition—that individual rights must take a back seat to states' rights—implying that Western notions of individual freedom are incompatible with Chinese Confucian values.[126] In addition, the Asian regional preparatory meeting for the Vienna Conference on Human Rights adopted the Bangkok Declaration, which asserted that "while human rights are universal in nature, they must be considered in the context of a dynamic and evolving process of international norm-setting, bearing in mind the significance of national and regional particularities and various historical, cultural and religious backgrounds."[127] The last quoted phrase creates the opening for nationalists to defend and promote practices that are antithetical to development—development as enhancing freedom and human capability—on cultural and national self-determination grounds.

The particularist or regionalist approach referenced above maintains that some values (often supposedly Western values) are incompatible with other cultural values. Supported by other Asian leaders, Lee Kuan Yew, the former prime minister of Singapore, claimed that Asian values emphasized obligation to the community rather than rights owed to the individual and as such are not compatible with Western notions of human rights.[128] The argument goes something like this: Confucian values prioritize order and discipline over individual rights.[129] Thus Lee incorporated Confucian values into his method of government as a benevolent dictator and father figure in the Confucian model of social relationships.[130] His defenders noted that Lee was instrumental in the rise of Singapore, creating one of the wealthiest city states in the world. While "[c]ontradicting Lee became synonymous with being disloyal to Singapore," Lee did invite foreign investment, improve infrastructure, education, and health, reduce crime rates, and institute a social security system.[131] Despite Lee's achievements in Singapore, it is important to note that positions like those taken up by Lee usually convince mostly those they serve best. For instance, Lee tolerated a society that had some unfair practices—like excluding women from certain positions—as long as it is done in the name of furthering a well-ordered society like Singapore.[132]

Today Singapore is one of the world's economic powerhouses, arguably thanks to Lee Kuan Yew's adherence to a Confucian cultural model. For his defenders, the question

---

[126] *Id.* at 9–10.

[127] Merry, *supra* note 6, at 66; *see also* World Conference on Human Rights, Bangkok, Thai., Mar. 29–Apr. 2, 1993, *Report of the Regional Meeting for Asia of the World Conference on Human Rights, Bangkok* Declaration, ¶ 8, U.N. Doc. A/CONF.157/PC/59 (Apr. 7, 1993).

[128] Merry, *supra* note 6, at 66.

[129] Sen, *supra* note 125, at 9.

[130] *Id.* at 10–14, 28.

[131] Terry McCarthy, *Lee Kuan Yew*, TIME (Aug. 23, 1999), http://www.time.com/time/world/article/0,8599,2054444,00.html.

[132] Stephen Macedo, *What Self-Governing Peoples Owe to One Another: Universalism, Diversity, and the Law of Peoples*, 72 FORDHAM L. REV. 1721, 1732–33 (2004).

is, why should Singapore adopt a different, arguably more Western style of governance, especially if it achieved similar (or better) results in its own way?

Yet, such a culturally particularistic approach "is in direct conflict with the idea of an international system of human rights, a conception which grew out of the Holocaust and the conviction that states' treatment of their citizens was no longer a purely domestic concern."[133] Indeed, once defined in this culturally specific way, human rights become dependent on regional politics and state sovereignty—countries will only enforce the human rights they feel are compatible with their cultural background. For nationalists, international human rights agreements are often framed as butting into areas that should be under state sovereignty. Culture change is therefore an often futile pursuit and even normatively offensive.

Take once again Lee Kuan Yew's Asian-values approach to human rights. Sen has rightly argued that Lee's particularist position misinterprets (perhaps purposefully) Confucius' message.[134] "The . . . issue is not whether [Confucianism is necessarily authoritarian] but whether the freedom-oriented perspectives are absent [from Confucian values]."[135] Sen argued that such freedom-oriented perspectives are not absent from Confucian values—even Confucius did not advocate "blind allegiance to the state."[136] Confucian values create mutual obligations between dominants and subordinates; dominants protect and give consideration, subordinates give obedience and respect.[137] Confucian values do not necessarily mandate total obedience to a superior. When a disciple asked Confucius how best to serve his liege lord, Confucius replied, "Tell him the truth even if it offends him."[138] Sen noted that Confucius was aware of the tension between individual rights and the state's needs; yet while Confucius was not a champion of individual liberty, it would be mistaken to read a justification for authoritarianism in his writings in the way certain politicians in Asia self-servingly do.[139] Authoritarian leaders are all too willing to "assert that human rights violate the fundamental cultural principles of a nation or a religion and therefore cannot be adopted."[140] Again, internationalists are caught in a sometimes self-imposed paradoxical bind—bound as they are to the principles of self-determination and domestic jurisdiction enshrined in public international law (but increasingly pierced by an international human rights movement equipped to pierce state sovereignty but, alas, ill equipped to pierce claims of cultural sovereignty). Similar positions have been used to oppose campaigns for women's rights, for example, because such

---

[133] Merry, *supra* note 6, at 66.

[134] Sen, *supra* note 125, at 17.

[135] *Id.*

[136] *Id.*

[137] Geert Hofstede & Michael Harris Bond, *The Confucius Connection: From Cultural Roots to Economic Growth*, ORG. DYNAMICS, Spring 1988, at 5, 8.

[138] Sen, *supra* note 125, at 17–18.

[139] *Id.* at 18.

[140] MERRY, *supra* note 65, at 14.

change would cause social upheaval, while simultaneously disrupting "a wide range of patriarchal privileges."[141]

Sen's position highlights an important point—how we approach cultural questions and considerations is very much based on how we define culture and values. If we (the international community or the law and development universe) allow certain cultural values to be defined too narrowly in one specific way, we allow little space for dissent within the cultural framework, and we risk ignoring legitimate dissenting voices. If we define our certain cultural values too broadly, we risk losing a sense of cultural identity and uniqueness. Sen also implied that the individual or group in power in a society often has a monopoly on that society's cultural narratives (which is not to deny that in many instances, the masses themselves may share those narratives as well, which in turn lead to the issue, discussed below, of private preferences). Lee Kuan Yew is a mild example of a "benevolent dictator," yet others who are not as benevolent (such as the Pol Pot, or Kim Il Sung, or Kim Jong Il) also exist. As I discuss below, it is important to examine who has social control in a culture, especially control of a society's cultural narratives.

As many scholars have observed, controlling cultures by patrolling cultural boundaries and expelling so-called trespassers has a direct and deleterious impact on development.[142] A constricted conception of culture allows "the self-proclaimed guardians of culture [to exclude] other members of the culture from making and contesting cultural meanings."[143] Self-interested elites marginalize equality, reason, and freedom,[144] characterizing efforts to incorporate them as illegitimate external imposition. Consequently, liberals and feminists have critiqued cultural rights on many grounds, for example, that they preserve the status quo at the expense of women and children;[145] that they tend to enforce cultural orthodoxy over progressive cultural dissent;[146] and that they are preserved often by suppressing individual autonomy.[147]

I examined the relationship between culture and development in Chapter 3. Timur Kuran has argued convincingly that the urgency to simply "preserve" culture may have

---

141 *Id.* In Somalia, the government encountered opposition when it banned female genital mutilation. Many Somali elders felt the practice a part of the culture and necessary to ensure female purity. *Somalia: Activists Laud Ban on FGM/C, Say Implementation Will Require More*, IRINNews.org (Aug. 13, 2012), http://www.irinnews.org/report/96092/somalia-activists-laud-ban-on-fgm-c-say-implementation-will-require-more.

142 Timur Kuran, *Cultural Obstacles to Economic Development: Often Overstated, Usually Transitory*, *in* Culture and Public Action 115, 115–17 (Vijayendra Rao & Michael Walton eds., 2004).

143 Sunder, *supra* note 115, at 504.

144 *See* Madhavi Sunder, *Enlightened Constitutionalism*, 37 Conn. L. Rev. 891, 899 (2004). *See also* Sen, *supra* note 113, at 53.

145 Janet E. Halley, *Culture Constrains*, *in* Susan Moller Okin, Is Multiculturalism Bad for Women? 100, 100–04 (Joshua Cohen et al. eds., 1999); Susan Moller Okin, *Is Multiculturalism Bad for Women?*, *in* Susan Moller Okin, Is Multiculturalism Bad for Women? 7 (Joshua Cohen et al. eds., 1999).

146 Yael Tamir, *Siding with the Underdogs*, *in* Is Multiculturalism Bad for Women?, *supra* note 145, at 47, 48.

147 Halley, *supra* note 145, at 100.

a negative effect on development. Kuran categorized the debate on economic development into two broad categories: multiculturalism and globalism.[148] Multiculturalists believe that globalization, "by destroying local cultures, harms the affected communities, even humanity as a whole."[149] Thus, there is a need to resist the "homogenizing influences of modern civilization by nurturing cultural differences."[150] Globalists on the other hand, view culture change as inevitable.[151] Notably, globalists generally maintain that it is "harmful to block cultural diffusion for the sake of protecting traditional values and practices."[152] Kuran argued that "cultural lock-in," or this tendency to resist cultural diffusion, is among one of the causes of persistent underdevelopment.[153] As I have discussed throughout the book, the traits that define a culture also influence economic performance, and at times these cherished customs harm economic productivity.[154] Kuran stated, "[t]here are sound reasons, then, for denying present cultures the *blanket* protections often demanded in the name of multiculturalism."[155] Indeed, for globalists, culture change is deemed not just inevitable but even normatively desirable.[156]

In Section B below, I discuss works by scholars who defend a particular understanding of culture and from such an understanding, show that culture is not immutable. Within this framework, I argue that culture change can be both good and feasible.

B. The Stickiness of Culture, Cultural Biases, and Cultural Framing

This part supplements other parts of the book that explored various conceptions of culture.[157] Culture is ubiquitous—we all live in a culture, and we see other cultures all around us. Are cultures unchangeable? Or are cultures much more malleable and resilient than critics of culture change would recognize or concede? Can the difficulties related to culture change be analyzed and understood? Chapter 4 demonstrated the withering away of even widely accepted international law norms such as conquest norms and the emergence

---

148 Kuran, *supra* note 142, at 115.

149 *Id.*

150 *Id.*

151 *Id.*

152 *Id.*

153 *Id.* at 117; *see* Mary Douglas, *Traditional Culture: Let's Hear No More About It*, *in* CULTURE AND PUBLIC ACTION 85, 100 (Vijayendra Rao & Michael Walton eds., 2004).

154 Kuran, *supra* note 142, at 116.

155 *Id.* at 117.

156 I argue that the rationale for culture change is strongest when the cultural norms at issue are antithetical to human freedom and capability. This is the universalist claim. Enhancing human freedom and human capability are staked on universalism grounds. By contrast, all other cultural norms that do not implicate universalist values (but that may be outlier norms or that may decrease market efficiency) may survive cultural relativism claims. This is so especially if, as Amartya Sen observed, these norms are the product of an inclusive and deliberative process.

157 *See* Introduction and Chapter 2.

and evolution of new norms such as the Geneva Convention norms; Chapter 5 discussed culture change in historical and current development framework.

This section builds on those prior chapters. Culture is not static but fluid. There are differences across cultures as well as within cultures, which means that assertions of cultural authenticity should not be automatically validated by law and development, especially if the cultural claims at issue are antidevelopment. Not only should law and development not defer to such cultural claims under the "self-determination" rubric. It should, rather, engage in culture change.

This conception of culture, as fluid, changing, and changeable, relies in part on scholarship that asks how cultures vernacularize and frame new or foreign ideas. An important factor is who has social control or control of a culture's frame. Thus armed, a culture change campaign can find support within a culture. Part B thus examines the complex background against which culture change may be implemented, focusing on the pragmatic, "how to" aspects of the project.

Several theorists, among them Herman Kahn, posit that although culture is a tricky, amorphous, and unquantifiable concept, it is ever changing and ultimately can be changed. "[Kahn held] the belief that culture is rather sticky and difficult to change in any basic fashion, although they can often be modified."[158] Kahn believed culture change in the context of modernization may be difficult, but possible.[159] "[The] ability to modernize often depends upon time and place."[160] Footbinding in China, discussed in Chapter 5 and later in this chapter, is an example of a cultural practice that withstood over a thousand years of criticism within imperial China, surviving even the imperial edicts attempting to abolish it.[161] For centuries Chinese women with bound feet were prized, and bound feet were considered beautiful.[162] This long-standing custom had a sense of inevitability and immutability attached to it. Yet, footbinding fell into quick decline at the turn of the twentieth century.[163] Kwame Anthony Appiah argued that the end of this cultural practice makes sense if viewed within the context of the waning days of the Qing dynasty and the modernization of China.[164] The end of footbinding came at a specific time and place in Chinese history—a time when China was catching up to the industrialized West, and footbinding became a source of national shame to China.[165] Framed in national development terms, the cultural norms supporting footbinding were both malleable and susceptible to change.

---

[158] Hofstede & Bond, *supra* note 137, at 6; THE ESSENTIAL HERMAN KAHN: IN DEFENSE OF THINKING 132 (Paul Dragos Aligica & Kenneth R. Weinstein eds., 2009).

[159] KAHN, *supra* note 158, at 132.

[160] *Id.*

[161] APPIAH, *supra* note 59, at 69.

[162] *Id.* at 70.

[163] *Id.* at 82–93.

[164] *Id.* at 72.

[165] *Id.* at 91–92.

Other theorists also acknowledge the "stickiness" of culture and complexities of changing cultural attitudes. Geert Hofstede and Michael Harris Bond observed that oftentimes, "[c]ulture's grip on us is complete."[166] "It not only affects our daily practices . . . it also affects the theories we are able to develop to explain our practices."[167] Thus, it is not surprising that our own cultural backgrounds limit our ability to understand other cultures. But being aware of and admitting our own cultural biases allow us to understand this limitation and minimize potential concerns about insensitivity or even imperialism. The Chinese emperors, for example, considered themselves the rulers of the world's most advanced civilization. From that standpoint, "if you regard yourself as humanity's overlord . . . with other countries as tributaries with nothing to teach you, why trouble to see what the modern barbarians had to offer?"[168] Of course this perspective is to be avoided, particularly in a culture change project.

As discussed below, given our inherent cultural limitations, there are at least four factors to consider when engaging in culture change. First, whenever a culture encounters a new idea or concept, that idea or concept will automatically be viewed from that individual culture's subjective context. In other words, new ideas are automatically reframed first and related to something familiar, not rejected out of hand. Even the Chinese emperors reframed new ideas in their own context, and then rejected them as offerings of lesser civilizations. Second, this automatic reframing process shows that cultures are not intrinsically resistant to change, and it also shows why they can be subject to purposive change. In other words, the reframing process shows why culture change is possible, as well as how it can be "sticky and difficult" at the same time. Third, because cultural biases play a part in this reframing process, culture change is complex albeit feasible. To change cultural attitudes, it is crucial to understand how any individual culture tends to react to new ideas. How a culture reacts to new ideas is often heavily dependent on how those ideas are framed or (as with the Chinese emperors) who has social control. Finally, if individuals and cultures truly reframe new ideas to fit into their own perspectives, then cultural erasure or whitewashing is unlikely to occur. Cultures are changed by new ideas, but are not destroyed (at least not by the ideas defended in this book).

Other commentators, among them Peggy Levitt and Sally Engle Merry, have focused on how cultural biases or assumptions within cultures affect how such cultures process new ideas. Levitt and Merry describe vernacularization as the "process of appropriation and local adoption" of global concepts.[169] As Merry explained, "[t]he concept of vernacularization was developed to explain the nineteenth-century process by which national

---

166 Hofstede & Bond, *supra* note 137, at 19.

167 *Id.*

168 George Walden, *George Walden Welcomes an Informed and Prudently Optimistic View of "China Versus the Rest,"* SUN. TELEGRAPH, May 22, 2011, at 28, *available at* http://www.telegraph.co.uk/culture/8512275/On-China-by-Henry-Kissinger-review.html.

169 Peggy Levitt & Sally Engle Merry, *Vernacularization on the Ground: Local Uses of Global Women's Rights in Peru, China, India and the United States*, 9 GLOBAL NETWORKS 441, 446 (2009).

languages in Europe separated, moving away from the medieval transnational use of Latin and creating a new and more differentiated sense of nationhood in Europe. Human rights language is similarly being extracted from the universal and adapted to national and local communities."[170] Universal norms can be localized. "Vernacularizers take the ideas and practices of one group and present them in terms that another group will accept" by "adapting and reframing them from the way they attach to a source context to one that resonates with the new location."[171] Vernacularization assumes a degree of engagement with local culture while simultaneously introducing global norms. This engagement—even if to prod, poke, and ultimately change some aspects of local culture—is important because engagement with local culture is crucial to maximize the chances of positive outcome.

Vernacularization is an important part of a culture change agenda. As discussed in the Introduction and Chapter 1, blanket reforms that rely on only law, via international treaties or newly drafted legislation, merely attempt to control, modify, or eradicate practices in societies without separately altering the local cultural fabric needed to effectuate such reforms.[172] Reform cannot be about global declarations that impose generic rules.[173] Even if for no other reason than a strategic one, it is important to think in terms of "how to" best implement culture change or cultural modification projects. In this respect, it is important to examine the competing interests of local movements and to analyze the degree of control that should be afforded to the society in which the reform is implemented.

At the very least, engaging local culture and local communities to allow local participation means that it is less likely culture change efforts will be resisted. A distinct weakness of this approach, however, is that local directives meant to address, for example, gender problems may be softened to allow for cultural traditions, and therefore fail to protect women.[174] Vernaculization, however, allows global norms to be mediated within a cultural framework, using language that would appeal to and be palatable to local communities. Vernacularization "translates" universal declarations into local language. "Successful domestic enforcement entails an adoption and adaptation process"[175] adopting international human rights norms and adapting them to local circumstances "through the use of strategic frames."[176]

---

[170] MERRY, *supra* note 65, at 219.

[171] Levitt & Merry, *supra* note 169, at 446, 449.

[172] Sally Engle Merry, *Women, Violence, and the Human Rights System*, *in* WOMEN, GENDER, AND HUMAN RIGHTS: A GLOBAL PERSPECTIVE 83, 90 (Marjorie Agosín ed., 2001). Relying on the treaty method for change has other drawbacks. If an issue is not one that is in "the interests of powerful nations in pressing for human rights of various kinds," then some norms that may be extremely detrimental to women will go unaddressed. Further, the heavy dependence upon what powerful and progressive nations think gives an imperialistic air to the entire process, which contributes to societal resistance. *Id.* at 93.

[173] *Id.* at 89.

[174] *Id.* at 92.

[175] Angela M. Banks, *CEDAW, Compliance, and Custom: Human Rights Enforcement in Sub-Saharan Africa*, 32 FORDHAM INT'L L.J. 781, 783 (2009).

[176] *Id.* at 795. *See* MERRY, *supra* note 65, at 1.

Framing is "one way that individuals and organizations align [to a social issue] . . . [in order] to gain adherents and constituents."[177] Frames are constructed from "a variety of cultural norms and values."[178] Frames, at least for Levitt and Merry, "are not themselves ideas, but ways of packaging and presenting ideas that generate shared beliefs, motivate collective action, and define appropriate strategies of action" as well as "channel the way a global values package attaches to pre-existing ideas and institutions."[179]

Levitt and Merry offer three types of "change projects"—one of a neoliberal flavor, one of a fundamentalist, religious flavor, and one of an antiglobalization flavor to appease the needs and desires of the communities that are approached.[180] Although change projects can target any cultural norms, the discussion below focuses on those norms that diminish women's rights and lives precisely because those are the norms that are likely most resistant to change.

The authors note that all three types of projects are meant, in the case of women's rights, to "redefine and adapt the ideas to facilitate understanding and assimilation. They modified aspects of women's human rights in an effort to make them comprehensible and appropriate in a particular context."[181] The first, and most characteristically neoliberal, uses the language of human rights to tackle issues in the culture. English words are used to "describe local narratives and symbols," and the words are then connected to human rights.[182] The second project, which mirrors the fundamentalist, religious approach, is an imaginative discourse in which the local population is encouraged to discuss aspirations of what rights they feel are essential human rights; the population makes connections between their own symbols to the outside world and the international view of human rights.[183] The final application involves the translation of human rights concepts directly to appropriate discourse within the culture.[184]

Although the above vernacularizations vary greatly in their strategies to teach and implement women's rights, Merry notes that "activists in each country are committed to developing models suited to their distinctive history and social conditions, yet the strategies they have adopted are all fairly similar."[185] Although the cultural histories and traditions may modify the dialogue to adapt "the rhetoric and structure of these programs or interventions to local circumstances,"[186] there are four main areas that Merry asserts must

---

177 Banks, *supra* note 175, at 793.

178 *Id.* at 794.

179 Levitt & Merry, *supra* note 169, at 452.

180 Peggy Levitt & Sally Engle Merry, *Making Women's Human Rights in the Vernacular: Navigating the Culture/Rights Divide*, *in* Gender and Culture at the Limit of Rights 81, 89 (Dorothy L. Hodgson ed., 2011).

181 *Id.* at 91.

182 *Id.*

183 *Id.* at 91–92.

184 *Id.* at 92.

185 Merry, *supra* note 65, at 135.

186 *Id.*

always be addressed no matter what the vernacularization.[187] These areas include criminalization, provision of social services, public education, and survey research.[188]

Take the example of violence against women. An approach that focuses on criminalization would involve training the executive branch to properly address violence against women, and training judges to allot strict punishment and avoid lenience based on religious or traditional justifications.[189] As discussed above, however, the legal method alone is not effective "[b]ecause the implementation of [these] laws lags well behind the passage of these laws, [and] activists devote considerable energy to implementation strategies."[190] Thus, the need arises for social services, which "seek to improve the woman's safety rather than to punish the offender."[191] Once women are provided with some safety, or well-being, they can then begin to develop agency to advocate for the criminalization of violence against women. In India, for instance, some women have developed women's courts, which meet close to the buildings of local authorities and "use humor and shaming to pressure litigants, adjust their meeting times to the rhythms of village life, and use their knowledge of local practices, customs, and social networks to gather evidence and negotiate agreements."[192]

A major problem with respect to the provision of social services is a lack of shelters, not necessarily due to resistance, but due to resource deficits.[193] Moreover, most programs tend to be located in cities, leaving rural victims with few options.[194] To combat these deficits and to combat apathy or resistance, general education, the third factor, is perhaps one of the most effective ways to decrease violence against women and maximizing their agency. General education has focused on "public awareness campaigns in the media, curricular development in schools, gender training, and public events such as marches and demonstrations."[195]

Academic survey and research, the fourth factor, helps insiders and outsiders to understand the problems that the specific society, and subsets of society, face in relation to gender violence.[196] Communication remains an entrenched problem: how to translate the language of social movements, the language of international human rights and women's rights into the local vernacular.[197] As already observed, advocates in civil societies must strive to frame seemingly or nominally Western feminist ideas within their own

---

[187] *Id.* at 139.

[188] *Id.*

[189] *Id. See also* Banks, *supra* note 175, at 790.

[190] Merry, *supra* note 65, at 139.

[191] *Id.* at 151.

[192] *Id.* at 157.

[193] *Id.* at 152.

[194] *Id.* at 154.

[195] *Id.* at 158.

[196] *Id.* at 159.

[197] *Id.* at 161.

constructs. For instance, "[e]xamples of independent women are drawn from Chinese history and Confucianism in a process one scholar described as 'Chinese packaging.'"[198] Advocates in India have also used images of strong, independent women from Hindu mythology to personify women in their culture.[199] The process is designed to help people internalize values of their own culture in a different context than has been presented to them and apply them positively, in this case, to women's rights.

While vernacularization and the four factors will still be important in the holistic approach, looking at all factors—social, economic, urbanism, rural issues, and so forth—can lead to "[a] more nuanced, dynamic understandings of the relation of culture, power and rights in the context of history and socio-economic change."[200] Historical and situational context are essential to bring about any kind of change that will not immediately be rejected. Various groups may mobilize to enact human rights, "but how they work depends on the context."[201] A prevalent issue is the lack of availability of a reliable source or history for many of these countries, and therefore finding the truth as to how and why the cultural practice is embedded within the social or economic sphere is difficult.[202] Once that can be determined, advocates then face the issue of how to meld that cultural practice into something that is still acceptable to the populace, but does not impinge on basic rights.

The question of popular or local acceptance of global norms is relatedly dependent on at least two factors—whether the local population internalizes the norms and thus accept them as fully legitimate, or whether the population can simply be acculturated to the norms.[203] The difference between these two concepts is distinct in that internalization requires interaction, interpretation, and internalization of the desired norms, while acculturation simply requires that the state adopt the norms as a result of peer pressure from other nations.[204] Those who push for internalization, such as Lynn Stout, believe that conscience is not cultivated simply through the threat of punishment.[205] To induce good behavior, we must focus on good behavior and how good behavior can create a positive society.[206] Stout explained that if society wishes to inculcate unselfish behavior, such unselfish behavior can be induced when certain conditions exist, that is, when there are "at least three important social influences: (1) instructions from authority; (2) beliefs

---

198 *Id.* at 162.

199 *Id.*

200 Dorothy L. Hodgson, *"These Are Not Our Priorities": Maasai Women, Human Rights, and the Problem of Culture*, *in* GENDER AND CULTURE AT THE LIMIT OF RIGHTS 138, 157 (Dorothy L. Hodgson ed., 2011).

201 MERRY, *supra* note 65, at 132.

202 *Id.*

203 Banks, *supra* note 175, at 798.

204 *Id.* at 802.

205 Lynn Stout, *Cultivating Conscience: How Good Laws Make Good People*, ISSUES IN GOVERNANCE STUD. (Brookings Inst., Wash., D.C.), Dec. 2010, at 1, http://www.brookings.edu/~/media/research/files/papers/2010/12/conscience%20stout/12_conscience_stout.pdf.

206 *Id.*

about others' selfishness or unselfishness; and (3) perceptions about the magnitude of the benefits to others from one's unselfish actions."[207] With respect to the first variable, "people tend to do what they are told to do. This instinct for obedience, it turns out, can also be employed for more prosocial purposes. When asked to do so, subjects in experimental games routinely act prosocially—even when it is personally costly for them to do so."[208] With respect to the second variable, humans are social or herd animals; when we see others acting unselfishly, we do so as well. Regarding the third variable, "people seem more inclined to behave unselfishly in experiments when they believe others will enjoy large gains, not small, from their unselfishness. We seem to be 'intuitive utilitarians' who are willing to sacrifice more when we believe others will benefit more from our sacrifice."[209] Behavioral scientists have been able to change the behaviors of research subjects by manipulating those social variables and hence facilitate the "cultural habits of unselfish prosocial behavior [that] are essential to both economic growth and psychological wellbeing."[210]

Scholars who accept acculturation as an adequate resolution to implementing human rights insist that even though decoupling may occur—the instance in which there is a significant difference in what policies the state espouses and what the state actually does—there will never be a permanent divide between policies and actions.[211] This is because the structural transformations that take place as a result of compliance with human rights norms will open up avenues to "empower new actors and increase the likelihood of a tighter connection between the state's actions and its commitments."[212] Thus, acculturation is a method (albeit imperfect) of developing agency for women while not forcing internalization of norms that some in the culture may find offensive or irreconcilable with traditional beliefs.[213] Some scholars believe that internalization creates a more lasting and legitimate relationship between the societal conscience and the introduced practice. Others, however, assert that they are "agnostic" as to whether the society must actually internalize the gender norms or whether they may just become acculturated.

Whether acculturation or internalization, the goal is simply to put in place an adaption process[214] that requires connection of international human rights norms "to the local context, which includes the local meaning-making institutions, and understanding

---

207 *Id.* at 5.

208 *Id.* at 4.

209 *Id.*

210 *Id.* at 6.

211 Banks, *supra* note 175, at 803.

212 *Id.*

213 *Id.* at 798–803 (highlighting that regardless of whether the accepted process is acculturation or internalization, the focus should be to change state preferences for given norms, not on constraining states' actions).

214 Angela Banks recognizes that after the rule of law process of adoption of international legal rules into the domestic legal system, a process of adaption also needs to occur for any successful preservation of the norms within the society. *Id.* at 783.

the power dynamics of these institutions and actors."[215] In both instances, the gender norms must be framed so that they "resonate with the broader culture and existing values to enable the frame to appear natural and familiar."[216]

The principle that ideas themselves should be framed in locally appealing ways is not new. There are many historical examples of how some rulers redefined themselves and their policies to promote what we would call progressive reforms. The Persian emperor Cyrus, for example, issued edicts announcing a policy of religious tolerance after his conquests; such edicts of religious tolerance were designed to make subjugated nations more amenable to his rule.[217] The Mauryan emperor Ashoka followed a similar path in India, issuing an edict promoting religious tolerance following the conquest of Kalinga: "A man must not do reverence to his own sect or disparage that of another man without reason . . . the sects of other people all deserve reverence for one reason or another. By thus acting, a man exalts his own sect, and at the same time does service to the sects of other people."[218] Cyrus's own edict not only established a policy of religious tolerance but also sought wide and diverse religious support for his government, specifically beseeching his subjects to pray to their own gods to bless his reign.[219] This appeal for support from different religious sects within his empire combined with his general religious tolerance won Cyrus legitimacy among Jewish communities, who accorded Cyrus great esteem and reverence, especially after he freed and permitted Jewish captives to return to Israel.[220] Cyrus and Ashoka both illustrate how culture, specifically cultural narratives, have been used since antiquity to achieve social control or carry out some sort of social (or cultural) agenda. Cyrus and Ashoka ruled vast empires with diverse populations. Direct control was impractical, if not impossible. Prudence and perhaps necessity guided their actions. Instead of enforcing their own beliefs on the conquered, Cyrus appealed to the narratives of the conquered. These methods were not uniquely Western, nor were they modern. These examples illustrate that some concepts often touted as Western constructions were independently practiced by cultures isolated from (or predating) what we call the West.

There are also many contemporary examples of cultural reframing. In Rwanda, women's participation in politics was reframed as "a necessary component of unity and reconciliation in post-genocide Rwanda."[221] From a strategic standpoint, framing women's rights in terms that are compatible with traditional Rwandan culture was deemed most likely to be effective. Traditional culture in Rwanda generally relegated women to the

[215] *Id.*

[216] *Id.* at 794.

[217] *Cyrus Cylinder*, The Brit. Museum, http://www.britishmuseum.org/explore/highlights/highlight_objects/me/c/cyrus_cylinder.aspx (last visited June 6, 2012, 11:50 AM).

[218] Sen, *supra* note 125, at 19.

[219] *Cyrus Cylinder, supra* note 217.

[220] *Id.; Ezra* 1:1–6.

[221] Banks, *supra* note 175, at 793.

home. To promote Rwandan women's political participation, representation was couched in terms of home life and the family. A woman, especially a mother, has a good sense of what is going well with the family. A Rwandan mother can accurately represent not just her needs, but the needs of her entire family and other Rwandan families as well. This unique ability among women translates into a better public servant. One voter put it this way: "[T]he real problems of a family are known by a woman and when . . . [women participate in politics], they help a country to get much better."[222] Today Rwanda has the highest proportion of female representation in the world and was the first country in the world to have a parliament with a female majority.[223]

In addition, women's rights groups successfully situated the call for women's rights and political participation within the tragic context of Rwanda's genocide. First, women's rights advocates pointed out that unlike ethnicity, gender was not a difference that would inflame or divide society. Second, they also argued that a postgenocide Rwanda would benefit from having greater women's participation because women can serve as a moderating influence due to their more peaceful and reconciliatory nature.[224]

In Hong Kong, efforts to curtail domestic violence by men against women was framed not in feminist but rather in Confucian terms because, again, how successful a framing effort can be "depends on features of social class, gender, race, and ethnicity that make up the social hierarchies of modern states."[225] Battering was framed as something that was antithetical to Confucian ideas about marriage.

Relatedly, South Africa, for instance, has long had traditional tribal/customary courts coexisting with modern statutory courts.[226] In 2003, the South African Law Commission issued a report urging the expansion of customary courts.[227] The report recommended that the composition of the courts "be in accordance with the customary law of the area" but regard should be given to "the constitutional values of democracy and equality."[228] This approach recognizes that the vocabulary of human rights, democracy, and equality in this case can be localized and can be geared toward the realities on the ground locally to produce just outcomes.

Take again the example of footbinding in China. The practice arguably began fifteen hundred years after the death of Confucius.[229] Footbinding was a sign of elevated status.[230]

---

[222] *Women to Rule Rwanda Parliament*, BBC NEWS (Sept. 17, 2008, 12:40 PM), http://news.bbc.co.uk/2/hi/7620816.stm.

[223] *Id.*

[224] *See* Angela M. Banks, *Challenging Political Boundaries in Post-Conflict States*, 29 U. PA. J. INT'L L. 105, 157 (2007).

[225] MERRY, *supra* note 65, at 222.

[226] SOUTH AFRICAN LAW COMMISSION, PROJECT 90, CUSTOMARY LAW: REPORT ON TRADITIONAL COURTS AND JUDICIAL FUNCTIONS OF TRADITIONAL LEADERS (2003), *available at* http://www.justice.gov.za/salrc/reports/r_prj90_tradlead_2003jan.pdf.

[227] *Id.*

[228] *Id.* at xi.

[229] APPIAH, *supra* note 59, at 65.

[230] *Id.* at 65 (citing Howard Levy's study of footbinding and its role in Chinese society).

When the Qing dynasty came to power in 1644 it attempted to do away with the practice of footbinding. However the practice spread even further and became ever more entrenched.[231] The practice inflicted much pain but remained entrenched for over a millennium despite imperial edicts banning it.[232] Kwame Anthony Appiah argued that the practice fell out of favor (in part) because of China's engagement with the outside world during the late nineteenth century.[233] Even though Christian missionaries played a role in the end of the practice, members of the Chinese cultural elite argued for its end "because it was a source of national shame."[234] Put another way, footbinding was reframed to be against China's interests and honor in the international arena.[235] The mangled bound foot represented the sickly, decrepit state of China, while the natural foot represented the healthy future of China.[236] This strategic reframing of footbinding, along with heavy enforcement by the Chinese Communist Party, led to the practice's downfall.[237]

From these examples we can see that not only are cultures fluid but they are also changeable by internal and external participants often acting together. Authenticity, internalization, and adaptation all hinge on how a cultural issue is framed. In Rwanda, women and motherhood became frames for accepting women as political participants in postgenocide Rwanda. In South Africa, traditional courts and traditional narratives can be used to frame and apply just outcomes. In the waning days of the Qing dynasty, the progress of China as a power in Asia became a frame for analyzing the practice of footbinding. Without a doubt these changes had external stakeholders; however, to label these changes as inauthentic would be incorrect. These changes are organic, and as Appiah suggested, the proponents of these changes already existed within their respective cultures.[238] What changed was the strategic frame of the cultural practices in question.[239]

Analyzed in this light, culture ceases to be a pure and monolithic concept that is inherently resistant to change. Culture is fluid, fairly fungible, and exploitable. This definition of culture avoids the intractable problems created by a particularist definition while providing a solid foundation for further analysis. Whoever gains social control gains control of the cultural narrative and, in essence, gains control of the culture's frames. This allows them to redefine culture to be compatible with other ideologies, or compatible with nothing at all.[240] Lee Kuan Yew accomplished this when he claimed that Confucian values are

---

231 *Id.* at 69.

232 *Id.*

233 *Id.* at 82–83.

234 *Id.* at 91–92.

235 *Id.* at 92.

236 Wang Ping, Aching for Beauty: Footbinding in China 41 (2000).

237 Fan Hong, Footbinding, Feminism and Freedom: The Liberation of Women's Bodies in Modern China 198 (1997).

238 Appiah, *supra* note 59, at 71–72.

239 Banks, *supra* note 175, at 795.

240 Levitt & Merry, *supra* note 169, at 444–45.

inconsistent with Western ones.[241] No one could easily dispute him when "[c]ontradicting Lee became synonymous with being disloyal to Singapore."[242] Another tragic example comes from the Rwandan genocide. During the genocide, radio broadcasts from Radio Télévision Libre des Mille Collines (RTLM) urged the Hutu population to target and kill Tutsis.[243] The perpetrators of the genocide framed the cultural narrative in a very specific way; one which dehumanized Tutsis, placed Hutus as superior, and urged Hutus to "exterminate the cockroaches."[244] The notorious "Ten Hutu Commandments" were broadcast on RTLM during the killings, exhorting Hutus to shun, avoid, and eventually kill all Tutsis.[245] As one commentator has noted, "[the] media [is] manipulated into serving as instruments of political and ideological propaganda. This goes without saying. The electronic media in particular are in some cases fashioned into tools of terror. . . ." [246] None of the commandments actually call for the extermination of the Tutsi, but Hutu Commandment number 8 says, "The Bahutu [Hutu] should stop having mercy on the Batusti [Tutsi)."[247] Clearly the meaning of the eighth Hutu Commandment was not lost on the perpetrators of the genocide. However, as we have seen with the examples of Cyrus and Ashoka, using a cultural frame in a specific way can also achieve arguably positive social outcomes.

These examples illustrate why it is important to understand who controls the cultural narrative. Merry echoed Sen, arguing that we must pay attention to the question of who speaks for a culture and who gets to define what a culture's values are—in other words, it is important to know who controls the frame.[248] Understanding who controls what can fit into the cultural frame can help reveal where a cultural practice comes from, whom it hurts, whom it benefits, and why it exists. Resistance often materializes because the current (unfair) status quo benefits a vocal segment of a society, or a powerful segment of a society. What is claimed to be a culturally relative notion of justice is often specifically advantageous for certain groups or interests within a culture. What this chapter defends is culture change that promotes prevailing objectives of law and development as I have discussed throughout the book.

C. Responding to Critics of Culture Change

Assuming, as Part B does, that changing cultural norms is feasible, is it normatively defensible?

---

241 Merry, *supra* note 65, at 14.

242 McCarthy, *supra* note 131.

243 Russell Smith, *The Impact of Hate Media in Rwanda*, BBC News (Dec. 3, 2003), http://news.bbc.co.uk/2/hi/africa/3257748.stm.

244 *Id.*

245 Julienne Munyaneza, *Africa: Hate Media, Peace Media*, MEDIAFORUM, no. 3/4 2009, at 35, 37 (1999), *available at* http://www.cameco.org/mediaforum_pdf/mf_spe6.pdf.

246 *Id.* at 36.

247 *Id.* at 37.

248 Merry, *supra* note 65, at 16.

The West in particular has had a strained history with large parts of the developing world. As a result, some outreach campaigns by the West have been met with heavy skepticism. To point to a relatively small but well-known incident, Malawi was on the verge of famine for many years. After a corn harvest disaster in 2005, almost five million people needed emergency food aid. For almost two decades, the World Bank and Western countries on whom Malawi depended for aid pushed Malawi to eliminate fertilizer subsidies and rely on free market policies for the buying and selling of fertilizer, "even as the United States and Europe extensively subsidized their own farmers."[249] The resulting increase in fertilizer prices led to decreased usage of fertilizers, soil depletion, and food shortages.[250] But after the 2005 corn harvest disaster, the Malawi's government ignored pressure from the World Bank and Western countries and "decided to follow what the West practiced, not what it preached."[251] The government reinstated fertilizer subsidies. As of 2007, it is a net exporter of grain.[252] Indeed, "a nation that has perennially extended a begging bowl to the world is instead feeding its hungry neighbors. It is selling more corn to the World Food Program of the United Nations than any other country in southern Africa and is exporting hundreds of thousands of tons of corn to Zimbabwe."[253] "The country's successful use of subsidies is contributing to a broader reappraisal of the crucial role of agriculture in alleviating poverty in Africa and the pivotal importance of public investments in the basics of a farm economy: fertilizer, improved seed, farmer education, credit and agricultural research."[254]

The implications of the International Monetary Fund's failure in Malawi are numerous. If the West can't even get food distribution right, how can they tell anyone how to structure a government? Or more controversially, a culture? Instances like these help create skepticism about international programs spearheaded by the West. Often this skepticism is outright pessimism and mistrust—some groups still stinging from the colonial era are wary of trusting the West's overtures. Western help is seen as foreign domination by other means.

And yet, culture change for the purpose of achieving development objectives, as advocated by Sen and Appadurai and Nussbaum, is necessary and desirable. Return once more to Lee Kuan Yew who argued that Western values are inconsistent with Asian (specifically Confucian) values.[255] The unspoken assumption proffered by this argument is that an individual culture is "smooth"—as in there is little to no deviation from the cultural orthodoxy. Cultural differences come from outside influences, or so this argument

---

[249] Celia W. Dugger, *Ending Famine, Simply by Ignoring the Experts*, N.Y. Times, Dec. 2, 2007, http://www.nytimes.com/2007/12/02/world/africa/02malawi.html?hp.

[250] *Id.*

[251] *Id.*

[252] *Id.*

[253] *Id.*

[254] *Id.*

[255] Merry, *supra* note 65, at 14.

claims. This assumption about culture assumes that whoever is speaking for a certain culture (call it Culture A) is an accurate and complete representative of Culture A. In the case of Singapore, or at least Lee Kuan Yew, we are to take it at face value that Lee is accurately representing Asian values and their contrasts with Western values. From that narrow perspective, cultural diversity is lost when human rights are universalized without considering cultural ramifications.[256]

This position misrepresents and misunderstands culture. Indeed, as discussed in Chapter 2, even anthropologists who once saw culture as hermetically sealed and unchanging, reflecting distinct value systems of a nation, have now abandoned this rigid view of culture for something more nuanced and complex. Culture is no longer conceptualized as mere traditions and habits, which reflect an understanding of culture in static terms. "The contemporary anthropological understanding of culture envisions a far more fluid, contested, and changing set of values and practices than that provided by the idea of culture as tradition."[257] "Its boundaries are fluid, meanings are contested, and meaning is produced by institutional arrangements and political economy. Culture is marked by hybridity and creolization rather than uniformity or consistency. Local systems are analyzed in the context of national and transnational processes and are understood as the result of particular historical trajectories. This is a more dynamic, agentic, and historicized way of understanding culture."[258]

Indeed, because anthropologists have been heavily influenced by the processes of "modernization, colonialism, and globalization,"[259] they have "shifted their focus from studying distinct cultures that survive over time to the effects of *modernity* on internal processes of culture change."[260] Cultures mix, mingle, and borrow from each other. Culture change is a fact of the modern condition and the question is not whether it exists or occurs but how and when. This has important implications for the project I propose because if culture is contested, interpreted, and reinterpreted even by those within a culture, then anthropology (as well as law and development) should not be primarily concerned about preventing the dilution of or preserving cultural mores and tradition from change. In fact, unlike international law, anthropology has evolved to reflect a more nuanced and hybrid understanding of culture, not as something homogeneous and traditional, to be protected and insulated from unsavory forces internally and externally; nor, as discussed in Chapter 2, as something so messy, particularized, and politicized that it should be cabined from international markets or from the universalism of public international law. Like modern anthropology, law and development should similarly shed its traditional reluctance to engage with culture. Law and development should not ally itself

---

256 Sen, *supra* note 125, at 9.

257 Merry, *supra* note 6, at 67.

258 *Id.*

259 Sunder, *supra* note 108, at 77.

260 *Id.*

with cultural elites who oppose culture change in the name of cultural authenticity. It should understand that "rights can emerge through culture, not just in opposition to it. The strategic use of culture includes challenging the authority of cultural leaders who claim to speak for the community as a whole, as well as formulating new cultural conceptions that are compatible with modernity and human rights."[261] Hence the need for culture change.

Lee Kuan Yew's argument about Asian versus Western values is doubly ironic because Singapore, as one of the world's biggest port cities and a former colony, is a melting pot of different cultures. Singapore's population is an eclectic mix of cultures, languages and ethnicities.[262] Lee himself spoke English, Chinese, Malay, and Japanese.[263] It is impossible to distill a culture to its purest essence, or to identify which cultural aspects are truly authentic. Arguments like Lee's also miss what actually happens when cultures engage with new concepts and ideas. Certainly there can be resistance, and Merry argued that very often cultural reinterpretation of an international norm can be a barrier as well as an asset to culture change.[264] "Cultures are not . . . pure," Merry argued; they are formed by hybridization and creolization.[265]

In fact, cultures throughout history have evolved and their evolution can be traced to many causes, including foreign. Human beings borrow from each other, and what they borrow includes ideas. "The ideas of Marxism, which originated in the British Library, have influenced conduct in Cuba, China and Cambodia. The ideas of democracy, which are not original to China, are by now extremely important Chinese ideas. The ideas of Christianity, which originated in a dissident sect of Judaism in a small part of Asia Minor, have by now influenced conduct in every region of the globe, as have the ideas of Islam."[266] Timur Kuran argued that culture is a "living organism" subject to change. Mary Douglas went so far as to state that there is no such thing as "traditional culture," only a "dynamically interactive and developing sociopsychic system."[267] "The ideas of feminism, of democracy, of egalitarian welfarism, are now 'inside' every known society."[268] Indeed, even encounters initially viewed as threats may transform one's very perceptions and preferences. Something deemed foreign in origin may in fact be adopted as domestic and indigenous over time; Turks, for example, no longer view as un-Turklike French transplants such as specialized secular courts to hear commercial disputes.[269] Although

---

[261] Sunder, *supra* note 108, at 83.

[262] Pankaj Mishra, *Beyond the Melting Pot*, N.Y. TIMES, May 22, 2011, at M2.

[263] McCarthy, *supra* note 131.

[264] MERRY, *supra* note 65, at 16.

[265] *Id.* at 15.

[266] NUSSBAUM, *supra* note 4, at 48–49.

[267] *See* Douglas, *supra* note 153, at 88.

[268] NUSSBAUM, *supra* note 4, at 49.

[269] Kuran, *supra* note 142, at 131–32; Sen, *supra* note 113, at 49. *See also* Niezen, *supra* note 117, at 2.

chili is not an indigenous Indian spice but was brought to India by the Portuguese in the sixteenth century, it is now considered very much Indian.[270]

As Sen remarked, culture is not "independent, unchanging and unchangeable" and is instead quite "nonhomogeneous, nonstatic, and interactive."[271] It is often presumed when referring to a particular culture, "Indonesian," for example, that it is homogeneous and monolithic. Yet, history shows the opposite in many cases. Indonesian history reveals not just Islamic tradition but strong Hindu, Buddhist, and Confucian cultural presence and influence.[272] Similarly, contrary to claims by Hindu nationalists, India has had a long history of cultural diversity—a thousand years of Buddhist dominance, with Christian presence since the fourth century and Parsees and Muslims since the eighth. Thus, even when one invokes a national culture as an identity issue to be defended, it is important to realize that the term often embodies great historical variations and heterogeneity even within an individual culture itself.[273]

Culture has historically been "nonstatic and interactive" and even all the more so in today's globalized world. Cultural interactions are increasing and cultural barriers collapsing. A noted anthropologist accurately described the modern world as one no longer "tightly territorialized, spatially bounded . . . [and] culturally homogeneous."[274] Thus, "the boundaries of cultural systems are leaky, and that traffic and osmosis are the norm, not the exception."[275] It is not only historically that cultures accumulate like layers of an onion onto a particular national identity—with Hinduism, Buddhism, Islam, for example, embedded in a span of several centuries in India. In today's world, borders are porous, communication fast and furious, and cultures, already less homogeneous than fundamentalists claim, collide. Cultures move and interact and from this process, undergo change. Indeed, as I showed in Chapter 2, opponents of globalization recognize and rail against this basic fact, condemning, for example, the World Trade Organization (WTO) and its "unprecedented powers . . . to rule on whether laws of nations—concerning public health, food safety, . . . culture, human rights, or anything—are 'barriers to trade' by WTO standards."[276] Modern cultures are characterized by cracks, fissures, change, and transformation. As Salman Rushdie described the mongrelized selves spawned from this modern condition:

[270] Sen, *supra* note 113, at 44.

[271] *Id.*

[272] *Id.* at 42.

[273] *Id.* at 43 ("Cultural determinists often underestimate the extent of heterogeneity within what is taken to be 'one' distinct culture.").

[274] Arjun Appadurai, Modernity at Large: Cultural Dimensions of Globalization 48 (1996).

[275] Appadurai, *supra* note 56, at 61.

[276] Lan Cao, *Corporate and Product Identity in the Post-National Economy: Rethinking U.S. Trade Laws*, 90 Calif. L. Rev. 401, 425 (2002).

> I was born an Indian, and not only an Indian, but a Bombayite—Bombay, most cosmopolitan, most hybrid, most hotchpotch of Indian cities. My writing and thought have therefore been as deeply influenced by Hindu myths and attitudes as Muslim ones . . . Nor is the West absent from Bombay. I was already a mongrel self, history's bastard, before London aggravated the condition.[277]

That culture exhibits cracks and fissures should not be surprising because despite the facade of unity and homogeneity, "dissensus . . . is part and parcel of culture and that a shared culture is no more a guarantee of complete consensus than a shared platform in the democratic convention."[278] Traditional communities are "internally contested, heterogeneous, and constantly evolving over time through internal debate and interaction with outsiders."[279] For example, protests by Indian women against male oppression is not a recent or Western-induced phenomenon. It is, rather, "a very old theme in Indian tradition, going straight back to Draupadi's eloquent protest against sexual harassment in Mahabharata, book 2"[280] when she managed to keep herself fully clothed by miraculously growing new yards of cloth on her sari despite persistent attempts to undress her. The women of SEWA (Self-Employed Women's Organization),[281] particularly its founder, find inspiration in this tale of women's protest and human dignity.

If Draupadi's protest against sexual harassment—the miraculous lengthening of her sari—is deemed problematic because it is arguably based on the deep-seated custom of female purity, one can find other forms of female protest, in both Hindu and Muslim traditions, that are founded on norms of female independence. For example, in a story by the Indian writer, the Nobel Laureate Rabindranath Tagore, the heroine, Mrinal, left her husband and in the process, invoked a historical figure in Indian history, the sixteenth-century Rajput queen Meerabai who also left her royal marriage to become a singer to sing "joyfully rebellious songs."[282]

Similar protests can be found in the Muslim tradition as well. Muslim feminist Rokeya Sakhawat Mossain's work, *The Sultana's Dream*, published in 1905, suggested that men should be in purdah, not women, because those who do harm are the ones that should be put in seclusion.[283]

Religious traditions can also be a source of freedom even for women. As Nussbaum explained, "[r]eligious traditions have indeed been powerful sources of oppression for women; but they have also been powerful sources of protection for human rights, of

---

[277] SALMAN RUSHDIE, *In Good Faith*, *in* IMAGINARY HOMELANDS 393, 404 (1991).

[278] Appadurai, *supra* note 56, at 61.

[279] Sunder, *supra* note 111, at 1403.

[280] NUSSBAUM, *supra* note 4, at 44.

[281] *See* Chapter 5 for a discussion of SEWA and its role in culture change projects.

[282] NUSSBAUM, *supra* note 4, at 44–45.

[283] *Id.* at 45–46.

commitment to justice, and of energy for social change."[284] In the same way that there is much cultural dissent, there is also religious dissent. There is diversity of beliefs and dissent within every religious tradition, from Judaism to Roman Catholicism to Hinduism and Islam.[285] For example, Mahatma Gandhi himself considered the essence of Hinduism to be "the pursuit of truth by nonviolent means," which in turn provides the foundation upon which Hindus and others can launch a concerted effort to eradicate the caste hierarchy.[286]

That culture (and religious tradition) is not only about affiliation or loyalty but also about dissensus or dissent[287] suggests that culture may be challenged by members who seek to contest and reinterpret traditional cultural norms.[288] What these challengers of cultural orthodoxy need is support from, not marginalization by, the international community.

Indeed, it is significant that often, critics are not foreigners but "natives" who inhabit the tradition but wish to push against its constraining boundaries. Many are women who are "claiming their rights to challenge religious and cultural authorities"[289] and "demanding more reason, choice, liberty, and equality within their religious and cultural communities."[290] What constitutes "tradition" is often oversimplified. Traditionalist purveyors of so-called authentic cultural norms often suppress "countertraditions of female defiance and strength,"[291] creating the impression that the historical context has been smooth and frictionless. Dissenters are also seeking to have law recognize their claim for dissent and their struggle for change within their normative community. For example, "the claims of women reformers in Muslim communities offer important new takes on traditional law and its attendant notions of cultural relativism, multiculturalism, [and] imposed identity. . . ."[292]

Thus, these dissenters reject "culturally relativist arguments that cultural groups ought to be let alone and allowed to continue their discriminatory ways. . . ."[293] Their struggle is one for voice and loyalty within a culture, not exit from it. In other words, as Madhavi

---

[284] NUSSBAUM, *supra* note 4, at 178.

[285] For a brief account of the variations of dissent within these religious traditions, *see* NUSSBAUM, *supra* note 4, at 181–87.

[286] NUSSBAUM, *supra* note 4, at 222.

[287] Appadurai, *supra* note 56, at 61.

[288] Sunder, *supra* note 115, at 498. *See also* Seyla Benhabib, *Cultural Complexity, Moral Interdependence, and the Global Dialogical Community*, *in* WOMEN, CULTURE, AND DEVELOPMENT: A STUDY OF HUMAN CAPABILITIES 240 (Martha C. Nussbaum & Jonathan Glover eds., 1995); Thomas L. Friedman, Op-Ed., *Brave, Young and Muslim*, N.Y. TIMES, Mar. 3, 2005, at A31, *available at* http://www.nytimes.com/2005/03/03/opinion/03friedman.html?_r=0.

[289] Sunder, *supra* note 111, at 1403.

[290] *Id.* at 1408.

[291] NUSSBAUM, *supra* note 4, at 42.

[292] Sunder, *supra* note 111, at 1457.

[293] *Id.* at 1458.

Sunder coined the term, these are "cultural dissenters"[294] who believe that "traditional liberalism takes too lightly the ease of exit from one's community"[295] and thus wish to stay within their culture and community but seek more voice within it. Shirin Ebadi, for example, received the Nobel Peace Prize in 2003 for her efforts to achieve freedom and equality for women within Islamic Iran.[296] As Ebadi wrote in her book, "[i]n the last twenty-three years, from the day I was stripped of my judgeship to the years doing battle in the revolutionary courts of Tehran, I had repeated one refrain: an interpretation of Islam that is in harmony with equality and democracy is an authentic expression of faith. It is not religion that binds women, but the selective dictates of those who wish them cloistered. That belief, along with the conviction that change in Iran must come peacefully and from within, has underpinned my work."[297]

Ironically, although nationalists are obsessed with defending traditional cultures from Western encroachment and see their anti-Western posture as bravely standing up to Western domination, the nationalist position is in fact "deeply foreign-dependent—in a negative and contrary form."[298] In other words, by reflexively opposing the West, this movement ironically defines itself as the "Other," that which the West is not. In this way, it is not much different from the phenomenon Edward Said critiqued in Orientalism, in which the East is seen by the West as the West's negative Other. In the language of today's nationalists, local culture or national culture is to be heralded and protected from its Western Other. Indeed, local culture is reflexively understood to be oppositional to or different from whatever Western culture is deemed to be. As Sen observed, however, this is hardly a trend to be celebrated. Quite simply, "seeing oneself as 'the other' does less than justice to one's free and deliberative agency."[299]

Exclusion of so-called foreign cultural influences also results in fewer choices for the local citizenry. Under the banner of protecting local culture, these defenders "rule out certain choices, on traditionalist grounds, because of their 'foreignness' (irrespective of what people decide to choose, in an informed and reflected way)."[300] Citizens thus are denied the exercise of cultural options by "political authorities, or by religious establishments, or by grand guardians of taste."[301]

---

[294] Sunder, *supra* note 115, at 498–551.

[295] Sunder, *supra* note 111, at 1409.

[296] *See Shirin Ebadi Fast Facts*, CNN (Dec. 18, 2014, 6:23 PM), http://www.cnn.com/2013/01/01/world/meast/shirin-ebadi---fast-facts.

[297] Shirin Ebadi with Azadeh Moaveni, Iran Awakening: A Memoir of Revolution and Hope 204 (2006). For additional examples of internal challenges to cultural orthodoxy, *see also* UN Dev. Programme, Arab Human Development Report 2003: Building a Knowledge Society 121 (2003) (proclaiming pluralism to be vital to human development); Friedman, *supra* note 288; Neil MacFarquhar, *Unexpected Whiff of Freedom Proves Bracing for the Mideast*, N.Y. Times, Mar. 6, 2005, at A1.

[298] Sen, *supra* note 113, at 54.

[299] *Id.*

[300] *Id.* at 53.

[301] *Id.*

This understanding of culture as pure, immutable, and homogeneous is radically different from the view of culture as dynamic and internally heterogeneous. Law and development should not start from the assumption that traditional culture is monolithic and incontestable; or that contesting tradition is illegitimate because the desired values are deemed foreign. Indeed, to do so would be to concede, falsely, that certain values, such as egalitarianism, are external and hence alien to certain societies;[302] or that certain societies are uniformly characterized by certain values only and not other values.[303] Critics of the international human rights movement have argued that the very notion of rights is itself a Western concept. But although it is true that "rights" per se are associated with the European Enlightenment, it is not true that the underlying components of the movement exist only in the West. This assumption that the world is divided into "impenetrable civilizational camps" viewed in oppositional terms, such as an Islamic versus a Western camp, obscures the fact that certain values are shared by both.[304] Indeed, many ideas associated with the international human rights movement have roots in many traditions.[305]

Other societies, for example, have had a history of celebrating religious freedom, tolerance, and pluralism. Even separate and apart from the validation of rights language in India's constitution, the principle of religious freedom developed much earlier in Indian thinking. In the third century BC, Emperor Ashoka renounced armed conquest after witnessing the carnage caused when his army conquered Kalinga country and adopted Buddhism, mandating a policy of respect toward all religious sects and guaranteeing them the freedom to live in accordance with their own religious principles. Emperor Ashoka also exhorted his officials to adopt the principles of judicial independence and impartiality when dispensing justice. He appointed "dharma ministers" to do good work, pushing them to pay attention to the needs of women and those in marginal communities, particularly religious communities.[306]

In the 1500s, Akbar, a Muslim emperor of India, for example, ordered that no one "should be interfered with on account of religion" and that "anyone is to be allowed to go over to a religion that pleases him."[307] During his reign, marriages between Muslims and Hindus were permitted without requiring Hindus to renounce their religion. Hindus

---

302 Sunder, *supra* note 144, at 891–92.

303 Amartya Sen, Op-Ed, *A World Not Neatly Divided*, N.Y. TIMES, Nov. 23, 2001, at A39, *available at* http://www.nytimes.com/2001/11/23/opinion/a-world-not-neatly-divided.html.

304 *Id.*

305 NUSSBAUM, *supra* note 4, at 99 & n.117.

306 Amulya Chandra Sen, *Ashoka*, ENCYCLOPEDIA BRITTANICA, http://www.britannica.com/EBchecked/topic/38797/Ashoka (last visited May 5, 2015); *Rulers, Policy, and Empire: The Edicts of Asoka*, BILL OF RIGHTS IN ACTION (Const. Rts. Found., L.A. Cal.), Fall 1998, *available at* http://www.crf-usa.org/bill-of-rights-in-action/bria-14-4-b-the-edicts-of-asoka. *See also* Edict XII of Ashoka, quoted in NUSSBAUM, *supra* note 4, at 195 (ordering that "the sects of other people all deserve reverence for one reason or another. By thus acting, a man exalts his own sect, and at the same time does service to the sects of other people.").

307 Sen, *supra* note 303. *See also* JAVAID REHMAN, THE WEAKNESSES IN THE INTERNATIONAL PROTECTION OF MINORITY RIGHTS 36 (2000).

were promoted to positions of authority within the administration. To demonstrate respect to Hindus, laws were passed to prohibit the slaughter of cows. Akbar's actions were in accordance with the principle of Sulaakins, enshrining universal tolerance and respect for the rights of all, regardless of religion and creed. During the same time period in the 1590s, Europe was in the midst of the Inquisitions. Given this history, it would be inaccurate to characterize pluralism as solely a Western value[308] and to reject attempts to influence the development of pluralism in Muslim societies as illegitimate external imposition.[309] The point is this: Not only is pluralism part of Islam's history, it is currently part of the "internal struggle within Islam to re-examine its texts and articulate a path for how one can accept pluralism and modernity."[310]

Many women in the Muslim world, for example, strive to promote liberty and democracy on the basis that those principles have universal appeal. There are many works that have explored the universality of basic human rights and have shown that "human rights are not a set of imposed western ideas, but are of universal application, speaking to the human condition."[311] Kofi Annan, former Secretary-General of the United Nations, bemoaned "the idea that different societies and cultures view fundamental human rights differently" and characterized it as "truly demeaning. . . of the yearning for human dignity that resides in every African heart."[312] Are notions of equality and liberty alien to a country if those notions have been incorporated into the constitution of that country, as it has, for example, into the Indian constitution?[313] The founders of India's constitution included basic liberties and principles of equality, including women's equality, into the constitution not because they were colonial values but because they are human values. Nehru declared that "it is the inalienable right of the Indian people, as of any other people, to have freedom. . . ."[314]

The drafters of India's constitution, for example, viewed certain basic values as universal and worked to incorporate egalitarian and pluralistic commitments into the governing document. The constitution of India incorporated rights and reflected values that were drawn from so many constitutions in the world that it prompted some critics to charge that as such, it "will 'break down soon after being brought into operation.'"[315] But many of India's constitution drafters insisted that "India should be rightfully able to

---

308 *See generally* NOAH FELDMAN, AFTER JIHAD: AMERICA AND THE STRUGGLE FOR ISLAMIC DEMOCRACY (2003).

309 Noah Feldman, *Imposed Constitutionalism*, 37 CONN. L. REV. 857, 888 (2005).

310 Thomas L. Friedman, Op-Ed, *Foreign Affairs; The Real War*, N.Y. TIMES, Nov. 27, 2001, at A19, *available at* http://www.nytimes.com/2001/11/27/opinion/foreign-affairs-the-real-war.html.

311 THOMAS M. FRANCK, THE EMPOWERED SELF: LAW AND SOCIETY IN AN AGE OF INDIVIDUALISM 148 (1999).

312 *Id.*

313 NUSSBAUM, *supra* note 4, at 37.

314 *Id.* at 39 n.9.

315 Sunder, *supra* note 144, at 899.

benefit from the world's intellectual heritage."[316] Whether a precedent or value is foreign isn't as important as whether it is a desirable one. "What the Indian Constitutionalists recognized is that the Enlightenment ideals of democracy, equality, reason, and dissent are not and cannot be the intellectual properties of Western nations alone, but are rightfully the treasures of the world."[317] In this sense, culture is understood and judged not by its source or geography but "by its manifest use and enjoyment."[318]

After many years of field studies on women's rights in developing countries, Martha Nussbaum remarked that "we can hardly be charged with imposing a foreign set of values upon individuals or groups if what we are doing is providing support for basic capacities and opportunities that are involved in the selection of any flourishing life and then leaving people to choose for themselves how they will pursue flourishing."[319] Her conclusion is that "[a]ny universalism that has a chance to be persuasive in the modern world must . . . be a form of political liberalism."[320] Different cultural communities may find that these principles of justice, equality, and democracy resonate differently within their specific cultural context and may "seek to apply these concepts within explicitly religious and cultural contexts."[321] Indeed, "attunement to cultural variety and particularity"[322] is important to avoid mistakes. For example, the assumption, often a Western assumption, that the nuclear family is foundational would not hold true in societies where group membership is paramount. Development projects that ignore the local tradition of "female group solidarity" may be blind to the economic and cultural potential of creating or facilitating women's collectives,[323] which can be potent platforms for women's empowerment.

However, although one undoubtedly needs to be aware of local arrangements, local varieties, and local history, sensitivity to local variations does not mean that there are no universal values or basic norms, such as "the dignity of the person, the integrity of the body, basic political rights and liberties, basic economic opportunities, and so forth."[324]

The ultimate issue is not whether a value is internal or external to a society, or promoted by insiders or outsiders. Salman Rushdie put it this way:

> [I]f by chance there were a universal value that might, for the sake of argument, be called freedom, whose enemies—tyranny, bigotry, intolerance, fanaticism—were the enemies of us all; and if this "freedom" were discovered to exist in greater quantity in the countries of the West than anywhere else on earth; and if, in the world

---

[316] *Id.*
[317] *Id.*
[318] Sen, *supra* note 113, at 54.
[319] Martha C. Nussbaum, Sex and Social Justice 9 (1999).
[320] *Id.* at 9.
[321] Sunder, *supra* note 111, at 1459.
[322] Nussbaum, *supra* note 4, at 40.
[323] *Id.*
[324] *Id.* at 41.

as it actually exists rather than in some unattainable Utopia, the authority of the United States were the best current guarantor of that "freedom"; then might it not follow that to oppose the spread of American culture would be to take up arms against the wrong foe?[325]

Similarly, as Rabindranath Tagore, who received the Nobel Prize in literature in 1913 put it: "Whatever we understand and enjoy in human products instantly becomes ours, wherever they might have their origin. I am proud of my humanity when I can acknowledge the poets and artists of other countries as my own. Let me feel with unalloyed gladness that all the great glories of man are mine."[326] Referring to Tagore, Amartya Sen noted the following: "His universalist, tolerant and rationalist ideals were a strong influence on my thinking, and I often recollect them in these divisive times."[327] Tagore firmly believed in the "non fragility" of Indian culture, that it was broad and of many parts, each related to and influenced by the other. Tagore, said Sen, did not believe that there was a conflict between the cultures and civilizations of the East and the West, and opposed barring outside influence.[328] After all, "[t]he exclusion of slaves in one society, untouchables in another, and women in still another may be much harder to sustain when other societies show the way to different types of social arrangements."[329]

---

[325] SALMAN RUSHDIE, STEP ACROSS THIS LINE: COLLECTED NONFICTION 1992–2002, at 268–69 (2002).

[326] Amartya Sen, *Tagore and His India*, NOBEL PRIZE (Aug. 28, 2001), http://www.nobelprize.org/nobel_prizes/literature/laureates/1913/tagore-article.html.

[327] Amartya Sen, Banquet Speech at the Nobel Banquet (Dec. 10, 1998), http://www.nobelprize.org/nobel_prizes/economics/laureates/1998/sen-speech_en.html. *See also* Parvathi Menon, *A Special Homecoming*, FRONTLINE (Jan. 2–15, 1999), http://www.frontline.in/static/html/fl1601/16011300.htm.

[328] Sen, *supra* note 327.

[329] Martha C. Nussbaum & Amartya Sen, *Internal Criticism and Indian Rationalist Traditions*, *in* RELATIVISM, INTERPRETATION AND CONFRONTATION 299, 320 (Michael Krausz ed., 1989).

Conclusion

IN MANY WAYS, this is a pessimistic book. Law and development has been marred by failures. There are many reasons for such failures. Volumes of books and articles have attempted to explain the rise and fall of the field. Few, however, have looked at the neglect of culture by the field as a significant reason, though certainly not the only reason, for its failures. Chapter 1 of this book examined the field's history, showing that law and development has ignored culture and opted to focus on more quantifiable factors instead. Much of law and development has historically been about legal transplantation—legal development inspired and implemented by importing foreign laws into developing countries. Scholars and practitioners of the field favor this approach in the hope that legal development is either a good in itself or that it can serve to facilitate or foster other forms of development—for example, economic and political development.

The first wave of law and development, which was birthed during the Cold War period of the 1960s, focused on legal development and the role of law in the political and economic development of Third World states. The hope was that the state would be a partner in the political and economic development of the country. Law reform such as the institution of contract and property laws was seen as necessary to support markets and consequently economic growth. The first wave received funding from many sources, such as national governments and financial institutions. "Law and development was part of the West's answer to communism, part of the promise, often not fulfilled, that a Western-led economic system could deliver economic growth with freedom."[1] For reasons discussed

[1] David Trubek, *The "Rule of Law" in Development Assistance: Past, Present, and Future*, *in* THE NEW LAW AND ECONOMIC DEVELOPMENT: A CRITICAL APPRAISAL 74, 82 (David M. Trubek & Alvaro Santos eds., 2006).

in Chapter 1, the first wave's promises failed to deliver. Legal transplantation did not yield legal development, market development, or political development. Authoritarian governments used law to entrench themselves and legal liberalism failed to take root in Third World countries. First wave scholars bemoaned the field's naiveté and ethnocentricism.

The first wave, however, implicitly adopted many of the assumptions of modernization theory which guided the works of first wave scholars. This included the notion that the implementation of modern laws required more than just wholesale transplantation of Western laws into the Third World. It necessarily required something deeper, for example, changing the legal culture of Third World legal systems, so that laws are not formalistically and mechanically implemented. For law to have an instrumental component and serve a desired instrumental purpose, legal culture should be changed. The first wave of law and development at least addressed the importance of culture as undergirding law, although its focus was limited to legal culture. The first wave also understood, correctly, that law and development is a long-term project, not always amenable to benchmarks and yardsticks nor is it subject to quick solutions.

The second wave of law and development began with the demise of the Soviet Union and the collapse of the Berlin Wall. It ushered in a frantic new effort to bring formerly Communist countries into the Western, capitalist fold. This involved decentralizing the state, liberalizing the economy, and strengthening institutions. Good governance and democracy-building initiatives were crucial to second wave development projects. While the first wave should be understood within the context of the Cold War, the second wave should be understood within the context of the post-Soviet era. While the first wave focused on the state's role in development, formal laws, and legal culture, the second wave focused on decentralizing the state, supplementing the development of formal laws with the development of formal institutions and ensuring that post-Communist states are integrated into the global market. The World Bank's Comprehensive Development Framework also expanded the development framework, emphasizing linkages between the political and economic (though not explicitly cultural) dimensions of development.

Following the first and second waves of law and development, noted scholars from other fields such as the economist Amartya Sen, the philosopher Martha Nussbaum, and the anthropologist Arjun Appadurai, among others, argue for a more holistic understanding of development. Whereas legal scholars have adopted a law-centrality approach to development, others have proposed studying the interrelationship between the different spheres of development—economic, political, legal, social, and cultural. Under this view, development is to be thickly understood to encompass not just the institution of formal laws and institutions but also human rights and poverty reduction. Sen, Nussbaum, and Appadurai favor inserting a culturally based inquiry into development; they understand that development is not just a legal process but also a cultural one. Sen and Nussbaum stake their view of human development on a capability approach which asks not what people want or prefer (as preferences are problematic indicators of the good life); what resources they consume; but rather, what certain indicators reveal about human capability, that is, whether they promote and expand, or denigrate and restrict, human capability. Indeed, their works provide direct support for the main thesis proposed in this book: that cultural norms have an impact on development and that those cultural norms which perpetuate underdevelopment should be addressed.

This observation, however, is highly controversial. There are at least two reasons for this controversy—one is from a disciplinary standpoint and the second is from a normative standpoint. From a disciplinary standpoint, law and development has long neglected culture, and this neglect, as I have shown in the book, is the result of entrenched disciplinary biases. I have provided several explanations for the utter neglect of culture in the law and development field. First, other scholarly fields that are most directly connected to law and development have systematically shunned culture. International law, including specifically public international law and private international law, has historically avoided dealing with culture. For public international law, culture is something that is subsumed within each state's domestic jurisdiction. Public international law is supposed to articulate universal rules and standards applicable to the entire community of nations; as culture is particularistic, reflecting individual state's history and tradition, public international law believes that it should abstain from culture. Cultural issues are thus deemed to be within the domestic jurisdiction of member states and, for the most part, beyond the reach of international law.

Private international law, or international economic law, also disregards culture, but on different grounds. Private international law is about business and economics; its stated aim is to establish an international economic framework that is stable, predictable, and rational. To the extent that culture is generally considered "messy," nontangible, or arbitrary, inherited and not freely chosen, it is not equated with rationality and thus not a matter private international law wishes to address or incorporate in its domain. To the contrary, private international law would prefer that culture be "cabined" and segregated from economic deliberations.

Law and development as a scholarly field inherits the framework erected by international law and thus is similarly reluctant to address cultural issues. In addition, most law and development scholars are from the liberal or critical tradition and thus are all too aware of the, at best, historical attempts to belittle non-European cultures, thus laying the foundation for a "blame-the-culture" school of development, that is, an assertion that culture is everything and history, politics, for example, count for little in explaining underdevelopment in the Third World.

International neglect of culture has paradoxically extended even into the field of international human rights. Although international human rights has managed to pierce the veil of state sovereignty, it has not done so with respect to the veil of culture. Thus, even though certain human rights violations are rooted in cultural traditions, international human rights law has not confronted such violations because it wishes to sidestep cultural issues. Such traditions must be altered. Ratified by more than 185 states, the Convention on the Elimination of All Forms of Discrimination Against Women (CEDAW), for example, requires that signatory states promote equality by passing any necessary laws to eliminate discrimination against women and to promote the principle of the equality of men and women.[2] But it also requires states to "modify the social and cultural patterns of conduct of men and women, with a view to achieving the elimination of prejudices and customary and all other practices which are based on the idea of the inferiority or the superiority of either of the sexes. . . ."[3] Indeed, the fact that CEDAW itself explicitly obligates ratifying states to take steps to change cultural patterns of conduct that contribute to the inequality of women shows that the notion of culture change itself is normatively acceptable and necessary in international law. CEDAW, however, ironically also allows ratifying states to exempt themselves from taking such changes on cultural grounds. As I have argued in the book, this very paradoxical stance contained in CEDAW is emblematic and reflective of how international human rights (and international law) have negotiated the explosive issue of culture.

Because international law has had such an ambivalent if not troubled relationship with culture, there has been much resistance to incorporating culture into the field of international law and related subfields—international human rights, international relations, and law and development. Thus, I devoted two chapters to exploring this issue. Chapter 2 showed that public and private international law and international relations have sidestepped and marginalized culture from their scholarly frames, focusing on states, state power, and state sovereignty. Chapter 2 also discussed how private international law relegated culture to the margin, developing rules that predominantly address markets instead. It is important to understand the degree to which aculturalism is entrenched in these scholarly disciplines. A proposal that runs head-on against the deeply entrenched historical inclinations of the field will be met with much resistance from those within the field.

Nonetheless, international law is not static. Chapter 4 showed that both international law and international relations have evolved from their initial preoccupations with state power and state sovereignty to include an array of other concerns, for example, human rights, environment, trade, and other nonsecurity issues. Values and norms which previously were outside the lens of international law and relations are now increasingly incorporated. A more pluralist vision of international law has emerged via the New Haven School of international law. Various theories within the field of international relations focus on norms and the process of norm change, demonstrating that even hard-core concerns such as power and security are informed and influenced by the values and norms that constitute a particular state's sense of identity. Correspondingly, although states remain the central actors in international law and international relations, other actors have been ushered onto the international stage. Non-state actors such as nongovernmental

---

[2] Convention on the Elimination of All Forms of Discrimination Against Women (CEDAW), art. 2, 1249 U.N.T.S. 13 (1979).

[3] *Id.* at art. 5.

organizations (NGOs), individuals, and commercial actors are all significant players with the capacity to engage state actors and, in the process, participate in the evolution of international norms. The Red Cross, for example, was instrumental in shaping the norms that underlie the now widely accepted Geneva Conventions. The World Bank under its President Robert McNamara successfully pushed against a state-centric view of development to promote antipoverty norms, challenging the then prevailing notion that states and their core economic interests are central to the development process.

Changes within international law have created openings that accommodate a more robust incorporation of norms into the field. By showing that international law has evolved and by showing that non-state actors are now significant players in the discipline, I argue that from a disciplinary standpoint, the inclusion of cultural values and norms into the framework of international law and law and development should not be deemed heretical. Indeed, my argument goes further than simply cultural inclusion. The arguments laid out in Chapter 4 which demonstrate that the scope of international law has expanded to include norms and values also demonstrate that such norms and values have changed and evolved over the years. Countless works have dissected the formation of custom in customary international law. States have consciously strived to alter custom and to influence the evolution of custom. Constructivist theory and other theories, such as the norm-cycle theory of international relations have shown how international norms have been changed by states and even non-state actors. In this way, Chapter 4 supports the argument that culture can be not only included in the international law and law and development framework but can also be changed. As the boundaries between the domestic and the international have blurred, transnational networks of international and domestic actors often operate at both domestic and international levels, sometimes pushing states to adopt new norms or new custom, other times working in conjunction with states to diffuse universal norms into the subnational sphere to trigger domestic culture change. Consequently, insights from international law and international relations regarding how international custom and international norms have evolved are useful for the culture change project advocated in this book.

Although openings and developments in international law should now support the inclusion of culture, norms, and values in international law and related fields, such as law and development, there is still resistance to the notion that any culture should be evaluated, much less changed. It is one thing to examine culture; it is another to take the position proposed in this book—to change culture.

Indeed, when one advocates for a culturally informed framework, or when one argues that culture should be engaged, what is usually meant is the need to be cognizant of or to take into account local culture, not to disrupt it, critically examine it, or transform aspects of it. There are indeed many good reasons for the need to be "culturally sensitive." For example, because culture influences how receptive a society is to outside efforts at legal transplantation, it is important to take into consideration local cultures. Local communities should be brought into the development process, from the planning stages to the implementation stages. The intended recipients of development efforts should ideally be not just passive recipients but active participants as well, as partners with a significant voice in the agenda-setting dimensions of reform. Naturally, community buy-in is important. Participatory development is important, not just because bottom-up participation is normatively good but also because it is more likely to yield positive results. Thus, these observations seem obvious and intuitive. Why impose top down when the alternative, bottom-up or grassroots reform, is likely to be more just and more effective?

A study conducted by Daniel Berkowitz regarding the effectiveness of legal transplant efforts regularly promoted by law and development concluded as follows:

> Our basic argument is that for legal institutions to be effective, a demand for law must exist so that the law on the books will actually be used in practice and legal intermediaries responsible for developing the law are responsive to this demand. If the transplant adapted the law to local conditions, or had a population that was already familiar with basic legal principles of the transplanted law, then we could expect that the law would be used. However, if the law was not adapted to local conditions, or if it was imposed via colonization and the population within the transplant was not familiar with the law, then we would expect that initial demand for using these laws to [*sic*] be weak.[4]

This intuition is supported by the work of the economist Dani Rodrik as well. Professor Rodrik stated that external blueprints should not be rigidly applied. Instead, law and development projects should tap into local knowledge and encourage local participation and local experimentation.[5] Similarly, Michael Trebilcock and Kevin Davis observed that "optimal institutions generally, including legal institutions in particular, will often be importantly shaped by factors specific to given societies, including history, culture, and long-established political and institutional traditions. This in turn implies some degree of modesty on the part of the external community in promoting rule of law or other legal reforms in developing countries and correspondingly a larger role for 'insiders' with detailed local knowledge."[6]

Indeed, projects that bypass local communities are doomed to fail and stories about their spectacular failures abound. As I described in my novel *Monkey Bridge*,[7] an American-funded development project donated modern stoves to peasants in a village

---

[4] Daniel Berkowitz et al., *Economic Development, Legality, and the Transplant Effect*, 47 Eur. Econ. Rev. 165, 166–67 (2003).

[5] Dani Rodrik, *Institutions for High-Quality Growth: What They Are and How to Acquire Them*, 35 Stud. Comp. Int'l. Dev. 3, 3–31 (2000).

[6] Kevin E. Davis & Michael J. Trebilcock, *The Relationship Between Law and Development: Optimists Versus Skeptics*, 56 Am. J. Comp. L. 895, 945 (2008).

[7] Lan Cao, Monkey Bridge 238 (1998).

in the Mekong Delta as part of the effort to win "hearts and minds." The stoves the peasants had been using were old, traditional clay stoves that emitted a lot of smoke. The new stoves, sleek and metallic, emitted much less smoke. The Americans left after giving a lecture about the new and improved stoves to a seemingly receptive audience. But when they returned to the village a few months later, they discovered that their new stoves lay in an abandoned heap. After a period of astonishment and dismay, they learned that the villagers had discarded the modern stoves because people in the Mekong Delta lived in thatched huts. Their roofs were made of thatch, not tiles or corrugated steel. Smoke and fumes from their old stoves had a fumigating effect. Smoke killed termites and other pests that thrived in the roofs. The new stoves emitted no smoke. Termites were not exterminated and survived to destroy their roofs and even the structures of their houses.

If someone had talked to the villagers and found out what they needed, rather than given them expensive stoves they didn't want or need because the stoves were not the right stoves given the circumstances of their living condition, a different project could have been conceived and implemented.

If something as seemingly simple as donating new stoves is so riddled with complications and unintended consequences, then one would expect that the law and development business of exporting laws will not be without complications. And if exporting laws is uncomplicated, exporting self-proclaimed universal norms of human rights, women's rights, equality, and economic and political development seem all the more difficult and complicated.

This book, however, has shown that culture does indeed influence development. Culture has market as well as human rights implications, particularly for women and the poor. If that premise is accepted, then the question should be, how could law and development *not* be concerned with culture?

As I noted in the Introduction, that cultural norms have an impact on law and development, even if one subscribes to a thin conception of the rule of law, have been noted by legal scholars. Yet, those very critics who bemoan the failure of law and development to address the background cultural norms of societies where law and development projects have been implemented go no further than make critical observations about the apparent cultural void.

Rosa Brooks has articulated the need for culture to figure more prominently in rule of law initiatives. "The rule of law is not something that exists 'beyond culture' and that can be somehow added to an existing culture by the simple expedient of creating formal structures and rewriting constitutions and statutes. In its substantive sense, the rule of law is a culture, yet the human-rights-law and foreign-policy communities know very little—and manifest little curiosity—about the complex processes by which cultures are created and changed."[8] Professor Brooks has also argued in favor of some form of cultural intervention.

---

[8] Rosa Ehrenreich Brooks, *The New Imperialism: Violence, Norms, and the "Rule of Law,"* 101 MICH. L. REV. 2275, 2285 (2003).

> [W]hile a good deal of recent work on domestic legal issues takes on the descriptive project of analyzing how norms and law interact, only a few legal scholars have addressed the question of how purposive governmental or nongovernmental norm-creation projects might actually work. This lacuna is even more noticeable in the domain of international and comparative law. . . . [T]hese issues of norm creation in the complex context of modern, international interventions are located at the interstices of international law, comparative law, and domestic law, traditionally conceived. They have found no disciplinary home, and tend to slip through the cracks, always at the periphery, never at the center of attention.[9]

Brooks exhorted as follows: "Those who care about human rights and the rule of law cannot afford to leave all of the creative insights about norm creation to the anthropologists or to Hollywood—and we certainly cannot afford to leave them to the bad guys. Yet so far, that is precisely what most of us have done, and this has to change."[10]

This book is one of the first comprehensive attempts to address this glaring cultural gap in law and development. Although at the outset, the call to engage in culture change may seem radical, draconian, or normatively problematic, it is important to note that even law and development projects that subscribe to a thin or minimalist conception of the rule of law, for example, requiring "only" minimum due process or an independent judiciary, involve more than simply exporting laws and are necessarily entwined with culture change. Similarly, a rule of law approach that is formalistic rather than substantive, that is, "only" reforming institutions (reforming the criminal justice system) or "only" passing the right laws, be it contract or property or criminal laws, without regard to the substantive desired end points (human rights, individual freedom) entails some not insignificant degree of culture change as well. In other words, as I showed in the Introduction, exporting laws and reforming institutions—now part of the usual reform menu—are not culture-free or culture-neutral tasks.

When I visited Vietnam in 1996 and gave a lecture on American contract law at Ho Chi Minh University in Saigon, a professor came to me after my lecture and made the following observation. He understood that state enforcement of contracts facilitated exchanges between strangers because no longer did people need to contract only with people they trusted. Yet, he still hung on to the traditional Vietnamese view of personalistic relationships. He still preferred the Vietnamese method of screening as a way of lowering transaction costs. As he explained, "before I enter into a contract with someone, I am interested less in whether contracts are enforced by the state, or what damages I would get if there is a breach. I am more interested in seeing how they have treated their parents when the parents are old and sick." The professor clearly believed that screening,

---

[9] *Id.* at 2325–26.

[10] *Id.* at 2327.

monitoring, and enforcement costs are likely to be less if he transacted with someone who could be trusted, that is, those who abided by the implicit bargain that one cares for one's parents in their old age.

The institution of contract law is designed precisely to facilitate transactions between and among unaffiliated parties with common commercial interests. Whether someone adheres to the traditional covenant between children and parents matters less if one is in a society where the rule of law exists and freely bargained for contracts are enforced. In this way, commerce no longer needs to be restricted to a close circle of clan members or individuals connected by birth and family. Indeed, contract law is a crucial factor in the transformation of economies based on *gemeinschaft* to *gesellschaft*, that is, community to society.[11] Historically, *gemeinschaft* connotes closely knit, often agrarian communities, while *gesellschaft* connotes more open, often urban societies.

The point is that when law and development exports contract law and other laws that support commercial transactions regularly entered into in market economies, it is not simply exporting law. It is also molding the transformation of perhaps traditionally closed, personalistic communities to more open, market-based societies, for example. It would be a mistake to pretend that it is acceptable to engage in legal development, to modernize laws, to establish the requisite legal system that is needed for a market economy or to reform institutions like the judiciary or law enforcement or legal education only because somehow such efforts are clearly demarcated efforts limited to laws and institutions. The assumption of law and development is that laws and institutions can and should be shaped and reformed; culture should not be shaped and reformed and should be left alone. Except for the experiment with changing legal culture in the first wave of reforms, law and development has been essentially agnostic about whether legal and institutional reform will spill over into more sensitive areas such as the cultural sphere. Yet, as I have discussed, by changing laws, law and development has also been engaging in transforming the cultural fabric of the importing country. Culture change has always been there, whether consciously or unconsciously, explicitly or implicitly. Indeed, the first wave development scholars understood this and hoped that legal development would result in development in other spheres, social, political, and economic. Influenced by modernization theory, the first wave sought to use law for instrumental purposes, for example, to change the legal culture of traditional society, to forge modern law and modern culture.

And yet it is unclear why for critics of culture change, transplanting formal laws and reforming institutions through an externally imposed law and development regime is defensible but reforming culture is not; some critics of culture change fear that culture will be used to blame the victim or to argue that culture is the "root" cause of poverty or of whichever ailment is at issue. I make no such claim. There are many causes of

---

[11] Ferdinand Tonnies, *Gemeinschaft and Gesellschaft*, *in* The Sociology of Community: A Selection of Readings 7 (Colin Bell & Howard Newby eds., 1974).

underdevelopment, and I make no argument as to which is the root cause or even the primary cause. Given the number of books and articles that have been written about myriad causes of underdevelopment, from geography to colonialism and structural inequities in the international system, it is unlikely that an argument that cultural norms may be one additional factor could possibly serve to crowd out other likely causes.

Much of the book is devoted to the question of whether cultural norms that support practices that constitute human rights violations or the subordination of women and girls or market inefficiencies are problematic and should be altered. To provide a concrete anchoring to these questions, examples drawn from the historical record as well as from current projects are included throughout the book. Each country-specific case study chosen, for example, Germany, Japan, Iraq, certainly merits its own full-length exegesis and a general law and development book such as this one will surely fail to present each country in all its rich historical complexities. Nonetheless, to pair theory and seemingly abstract proposals with pragmatic proposals, I have included specific examples, particularly in Chapter 5, to illustrate that culture change has been accomplished in different historical, national, and cultural settings. Certain culture change projects (such as those to boost market efficiency) may be less problematic for some than other culture change projects (such as those to protect human capability and freedom). Amartya Sen, Martha Nussbaum, and Arjun Appadurai support critically addressing cultural norms that perpetuate poverty and women's subordination, for example. Moreover, CEDAW itself specifically supports and requires state parties to take concrete steps to affirmatively change cultural norms that oppress women and perpetuate women's subordination. Presumably critics of culture change would also be critical of CEDAW's call for culture change, as well as attempts by others to alter cultural norms that support a host of practices that marginalize and oppress women, all presumably because culture cannot be tinkered with.

In recent years, the idea of culture change has become more acceptable and legitimate, at least in certain civil society sectors. In December 2014, the Ford Foundation, for example, invited "more than 75 pop culture and social change thought leaders to take part in CULTURE/CHANGE, a rare convening to explore the present—and shape the future—landscape of the culture change field."[12] The conference highlighted three key turning points in the field: commitment of the "social change sector to support and implement long-term culture change initiatives,"[13] efforts by the pop culture artists "to integrate social change values into popular content,"[14] and integration and collaboration between different disciplines and fields.

Questions examined by conference attendees are similar to those addressed throughout this book. For example, how can norm entrepreneurs or change advocates influence

---

[12] Ford Foundation, *Culture Change: Insights and Priorities* (Final Report), Dec. 17, 2014, at 3, *available at* http://www.slideshare.net/tracyvs1/culturechange-insights-and-priorities-v3.

[13] *Id.* at 4.

[14] *Id.*

culture? Who controls culture and how can it be influenced? Conference organizers boldly declared that "[t]he field has firmly moved past the debate of IF and WHY culture change is needed to achieve widespread change within social movements. We have entered the stage of experimentation to find the best strategies, relationships, and investments to leverage pop culture to create the shifts in cultural narratives, believes and values we seek."[15] Above all, participants emphasized the need to make connections across different areas: "Culture change work must not be seen as separate program or a specific campaign strategy, but as the practice which guides the organization's overall storytelling, media and engagement strategy."[16] And foundations were encouraged to fund culture change projects, as well as to create an organizational roadmap of "all the various strands of culture change work being undertaken by their respective grantees."[17] Organizers stressed the need to use "social impact storytelling" (presumably similar to framing strategies discussed in Chapter 6).

Many of the conclusions drawn by participants at the conference again reflect observations similarly made in this book. First, culture change is a long-term strategy and project;[18] by its nature, the process of culture change, its evolution and shifts, do not coincide with quantitative measurements and benchmarks.[19] Second, culture change involves cross-sector work and informal as well as formal networks of culture change workers.[20] "Breaking down sector silos is incredibly important to advancing the culture change field."[21] As noted throughout this book, norm change activists and NGOs that work at the international level to change international criminal norms and to push states to adopt such norms have much in common with those that work at the subnational level to transport and diffuse international or universal norms into the domestic level. Formal and informal practitioners and realms, domestic and international spheres, the evolution of customary law at the international level and culture change at the subnational, domestic level are more intertwined and related than demarcated and separate in their respective silos.

Breakthrough, an NGO founded by an Indian American to create a culture of international human rights supportive of human dignity and justice, is another organization that emphasizes culture change. In April 2015, Breakthrough organized a global session called "Using Culture to Change Culture."[22] The session was dedicated to translating international human rights norms into not just the legal framework but also the accompanying

---

15 *Id.* at 8.
16 *Id.* at 10.
17 *Id.* at 17.
18 *Id.* at 14.
19 *Id.* at 18.
20 *Id.* at 15.
21 *Id.* at 8.
22 Skoll World Forum 2015, *Using Culture to Change Culture*, Apr. 15, 2015, at 1, *available at* http://skollworldforum.org/2015/04/21/forum2015-how-to-use-storytelling-to-change-culture/.

cultural framework. The purpose of the session was to convene advocates, from filmmakers to technologists, "to explore how to more effectively create culture change through storytelling, media, arts, technology, and other tools."[23] Participants discussed the role of storytelling—through different vehicles such as the performing arts, documentary, radio, videos, the written word—in empowering the storyteller. "Storytelling enables people negatively affected by an issue to process their experiences and heal their way into becoming leaders for change. This in turn can engage multiple constituencies in the journey of transformation and build movements that can shift us beyond advocacy to real culture change."[24] Ideas discussed at the session are similar to the broad themes examined in this book, that is, how "to identify and engage underlying cultural and spiritual beliefs and engage with them at the community level to shift and create new norms."[25]

Certainly, culture change projects, like other law and development projects, may be poorly implemented and may fail, like countless other law and development projects. Culture change projects may be inapplicable in certain situations. And there is no formula that will guarantee culture change success, just as there is no formula to guarantee rule of law success. There may also be unintended consequences.

However, the basic thesis of this book, that law and development is inherently not just a legal, political, or economic process but also a cultural one stands. As such, if law and development continues to be pursued, it must engage cultural norms. Where those norms are at odds with the substantive norms of law and development—women's rights, human rights, the eradication of poverty or practices that constrain human capability—culture change is normatively staked on the universalism of human dignity, whether in developing or developed countries.

---

[23] *Id.*

[24] *Id.*

[25] *Id.* at 2.

Index

Surnames started with "al-" are alphabetized by the following part of the name.